TERRORISM

Documents of International and Local Control

VOLUME 82

Related titles in ***Terrorism: Documents of International and Local Control, Second Series:***

Compensation for Victims of Terrorism
Marshall Shapo

The Law of Sovereign Immunity and Terrorism
James Cooper-Hill

TERRORISM

Documents of International and Local Control

VOLUME 82

U.S. PERSPECTIVES

Oceana®
NEW YORK

OXFORD
UNIVERSITY PRESS

Oxford University Press, Inc., publishes works that further Oxford University's objective of excellence in research, scholarship, and education.

Published by Oxford University Press, Inc.
198 Madison Avenue, New York, New York 10016

Cataloging-in-Publication information is available from the Library of Congress.

ISSN 1062-4007
Terrorism: Documents of International and Local Control

ISBN: 978-0-19-533873-7 (v. 82)

Note to Readers:

This publication is designed to provide accurate and authoritative information in regard to the subject matter covered. It is based upon sources believed to be accurate and reliable and is intended to be current as of the time it was written. It is sold with the understanding that the publisher is not engaged in rendering legal, accounting, or other professional services. If legal advice or other expert assistance is required, the services of a competent professional person should be sought. Also, to confirm that the information has not been affected or changed by recent developments, traditional legal research techniques should be used, including checking primary sources where appropriate.

(Based on the Declaration of Principles jointly adopted by a Committee of the American Bar Association and a Committee of Publishers and Associations.)

TABLE OF CONTENTS

VOLUME 82

DOCUMENTS

INFRASTRUCTURE SECURITY

MARITIME SECURITY

INFRASTRUCTURE SECURITY

DOCUMENT NO. 1

PORT RISK MANAGEMENT: ADDITIONAL FEDERAL GUIDANCE WOULD AID PORTS IN DISASTER PLANNING AND RECOVERY

GAO Report
(GAO-07-412)

March 28, 2007

Highlights

Why GAO Did This Study

U.S. ports are significant to the U.S. economy, handling more than 2 billion tons of domestic and import/export cargo annually Since Sept 11, 2001, much of the national focus on ports' preparedness has been on preventing potential acts of terror, the 2005 hurricane season renewed focus on how to protect ports from a diversity of threats, including natural disasters. This report was prepared under the authority of the Comptroller General to examine (1) challenges port authorities have experienced as a result of recent natural disasters, (2) efforts underway to address these challenges, and (3) the manner in which port authorities plan for natural disasters GAO reviewed documents and interviewed various port stakeholders from 17 major U.S. ports.

What GAO Recommends

To ensure that ports achieve adequate planning for natural disasters, GAO recommends that the Secretary of Homeland Security encourage port stakeholders to use existing forums for discussing all-hazards planning.

DHS, DOT and DOD generally agreed with the facts presented in the report However, DHS expressed concern about using existing forums for planning. Our work showed that these forums are already being used for planning in several cases which should be further encouraged.

What GAO Found

Ports, particularly those impacted by the 2005 hurricane season, experienced many different kinds of challenges during recent natural disasters. Of the 17 U.S. ports that GAO reviewed, port officials identified communications, personnel, and interagency coordination as their biggest challenges.

Many port authorities have taken steps to address these challenges Individually, ports have created redundancy in communications systems and other backup equipment and updated their emergency plans. Collectively, the American Association of Port Authorities developed a best practices manual focused on port planning and recovery efforts, as well as lessons learned from recent natural disasters. Even ports that have not experienced problems as a result of recent disasters, but are nonetheless susceptible to disaster threats, have responded to lessons learned by other ports. Additionally, federal maritime agencies, such as the U.S. Coast Guard, the Maritime Administration, and the U.S. Army Corps of Engineers have increased their coordination and communication with ports to strengthen ports' ability to recover from future natural disasters and to build stakeholders' knowledge about federal resources for port recovery efforts.

Most port authorities GAO reviewed conduct planning for natural disasters separately from planning for homeland security threats. Unlike security efforts, natural disaster planning is not subject to the same type of specific federal requirements and, therefore, varies from port to port. As a result of this divided approach, GAO found a wide variance in ports' natural disaster planning efforts, including:

- the level of participation in disaster forums, and
- the level of information sharing among port stakeholders

In the absence of appropriate forums and information sharing opportunities among ports, some ports GAO contacted were limited in their understanding of federal resources available for predisaster mitigation and postdisaster recovery. Other ports have begun using existing forums, such as their federally mandated Area Maritime Security Committee, to coordinate disaster planning efforts. Port and industry experts, as well as recent federal actions, are now encouraging an all-hazards approach to disaster planning and recovery. That is, disaster preparedness planning requires that all of the threats faced by the port, both natural (such as hurricanes) and man-made (such as terror events), be considered together. The Department of Homeland Security, which through the Coast Guard oversees the Area Maritime Security Committees, provides an example of how to incorporate a wider scope of activity for ports across the country. Additionally, the Maritime Administration should develop a communication strategy to inform ports of the maritime resources available for recovery efforts.

Abbreviations

AAPA	American Association of Port Authorities
AMSC	Area Maritime Security Committee
COTP	Captain of the Port
DHS	Department of Homeland Security
DOD	Department of Defense
DOT	Department of Transportation
FEMA	Federal Emergency Management Agency
GICA	Gulf Intracoastal Canal Association
LEA	Local Emergency Management Agency
MIRP	Maritime Infrastructure Recovery Plan
MSRAM	Maritime Security Risk Assessment Model
MTSA	Maritime Transportation Security Act of 2002
NIMS	National Incident Management System
NRP	National Response Plan
SAFE Port Act	Security and Accountability for Every Port Act of 2006

Congressional Committees:

U.S. ports and waterways handle more than 2 billion tons of domestic and import/export cargo annually, and more than 95 percent of U.S. international trade moves by water. As such, ports are a global gateway to world markets and significant engines in the U.S. economy. As important as they are, virtually every major U.S. port faces one or more types of natural disasters with potentially devastating consequences Ports throughout the eastern seaboard and the Gulf Coast face the possibility of hurricanes, and ports on the West Coast are in areas that are highly susceptible to earthquakes. Losing a major port, even for a few weeks or months, could have a national economic impact, making effective recovery a concern not only for the local area but for the federal government as well.

Ports' complexities exacerbate the difficulty of taking adequate steps to deal with possible natural disasters. Ports are often sprawling enterprises, and each port is unique. Further, a "port" is seldom a single entity. Rather, a port is usually a collection of varied maritime stakeholders. Ports usually include a public entity, such as a port authority. The role of port authorities varies from port to port. For example, the Port of Mobile operates a coal plant in the port, but it also has tenants that lease and operate their own facilities in the port area. Other ports, such as the Port of Miami, are owned and managed by county government,[1] but terminal operators are responsible for the day-to-day maintenance and repair of the terminal area. Besides port authorities, port stakeholders include shipping companies and other tenants that may be leasing port authority facilities, factories and other industries located in the area, and local and state law enforcement and emergency management agencies. Terminals or facilities may also be privately owned Federal agencies also have a role at ports including the U.S. Coast Guard (Coast Guard), U.S. Army Corps of Engineers, and the Maritime Administration.[2] Despite these complexities, ports have various forums in which these maritime stakeholders can coordinate on issues that affect the port as a whole. For terrorism concerns, for example, major U.S. ports have a Area Maritime Security Committee (AMSC)[3] that provides a venue for discussing security concerns For disaster relief concerns, U.S. ports would work with the Federal Emergency Management Agency (FEMA) regarding disaster assistance.

Since the terrorist attacks of September 11, 2001, much of the focus on emergency preparedness has been on preparedness for preventing, mitigating the effects of, and responding to terrorist attacks. Through legislation and presidential directives, the Department of Homeland Security (DHS) is the primary federal organization responsible for preparing the nation both for terrorist attacks and for major disasters. Homeland Security Presidential Directives 5 and 8 require that DHS establish a single, comprehensive approach to and plans for the management of emergency events whether the result of terrorist attacks or large-scale natural or accidental disasters.[4] As we have previously reported, the capabilities needed to respond to major disasters, whether the result of a terrorist attack or nature, are similar in many ways. The devastating hurricane season of 2005, which included Hurricanes Katrina, Rita, and Wilma, focused renewed attention on the potential effects that natural disasters could pose to port operations. The numerous vulnerabilities port operations face, together with the limited resources available to deal with them, have also initiated a renewed look at how to protect ports from a variety of threats.

In light of the continued attention both to port security and to federal natural disaster response, we are providing a comprehensive view of steps ports have taken to prepare and mitigate the impacts of natural disasters. Consequently, we conducted this review, initiated under the Comptroller General's authority, to examine port disaster preparedness measures and to examine the federal role in helping ports plan and recover from natural disaster impacts. More specifically, this report examines (1) the challenges port authorities have experienced as a result of recent natural disasters, (2) the efforts under way to address challenges from these disasters, and (3) the manner in which port authorities plan for natural disasters and the effect of this approach on their ability to share information with port stakeholders and access federal resources.

To address the challenges port authorities experience as a result of recent disasters and the efforts to address these challenges, we selected 17 U.S.

ports for review (see fig. 1) We focused primarily on commercial ports and various commercial aspects of these ports. The criteria we used included selecting ports that (1) varied in size (based on cargo value) and (2) varied in the degree to which they had experienced some type of natural disaster since 1998.[5] Based on guidance from DHS regarding the most significant natural disaster threats to ports, we limited the natural disasters we considered to earthquakes and hurricanes. In particular, we focused on ports impacted by the 2005 hurricane season; in all, 11 of the 17 ports we selected were affected by hurricanes that year. We conducted site visits at 7 of the 17 ports, where we interviewed various maritime stakeholders, including officials from the port authorities, emergency management agencies, and federal agencies such as the Coast Guard, U.S. Army Corps of Engineers, Maritime Administration, and FEMA. We contacted the remaining 10 ports by telephone and conducted a more limited range of interviews For all 17 ports, we reviewed numerous planning documents, including emergency operations plans, business continuity plans, and hurricane plans.

Figure 1: Ports Selected for Case Studies and Phone Interviews

Sources: GAO, Map Resources (map)

To determine the manner in which port authorities prepare for disasters and its effect on information sharing and access to federal resources, we relied primarily on information obtained from our 17 case studies and phone interviews, supplementing it as necessary with other information related to risk management and disaster planning. For perspective on risk management, we used our body of work related to risk management throughout the federal government[6] and supplemented it with additional risk management models and tools from a wide range of federal, professional, and academic stakeholders, as well as interviews and documents from the Coast Guard and offices within DHS. We did not include any separate planning efforts conducted by private operators, for two key reasons: their roles and responsibilities vary greatly from port to port and; unlike their planning efforts for homeland security, their efforts for natural disasters are not subject to the same type of federal requirements or guidelines. We performed our work from December 2005 through March 2007, in accordance with generally accepted government auditing standards See appendix I for more detail regarding our objectives, scope, and methodology.

Results in Brief

Port authorities reported experiencing many different kinds of challenges during recent natural disasters, with communication, personnel, and interagency coordination reported as the most problematic challenges. This was particularly true for ports that were impacted by the 2005 hurricane season. Twelve of the 17 ports we reviewed had experienced at least one hurricane or earthquake since 1998, and of these, 8 reported one or more types of challenges in responding (see fig. 2). The most visibly apparent challenge port authorities experienced was dealing with damaged infrastructure, including structural damage to buildings and piers, and silting and debris clogging key waterways. Port authorities also reported difficulties restoring power, water, and other utilities. However, the greatest challenges port officials said they experienced—and in many cases did not anticipate—were in the following other areas:

- *Communications* Many ports experienced difficulties in communicating both outside the port and with port personnel and other port stakeholders. Phone outages were extensive and cell phone reception was limited. For example, one port was without services for 2 to 4 weeks following Hurricane Katrina.
- *Personnel* When many port personnel around the Gulf area were evacuated from their homes, the evacuation caused problems both in locating personnel and also in letting them know they should return to work.
- *Coordination* Officials reported difficulties coordinating with local, state, and federal stakeholders, especially for planning and recovery efforts. For example, in some cases, port officials had difficulty re-entering the port because they lacked the credentials required by local police and other emergency management officials Some ports also reported difficulty accessing federal resources for recovery efforts. For example, officials at some ports said they had problems understanding the process in filing for disaster assistance and coordinating damage assessments with FEMA or were unaware of resources available through the Maritime Ad-

ministration, such as ships that could be used for housing or for conveying supplies.

Figure 2: Port Experiences with Natural Disasters Since 1998

Source: GAO

Port authorities and other stakeholders reported taking a variety of steps to address these challenges. Port authorities have replaced, repaired, and created redundancies for a variety of communications systems and physical infrastructure—for example, purchasing backup phone systems and power generators, creating alternative administrative sites, and developing alternative storage for computer information. Though the 2005 hurricane season primarily affected Gulf ports, port authority officials elsewhere said the results of that season prompted them to improve their preparation as well One key effort was undertaken by the American Association of Port Authorities (AAPA), an industry group. It convened work groups to discuss lessons learned and, based on the input, issued a manual with guidance for ports on such issues as developing alternative communications, setting up an emergency operations center, and identifying federal resources for recovery efforts. Port authorities reported their changes often extended to improving coordination with other stakeholders. Some ports adapted forums intended for security planning, such as their AMSC, while others with existing natural disaster forums took steps to strengthen them. Some port authorities also established plans for coordinating with neighboring ports. Actions have also been taken at the federal level. For example, the Maritime Administration contributed to a one-time plan developed by FEMA—the Federal Support Plan. This plan was specifically cited for the 2006 Hurricane Season and was specific to the federal government's response to support the State of Louisiana. The Maritime Administration contributed to this plan by identifying government and commercial maritime capabilities that could be employed in response to a disaster. To date, while the Maritime Administration plans to provide a directive regarding capabilities to all of their regional offices in June 2007, no plan exists for communicating this information to ports.

Port authorities we reviewed generally conducted their natural disaster planning separately from planning for homeland security threats, and this approach has reduced their ability to facilitate sharing natural disaster planning information among key stakeholders and to access federal resources. Planning for homeland security, an activity that is governed by federal law, tends to be consistent from port to port. By contrast, natural disaster planning, which is not subject to the same type of specific federal requirements, varied considerably at the ports we reviewed in its extent and thoroughness. Separate planning for these two threats means that ports are not able to effectively estimate the impact of mitigation alternatives and optimize their investments in these alternatives based on costs and benefits. Industry experts and port stakeholders, such as the Coast Guard, are now encouraging unified consideration of all risks faced by ports, but we found few port authorities were taking a unified approach. One consequence of divided planning is that key stakeholders were not necessarily participating in natural disaster planning. Unlike security planning, where the Secretary of Homeland Security can establish an AMSC with broad representation across port stakeholders, natural disaster planning carries no such requirement During our review, we found substantial variation in the maturity of, and participation in, natural disaster planning forums at ports In particular, one port had no forum that brought together the port authority and the local disaster planning agency, which had knowledge of available federal resources, such as FEMA grant programs, as well as the expertise to deal with grant requirements. In the absence of such a forum, it is not surprising that some ports were limited in their understanding of federal resources available for predisaster mitigation and postdisaster recovery. To help improve information sharing, some ports have begun using their federally authorized AMSC, or some other similar forum with wide representation, in disaster planning efforts DHS, which through the Coast Guard coordinates the AMSCs, provides an example of how to incorporate a wider scope of committee activity for ports across the country.

To help ensure that ports achieve adequate planning for natural disasters and effectively manage risk to a variety of threats, we are recommending that the Secretary of the Department of Homeland Security encourage port stakeholders to use existing forums for discussing their all-hazards planning efforts and include appropriate representatives from DHS, the port authority, representatives from the local emergency management office, the Maritime Administration, and vessel and facility owner/operators. To help ensure that ports have adequate understanding of maritime disaster recovery resources, we recommend that the Secretary of the Department of Transportation direct the Administrator of the Maritime Administration to develop a communication strategy to inform ports of the maritime resources available for recovery efforts.

In commenting on a draft of this report, DHS, the Department of Transportation (DOT), and the Department of Defense (DOD) generally agreed with the facts presented. In its letter, DHS did not endorse placing responsibility for disaster contingency planning on existing committees in ports and said these responsibilities should remain with state and local emergency management planners. Our recommendation was not to place responsibility for such planning within port committees, but rather to use these existing forums as a way to engage all relevant parties in discussing natural disaster planning for ports. DOT officials provided a number of comments and clarifications, which we incorporated as appropriate to ensure the accuracy of our report. The DOT generally concurred with GAO's recommendation. The DOD provided technical comments and clarifications.

Background

Port Activities Involve Many Different Entities

Ports comprise many different stakeholders, both public and private Port authorities also may have jurisdiction over some or all of the geographical area of a port. The port authority can be an agency of the state, county, or city in which the port is located. In most ports in North America, the actual task of loading and unloading goods is carried out by private operators who lease space or equipment from the port authority. (In some ports, the port authority also manages some of these stevedoring activities.) The percentage of the port area over which the port authority has jurisdiction, and the level of involvement of the port authority in the port's operations, is different from port to port. This variability in port authority jurisdiction and operational involvement has direct consequences for portwide disaster preparedness. Even though a port authority may have a thorough disaster plan in place, that plan may not be binding on any of the private operators in the port.

The stakeholders involved at any given port can vary but, in general, they include port authorities, private-sector operators doing business within the port, government agencies, and information-sharing forums. Table 1 summarizes these basic participants and their roles.[7]

Table 1: Port Stakeholder Roles

Port stakeholder	Stakeholder role
Quasi-governmental	
Port authority	• Provides a limited governance structure for the port.
	• Sometimes owns port assets such as cranes and pier space.
	• The role of the port authority varies from port to port Some ports own and operate cargo terminals, while others lease their equipment and pier space to private operators. Others engage in a combination of both activities.
Private sector	
Facility/service operators	• Ship owners and operators
	• Stevedoring companies
	• Rail carriers/operators
	• Trucking and shipping companies
	• Other operators to support the day-to-day activities of the port
State and local governments	
State or local emergency management	• May assist port in planning for natural disasters and security threats. May also help to agency coordinate disaster response services such as police, fire, and medical teams for the port.
Information sharing forums	
Area Maritime Security Committee	• Federally established forum at all ports for all stakeholders to share information on security issues through regularly scheduled meetings, electronic bulletins on suspicious activities around seaport facilities, and sharing of key documents.[a]
	• The U.S. Coast Guard Captain of the Port (COTP)[b] is authorized to establish and coordinate the AMSC and appoint members along with other duties as prescribed by regulation.
Harbor Safety Committee	• Forum at many ports for all stakeholders to advise on regulatory and nonregulatory safety-related issues, including disaster preparedness. Only two Harbor Safety Committees , at Ports of Houston, Texas, and New Orleans, Louisiana, are federally mandated[C]
	• Committees, at the Ports of Houston, Texas, and New Orleans, Louisiana, are federally mandated.[c]

Port stakeholder	Stakeholder role
Gulf Intracoastal Canal Association	The Gulf Intracoastal Canal Association (GICA) is maritime trade association that is an advocate for issues regarding the Gulf Intracoastal Waterway, which is an inland navigable waterway located along the Gulf Coast. One of GICA's missions is to work with its members, as well as the Coast Guard and Corps, to identify opportunities to improve the safety and efficiency of the Gulf Intracoastal Waterway.
American Association of Port Authorities	A trade association that represents more than 150 public port authorities in the United States, Canada, the Caribbean, and Latin America.
	Coordinated a series of working groups to develop best practices for disaster preparation and recovery.

Source: GAO

[a] Maritime Transportation Security Act of 2002 (MTSA), Pub L No 107-295, 116 Stat 2064, contains many of the homeland security requirements related specifically to port security The Area Maritime Security Committees are authorized by section 102 of MTSA, as codified at 46 U.S.C. § 70112(a)(2).

[b] A Coast Guard officer designated as the lead official to facilitate execution of Coast Guard duties in that area 14 U.S.C. § 634.

[c] Coast Guard Authorization Act of 1991, Pub L No 102-241, § 18 and § 19, 105 Stat 2208.

These various stakeholders interact in a variety of ways. The port authority provides a limited governance structure for the port. Many port authorities lease piers, or "terminals," and equipment to stevedoring companies and shipping lines that are responsible for the actual loading and transport of cargo. Some port authorities also operate cargo terminals alongside the private operators. Figure 3 depicts the main elements of a typical port. Individual ports may not include all of these elements, or may include some not depicted here.

Figure 3: Port Elements

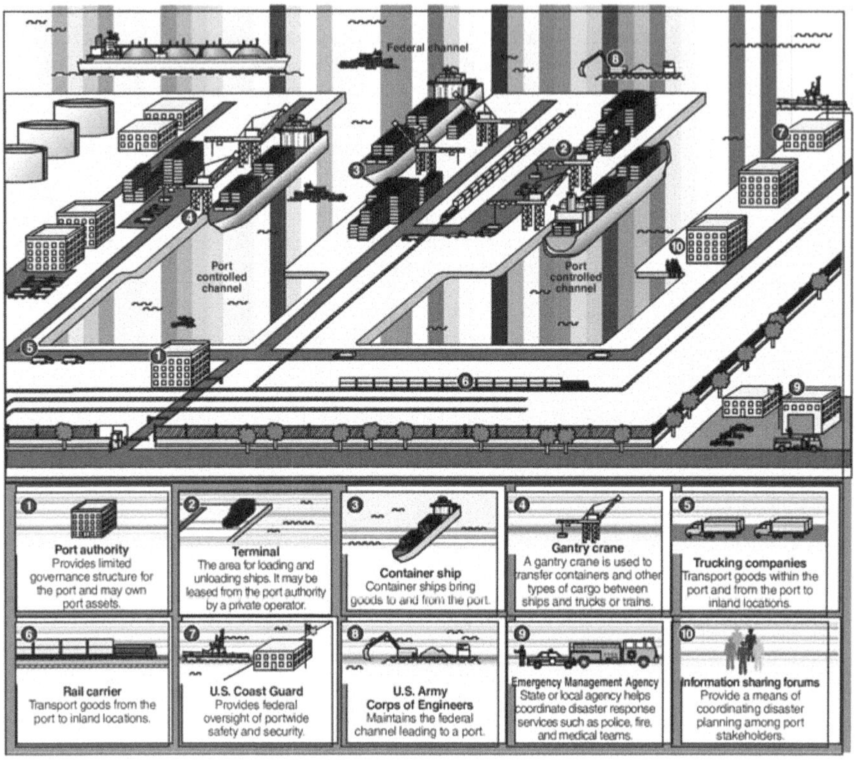

Source: GAO

Federal Role in Port Activities Is Extensive

Several federal agencies provide support to ports in natural disaster planning, response, and recovery (see table 2). These agencies have different missions that relate to port operations, including natural disaster planning and response. For example, the Coast Guard is the agency responsible for most federal oversight related to portwide safety and security. It plays the primary role in coordinating efforts for homeland security efforts FEMA plays a role in homeland security planning and also administers several assistance programs for disaster preparation and recovery. The Maritime Administration plays a general role in coordinating efforts to strengthen the maritime system and also has the ability to provide maritime assets that could be used to support homeland security interests. These vessels are part of the country's National Defense Ready Reserve Fleet, including ships and barges, which could be used for housing, power generation, or the movement of water and other supplies.

Table 2: Federal Agency Role at Ports

Stakeholders	Selected mission-related activities
Department of Homeland Security	
U.S. Coast Guard	Promotes and carries out five operating goals at every U.S. port: Maritime Safety, Protection of Natural Resources, Mobility (i.e., facilitation of the movement of people and goods), Maritime Security, and National Defense . Coordinates the AMSC where they have been created. Responsible for closing the port to vessel traffic before or during a disaster and reopening the port to traffic following the incident. Reviews facility security plans and oversees compliance with these plans.
FEMA	Administers the Public Assistance Grant Program that provides funds for the repair, replacement, or restoration of disaster-damaged, publicly owned facilities. Few ports have received funding for post-disaster recovery under this program. Administers the Hazard Mitigation Grant Program that provides funds to state and local governments to implement long-term hazard mitigation measures after a major disaster declaration. Ports may be included as sub-applicants on a state or local government application Very few ports have applied for and received hazard mitigation grants. Administers the Predisaster Mitigation Program that provides technical and financial assistance for hazard mitigation planning and the implementation of mitigation projects prior to a disaster event.
Preparedness Directorate–Office of Grants and Training	Administers the Port Security Grant Program that provides funds each year to mitigate security threats to ports. Both port authorities and private operators may apply. The program has distributed $876,394,146 since its inception, and $168,052,500 in the fiscal year 2006 program.
Maritime Administration	• Seeks to improve and strengthen the U.S. marine transportation system—including infrastructure, industry and labor—to meet the economic and security needs of the nation. • Provides ready reserve vessels that could be used to support vital homeland and national security interests.[b]

Stakeholders	Selected mission-related activities
	• Publishes a Port Risk Management and Insurance Guidebook that is currently being revised to include disaster preparedness guidance for ports.
Department of Defense	
U.S. Army Corps of Engineers	• Maintains any federal channels leading to a port Following disasters, surveys the channel, removes debris, and oversees any necessary dredging.

Source: GAO

[a] The U.S. Army Corps of Engineers maintains more than 12,000 miles (19,200 km) of inland waterways and operates 235 locks.

[b] The Maritime Administration manages this inactive inventory for the Department of Defense.

Federal Disaster Planning Guidance

The terrorist attacks of September 11, 2001, prompted additional federal efforts to address a broad spectrum of emergencies. The Homeland Security Act of 2002[8] required DHS to develop a comprehensive National Incident Management System (NIMS),N IMS is intended to provide a consistent framework for incident management at all jurisdictional levels regardless of the cause, size, or complexity of the situation and to define the roles and responsibilities of federal, state, and local governments, and various first responder disciplines at each level during an emergency event. To manage all major incidents, NIMS has a standard incident management system, called the Incident Command System, with five functional areas—command, operations, planning, logistics, and finance and administration NIMS also prescribes interoperable communications systems and preparedness before an incident happens, including planning, training, and exercises.

In December 2004, DHS issued the National Response Plan (NRP), intended to be an all-discipline, all-hazards plan establishing a single, comprehensive framework for the management of domestic incidents where federal involvement is necessary. The NRP includes planning assumptions, roles and responsibilities, concept of operations, and incident management actions. The NRP also includes a Catastrophic Incident Annex, which provides an accelerated, proactive national response to a "catastrophic incident," defined as any natural or man-made incident, including terrorism, resulting in extraordinary levels of mass casualties, damage, or disruption severely affecting the population, infrastructure, environment, economy, national morale, or government functions.

Developing the capabilities needed to deal with large-scale disasters is part of an overall national preparedness effort that should integrate and define what needs to be done, where, based on what standards, how it should be done, and how well it should be done. Along with the NRP and NIMS, DHS has developed the National Preparedness Goal. Considered as a group, these three documents are intended to guide investments in emergency preparedness and response capabilities. The NRP describes what needs to be done in response to an emergency incident, either natural or man-made, the NIMS describes how to manage what needs to be done, and the National Preparedness Goal describes how well it should be done. The National Preparedness Goal is particularly useful for determining what capabilities are needed, especially for a catastrophic disaster. The interim goal addresses both natural disasters and terrorist attacks. It defines both the 37 major capabilities that first responders should possess to prevent, protect from, respond to, and recover from disaster incidents and the most critical tasks associated with these capabilities.[9] An inability to effectively perform these critical tasks would, by definition, have a detrimental impact on effective protection, prevention, response, and recovery capabilities.

The Maritime Infrastructure Recovery Plan (MIRP), released by DHS in April 2006, applies these disaster preparedness documents to the maritime sector. The MIRP is intended to facilitate the restoration of maritime commerce after a terrorist attack or natural disaster and reflects the disaster management framework outlined in the National Response Plan. The MIRP addresses issues that should be considered by ports when planning for natural disasters. However, it does not set forth particular actions that should be taken at the port level, leaving those determinations to be made by the port operators themselves.

The 9/11 Commission pointed out that no amount of money or effort can fully protect against every type of threat. As a result, what is needed is an approach that considers the relative risks these various threats pose and determines how best to use limited resources to prevent threats, where possible, and to respond effectively if they occur. While the Homeland Security Act of 2002 and Homeland Security Presidential Directive 7 call for the use of risk management in homeland security, little specific federal guidance or direction exists as to how risk management should be implemented In previous work examining risk management efforts for homeland security and other functions, we developed a framework summarizing the findings of industry experts and best practices.[10] This framework, shown in figure 4, divides risk management into five major phases: (1) setting strategic goals and objectives, and determining constraints; (2) assessing the risks; (3) evaluating alternatives for addressing these risks; (4) selecting the appropriate alternatives; and (5) implementing the alternatives and monitoring the progress made and results achieved.

Figure 4: GAO Risk Management Framework

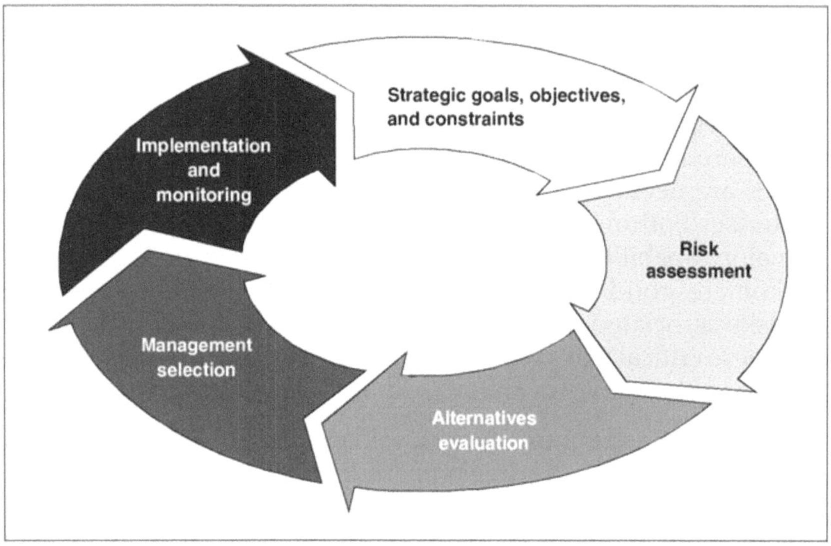

Source: GAO

Recent Natural Disasters Created a Variety of Challenges; Some Recovery Efforts Were More Difficult Than Expected

Recent natural disasters—particularly Hurricanes Katrina, Wilma, and Rita in 2005—challenged affected ports on several fronts, according to port authority officials. Since 1998, hurricanes have damaged buildings, cranes, and other equipment owned by seven of the port authorities we interviewed. Ports also reported damage to utility systems and experienced delays in water, sewer, and power restoration. Port authorities cited clearing waterways and debris removal as another difficulty. In the case of Hurricane Katrina, some ports, such as Gulfport and New Orleans, have not yet returned or took about 6 months to return to predisaster operational levels, respectively. Separate from the physical impact of the disasters, challenges occurred with personnel, communications and coordination issues and, according to port authority officials, these challenges proved more difficult than anticipated. In some cases, personnel had evacuated the area, and port officials were unsure when staff would be able to return to work. Given that many phone lines were down, there were delays in restoring phone service and, in most cases, ports did not have communications alternatives in place. Some port authorities also reported difficulties in working with local, state, and federal entities during the recovery process, including coordinating re-entry to the port of port personnel and filing for FEMA disaster recovery assistance.

Damage to Infrastructure Affected Operations at Most Ports Experiencing Recent Natural Disasters

Even though most ports anticipated and had plans in place to mitigate infrastructure damage from natural disasters, over half of the port authorities we contacted reported that the disasters created infrastructure challenges. Twelve of the 17 ports we reviewed had experienced a hurricane or earthquake since 1998, and among those 12 port authorities, 7 reported challenges in restoring infrastructure (see fig. 2). While we were unable to review a complete list of disaster assistance estimates, some port authorities were able to provide specific dollar amounts for repair damage to buildings, cranes, or other equipment. For instance, the Port of Miami reported spending more than $6 million on repairs as a result of Hurricanes Katrina, Wilma, and Rita, including damage to facilities, signage, sea wall and storm drainage system. Likewise, The Port of Houston reported spending $200,000 for facility repairs following Hurricane Rita Ports were still faced with these repair costs even though a majority of the port plans we reviewed included infrastructure damage mitigation. As a way to work around the damaged structures, ports also utilized temporary trailers for administrative and operational functions. For example, this occurred at the Port of Port Arthur, where the strategy of reserving backup equipment with appropriate vendors was included in that port's Hurricane Readiness Plan.

Besides the repair costs involved, another indication of the significance of damage to infrastructure was the effect on port operations. In several cases, tenants left the port and moved elsewhere. For example, Port of New Orleans officials said that because they are unsure if departed tenants at the port will return, they have been reluctant to replace three severely damaged container cranes. Operations have been even more curtailed at the Port of Gulfport, also because of Hurricane Katrina, Port authority officials report that they have been able to repair only 3 of their 12 warehouses, which limited their ability to accommodate storage for some of their major operators. These operators have since moved their operations to other nearby ports, such as Pascagoula, Mississippi, or Mobile, Alabama.

Besides damage to buildings, cranes, and other equipment involved specifically in moving cargoes, port authorities also reported damages to their utility systems, including water, sewer, and power. For example, following Hurricane Katrina, the Port of Port Arthur was without power for approximately 2 weeks. Because of a lack of on-site generators, port officials limited port operations to daylight hours only. The power outage also limited operation of certain hangar doors that required electrical power to be opened Ports with damage to water and sewer included Gulfport, where 2 months were needed to restore its sewer and water capacity. Similarly, the Port of Pascagoula had three damaged water wells as a result of Hurricane Katrina. Port officials told us one of those wells was still not operational almost a year later. While some ports included backup water and power resources in their contingency utility plans, officials at one port said their backup resources may not be adequate to address long-term or extensive outages. In fact, 10 of the 17 ports we reviewed did not have plans for utility system restoration The lack of anticipation of these vulnerabilities was particularly apparent for ports affected by Hurricanes Katrina, Wilma, and Rita; only 4 of the 10 ports impacted by those storms had planned for utility challenges. For example, Port of New Orleans officials said their supply of 5 to 10 days of water and 3 to 5 days of power through generators was not enough to sustain them through the outages caused by Hurricane Katrina.

While many ports indicated that several federal agencies were eventually able to effectively aid in clearing the waterways and restoring aids to navigation, ports' experiences varied. Their experiences also demonstrated that rapid clearing of waterways is key to reestablishing port operations and emphasizes the need for ports to coordinate and arrange for debris removal and restoring aids to navigation ahead of time. Following are some examples:

- Following Hurricane Katrina, the Port of Gulfport had to remove large amounts of debris, such as tree limbs that were hanging and leaning over roads, as well as containers, cargo, and other equipment that winds had scattered into the roadways. Port officials said that clearing these obstructions was essential to re-establishing port operations. Immediately after the hurricane, the local Navy construction battalion (called Seabees) volunteered to assist the port by clearing roads with their large bulldozers, which enabled supplies and cargo to move in and out of the port. The Seabees also cleared boat ramps so that Coast Guard search and rescue vessels could safely enter the waterway. Port officials estimated that, over a period of 3 weeks, the Seabees cleared about 30 percent of the debris in the port area. After the Seabees were called to other duties, Port of Gulfport officials hired a contractor to remove the remaining debris at a cost of about $5 million. Port of Gulfport officials said that they applied for FEMA reimbursement of these costs. Further, they explained that the use of and planning for existing federal resources for debris removal, such as the Navy Seabees, could have saved even more time and possibly federal dollars that would later be paid to the port in the FEMA reimbursement process.
- Inside the port area, the Port of Mobile experienced challenges with debris removal that federal agencies such as the Corps or the Coast Guard were not responsible for removing. These challenges may have caused additional delays in restoring port operations. For instance, port officials explained that storm surge waters from Katrina loosened several oil rigs in the Gulf, one of which made its way into the port's pier area and damaged several piers. They said the port is currently in litigation to resolve who will pay for the damages. Port of Mobile officials also estimated that dredging expenses, including the removal of branches, sand, and silt

from pier areas will be more than $7.5 million. Because the rig obstruction and other pier damages were not in the federal waterway or jurisdiction, Port of Mobile officials said they were only able to receive limited assistance from federal agencies in resolving their internal damage issues.

Difficulties with Personnel, Communication, and Coordination Issues Were Greater Than Expected during Recovery Efforts

Officials of eight port authorities we contacted reported challenges related to personnel, communications, or coordination with port stakeholders as a result of hurricanes since 1998 and, in conversations with us, they indicated that these challenges were more difficult than anticipated. Port plans we reviewed addressed some of these types of vulnerabilities to natural disasters. However, ports still identified such vulnerabilities as a significant obstacle to their ability to return to predisaster operational levels. Several ports cited examples about how their personnel had evacuated and, for numerous reasons, were unable to return to work. For example, several Port of Gulfport employees lost their homes during Hurricane Katrina and had no local living arrangements for themselves or their families. Likewise, the Port of New Orleans said its operations were stifled by the lack of personnel and labor in both Hurricane Katrina and Hurricane Rita. At the Port of Port Arthur, lack of power for area homes kept employees from returning immediately, causing temporary delays in port operations.

Port authorities also did not anticipate the extent to which their communications systems would be impacted. High winds and flooding from the hurricanes rendered phone lines out of service. With phones lines down, port authorities were unable to get in touch with their staff or other port stakeholders to share information. For instance, we learned that approximately 50 percent of phones at the Port of Mobile were out of service for about 2 to 4 weeks. Other ports, including New Orleans, Pascagoula, and Port Arthur, also experienced phone outages and reported limitations in cell phone reception.

Ports also identified coordination challenges with local, state, and federal stakeholders while planning for and recovering from natural disasters. At the local level, one coordination problem port officials experienced was in re-entering the port after the storm. For example, in Gulfport, port officials were denied entry to port property for the first 2 weeks following Hurricane Katrina. Similarly in Houston, law enforcement agencies blocked roads for access back into Houston after the Hurricane Rita evacuation. In some cases, port officials did not have the proper credentials required by local police and other emergency management officials to be allowed roadway access through the city to their port.

In other instances, we found that ports experienced varied levels of coordination with local emergency management agencies, especially regarding planning efforts. For example, Mobile County Emergency Management officials affirmed that they have a close working relationship with the Port of Mobile, where they have helped the port conduct risk assessments and emergency planning activities, and where they coordinate with port officials on other plans involving safety, security, and the environment. Conversely, Port of Gulfport and Harrison County Emergency Management officials in Mississippi said they had limited contact and coordination regarding emergency recovery. One county emergency management official said that although the agency has made efforts to share planning documents with the port, the agency is required to work through the Mississippi Emergency Management Agency and follow any guidance in the state emergency plan to request resources from or provide assistance to the port.

At the federal level, one coordination issue reported by port stakeholders involved difficulties in coordinating with FEMA for recovery resources. Some local emergency management officials and port officials that we interviewed expressed concerns about the level of interaction with FEMA officials before an incident occurs. For example, Port of Jacksonville officials said they would like to see FEMA take a more active role in the disaster planning process, such as participation on the AMSC at the local level or coordinating with the Florida State Department of Community Affairs at the state level.[11] Similarly, Port of Los Angeles officials said effective communication with FEMA is essential and that they would like to communicate more clearly with FEMA about reimbursement policies before a disaster takes place. In fact, in November 2006, port officials from Los Angeles and Oakland held a joint meeting with FEMA and the California Office of Emergency Services to discuss the current federal and state regulations and practices regarding disaster relief fund and reimbursement policy.

Port stakeholders also expressed concerns about coordinating with FEMA after an incident occurred, including inconsistencies in information and difficulty in appropriately completing FEMA forms and other documents required for reimbursement. At the county emergency management level, one agency official cited an inconsistency of the interpretation of FEMA policies and changing personnel as some of the challenges in working with FEMA. This official suggested that interacting with FEMA officials more frequently before a disaster would help the port authority better understand which personnel to contact in an emergency situation. The official said this coordination problem became obvious during the Hurricane Katrina recovery effort when, after the port had made several requests, FEMA did not send a representative to the area Port officials in Gulfport also found it difficult to reconcile their damages using FEMA's cost estimate process. To resolve the paperwork confusion, the Port of Gulfport hired an outside company to deal with FEMA directly and to handle all reimbursement-related issues on their behalf. While Port of Gulfport officials recognized that FEMA's attention to detail was an effort to prevent fraud and abuse, they also said FEMA staff could have done a better job in providing guidance about the reimbursement process.

Besides having coordination challenges with FEMA, we learned that several ports were unclear about resources that were available for recovery from the Maritime Administration. Immediately following Hurricane Katrina, the Gulf area was in need of critical resources such as power, water, and personnel. However, due to infrastructure damages around the area, it was difficult to get these resources into ports. As such, The Maritime Administration provided, with the concurrence of the Department of Defense, ready reserve vessels for FEMA's use. These ready reserve vessels are strategic sealift assets usually used for defense purposes that could be used for command and control, housing, power generation, or the movement of water and other supplies. We found that ports' knowledge about these assets and how to request them was limited. For example, port authority officials at one port turned down the Maritime Administration's offer for a housing vessel. The port determined that the deep draft and large size of the vessel might impede commercial traffic and block other vessels from entering their port. Port officials reached this determination without the knowledge that smaller vessels for the same purpose could have been provided by the Maritime Administration. The vessel offered by the Maritime Administration, however, was instead deployed to the Port of New Orleans area to house first responders.

Port Authorities Have Various Efforts Under Way to Mitigate Challenges

Many port authorities have taken steps to address the challenges resulting from recent natural disasters. Individually, they have taken such steps as upgrading communications equipment, adding backup communications approaches and power equipment, and creating alternative sites for administrative operations and storage of computer data. Collectively, they have shared best practices for disaster planning and response, most notably through an industry-wide publication with detailed planning steps and guidelines. Port authorities that were not directly impacted by recent disaster events have also taken steps to revise their planning efforts, including greater coordination with other port stakeholders. Many port authorities have adapted or improved existing stakeholder forums to assist in facilitating port planning for natural disasters. At the federal level, agencies such as the Maritime Administration have taken steps to assist ports in identifying federal resources available for disaster response and recovery.

Steps Taken Include Port-Specific and Industry-Wide Actions

As a result of the lessons learned from recent natural disasters, port authorities report taking many steps to mitigate vulnerabilities. One mitigation tactic reported by many port authorities is to add equipment and develop redundant systems to help during any recovery efforts. The most frequent redundancy added was in creating communications alternatives. Various port authorities reported purchasing communications equipment that does not necessarily rely on traditional land lines for calling, such as analog pagers, wireless handheld devices, CB radios, and satellite phones. They also integrated more sophisticated communications hardware and software programs. Some ports, such as Houston and San Diego, implemented 1-800 phone numbers to receive calls from port personnel. As an additional precaution, the Port of Houston utilizes call centers located out of state in areas that are less likely to have been impacted by the same storm. In another effort to route calls out of the impacted area, the Port of New Orleans has also been assigned phone numbers with alternative area codes.

Besides making improvements to communications systems, many port authorities took steps related to power and administrative operations. Seven port authorities reported purchasing or arranging for alternative power supplies that could be used during an outage. For example, the Port of New Orleans purchased generators after the 2005 hurricane season. Ports also recognized the need for administrative and information technology location alternatives. Four port authorities reported changing their alternative administrative sites since recent storms Port authorities also told us that they have changed the way they back up and store their electronic data and equipment. For example, the Port of New Orleans previously had its alternative work site only 3 miles away from its regular operations location. Since both operations sites could be susceptible to the same disaster event, Port of New Orleans officials have partnered with the Port of Shreveport, Louisiana, almost 200 miles away, to use Shreveport's facilities as an alternate operations site if the Port of New Orleans is out of business for more than 5 days Further, the two ports have prepared a mutual agreement, which includes cost sharing efforts for information technology infrastructure upgrades at the Port of Shreveport, to better accommodate New Orleans' needs in a disaster.

Another mitigation tactic by ports has been the sharing of best practices and lessons learned from recent natural disasters. Through efforts by the AAPA, a nationwide industry group, ports from across the U.S. and Canada participated in the development of an industry best practices document.[12] In developing this document, AAPA organized various working groups, which included port officials from ports that had been affected by recent natural disasters, as well as ports that had not been affected. Acting as a forum for port officials to share their experiences with natural disasters, these working groups were able to develop a manual focused on port planning and recovery efforts. Vetted by AAPA members, the manual includes planning for emergency operations, communications, damage assessments, insurance and FEMA claims processes, coordinating with federal agencies, and overall emergency planning objectives.

Another industry group, the GICA,[13] has worked closely with the Corps, Coast Guard and other maritime agencies to implement new practices for a more efficient response to maritime related incidents. Many of these efforts have been implemented as result of recent hurricanes. For example, a special Logistics Support Center is set up during response times for the sole purpose of assisting the Corps and Coast Guard with contracting special equipment, including water, fuel and crane barges, towing vessels, pumps, and generators. Regarding clearing the waterways, GICA barge members have provided knowledgeable waterway operators and state-of-the-art boats to assist Coast Guard personnel in conducting channel assessments immediately following a storm. In an effort to restore aids to navigation, GICA contacts also towed 50 temporary buoys and supplied aircraft for aerial surveillance of the waterways. Moreover, the Corps, Coast Guard, and GICA formed the Gulf Coast Inland Waterways Joint Hurricane Team to develop a protocol for storm response Finalized in July 2006, the Joint Hurricane Response Protocol[14] is an effort to more fully develop lessons learned from previous hurricane seasons and waterways management practices, with the goal of implementing an effective restoration of Gulf Coast maritime commerce following future storms.

Ports that have not experienced problems as a result of recent disasters but that are nonetheless susceptible to disaster threats have also responded to these lessons learned by other ports. For example, the Port of Tacoma hired a consultant to assist in developing a business continuity plan. The Port of Jacksonville has also undertaken a comprehensive enhancement to its continuity of operations plan. Likewise, as a result of lessons learned from the Loma Prieta Earthquake in Oakland, the Port of Los Angeles developed more stringent seismic building codes. Additionally, Port of Savannah officials told us that they, too, have changed their prehurricane crane operations based on lessons learned from hurricanes in the Gulf region.

Ports Have Taken Steps to Improve Stakeholder Coordination

We found several examples of port efforts to improve stakeholder coordination, including utilizing existing forums to coordinate disaster planning, as well as realigning and enhancing their current plans. Regarding the use of existing forums, port authorities in both New Orleans and Mobile said they were using their AMSC to coordinate response and recovery efforts. Moreover, GAO has previously reported that in the wake of Hurricane Katrina, information was shared collaboratively through AMSCs to determine when it was appropriate to close and then reopen the port.[15] Port-specific coordination teams, such as those at the Port of Houston, have also used their lessons learned to improve coordination for natural disaster planning Houston's port coordination teams are an outgrowth of the port's relationships with other maritime stakeholders in the Houston-Galveston Navigation Safety Committee,[16] which includes a wide variety of waterway users and operators In another example, the Port of Oakland works closely with the City Disaster Council on emergency planning and participates in various exercises with city, county, and state officials.

We also found several examples of how ports have aligned their local planning with the national planning structure and have identified various ways to enhance their current coordination plans. The national structure, which includes NIMS and NRP, is designed to provide a consistent framework and approach for emergency management Port plans that we reviewed, in particular those from ports in hurricane impacted areas, have identified the importance of adapting to this national structure and emergency response system For example, the Port of Mobile's emergency operations plan explains that the complexity of incident management and the growing need for stakeholder coordination has increased its need for a standard incident management system. Therefore, the Port of Mobile's emergency operations plan outlines the use of an incident management framework from which all agencies can work together in an efficient and effective manner Some port authorities making changes have not experienced any significant impact from recent disasters For instance, Port of Jacksonville officials reported that Hurricane Katrina impacts in the Gulf region prompted them to revise their disaster preparedness plans, including reorganizing the plans to reflect NIMS language and alignment with NRP guidelines. Similarly, Port of San Diego officials said they hired a consultant to assist them with drafting their emergency response and business continuity plan San Diego's plan prioritized risks, clarified roles and responsibilities of key departments, and laid out directions on how to better coordinate with local emergency management officials during a disaster event.

Federal Agencies Have Attempted to Help Ports Strengthen Recovery Efforts

Since the 2005 hurricane season, federal agencies have also taken steps to help port authorities strengthen ports' ability to recover from future natural disasters These efforts have focused on increased coordination and communication with stakeholders and also on building stakeholders' knowledge about federal resources for port recovery efforts The efforts primarily involve four federal agencies that in some fashion work directly with ports—the Maritime Administration, the Coast Guard, FEMA and the U.S. Army Corps of Engineers Efforts for those four agencies are as follows:

Maritime Administration Efforts: The Maritime Administration has taken two main steps: developing an approach for activating maritime assets in disaster recovery, and updating a risk management guidebook During the 2005 hurricane season, the Maritime Administration emerged as a critical resource for the Gulf area by providing vessels from the nation's National Defense Ready Reserve Fleet to enable recovery operations and provide shelter for displaced citizens Since that time, FEMA developed a one-time plan—the Federal Support Plan, which was cited specifically for the 2006

Hurricane Season and specific to the federal government's response efforts in the State of Louisiana The Maritime Administration contributed to this plan by identifying government and commercial maritime capabilities that could be employed in response to a disaster.[17] According to Maritime Administration officials, while the information is focused on the Gulf area, it could be easily adapted to other areas in the United States if a disaster occurred To date, the Maritime Administration is completing the process of identifying needs and capabilities and plans to provide a directive regarding capabilities to its regional offices in June 2007. However, no strategy exists for communicating this information to ports.

The Maritime Administration is also currently updating its publication titled *Port Risk Management and Insurance Guidebook* (2001). This publication is the Maritime Administration's "best practices" guide for port risk management Developed primarily to assist smaller ports in conducting risk management, it includes information on how ports can obtain insurance coverage, facilitate emergency management and port security, and apply risk management The Maritime Administration began updating the guidebook after the 2005 hurricane season According to officials from the Maritime Administration, ports are actively using this guidebook, especially since many of the contributors are port directors and risk managers at the ports.

While these efforts demonstrate the Maritime Administration's increased involvement in assisting ports in planning for future disasters, we also observed that Maritime Administration regions vary in their level of communication and coordination with ports According to a Maritime Administration official, the Gulf and East Coast regions have been working with FEMA regional offices to quickly activate needed assets in case of a disaster However, while the Gulf and East Coast regions have been strengthening these relationships, other regions may not have the same level of coordination We found, in general, port authorities' interaction with the Maritime Administration was limited for natural disaster planning, and the ports we spoke to said they usually did not work directly with the agency in disaster planning.[18] This view was echoed by Maritime Administration officials who said that the relationship between the agency's regional offices and the ports in their respective areas varied across the country.

Coast Guard efforts: Coast Guard efforts in natural disaster planning varied considerably from port to port and were most extensive in the Gulf. While in general, the Coast Guard was considered successful in its missions during the 2005 hurricane season, its officials said they were taking additional steps in improving planning for recovery efforts with port stakeholders based on their experiences with recent natural disasters. For example, at the Port of Mobile, Coast Guard officials said that participating in an actual Incident Command System[19]emergency centers has been as helpful as exercises and, since the 2005 hurricane season, they have utilized such a unified command at least 10 times in preparation for potential hurricane landfalls in the region. At other ports, the Coast Guard had a more limited role in assisting ports in planning for natural disasters.

Even at ports that had not experienced substantial damage from a recent natural disaster, however, Coast Guard units were applying lessons learned from other ports' experiences and increasing their level of involvement For example, the Port of Houston sustained minimal damage from Hurricane Rita; however, Coast Guard officials said that they identified areas where they could make improvements. The Coast Guard at the Port of Houston leads a recovery planning effort through port coordination teams, which include stakeholders such as the port authority, Coast Guard, and private operators, working together during disaster recovery efforts. These teams are all-hazards focused and are activated differently for terrorist incidents or natural disasters Coast Guard officials said that although the teams were successful in planning for Hurricane Rita, there were areas for improvement, including outreach and training with port stakeholders and communication. Further, Coast Guard officials at the Port of Tacoma said that other ports' experiences with recent natural disasters has generated interest in them becoming more involved in the planning and coordination of natural disasters. They also indicated they were interested in adapting, in some form, a planning forum similar to the Port of Houston's port coordination teams.

FEMA efforts: While state and local emergency management agencies assist in facilitating FEMA disaster planning at the port level, FEMA has several efforts underway to improve its assistance to ports for disaster recovery For instance, FEMA officials said that through the Public Assistance Program, FEMA is able to provide assistance to ports that are eligible applicants after a major disaster or emergency Based on lessons learned from Hurricane Katrina, FEMA is also reviewing and updating its policies and guidance documents associated with this program. To administer the program, FEMA will coordinate closely with federal, state, and local authorities (including emergency management agencies) through its regional offices. Officials also said that through planning, training, and exercise activities sponsored by DHS, they hope to have greater opportunities to interact and coordinate with port authorities and other local agencies before disasters occur. Further, officials agree that coordination with their local counterparts is an important part of emergency management and disaster recovery efforts.

U.S. Army Corps of Engineers efforts: Although the U.S. Army Corps of Engineers generally does not conduct natural disaster planning with ports, staff at the district level have made some efforts to increase their level of involvement in this process, particularly in the Gulf region. For example, district U.S. Army Corps of Engineers staff have (1) organized and chaired yearly hurricane planning forums to which all ports in the region are invited; (2) organized prestorm teleconferences for port stakeholders, National Oceanic and Atmospheric Administration, U.S. Navy, and in some instances, the media; (3) participated in the Coast Guard's Partner Emergency Action Team, which specifically address disaster preparedness; (4) geographically aligned with the Coast Guard to better facilitate coordination during an emergency; and (5) implemented informational training on planning for hurricanes to ports and other maritime stakeholders. Many of these improvements were implemented as a result of Hurricane Ivan (2001) and the hurricanes from the 2005 season. However, the extent of the U.S. Army Corps of Engineers participation in natural disaster planning with ports varies For instance, U.S. Army Corps of Engineers representatives in Savannah said they do not play a significant role in the port's natural disaster planning for recovery efforts. Similarly in Jacksonville, U.S. Army Corps of Engineers officials explained that their primary natural disaster recovery duty at the Port of Miami is to repair the federal channel and they do not participate in the port authority's disaster planning efforts. However, the Jacksonville U.S. Army Corps of Engineers does cooperate with the Coast Guard's Marine Safety Office in Jacksonville in the development of their hurricane preparedness plan. For this effort, it assisted in determining what vessels could remain in port during a hurricane and what vessels would be required to leave.

Current Planning Approach Lessens Effective Coordination among All Port Stakeholders

Most port authorities we reviewed conduct planning for natural disasters separately from planning for homeland security threats Federal law established security planning requirements that apply to ports Similar requirements do not exist with regard to natural disaster planning. The ports we contacted used markedly different approaches to natural disaster planning, and the extent and thoroughness of their plans varied widely. A few ports have integrated homeland security and natural disaster planning in what is called an all-hazards approach, and this approach appeared to be generating benefits and is in keeping with experts' recommendations and with the newest developments in federal risk management policy. A consequence of the divided approach was a wide variance in the degree to which port stakeholders were involved in natural disaster planning and the degree to which port authorities were aware of federal resources available for disaster recovery. For homeland security planning, federal law provides for the establishment of AMSCs with wide stakeholder representation, and some ports are using these committees or another similar forum with wide representation in their disaster planning efforts DHS, which through the Coast Guard oversees the AMSCs, provides an example of how to incorporate a wider of scope of committee activity.

Port-Level Natural Disaster Planning Is Primarily Conducted Separately from Other Threats

Of the ports we visited, more than half developed plans for natural disasters separately from plans that address security threats This is likely due to the requirement that port authorities carry out their planning for homeland security under the federal framework created by the Congress in the Maritime Transportation Security Act (MTSA),[20] under which all port operators are required to draft individual security plans identifying security vulnerabilities and approaches to mitigate them. Under the Coast Guard's implementing regulations, these plans are to include such items as measures for access control, responses to security threats, and drills and exercises to train staff and test the plan.[21] The plans are "performance-based"; that is, the security outcomes are specified, but the stakeholders are free to identify and implement appropriate solutions as long as these solutions achieve the specified outcomes Because of the similarities in security and natural hazard planning these plans can be useful for guiding natural disaster response.

MTSA also provided the Secretary of Homeland Security with the authority to create AMSCs at the port level. These committees—with representatives from the federal, state, local, and private sectors—offer a venue to identify and deal with vulnerabilities in and around ports, as well as a forum for sharing information on issues related to port security. The committee assists the Coast Guard's COTP in developing an area maritime security plan, which complements the facility security plans developed by individual port operators. The plan provides a framework for communication and coordination among port stakeholders and law enforcement officials and identifies and reduces vulnerabilities to security threats throughout the port area.

In contrast, port authority and operator natural disaster planning documents are generally not required by law and vary widely. According to one member from the AAPA, ports will have various interrelated plans, such as hurricane readiness plans, emergency operations plans, engineering plans, and community awareness and emergency response plans. Taken as a whole, the distinct plans for a particular port may represent the port's risk management approach to disaster planning.

In addition, port natural disaster plans are not reviewed by the Coast Guard. Representatives of the Coast Guard at locations we visited confirmed they do not review port authority or port operator planning documents pertaining to natural disaster planning. For example, officials at the Port of Oakland and the Port of Tacoma said they do not review the port or port stakeholders planning documents for natural disaster planning. Coast Guard officials at the Port of Savannah also noted that they do not review the hurricane plans for port operators. They contended that they do not have the expertise to advise the operators on how to protect or restart their particular operations. Moreover, natural disaster plans developed by port authorities generally do not apply to the port's private operators. Only in one case did a port authority state that it required its private operators' to draft a natural disaster plan.

Under the Separate Approach, Disaster Plans Show Wide Variation

We found that the thoroughness of natural disaster plans varied considerably from port to port. For instance, the Port of Mobile had a relatively thorough plan. The Port of Mobile was affected by three major hurricanes in 2005-2006 Roughly a year after Hurricane Katrina, the Alabama State Port Authority completed an extensive emergency operations plan, based on an analysis that considered natural, man-made, and security-related hazards. The operations plan describes preparedness, response, recovery, and mitigation procedures for each identified threat, establishes requirements for conducting exercises, and establishes a schedule for regular plan reviews and updates.[22] In contrast, the Port of Morgan City does not have a written plan for preparing for natural disaster threats, but instead relies on port personnel to assess disaster risk and prepare appropriately. Following a disaster, the port authority relies on senior personnel to direct recovery efforts as needed.

In the absence of uniform federal guidance for port disaster planning, some local governments have instituted local planning requirements. The differences in these local guidelines account for some of the variation in the content and thoroughness of port disaster plans. For example, the Miami-Dade County Emergency Management Office helps to coordinate disaster preparedness for all county agencies, including the Port of Miami. As such, the port submits its hurricane plans and continuity of operations plan to the office each year for review, which provides a certain level of quality assurance. By comparison, the Port of Los Angeles found local seismic building codes were insufficient to reach the desired level of preparedness, so the port developed its own seismic codes to guide infrastructure construction and repair.

Combined All-Hazards Approach Shows Promise for Improved Planning

In contrast to the disjunctional planning for both natural disasters and security at ports, industry experts encourage the unified consideration of all risks faced by the port. Unified disaster preparedness planning requires that all of the threats faced by the port, both natural and man-made, be considered together. This is referred to as an all-hazards approach. Experts consider it to offer several advantages:

- *Application of planning resources to both security and natural disaster preparedness* Because of the similarities between the effects of terrorist attacks and natural or accidental disasters, much of the planning, personnel, training, and equipment that form the basis of protection, response, and recovery capabilities are similar across all emergency events. As we have previously reported, the capabilities needed to respond to major disasters, whether the result of terrorist attack or nature, are similar in many ways.[23] Unified risk management can enhance the efficiency of port planning efforts because of the similarity in recovery plans for both natural and security-related disasters. One expert noted that responding to a disaster would likely be the same for a security incident and a natural disaster incident from an operational standpoint.

- *Efficient allocation of disaster-preparation resources* An all-hazards approach allows the port to estimate the relative impact of mitigation alternatives and identify the optimal mix of investments in these alternatives based on the costs and benefits of each. The exclusion of certain risks from consideration, or the separate consideration of a particular type of risk, gives rise to the possibility that risks will not be accurately assessed or compared, and that too many or too few resources will be allocated toward mitigation of a particular risk. Port risk management experts noted that, in the absence of an all-hazards risk management process, it is difficult to accurately assess and address the full spectrum of threats faced by a port.

Federal Actions Reflect Movement Toward All-Hazards Approach

At the federal level, the Congress has introduced various elements of an all-hazards approach to risk management and assistance to ports. Examples are as follows:

- *Single response approach to all types of emergency events* NIMS and NRP, which were implemented by DHS, provide a unified framework for responding to security and natural disaster events. NIMS is a policy document that defines roles and responsibilities of federal, state, and local first responders during all types of emergency events. The NRP is designed to integrate federal government domestic prevention, protection, response, and recovery plans into a single operational plan for all-hazards and all-emergency response disciplines. Using the framework provided by NIMS, the NRP describes operational procedures for federal support to emergency managers and organizes capabilities, staffing, and equipment resources in terms of functions that are most likely to be needed during emergency events. In addition, along with the NRP and NIMS, DHS has developed the National Preparedness Goal, as required by Homeland Security Presidential Directive 8. Considered as a group, these three documents are intended to guide investments in emergency preparedness and response capabilities for all hazards. An inability to effectively perform these critical tasks would, by definition, have a detrimental impact on effective protection, prevention, response, and recovery capabilities.
- *Broadened focus for risk mitigation efforts* Security and Accountability for Every Port Act, passed in October 2006, contains language mandating

that the Coast Guard institute Port Security Training and Exercise Programs to evaluate response capabilities of port facilities to respond to acts of terrorism, natural disasters, and other emergencies.[24]

Officials from the DHS Preparedness Directorate's Grants and Training Office also noted that the criteria for the Port Security Grant Program is beginning to reflect the movement toward all-hazards planning in the future DHS officials stated that the program may evolve to focus more on portwide risk management, rather than on risk mitigation for particular assets Furthermore, grant applications that demonstrate mitigation of natural hazard risks in addition to security risks may be more competitive. Other officials noted that while the program may focus more on all hazards in the future, it will remain focused on security priorities for now.

Another agency-level movement toward the all-hazards approach is occurring in the Coast Guard's improvement of a computer tool it uses to compare security risks for targets throughout a port, including areas not under the jurisdiction of a local port authority. This tool, called the Maritime Security Risk Assessment Model (MSRAM), provides information for the U.S. Coast Guard COPT to use in deciding the most efficient allocation of resources to reduce security risks at a port. The Coast Guard is developing an all-hazards risk assessment and management system, partially fed by MSRAM, which will allow comparison of risks and risk-mitigation activities across all goals and hazards The Coast Guard directs the Area Maritime Security Committee to use MSRAM in the development of the Area Maritime Security Plan Given that the Coast Guard is enhancing the MSRAM with a tool that will incorporate natural hazards, the risks addressed in the Area Maritime Security Plan could likely include both natural and security threats in the future.

An all-hazards approach is in many ways a logical maturation of port security planning, which saw an aggressive homeland security expansion in the wake of the terrorist attacks of September 11, 2001. One expert in seismic risk management we spoke with said port officials he contacted indicated that they were not focused on natural disaster risk because, in their view, the federal government wanted them to focus on security risks instead. At some ports, hurricanes or earthquakes may be a greater threat than terrorism, and a case can be made that overall risk to a port might be more effectively reduced through greater investment in mitigating these risks. While federal law provides guidance on addressing security risks through MTSA[25] and its implementing regulations, it does not provide similar guidance pertaining to mitigation of natural disaster threats.

Our previous work on risk management has examined the challenges involved in comparing risk across broader threat categories.[26] A risk management framework that analyzes risks based on the likelihood that they will occur and the consequences of their occurrence is a useful tool for ensuring that program expenditures are prioritized and properly focused. In light of the competition for scarce resources available to deal with the threats ports face, a clear understanding of the relative significance of these threats is an important step.

Port Authorities Using an All-Hazards Approach Indicate Benefits Resulted

Two port authorities we reviewed have begun to take an all-hazards approach to disaster planning by developing planning documents and structures that address both security risks and natural disasters, and officials at both ports said this approach yielded benefits.[27] At the Port of Houston, the Coast Guard used its authority to mandate the creation of port coordination teams by creating teams that include all port stakeholders and combine planning and response efforts for both security and natural disaster threats. This unified approach to risk management has allowed the port to respond efficiently to disasters when they occur, according to port officials. In particular, they said, the organization of the team changes to match the nature of the threat. For security threats, the teams are organized geographically and do not require that the entire port close down, thereby appropriately matching resources to the threat being faced. For natural disasters, the teams are organized functionally because of the more dispersed nature of the threat.

Following the 2005 hurricane season, the Port of Mobile convened a task force to reorganize its disaster planning to address both security incidents and natural disasters. The task force, which recently completed its emergency operations plan, included the Port Authority Police Chief; Harbormaster; Environmental, Health and Safety Manager; and representatives of the port's rail, cargo, intermodal and development divisions. A member of the county emergency management agency also served on the task force to provide expert guidance on emergency response planning.

Port stakeholders in other ports that had not moved to an all-hazards approach also said preparedness and response practices for security incidents and natural disasters are sufficiently similar to merit combined planning. Officials in several ports said that although they are required to allocate certain resources to security risk mitigation, overall risk to the port would be more effectively reduced if they had the flexibility to allocate some of those resources to mitigating natural disaster risk.

Under the Separate Approach, Gaps Exist in Coordinating Maritime Stakeholders and Obtaining Information about Federal Resources

We have previously reported that, for homeland security planning, the AMSCs established under federal law have been an effective coordination tool.[28] These committees have provided a structure to improve the timeliness, completeness, and usefulness of information sharing between federal and nonfederal stakeholders. Port stakeholders said that the committees were an improvement over previous information-sharing efforts because they established a formal structure for communicating information and new procedures for sharing information. Stakeholders stated that, among other things, the committees have been used as a forum for sharing assessments of vulnerabilities, providing information on illegal or suspicious activities, and providing input on Area Maritime Security Plans. Stakeholders, including private operators, said the information sharing had increased their awareness of security issues around the port and allowed them to identify and address security issues at their facilities. Likewise, Coast Guard officials said the information they received from nonfederal participants had helped in mitigating and reducing risks.

In contrast to the regulatory requirements for the establishment of AMSCs, there are no nationwide federal mandates for all-hazards planning forums that involve a broad spectrum of stakeholders in disaster planning. In the absence of any consistent requirement or approach, we found substantial variation in the maturity of, and participation in, natural disaster planning forums at ports. As table 3 shows, the level of activity and the participants varied considerably. Some ports utilized their AMSC for both types of planning, while others conducted natural disaster planning efforts primarily within the local area's broader emergency management forums, and still others conducted their planning piecemeal, with various entities meeting separately and not in one coordinated forum.

Table 3: Natural Disaster Planning Forums at Ports GAO Visited

Port	Description of forum
Tacoma	The port does not have a central forum for coordinating stakeholder natural disaster planning efforts. Instead, occasional disaster preparedness exercises with the county emergency management agency and the Coast Guard provide stakeholders with opportunities to share lessons learned. However, the Port of Tacoma conducts planning activities with the county emergency management department.
Oakland	The port is an active member of the City's Emergency Management Board (Disaster Council) which works closely with the Port of Oakland on emergency planning and testing of plans/exercises. The port is also involved in a number of city, county, and statewide exercises.
Houston	The port has an all-hazards forum through the Port Coordination Team and its constituent Port Coordination Centers. These centers and team include representatives from the port authority and the Coast Guard and a range of stakeholders from private entities. The forum plans for natural disasters and security threats and is activated differently depending on the type of event. However, the forum does not include representatives from the local emergency management office.
Mobile	The port's AMSC is the most significant forum for disaster planning. Following the 2005 hurricane season, the port authority convened a task force to reorganize its disaster planning to address both security incidents and natural disasters. The task force included stakeholders from across the port area The port also works with the county emergency management agency.
Gulfport	The port authority meets once a year with customers and tenants to discuss hurricane preparedness and review the hurricane plan. The port provides training on transporting cargo during hurricanes and participates in separate response and recovery planning meetings with other maritime stakeholders, such as the U.S. Army Corps of Engineers.

Port	Description of forum
Miami	The primary forum used to discuss natural disaster planning is the Safety First Committee, which discusses a variety of safety issues. The committee is led by the Port of Miami and meets monthly. To address individual private sector stakeholders, a subcommittee meets with individuals as needed.
Savannah	The port authority is involved in several port forums that discuss a variety of issues; emergency issues may be addressed in these forums if they are imminent. Externally, the port authority's primary interactions are with the state for hazard mitigation programming and with the local emergency management office for response and evacuation. Until recently, interaction with the local emergency management office was limited.

Source: GAO

[a] According to port officials, the Port of Houston does coordinate with the local emergency management agency during a disaster event.

The Port of Savannah provides an example of how separate planning for natural disasters and security can lead to a lack of coordination and information-sharing. While officials from the local emergency management agency said they reviewed and provided comments on the Georgia Port Authority's most recent Hurricane Plan and Draft Emergency Operations Plan, this had not traditionally been the case over the past several years. According to a representative from the emergency management agency, if the port is not sharing its emergency operations plans, it makes it difficult for responders in the local area to understand what is happening within the port in terms of planning for natural disasters. Additionally, while the local EMA is enjoying an ongoing productive dialogue with port representatives in developing the Emergency Operations Plan and working on port safety and security issues, they are not having the same level of success with port representatives responsible for hurricane planning. Even so, officials said that they had seen marked improvement in the area of portwide cooperation and involvement among stakeholders.

Port authorities' lack of familiarity with FEMA's programs is another example of the gaps that exist. We found that port authorities' understanding of FEMA's assistance was dependent on their relationship with the local or state emergency management office—a stakeholder that is not necessarily involved in the forums where the port's natural disaster planning occurs. We discussed three FEMA programs with officials from our seven case study ports: the Public Assistance Program, Hazard Mitigation Grant Program and the Predisaster Mitigation Grant Program (see table 4 for brief descriptions). These programs provide ports with funds for disaster mitigation efforts before and after disaster events and assist ports in avoiding costly damages. Of the three programs, port authorities were most knowledgeable about, and most involved with, the Public Assistance Program, although even with this program, some port authorities reported encountering challenges with the process during the 2005 hurricane season. Their knowledge and participation in the two hazard mitigation grant programs was dependent on their involvement with the emergency planning office. FEMA officials told us that no ports have applied as an applicant or subapplicant for the Predisaster Mitigation Program,[29] and only a few had received assistance through the Hazard Mitigation Grant Program since 1998. AAPA officials made the same point—that many ports are unaware, unsure how to navigate or do not understand the resources that are available to them for disasters. In its new best practices manual for natural disaster planning, AAPA included a section regarding various federal resources available, including FEMA.

Table 4: Key FEMA Disaster Assistance Programs

Public Assistance Program [a]	Provides grants for the repair, replacement, or restoration of disaster-damaged, publicly owned facilities and the facilities of certain private nonprofit organizations The federal share is not less than 75 percent of the eligible cost for emergency measures and permanent restoration. The state determines who pays the nonfederal share.
Hazard Mitigation Grant Program[b]	Provides grants to states and local governments to implement long-term hazard mitigation measures after a major disaster declaration. The purpose of program is to reduce the loss of life and property due to natural disasters and to enable mitigation measures to be implemented during the immediate recovery from a disaster. Provides up to 75% of the cost of hazard mitigation measures The State or grantee must provide a 25% match
Predisaster Hazard Mitigation Program[c]	The program provides funds on a competitive basis to states, territories, Indian tribal governments, and communities for hazard mitigation planning and the implementation of mitigation projects prior to a disaster event. Funding these plans and projects reduces overall risks to the population and structures, while also reducing reliance on funding from actual disaster declarations. The nonfederal share of the grant is at least 25. Eligibility for a project grant is dependent on the applicant and sub-applicant having a FEMA approved hazard mitigation plan. States are eligible as applicants for grants and ports are eligible as a subgrantee of the state.

Source: GAO

[a] Established by Robert T Stafford Disaster Relief and Emergency Assistance Act Pub L No 93-288, 88 Stat.143 (1974), codified in 42 U.S.C. ch 68.

[b] Authorized in 42 U.S.C. § 5170c.

[c] Authorized in 42 U.S.C. § 5133.

Conclusions

The 2005 hurricane season emphasized the need for ports to plan for other threats in addition to security. Since the terrorist attacks of September 11, 2001, the country has focused on enhancing its security measures, and ports in particular have been targeted due to their vulnerability and their criticality to the U.S. economy While ports have long prepared to some degree for hurricanes and earthquakes, the hurricanes of 2005 highlighted key areas in which natural disaster planning was often inadequate. Even ports that were not directly impacted by the hurricanes recognized their own vulnerabilities and took additional actions. As ports continue to revise and improve their planning efforts, available evidence indicates that, if ports take a system-wide approach, thinking strategically about using resources to mitigate and recover from all forms of disaster, they will be able to achieve the most effective results. The federally established framework for ports' homeland security planning appears to provide useful elements for establishing an all-hazards approach and adopting these elements appears to be a logical starting point for an all-hazards approach for port authorities. In particular, greater coordination between stakeholders appears important to ensure that available federal resources can be most effectively applied. A forum for sharing information and developing plans across a wide range of stakeholders, as occurs with a port's AMSC, is critical for ensuring that local stakeholders can use federal resources effectively. This is especially the case for mitigation grants administered by the Federal Emergency Management Agency and the Maritime Administration's communication of information regarding making ships and other maritime resources available for disaster recovery.

Recommendations for Executive Action

To help ensure that ports achieve adequate planning for natural disasters and effectively manage risk to a variety of threats, we are recommending that the Secretary of the Department of Homeland Security encourage port stakeholders to use existing forums for discussing all-hazards planning efforts and include appropriate representatives from DHS, the port authority, representatives from the local emergency management office, the Maritime Administration, and vessel and facility owner/operators.

To help ensure that ports have adequate understanding of maritime disaster recovery resources, we recommend that the Secretary of the Department of Transportation direct the Administrator of the Maritime Administration to develop a communication strategy to inform ports of the maritime resources available for recovery efforts.

Agency Comments and Our Evaluation

We provided a draft of this report to DHS, DOT, and DOD for their review and comment.

In DHS's letter, the department generally agreed existing forums provide a good opportunity to conduct outreach to and participation by stakeholders from various federal, state, and local agencies and, as appropriate, industry and nongovernmental organizations. However, the department said it did not endorse placing responsibility for disaster contingency planning on existing committees in ports and said these responsibilities should remain with state and local emergency management planners. Our recommendation was not to place responsibility for such planning within port committees, but rather to use these existing forums as a way to engage all relevant parties in discussing natural disaster planning for ports. The problem we found at various locations we visited was that all parties have not been involved in these efforts. In our view, these committees represent a ready way to accomplish this task. While we understand Coast Guard's concern with diluting existing statutorily mandated port-related committees, we found during the course of our fieldwork that some ports were already using existing port committees effectively to plan for all hazards. Further, we believe that the unique nature of ports and their criticality to goods movement warrants that all ports be encouraged to have a specific forum for all-hazard planning. DHS's letter is reprinted in appendix II. DHS officials provided technical comments and clarifications, which we incorporated as appropriate to ensure the accuracy of our report.

In general, DOT agreed with the facts presented in the report Department officials provided a number of comments and clarifications, which we incorporated as appropriate to ensure the accuracy of our report. The department generally concurred with GAO's recommendation.

Additionally, DOD generally agreed with the facts presented in the report Department officials provided some technical comments and clarifications, which we incorporated as appropriate to ensure the accuracy of our report.

We will send copies of this report to the interested congressional committees, the Secretary of Transportation, and other interested parties. We also will make copies available to others upon request. In addition, the report will be available at no charge on the GAO Web site at http://www.gao.gov.

If you or your staff has any questions about this report, please contact me at (202) 512-6570 or sigerrudk@gao.gov. Contact points for our Offices of Congressional Relations and Public Affairs may be found on the last page of this report. GAO staff who made major contributions to this report are listed in appendix III.

Katherine Siggerud Director,
Physical Infrastructure

List of Committees

The Honorable Daniel K. Inouye
Chairman
Committee on Commerce, Science and Transportation
United States Senate

The Honorable Joseph I. Lieberman
Chairman
The Honorable Susan M. Collins
Ranking Member
Committee on Homeland Security and Governmental Affairs
United States Senate

The Honorable Robert C. Byrd
Chairman
Committee on Appropriations
United States Senate

The Honorable James Oberstar
Chairman
Committee on Transportation and Infrastructure
House of Representatives

The Honorable Bennie G. Thompson
Chairman
Committee on Homeland Security
House of Representatives

The Honorable David E. Price
Chairman
Subcommittee on Homeland Security
Committee on Appropriations
House of Representatives

Endnotes

[1] The Dante B. Fascell Port of Miami-Dade is owned and managed by the local government, Miami-Dade County.

[2] In this report, "port" usually refers to one of two things: (1) the port authority, or (2) the collective group of stakeholders. We have taken care to ensure that the reference intended is clear. Where necessary, we have inserted clarifying language (such as "port authority") to help ensure clarity.

[3] Maritime Transportation Security Act of 2002, Pub L No 107-295, 116 Stat 2064.

[4] GAO, *Homeland Security: DHS' Efforts to Enhance First Responders' All-Hazards Capabilities Continue to Evolve,* GAO-05-652 (Washington, D.C.: July, 11, 2005).

[5] We chose 1998 as the cutoff date for recent disasters based on the available data from FEMA.

[6] See, for example, GAO, Risk Management: Further Refinements Needed to Assess Risks and Prioritize Protective Measures at Ports and Other Critical Infrastructure, GAO-06-91 (Washington, D.C.: Dec 15, 2005).

[7] See table 2 for federal agencies involved.

[8] Pub L No 107-296, 116 Stat 2135 (2002).

[9] Homeland Security Presidential Directive 8 (HSPD-8).

[10]GAO-06-91.

[11] The Florida State Department of Community Affairs is the department that houses the state emergency management agency.

[12] Emergency Preparedness and Continuity of Operations Planning: *Manual for Best Practices*, American Association of Port Authorities, Prepared by: Phyllis Saathoff, Managing Director, Port Freeport September 2006.

[13] GICA is maritime trade association that is an advocate for issues regarding the Gulf Intracoastal Waterway, which is an inland navigable waterway located along the Gulf Coast

One of GICA's missions is to work with it members, as well as the Coast Guard and Corps, to identify opportunities to improve the safety and efficiency of the Gulf Intracoastal Waterway.

[14] Gulf Coast Inland Waterways Joint Hurricane Response Protocol: Prepared by the Gulf Coast Joint Hurricane Team July 2006.

[15] GAO, *Maritime Security: Information Sharing Efforts are Improving*, GAO-06-933T (Washington, D.C.: July 10, 2006).

[16] Also known as HOGANSAC, this committee's 19 members include pilots associations, operators, and environmental and academic interests. The committee addresses a wide range of topics affecting navigation in the area. Other individuals with experience and interest in navigation safety issues serve on working groups established by the committee to examine other issues of local interest.

[17] The primary planning instrument for DOT remains the Emergency Support Function #1 Annex to the National Response Plan; however, the annex does not detail site specific information as was done for this plan.

[18] According to officials from MARAD, the DOT Regional Emergency Transportation Coordinator and Representatives may play a supporting role with regards to communicating and coordinating department response processes and building relationships with local authorities.

[19] The Incident Command System, established under NIMS, is a system for managing all types of major incidents It defines the operating characteristics, interactive management components and structure of incident management and emergency response organizations engaged throughout the life cycle of an incident.

[20] The Maritime Transportation Security Act of 2002 (MTSA), Pub L No 107-295, 116 Stat 2064 contains many of the homeland security requirements related specifically to port security The Area Maritime Security Committees are authorized by section 102 of MTSA, (46 U.S.C. § 70112(a)(2)).

[21] The requirements for security plans are found in 33 C.F.R Part 104, Subpart D for vessels, and 33 C.F.R Part 105, Subpart D for facilities.

[22] Mobile's plan, while relatively thorough, still has gaps in coordination with port stakeholder. Port authority officials noted that they do not share their emergency plans with tenants or outside partners. While many tenants develop their own emergency plans, the port authority does not require them.

[23] GAO-05-652.

[24] Security and Accountability for Every Port Act of 2006, Pub L No 109-347, §113(a) 114(a) 120 Stat 1884 (SAFE Port Act).

[25] Pub L No 107-295, 116 Stat 2064 (2002).

[26] GAO-06-91.

[27] A third port, the Port of Oakland has taken a step toward employing an all-hazards approach The Area AMSC elected to add natural disaster planning information to their Area Maritime Security Plan as a set of appendixes.

[28] GAO-06-933T.

[29] Recently, the Port of Tacoma began participating in the Predisaster Hazard Mitigation Program as a subgrantee of the county.

Appendix I:
Objectives, Scope, and Methodology

This report, initiated under the Comptroller General's authority to examine government operations, examines (1) the challenges port authorities have experienced as a result of recent natural disasters, (2) the efforts under way to address challenges from these disasters, and (3) the manner in which port authorities prepare for disasters and the effect of this approach on their ability to share information with port stakeholders and access federal resources.

To address these objectives, we focused much of our work on 17 U.S. ports We focused primarily on commercial ports and various commercial aspects of these ports. The main criteria we used to select ports for study were as follows:

- *Size of port, based on the value of imported cargo* To ensure a varied size of ports, we selected ports that were among the top 50 in size, but within these 50, we chose ports whose total cargo values were greater than and less than the average cargo value for all 50 top ports.
- *Experience with recent natural disasters* We focused our efforts primarily—but not exclusively—on ports that had some degree of experience with a natural disaster since 1998. Based on Department of Homeland Security (DHS) guidance about the most significant disaster threats and potential hazards, we limited our focus to ports that have hurricane or seismic threats. In particular, we included a number of ports affected by the 2005 hurricane season—primarily hurricanes Katrina, Wilma, and Rita. In all, 10 of the 17 ports we selected were affected by hurricanes that year.
- *Operational type* We chose ports that reflected a range of operating types, including those that (1) manage port operations and provide all services, (2) act as a landlord and lease operations and facilities to tenants, and (3) conduct limited operations in the port and lease facilities to others.
- *Region of the United States* We selected ports from the East, Gulf, and West Coasts. There is an overrepresentation of Gulf region ports to ensure adequate coverage of hurricane affected ports.

In making our selections, we used information from the Maritime Administration, including port demographics operational, legal type, and region from the Public Port Finance Survey Report and Maritime Administration waterborne statistics which report the top 50 ports in terms of total cargo value. We determined that what we found at those ports is not generalizable to all U.S. ports. We used disaster data from Federal Emergency Management Agency (FEMA) to assess how many natural disasters had affected the counties in which each port was located. Based on our review of data documentation, we determined that the data we used in applying our criteria for port selection were sufficiently reliable for our purposes.

We took two approaches to reviewing these ports—site visits and telephone interviews. We conducted site visits at seven ports, as follows:

- Tacoma, Washington
- Houston, Texas
- Oakland, California
- Gulfport, Mississippi
- Mobile, Alabama
- Miami, Florida
- Savannah, Georgia

During these visits, we gathered information from various maritime stakeholders, including officials from port authorities, emergency management agencies, the U.S. Coast Guard, the U.S. Army Corps of Engineers, and the Maritime Administration. Although we talked to four private operators, we excluded interviewing other private operators because their roles and responsibilities vary greatly from port to port and because their efforts for natural disasters, unlike their efforts for homeland security, are not subject to federal requirements or guidelines. We designed our case study interview questions to provide insight on (1) general governance and operations of the port, (2) impacts from recent natural disasters, (3) lessons learned from previous natural disasters, (4) risk management procedures, and (5) stakeholder collaboration.

We conducted telephone interviews with officials at 10 ports, as follows:

- Freeport, Texas
- Jacksonville, Florida
- Los Angeles, California
- Morgan City, Louisiana
- New Orleans, Louisiana
- Pascagoula, Mississippi
- Port Arthur, Texas
- Richmond, Virginia
- San Diego, California
- Wilmington, North Carolina

At these ports, we limited our telephone interviews to port authorities only These semi-structured interviews addressed the same topics as the case study but focused more on damages and lessons learned as a result of recent natural disasters. For both sets of ports, we also reviewed numerous planning documents from port stakeholders including emergency preparedness plans, disaster recovery plans, hurricane operations, hurricane manuals, seismic guidelines, and business continuity plans.

To assess the challenges port authorities experienced as a result of recent natural disasters, we used the interviews we conducted and the documents we obtained from officials at the 17 ports. To determine the efforts under way to address these challenges, we reviewed information from our interviews with and documents from American Association of Port Authorities (AAPA) officials and various federal agencies In particular, we reviewed the *Emergency Preparedness and Continuity of Operations Planning: Manual for Best Practices* that was developed through several working groups coordinated by the AAPA. The working groups provided a forum for port officials across the United States and Canada to share their experience in planning for the impacts of recent natural disasters and to share their best practices. We conducted interviews with the Chair of the working groups and other AAPA officials to gather more information about the working group's procedures and vetting process. Additionally, we interviewed various regional and headquarter officials of the Maritime Administration, U.S. Coast Guard (Coast Guard), Department of Transportation, U.S. Army Corps of Engineers, FEMA, and DHS. We reviewed the following federal risk management plans:

- The draft appendix for maritime resources for the Federal Support Plan The appendix is part of a one-time joint planning document between the Department of Transportation and FEMA for the state of Louisiana (2006 Hurricane Season). The Maritime Administration, an agency within the Department of Transportation, developed this appendix to assist in future recovery efforts by identifying resources, protocols, and organizations for maritime resources.
- The *Port Risk Management and Insurance Guidebook*, developed by the Maritime Administration. This publication is a best practices guide for port risk management, including information on how ports obtain insurance coverage and facilitate emergency management.

To determine how port authorities plan for natural disasters and the effects of that approach on information-sharing among port stakeholders and access to federal resources, we reviewed port and federal disaster planning documents collected from various port stakeholders at each of the seven ports we visited in person. In order to gain an understanding of best practices for such planning efforts, we interviewed academic, industry, and government experts.[1] In particular, we interviewed risk management experts from the following organizations:

- Georgia Institute of Technology's Port Seismic Risk Management Team conducted damage assessments at seven ports in south Louisiana in October 2005 immediately following Hurricane Katrina.

- ABS Consulting has worked with a variety of clients including the Coast Guard, Maritime Administration, and FEMA and thus helped develop several port risk management tools.
- The Office of Grants and Training at DHS administers both Port Security and Homeland Security Grants.
- The Coast Guard has expertise in utilizing the Maritime Security Risk Assessment Model (MSRAM) to assess security risk and has plans to incorporate natural disaster risks into the model.

We also reviewed related laws and mandates that provide federal oversight to ports—namely the Maritime Transportation Security Act of 2002 [2] and its implementing regulations and other applicable law. We also reviewed the Puget Sound area maritime security plan and attended an Area Maritime Security Committee meeting at the Port of Houston-Galveston. To determine steps that federal agencies were taking with regard to all-hazards risk management, we reviewed (1) the Security and Accountability for Every Port Act (SAFE Port Act),[3] which addresses risk mitigation of transportation disruptions, including disruptions caused natural disasters and (2) policy documents including the National Response Plan and the National Incident Management System. We also reviewed a presentation on the Coast Guard's MSRAM.

Our work, which we conducted from December 2005 through February 2007, was conducted in accordance with generally accepted government auditing standards.

Endnotes

1 For risk management, which is a central component of best practices, we limited our investigation to the context of emergency planning and did not address insurance-related risk management.

2 Pub L No 107-295, 116 Stat 2064 (2002).

3 Security and Accountability for Every Port Act of 2006 (SAFE Port Act), Pub L No 109-347, 120 Stat 1884. We also reviewed the SAFE Port Act Conference Report—House Report 109-711.

Appendix II: Comments from the Department of Homeland Security of Homeland Security

U.S. Department of Homeland Security
Washington, DC 20528

Homeland Security

March 13, 2007

Ms. Katherine Siggerud
Director, Physical Infrastructure
U.S. Government Accountability Office
441 G Street, NW
Washington, DC 20548

Dear Ms. Siggerud:

RE: Draft Report GAO-07-412, Port Risk Management: Additional Federal Guidance Would Aid Ports in Disaster Planning and Recovery (GAO Job Code 542083)

The Department of Homeland Security (DHS) appreciates the opportunity to review and comment on the draft report referenced above. The Government Accountability Office (GAO) recommends that the Secretary encourage port stakeholders to use existing forums for discussing all hazards planning efforts and include appropriate representatives from DHS, the port authority, representatives from the local emergency management office, the Maritime Administration, and vessel and facility owner/operators. The intent of the recommendation is to ensure or otherwise encourage ports to adequately plan for natural disasters and effectively manage risk associated with a variety of threats.

Across the nation, the U.S. Coast Guard serves a leadership role in a wide variety of port level committees. Some of these committees specifically address contingency planning such as Area Committees and Area Maritime Security Committees (AMSC), which focus on oil/hazardous material preparedness and response, and port security respectively. Additionally, where applicable, the Coast Guard is formally involved in Harbor Safety Committees that primarily focus on ports and waterways management issues. Each of these committees involves extensive outreach to and participation by stakeholders, including various federal, state, and local agencies, and, as appropriate, industry and non-governmental organizations to address their specific focus areas. At the national level, the Coast Guard provides forums such as the Towing Safety Advisory Committee so that specific maritime stakeholder groups can communicate with the Coast Guard. The National Response Plan establishes a comprehensive all-hazards approach to enhance the ability of the United States to manage domestic incidents. Collectively these various committees and organizations may provide extensive opportunities for stakeholder involvement in contingency planning.

We agree that existing forums provide a good opportunity for the agency/agencies responsible for disaster planning to engage an appropriate array of port stakeholders to ensure the ports are adequately represented. DHS does not, however, endorse placing the responsibility for disaster contingency planning on existing committees as those responsibilities should properly remain with state and local emergency management planners and other responsible government agencies. Additionally, many of the existing port-related committees were statutorily mandated to fulfill specific responsibilities and we must caution against diluting their ability to effectively carry out those missions.

GAO's recommendation does align well with DHS Preparedness Directorate's Office of Grants and Training initiative to, in conjunction with the United States Coast Guard, reach out to appropriate port stakeholders to foster the concept of Port Wide Risk Management. This concept, based on the risk management framework identified in the National Infrastructure Protection Plan, will assist the ports in the management of resources (including federal grant funds) to address all risks encountered in their ports.

A port-wide risk management program will also be fully integrated into the broader regional planning construct that forms the core of the Urban Area Security Initiative (UASI), as well as applicable statewide initiatives. Adoption of a deliberate risk management planning process, consistent with that employed in the UASI and state programs, is also a key focus of the recently signed Security and Accountability For Every Port (SAFE Port) Act.

Sincerely,

Steven J. Pecinovsky

Steven J. Pecinovsky
Director
Departmental GAO/OIG Liaison Office

Appendix III:
GAO Contact and Staff Acknowledgments

GAO Contact

Katherine Siggerud, (202) 512-6570, siggerudk@gao.gov

Staff Acknowledgments

In addition to the individual named above, Sally Moino, Assistant Director; Casey Hanewall; Lindsey Hemly; Christoph Hoashi-Erhardt; Bert Japikse; Erica Miles; Sara Ann Moessbauer; Jamilah Moon; Sharon Silas; Stan Stenerson; and Randall Williamson made key contributions to this report.

DOCUMENT NO. 2

FOREIGN OWNERSHIP: DISCUSSION OF CHALLENGES POSED BY FOREIGN OWNERSHIP TO USING CRITICAL INFRASTRUCTURE

Hearing Before the Subcommittee on Transportation Security and Infrastructure Protection

March 23, 2007

Statement of Sheila Jackson-Lee Subcommittee Chairwoman

I would like to take this opportunity to thank you all for joining us this morning so that we can begin our exploration of the topic of foreign ownership and how it intersects with national security.

A little over a year ago, Congress united to oppose the Administration's failure to conduct adequate oversight when there was a proposal by Dubai Ports World to enter into a deal that would have put Dubai Ports in charge of managing many of our U.S. sea ports. The issue became of particular concern not because Dubai Ports was a foreign company, but because it was one that was controlled by a foreign government.

On the heels of September 11th, this deal raised well-deserved skepticism of how the United States monitors and evaluates foreign ownership of our critical infrastructure. Today, more than a year later, we continue to monitor this issue closely by holding this hearing and others that will explore the Department of Homeland Security's involvement with the Committee on Foreign Investment in the United States, or CFIUS as some call it.

Before 9/11, the CFIUS process was not a strong focus of many Americans. As we know, this country relies on foreign investment. As a recent Congressional Research Service (CRS) publication indicates, foreign investment in the United States could top $160 Billion dollars for 2006. Thus, while foreign investment is a great resource and indicator of our strength in the global economy, we must be vigilant that we do not compromise security. After 9/11, our outlook on foreign investment and especially ownership of critical infrastructure changed. Americans, including myself, began to wonder who's watching what foreign investment is being made in the U.S. and where is it being made.

I, like most Americans, whole-heartedly support capitalism and free trade, yet as events have shown, we need to pursue a vigorous oversight agenda, especially in the area of foreign investment in critical infrastructure. Dubai Ports taught us that we need not just focus in one area of infrastructure, but we need to focus on all areas As the Chairwoman of this Subcommittee which bears the term "infrastructure protection" in its title—I intend to do just that—evaluate how infrastructure is being protected to ensure its here and available when America needs it most.

As we all know, terrorists don't signal or call ahead before they attack. We saw this in Madrid and London, amongst other horrible incidents Terrorists are creative, especially in the ways in which they will attack us . t's not inconceivable that a terrorist might not try and attack us with brute force, but simply by pressing a computer button or by crippling a key asset.

It is with this notion, that I, along with other members of this subcommittee, am seriously committed to protecting critical infrastructure and understanding how the Administration is protecting our vital assets.

One example of how serious we are taking this role in this Committee is by supporting HR 556, Committee on Foreign Investment in the U.S. (CFIUS) Reform Bill. This bill provides needed reform by formalizing and streamlining the structure and duties of the Committee on Foreign Investment in the United States. I am happy to say that I voted to support this bill, along with more than 400 of my colleagues on both sides of the aisle.

This bill addresses many of the concerns raised about CFIUS, especially its current lack of transparency and oversight and Congressional reporting and accountability. This bill adds much clarity to a relatively murky process.

This bill rectifies concerns from the business community by formally establishing CFIUS, its membership, and time lines as to how and when a CFIUS review will be conducted. According to the Congressional Research Service's analysis of HR 556, the bill increases the role of congressional oversight by requiring greater reporting by CFIUS on its actions and allowing for a greater amount of detailed information about CFIUS' operations.

Today, we want to continue exploring the role that the Department of Homeland Security has with CFIUS and how it's accomplishing its goal of overall infrastructure protection. I look forward to the witnesses' testimony and learning about how the CFIUS process and the Department's role can be fortified while protecting the United States' interests in international commerce.

Statement of Stewart A. Baker
Assistant Secretary for Policy
Department of Homeland Security

Madam Chairman, Ranking Member Lungren, Chairman Thompson, Ranking Member King and distinguished members of this Subcommittee, I am pleased to appear before you today to discuss the Committee on Foreign Investment in the United States (CFIUS)—of which the Department of Homeland Security is a member—and about the challenges posed by foreign ownership of critical infrastructure.

Background

I should emphasize at the outset that the CFIUS process is one of DHS's highest priorities. We have significantly increased staff and other resources and have a very robust review process that enables our Department to bring to CFIUS a diversity of viewpoints, expertise, and skills from across our constituent components. The government agencies from which we were formed give us a broad perspective, informed by a thorough understanding of infrastructure threats, vulnerabilities, and consequences.

Since the Department began functioning in March 2003, we have participated in the review of hundreds of foreign acquisitions, many of which have involved the nation's most critical infrastructure, technology, and other assets vital to our national security. In 2006, CFIUS reviewed over 100 transactions. DHS plays a particularly important role in CFIUS reviews of transactions involving critical infrastructure, and when DHS requests mitigation agreements in those cases—a topic to which I'll return in a few minutes—DHS has a leading role in monitoring compliance with those agreements to which they are a party.

DHS interprets its security mandate broadly DHS's implementation of this mandate sometimes gives rise to debate within CFIUS, but it is a healthy debate that ultimately enhances both national security and an open investment climate—twin objectives DHS does not believe can be properly divorced from each other and which DHS always seeks to promote.

Jurisdiction

I want to highlight, however, that CFIUS is not a silver bullet capable of securing all critical infrastructure. In particular, Congress explicitly—and appropriately—limited CFIUS's legal authority to investigations of mergers, acquisitions or takeovers by or with foreign persons that could result in foreign control of persons engaged in interstate commerce in the United States. All CFIUS jurisdictional decisions are made based on a thorough evaluation of the specific facts presented by a given transaction.

Within CFIUS's statutory mandate,—that is, mergers or acquisitions that result in foreign control of U.S. businesses—our review is a searching one.

Our Review Process

DHS generally analyzes the incremental risk presented by an acquisition in three parts: (1) vulnerability; (2) threat; and (3) consequences.

The vulnerability analysis focuses on the assets being acquired. We ask, "what vulnerabilities are exposed by the transaction that may be exploited by someone with bad intent and significant capabilities" (this includes the company acquiring the U.S. operations as well as others who may take advantage of the new management). If a chemical plant is being acquired, for example, we want to know whether the chemicals produced are dangerous and, if so, whether there are significant vulnerabilities and if adequate security plans are in place to protect the physical facility and any sensitive data, systems, and networks.

The threat analysis then asks whether the acquirer has significant capabilities for exploiting the target and has intent to do so. Here we're looking for derogatory information about the buyer. The DNI coordinates preparation of a National Security Threat Assessment for each transaction by the intelligence community (including elements within DHS), which generally serves as the principal source of our threat analysis.

Finally, we ask what the consequences could be if the acquirer successfully exploited the target. To go back to the chemical plant example, we would want to know what would happen if someone exploited critical assets within the plant to cause an explosion or chemical release—how would that affect the surrounding communities? And we may need to know whether theft or exploitation of data, systems, and networks also could present a problem (e.g., within the chemical plant example: could the business systems be exploited to reveal HAZMAT routing information, or could the control systems be compromised to cause a dangerous chemical release?)

We then weigh these three factors—vulnerability, threat, and consequences—to come up with an assessment of the incremental risk presented by the transaction.

Background on Mitigation Agreements

In most transactions that CFIUS reviews, the increase in risk as a result of the foreign acquisition is either non-existent or sufficiently low that CFIUS needs to take no formal action. In other instances, we may see an increase in risk, but we may believe that existing authorities other than Exon-Florio and the International Emergency Economic Powers Act are sufficient to address the risk.

Occasionally, however, we come to the conclusion that the transaction may impair national security, that the incremental risk posed by the transaction cannot be adequately addressed by existing law, and that the risk can and should be mitigated through a CFIUS agreement, as a condition to concluding the review or investigation without further action by the President.

A CFIUS mitigation agreement is an agreement between (I) companies undergoing a CFIUS review and (ii) and one or more of the CFIUS agencies. The purpose of such an agreement is to reduce the perceived national security risks associated with a foreign acquisition, merger, or takeover of a U.S. company subject to review by CFIUS. When the parties come to terms, a mitigation agreement generally will pave the way for the CFIUS agency or agencies involved to recommend that CFIUS allow the transaction to proceed.

Consistent with Exon-Florio and the important U.S. policy interest in maintaining an open investment climate, a CFIUS agency entering into a mitigation agreement seeks to mitigate national security risks using the means least onerous to accomplishing that end. Where CFIUS determines there is a risk to be mitigated, it takes a variety of approaches to mitigation agreements dictated by the particular circumstances of an individual transaction. They range from commitment letters on a specific issue of concern to formal mitigation agreements with detailed commitments including cooperation in the development and execution of security plans. As you would expect, agreements deemed necessary in transactions involving significant risks to critical infrastructure often are the most substantial. These agreements often include some combination of the following:

- Security plan and designated security officer
- Background checks for key personnel
- Limitations on foreign personnel's involvement in certain sensitive tasks
- Certification of export control compliance
- Customer lists
- Notifications of certain security incidents, such as cyber attacks
- Compliance with various appropriate international, industry, and/or Federal standards, guidelines, and recommended practices
- Right to site visits and access to books and records
- Audits
- Notification of changes to key management positions
- Liquidated damages for breach

Often the elements of these agreements—e.g., the requirements to have a security plan, security officer, conduct background checks, and comply with appropriate standards and recommended practices—reinforce measures already taken by the companies involved.

In rare cases, CFIUS agencies have asked the companies involved to agree to an "evergreen CFIUS" provision—i.e., the right to re-open a CFIUS case if the companies materially breach the mitigation agreement. The decision to re-open would be made by CFIUS consensus at the highest levels of each agency DHS believes that this extraordinary remedy is appropriate in rare circumstances where the transaction presents significant national security risks, existing remedies will not be adequate to protect the national security, and we anticipate that standard commercial incentives will not be sufficient to compel compliance with the agreement.

Increase in Mitigation Agreements and Compliance Monitoring Work

Given the range of its responsibilities, DHS is often among the agencies which identifies the need to consider a mitigation agreement. Reflecting the increase in filings and other factors there has been a notable increase in the number of mitigation agreements.

Let me give you a few demonstrative statistics. From 2003-2005, the first three years of DHS's existence, we were a party to 13 mitigation agreements. In 2006 alone, DHS was a party to 15 mitigation agreements.

Of course, we recognize that when we enter into these agreements, we assume an obligation to monitor compliance. Our compliance monitoring is not new—GAO credited DHS's efforts in this regard two years ago. For some time DHS has:

- monitored to ensure that companies provide all reports and other deliverables required by mitigation agreements;
- reviewed all reports and other deliverables to ensure that they are accurate, complete, and otherwise satisfy the requirements of the agreements;
- occasionally conducted on-site visits and audits; and
- met with companies to discuss issues of compliance and non- compliance.

What is new, though, is that we've significantly increased the resources devoted to monitoring compliance. For example, whereas site visits previously were sporadic, DHS now has a program in place to conduct regular site visits.

We believe that DHS's CFIUS program represents a success story about the protection of critical infrastructure and other assets, and I would be happy to answer any questions you might have about the program

Statement of Robert B. Stephan
Assistant Secretary for Infrastructure Protection
Department of Homeland Security

Madam Chairman, Ranking Member Lungren, Chairman Thompson, Ranking Member King and distinguished members of the Subcommittee, I appreciate the opportunity to briefly address you on our role in the Committee of Foreign Investment in the United States (CFIUS). Within the Office of Infrastructure Protection, we carefully monitor and analyze the risks posed to the Nation's critical infrastructure and key resources (CI/KR). Part of that analysis includes an assessment of foreign ownership, control and influence over CI/KR Responsibility for that analysis rests with the Department's Homeland Infrastructure Threat and Risk Analysis Center (HITRAC).

HITRAC, a joint infrastructure-intelligence fusion center between the Office of Infrastructure Protection (OIP) and the Office of Intelligence and Analysis (I&A), provides tailored CI/KR threat and risk products to the private sector and our Federal, State, and local security partners. It monitors changes to the threats, vulnerabilities, and consequences associated with the Nation's infrastructure that could affect the national risk profile Significant changes in the CI/KR risk profile will naturally drive changes in our focus, plans, and programs HITRAC helps set the priorities for our collective critical infrastructure protection efforts.

HITRAC also provides focused analytical support directly to the Office of Policy as part of the Department's role on CFIUS. As you know, CFIUS is the interagency committee established in 1975 to review the national security impact of acquisitions, mergers, and takeovers of U.S. assets by foreign persons.-DHS was added as a full member of the committee in February 2003 and joined eleven other members who deliberate each case in accordance with the Exon-Florio statute and applicable Treasury regulations.

Although the DHS Office of Policy has overall responsibility for the Department's CFIUS-related reviews and for making recommendations to the Secretary on how to approach each case, dedicated staff in HITRAC support departmental decision making by preparing risk assessments of every filing that are provided directly to the Office of Policy. These assessments, prepared by a special CFIUS Support Team of OIP and I&A analysts within HITRAC, provide policy makers within the Department with an understanding of how these acquisitions can impact U.S. infrastructure.

HITRAC analysts conduct detailed reviews of all classified and unclassified information related to the foreign company and subsidiaries involved in the transaction, and look for any indication that the foreign company or senior personnel might, as the statute says, "take action that threatens to impair the national security."

This research is supported by our law enforcement partners such as Immigration and Customs Enforcement (ICE) and Customs and Border Protection (CBP), which can provide evidence of potentially illegal trade practices and reach back to the broader law enforcement community.

An assessment of the threat posed by the transfer of control to foreign persons is, however, only part of HITRAC's analysis HITRAC's CFIUS analysts work with subject matter experts in the infrastructure sector affected by a transaction to analyze the vulnerabilities in U.S. infrastructure that the transaction may expose. Obviously, situations in which the potential vulnerabilities can be exploited by identified threats raise the most serious concern HITRAC coordinates its analysis with relevant Sector Specific Agencies, such as the DHS Office of Cyber Security and Telecommunications, the Transportation Security Administration, the U.S. Coast Guard, and the Department of Energy.

The final risk assessment informs the Office of Policy's recommendation to the Secretary by highlighting areas of increased risk and proposing potential mitigation strategies the Department can use to manage any risk posed by the transaction. Under DHS Chief Intelligence Officer Charlie Allen's leadership, HITRAC's assessments also inform the Director of National Intelligence's reviews of each CFIUS case, in collaboration with the rest of the Intelligence Community.

HITRAC continues to provide analytical support and advice to the Office of Policy during negotiations on mitigation agreements that the U.S. Government uses, in some cases, to manage risk It should be noted that HITRAC produces its assessments in a very compressed timeframe to allow policymakers maximum time to take appropriate actions within the statutory 30-day timeframe mandated for initial CFIUS reviews.

HITRAC also performs similar analytical reviews of FCC license transfers to foreign entities through an interagency group made up of the Departments of Justice, Homeland Security and Defense.

In 2006, HITRAC analysts reviewed 113 CFIUS cases, writing coordinated assessments on each one. The Exon-Florio statute prevents us from disclosing information about specific cases, but HITRAC's CFIUS assessments have covered a range of infrastructures, from the chemical, energy and nuclear power sectors, to the information technology industry, to the defense industrial base.

The Office of Infrastructure Protection and HITRAC recognize that thorough scrutiny of the potential risks posed by foreign ownership of critical infrastructure is vital to protecting the Nation's security and economic strength. We will continue to closely monitor CFIUS cases for the emergence of adverse trends, and we will continue to work with our Federal partners to ensure that performance of this mission meets with the highest standards.

Thank you for the opportunity to appear before this Subcommittee today and I would be happy to answer any questions you may have at this time.

Statement of Gregory Garcia
Assistant Secretary for Cyber Security and Telecommunications
Department of Homeland Security

Madam Chairman, Ranking Member Lungren, Chairman Thompson, Ranking Member King and distinguished members of the Subcommittee, I appreciate the opportunity to briefly address you on our role in the Committee on Foreign Investment in the United States (CFIUS).T he Office of Cyber Security and Telecommunications helps to ensure the security, integrity, reliability and availability of our information and communications networks.

One area of particular emphasis for us is emerging cyber security threats. The Department reviews transactions notified to CFIUS for cyber security and communications threats and vulnerabilities. Leveraging the subject matter expertise in our Office of Cyber Security and Communications (CS&C), we evaluate transactions for potential vulnerabilities and ensuing risk to the cyber and communications sectors, as well as other critical infrastructures sectors. As appropriate given the nature of the transaction and subsequent risk, we assess vulnerabilities, participate in risk assessments, provide risk mitigation advice and participate in post-action compliance review. This can include developing specific provisions in risk mitigation agreements with the companies engaged in the transaction.

Our role in cyber security and infrastructure protection makes CS&C a logical partner in the CFIUS process. CS&C is engaged with the Office of Infrastructure Protection in supporting the cyber security and communications components of the National Infrastructure Protection Plan, which requires each of the 17 critical infrastructure and key resources sectors identified in HSPD-7 to develop Sector Specific Plans that address the physical, human, and cyber elements critical to the proper functioning of the sector. DHS/CS&C has a role in developing cyber portions of risk management methodologies and in supporting protective programs that cut across all sectors (e.g., US-CERT, the Control Systems Security Program) DHS/CS&C also is responsible for the development and implementation of the Information Technology and Telecommunications Sector Specific Plans in coordination private and public sector security partners.

Thank you for the opportunity to appear before this Subcommittee today and I would be happy to answer any questions you may have at this time.

Statement of Ann M. Calvaresi-Barr
Director Acquisition and Sourcing Management
Government Accountability Office

Defense Trade: National Security Reviews of Foreign Acquisitions of U.S. Companies Could Be Improved

GAO Report
(GAO-07-661T)

Madam Chairwoman and Members of the Subcommittee:

I am pleased to be here today to take part in this hearing on issues related to foreign ownership of U.S. assets and potential effects on national security. As you know, U.S. export control laws, national disclosure policy, the National Industrial Security Program, and other processes and programs have been established to protect defense technologies and other critical assets from falling into the wrong hands, and for other reasons. Similarly, the Exon-Florio amendment to the Defense Production Act of 1950,[1] enacted in 1988, authorized the President to suspend or prohibit foreign acquisitions, mergers, or takeovers[2] of U.S. companies that pose a threat to national security. Exon-Florio is meant to serve as a safety net when laws other than the International Emergency Economic Powers Act[3] may be ineffective in protecting national security.

Exon-Florio is administered by the Committee on Foreign Investment in the United States, currently made up of 12 members: the Department of the Treasury, which serves as Chair; the Departments of Commerce, Defense, Homeland Security, Justice, and State; and six offices in the Executive Office of the President. On the surface, the Exon-Florio review process is fairly straightforward According to regulations, after a company voluntarily files a notice of a pending or completed acquisition by a foreign concern, the Committee conducts a 30-day review to determine whether there are any national security concerns. If the Committee is unable to complete its review within 30 days, the Committee may either allow the companies to withdraw the notification and refile or initiate a 45-day investigation. If a case undergoes an investigation, the Committee submits a report to the President, including a recommendation for action. Cases that result in a presidential decision are reported to the Congress.

As requested, my comments today will summarize our reports on weaknesses in the Exon-Florio process that GAO has identified over the past decade. Before I begin, however, it is important to provide some context to Exon-Florio. Specifically, implementing Exon-Florio can pose a significant challenge for the federal government because of the potential for conflict with U.S. open investment policy—a policy that, in recognizing the economic benefits associated with foreign investments, calls for foreign investors to be treated no differently than domestic investors. This challenge has increased significantly since September 2001, when threats facing the nation were fundamentally redefined to include threats against the homeland, including those to our critical infrastructure. At the same time, the economy has become increasingly globalized, as countries open their markets and communicate regularly through the Internet. Government programs established decades ago are often ill-equipped to grapple with these emerging complexities. GAO, therefore, designated the effective identification and protection of critical technologies as a government-wide high-risk area, which warrants a strategic reexamination to identify needed changes.[4] In terms of Exon-Florio, legislation has been introduced to reform the Exon-Florio process.

Our understanding of the Committee's process is based on our 2005 work, but built on our review of the process and our discussions with agency officials for our 2002 report. For our 2005 review, and to expand our understanding of the Committee's process for reviewing foreign acquisitions of U.S. companies, we met with officials from the Departments of Commerce, Defense, Homeland Security, Justice, and the Treasury—the agencies that are most active in the review of acquisitions—and discussed their involvement in the process. Further, we conducted case studies of nine acquisitions that were filed with the Committee between June 28, 1995, and December 31, 2004. We conducted our review from April 2004 through July 2005 in accordance with generally accepted government auditing standards.

To summarize our work in this area, we have found that several aspects of the Committee's process for implementing Exon-Florio may have weakened the law's effectiveness. First, we found a lack of agreement among Committee members about the scope of Exon-Florio—specifically, what defines a threat to national security. Neither the statute nor the implementing regulation defines "national security." However, the statute provides factors that may be considered in determining threats to national security. Despite these factors, some Committee members argued to apply a more traditional definition—one limited to concerns about export-controlled technologies or items, classified contracts, and the existence of specific derogatory intelligence on a foreign company. Other Committee members have argued that a broader view is warranted, and in analyzing the effects of an acquisition, considered the potential vulnerabilities that an acquisition can create with regard to U.S. critical infrastructure, defense supply, and defense technology superiority. These disagreements may have limited the Committee's analyses of proposed or completed acquisitions.

Second, Committee members also had differing opinions on the criteria that should be used to determine whether an investigation was warranted. The criteria used by Treasury as the Committee Chair and others were essentially the same criteria established in the current law for the President to suspend or prohibit a transaction, or order divestiture—that is, there is credible evidence that the foreign controlling interest may take action that threatens national security and that no laws other than Exon-Florio and the International Emergency Economic Powers Act are adequate to protect national security. Some Committee members have argued that applying these criteria is inappropriate because the purpose of an investigation is to determine whether or not credible evidence of a threat exists.

Third, while most acquisitions are not problematic and the Committee's review can be completed within the 30-day period allowed by Exon-Florio, some more complex acquisitions required more analysis or consideration than the 30-day review period could accommodate. However, the Committee has been reluctant to use the additional 45 days allowed by the legislation because it would require initiating an investigation. The Committee's concern was that the negative perceptions surrounding an investigation could discourage foreign investment in the United States, thereby conflicting with U.S. open investment policy. To avoid investigations, the Committee has in the past encouraged companies to withdraw their notifications of proposed or completed acquisitions and refile them at a later date. Between 1997 and 2004, companies involved in 18 acquisitions were allowed to withdraw their notification and refile at a later time. The new filing is considered a new case and restarts the 30-day clock. While withdrawing and refiling provides additional time for Committee members to review a foreign acquisition while minimizing the risk of chilling foreign investment, it may also heighten the risk to national security in transactions where there are concerns and the acquisition has been completed or is likely to be completed during the withdrawal period. This was the situation in 4 of the 18 acquisitions cited above. One company did not refile for 9 months, another did not refile for 1 year, and 2 had yet to refile at the time of our review.[5]

Finally, because very few cases required a presidential decision—the criterion for reporting to the Congress on specific cases—the Congress had little insight into the Committee's process. Further, a 1992 amendment to the legislation requires a report to the Congress every 4 years on certain trends in foreign acquisitions. However, at the time of our work only one report had been submitted, in 1994 I understand that another report, in response to that requirement, has been issued.

Since our 2005 report, the Committee has taken some actions to reform the process, such as increasing communication to interested congressional committees. However, we have not examined how these changes are working. It should be noted that because the law provides for confidentiality of information filed under Exon-Florio, our ability to discuss details of cases we examined is limited.

Background

Enacted in 1988, the Exon-Florio amendment to the Defense Production Act authorized the President to investigate the effects of foreign acquisitions of U.S. companies on national security and to suspend or prohibit acquisitions that might threaten national security. The President delegated investigative authority to the Committee on Foreign Investment in the United States, an interagency group responsible for monitoring and coordinating U.S. policy on foreign investment in the United States.[6] Since the Committee's establishment in 1975, membership has doubled, with the Department of Homeland Security being the most recently added member. In addition to the Committee's 12 standing members, other agencies may be called on when their particular expertise is needed.

In 1991, the Treasury Department, as Chair of the Committee, issued regulations to implement Exon-Florio. The law and regulations establish a four-step process for reviewing foreign acquisitions of U.S. companies: (1) voluntary notice by the companies;[7] (2) a 30-day review to identify whether there are any national security concerns; (3) a 45-day investigation period to determine whether those concerns require a recommendation to the President for possible action; and (4) a presidential decision to permit, suspend, or prohibit the acquisition (see fig. 1).

Figure 1: Process Used by the Committee on Foreign Investment in the United States to Implement the Exon-Florio Amendment

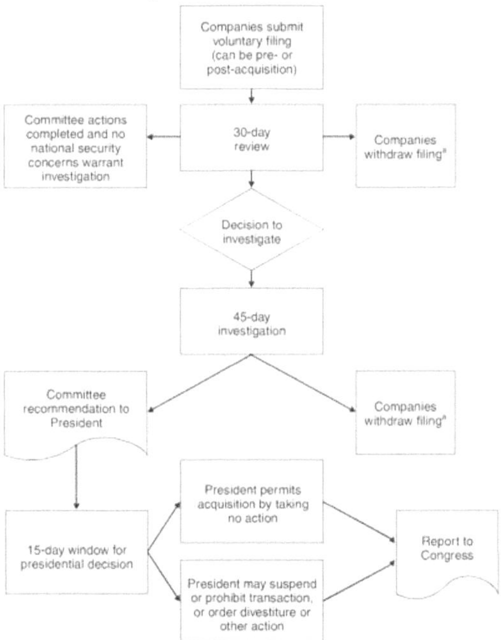

Source: GAO analysis based on 50 U.S.C app § 2170 and 31 C.F.R Part 800 and case file reviews

[a] At any point prior to a presidential decision, companies can request to withdraw a notification.

In most cases, the Committee completes its review within the initial 30 days because there are no national security concerns or concerns have been addressed, or the companies and the government agree on measures to mitigate identified security concerns. In cases where the Committee is unable to complete its review within 30 days, it may initiate a 45-day investigation or allow companies to withdraw their notifications. The Committee generally grants requests to withdraw. When the Committee concludes a 45-day investigation, it is required to submit a report with recommendations to the President. If Committee members cannot agree on a recommendation, the regulations require that the report to the President include the differing views of all Committee members.[8] The President has 15 days after the investigation is completed to decide whether to prohibit or suspend the proposed acquisition, order divestiture of a completed acquisition, or take no action.[9] Table 1 provides a breakdown of notifications and committee actions taken from 1997 through 2004 (the latest date for which data were available at the time of our 2005 review).

Table 1: Notifications to the Committee on Foreign Investment in the United States and Actions Taken, 1997 through 2004

Year	Notifications	Acquisitions[a]	Investigations[b]	Notices withdrawn after investigation begun	Presidential decisions
1997	62	60	0	0	0
1998	65	62	2	2	0
1999	79	76	0	0	0
2000	72	71	1	0	1
2001	55	51	1	1	0
2002	43	42	0	0	0
2003	41	39	2	1	1
2004	53	50	2	2	0
Total	**470**	**451**	**8**	**6**	**2[c]**

Source: Department of the Treasury

[a] Acquisitions that were withdrawn and refiled are shown in the year of initial notification.

[b] Investigations are shown in the year of their notification.

[c] In both cases the President took no action, thereby allowing the transaction, and sent a report to Congress.

Over the past decade, GAO has conducted several reviews of the Committee's process and actions and has found areas where improvements were needed. In 2000, we found that gaps in the notification process raised concerns about the Committee's ability to ensure transactions are notified.[10] Our 2002 review, prompted by a lack of congressional insight into the process, again found weaknesses in the process. Specifically, we reported that member agencies could improve the agreements they negotiated with companies under Exon-Florio to mitigate national security concerns. We also questioned the use of withdrawals to provide additional time for reviews.[11] While our most recent work indicated that member agencies had begun to take action to respond to some of our recommendations, concerns remained about the extent to which the Committee's implementation of Exon-Florio had provided the safety net envisioned by the law.[12]

Views Differed over What Constitutes a National Security Threat and When an Investigation Is Warranted

In 2005, we reported that a lack of agreement among Committee members on what defines a threat to national security and what criteria should be used to initiate an investigation may have limited the Committee's analyses of proposed and completed foreign acquisitions. From 1997 through 2004, the Committee received a total of 470 notices of proposed or completed acquisitions,[13] yet it initiated only 8 investigations.

While neither the statute nor the implementing regulation defines "national security," the statute provides a number of factors that may be considered in determining a threat to national security (see fig. 2).

Figure 2: Exon-Florio Factors That May Be Considered When Determining a Threat to National Security

- Domestic production needed for projected national defense requirements.
- The capability and capacity of domestic industries to meet national defense requirements, including the availability of human resources, products, technology, materials, and other supplies and services.
- The control of domestic industries and commercial activity by foreign citizens as it affects the capability and capacity of the United States to meet national security requirements.
- The potential effects of the proposed or pending transaction on sales of military goods, equipment, or technology to any country identified under applicable law as (a) supporting terrorism or (b) a country of concern for missile proliferation or the proliferation of chemical and biological weapons.
- The potential effects of the proposed or pending transaction on U.S. international technological leadership in areas affecting national security.

Source: 50 U.S.C app § 2170(f)

Some Committee member agencies argued for a more traditional and narrow definition of what constitutes a threat to national security—that is, (1) the U.S. company possesses export-controlled technologies or items; (2) the company has classified contracts and critical technologies; or (3) there is specific derogatory intelligence on the foreign company Other members, including the Departments of Defense and Justice, argued that acquisitions should be analyzed in broader terms. According to officials from these departments, vulnerabilities could result from foreign control of critical infrastructure, such as control of or access to information traveling on networks. Vulnerabilities can also result from foreign control of critical inputs to defense systems, such as weapons system software development[14] or a decrease in the number of innovative small businesses researching and developing new defense-related technologies.

While these vulnerabilities may not pose an immediate threat to national security, they may create the potential for longer term harm to U.S. national security interests by reducing U.S. technological leadership in defense systems. For example, in reviewing a 2001 acquisition of a U.S. company, the Departments of Defense and Commerce raised several concerns about foreign ownership of sensitive but unclassified technology, including the possibility of this sensitive technology being transferred to countries of concern or losing U.S. government access to the technology. However, Treasury argued that these concerns were not national security concerns because they did not involve classified contracts, the foreign company's country of origin was a U.S. ally, or there was no specific negative intelligence about the company's actions in the United States.

In one proposed acquisition, disagreement over the definition of national security resulted in an enforcement provision being removed from a mitigation agreement between the foreign company and the Departments of Defense and Homeland Security Defense had raised concerns about the security of its supply of specialized integrated circuits, which are used in a variety of defense technologies that the Defense Science Board had identified as essential to our national defense—technologies found in unmanned aerial vehicles, the Joint Tactical Radio System, and cryptography and other communications protection devices. However, Treasury and other Committee members argued that the security of supply issue was an industrial policy concern and, therefore, was outside the scope of Exon-Florio's authority. As a result of removing the provision, the President's authority to require divestiture under Exon-Florio was eliminated as a remedy in the event of non-compliance.[15]

Committee members also disagreed on the criteria that should be applied to determine whether a proposed or completed acquisition should be investigated. While Exon-Florio provides that the "President or the President's designee may make an investigation to determine the effects on national security" of acquisitions that could result in foreign control of a U.S. company, it does not provide specific guidance for the appropriate criteria for initiating an investigation of an acquisition.[16] At the time of our work, Treasury, as Committee Chair, applied essentially the same criteria established in the law for the President to suspend or prohibit a transaction, or order divestiture: (1) there is credible evidence that the foreign controlling interest may take action to threaten national security and (2) no laws other than Exon-Florio and the International Emergency Economic Powers Act are adequate and appropriate to protect national security.[17] However, the Defense, Justice, and Homeland Security Departments argued that applying these criteria at this point in the process is inappropriate because the purpose of an investigation is to determine whether or not credible evidence of a threat exists. Notes from a policy-level discussion of one particular case further corroborated these differing views.

Committee Allowed Withdrawal of Notifications to Avoid Investigations

Committee guidelines required member agencies to inform the Committee of national security concerns by the 23rd day of a 30-day review—further compressing the limited time allowed by legislation to determine whether a proposed or completed foreign acquisition posed a threat to national security. According to one Treasury official, the information is needed a week early to meet the legislated 30-day requirement. While most reviews are completed in the required 30 days, some Committee members have found that completing a review within such short time frames can be difficult—particularly in complex cases. One Defense official said that without advance notice of the acquisition, time frames are too short to complete analyses and provide input for the Defense Department's position. Another official said that to meet the 23-day deadline, analysts have only 3 to 10 days to analyze the acquisition. In one instance, Homeland Security was unable to provide input within the 23-day time frame.

If a review cannot be completed within 30 days and more time is needed to determine whether a problem exists or identify actions that would mitigate concerns, the Committee can initiate a 45-day investigation of the acquisition or allow companies to withdraw their notifications and refile at a later date.[18] According to Treasury officials, the Committee's interest is to ensure that the implementation of Exon-Florio does not undermine U.S. open investment policy. Concerned that public knowledge of investigations could devalue companies' stock, erode confidence of foreign investors, and ultimately chill foreign investment in the United States, the Committee has generally allowed and often encouraged companies to withdraw their notifications rather than initiate an investigation.

While an acquisition is pending, companies that have withdrawn their notification have an incentive to resolve any outstanding issues and refile as soon as possible. However, if an acquisition has been concluded, there is less incentive to resolve issues and refile, extending the time during which any concerns remain unresolved. Between 1997 and 2004, companies involved in 18 acquisitions withdrew their notification and refiled 19 times. In four cases, the companies had already concluded the acquisition before filing a notification. One did not refile until 9 months later and another did not refile for 1 year. Consequently, concerns raised by Defense and Commerce about potential export control issues in these two cases remained unresolved for as much as a year—further increasing the risk that a foreign acquisition of a U.S. company would pose a threat to national security.

For the other two cases, neither company had refiled at the time we completed our work. In one case, the company had previously withdrawn and refiled more than a year after completing the acquisition. The Committee allowed it to withdraw the notification to provide more time to answer the Committee's questions and provide assurances concerning export control matters. The company refiled, and was permitted to withdraw a second time because there were still unresolved issues. When we issued our report in 2005, 4 years had passed since the second withdrawal without a refiling. In the second case, the company—which filed with the Committee more than 6 months after completing its acquisition—was also allowed to withdraw its notification. At the time we issued our report, 2 years had passed without a refiling.

Lack of Reporting Contributed to the Opaqueness of the Committee's Process and Diminished Oversight

In response to concerns about the lack of transparency in the Committee's process, the Congress passed the Byrd Amendment to Exon-Florio in 1992, requiring a report to the Congress if the President made any decision regarding a proposed foreign acquisition. In 1992, another amendment also directed the President to report every 4 years on whether there was credible evidence of a coordinated strategy by one or more countries to acquire U.S. companies involved in research, development, or production of critical technologies for which the United States is a leading producer, and whether there were industrial espionage activities directed or assisted by foreign governments against private U.S. companies aimed at obtaining commercial secrets related to critical technologies.

While the Byrd Amendment expanded required reporting on Committee actions, few reports have been submitted to the Congress because withdrawing and refiling notices to restart the clock has limited the number of cases that result in a presidential decision. Between 1997 and 2004, only two cases—both involving telecommunications systems—resulted in a presidential decision and a subsequent report to the Congress. Infrequent reporting of Committee deliberations on specific cases provides little insight into the Committee's process to identify concerns raised during investigations and determine the extent to which the Committee has reached consensus on a case. Further, despite the 1992 requirement for a report on foreign acquisition strategies every four years, at the time of our work there had been only one report—in 1994. However, another report, in response to this requirement, was recently delivered to the Congress.

In conclusion, the effectiveness of Exon-Florio as a safety net depends on how the broad scope of its authority is implemented in today's globalized world—where identifying threats to national security has become increasingly complex. While Exon-Florio provides the Committee on Foreign Investment in the United States the latitude to define what constitutes a threat to national security, the more traditional interpretation fails to fully consider factors currently embodied in the law. Further, the Committee guidance requiring reviews to be completed within 23 days to meet the 30-day legislative requirement, along with the reluctance to proceed to an investigation, limits agencies' ability to complete in-depth analyses. However, the alternative—allowing companies to withdraw and refile their notifications—increases the risk that the Committee, and the Congress, could lose visibility over foreign acquisitions of U.S. companies. The criterion for reporting specific cases to the Congress only after a presidential decision contributes to the opaque nature of the Committee's process.

Our 2005 report laid out several matters for congressional consideration to (1) help resolve the differing views as to the extent of coverage of Exon-Florio, (2) address the need for additional time, and (3) increase insight and oversight of the process. Further, we suggested that, when withdrawal is allowed for a transaction that has been completed, the Committee establish interim protections where specific concerns have been raised, specific time frames for refiling, and a process for tracking any actions being taken during a withdrawal period. We have been told that some of these steps are now being taken.

Madam Chairwoman, this concludes my prepared statement I will be happy to answer any questions you or other Members of the Subcommittee may have.

For information about this testimony, please contact Ann M. Calvaresi-Barr, Director, Acquisition and Sourcing Management, at (202) 512-4841 or calvaresibarra@gao.gov. Other individuals making key contributions to this product include Thomas J Denomme, Gregory K. Harmon, Paula J. Haurilesko, John J. Marzullo, Russell Reiter, Karen Sloan, and Marie Ahearn.

Scope and Methodology

Our understanding of the Committee's process is based on our 2005 work but built on our review of the process and our discussions with agency officials for our 2002 report. For our 2005 review, and to expand our understanding of the Committee's process for reviewing foreign acquisitions of U.S. companies, we met with officials from the Departments of Commerce, Defense, Homeland Security, Justice, and the Treasury—the agencies that are most active in the review of acquisitions—and discussed their involvement in the process. Further, we conducted case studies of nine acquisitions that were filed with the Committee between June 28, 1995, and December 31, 2004. We selected acquisitions based on recommendations by Committee member agencies and the following criteria: (1) the Committee permitted the companies to withdraw the notification; (2) the Committee or member agencies concluded agreements to mitigate national security concerns; (3) the foreign company had been involved in a prior acquisition notified to the Committee; or (4) GAO had reviewed the acquisition for its 2002 report. We did not attempt to validate the conclusions reached by the Committee on any of the cases we reviewed. To determine whether the weaknesses in provisions to assist agencies in monitoring agreements that GAO had identified in its 2002 report had been addressed, we analyzed agreements concluded under the Committee's authority between 2003 and 2005. We conducted our review from April 2004 through July 2005 in accordance with generally accepted government auditing standards.

Endnotes

1 50 U.S.C app § 2170.

2 In the remainder of this statement, acquisitions, mergers, and takeovers are referred to as acquisitions.

3 The International Emergency Economic Powers Act gives the President broad powers to deal with any "unusual and extraordinary threat" to the national security, foreign policy, or economy of the United States (50 U.S.C. §§ 1701-1706). To exercise this authority, however, the President must declare a national emergency to deal with any such threat. Under this legislation, the President has the authority to investigate, regulate, and, if necessary, block any foreign interest's acquisition of U.S. companies (50 U.S.C. § 1702(a)(1)(B)).

4 *High Risk Series: An Update*, GAO-07-310 (Washington D.C.: Jan 2007).

5 Given the immediacy of this hearing, we were unable to gather and verify data on the disposition of these cases. However, even if the companies refiled subsequent to our 2005 reporting, the refilings were not timely.

6 Executive Order 11858 (May 7, 1975), as amended by Executive Order 12188 (Jan 2, 1980), Executive Order 12661 (Dec 27, 1988), Executive Order 12860 (Sept 3, 1993), and Executive Order 13286 (Feb 28, 2003).

7 Notification is not mandatory. However, any member agency is authorized to submit a notification of an acquisition if the companies have not done so. As of our 2005 report, no agency has submitted a notification of an acquisition. Instead, member agencies have informed Treasury of acquisitions that may be subject to Exon-Florio, and Treasury has contacted the company to encourage them to officially notify the Committee of the acquisition to begin a review.

8 31 C.F.R § 800.504(b).

9 In 1990, the President ordered a Chinese aerospace company to divest its ownership of a U.S. aircraft parts manufacturer. To date, this is the only divestiture the President has ordered.

10 *Defense Trade: Identifying Foreign Acquisitions Affecting National Security Can Be Improved*, GAO/NSIAD-00-144 (Washington, D.C.: June 29, 2000).

11 *Defense Trade: Mitigating National Security Concerns under Exon-Florio Could Be Improved*, GAO-02-736 (Washington, D.C.: Sept 12, 2002).

[12] *Defense Trade: Enhancements to the Implementation of Exon-Florio Could Strengthen the Law's Effectiveness*, GAO-05-686 (Washington, D.C.: Sept 28, 2005).

[13] Nineteen of these notices were refilings.

[14] *Defense Acquisitions: Knowledge of Software Suppliers Needed to Manage Risks*, GAO-04-678 (Washington D.C.: May 25, 2004).

[15] The regulations provide that the Committee may reopen its review or investigation and revise its recommendation to the President if it determines that the companies omitted or provided false or misleading material information to the Committee (31 C.F.R § 800.601(e)).

[16] 50 U.S.C. app § 2170(a) Under the statute, investigations are mandatory in those cases in which the acquiring company is "controlled by or acting on behalf of a foreign government" and the acquisition could result in control of the U.S. company and could affect the national security of the United States (50 U.S.C.. app § 2170(b)).

[17] 50 U.S.C. app § 2170(e).

[18] Exon-Florio's implementing regulations permit companies to request to withdraw notifications at any time up to a presidential decision. After the Committee approves a withdrawal, any subsequent refiling is considered a new, voluntary notice.

MARITIME SECURITY

DOCUMENT NO. 3

SECURING LNG TANKERS TO PROTECT THE HOMELAND

Hearing Before the Committee on Homeland Security

March 21, 2007

Statement of Jim Wells, Director
Natural Resources and Environment
Government Accountability Office

Maritime Security: Public Safety Consequences of a Liquefied Natural Gas Spill Need Clarification

GAO Report
(GAO-07-633T)

Highlights

Why GAO Did This Study

Liquefied natural gas (LNG) is a supercooled liquid form of natural gas. U.S. LNG imports are projected to increase to about 17 percent of natural gas supplies by 2030, from about 3 percent today. To meet this increase, energy companies have submitted 32 applications for new terminals. If a terrorist attack on an LNG tanker caused a spill, potential hazards, such as fire, asphyxiation, and explosions, could result. The Department of Energy (DOE) recently funded a study to conduct small- and large-scale experiments to refine and validate models that calculate how heat from large LNG fires would affect the public.

This testimony is based on GAO's recently released report, *Maritime Security: Public Safety Consequences of a Terrorist Attack on a Tanker Carrying Liquefied Natural Gas Need Clarification* (GAO-07-316). To prepare this report, GAO examined the results of six recent unclassified studies on the effects of an LNG spill and convened a panel of 19 experts to identify areas of agreement on the consequences of a terrorist attack on an LNG tanker.

What GAO Recommends

GAO recommended that DOE incorporate the key issues GAO's expert panel identified, particularly the potential for cascading failure, into its current LNG study. DOE concurred with this recommendation.

What GAO Found

The six studies GAO reviewed examining the potential effect of a fire resulting from an LNG spill produced varying results; some studies also examined other potential hazards of a large LNG spill and reached consistent conclusions on explosions. Specifically, the studies' conclusions about the distance at which 30 seconds of exposure to the heat (heat hazard) could burn people ranged from less than 1/3 of a mile to about 1-1/4 miles. Sandia National Laboratories (Sandia) conducted one of the studies and concluded, based on its analysis of multiple attack scenarios, that a good estimate of the heat hazard distance would be about 1 mile. Federal agencies use this conclusion to assess proposals for new LNG import terminals. The variations among the studies occurred because, with no data on large spills from actual events, researchers had to make numerous modeling assumptions to scale up the existing experimental data for large LNG spills. Three of the studies also examined other potential hazards of an LNG spill, including LNG vapor explosions and sequential failure of multiple tanks on the LNG vessel (cascading failure). All three studies considered LNG vapor explosions unlikely unless the vapors were in a confined space. Finally, the Sandia study examined the potential for cascading tank failure and concluded that only three of the five tanks in a typical tanker would potentially be affected, and that such failure would increase the duration of the LNG fire.

GAO's panel of experts generally agreed on the public safety impact of an LNG spill caused by a terrorist attack, disagreed on specific conclusions of the Sandia study, and suggested future research priorities. Experts agreed that the most likely public safety impact of an LNG spill is the heat impact of a fire and that explosions are not likely to occur unless LNG vapors are in confined spaces. However, the experts did not all agree with the heat hazard and cascading failure conclusions reached by the Sandia study. Finally, they suggested priorities to guide future research aimed at clarifying uncertainties about heat impact distances and cascading failure. DOE's recently funded study involving large-scale LNG fire experiments addresses only some of the research priorities the expert panel identified.

Mr. Chairman and Members of the Committee:

I am pleased to be here to discuss the results of our recently released report on the public safety consequences of a terrorist attack on a tanker carrying liquefied natural gas (LNG).[1] As you know, LNG is a supercooled liquid form of natural gas, which, if spilled, poses potential hazards, such as fire, asphyxiation, and explosions. U.S. imports of LNG, now about 3 percent of total U.S. natural gas supplies, are projected to be about 17 percent of U.S. supplies by 2030. To meet this increased demand, energy companies have submitted 32 applications to federal regulators to build new terminals for importing LNG in 10 states and 5 offshore areas. Access to accurate information about the consequences of LNG spills is crucial for developing risk assessments for LNG siting decisions. Despite several recent modeling studies of the consequences of potential LNG spills, uncertainties remain about the risks such spills would pose to the public. One of these studies, conducted by Sandia National Laboratories (Sandia) in 2004, is used by the Coast Guard to assess the suitability of waterways for LNG tankers traveling to proposed LNG facilities. In this context, DOE has recently funded a new study that will conduct small- and large-scale LNG fire experiments to refine and validate existing models that calculate how heat from large LNG fires would affect the public.

My testimony today summarizes the results of our report. Specifically, I will (1) describe the results of recent unclassified studies on the consequences of an LNG spill and (2) identify the areas of agreement and disagreement among experts concerning the consequences of a terrorist attack on an LNG tanker. To address these issues, we examined six unclassified studies of the consequences of LNG spills. We also convened a Web-based panel of 19 experts to identify areas of agreement and disagreement on LNG spill consequence issues. Because some additional studies are classified, we will be issuing a separate classified report with related findings at a later date.

Summary

The six unclassified studies we reviewed all examined the heat impact of an LNG fire but produced varying results; some studies also examined other potential hazards of a large LNG spill and reached consistent conclusions on explosions. Specifically, the studies' conclusions about the distance at which 30 seconds of exposure to the heat could burn people—also termed the heat impact distance—ranged from less than 1/3 of a mile to about 1-1/4 miles. These variations occurred because, with no data on large spills from actual events, researchers had to make numerous modeling assumptions to scale up the existing experimental data for large LNG spills. These assumptions involved the size of the hole in the tanker, the number of tanks that fail, the volume of LNG spilled, key LNG fire properties, and environmental conditions, such as wind and waves. Three of the studies also examined other potential hazards of an LNG spill, including LNG vapor explosions, asphyxiation, and the sequential failure of multiple tanks on the LNG vessel (cascading failure). All three studies considered LNG vapor explosions unlikely unless the vapors were in a confined space. Only the Sandia study examined asphyxiation and concluded that asphyxiation did not pose a hazard to the general public. Finally, only the Sandia study examined the potential for cascading failure of LNG tanks and concluded that only three of the five tanks on a typical LNG vessel would be involved in such an event and that this number of tanks would increase the duration of the LNG fire.

Our panel of 19 experts generally agreed on the public safety impact of an LNG spill, disagreed on specific conclusions of the Sandia study, and suggested future research priorities. Experts agreed on three main points: (1) the most likely public safety impact of an LNG spill is the heat impact of a fire; (2) explosions are not likely to occur in the wake of an LNG spill unless the LNG vapors are in confined spaces; and (3) some hazards, such as freeze burns and asphyxiation, do not pose a hazard to the public. However, the experts disagreed with a few conclusions reached by the Sandia study that the Coast Guard uses to assess the suitability of waterways for LNG tankers going to proposed LNG terminals. Specifically, all experts did not agree with the study's 1-mile estimate of heat impact distance resulting from an LNG fire: 7 of 15 thought Sandia's distance was "about right," 8 were evenly split on whether the distance was "too conservative" or "not conservative enough," and 4 did not answer this question. Experts also did not agree with the Sandia National Laboratories' conclusion that only three of the five LNG tanks on a tanker would be involved in a cascading failure. Finally, experts suggested priorities to guide future research aimed at clarifying uncertainties about heat impact distances and cascading failure, including large-scale fire experiments, large-scale LNG spill experiments on water, the potential for cascading failure of multiple LNG tanks, and improved modeling techniques. DOE's recently funded study involving large-scale LNG fire experiments addresses some, but not all, of the research priorities the expert panel identified.

Background

As scientists and the public have noted, an LNG spill could pose potential hazards. When LNG is spilled from a tanker, it forms a pool of liquid on the water. As the liquid warms and changes into natural gas, it forms a visible, foglike vapor cloud close to the water. The cloud mixes with ambient air as it continues to warm up, and eventually the natural gas disperses into the atmosphere. Under certain atmospheric conditions, however, this cloud could drift into populated areas before completely dispersing. Because an LNG vapor cloud displaces the oxygen in the air, it could potentially asphyxiate people who come into contact with it. Furthermore, like all natural gas, LNG vapors can be flammable, depending on conditions. If the LNG vapor cloud ignites, the resulting fire will burn back through the vapor cloud toward the initial spill. It will continue to burn above the LNG that has pooled on the surface—this is known as a pool fire. Small-scale experiments to date have shown that LNG fires burn hotter than oil fires of the same size. Both the cold temperatures of spilled LNG and the high temperatures of an LNG fire have the potential to significantly damage the tanker, causing a cascading failure. Such a failure could increase the severity of the incident. Finally, concerns have been raised about whether an explosion could result from an LNG spill.

The Federal Energy Regulatory Commission is responsible for approving applications for onshore LNG terminal sitings, and the U.S. Coast Guard is responsible for approving applications for offshore sitings. In addition, the Coast Guard reviews an applicant's Waterway Suitability Assessment, reaches a preliminary conclusion on whether the waterway is suitable for LNG imports, and identifies appropriate strategies that reduce the risk posed by the movement of an LNG tanker.

Studies Identified Different Distances for the Heat Effects of an LNG Fire, but Agreed on Other LNG Hazards

The six studies we examined identified various distances at which the heat effects of an LNG fire could be hazardous to people. The studies' results about the distance at which 30 seconds of exposure to the heat could burn people ranged from less than 1/3 of a mile (about 500 meters) to about 1-1/4 miles (more than 2,000 meters). The studies' variations in heat effects occurred because (1) different assumptions were made in the studies' models about key parameters of LNG spills and (2) the studies were designed and conducted for different purposes. Since no large-scale data are available for LNG spills, researchers made numerous modeling assumptions to scale up the existing experimental data for large spills. Key assumptions made included hole size and cascading failure, waves and wind, the volume of LNG spilled, and the amount of heat radiated from the fire. For example, studies made assumptions for the size of the hole in the LNG tanker that varied from less than 1 square meter up to 20 square meters. Additionally, the studies were conducted for different purposes. Two studies were academic analyses of the differences between LNG and oil spills; three specifically addressed spills caused by terrorist attacks, which was a concern in the wake of the September 11 attacks; and the final study developed appropriate methods for regulators to use to estimate heat hazards from LNG fires. Results of these studies can be found in our report being released today.

Some studies also examined other potential hazards, such as explosions, asphyxiation, and cascading failure, and identified their potential impacts on public safety. Three studies examined the potential for LNG vapor explosions, and all agreed that it is unlikely that LNG vapors could explode if the vapors are in an unconfined space. Only one study examined the potential for asphyxiation following an LNG spill if the vapors displace the oxygen in the air. It concluded that fire hazards would be the greatest problem in most locations, but that asphyxiation could threaten the ship's crew, pilot boat crews, and emergency response personnel. Finally, only the Sandia study examined the potential for cascading failure of LNG tanks and concluded that only three of the five tanks would be involved in such an event and that this number of tanks would increase the duration of the LNG fire.

Experts Generally Agreed That the Most Likely Public Safety Impact of an LNG Spill Is the Heat Effect of a Fire, but That Further Study Is Needed to Clarify the Extent of This Effect

The 19 experts on our panel generally agreed on the public safety impact of an LNG spill, disagreed with specific conclusions of the Sandia study, and suggested future research priorities.[2] Specifically:

- Experts agreed that the main hazard to the public from a pool fire is the heat from the fire, but emphasized that the exact hazard distance depends on site-specific weather conditions; composition of the LNG (relative percentages of methane, propane, and butane); and the size of the fire.
- Eighteen of 19 experts agreed that the ignition of a vapor cloud over a populated area could burn people and property in the immediate vicinity of the fire. Three experts emphasized in their comments that the vapor cloud is unlikely to penetrate very far into a populated area before igniting.
- With regard to explosions, experts distinguished between explosions in confined spaces and in unconfined spaces. For confined spaces, such as under a dock or between the hulls of a ship, they agreed that it is possible, under controlled experimental conditions, to induce explosions of LNG vapors; however, a detonation—the more serious type of vapor cloud explosion—of confined LNG vapors is unlikely following an LNG spill caused by a terrorist attack. For unconfined spaces, experts were split on whether it is possible to induce such explosions under controlled experimental conditions; however, even experts who thought such explosions were possible agreed that vapor cloud explosions in unconfined spaces are unlikely to occur following an LNG spill caused by a terrorist attack.

Our panel of 19 experts disagreed with a few of the Sandia study's conclusions and agreed with the study authors' perspective on risk-based approaches to dealing with the hazards of potential LNG spills. For example:

- Seven of 15 experts thought Sandia's heat hazard distance was "about right," and the remaining 8 experts were evenly split as to whether the distance was "too conservative" (i.e., larger than needed to protect the public) or "not conservative enough" (i.e., too small to protect the public). Officials at Sandia National Laboratories and our panel of experts cautioned that the hazard distances presented cannot be applied to all sites because of the importance of site-specific factors. Additionally, two experts explained that there is no "bright line" for hazards—that is, 1,599 meters is not necessarily "dangerous," and 1,601 meters is not necessarily "safe."

- Nine of 15 experts agreed with Sandia's conclusion that only three of the five LNG tanks on a tanker would be involved in cascading failure. Five experts noted that the Sandia study did not explain how it concluded that only three tanks would be involved in cascading failure.
- Finally, experts agreed with Sandia's conclusion that consequence studies should be used to support comprehensive, risk-based management and planning approaches for identifying, preventing, and mitigating hazards from potential LNG spills.

The experts also suggested priorities for future research—some of which are not fully addressed in DOE's ongoing LNG research—to clarify uncertainties about heat impact distances and cascading failure. These priorities include large-scale fire experiments, large-scale LNG spill experiments on water, the potential for cascading failure of multiple LNG tanks, and improved modeling techniques. As part of DOE's ongoing research, Sandia plans to conduct large-scale LNG pool fire tests, beginning with a pool size of 35 meters—the same size as the largest test conducted to date. Sandia will validate the existing 35-meter data and then conduct similar tests for pool sizes up to 100 meters. Of the top 10 LNG research priorities the experts identified, only 3 have been funded in the DOE study, and the second highest ranked priority, cascading failure, was not funded. One expert noted that although the consequences of cascading failure could be serious, because the extreme cold of spilled LNG and the high heat of an LNG fire could damage the tanker, there are virtually no data looking at how a tanker would be affected by these temperatures.

Conclusions

It is likely that the United States will increasingly depend on LNG to meet its demand for natural gas. Consequently, understanding and resolving the uncertainties surrounding LNG spills is critical, especially in deciding where to locate LNG facilities. While there is general agreement on the types of effects of an LNG spill, the study results have created what appears to be conflicting assessments of the specific heat consequences of such a spill. These assessments create uncertainty for regulators and the public. Additional research to resolve some key areas of uncertainty could benefit federal agencies responsible for making informed decisions when approving LNG terminals and protecting existing terminals and tankers, as well as providing reliable information to citizens concerned about public safety.

To provide the most comprehensive and accurate information for assessing the public safety risks posed by tankers transiting to proposed LNG facilities, we recommended that the Secretary of Energy ensure that DOE incorporates the key issues the expert panel identified, particularly the potential for cascading failure, into its current LNG study.

DOE concurred with our recommendation.

Mr. Chairman, this concludes my prepared statement. I would be happy to respond to any questions that you or Members of the Committee may have.

Contacts and Acknowledgments

For further information about this testimony, please contact me at (202) 512-3841 or wellsj@gao.gov. James W. Turkett, Janice M. Poling, and Carol Herrnstadt Shulman also made key contributions to this statement.

Endnotes

[1] GAO, *Maritime Security: Public Safety Consequences of a Terrorist Attack on a Tanker Carrying Liquefied Natural Gas Need Clarification,* GAO-07-316 (Washington, D.C.: Feb. 22, 2007). This report was prepared at the request of this Committee, the House Committee on Energy and Commerce, and Representative Edward J. Markey.

[2] We considered experts to be "in agreement" if more than 75 percent of them indicated that they completely agreed or generally agreed with a given statement. Not all experts commented on every issue discussed.

Statement of RDML Brian Salerno
Director
Inspection and Compliance
U.S. Coast Guard
Department of Homeland Security

Introduction

Good morning Mr. Chairman and distinguished members of the Committee. I am Rear Admiral Brian Salerno, the Director of the Inspection and Compliance Directorate at U.S. Coast Guard Headquarters. It is my pleasure to appear before you today to discuss the Coast Guard's role in providing for the safety and security of Liquefied Natural Gas (LNG) vessels and facilities, and how the Coast Guard is cooperating with other Federal Agencies on this important national issue.

As the Federal Government's lead agency for Maritime Homeland Security, the Coast Guard plays a major role in ensuring all facets of marine transportation of LNG, including LNG vessels, shoreside terminals and LNG deepwater ports, are operated safely and securely, and that the risks associated with the marine transportation of LNG are managed responsibly. Today, I will briefly review the applicable laws and regulations that provide our authority and the requirements for the safe and secure operation of the vessels, shoreside terminals and deepwater ports. I will also describe how the Coast Guard is working with the other Federal entities here today, as fellow stakeholders in LNG safety and security.

LNG Vessel Safety

The Coast Guard has long recognized the unique safety and security challenges posed by transporting millions of gallons of LNG or "cryogenic methane." LNG vessels have had an enviable safety record over the last 45 years. Since international commercial LNG shipping began in 1959, tankers have carried over 40,000 LNG shipments and while there have been some serious accidents at sea or in port, there has never been a breach of a ship's cargo tanks. Insurance records and industry sources show that there were approximately 30 LNG tanker safety incidents (e.g. leaks, groundings or collisions) through 2002. Of these incidents, 12 involved small LNG spills which caused some freezing damage but did not ignite. Two incidents caused small vapor vent fires which were quickly extinguished.

Today, there are over 200 LNG vessels operating worldwide and another 100 or so under construction. While there are no longer any U.S. flag LNG vessels, all LNG vessels calling in the U.S. must comply with certain domestic regulations in addition to international requirements. Our domestic regulations for LNG vessels were developed in the 1970s under the authority of the various vessel inspection statutes now codified in Title 46 United States

Code. Relevant laws providing the genesis for LNG vessel regulation include the Tank Vessel Act (46 U.S.C. 391a) and the Ports and Waterways Safety Act of 1972, as amended by the Port and Tanker Safety Act of 1978 (33 U.S.C. 1221, *et. seq*). Regulations located in Title 46, Code of Federal Regulations (CFR) Part 154, "Safety Standards for Self-Propelled Vessels Carrying Bulk Liquefied Gasses," specify requirements for the vessel's design, construction, equipment and operation. Our domestic regulations closely parallel the applicable international requirements, but are more stringent in the following areas: the requirements for enhanced grades of steel for crack arresting purposes in certain areas of the hull, specification of higher allowable stress factors for certain independent type tanks and prohibiting the use of cargo venting as a means of cargo temperature or pressure control.

All LNG vessels in international service must comply with the major maritime treaties agreed to by the International Maritime Organization (IMO), such as the International Convention for the Safety of Life at Sea, popularly known as the "SOLAS Convention" and the International Convention for the Prevention of Pollution from Ships, popularly known as the "MARPOL Convention." In addition, LNG vessels must comply with the International Code for the Construction and Equipment of Ships Carrying Liquefied Gases in Bulk, known as the "IGC Code."

Before being allowed to trade in the United States, operators of foreign flag LNG carriers must submit detailed vessel plans and other information to the Coast Guard's Marine Safety Center (MSC) to establish that the vessels have been constructed to the higher standards required by our domestic regulations. Upon the MSC's satisfactory plan review and on-site verification by Coast Guard marine inspectors, the vessel is issued a Certificate of Compliance. This indicates that it has been found in compliance with applicable design, construction and outfitting requirements.

The Certificate of Compliance is valid for a two-year period, subject to an annual examination by Coast Guard marine inspectors, who verify that the vessel remains in compliance with all applicable requirements. As required by 46 U.S.C. 3714, this annual examination is required of all tank vessels, including LNG carriers.

LNG Vessel Security

In addition to undergoing a much more rigorous and frequent examination of key operating and safety systems, LNG vessels are subject to additional measures of security when compared to crude oil tankers, as an example. Many of the special safety and security precautions the Coast Guard has long established for LNG vessels derived from our analysis of "conventional" navigation safety risks such as groundings, collisions, propulsion or steering system failures. These precautions pre-dated the September 11, 2001 tragedy, and include such measures as special vessel traffic control measures that are implemented when an LNG vessel is transiting the port or its approaches, safety zones around the vessel to prevent other vessels from approaching nearby, escorts by Coast Guard patrol craft and, as local conditions warrant, coordination with other Federal, state and local transportation, law enforcement and/or emergency management agencies to reduce the risks to, or minimize the interference from other port area infrastructure or activities. These activities are conducted under the authority of existing port safety and security statutes, such as the Magnuson Act (50 U.S.C. 191 *et. seq.*) and the Ports and Waterways Safety Act, as amended.

Since September 11, 2001, additional security measures have been implemented, including the requirement that all vessels calling in the U.S. must provide the Coast Guard with a 96-hour advance notice of arrival (increased from 24 hours advance notice pre-9/11). This notice includes information on the vessel's last ports of call, crew identities and cargo information. In addition, the Coast Guard now regularly boards LNG vessels at-sea, where Coast Guard personnel conduct special "security sweeps" of the vessel and ensure it is under the control of proper authorities during its port transit. In order to protect the vessel from external attack, LNG vessels are escorted through key port areas. These armed escorts afford protection to the nearby population centers by reducing the probability of a successful attack against an LNG vessel. These actions are in addition to the safety and security oriented boardings previously described.

Of course, one of the most important post-9/11 maritime security improvements has been the passage of the Maritime Transportation Security Act of 2002 (MTSA). Under the authority of MTSA, the Coast Guard developed a comprehensive new body of security measures applicable to vessels, marine facilities and maritime personnel. Our domestic maritime security regime is closely aligned with the International Ship and Port Facility Security (ISPS) Code. The ISPS Code, a mandatory requirement of the SOLAS Convention, was adopted at the IMO in December 2002 and came into effect on July 1st 2004. Under the ISPS Code, vessels in international service, including LNG vessels, must have an International Ship Security Certificate (ISSC). To be issued an ISSC by its flag state, the vessel must develop and implement a threat-scalable security plan that, among other things, establishes access control measures, security measures for cargo handling and delivery of ships stores, surveillance and monitoring, security communications, security incident procedures, and training and drill requirements. The plan must also identify a Ship Security Officer who is responsible for ensuring compliance with the ship's security plan. The Coast Guard rigorously enforces this international requirement by evaluating security compliance as part of our ongoing port state control program.

Shoreside LNG Terminal Safety and Security

Presently there are six shoreside LNG terminals in the U.S. and U.S. Territories: the export facility in Kenai, AK; and, import terminals in Everett, MA; Cove Point, MD; Elba Island, GA; Lake Charles, LA; and Penuelas, PR. Under Title 33, CFR Part 127, the Coast Guard has responsibility for the facility's waterside "marine transfer area" and the Department of Transportation's Pipeline and Hazardous Materials Safety Administration has responsibility for shoreside portion of the facility. The safety requirements regulated by the Coast Guard in the marine transfer area include electrical power systems, lighting, communications, transfer hoses and piping systems, gas detection systems and alarms, firefighting equipment, and operational matters such as approval of the terminal's Operations and Emergency Manuals and personnel training.

The recently promulgated "Maritime Security Regulations for Facilities," found in Title 33 CFR Part 105, were developed under the authority of MTSA. These regulations require the LNG terminal operator to conduct a facility security assessment and develop a threat-scalable security plan that addresses the risks identified in the assessment. Much like the requirements prescribed for vessels, the facility security plan establishes access control measures, security measures for cargo handling and delivery of supplies, surveillance and monitoring, security communications, security incident procedures and training and drill requirements. The plan must also identify a Facility Security Officer who is responsible for ensuring compliance with the facility security plan. The six existing U.S. LNG terminals were required to submit their security plans to the Coast Guard for review and approval in 2003 and full implementation of the plans was required by July 1, 2004. These reviews have been completed, and the terminals' compliance with the plans has been verified by local Coast Guard port security personnel through on-site examinations. In contrast to our safety responsibility, whereby our authority is limited to the "marine transfer area," our authority regarding the security plan can, depending upon the particular layout of the terminal, encompass the entire facility.

Shoreside LNG Terminal Siting

The issue of constructing new shoreside LNG terminals has been controversial, due in large part to public concerns over both perceived and actual risks to the safety and security of LNG vessel operations. Under the Natural Gas Act, the Federal Energy Regulatory Commission (FERC) has permitting authority, including safety review of facility siting, for LNG terminals onshore and within state waters. The Coast Guard is not involved in any aspect of determining or approving the shoreside facility's location.

However, the Coast Guard plays an important role in the siting process once it has begun. Along with an application to the FERC, an owner or operator who intends to build a new shoreside LNG facility, or who plans new construction on an existing facility, must submit a "Letter of Intent" to the Coast Guard Captain of the Port (COTP) in whose zone the facility is located (in accordance with by 33 CFR 127.007). This letter must provide information on: the physical location of the facility; a description of the facility; the characteristics of the vessels intended to visit the facility and the frequency of visits; and, charts that show waterway channels and identify commercial, industrial, environmentally sensitive and residential areas in and adjacent to the waterway to be used by vessels enroute to the facility, within 15.5 miles of the facility.

The COTP reviews the information provided by the applicant and makes a determination on the suitability of the waterway for LNG vessels. Factors considered include: density and characteristics of marine traffic in the waterway; locks, bridges or other man made obstructions in the waterway; the hydrologic features of the waterway, e.g., water depth, channel width, currents and tides, natural hazards such as reefs and sand bars; and underwater pipelines and cables. If the waterway is found suitable and after the Coast Guard meets all of its National Environmental Policy Act (NEPA) requirements, the COTP will issue a Letter of Recommendation (per 33 CFR 127.009).

Both the Coast Guard and the FERC recognize that the "Letter of Recommendation" process, which dates from 1988, does not, in its current form, adequately take into account the security concerns of our post 9/11 environment. Also, the existing regulations are focused primarily on conventional navigation safety risk management issues such as traffic density, hydrologic characteristics of the waterway, etc. They do not focus on port security risk management issues, and in particular, they do not directly require an analysis of the consequences of an LNG spill on the waterway proposed for vessel transits.

To address this problem, on February 10, 2004, the Coast Guard entered into an Inter-Agency Agreement (IAA) with FERC and RSPA to work in a coordinated manner to address issues regarding safety and security at shoreside LNG facilities, including terminal facilities and tanker operations, to work together, avoid duplication of effort, and to maximize the exchange of relevant information related to the safety and security aspects of LNG facilities and the related maritime concerns.

Soon after the completion of the IAA, work began on a more detailed guidance document for use by the involved agencies. On 14 Jun 05, the Navigation and Vessel Inspection Circular (NVIC) 05-05, "*Guidelines on Assessing the Suitability of a Waterway for LNG Marine Traffic*," was published to provide guidance on how to conduct and validate a Waterway Suitability Assessment so that full consideration is given to the safety and security of the port, the facility, and vessels transporting the LNG. Simply put, it established a uniform national process for conducting port-specific risk and waterway suitability assessments.

Under the NVIC 05-05 guidelines, since the Coast Guard is also a cooperating agency for the preparation of the FERC's Environmental Impact Statement, this guidance assists the Coast Guard in obtaining all information needed to assess the proposed LNG marine operations and fulfill its commitment to FERC to provide input to their Environmental Impact Statement (EIS). Once completed, the Coast Guard can adopt FERC's EIS to meet its NEPA obligations associated with the subsequent issuance of the COTP Letter of Recommendation.

The Waterway Suitability Assessment (WSA) process put forth in the NVIC uses a risk management approach to developing mitigation measures for the hazards introduced to the affected waterway due to the nature of LNG. The NVIC requires the applicant to conduct a risk analysis of the waterway and propose mitigating measures. In addition, the applicant is required to do an analysis of the resources necessary to perform the proposed mitigation measures. This WSA process usually begins very early in the process, typically during the FERC's pre-filing period.

In addition to an evaluation of conventional navigation safety risks, a critical part of the WSA is an analysis of an LNG spill on the waterway and the thermal effects from a resulting pool fire. The analysis includes the application of the hazard distances and zones of concern established by the spill consequence models described in the 2004 Sandia National Labs Report.

Once the WSA is completed by the applicant, it is submitted to the Coast Guard and reviewed and validated by key stakeholders at the port, such as the Area Maritime Security Committee and the Harbor Safety Committee, and other local port stakeholders. In previous cases, there have even been public meetings and workshops during the development and validation of the WSA and the public is encouraged to provide comments.

When the Coast Guard's WSA validation process is complete, the COTP makes a preliminary determination regarding the suitability of the waterway, whether the waterway can accommodate the proposed traffic and whether there is sufficient capability within the port community to responsibly manage the safety and security risks of the project. This preliminary determination is communicated to the FERC in a Waterway Suitability Report (WSR).

The WSR report conveys the assessment and analysis conducted by the applicant during the WSA process and it usually includes risk mitigation measures that the COTP determines is necessary for the vessel to safely and securely transit to the proposed facility. Once FERC receives the WSR, the report is incorporated into the EIS. FERC addresses the environmental impacts of the proposed vessel transits on the waterway, the environmental impacts of the proposed risk mitigation measures and the public safety and environmental impacts of a LNG spill and fire on the waterway.

Once the FERC's EIS is published, it is subsequently reviewed by the Coast Guard's environmental specialists. If it is acceptable and meets all of the Coast

Guard's NEPA requirements, the Coast Guard issues a Record of Decision that adopts the EIS for our Letter of Recommendation process.

Upon completion of the Record of Decision, the COTP issues a "Letter of Recommendation" to the owner or operator of the proposed facility, and to the state and local government agencies having jurisdiction, as to the suitability of the waterway for the proposal (33 CFR 127.009).

The Coast Guard is also working on the regulatory changes in 33 CFR Part 127 necessary to bring the existing "Letter of Intent" and "Letter of Recommendation" regulations up to date, specifically by requiring the waterways management information to be submitted to the COTP at the time of FERC "pre-filing" or conventional application, and adding specific requirements for a port security assessment, in addition to the waterways management information, to be presented to the COTP for evaluation.

LNG Deepwater Ports: Authority and Agency Relationships

The Coast Guard's authority to regulate Deepwater Ports (DWPs) derives from the Deepwater Port Act of 1974 (DWPA). The regulations pertaining to the licensing, design, equipment and operation of DWPs are found in Title 33 CFR Subchapter NN (Parts 148, 149 and 150). Originally pertaining only to oil, MTSA amended the DWPA to include natural gas. This Act allows for the licensing of DWPs in the Exclusive Economic Zone, outside of state waters, along all maritime coasts of the United States. The Secretary of the Department of Homeland Security (DHS) and the Secretary of DOT delegated the processing of DWP applications to the Coast Guard and the Maritime Administration (MARAD), respectively. MARAD is the license issuing authority and works in concert with the Coast Guard in developing the Environmental Impact Statement, while the Coast Guard has primary jurisdiction over design, equipment and operations and security requirements. The DWPA established a specific time frame of 330 days from the date of publication of a Federal Register notice of a "complete" application to the date of approval or denial of a DWP license. Among other requirements, an applicant for a DWP license must demonstrate consistency with the Coastal Zone Management Plan of the adjacent coastal States.

The Coast Guard and MARAD, in cooperation with other Federal agencies, must comply with the requirements of the National Environmental Policy Act in processing DWP applications within the timeframes prescribed in the Deepwater Port Act. To date the Coast Guard has received a total of 15 DWP applications, including four that have already been licensed: Louisiana Offshore Oil Platform, Chevron-Texaco's Port Pelican project, Excelerate Energy's Gulf Gateway project, and Shell's Gulf Landing. Recently, the Maritime Administrator has issued Records of Decisions for three others: Freeport McMoRan's Main Pass Energy Hub, Suez's Neptune project and Excelerate Energy's Northeast Gateway. The latter two are off the coast of Massachusetts and the others are all offshore of Louisiana. Only the Gulf

Gateway has been built so far. Three have been withdrawn and six others are in various stages of processing. We are anticipating between two and four additional applications within the next several months.

To expedite the application review process, and more efficiently coordinate the activities of the numerous stakeholder agencies, the Coast Guard entered into a Memorandum of Understanding (MOU), involving more than a dozen agencies, including FERC, NOAA, the Army Corps of Engineers and the Environmental Protection Agency. The MOU obliges the participating agencies to work with each other and with other entities as appropriate, to ensure that timely decisions are made and that the responsibilities of each agency are met. These responsibilities include: assessing their particular role in the environmental review of DWP licenses; meeting with prospective applicants and other agency representatives to identify areas of potential concern and to assess the need for and availability of agency resources to address issues related to the proposed project.

LNG Deepwater Ports Safety and Security

While conventional crude oil DWPs have been in operation around the world for many years, LNG DWPs are an emerging concept. Currently, there is only one in operation, off the coast of Texas. There are a variety of different designs under development that borrow from designs and technology that have been time-tested in the offshore energy and the LNG industries. Proposals include ship-shaped hull designs similar to existing Floating Production, Storage and Offloading (FPSO) units, platform based storage and regasification units, gravity based structures, and innovative docking structures that attach directly to the LNG carrier to serve as both a mooring and offloading system. Because this is a new concept, the Coast Guard's regulations apply a "design basis" approach, rather than mandate a series of prescriptive requirements. Under a "design basis" approach, each concept is evaluated on its own technical merits, using relevant engineering standards and concepts that have been approved by recognized vessel classification societies and other competent industrial and technical bodies. In addition, the Coast Guard's DWP regulations require that all LNG DWPs develop and implement a security plan that, at a minimum, will addresses the key security plan elements provided in Title 33 CFR Part 106, "Maritime Security: Outer Continental Shelf Facilities." A risk and consequence analysis is completed as part of the risk mitigation strategy and security measures are developed between the applicant and the Coast Guard local Captain of the Port.

Thank you for giving me this opportunity to discuss the Coast Guard's role in LNG safety and security and our relationships with other stakeholder agencies. I will be happy to answer any questions you may have.

Statement of H. Keith Lesnick
Director
Office of Deepwater Port Licensing
Maritime Administration
Department of Transportation

Good morning, Mr. Chairman and Members of the Committee. I am pleased to have the opportunity to testify before you today and to discuss the dramatic growth in U.S. Liquefied Natural Gas (LNG) imports, the deepwater licensing program, and the Department of Transportation and the Maritime Administration's plans to increase the employment of U.S. mariners within this highly specialized and vital energy sector.

While worldwide natural gas is in plentiful supply, the United States holds less than 4 percent of world reserves. During 2006, about 84 percent of all natural gas consumed in the United States was domestically produced. By the year 2025, as demand increases, domestic production is only expected to account for 79 percent of consumption. To accommodate this shortfall, LNG imports are projected to increase eight-fold to 4.4 trillion cubic feet per year.

Importing LNG will serve to relieve the Nation's growing energy needs by diversifying energy sources. Deepwater ports are necessary to enhance the Nation's ability to import LNG from world wide sources. The Energy Information Administration's recently released *Annual Energy Outlook 2007* states U.S. energy consumption projected for the year 2025 will be about 23 percent higher than it was in 2006.

As a consequence, the United States finds itself in a situation unlike any we have experienced before. There is strong international competition from China, Japan, and Korea for energy resources. Advances in vessel size to transport oil and LNG, the number of LNG carriers, and advances in LNG transfer technology have made importing energy ever more efficient and cost effective.

Numerous logistical hurdles remain, however. Local opposition to the construction of LNG terminals is growing, compounding the already difficult task of locating suitable gas receiving sites. At present, the continental United States has 5 operational LNG import terminals—1 is a deepwater port located 116 miles off the coast of Louisiana. The combined capacity of the five terminals is equal to six percent of the Nation's gas consumption. Clearly, the Nation's growing need for imported natural gas necessitates a greater investment in the infrastructure required to accommodate energy needs. As such, the Maritime Administration's Deepwater Port licensing program is designed to facilitate the licensing, construction, and operation of deepwater oil and LNG terminals located seaward of U.S. territorial waters.

In 2002, the Deepwater Port Act was amended to expand the Secretary of Transportation's existing authority to include authority to issue licenses for offshore natural gas terminals. (The permitting of LNG facilities onshore and in state waters remain under the jurisdiction of the Federal Energy Regulatory Commission.) The Maritime Administration, by delegation from the Secretary of Transportation, is the lead federal agency for licensing offshore LNG and oil terminals. The Secretary of Transportation delegated authority over "pipeline maters" to the Pipeline and Hazardous Materials Safety Administration. In processing of Deepwater Port license applications, the Maritime Administration works in concert with the U.S. Coast Guard, numerous federal agencies, and state and local governments. At the conclusion of the application's environmental review process, the Maritime Administration makes a final license approval determination through the issuance of a Record of Decision. The Record of Decision incorporates the reasons behind the Maritime Administration's decision to issue or deny a license. The Record of Decision also enumerates the various conditions of licensure that govern the operation of the deepwater port facility.

To date, 15 LNG Deepwater Port applications have been filed and 4 licenses have been issued. If all applications under consideration by the Maritime Administration were constructed and operating at full capacity, they would represent over a quarter of the Nation's total gas capacity.

Congress amended the Deepwater Port Act through the Coast Guard and Maritime Transportation Act of 2006, to direct the Secretary of Transportation to develop and implement a program to promote the transportation of LNG to the United States on U.S.-flag vessels. The Act further directed the Secretary to give top priority to applications that use U.S.-flag vessels in their operations. The Act also requires that applicants provide the nation of registry for, and the citizenship of officers and crew members serving on vessels transporting LNG to U.S. deepwater ports. The Maritime Administration interprets this requirement to include those international LNG tankers providing gas to the deepwater facilities licensed by the Agency.

Therefore, in responding to these legislative directives, the Maritime Administration is in the process of developing a voluntary deepwater port manning program to encourage employing highly trained and skilled U.S. mariners to meet the current and forecasted demand for professional mariners in the international LNG shipping industry.

We are already seeing results from our efforts. Last December, the Maritime Administration announced an innovative public-private partnership with SUEZ Energy—the first official partnership of its kind within the international LNG industry. Under this agreement, SUEZ will provide training and employment opportunities for U.S. citizen officers, cadets, and unlicensed mariners aboard their tanker fleet and at both of their planned deepwater port terminals off the coasts of Boston and Florida. Additionally, Excelerate Energy has entered into a similar agreement for the Northeast Gateway deepwater port facility in Massachusetts Bay and for its existing facility in the Gulf of Mexico. In January 2007, a Louisiana-based applicant, Freeport-McMoRan Energy, also committed to work with the Maritime Administration to develop programs to train and employ U.S. mariners on LNG vessels servicing their Main Pass Energy Hub facility being planned off the coast of Louisiana.

These agreements represent sound public policy—increased safety, security, and improved transportation efficiencies—and they open up vital training and employment opportunities for U.S. mariners in the LNG industry. The Maritime Administration intends to continue to reach similar voluntary agreements with our pending and future deepwater port applicants and all energy companies serving the Nation's international maritime markets.

It is estimated that as many as 3,700 to 5,000 additional mariners may be needed by next year. The magnitude of this manpower shortage will only serve to negatively impact this industry's excellent safety record. Over the last 5 years the global LNG carrier fleet grew by 73 percent, from 128 to 222 vessels. And, an additional 133 LNG vessels are scheduled for delivery to service the global LNG trades by 2010. This expanded fleet will require as many as 10,000 additional seafarers, of whom almost 3,000 will be licensed officers—and, offers tremendous employment opportunities for both licensed and unlicensed U.S. mariners. This dramatic increase also comes at a time when we are already experiencing a greater demand for seafarers in general due to a dramatic increase in international trade.

The worldwide LNG tanker fleet currently lacks a single U.S.-flag vessel. As a direct result, few U.S. mariners have the opportunity to gain vital hands-on experience in this growing industry. Clearly, the lack of U.S.-flag LNG tankers translates into a lack of job opportunities for U.S. citizens. It is the Maritime Administration's goal to help correct this situation and provide U.S. mariners opportunities in an industry vital to our energy and security needs.

The Maritime Administration strives to ensure a reliable supply of U.S. citizen mariners to serve on LNG vessels calling at U.S. energy receiving facilities. The Agency is working with the U.S. Merchant Marine Academy, state maritime academies, and other training facilities to develop and expand innovative educational programs. Specifically, the goal is to provide immediate employment for entry level mariners, both licensed and unlicensed, into the LNG industry upon graduation and courses for the retraining and/or recertifying of current mariners who are sailing on vessels other than LNG—permitting them to transition into LNG service.

Ultimately, employing highly trained and skilled licensed U.S. mariners will help alleviate the growing worldwide shortage of professional mariners confronting the international LNG shipping industry. It will also serve to help maintain the industry's excellent safety record by maintaining the LNG officer pool. U.S. mariners are highly skilled in the operation of steam plants used on the majority of LNG vessels and are experts in operating other marine main propulsion systems, such as diesel, diesel electric, and gas turbines. In addition, America's maritime officers unions continue to train their members to the highest industry standards in LNG technologies.

It is also important to note that from an economic and competitive perspective, the growing worldwide shortage of trained and qualified LNG ships' officers has created an opportunity for U.S. officers to work aboard foreign-flag LNG vessels. International vessel operators are dramatically increasing the wages and benefits offered to foreign officers to keep or attract their services, thus narrowing the gap between the wages and benefits paid to Americans and those paid to their foreign counterparts.

The licensing of deepwater ports also contributes to the Department of Transportation's strategic goal of improved mobility and reduced congestion by limiting the number of mega LNG tankers entering our Nation's port facilities. The construction of deepwater port terminals enhances transportation safety by isolating terminals away from congested population areas.

The Maritime Administrator is required to consider the national interests in the issuance of a deepwater port license. The Maritime Administration considers the safe, secure, and efficient importation of an environmentally friendly source of energy vital to the Nation's economic growth.

We are proud of the Deepwater Ports Licensing Program and our efforts to encourage employing qualified U.S. citizens to work aboard the vessels serving the energy sector.

I want to thank the Members of the Committee and Chairman Thompson in holding this hearing today and I am happy to respond to any questions that you may have.

Statement of J. Mark Robinson
Director
Office of Energy Projects
Federal Energy Regulatory Commission

My name is J. Mark Robinson and I'm Director of the Office of Energy Projects (OEP) at the Federal Energy Regulatory Commission (FERC or Commission). I am here as a staff witness and do not speak on behalf of any Commissioner. Our office is responsible for non-federal hydroelectric licensing, administration, and safety; siting of electric transmission lines; certification of interstate natural gas pipelines and storage facilities; and, more significantly for today's session, authorization and oversight over the construction, operation, and safety of on-shore and near-shore Liquefied Natural Gas (LNG) terminals. We also share security responsibilities for these facilities with the U.S. Coast Guard (Coast Guard), which has primary responsibility under the Maritime Transportation Security Act of 2002.

I want to thank you for this opportunity to speak today and to specifically address how we ensure the safety and security of LNG import facilities and the related LNG shipping. Overall, the safety record of the industry is commendable. LNG terminals in the United States have never had an LNG safety-related incident that harmed the public or the environment. Similarly, no shipping incidents have occurred worldwide that resulted in a significant loss of cargo during the almost 50 years of LNG transport. I will first describe the measures we use to provide for safe and secure LNG import terminal siting, construction and operation. Next, I will briefly address the measures taken to ensure the continuing safe history of LNG shipping. And finally, I will comment on the GAO report.

Safety, Security and Siting of LNG Import Terminals

Be assured that consideration of public safety is our highest priority when fulfilling our Congressional mandate under the Natural Gas Act to regulate facilities for the importation of natural gas. The Commission has been proactive in addressing safety concerns and rigorously applies high safety standards to these projects. When projects meet our safety standards and are found to be in the public interest, the Commission will approve them. If a proposed project falls short of these standards, the Commission will reject it, as was done with the proposed Keyspan LNG Terminal Project in Providence, Rhode Island.

The excellent safety record of the LNG import facilities in the U.S. extends over the past 35 years. The siting and oversight of LNG facilities is governed by a comprehensive scheme of federal regulation that guarantees that the FERC and other federal agencies work together to ensure public safety. The FERC's LNG project review process works to address all siting and operational issues with the full participation of the federal and state agencies, and the public, and, only after that comprehensive review, attempts to ensure the timely development of necessary energy infrastructure. Once in operation, FERC oversight and inspection is an on-going process for the life of the facility.

Every aspect of our engineering and siting review, and our coordination with the Coast Guard and the U.S. Department of Transportation (DOT), is geared toward assuring that a facility will operate safely and securely. This review may be broken into three distinct phases: pre-authorization review; pre-construction review; and pre-operation review.

Pre-Authorization Review—During the pre-authorization phase, Commission staff addresses the safety and security of an LNG import terminal by reviewing facility designs and ensuring that the proposal includes a number of design and operational features. FERC regulations require that from the early stages of project development, potential applicants meet with FERC staff to describe the proposal and solicit guidance on required design features. At this point, we make sure that DOT and the Coast Guard are aware of new projects or proposed expansions. These meetings provide the opportunity for FERC staff to offer suggestions related to the environmental, engineering and safety features of the proposal and review conceptual designs. These activities occur over at least a six month time span during the mandatory pre-filing period required by the Energy Policy Act of 2005 and are detailed in the FERC's regulations under Title 18 of the Code of Federal Regulations (CFR), § 157.21.

Based on this input from FERC staff, the project sponsors continue to develop the front-end-engineering-design (FEED) to be filed as part of the formal application for the proposed LNG facility. The design information, which must be contained in the formal application, is extensive and is specified by 18 CFR § 380.12 (m) and (o). In order to ensure that the filings are complete, FERC publicly issued "Draft Guidance For Filing Resource Reports 11 (Reliability and Safety) & 13 (Engineering and Design) For LNG Facility Applications" in December 2005. This document clarified the level of detail required for the engineering submittal so FERC staff can adequately assess the safety, operability, and reliability of the proposed design. Areas for specific guidance and clarification include:

- the level of detail, including a requirement for a hazard design review, necessary for the FEED submitted to the FERC;
- LNG spill containment sizing and design criteria for impoundments, sumps, sub-dikes, troughs or trenches;
- design spills to be used in the calculation of thermal and flammable vapor exclusion zones; and
- use of the Coast Guard's Navigation and Vessel Inspection Circular 05-05 and the waterway suitability assessment process.

The level of detail required to be submitted in the proposed design will require the project sponsor to perform substantial front-end engineering of the complete facility. The design information is required to be site-specific and developed to the extent that further detailed design will not result in changes to the siting considerations, basis of design, operating conditions, major equipment selections, equipment design conditions, or safety system designs considered by the FERC during the review process. The required information must include all features necessary for commissioning, start-up, operation and maintenance of the facility, including details of the utility, safety, fire protection and security systems. Novel designs require additional detail for proof of concept.

A complete FEED submittal will include up-to-date piping and instrumentation diagrams (P&IDs). Information on these drawings allows FERC staff to begin assessing the feasibility of the proposed design. Adequate P&IDs will include:

- equipment duty, capacity and design conditions;
- piping class specifications;
- vent, drain, cooldown and recycle piping;
- isolation flanges, blinds and insulating flanges;
- control valves and operator types (indicating valve fail position);
- control loops including software connections;
- alarm and shutdown set points;
- shutdown interlocks;
- relief valve set points; and
- relief valve inlet and outlet piping size.

Once an application is formally made to the Commission, FERC staff performs a detailed review of the information supporting the proposed LNG facility design. Since the enactment of the Energy Policy Act of 2005, no later than 30 days after the application filing, the agency designated by the Governor of the state where the terminal is proposed may file an advisory report on state and local safety considerations. Before issuing an order authorizing an applicant to site, construct, expand, or operate an LNG terminal, the Commission shall review and respond specifically to the issues raised.

During the analysis of the application, FERC staff compiles pertinent technical information to assess the design of the LNG facility. Although operability and reliability of the proposed design are considered, our primary focus is on the safety features that must be built into the system. This review is performed prior to any Commission approval and evaluates the safety of:

- the LNG transfer systems;
- storage tanks and process vessels;
- pumps and vaporizers;
- pressure relief, vent and disposal systems;
- instrumentation and controls;
- spill containment systems;
- hazard detection and control systems; and
- emergency shutdown systems.

Each LNG import terminal must have an extensive array of hazard detection devices to provide an early warning for the presence of combustible gases, fires, or spills of LNG and activate emergency shut-down systems. Using the submitted design, FERC staff assesses the conceptual hazard detection system, which typically consists of combustible-gas detectors, fire detectors, heat detectors, smoke or combustion product detectors, and low temperature detectors. Typically, each facility will have over 100 of these types of detectors.

Use of these active systems to automatically shutdown equipment, and other passive safety protections, such as impoundments, are reviewed to ensure that appropriate safety provisions are incorporated in the plant design. A detailed layout of the passive spill containment system showing the location of impoundments, sumps, sub-dikes, channels, and water removal systems is evaluated to allow FERC staff to assess the feasibility of the location, design configuration, dimensions, capacity and materials of construction for this system. In accordance with Title 49 of the Code of Federal Regulations, § 193.2181, these spill containment systems must accommodate 110 percent of an LNG tank's maximum liquid capacity.

Active hazard control systems consisting of strategically placed dry chemical extinguishers; carbon dioxide or nitrogen snuffing equipment; high expansion foam systems; and fire-water systems throughout the terminal are evaluated in accordance with Federal regulations and good engineering practices. A detailed layout of the fire water system showing the location of fire water pumps, piping, hydrants, hose reels, and auxiliary or appurtenant service facilities is reviewed for adequacy.

In addition, each storage or process area containing LNG must be surrounded by an impoundment structure to contain and limit potential spills associated with that equipment. Based on the size and location of these impoundments, the project sponsor must establish exclusion zones around the facility so that the effects from potential LNG pool fires and flammable vapors from an unignited LNG spill do not pose a hazard to the public. In accordance with Title 49 CFR § 193.2057 and 193.2059, and in conjunction with the National Fire Protection Association 59A LNG Standards, thermal radiation and vapor dispersion exclusion zones are calculated by FERC staff based on spill scenarios and heat flux levels. The operator must be able to legally control land uses within any portion of these zones extending beyond the terminal site to prevent damaging effects of an LNG pool fire or a flammable vapor mixture from impacting public safety.

Further, during the pre-authorization phase and beyond the cryogenic design review, each application for an LNG facility is subject to a detailed review by the FERC staff of numerous other studies and reports that the applicants are required to complete. These include:

- seismic analyses;
- fire protection evaluations;
- threat and vulnerability assessments; and
- Operation and Maintenance manuals.

The information used for the pre-authorization review is gathered from the application, data requests, and a *Cryogenic Design Technical Conference* held with the applicant's design team. This meeting allows FERC staff and company engineers to discuss specific engineering-related issues. Representatives from the Coast Guard and DOT, as well as state and local fire marshals, are invited to attend. Although the Coast Guard is generally in attendance to address facility issues, the issues specifically related to LNG vessel transit are dealt with during the Coast Guard's separate waterway suitability assessment (WSA) process.

The staff's conclusions and recommendations on the proposed design, including all safety measures, are presented in the Safety section of the publicly-released FERC environmental assessment or environmental impact statement (EIS). Ultimately, these recommendations have appeared as conditions in Commission Order approving the project. In addition to design considerations, the Order may also contain other LNG-specific standard conditions that pertain to the safe operation and security of the facility. If the Commission decides that a project would be safe, is in the public interest, and authorizes it, continued review would occur during the pre-construction phase.

Pre-Construction Review—If a project sponsor receives a Commission Order and decides to pursue the project, it will engage the services of an Engineering, Procurement, and Construction (EPC) firm to commence detailed engineering of the facility. This process results in a "final design" that usually contains further development or minor refinements to the approved FEED on file with the FERC. For these modifications, the FERC Order requires the project sponsor to request approval for the change, justify it relative to site-specific conditions, explain how that modification provides an equal or greater level of protection than the original measure; and receive approval from the Director of OEP before implementing that modification. For more significant changes, the project sponsor would be required to file an amendment or a new application, initiating another extensive review at the Commission.

The final design will typically include hundreds of pages of detailed engineering drawings and specifications for every area and piece of equipment in the facility including the marine platform, transfer lines, tanks, sumps, pumps, compressors, vaporizers, and blowers. Only after FERC staff has reviewed the final design for a particular facility component to ensure it complies with all the safety conditions of the Order and that it conforms to the approved design on file, will authorization to construct that component be granted. We review large scale issues such as the facility's final plot plan and location of equipment, tanks, and impoundments to verify that all exclusion zones remain in compliance with siting regulations. These final review checks will also confirm that the number, location, type, and size of hazard detection and hazard control equipment match or improve upon the approved design and that redundancy, fault detection, and fault alarm monitoring exist in all potentially hazardous areas and enclosures.

Prior to entering the detailed design phase, project sponsors perform a hazard and operability study of the initial design. This study is intended to identify potential process deviations that could occur during operation and lead to personnel injury or equipment damage. The analysis proceeds by systematically identifying possible causes for operational deviations and the consequences of these deviations at numerous locations in the regasification process. Areas of concern typically include equipment failures, human failure, external events, siting issues, previous incidents, and safeguard or control failures. These causes and consequences are in turn used to evaluate the inherent safeguards in the design and to identify suitable design modifications as required. Examples of the additional safeguards that are required are: detection systems, prevention systems, procedural safeguards, active and passive safety equipment, emergency response procedures, and secondary containment.

During the pre-construction phase, FERC staff will review this study as well as review all piping and instrumentation diagrams, including every valve and thermocouple, to make sure that the overall safety of the final design provides an equal or greater level of protection as the original design approved by the FERC.

Furthermore, the design of some facility components such as the foundation of the LNG tanks will be reviewed by geotechnical experts who determine if the foundation structure is capable of safely supporting the load of a full LNG tank, even during seismic events.

In accordance with the Energy Policy Act of 2005, Commission Orders authorizing an LNG import terminal require the project sponsor to develop an Emergency Response Plan (ERP) in consultation with the U.S. Coast Guard and state and local agencies. Prior to any construction at the facility, this plan, which must also include cost-sharing provisions for safety and security, must be approved by the Commission. The ERP must include written procedures for responding to: emergencies within the LNG terminal; emergencies that could affect the public adjacent to an LNG terminal; and emergencies that could affect the public along the LNG vessel transit route. The ERP must be prepared in consultation with the Coast Guard and state and local agencies, and it must be approved by the Commission prior to any final approval to begin construction at the terminal site.

Commission engineering staff reviews each ERP to ensure that the appropriate state and local agencies have been involved in preparing the plan, that the local Coast Guard Marine Safety Office has been consulted and concurs, and that the following topics are completely addressed:

- Structure of the incident management organization of the LNG terminal; and name, title, organization, and phone number of all required agency contacts;
- Procedures for responding to emergencies within the LNG Terminal—identification of the types and locations of specific emergency incidents that may reasonably be expected to occur at the LNG terminal due to operating malfunctions, structural collapse, personnel error, forces of nature and activities adjacent to the terminal;
- Procedures for emergency evacuation adjacent to the LNG Terminal and along LNG vessel transit route; detailed procedures for recognizing an uncontrollable emergency and taking action to minimize harm to terminal personnel and the public; procedures for the prompt notification of appropriate officials and emergency response agencies based on the level and severity of potential incidents; and the sequence of such notifications;
- Plans for initial and continuing training of plant operators and local responders; and provisions for annual emergency response drills by terminal emergency personnel, first responders, and appropriate federal, state and local officials and emergency response agencies; and
- Documentation that the required consultation with the Coast Guard and state and local agencies has been completed through correspondence with consulting agencies, and minutes or notes of coordination meetings.

In addition, both the Energy Policy Act of 2005 and Commission Orders authorizing LNG terminals require that the ERP include a Cost-Sharing Plan identifying the mechanisms for funding all project-specific security costs and safety/emergency management costs that would be imposed on state and local agencies. The cost-sharing plan must specify what the LNG terminal operator will provide to cover the cost of the state and local resources required to manage the security of the LNG terminal and LNG vessel, and the state and local resources required for safety and emergency management, including:

- Direct reimbursement for any per-transit security and/or emergency management costs (for example, overtime for police or fire department personnel);
- Capital costs associated with security/emergency management equipment and personnel base (for example, patrol boats, fire fighting equipment); and
- Annual costs for providing specialized training for local fire departments, mutual aid departments, and emergency response personnel; and for conducting exercises.

The cost-sharing plan must include the LNG terminal operator's letter of commitment with agency acknowledgement for each state and local agency designated to receive resources.

FERC and other federal agencies work with state and local entities, as well as the general public, to ensure that all public interest considerations are carefully studied and weighed before a facility is permitted and allowed to begin construction and operate, and that public safety and the environment are given high priority. No construction may commence until the Director of OEP finds that all safety requirements have been met.

Pre-Operation Review—Once construction of the project has been authorized to begin, Commission staff inspects each site at least once every eight weeks to ensure that project construction is consistent with the designs approved during the pre-authorization and pre-construction review phases.

During these inspections, Commission staff physically examines the entire site to verify the ongoing construction activities in each area. Staff confirms that the locations of individual process equipment under construction are in accordance with the approved site design, ensuring that the safe distances required between property lines, equipment, and facilities are being maintained. Staff verifies that all site activity and equipment under construction comply with the conditions of the Order that are applicable for that phase of the project. Commission engineers also meet with the owner's project design engineers to discuss any modifications or design refinements that may result from the detailed design phase of development—for example, adjustments considered necessary as a result of equipment vendor specifications or other insights realized during construction.

In addition, staff reviews both the owner's and the EPC firm's quality assurance plans to verify that rigorous and stringent quality control inspections are being conducted by both parties during all phases of the construction process. Inspections must apply to equipment and components being fabricated at manufacturing sites, material and equipment received at the construction site, specific assembly or fabrication methods employed during construction, and also the continuous verification of the precision and quality of all structural work carried out during the construction process.

Staff reviews all of the non-conformance reports generated by the project's quality control inspectors and how these incidents have been satisfactorily resolved. These deviations from the intended quality of work are evaluated by FERC staff to ensure that the final quality of the work will meet or exceed design requirements. Problems of significant magnitude are required to be reported to the Commission within 24 hours.

During the later stages of the typical three-year construction period, FERC staff monitors the EPC contractors' efforts to commission (*i.e.*, test and start-up) the various process systems and equipment throughout the terminal in preparation for the commencement of commercial operations. Commission staff is actively involved in the commissioning phase to verify that the final, constructed facility complies with the design authorized by the Commission Order, and that the project sponsor has complied with all conditions. This review includes verification that all of the cryogenic design recommendations in the Order applicable to the facility's pre-construction and construction phases have been fulfilled. Multiple on-site inspections are performed to confirm the construction and location of all plant equipment, process systems, and safety systems, including:

- Verifying LNG spill containment structures for completion of walls, piping, correct slope, size, materials used, sump pumps, and instrumentation for cold detection shutoff, and confirmation that proper materials have been used to complete containment;
- Checking critical instrumentation against the P&IDs with the actual piping, valves, and controls; and the instrument readouts, controls, and alarm/shutdown functions in the plant control room;
- Confirming that all required hazard detection devices (combustible gas, fire, smoke, low temperature) have been installed, including an examination of the cause and effect diagrams and instrument locations for appropriate redundancy and "alarm" and "shutdown" conditions. The physical inspection also evaluates detector location and orientation for blind spots that may require additional hazard detection devices;
- Confirming that all dry chemical, carbon dioxide, or other fire extinguishing units/bottles have been installed. The devices are checked to confirm proper weight and areas have been covered;
- Confirming that all critical pressure relief valves have been installed, have proper discharge orientation, and vent collection systems are operable;

- Confirming that the entire firewater system is in place, including monitors, hydrants, pumps, screens, deluge and water supply, and has been tested for operation;
- Checking each LNG storage tank's equipment including elevation bench marks, rotational devices, liquid level gauges, pressure and vacuum relief valves, and discretionary relief valves for proper installation and confirming that all permanent covers have been installed. After cool-down, the fill lines and tank penetrations are inspected for presence of excessive low temperature conditions;
- Checking critical, required alarms and shutdowns, including set points (*e.g.*, tank foundation temperatures, send-out temperature shutdown set points) within the plant's Control Room and satellite control centers;
- Confirming that all temporary construction structures have been removed and the facility complies with National Electrical Code Division requirements; and
- Confirming that the plant's Emergency Shutdown System has been tested and is fully operational, including that all required systems have been tied into it.

Prior to operation, each LNG tank is hydrostatically tested to gauge the tank's ability to handle expected loads. During the hydrostatic test, the FERC Order will require the project sponsor to include a reliable measurement system to monitor any deflections in the tank foundation or structure during the hydraulic test. At a minimum, this system must include as many monitoring points as is necessary so that sag, warping, tilt, and settlements can be monitored. Tolerances for sag, tilt, and shell warping must meet or exceed the limits specified by the tank manufacturer. In this manner, the strength of the tank is thoroughly examined under loads similar to what will be experienced in actual operation. The final design review will ensure that adequate plans for such testing are in place for all facility components.

As part of the pre-commission inspection, FERC staff also reviews the Start-up Manual, Safety Plan Manual, and Operations and Maintenance Manuals applicable to the installation. This review includes verifying that the terminal staff has received the necessary training to operate the plant or new systems, if an existing plant is being expanded. We confirm that the plant has employed the required staffing with a level and function appropriate for the facility.

FERC staff confirms that all plant security systems are in place (personnel, cameras, and other equipment), and that the Facility Security Plan is current. This review also includes confirming that all spare equipment that was authorized is on site and properly installed.

FERC staff also checks the entire facility site to ensure that all recommended environmental mitigation measures including erosion and sediment controls are in place, are being properly maintained, and that the company is making prudent steps to ensure that the site is properly stabilized for the operational life of the facility (*e.g.*, installation of shore line stabilization mats and rip rap).

Prior to operation, FERC staff also reviews the facility security to ensure compliance with the authorized design. Principal concerns are compliance with the DOT regulations, as well as sufficient levels of security provided by surveillance cameras; intrusion detection systems; security fencing; and on-site access control plans.

Only after all of the above-identified inspections and reviews have been successfully completed would FERC staff recommend that the terminal is ready for operations. The Director of OEP must issue a letter to the company that authorizes commencement of service from the facility.

Prior to operation, the terminal must also satisfy other federal agency requirements. For example, the facility must have a Facility Security Plan approved by the Coast Guard and a Vessel Transit Management Plan prepared by the Coast Guard and port stakeholders.

FERC oversight continues after an LNG import terminal project commences commercial operations. In fact, the Office of Energy Projects was reorganized to specifically create a Branch that is dedicated to ensuring that all FERC requirements, including safety and security measures, are complied with throughout the life of the project. Each LNG facility under FERC jurisdiction is required to file semi-annual reports to summarize plant operations, maintenance activity and abnormal events for the previous six months. LNG facilities are also required to report significant, non-scheduled events, including safety-related incidents (*e.g.*, LNG or natural gas vapor releases, fires, explosions, mechanical failures, unusual over-pressurization, major injuries) and security-related incidents (*e.g.*, attempts to enter site, suspicious activities near the plant site or around the marine terminal), as soon as possible but no later than within 24 hours. In addition, FERC staff conducts annual on-site inspections and technical reviews of each import terminal throughout its entire operational life. The inspection reviews the integrity of all plant equipment, operation and maintenance activities, safety and security systems, any unusual operational incidents, and non-routine maintenance activities during the previous year. Ultimately, the Director of the Office of Energy Projects has the authority to take whatever measures are necessary to protect life, health, property or the environment.

We are proud of our track record working with DOT, the Coast Guard, states agencies, and with all interested stakeholders on these projects, and we are committed to continuing LNG's outstanding operational performance.

The Safe History of LNG Shipping

In addition to ensuring safe and secure terminal sites, FERC coordinates closely with the Coast Guard to ensure the safety and security of the LNG vessel transit to the import facility. Under our pre-filing regulations, applicants are required to prepare a WSA, which is reviewed by the Coast Guard and members of the local Area Maritime Security Committee. The Coast Guard convenes a working group consisting of members of the local Area Maritime Security Committee, federal agencies, state and local law enforcement, state and local firefighters, maritime and security professionals, and key port stakeholders throughout the port area.

Under Coast Guard supervision, this group, through a series of focused meetings, brings together its viewpoints to form a consensus on appropriate measures and mitigation needed to manage responsibly the safety and security risks posed by LNG marine traffic. At these meetings, FERC staff serves as the LNG technical advisor to the working group, provides insight from our participation in other waterways, and assists in identifying credible hazard scenarios. The group's detailed recommendations from the meetings are presented to the Coast Guard to assist in the Captain of the Port's review of the applicant's WSA. Based on its review, the Captain of the Port will make a preliminary determination on the suitability of the waterway. This determination will be presented to the FERC in the Coast Guard's Waterway Suitability Report.

The Waterway Suitability Report, filed with the Commission, preliminarily determines whether the waterway is suitable for LNG vessel transits, from both a safety and security perspective, and identifies additional resources that may be required. The results of this analysis are incorporated into the draft EIS and released for public comment. The 45-day comment period usually includes a public meeting near the proposed facility and along the pipeline route. In this manner, after public comment has been received and the final EIS is published, the Commission has a complete record on the suitability of the waterway and potential resource requirements prior to deciding whether to approve a particular LNG import terminal.

Since the beginning of commercial operations in 1959, LNG carriers have made over 46,000 voyages worldwide without a significant release of cargo or a major accident involving an LNG carrier. In no instance has an LNG cargo tank been breached either by an accidental or intentional event.

Any LNG carriers used to import LNG to the United States must be constructed and operated in accordance with the International Maritime Organization's (IMO) *Code for the Construction and Equipment of Ships Carrying Liquefied Gases in Bulk*, the *International Convention for the Safety of Life at Sea*, as well as 46 CFR Part 154, which contain the United States safety standards for vessels carrying bulk liquefied natural gas. Foreign flag LNG carriers are required to possess a valid IMO Certificate of Fitness and a Coast Guard Certificate of Compliance.

LNG carriers are well-built, robust vessels employing double-hull construction, with the inner and outer hulls separated by about 10 feet. The LNG cargo tanks are further separated from the inner hull by a layer of insulation approximately one-foot thick. As required by the IMO conventions and design standards, hold spaces and insulation areas on an LNG carrier are equipped with gas detection and low temperature alarms. These devices monitor for leaks of LNG into the insulation between primary and secondary LNG cargo tank barriers. In addition, hazard detection systems are also provided to monitor the hull structure adjacent to the cargo tank, compressor rooms, motor rooms, cargo control rooms, enclosed spaces in the cargo area, specific ventilation hoods and gas ducts, and air locks.

Even in the few instances worldwide where there have been incidents, the integrity of LNG vessel construction and safety systems has been demonstrated. One of the more significant incidents involved the *El Paso Paul Kayser* which grounded on a rock in the Strait of Gibraltar during a loaded voyage from Algeria to the United States in June 1979. Extensive bottom damage to the outer hull and the ballast tanks resulted; however, the cargo tanks were not damaged, and no cargo was released.

There have been a few other instances where LNG ships have grounded. In 1980, the *LNG Taurus* grounded near the entrance to Taboata Harbor, Japan. The grounding resulted in extensive bottom damage, but the cargo tanks were not affected and no cargo was released. The ship was refloated and the cargo was unloaded. In 2004, the *Tenaga Lima* was grounded on rocks, due to a strong current while proceeding to open sea East of Mopko, South Korea. The ship's shell plating was torn open and fractured over an approximate area of 20- by 80-feet. Internal breaches allowed water to enter the insulation space between the primary and secondary membranes. However, the ship was refloated, repaired, and returned to service. Although damage was incurred when these LNG ships were grounded, their cargo tanks were never penetrated and no LNG was released.

In another incident, the *Norman Lady* was struck by the nuclear submarine *USS Oklahoma City* while the submarine was rising to periscope depth near the Strait of Gibraltar in November 2002. The LNG carrier sustained only minor damage to the outer layer of its double hull but no damage to its cargo tanks.

More recently, the *Khannur* had a cargo tank overfill into the ship's vapor handling system during unloading at Everett, Massachusetts, in 2001. Approximately 100 gallons of LNG were vented onto the protective decking over the cargo tank dome resulting in several cracks. After inspection by the Coast Guard, the *Khannur* was allowed to discharge its cargo. In 2002, the *Mostaefa Ben Boulaid* had LNG spill onto its deck during loading operations in Algeria. The spill, which was believed to be caused by overflow, caused brittle fracturing of the carbon steelwork. The ship was required to discharge its cargo and proceed to dock for repairs. Although all these incidents resulted in an LNG release, there were no injuries in any of these incidents.

The most recent incident occurred in 2006 when the *Golar Freeze* moved away from its docking berth during unloading in Savannah, Georgia. The powered emergency release couplings on the unloading arms activated as designed, and transfer operations were shut down, preventing release of significant amounts of LNG or any structural or environmental damage.

After inspection and onsite clearance by FERC staff and the Coast Guard, the arms were reactivated and transfer operations resumed without incident.

The low number of LNG tanker incidents can be attributed to the careful handling of the tankers, as well as safety and security procedures used in the ports. The transit of an LNG vessel through a waterway is strictly controlled by the Coast Guard to prevent accidental or intentional incidents that could damage the vessel or endanger the public. Entry into a port typically involves Coast Guard requirements such as:

- 96 hours advance notification of arrival and the vessel crew manifest;
- Coast Guard boarding of the LNG Vessel for an inspection of the ship safety system;
- Moving safety/security zones around the LNG vessel;
- Armed and unarmed escorts;
- Tug escort to assist with turning and mooring operations;
- Safety and security zones around the terminal dock while the vessel is berthed;
- Accompaniment by a state-licensed pilot; and
- Inspection of the dock safety systems before commencing cargo transfer.

With these operational measures, the transit of LNG carriers has been demonstrated to be safe along the waterway from the berthing area to the territorial sea.

GAO Report [No GAO-07-316]: "Public Safety Consequences of a Terrorist Attack on a Tanker Carrying Liquefied Natural Gas Need Clarification."

I am encouraged that the GAO report reached many of the same conclusions on LNG hazards which we have published in each FERC environmental impact statement. The findings of the GAO expert panel concur with FERC staff's assessment of the potential public safety consequences of a terrorist attack on an LNG tanker regarding:

- unconfined vapor cloud explosions;
- freeze burns;
- asphyxiation; and
- rapid phase transitions (RPTs).

These phenomena do not pose a significant hazard to the on-shore public during a large-scale LNG spill. Natural gas vapors (primarily methane) can detonate if contained within a confined space, such as a building or structure, and ignited. However, unconfined methane-air mixtures have been ignited but not detonated in experiments. Although the addition of heavier hydrocarbons influences the tendency of an unconfined vapor cloud to detonate, the possibility for detonation of a large unconfined vapor cloud is unrealistic due to precise timing, necessary mixing, and required amount of initiating explosives.

Similarly, the public is not at risk from freeze burns or asphyxiation. Clouds from an LNG spill would be continuously mixing with the warmer air surrounding the spill site. Dispersion modeling estimates that the majority of the cloud would be within 25 degrees Fahrenheit of the surrounding atmospheric temperature, with colder temperatures closest to the spill source and away from the public. In addition, the majority of the cloud would be below concentrations which could result in oxygen deprivation effects, including asphyxiation, with the highest methane concentrations closest to the spill source.

The report also focused on potential impacts from RPTs. Our project-specific EISs include a discussion of this issue. While RPTs can occur during a spill on water, impacts would be limited to the area within the pool and would be unlikely to affect the public. The overpressure events observed during experimentation have been relatively small, estimated to be equivalent to several pounds of TNT. Although such an event is not expected to cause significant damage to an LNG vessel, it could increase the rate of LNG pool spreading and the LNG vaporization rate for a spill on water.

FERC staff also concur with the GAO report on the potential for a boiling liquid expanding vapor explosion (BLEVE). While it may be theoretically possible, the low storage pressure, use of insulation, and installation of relief valves on both onshore LNG storage tanks and LNG carriers render the possibility of a BLEVE unlikely for LNG as it is normally transported and stored.

The report further states that the most likely public safety impact from an LNG spill would be from heat associated with a pool fire. FERC staff has also analyzed this issue in the course of project specific reviews and has reached that same conclusion. In its 2004 report, Sandia considered scenarios likely to breach an LNG cargo tank. Events ranged from accidental collisions, groundings, rammings, sabotage, hijackings, attacks with small missiles and rockets, and attacks with bulk explosives. These types of events which could potentially lead to a large LNG spill would likely be accompanied by a number of ignition sources. Surrounding impacts would be from an LNG pool fire, and subsequent radiant heat hazards, rather than the formation of a large unconfined vapor cloud. Each of our EISs describes those potential impacts on the local waterway.

As stated in the 2004 Sandia report, the most significant impacts to public safety and property exist within approximately 500 meters (1,640 feet) of a spill due to thermal hazards from a fire, with lower public health and safety impacts beyond 1,600 meters (approximately 1 mile). We believe the Sandia report and FERC's site-specific analysis are a reasonable and conservative basis to examine potential impacts from an LNG tanker fire.

The GAO study reports four experts thought the Sandia distance calculations were "too conservative"; four thought "not conservative enough"; seven thought "about right." Although the report characterizes this as disagreement, the majority of the panel (11 of 15) responded that the calculations were either accurate or overly conservative.

Although FERC staff generally agrees with the material presented in the GAO report, further explanation of some information is necessary. For instance, the report mentions that an LNG vapor cloud is visible, but natural gas vapors are colorless. The fog-like appearance usually associated with an LNG vapor cloud results from condensation of water vapor in the air due to the lower temperatures of the cloud. However, appearance of this visible water vapor does not necessarily reflect the flammable portion of the cloud. In addition, the report states that LNG fires burn hotter when the maximum flame temperature of methane is nearly the same as other fuels. Radiant heat from a large-scale LNG pool fire is assumed to be greater than other common hydrocarbon fuels based on the results of small-scale fire measurements. However, it has not been proven that this effect would scale up to larger fires. Oxygen deprivation and smoke generation in a larger fire may lead to lower surface emissive power.

In each EIS, FERC staff includes site-specific modeling done with the methodology developed for FERC by ABS Consulting. In areas of uncertainty due to the lack of large-scale field data, the FERC model uses conservative assumptions (*i.e.*, resulting in longer hazard distances). These conservative assumptions concern: calculation of the pool spread; determination of the pool fire flame height; and use of a higher surface emissive power. Our results have been in agreement with the Sandia guidance zones of concern, and support the conservative nature of the calculations.

Cascading failure of the LNG storage tanks, addressed by Sandia in its previous examination of currently operating LNG carriers, was another topic of disagreement among the experts. Sandia stated that the events would not likely involve more than two or three cargo tanks. As stated in the 2004 Sandia report, the nominal hole size of an intentional breaching scenario would be no more than 5- to 7-m2, which is the appropriate range we use in the FERC staff EIS for calculating potential hazards from spills. For a breach of a 7 m^2 in a single tank, the fire duration would be approximately 10 minutes. Whereas smaller hole sizes could result in fires lasting over 1 hour. While the expected fire duration from cascading tank failure would increase, the overall fire hazard was not expected by Sandia to increase by more than 20 to 30 percent. GAO recommended that further study of this issue could be undertaken by Sandia. We concur that further study on cascading mechanisms may clarify if the subsequent failure of the fourth and fifth cargo tanks would occur over time with the most probable consequence of further extending the duration of the fire.

Related to cascading failure mechanisms are the effects such an event may have on a pool fire (*i.e.*, whether it would increase the duration of the event, increase the size of the pool fire, or lower the radiant heat due to increased smoke generation). Current knowledge of the physical properties associated with an LNG spill are based on small-scale (<35 meter diameter pool) tests. How the data collected from small-scale pool fires can be extrapolated to the potentially large-scale cargo releases is a subject of much debate among the modeling community. Quantifying the physical properties of large-scale LNG spill should be a priority. This will allow analysts to refine the consequence models and generate more consistent results. Sandia currently has this effort underway with the Advanced LNG Pool Fire Testing Program.

Initial experimental results are expected in a few months, and the large-scale experiments are planned to be complete by August 2008. The initial results of these experiments will determine better correlations for the flame height and mass fire behavior which could be expected during larger fires. The large-scale tests will result in better data on vapor production rates, smoke generation, and surface emissive power. In a separate effort, Sandia is also applying its threat analysis and spill probability methodology to LNG tankers larger than those previously studied. The research is designed to provide an estimation of the sizes of breaches, including hole size, spill volume, and number of tanks breached, for membrane-designed ship classes ranging from 216,000 m^3 to 267,000 m^3. These are representative of LNG ships that are currently being designed, constructed and proposed for use at LNG facilities in the United States. Presently, each Order issued by the Commission requires the applicant to prove that staff's modeling of hazards for those large tankers is accurate. They must do this and get approval from the Director of OEP prior to accepting the larger size ships.

We will use this new data to enhance our modeling capabilities for determining possible consequence areas resulting from a successful intentional attack on an LNG tanker. FERC staff has always committed to modify our analyses, when appropriate, as new data and improved modeling technologies are developed.

I believe that this research is beneficial and necessary and will provide more exact information and technical details. Removing the uncertainty inherent in modeling phenomena will result in more accurate models. However, in current areas of uncertainty, we have made conservative assumptions. FERC staff believes the refined models will likely show smaller consequence areas. FERC, and along with it, the Coast Guard and DOT have a competent understanding of the risks and how to mitigate them effectively to ensure public safety.

In conclusion, LNG is a commodity which has been and will continue to be transported safely in the United States. The U.S. Coast Guard, the U.S. DOT and FERC are committed to ensuring that safety. As a matter of policy, the Commission is committed to continually raising the bar on energy infrastructure safety. As new safety measures, improved monitoring equipment, and enhanced safety and security protocols are developed, the Commission will ensure that LNG remains a safe and secure fuel source for the country.

Statement of Ron Davis
President
Marine Engineers' Beneficial Association

Thank you Chairman Thompson and Ranking Member King, and thank you to the rest of the Committee for inviting me to speak before you today. I would specifically like to thank you for allowing us the opportunity to discuss the unique issues we face in safely and securely transporting Liquefied Natural Gas to the United States.

My name is Ron Davis, and I am the President of the Marine Engineers' Beneficial Association. The MEBA is the nation's oldest maritime labor union, representing deck and engineering officers licensed by the United States Coast Guard. Our mariners serve in a variety of capacities in the commercial, government owned and operated, and domestic fleets, as well as in shore side employment.

The MEBA was proud to take a leading role in the development of the transportation of LNG by ocean tank vessel in the 1970s. Our members crewed U.S. flag LNG vessels until 2001. Today, however, not a single LNG tanker flies the American flag, and none of these vessels are crewed by Americans. We feel that this represents a serious threat to America, and we have been working to restore American mariners aboard this important segment of the maritime community.

Need for Shipboard Import of LNG to the United States

According to the Federal Energy Regulatory Commission, U.S. natural gas demand is expected to increase by 40% by 2025 to 30.7 trillion cubic feet (TCF).[I] However, domestic supply, which has not equaled demand for many years, will only increase by 14.5 %. Without intervention, our natural gas supply will not keep pace with industry and the public's demand. Mr. Jeff Wright, Chief of the Energy Infrastructure Group, Office of Energy Project, Federal Energy Regulatory Commission cites the following reasons for this situation:

- Decline in the United States' underground domestic gas reserves;[ii]
- Canada's problems with flattening gas production in the Western Canadian Sedimentary Basin (WSCB) and its need to fulfill its own demands;[iii] and
- Continuation of Mexico's growing economy with Mexico keeping an increasing share of its natural gas to meet its future demands.[iv]

This means the United States cannot rely solely on natural gas produced in North America. Therefore, LNG will need to be imported to the United States on oceangoing LNG tankships.

Thorough Vetting of U.S. Merchant Mariners Provides Unmatched Shipboard and Deepwater Port Security

All LNG entering the U.S. is carried on foreign flag ships operated by either non-U.S. citizen mariners, or aliens who are not lawfully admitted to the United States for permanent residence. Unlike foreign seamen:

- U.S. Merchant Mariners receive their credentials to work from the U.S. Coast Guard;
- U.S. Merchant Mariners undergo extensive background checks performed by the Federal Bureau of Investigation;
- U.S. Merchant Mariners are background checked through a National Driver (vehicle) Record database;
- U.S. Merchant Mariners will also be subject to jurisdiction of the Transportation Safety Administration (TSA) where they will be vetted through a terrorist watch database in order to receive a Transportation Worker Identification Card (TWIC).
- U.S. Merchant Mariners are citizens of the United States or aliens lawfully admitted for permanent residence.

American mariners undergo a stringent and thorough vetting and credentialing process. Our Coast Guard-issued license is considered accurate (with regard to identity of the holder) and valid with respect to the qualifications and ability of the individual mariner. Moreover, the document is relatively tamper-proof. Each mariner goes through an extensive background check by several federal agencies including the Coast Guard, Federal Bureau of Investigation and now with the TWIC coming into effect, the Transportation Security Administration.

While foreign mariners may be required to comply with their government's regulations as well as international standards, the validity of some of the credentials is suspect. A few years ago, International Transport Workers Federation President, David Cockroft, purchased an authentic Panamanian first officers certificate and sea book despite no practical maritime experience. The Seafarers' International Research Centre at the University of Wales investigated the issue of fraudulent qualifications. Its preliminary findings revealed 12,653 cases of forgery in 2001.

Federal and state government, local municipalities and the communities surrounding LNG import terminals can be assured, that with American mariners, the LNG vessels are manned by professional seafarers who have the integrity and the training necessary for the safe transport of LNG.

Congress Recognizes Need for U.S. Mariners

Congress has recognized the security that U.S. mariners bring to LNG vessels and has taken steps to promote enhanced security. Last year's Coast

Guard Authorization bill included language that gave priority application processing to companies seeking LNG terminal licenses if they commit to using American crews, and it also directed the Maritime Administration to find ways to promote the use of Americans in this sector.

Problems in Growth of Demand for LNG and with Incoming Generation of LNG Officers

On June 20, 2006, Reuters reported that a growing global demand for liquefied natural gas and tight supply of specialized tankers and crew create a risk of dangerous lapses in standards of security. See, *Darwin (Reuters), LNG Demand Growth Risks Fall in Shipping Standards, June 20, 2006.*

Setting aside the security issue of foreign mariners, the United States must take into consideration the risks involved with poorly trained, insufficiently qualified and questionably vetted mariners who may deliver LNG to its shores. For instance, Yea Byeon-Deok, professor and LNG initiative coordinator of the International Association of Maritime Universities, recently stated at a conference in Australia: "Nobody knows what would happen if a significant accident occurred on a large LNG carrier. All we can say is that a 100,000 ton tanker has four times the energy potential of the atomic bomb used to hit Hiroshima . . . Many sub-standard vessels have begun to appear as demand for LNG increases, while there is a chronic shortage of experienced crew."

New orders for construction of LNG vessels imply a need for 3,575 officers over the next three years, Professor Yea said, of which 60% would need to be at senior or experienced level. Yea warned that "recruitment and training were falling ***dangerously short of requirements to staff complicated vessels which could make dramatic targets for potential terror attacks.***" *Reuters, June 20, 2006*. Mr. Yea pointed out that the growth in "flag of convenience" ships which fly alternative flags to the country of ownership, allow the owners to avoid taxes, quality control and labor regulations which evidences deteriorating standards.

The younger generation of sea-going deck and engineering officers is withdrawing from the industry prematurely. These junior officers are showing less and less interest in continuing to go to sea and they are typically leaving for shore-side positions prior to taking on senior level seagoing positions. This has made it difficult for ship owners and operators to ensure a sustained supply of senior officers. There is as of yet no effective means to counter this tendency. This data is based on a report in the U.S. Coast Guard *Journal of Safety at Sea, Proceedings* regarding the international (non-U.S. Merchant Mariner) pool of shipboard officers.

The U.S. Merchant Marine was not considered in the aforementioned report. Indeed, had the U.S. Merchant Marine been considered, the resulting report would have shown that there is a vibrant and growing U.S. Merchant

Mariner pool resulting in part by investments made in the passenger, freighter and tanker vessel maritime sectors. Moreover, it makes sense to staff LNG vessels delivering cargo to the United States with U.S. merchant mariners. U.S. merchant mariners are true patriots and care about their country—they would not be "for hire" foreign personnel with little or no connection to America other than a job that provides a paycheck. U.S. Coast Guard licensed officers and crew provide answers and solutions to many of the safety and security concerns surrounding the importation of LNG.

Wide Scale Officer Shortage is Resulting in Foreign Ship Operators "Poaching" LNG Officers; Poor Training; Steep Decline in Safety and Security; and Violations of International Law

As reported in numerous articles and studies conducted by leading international maritime trade publications including Tradewinds and Fairplay, LNG owners and operators are lashing out at each other with allegations of "poaching", conducting insufficient training in violation of ISM Code as well as failing to properly check past employment references.

The sudden and sustained surge in global demand for liquefied natural gas and the worldwide shortage of mariners with LNG and steam experience is leading to predictable results. Ship managers seem willing to do whatever they can to get their ships fully crewed in the face of a growing wide-scale officer shortage. "The industry had previously grown slowly, so companies were able to train manpower and expand operations at a comfortable rate of two to three ships every two years," Keith Bainbridge, director of LNG Shipping Solutions, told Fairplay magazine in 2005 "But where an industry experiences 40-50% growth within a couple of years, it will split at the seems," he predicts.[v]

This manpower crisis is made even worse by new ship managers entering the LNG trade. A Fairplay article titled, *Poaching War for Crew Erupts*, cited the "voracious appetite for scarce manning resources, both at sea and onshore. This has created severe competition among LNG owners."[vi]

The Society of International Gas Tanker and Terminal Operators LTD (SIGTTO) has recognized the acute shortage and the reaction by some. "A short-term answer for an LNG vessel operator is to "poach" crew from another such operator but, clearly, the long-term answer is training, training, and further training. SIGTTO members, as much as anyone, wish for the quite unique safety record of LNG shipping to be preserved. The influx of new personnel into the industry is of concern, especially if there is a temptation by a minority of operators to "cut corners" and put officers into positions of responsibility on a LNG carrier before they have been properly trained."[vii]

In an article titled *Officer Crunch Sparks Safety Alarm*, Anglo Eastern Ship Management's training director Pradeep Chawla states that "intense pressure to promote more maritime officers is resulting in inexperienced officers making more mistakes and more dangerous situations on board. The training director noted that, "shortages have made it harder to retain officers because manning agents use higher wages to lure away experienced seafarers, especially in LNG/LPG and other specialized trades."[viii] Moreover, not all companies train officers, with many resorting to poaching.

The crewing crunch is giving rise to new and dangerous theories of crewing to meet the sustained demand. "Some operators are contemplating an airline-style approach, training their crew units to ever-higher standards and frequently rotating them among vessels. That would fly in the face of an industry that had, until last year, been characterized by its conservatism on crewing and had viewed rapid crew rotation as a threat to safety." The article mentions that with the shortage, there is an "increasing incidence of crews of strangers being cobbled together with precious little time to develop mutual trust and overcome their natural fear of blame."

In an article titled *Near Calamities in Cargo Operations, Fairplay* details two case studies, on international vessel crewing practices, to illustrate the dangers of new crew members who are unfamiliar with the vessel or on-board procedures. "In both incidents, one of the factors that contributed to the near calamities was the fact that one or more of the crewmembers involved were new to the ship and unfamiliar with all aspects of the vessel." "The importance of learning the idiosyncrasies of a particular vessel cannot be overstressed, and even when crew are transferred to sister ships they should not assume that every feature of the ships will be the same." As noted above, short cuts in manning and "inventive" solutions to crew shortages can prove to be a recipe for disaster.[ix]

The consequences of crewing instability and poaching can also lead to serious deterioration of the relationship between mariner and management. "There has to be a management team in which officers can pick up the phone and discuss problems openly, rather than hiding them until it is too late" says Simon Pressly, GM of Dorchester Marine, an LNG vessel operator in a Fairplay article. The author continues with the observation that, "Unfortunately, with poaching so rampant, the dangerous lack of crew continuity is likely to continue until operators start making the requisite investments in manpower training."[x]

Tradewinds states that the LNG-crewing shortage is giving rise to some serious shortcomings that are a direct threat to the industry's safety record and are in violation of the International Safety Management (ISM) Code. Some operators and ship managers are employing senior-level ship's officers that were terminated from employment by competing companies due to poor performance and substance abuse.[xi]

On another front, big international shipping companies and ship management firms are feeling the LNG crewing pinch. Some operators are enticing

LNG shipboard officers to switch companies by offering wages at 30-40% higher than what has been paid in the past—and officers are switching companies and leaving their former employer in crisis. Some companies are offering over $18,000 a month (in wages only, not including benefits) to attract qualified LNG officers.[xii]

All decision makers and stakeholders involved with the importation of LNG to the United States must take notice of what is going on in the international market. With growing natural gas demands and some 50-plus applications on the books for LNG import terminals, the American people need to be assured that the most highly trained and experienced personnel are transporting security sensitive LNG to the United States. There is no room for error when it comes to liquefied natural gas. Like no other time in history, the economics are in place whereby the U.S. Merchant Marine can economically and safely deliver LNG cargo; provide a stable pool of mariners for the long term; provide the highest amount of training; and comply with all U.S. and international laws.

International Consequence: Insurance Underwriters Deeply Concerned with Inexperienced Crews Aboard LNG Vessels

A recent article titled *LNG Ships Facing Premium Boost* details the nervousness of the insurance industry as the LNG fleet suffers through poorly managed growing pains. "Underwriters appear to be changing their view of LNG vessels, which have traditionally been regarded as particularly well managed, despite being costly and potentially hazardous." Now, higher insurance premiums are the prospect for LNG vessel owners as a result of "a big deterioration in the claims record of the world gas fleet." Marsh, the largest insurance brokering group issued a report concerning claims of more than $400 million run up by the LNG fleet.[xiii]

Higher insurance premiums are in prospect for owners of LNG carriers after a spate of claims including operational incidents have left insurance underwriters facing big losses according to Marsh.[xiv] Marsh reports that risk profile is increasing due to a shortage of crew with LNG experience.[xv]

With 200 LNG vessels in service and over 100 on order, Marsh identifies a number of factors associated with the rapid growth as adding to the risk profile of the gas-ship fleet including shortage of crews with LNG-carrier experience and new owners entering the market with the intention of trading vessels on the spot market rather than traditional long term charters.[xvi]

The shortage of mariners in the international fleet is dire. It is abundantly clear, therefore, that the U.S. Merchant Marine must enter the market.

International Reaction: Responsible Shipping Ministries React to Manning Shortcuts and Abuse; Use of National Flag Vessels Promoted By Major Importers

Some of the world's largest importers of LNG, Japan and Korea, are an increasingly powerful consumer of LNG, have made registry of LNG ships a matter of national maritime policy. "Japan transported about 43% of its total LNG import of 59.1 million tons in 2003 on Japanese owned and controlled ships. Similarly, Korea transported about 61% of its LNG imports of 19.3 million tons in the same year on Korean controlled ships. In the combined import of Japan and Korea, third-party owned ships constituted only 8.3 percent," says a shipping industry representative.[xvii] It is notable that Japanese and Korean controlled vessels are in respectable registries and do not cut corners on crewing in order to compete on the world market.

India's Shipping Ministry has attempted to rejuvenate its merchant marine by requiring Indian manning and Indian registry for LNG vessels importing to the Indian coastline. However, another branch of the Indian government, the Indian Ministries of Commerce and Petroleum & Natural Gas, has prevailed in the internal battle, handing India a set back in its efforts to build a domestic flagged LNG fleet.

Conclusion

With 97% of all cargo imported to United States being carried on vessels that are not registered under the American-Flag and not crewed by U.S. citizens, one would think that the safe and secure transportation of security sensitive cargo would be a serious concern. More to the point, at this time 100% of all Liquefied Natural Gas that enters the United States is carried on ships staffed by non-U.S. citizen mariners. The MEBA strongly believes that the use of American mariners is a critical component to the safe and secure importation of LNG to the United States.

With this in mind, some responsible corporate citizens in the LNG sector have recently agreed to expand their crewing practices to include U.S. citizen crews on LNG tankers. These companies, Suez LNG/Neptune, Excelerate/Northeast Gateway and Freeport-McMoRan, must be commended. We must also praise Maritime Administrator Sean Connaughton and the Maritime Administration for their efforts to promote American mariners on LNG tankers. Without their help, the progress made with these companies would have been much more difficult.

We look forward to working with Congress and the Administration moving forward to further protect our communities and maritime infrastructure.

Endnotes

[i] Annual Energy Outlook 2005, Energy Information Administration, U.S. Department of Energy, February 2005, Table 13.

[ii] Mr. Wright cites the Annual Energy Outlook 2005, Energy Information Administration, U.S. Department of Energy, Table 13, which reaches the conclusion that production from conventional underground gas deposits is projected to decline between now and 2025. This decline is somewhat offset by increased gas production from non-conventional domestic gas sources (most notably coal-bed methane), increased production from deep water sources (greater than 200 meters) in the Gulf of Mexico, and commencement of deliveries of Alaska gas to the lower 48 states. The Alaskan volumes are problematic according to Mr. Wright, because there has been no application to construct necessary infrastructure to transport the gas, and the timeline from application to first delivery is approximately 10 years.

[iii] The National Energy Board of Canada states, the Western Canadian Sedimentary Basin (WSCB) accounts for more than 90% of the gas production in Canada and for about 23% of North American natural gas production annually. In the last few years, gas production from the WSCB appears to have flattened after many years of growth, leading to increased uncertainty about the ability of industry to increase or even maintain current production levels from the basin over the longer term. See, Canada's Conventional Natural Gas Resources: A Status Report, National Energy Board, April 2004, pp. 9-10.

[iv] Exports of gas to Mexico have increased greatly in the last few years. These exports do not constitute a large out-flow of gas at present. However, the Mexican economy is growing and if it continues to grow, its demand for natural gas will increase and require the United States to import an increasing amount of gas to meet, not only domestic needs, but also the needs of Mexico. In other words, what Mexico imports and shares today by way of natural gas, Mexico may not be able share later. Jeff Wright, Chief, Energy Infrastructure Policy Group, Office of Energy Project, Federal Energy Regulatory Commission, Fall 2005.

[v] *Poaching War for Crews Erupts*, Fairplay International Shipping Weekly, February 24, 2005.

[vi] Id.

[vii] *SIGTTO News*, September 2005, p.5.

[viii] *Poaching War for Crews Erupts*, Fairplay International Shipping Weekly, February 24, 2005.

[ix] *Near Calamities in Cargo Operations*, Fairplay International Shipping Weekly, December 1, 2005.

[x] *Poaching War for Crews Erupts*, Fairplay International Shipping Weekly, February 24, 2005.

[xi] *LNG Crewing Shock*, Tradewinds, February 25, 2005.

[xii] *Philippines Dangles $18,000 Carrot*, Tradewinds, January 9, 2006; See also, *LNG Wage Anger*, Tradewinds, November 4, 2005; *Officer on $320,000 a year, claims Sigtto*, Tradewinds, November 4, 2005.

[xiii] Tradewinds, Insurers Get LNG Jitters, LNG Ships Facing Premiums Boost, March 17, 2006.

[xiv] Id.

[xv] Id.

[xvi] Id.

[xvii] *Foreign Flag Vessels May Bring Down LNG Import Costs*, The Hindu Business Line, December 13, 2005.

Statement of Dr. Phani K. Raj
President
Technology & Management Systems, Inc.
Burlington, MA

Mr. Chairman, Mr. King, Members of the Committee, it is a privilege and high honor for me to be invited to testify and share my knowledge on liquefied natural gas (LNG) safety related to accidental or intentional breach of cargo tanks in a LNG vessel.

1. Introduction

I come before you as a researcher in the field of LNG safety with over 30 years of experience in conducting experiments, analyzing the test results and developing mathematical models for the behavior of LNG upon its release into the environment and the hazards it may pose. My research projects related to LNG have been funded primarily by U.S. Federal agencies (U.S. Coast Guard and U.S. Department of Transportation) and to a lesser extent by the LNG industry. I was one of the members of the research team (and the principal author of the technical report) that conducted the field experiments in mid 1970s to understand the different behavior phenomena associated with the release of LNG on water, including that of the pool fire on water and its radiant heat emission characteristics. This series of tests, which to this day remains as the only comprehensive set of experiments on water, was funded by the United States Coast Guard, and conducted in the U.S. Navy testing facility in China Lake, CA. Many of the mathematical models used today are in one way or other based on the findings from this series of tests, though the test sizes were of a modest scale compared to sizes of postulated spills to which the models are being applied now. My recent research, sponsored jointly by the Pipeline & Hazardous Materials Safety Administration (PHMSA) of the U.S. Department of Transportation and Distrigas of Massachusetts, LLC (DOMAC), has been to evaluate the data from the largest LNG fire experiment to date and model the characteristics of very large LNG pool fires and their radiant heat effects. This research and the model developed are based on the data from larger size LNG fire tests conducted in France in 1987. The model and the findings, which have been published in a peer reviewed technical journal, indicate that large LNG fires behave quite differently than the smaller scale fires (used in China Lake tests) and, in fact, radiate less heat per unit fire area. Other research that I am currently involved in includes the determination of the tolerance (without injury) of human beings to LNG fire radiant heat exposure, and the degree of protection provided by ordinary civilian clothing and other intervening objects to the public from the effects of radiant heat from a large LNG fire.

In my capacity as a scientist and researcher in the field of LNG behavior modeling, I have (I) provided consulting support to the Government agencies, the LNG industry, Standards setting bodies, (ii) testified before administrative and regulatory proceedings, (iii) presented many scientific research findings before peer groups, responded to the safety questions from the public in public hearings, (iv) trained firemen and first responders on the properties and behavior of LNG, and (v) authored a number of technical publications in reputable journals. I also serve on the LNG Standards Committee of the National Fire Protection Association (NFPA), which has developed a consensus standard on LNG facility design, LNG handling and storage, and personnel training requirements. Parts of this standard, especially on LNG fire hazard assessment and protection, have been incorporated in federal regulations.

I review below some of the important questions that have been raised in scientific forums and public debate on LNG behavior and safety and provide my views on the subject. My testimony below will:

(i) Comment on the exemplary safety record of the LNG industry both in the U.S. and worldwide

(ii) Highlight some of the LNG properties that have an impact on potential hazards and compared them with properties of other common fuels,

(iii) Discuss the knowledge related to what is known and unknown in mathematical modeling to predict adverse public impact distances from LNG releases,

(iv) Identify immediate and near term research needs to fill the gaps in our knowledge, and,

(v) Argue that results based on risk analyses and not those based on the consideration of a single scenario (however large the hazard) should form the basis of policy decision-making related to LNG activities. This discussion includes, briefly, the current LNG regulatory requirements in the U.S. and potential for improvements in assessment techniques that may lead to a more balanced and efficient use of resources.

2. Safety Record of the LNG Industry

LNG industry has operated safely both in the U.S. and worldwide for over six decades. There is no technical or operational reason why this exemplary record will not continue. New technologies, application of results of careful research, and continued personnel training are expected to contribute to the enhancement of the safety record.

In the U.S., LNG has been used in peak shaving operations (liquefying pipeline natural gas during periods of low demand, storing the liquid, and re-gasifying it to meet peak demand, generally during winter months) for over 60 years. Trans-continental shipments of LNG in ocean-going tankers started in 1959. The worldwide demand for LNG has grown significantly since the 1960s and today over 150 LNG ships safely deliver the liquid to ports in many countries (including the U.S., Japan, France, et al) in some of the busiest and most congested ports of the world near population centers. The safety record of the LNG industry is enviable and unmatched by any other comparable industry—not a single injury or fatality to a member of the public for over 50 years and extremely low rates of injury even among the workers in the industry. Over 45,000 tanker shipments have occurred world wide to date, without any significant LNG spills (other than very minor leaks through pipe gaskets, overfilling of tanks, and spills during make and break of the unloading arms).

The industry is highly regulated in the U.S. and has to meet very strict mechanical design, personnel training and low public impact standards. The ships are built to international standards, are of double hull design (and have been from the very beginning of the industry). The U.S. Coast Guard inspects every LNG vessel that visits a U.S. port before it enters the port. This inspection includes a check of safety emergency systems, interview with personnel, review of ship's records and a security assessment. In addition, the U.S. Coast Guard (specifically, USCG Sector Boston) has mandated certain exclusion zones in the fore, aft and sides of an LNG ship in transit to minimize collision risks with other vessel traffic in the port. The shore-based operations and facilities of LNG terminals come under the purview of the U.S. DOT regulations and are inspected annually for safety. In addition, the design of storage tanks and other systems in the facility have to conform to the industry consensus standard, namely, the National Fire Protection Association's "Standard for the production, Storage, and Handling of Liquefied Natural Gas, (NFPA 59A)." The DOT regulations also stipulate the training requirements for industry personnel. Last but not the least, every one of the LNG terminal facilities in the U.S. has to prepare and follow a security plan to thwart any potential sabotage or terrorist acts. This level of scrutiny and regulatory oversight, in addition to the industry's self interest to operate extremely safely, has been the principal cause of the safety success story. As mentioned earlier, no other energy industry has such an outstanding safety record. However, the price for an exemplary safety record is eternal vigilance, personnel training and implementation of advanced technologies.

3. LNG properties that have an impact on potential hazards and comparison with properties of other common fuels

LNG burning properties are not very different compared to similar properties of other commonly used hydrocarbon fuels. Large LNG fires will be very similar in radiant heat emission characteristics to large fires of propane, gasoline, jet fuel, etc.

LNG is natural gas cooled at atmospheric pressure to a low temperature of –260 °F. It consists, mainly, of methane and few percent by volume of ethane and propane and traces of other hydrocarbons and nitrogen. Methane is a member of the saturated hydrocarbon group of chemicals, which includes ethane, propane, butane, pentane, octane (the principal constituent of gasoline). Each molecule of a hydrocarbon fuel consists of carbon and hydrogen atoms combined in specific proportions. The combustion properties of all hydrocarbon fuels are very similar. For example, the heat produced when a pound of any in air[1] one of these saturated hydrocarbons is burned is the about the same, namely 20,000 Btu (within ± 5%). Also, the pounds of air required to burn completely one pound of any of these fuels are also about the same, namely, 15.5 (± 3%), except for methane, which requires a larger quantity of air. The consequence of the similarity in combustion properties is that the fires all of these fuels should have, within ± 100 °F, the same temperature, methane fires being the least hot. This observation has been demonstrated by carefully conducted laboratory experiments with different fuels.

The implication of the above observation is that methane (LNG) fires are no different in temperature than other fuels that the industrial society uses. All fires emit heat in the form of radiant heat ("infrared radiation") and the amount of energy emitted is dependent on the fire temperature. The question, therefore, is why methane (or LNG) fires are considered to be more "hazardous" or "hot?" This has to do with one additional phenomenon that occurs in burning, namely, production of soot particles (unburned carbon) in a fire. The higher the number of carbon atoms in the fuel molecule (as in gasoline or diesel fuel) the greater is the production of soot particles during the process of burning. That is, a methane fire will, all other conditions being the same, produce a smaller amount of soot in a given size fire than in a fire burning a heavier oil. The soot particles produced tend to form a mantle or shroud around the fire. The larger the density of the soot particles in the mantle, the higher is the absorption of the radiant heat emitted from inside the fire and the lower is the magnitude of the heat emitted to the surroundings. The soot layer acts as a "heat blocker" much the same way as a smoked glass does to visible light. In the case of smaller fires, this blocking of heat emission is smaller because of the lower soot amount produced. The fire from the burning of methane -which has a single carbon atom in the fuel molecule and which produces the least amount of soot- will therefore appear "brighter" or "hotter" to an observer outside the fire. However, as the methane fire size increases a lot more soot is produced, forming a black shroud around the fire, like fires of "heavier" hydrocarbons.. This reduces the overall radiative heat emission to the outside. Therefore, when the fire sizes become large (such as hundreds of feet in diameter), the distinction between fires of different hydrocarbon fuels tends to diminish and they all look about the same (with small differences in the amount of radiant heat emitted to the outside). That is, LNG is clean burning in relatively small size fires but as its size becomes large it burns "dirty." Exhibit 1 [omitted] shows a 14 m diameter LNG fire on water observed in the tests conducted at China Lake. The smoky aspects of a large LNG fire is seen in Exhibit 2 [omitted], which shows the 35 m diameter LNG fire in the tests conducted in 1987 at Montoir, France. The latter fire is the largest LNG fire tested to date.

4. Immediate and near term research needs to fill the gaps in our knowledge

4A. What is known and unknown in mathematical modeling to predict adverse public impact distances from LNG releases

The models that are being currently used in LNG hazard assessment have layer upon layer of conservative calculations, making predicted distance to hazard substantially more than what it may be in reality. New sets of larger LNG pool fire tests and other equally important research will provide the necessary framework for the development of realistic models with which to assess the hazards from potential LNG release scenarios from ships.

To a large extent the fire hazard assessment models used currently are based on the data and findings from tests such as China Lake experiments. These test sizes were of a modest scale compared to sizes of postulated spills to which the models are being applied now. There is considerable uncertainly in the scale-up and applicability to larger LNG releases.

The extent of the potential hazard zone surrounding a LNG release depends upon a number of factors including the quantity and rate of LNG release, the location of release (onto water or land), the environmental conditions and mitigating circumstances and the type of behavior of interest (dispersion and subsequent ignition of a vapor cloud, a pool fire, or other type of behavior of concern). Our knowledge of and confidence in modeling some types of LNG behavior, even in the case of very large spills, are good and in other cases they are very limited or lacking. The gaps in our knowledge of applicability to larger LNG releases make it difficult to model the entire sequence of events as a system and estimate the magnitude of the final consequence.

There are four distinct steps in modeling the consequences of release of any hazardous material, including LNG. These steps include, (I) the quantitative description of the details of the source and the modification that the released material may undergo in the immediate vicinity of release location due to its interaction with air or water. (ii) the description of behavior of the released material in the environment (burning as a pool fire, dispersion of vapor in the atmosphere and later burning as a vapor fire, rapid phase transition-RPT, etc) and quantification of the hazardous effects caused by the behavior, (iii) the enhancement or reduction of the hazardous effects due to interaction with the atmosphere and, finally, (iv) calculation of the effects on people or structures using the appropriate susceptibility criteria for such hazards (or alternatively, calculating the distance from the release where the hazards are below acceptable levels).

In the case of scenarios of potential LNG release from tankers, there are significant uncertainties and unknowns in the first step itself, namely source modeling. This has a significant impact on the overall hazard prediction. The calculation of the rate of discharge of LNG from a specified size hole on the side of a ship's tank is relatively straight forward, when such a hole is above the water line. Other phenomena may also occur, which substantially reduce the overall flow rate. One such is the creation of a vacuum condition in the tank leading to intermittent discharge ("glug-glug" type of flow as from an inverted bottle). Our knowledge to calculate the LNG outflow and the water inflow rate in the case the hole is either at or below the water line should be supplemented. The physics of mixing of LNG outflow with the water inflow, and mixing of water entering the tank with the LNG inventory in the tank (causing rapid evaporation and exacerbating the tank pressure condition), are some of the potential phenomena that have not been studied carefully. The calculations of how fast LNG comes out and in what form (liquid, vapor, liquid drops) are extremely difficult and full of uncertainties. Currently, there are no experiments to guide us to model the flow when the hole is at or below water line. Performing a chain of calculations using only a single scenario of release cannot be the last word on the extent of the public hazard, however conservative the assumptions may be. A whole spectrum of events and their consequences needs to be considered.

The GAO report has identified cascading tank failures due to heat or the contact of cryogenic liquid and carbon steel as another issue. The conditions under which these cascading tank failures may occur and resultant effects on the hazards are not clearly understood. Therefore, there are considerable uncertainties in describing the rate and quantity of LNG released and the form in which it may be released depending upon the locations and sizes of holes in the two hulls of the ship.

The vapor formed by the release of LNG (into or on water) is most likely to be ignited, close to the ship, from hot metals or electrical sparks (static or cut cables). In all current generation models it is assumed that all released LNG will form an expanding-vaporizing pool on the water surface sustaining a pool fire. Modeling the spread of the pool given the volume of the liquid LNG in the pool (or the rate of volume entering the pool) is reasonably well established. However, what is not known precisely is how much of the LNG flowing out of the tank actually pools on the surface. A large jet of LNG pouring out from an elevated hole plunging into water can penetrate the water column to a significant depth, fragment by both mechanical and thermal interaction with water, form small droplets of LNG most of which will vaporize[2] by the time they rise to the surface leaving only a fraction of the release to form a floating liquid pool. There are two main consequences of this. One is that the large vapor volume released could burn as a fireball near the ship. (A fireball puts out significantly higher heat (per unit area) but for a considerably shorter duration than a pool fire). The second possible outcome is that the vapor produced within the water column together with the vapor produced by the spreading LNG pool on water burns in a pool fire. The diameter of this pool fire would be far less than if all released liquid pooled on the water surface. Both of these phenomena have direct effect on the calculated hazard distance. No experiments have been conducted to understand the effects of LNG jet plunging into the water and the consequent fireball, pool fire or other types of burning.[3]

A fire poses hazards due to the emitted radiant heat. Radiant heat is the heat felt by a person (or an object) outside the fire and at some distance from the fire so that the heat is not due to direct contact with the hot gases in the fire. This is the "heat" that one experiences when facing a fire in a home fireplace. The radiant heat emission from a fire is generally quantified by a parameter called the "emissive power," which is the average amount of heat energy "leaving" a unit nominal surface area of the fire and is expressed in units of kW/m^2 or Btu/hr ft^2. The higher the emissive power the brighter a fire will appear and the farther one needs to be from the fire to be safe. The emissive power of LNG fires has been measured in relatively small-scale field tests. Most of these small fires burn bright (as seen in Exhibit 1 [omitted]). It is known that emissive power value is fire size dependent. A large body of current generation models used for LNG fire hazard distance evaluations assume that irrespective of the fire size the emissive power remains essentially the same (and high), leading to the prediction of uncomfortably large hazard distances from large spills of LNG.

As argued earlier (and shown in Exhibit 2 [omitted]), large LNG fires become smoky, very similar to other fuel fires. All smoky fires have a region close to the bottom where the smoke mantle has not formed and where the hot "bright" parts of the fire are visible from which can emanate high radiant heat fluxes. The height of this region decreases as the size of the fire increases. The black (cold) smoke mantle enveloping the fire absorbs the radiant heat emission from the inner regions of the fire resulting in substantially less radiant heat energy being released to the areas outside the fire. In the case of large LNG pool fire on water the burning regions close to the water could be hot but the overall emissive power will be less than that from a smaller size fire. In addition, the hot region close to the water will result in inducing high vaporization of water, locally. The water vapor thus formed just around the base of the fire may contribute to absorbing the radiant heat emission in addition to, being sucked into the fire and affecting the combustion chemistry to make the fire cooler and less radiative. None of these phenomena have been studied quantitatively in any controlled, large-scale experiments. We do not know how smoky very large LNG fires will be and what the height of the lower "bright' burning zone would be or what the mean emissive power will be. A theoretical model developed using the principles of combustion physics and validated against the best available data from the 35 m LNG fire experiments (the largest fire to date) seems to indicate that the mean emissive power of large LNG fires from ship spills may be only about a 1/3 as radiative as smaller fires. If this is true, the hazard distances predicted from current models will have to be reduced by almost a factor of 2. Certainly, more research and large pool fire experiments on water are needed to get definitive data. I concur with the GAO recommendation on the need for this research.

Some people analyzing LNG hazards from ship releases are concerned with cascading failures of tanks due to external fires or interactions of the cryogenic LNG with metal structure of the ship. In fact, the GAO report recommends that research be conducted on this potential failure phenomenon. I agree with this recommendation, in principle, provided the types of research performed are realistic representations of the conditions following LNG release from a single tank. The heat from a pool fire may not result in further tank failures. The potential for cryogenic liquid-carbon steel interaction will depend upon a number of variables including the extent to which water is present, the location of contact between the hull plate and the liquid, whether such a contact will result in the immediate fracture of a part of the plate and the draining of the cryogenic liquid reducing the possibility of further contact, the engineered naval architectural designs that maintain the integrity of the ship structure even when a part of the structure fails, etc.

It is my opinion that heat from even a LNG pool fire impinging on the outer hull plate of the ship will be insufficient to cause further tank failures. This opinion is based on the following reasons; (I) there are at lest two historical records of incidents involving ships carrying refrigerated liquefied fuels which were exposed to intense and very long duration (hours) hydrocarbon fires impinging on the hulls and deck plates, yet suffered no failures of the cryogenic liquid tanks, (ii) the ships were of smaller size than current day LNG vessels; because of shorter dimensions, the smaller vessels are relatively more vulnerable to heat transfer from the fire to the tanks (and yet the tanks did not fail), (iii) the calculated lifetime of a LNG pool fire is of the order of minutes within which the total heat transfer to a massive ship structure would not affect the hull integrity (especially since the outer hull is also cooled by sea water), and (iv) the LNG and hydrocarbon fires have the same temperature as discussed earlier. The cases I cite are the incidents with "Yuyo Maru # 10" and the "Gaz Fountain."

In November 1974 the Yuyo Maru No10, a 47,300 m^3 tank capacity ship carrying refrigerated LPG in insulated tanks with ballast tanks filled with naptha (a fuel very similar to gasoline) was underway in Tokyo harbor. It was hit broadside by 15,500dwt steel products carrying ship "Pacific Ares," The collision resulted in one of the wing tanks of Yuyo Maru being punctured and releasing naptha on to both the water and the deck of the colliding ship.[4] The naptha pool ignited immediately and the resulting fire caused damage to both the LPG carrier and the colliding vessel. The naptha fire on the sea engulfed the ships for more than 4 hours. The LPG vapors were released through the normal relief valves and no boiling liquid expanding vapor explosion (BLEVE) occurred nor did a leak of liquid propane occur nor any tank failure.

The other incident refers to Gaz Fountain. This ship, designed to carry both LNG and LPG, was hit in the Persian Gulf during the Iran/Iraq war in October 1984 by three air-to-surface Maverick missiles, which caused extensive damage on the deck of the ship.[5] The ship at that time was carrying LPG. Intense and long lasting fire resulted on the deck. Propane vapors burned through a gash in the tank roof as a large vent fire. No tank failure or release of refrigerated liquid propane resulted nor did any of the tanks undergo a BLEVE type of failure.

Other researchers have postulated the failure of LNG ship tanks due to fire heat exposure leading to a LNG tank explosion (due to BLEVE). As indicated above, no such explosions have occurred in tanks of ships carrying refrigerated liquefied petroleum gas (LPG) even after being subjected to intense fires on the outside. For a BLEVE to occur the liquid in a tank must be heated to temperatures well beyond its normal boiling temperature (and therefore higher pressure in the tank) and the tank has to be suddenly depressurized by, say, the sudden rupture of the tank wall. The rapid depressurization results in the production of large volumes of vapor, which may ignite and form a large fireball and the pressure waves created may hurl pieces of the tank to some distance. The higher the pressure in the tank at rupture the worse will be the effect of a BLEVE including the throw of the pieces of the tank to distances up to ¼ mile. BLEVE incidents have occurred in pressurized (LPG) rail tank cars or relatively small LPG storage tanks in which the pressure is normally about 105 psig and the tank will withstand pressures up to 375 psig before rupturing. Large tanks have not exhibited the BLEVE type of explosive rupture;The smaller the tank and the higher the pressure it can withstand the greater is the likelihood for the occurrence of a BLEVE.

One can conclude that a BLEVE is extremely unlikely in a LNG ship tank when one considers the conditions necessary for such an event to occur. First, the volume of liquid in each tank of a LNG carrier is large (25, 000 m^3). To heat such a massive amount of liquid to any temperature significantly higher than its normal boiling temperature requires significant amount of heat to be input. The calculated lifetime of a LNG pool fire (caused by the rupture of another tank) generally ranges from a few minutes to, at best, 15 minutes. Over this burning time it is difficult to transfer significant quantity of heat to the LNG in the tanks. Second, the LNG tanks are well insulated and separated from the outer hull by a large (at least 2 m wide) inter-hull ballast space, which impedes heat transfer from the fire to the tank wall. Third, the tanks are provided with relief valves, which will ensure that no significant rise in the pressure occurs. Further more, because of the size of the LNG tank the roof of the tank will not be able to withstand any significant increase in pressure before being damaged. Last but not the least, actual experience with large ships carrying refrigerated fuels (LPG and butane) in tanks similar to those in LNG carriers indicates that even though they were subject to fires lasting several hours no BLEVE resulted. Therefore, in my opinion, the consideration of BLEVE as a potential public hazard phenomenon in the scenario of an accidental or intentional release from a LNG ship is addressing a non-problem.

4B. Areas that require additional research and why

Other research that may be as important as pool fire tests and modeling needs to be performed to determine the type and magnitude of other hazards, which may, under certain circumstances, become the dominant hazard scenario(s) rather than a pool fire. These include water-LNG interaction, water intrusion into LNG tanks and considerations of a fireball type of burning.

There are two most likely scenarios resulting from a large release from a LNG ship. These are (I) the formation of a LNG pool fire on water (initially expanding but reaching later a steady size) and, (ii) the potential formation of a large fireball type burning due to the immediate ignition of the large volume of vapor produced rapidly and locally from the LNG jet-water interaction. Whether such interaction could lead to localized and flameless rapid phase transition explosions, (RPT), should be investigated. A RPT together with LNG jet penetration into the water column together with the occurrence of a RPT can result in a very large volume of vapor bring thrown high up in the air leading to the formation of a fireball if ignited. The recent GAO report has recommended the investigation of the radiant heat emission and smoke production characteristics of large LNG pool fires on water. I am in agreement with GAO on this recommendation. However, the results of a pool fire test series alone will not provide all of the knowledge required to perform a credible public safety assessment. Therefore, I recommend the conduct of the following types of experiments followed by modeling to properly estimate the potential hazard areas from different types of similar magnitude phenomena. (These recommendations are complementary to those of the GAO).

1. Large LNG pool fire of sizes up to 100 m in diameter on (deep) water—the objective of these tests should be to understand the variation of the fire dynamics, smoke production characteristics and radiant heat emission change from bottom to top of LNG fires as the fire size increases.

2. Plunging LNG jet interaction with water (of significant depth) to understand the phenomenon of depth of penetration, jet fragmentation, rate of vaporization and fraction of liquid spilled that will eventually pool on the water surface. This is an equally important phenomenon to consider since in some situations most of the spilled LNG may evaporate in the water column and the pool formed may be so small as to not pose

significant pool fire hazard compared to, perhaps, other phenomena like a fireball type of burning.

3. Ignition tests with a plunging LNG jet into water to see if a fireball results (and if so the conditions under which it happens) or whether a fire similar to a pool fire but with substantially large fire plume results due to very high gas release rates in the "pool."

4. Viewing a LNG Pool fire (or even a large natural gas fire) from a distance of several hundreds of meters up to 2 km on a very large expanse of water and measuring the absorption of the radiant heat in the atmosphere. Current calculations of LNG heat absorption by the intervening atmosphere are based on the assumption that the fire radiates like an ideal black body. However, LNG fires are known to be band emitters of radiation in exactly the right frequency where the water vapor (and to some extent the carbon dioxide) in the atmosphere absorbs. Such a definitive test conducted on water will provide a basis for taking into consideration the beneficial (and mitigative) aspects of the atmosphere. Unfortunately, some of the models used in calculating hazard distances either incorrectly model the atmospheric absorption or do not consider it at all. Such omission is not excusable when the predicted hazard distances are in hundreds of meters (up to 2 km).

5. The interaction of the LNG outflow and the water inflow (simultaneously) to understand what may happen if the postulated hole location in the ship's tank is at or below the water line. The flow situation and the effects of large quantity of water intrusion into a tank filled with LNG are complex and need to be studied. Such a phenomenon may need to be considered in hazard calculations.

5. Results from risk assessments rather than from a single postulated scenario should be the basis of policy decision making.

Risk analysis as a tool is being increasingly utilized in the U.S. for decision-making, but only in bits and pieces. The single important reason for the lack of universal adoption of risk-based decision making is the lack of standards for the levels of risk that are acceptable to society.

It is my opinion that policy decisions should be made after evaluating all possible scenarios of releases, their likelihood of occurrence, the levels of consequences associated with each scenario and considering the effects of either natural mitigation processes or man made technological or procedural systems. Absent such an approach, the focus will always be on the largest, most incredible types of releases, whether they have ever a chance of occurrence or not. Preparing for and managing resources required to respond to emergencies involving events that occur with very low probabilities is a misapplication of resources.

It is very commendable that the report by Sandia[6] recognizes that risk analysis must be the basis of overall assessment rather than the consequences of a single worst-case event. In fact, this report has provided a template on how one should perform a risk assessment; unfortunately, since the process has not been quantified with a specific example, the public seems to be focusing on the results from the theoretical assessment of the consequences only. Many other federal agencies have long recognized the usefulness of risk-based approach. However, it has been slow in "permeating" to the LNG industry regulations. The U.S. Coast Guard requires the performance of Waterway Suitability Assessment, for LNG ship passage to a port, based on a risk consideration approach. The U.S. DOT has in its Pipeline Integrity Management regulations the requirements for performing risk based assessments. The NFPA LNG Committee is considering providing, as an alternative Standard for compliance, a risk based standard.[7] The European regulators have successfully used the risk-based approach to permitting LNG and other petrochemical facility siting for over a decade.

One of the important recommendations I would offer this August body is to consider setting up acceptability standards for levels of risk that are suitable for siting industrial activities and for continuing such operations. Risk cannot be considered in a vacuum; it has to be based on comparative scales. There is substantial body of literature on this topic.

6. Conclusions

1. LNG industry has operated safely both in the U.S. and worldwide for over six decades. There is no technical or operational reason why this exemplary record will not continue. New technologies, application of results of careful research, and continued personnel training are expected to contribute to the enhancement of the safety record.

2. LNG burning properties are not very different compared to similar properties of other commonly used hydrocarbon fuels. Large LNG fires will be very similar in radiant heat emission characteristics to large fires of propane, gasoline, jet fuel, etc.

3. The models that are being currently used in LNG hazard assessment have layer upon layer of conservative calculations, making predicted distance to hazard substantially more than what it would likely be in reality. New sets of larger LNG pool fire tests will provide the necessary framework for the development of realistic models with which to assess the fire hazards from potential LNG release scenarios from ships.

4. Other research that may be as important as pool fire tests and modeling needs to be performed to determine the type and magnitude of other hazards, which may, under certain circumstances, become the dominant hazard scenario(s) rather than a pool fire. These include water-LNG

interaction, water intrusion into LNG tanks and considerations of a fireball type of burning.

5. Focusing only on consequences of perceived worst cases rather than on the overall risk from an activity will result in poorly utilized and improperly allocated resources, not to speak of the economic penalties that may result.

6. Risk analysis as a tool is being increasingly utilized in the U.S. for decision-making, but only in bits and pieces. The single important reason for the lack of universal adoption of risk-based decision making is the lack of standards for the levels of risk that are acceptable to society.

Mr. Chairman and Members of the Committee, I thank you for the opportunity to testify before your Committee.

Endnotes

[1] In sufficient quantity of air which contains the chemically required amount of oxygen to react with the hydrocarbon for complete combustion (called the "stoichiometric" amount).

[2] My own recent analysis of the phenomenon of a LNG jet plunging into deep water indicates that depending upon the LNG plunging velocity into the water surface 50% or higher fraction of the released liquid could vaporize in the immediate vicinity of the release leaving only a smaller volume of liquid to spread on the water surface.

[3] I, however, noticed in the China Lake tests that the higher the spill rate (in gpm) of LNG the higher was the burning rate, the taller was the fire and the quicker it went out.

[4] William de Barry Thomas, "Spectacle Blurs Issues," Hazardous Cargo Bulletin, p 23, October 1984.

[5] J.A. Carter, "Salvage of Cargo from war damaged Gaz Fountain," paper presented at the 1985 Gastech Conference, Nice, France, 1985.

[6] Hightower, M, L. Gritzo, A. Luketa-Hanlin, J. Covan, S.Tieszen, G. Wellman, M. Irwin, M. Kaneshige, B. Melof, C.Morrow, and D. Ragland, "Guidance on Risk Analysis and Safety Implications of a Large Liquefied Natural Gas (LNG) Spill Over Water," Sandia National Laboratory Rep.# SAND2004-6258, U.S. Department of Energy, Washington, DC, Dec 2004.

[7] The full membership of this NFPA 59A Committee is considering this recommendation and verbiage provided by its sub-committee. If approved, this alternative standard would be incorporated into the 2009 edition of the NFPA 59A Standards.

DOCUMENT NO. 4

MARITIME SECURITY: POTENTIAL TERRORIST ATTACKS AND PROTECTION PRIORITIES

CRS Report
RL33787

January 9, 2007

Paul W. Parfomak and John Frittelli
Resources, Science, and Industry Division
Congressional Research Service

Summary

A key challenge for U.S. policy makers is prioritizing the nation's maritime security activities among a virtually unlimited number of potential attack scenarios. While individual scenarios have distinct features, they may be characterized along five common dimensions: perpetrators, objectives, locations, targets, and tactics. In many cases, such scenarios have been identified as part of security preparedness exercises, security assessments, security grant administration, and policy debate. There are far more potential attack scenarios than likely ones, and far more than could be meaningfully addressed with limited counter-terrorism resources.

There are a number of logical approaches to prioritizing maritime security activities. One approach is to emphasize diversity, devoting available counter-terrorism resources to a broadly representative sample of credible scenarios. Another approach is to focus counter-terrorism resources on only the scenarios of greatest concern based on overall risk, potential consequence, likelihood, or related metrics. U.S. maritime security agencies appear to have followed policies consistent with one or the other of these approaches in federally-supported port security exercises and grant programs. Legislators often appear to focus attention on a small number of potentially catastrophic scenarios.

Clear perspectives on the nature and likelihood of specific types of maritime terrorist attacks are essential for prioritizing the nation's maritime anti-terrorism activities. In practice, however, there has been considerable public debate about the likelihood of scenarios frequently given high priority by federal policy makers, such as nuclear or "dirty" bombs smuggled in shipping containers, liquefied natural gas (LNG) tanker attacks, and attacks on passenger ferries. Differing priorities set by port officials, grant officials, and legislators lead to differing allocations of port security resources and levels of protection against specific types of attacks. How they ultimately relate to one another under a national maritime security strategy remains to be seen.

Maritime terrorist threats to the United States are varied, and so are the nation's efforts to combat them. As oversight of the federal role in maritime security continues, Congress may raise questions concerning the relationship among the nation's various maritime security activities, and the implications of differing protection priorities among them. Improved gathering and sharing of maritime terrorism intelligence may enhance consistency of policy and increase efficient deployment of maritime security resources. In addition, Congress may assess how the various elements of U.S. maritime security fit together in the nation's overall strategy to protect the public from terrorist attacks.

This report will not be updated.

Introduction

Maritime security is a principal protective element of United States' global war on terrorism. The Bush Administrations' *National Strategy for Maritime Security* states that "the infrastructure and systems that span the maritime domain . . . have increasingly become both targets of and potential conveyances for dangerous and illicit activities."[1] Widely reported maritime attacks against the United States and its allies, such as the bombings of the U.S.S. *Cole* in 2000 and the French oil tanker *Limburg* in 2002, have focused Congressional attention on maritime threats.[2] In 2006, debate over the failed attempt by Dubai Ports World to operate marine terminals at some U.S. ports raised additional Congressional concerns about U.S. maritime security activities.[3] Questions have emerged regarding both the nation's overall strategy for maritime security and its level of commitment to specific components of that strategy.

As debate about U.S. maritime security continues, policy makers seek a better understanding of the nature and likelihood of potential terrorist attacks against the United States, and how federal programs prioritize their efforts to prevent such attacks. This report outlines the key dimensions of maritime terrorism and how these dimensions may characterize specific attacks in the global maritime domain. The report illustrates credible maritime attack scenarios based on actual past attacks or potential attacks developed for maritime security exercises or other U.S. counter terrorism activities. It discusses the challenge to maritime security planners of facing a virtually unlimited number of potential attack scenarios and how certain federal programs address this challenge. It also reviews various perspectives on the overall likelihood of maritime terror attacks on the United States. Finally the report discusses implications for homeland security policy.[4]

Characterizing Potential Maritime Terrorist Attacks

Maritime terrorism encompasses a wide range of potential attack scenarios. While individual scenarios have distinct features, for purposes of this report they may be characterized along five common dimensions: perpetrators, objectives, locations, targets, and tactics. These dimensions are useful for discussing both historical instances of maritime terrorism and potential scenarios for future maritime attacks.

Perpetrators

Identifying potential perpetrators is important in evaluating maritime attacks because perpetrator capabilities vary widely and, therefore, bear on the types of attacks they might attempt. Disgruntled shipping workers, for example, may exploit privileged port access to circumvent security safeguards and mount an "insider" attack on maritime infrastructure. An Al Qaeda cell, on the other hand, may mount an entirely different type of attack on the same type of infrastructure, exploiting sophisticated training in terrorist tactics and privileged access to weapons and explosives, especially overseas. Although many terrorist groups may pose a credible threat to the United States, not all may pose a *maritime* threat.

Al Qaeda and its affiliates have been a primary focus of U.S. maritime security policy given the terror network's hostility to U.S. interests and its record of past attacks. Al Qaeda or its operatives, for example, appear to have been responsible for both the *Cole* and *Limburg* bombings.[5] Likewise the Abu Sayyaf Group, Islamist separatists based in the Philippines and tied to Al Qaeda, appears to have been behind the bombing of the Philippine vessel *Superferry 14* in 2004.[6] Groups or individuals not necessarily affiliated with Al Qaeda may also attack the United States, however. It is noteworthy that the only sustained international terrorist campaign in U.S. waters over the last 40 years was carried out by anti-Castro Cuban groups between 1968 and 1976.[7] Independent Islamist terrorist cells may also emerge as Al Qaeda is disrupted or disaggregated by the U.S. war on terror. According to a State Department review of Al Qaeda activity in 2005, "what was once a relatively structured network appeared to be a more diffuse worldwide movement of like-minded individuals and small groups, sharing grievances and objectives, but not necessarily organized formally."[8] Given this evolution among terrorist groups, maritime terrorism scenarios increasingly require consideration of a broad spectrum of potential perpetrators.

Acts of maritime terrorism may have many objectives. They may seek to cause human casualties, economic losses, environmental damage, or other negative impacts, alone or in combination, of minor or major consequence.[9] If human casualties are the principal objective, passenger vessels such as cruise ships and ferries, which together account for less than 4% of U.S. commercial vessel inventory, may be more attractive terrorist targets than cargo and other vessels.[10] Consistent with this reasoning, federal agencies reportedly concluded in 2004 that the Washington state ferry system had been under surveillance as a possible terrorism target.[11] A weapon of mass destruction (WMD) attack on a heavily populated U.S. port could inflict the greatest number of human casualties. The Defense Department's Joint Task Force–Civil Support developed such a scenario in a 2005 exercise involving the smuggling and detonation of a 10-kiloton nuclear device in the port of Charleston, SC.[12]

If economic loss is the primary objective, terrorists may seek to carry out different types of attacks, with potentially few human casualties but significant impacts to critical infrastructure or commerce. The *Limburg* bombing may have been an attack of this type, threatening to disrupt the global oil trade and causing considerable consternation among tanker operators.[13] Although the bombing killed only one member of the *Limburg's* crew, it caused insurance rates among Yemeni shippers to rise 300% and reduced Yemeni port shipping volumes by 50% in the month after the attack.[14] The bombing also caused significant environmental damage, spilling 90,000 barrels of oil into the Gulf of Aden.[15] Other types of maritime attacks could disrupt more directly the shipping operations of key commercial ports. For example, in a 2005 Department of Homeland Security (DHS) exercise, terrorists hypothetically destroyed the International Bridge in Sault Ste.

Marie, MI, blocking the shipping channel below with debris, by exploding a fuel tanker truck on the bridge.[16]

The potential consequences of a terror attack are also an important consideration in evaluating terrorist objectives. Terrorists groups such as Al Qaeda appear to choose the scale (and timing) of their attacks in order to maximize media coverage, and hence, public awareness and psychological impact. As one academic study concluded,

> To make it into the news, terrorists operating in Western countries can commit some minor terror incident with few fatalities, whereas terrorists in developing countries need to "produce" a lot of blood to attract the attention of Western media.[17]

Accordingly, attack scenarios must consider consequences, and how such consequences would align with the objectives of potential perpetrators. The study cited above suggests that terrorists attacking the United States may achieve their media objectives even with relatively minor attacks.

Locations

Where a potential maritime attack could occur is also essential to defining a terrorism scenario. Examples above have already illustrated that maritime attacks targeting U.S. interests may occur in U.S. ports (of which there are over 360)[18] or among the ports of the nation's 165 maritime trading partners.[19] Specific types of attacks, such as the smuggling of WMDs in ship-borne cargo containers, may involve both a foreign port of departure and a U.S. port of entry. Maritime terror attacks may also occur at sea in areas of concentrated shipping like the Straits of Gibraltar where, in 2002, Al Qaeda operatives reportedly plotted to attack U.S. and British warships, and possibly commercial vessels.[20] The Straits of Malacca in southeast Asia is another location frequently identified by security analysts as a potential locus of maritime terrorism activity. In 2001, Jemaah Islamiyah terrorists reportedly had plans to attack U.S. navy vessels visiting the region.[21] The Organization for Economic Cooperation and Development (OECD) has identified nine similar shipping bottlenecks around the world where potential terrorist activities are a concern.[22]

Terrorist attacks in U.S. waters may have the greatest potential to injure U.S. citizens if they occur in populated areas. They may also have the greatest potential for economic impact in the event of the closure of a major U.S. port. Nonetheless, future attacks on U.S. interests in foreign ports, or on vessels at sea in transit to the United States, may be easier for terrorists to execute than attacks in U.S. waters.

Targets

Another key aspect of maritime terrorism scenarios is identifying potential targets. There are numerous possibilities, especially in and around ports. As a U.S. Government Accountability Office (GAO) analyst testified before Congress in 2006,

> Ports contain a number of specific facilities that could be targeted by terrorists, including military vessels and bases, cruise ships, passenger ferries, terminals, dams and locks, factories, office buildings, power plants, refineries, sports complexes, and other critical infrastructure.[23]

In addition to vessels and infrastructure, terrorists may seek to attack maritime communities using ships as delivery vehicles for WMDs or by exploiting chemicals or explosives in cargo ships or onshore storage tanks in populated port areas. The Homeland Security Council included terrorist attacks on ships carrying flammable and toxic chemical cargoes in a U.S. port among the hazard scenarios it developed in 2004 as the basis for U.S. homeland security national preparedness standards.[24] Because the characteristics of infrastructure targets or human targets may be unique to any specific category of target (e.g., propane tankers) or community (e.g., Charleston), understanding how target characteristics relate to terrorist capabilities and objectives may offer valuable insights into the credibility of particular attack scenarios.

Tactics

Maritime security analysts have discussed numerous potential tactics for terrorist attacks on U.S. maritime targets. The following passage from the *National Strategy for Maritime Security* summarizes many of the tactics most commonly mentioned in maritime security discussions:

> Terrorists can also develop effective attack capabilities relatively quickly using . . . explosives-laden suicide boats and light aircraft; merchant and cruise ships as kinetic weapons to ram another vessel, warship, port facility, or offshore platform; commercial vessels as launch platforms for missile attacks; underwater swimmers to infiltrate ports; and unmanned underwater explosive delivery vehicles. Mines are also an effective weapon. . . . Terrorists can also take advantage of a vessel's legitimate cargo, such as chemicals, petroleum, or liquefied natural gas, as the explosive component of an attack. Vessels can be used to transport powerful conventional explosives or WMD for detonation in a port or alongside an offshore facility.[25]

General tactics of maritime attacks like those above have been further described in security bulletins based on specific terrorism intelligence. For example, in 2004 the Federal Bureau of Investigation warned of possible improvised marine mines in "waterborne flotsam commonly seen around waterways" or attached to buoys.[26] More specific tactics have also been articulated as part of U.S. maritime security exercises discussed later in this report.

As the previous citations suggest, analysis of terrorist tactics must take into account the specifics of the attack in question. Some analysts believes that there is a "low probability" that terrorists would try to use a large ship as a weapon because of the complexity of doing so, but that attacks by small boats are more likely because they "satisfy the overwhelming terrorist requirement for simplicity."[27] Similarly, the Commandant of the U.S. Coast Guard (USCG) has reportedly stated that "there is a significant threat by vessel-borne improvised explosive devices" and that "vulnerability to small-boat attacks stood out" during a 2006 threat assessment.[28]

Unlimited Scenarios

The dimensions of maritime terrorism defined above may be used to characterize both historical terrorist attacks and potential future attacks against the United States. Table 1 provides a set of illustrative characteristics which could serve as the basis for the development of potential attack scenarios.

Table 1. Example Maritime Attack Characteristics

Dimensions	Example Characteristics	
Perpetrators	• Al Qaeda and affiliates • Islamist unaffiliated • Foreign nationalists	• Others • Disgruntled employees
Objectives	• Mass casualties • Port disruption	• Trade disruption • Environmental damage
Locations	• 360+ U.S. ports • 165 foreign trade partners	• 9 key shipping bottlenecks
Targets	• Military vessels • Cargo vessels • Fuel tankers • Ferries/cruise ships	• Port area populations • Ship channels • Port industrial plants • Offshore platforms
Tactics	• Explosives in suicide boats • Explosives in light aircraft • Ramming with vessels Ship-launched missiles • Harbor mines	• Underwater swimmers • Unmanned submarine bombs • Exploding fuel tankers • Explosives in cargo ships • WMDs in cargo ships

Source: CRS

What is apparent from Table 1 is the possibility of generating numerous unique, logically consistent, and operationally credible attack scenarios based on different combinations of perpetrators, objectives, locations, targets, and tactics. Doing so exhaustively, however, leads to far more potential attack scenarios than likely ones, and far more than could be meaningfully addressed with limited counter-terrorism resources. As one security analyst has articulated the problem,

> An accurate assessment of the current nature and scope of the global maritime terrorist threat should be driven by an assessment of what is probable, rather than merely possible. However, sober analysis of this issue has been clouded amid the anxiety created by the current global security climate, with much discussion turning on the notion that terrorists could potentially strike any target with virtually any means available. . . .[29]

A key challenge, therefore, for U.S. security analysts and policy makers is prioritizing the nation's maritime security activities among a virtually unlimited number of potential attack scenarios. How federal agencies have been addressing the "unlimited scenarios" problem is discussed in the following section.

U.S. Maritime Security Activities

A number of logical approaches to prioritizing maritime security activities exist given the unlimited number terrorism scenarios. One approach is to emphasize diversity, devoting available counter-terrorism resources to a broadly representative sample of credible scenarios. Another approach is to focus counter-terrorism resources on only the scenarios of greatest concern based on overall risk, potential consequence, likelihood, or related metrics. U.S. maritime security agencies appear to have followed policies consistent with one or the other of these approaches in federally-supported exercise and grant programs. These approaches lead to differing allocations of resources and levels of protection against specific types of attacks. How they ultimately relate to one another under a national maritime security strategy remains to be seen.

Maritime Security Exercises

The USCG, the U.S. Navy, and other federal agencies conduct ongoing port security training exercises domestically and overseas. Taken collectively, the terrorism scenarios in these exercises to date have spanned an extremely broad range of objectives, locations, targets, and tactics. Specific scenario characteristics are discussed below in the context of particular maritime security exercise programs.

PortSTEP Scenarios. In collaboration with the USCG, the Transportation Security Administration (TSA) has developed U.S. maritime terrorism scenarios under the agency's Port Security Training Exercises Program (PortSTEP).[30] PortSTEP fulfills the annual exercise requirements for Area Maritime Security Plans under the Maritime Transportation Security Act of 2002 (P.L. 107-295) through a combination of basic tabletop, advanced tabletop, and field exercises. The PortSTEP program began in 2005 and plans to complete exercises in 40 port areas by October 2007. According to the PortSTEP program office, the 25 exercises conducted through 2006 have involved chemical, biological, and radiological ("dirty bomb") attacks, as well as various kinds of explosives and improvised explosive devices. The scenarios have targeted or exploited cruise ships, container ships, a harbor truck, a barge, a rail yard, port industrial facilities, bridges, and a national landmark. Because the TSA is responsible for the security of all major surface transportation modes, it is a specific goal of the PortSTEP program to incorporate surface transportation modes such as rail and trucking into its maritime security exercises. While the list of ports in PortSTEP includes many of the largest U.S. ports, it covers a broad cross-section in terms of size and geography, including Buffalo, NY; Chicago, IL; Corpus Christi, TX; Juneau, AK; Long Beach, CA; Pittsburgh, PA; and Tampa, FL.[31]

AMSTEP Scenarios. The USCG has developed additional U.S. maritime terrorism scenarios under its Area Maritime Security Training and Exercise Program (AMSTEP), initiated in October 2005. Like the PortSTEP program, AMSTEP conducts tabletop and field exercises to fulfill annual exercise requirements for Area Maritime Security Plans under P.L. 107-295. AMSTEP differs from PortSTEP in that it emphasizes surface transportation modes less deliberately in its terrorism scenarios. The program plans to conduct up to 28 exercises through FY2007, specifically in ports not covered by the PortSTEP program. The AMSTEP program office states that its exercises are designed around Area Maritime Security Committee objectives in individual ports; there are no requirements to conduct exercises under any specific scenario.[32] According to the limited public information available, the program's exercise scenarios in 2006 involved terrorist stowaways on an inbound hazardous cargo vessel, an explosion at a jet fuel receiving terminal, a suspicious package at a port facility, surveillance of petrochemical terminals, a potential improvised explosive device (IED) attached to the hull of a freighter, theft of gasoline tanker truck, and explosion aboard an oil tanker in a shipping channel, among others.[33] The USCG has conducted AMSTEP exercises in port areas including Key West, FL; Duluth, MN; Long Island, NY; Charleston, SC; Corpus Christi, TX; Houston/Galveston, TX; and Washington, DC, among others.[34]

Asymmetric Warfare Initiative. Port security exercises have also been conducted jointly by the U.S. Navy, USCG, FBI, local law enforcement, and other agencies under the federally sponsored Asymmetric Warfare Initiative (AWI). The AWI exercises, carried out annually since 2003, have reportedly included the following terrorist attacks scenarios:

- Explosives attack on a chlorine storage tank in port
- Hostage-taking and executions aboard a vessel in port
- A marine mine attack on a Navy frigate in port
- Underwater explosive devices planted on multiple vessels in port
- A nuclear device aboard an incoming vessel in a 55-gallon drum
- Attack on a port with a biological disease agent[35]
- Detonation of a "dirty" bomb in a shipping container in port[36]
- Aircraft attack on a passenger ferry or cruise ship
- Ammonium nitrate bombs shipped by rail to a port[37]
- Sarin gas attack on a cruise ship in port[38]

The AWI has held its exercises in Port Hueneme, CA, Los Angeles, CA, San Diego, CA, and the Puget Sound, WA, and Hampton Roads, VA areas.

Other U.S. Attack Scenarios. In addition to the scenarios listed above, the USCG, the U.S. Navy, other government agencies, and security analysts have reportedly developed attack scenarios as part of other maritime security exercises or planning activities. These scenarios have included:

- Various types of an explosives attack on a ship in port[39]
- "Dirty" bombs in cargo containers at multiple U.S. ports[40]
- Radioactive materials carried on a cargo ship 90 miles offshore[41]
- Underwater and fishing boat explosives attacks on a riverboat[42]
- Bombing and sinking of a liquefied propane gas (LPG) tanker in a major commercial and naval shipping channel[43]
- Hijacking of a river tanker for use as a "floating bomb"[44]
- Ramming and "dirty" bombing a ferry with a hijacked cargo ship[45]
- Coordinated bombing of docks and bridges, and mining of the harbor at a major commercial port[46]
- Attack on a liquefied natural gas (LNG) terminal and tanker in port[47]

Again, although these exercises may have been conducted independently of one another, they encompass a broad range of potential attack scenarios.

Overseas Exercises. Apart from exercises in U.S. territorial waters, the U.S. Navy, USCG, and other federal agencies participate in maritime security exercises overseas, often in cooperation with other countries. For example, in 2006, the U.S. Navy and USCG joined with the Thai Navy and other international participants in simulating the hijacking of a vessel with military cargo in the Strait of Malacca.[48] In 2006, the U.S. Navy also participated in a multi-national maritime exercise involving the hypothetical placement of sea mines by terrorists in coastal waters of the South China Sea.[49] In 2003, the U.S., Japanese, Australian, and French Navies conducted an exercise involving the seizure of illegal WMD-related cargo aboard a commercial vessel in the Coral Sea.[50] These are only three illustrations of what appear to be numerous maritime counter-terrorism exercises carried out by U.S. agencies around the world over the past five years.

Emphasizing Scenario Diversity. Based on the scenario summaries above, it appears that the USCG, the U.S. Navy, and other agencies have structured their maritime terrorism exercises in a manner that addresses diverse terrorism scenarios across many ports. Given that the PortSTEP, AMSTEP, and AWI programs, in particular, are geared toward training and evaluation, there are logical reasons they would employ such diverse scenarios. The PortSTEP program, for example, states that its exercises "are scaled and tailored to each specific port's needs" based on the recommendations of individual Area Maritime Security Committees.[51] Since many aspects of terrorism prevention and response (e.g., communications) are common to a range of attack scenarios in a given port area, the choice of one scenario or another may reveal similar things about security plan performance. Scenario diversity also maximizes the operational and geographical experience among senior U.S. agency planners in an environment of great uncertainty about future maritime terror attacks. Emergency responders may therefore be more likely to have at least some level of preparedness for any kind of maritime attack, anywhere.

Terrorism scenario diversity is also relatively simple, with a limited need for complex and time consuming risk assessments to establish scenario priorities. The only key requirement common to all of the aforementioned scenarios appears to be credibility, or, as stated in USCG port security guidelines, that they be "within the realm of possibility and, at a minimum, address known capabilities and intents as evidenced by past events and available intelligence."[52] It may be sufficient, therefore, that scenarios are credible and meet the particular needs of local port security officials, not that they are demonstrably more or less critical than one another.[53] The principal disadvantage of a diverse scenarios approach is that it may devote too many security resources to relatively unlikely scenarios and not enough to more likely ones. An alternative approach, for example, might be to conduct repeated exercises involving only a few high-consequence scenarios (e.g., container WMDs) and only in the largest or most populous U.S. ports.

DHS Port Security Grants

The Department of Homeland Security (DHS) initiated its Port Security Grant Program (PSGP) in 2002 to provide competitive security enhancement grants to U.S. ports. The PSGP awarded approximately $870 million in port security grants by the end of 2006.[54]

The first four rounds of PSGP grants appear to have been awarded in a manner consistent with the "broad scenarios" approach described above. For example, the DHS awarded round two grants to over 125 U.S. port areas ranging from major ports such as Baltimore, MD, Houston, TX, and Long Beach, CA, to relatively minor ones, such as Christiansted, VI, Fernandina Beach, FL, and Homer, AK. These awards also appear to have been granted for protection of a wide range of potential terrorist targets, including container terminals, rail yards, sightseeing vessels, ferries, chemical plants, energy facilities, and port operations.[55] Consistent with this conclusion, a 2005 review of the PSGP by the DHS Inspector General determined, among other findings, that "the evaluation and selection process focused on awarding funds to as many applicants as possible."[56] According to the report, this focus was influenced by tension between the "fair and equitable" award criteria mandated under the MTSA and the competitive criteria mandated under TSA appropriations. The report also noted, that PSGP awards were not based on a national risk assessment because a mechanism to perform such an assessment did not yet exist within TSA.[57]

In 2005, the DHS began to award PSGP grants on a more selective basis as determined by the agency's new national assessment and ranking of port risk. For its fifth round in 2005, the DHS evaluated the 129 largest U.S. ports using a risk-based formula to identify 66 ports eligible to apply for the grants. DHS subject matter experts further reviewed and prioritized grant applications within this pool of eligible ports based on specific risk scenario, among other factors. Note that the PSGP round five grant application materials state that the program

> places a strong emphasis on prevention and detection relative to improvised explosive devices (IEDs), as well as chemical, biological, radiological, and nuclear devices. . . . Of great concern to port security are IEDs delivered via small craft, underwater and in vehicles on ferries. Areas of focus for grantees should include protection of facilities such as public cruise lines, ferry terminals, and vessels from tampering and attack.[58]

PSGP round five awards were granted to 36 ports, predominantly the largest U.S. ports in terms of cargo tonnage or passenger traffic. According to the DHS, this approach was intended to allocate grant resources according to the overall risk among eligible ports and to fund projects with the greatest potential to reduce the risk of "high-priority" threats.[59]

The PSGP's round six grant eligibility was expanded to what the DHS has determined are the nation's 100 "most critical" ports.[60] This was an apparent reversal of the program's strategic shift in round five which focused on larger ports. On the other hand, the PSGP round six grant application materials also appeared to focus on a smaller range of specific attack scenarios, placing a "strong emphasis" only on improvised explosive devices (IED) placed underwater, in vehicles on ferries, or in small craft and not on chemical, biological, radiological, and nuclear devices, as stated in round five.[61] According to press reports, the Coast Guard's Maritime Security Risk Assessment Model (MSRAM), which was used by the DHS to help evaluate its 2006 grant program applications, dealt only with "plausible" scenarios, such as small boat attacks on oil terminals, and did not attempt to evaluate the consequences of attacks using weapons of mass destruction.[62] Projects which demonstrated enhanced "Maritime Domain Awareness" such as access controls and standardized credentialing, command and control, communications, and intelligence sharing and analysis were added as an additional criteria for reviewing grant applications in round six. PSGP round six awards were granted to 50 ports of the 100 eligible to apply.

Emphasizing High Priority Scenarios. The PSGP's current focus on specific types of weapons and targets and on the nation's largest ports demonstrates an approach to the "unlimited scenarios" problem which emphasizes key scenarios. While not excluding other scenarios, the PSGP round six application materials appear to narrow down priority scenarios in terms of locations (major ports), targets (ferries and cruise ships), and tactics (IED's). Port Security officials have also focused on priority scenarios, although not necessarily the same stated by the PSGP.

> There are . . . a number of threat concerns that are believed to be more likely and therefore are the ones that most maritime security programs today are

> built around. These include the use of ports or vessels as a means to smuggle weapons of mass destruction or terrorist operatives into the United States, the use of ships as a weapon to attack critical infrastructure, the scuttling of ships in major shipping channels and terrorist attacks on ships such as ferries or oil tankers.[63]

As indicated by DHS, the priority scenarios approach has the advantage of applying the nation's limited maritime security resources against terrorism attack scenarios of greatest relative concern based on intelligence and risk assessment. The approach may also create potentially beneficial competition among grant applicants seeking funds for similar security activities in different ports. It reflects the DHS's move towards risk-based distribution of all homeland security grants, maritime and non-maritime, as recommended by the 9/11 Commission.[64]

One significant disadvantage of emphasizing priority scenarios is dependence upon intelligence and risk assessment in an environment where neither may be robust. As the President's *National Strategy for Homeland Security* stated in 2002, "the ambiguous nature of most intelligence on terrorist threats means that . . . decisions must often be made in conditions of great uncertainty."[65] To the extent that priority attack scenarios identified by DHS or port security officials are not the right ones, serious threats to U.S. maritime security may remain. Perhaps predictably, there appears to be disagreement among security analysts about the credibility and likelihood of specific attack scenarios frequently cited in maritime security policy discussions. Specific examples are discussed in the following section.

Likelihood of U.S. Maritime Terrorist Attacks

Clear perspectives on the likelihood of specific types of maritime terrorist attacks are essential for prioritizing the nation's maritime anti-terrorism activities. Especially when security policies seek to concentrate resources against a relatively limited number of terrorism scenarios, as appears to be the case for DHS port security grants, the responsible agencies must be confident that these scenarios are credible and do, indeed, pose the greatest threat to the United States. In practice, however, there has been considerable public debate about the likelihood of scenarios frequently identified as having high priority by federal policy makers. As a 2006 RAND study of maritime security concluded "many perceptions of maritime terrorism risks do not align with the reality of threats and vulnerabilities."[66] The following section discusses perceptions and uncertainties pertaining to three prominent maritime attack scenarios, including nuclear or "dirty" bombs smuggled in shipping containers, liquefied natural gas (LNG) tanker attacks, and attacks on passenger ferries.

The "Bomb in a Box" Scenario

Type of Bomb. The Bush Administration's *National Strategy for Maritime Security* states that "WMD issues are of the greatest concern since the maritime domain is the likely venue by which WMD will be brought into the United States."[67] One arms control expert believes that, under current maritime security practices, the likelihood of such an attack within the decade "is more likely than not."[68] According to a press report, the operations and emergency management director for the Port of Los Angeles has stated that the probability of a nuclear attack at his port is "not low," and that measures to prevent such an attack are the port's top priority.[69]

Although much attention is paid to the threat of nuclear terrorism, there are divergent opinions about the likelihood of a terrorist group such as Al Qaeda constructing or otherwise obtaining a workable nuclear weapon.[70] Expert estimates of the probability of terrorists obtaining a nuclear device have ranged from 50% to less than 1%.[71] Among other challenges to obtaining such a device, experts believe it unlikely that countries with nuclear weapons or materials would knowingly supply them to a terrorist group.[72] It also may be technically difficult to successfully detonate such a nuclear device. North Korea experienced technical failures in conducting its 2006 nuclear weapons test, and this test took place under highly controlled conditions.[73] Attempting to detonate a nuclear device in a maritime terror attack could pose even greater operational challenges. Consistent with these perspectives, Secretary of Homeland Security Michael Chertoff has stated, "I don't think that in the near term there's a significant likelihood of a traditional nuclear device being detonated" in the United States.[74]

Other experts concede that evaluating the likelihood of nuclear terrorism is inherently uncertain, but that such potential attacks warrant attention even if they are unlikely.

> The probability of a terrorist attack with an actual nuclear weapon cannot be reliably estimated, and it is surely lower than the probability of virtually any other type of terrorist attack. But the devastation from such an attack would be so overwhelming that, based on expected damages—the probability multiplied by the consequences—this threat must be considered one of the greatest dangers America faces . . ..[75]

Terrorist attacks on U.S. ports with radiological dispersion devices ("dirty" bombs) is also considered among the gravest maritime terrorism scenarios.[76] A 2003 simulation of a series of such attacks concluded that they "could cripple global trade and have a devastating impact on the nation's economy."[77] Many terrorism analysts view such a dirty bomb attack as relatively likely. In a 2005 survey, for example, nuclear non-proliferation experts expressed their beliefs (on average) that there was a 25% chance of a dirty bomb attack in the United States by 2010 and a 40% chance of such an attack by 2015.[78] Studies suggest that the materials required to make a dirty bomb may be widely available and poorly controlled internationally.[79] According to some press reports, U.S. and British intelligence agencies have reportedly concluded that Al Qaeda has succeeded in making such a bomb.[80] Port operators have testified before Congress that they believe "it is just a question of time" before terrorists with dirty bombs successfully attack a U.S. port.[81]

Although many experts consider attacks with dirty bombs among the most likely maritime terrorism scenarios, other experts dispute this conclusion. Scientists have long questioned whether terrorists could actually build a dirty bomb with catastrophic potential since handling the necessary radioactive materials could cause severe burns and would likely expose the builders to lethal doses of radiation.[82] Building and transporting such a bomb safely and to avoid detection would likely require so much shielding that it would be "nearly impossible" to move.[83] Weaker dirty bombs made from less radioactive (and more common) materials would be easier to build and deploy, but would have a much smaller physical impact and would likely cause few human casualties. Consequently, some analysts argue that terrorists will forego dirty bombs, restricting themselves to the use of more conventional explosives.[84] In support of this argument, analysts point to the fact that there have been no U.S. dirty bomb attacks, notwithstanding the supposed ease of perpetrating such attacks.[85] They also note that the 2005 U.S. indictment of alleged "dirty bomber" Jose Padilla, in fact, contained no evidence of, or references to, a dirty bomb plot.[86] Faced with contradictory perspectives on the likelihood of a dirty bomb attack scenario at a U.S. port, analysts and policy makers draw qualified conclusions about such an attack. If a "weak" dirty bomb attack is more likely than a "strong" one, but a weak attack will have limited effects, it is unclear whether such an attack would meet terrorist objectives. On the other hand, the effects on the general public of any dirty bomb attack, even a weak one, may be great enough to motivate potential attackers. As one analyst has stated, notwithstanding the challenges to dirty bombers, "the chances of a dirty bomb being deployed by al Qaeda cannot be discounted. . . Given the exponential psychological and economic effects of such a weapon, the benefits of deploying one may far outweigh the costs and difficulties entailed in its construction."[87]

Method of Delivery. The potential smuggling and detonation of a nuclear or dirty bomb device in a shipping container at a U.S. port is one of the threats most specifically and frequently mentioned by legislators in the context of maritime security.[88] Shipping containers may be particularly vulnerable to terrorist infiltration compared to other types of cargo for three reasons. First, shipping containers are relatively large. They come in standard sizes from 20 to 53 feet long, although the most common are 40 feet or longer—about the size of a truck semi-trailer. Second, the containers on any given ship are packed at the factories or warehouses of many different companies that can be dispersed far and wide from the loading port, making it impossible for government authorities to ensure that only legitimate cargo has been packed. Third, the containers are typically trucked to the port of loading, during which the integrity of the shipments rests entirely on the trustworthiness or due diligence of the truck drivers. A maritime security expert at the Council on Foreign Relations, who is a former Commandant of the U.S. Coast Guard, outlines a scenario that most concerns him:

> Let me share with you the terrorist scenario that most keeps me awake at night. . . . A container of athletic foot wear for a name brand company is loaded at a manufacturing plant in Surabaya, Indonesia. The container doors are shut and a mechanical seal is put into the door pad-eyes. These designer sneakers are destined for retail stores in malls across America. The container and seal numbers are recorded at the factory. A local truck driver, sympathetic to Al Qaeda picks up the container. On the way to the port, he turns into an alleyway and backs up the truck at a nondescript warehouse where a small team of operatives pry loose one of the door hinges to open the container so that they can gain access to the shipment. Some of the sneakers are removed and in their place, the operatives load a dirty bomb wrapped in lead shielding, and they then refasten the door.

Other analysts assert that, if terrorists were to attempt a nuclear or dirty bomb attack in a U.S. port, they would be unlikely to do so using a shipping container because it would put the device beyond a terrorist group's control. These analysts question whether the container shipping system offers the routing or scheduling precision required by terrorists to position the bomb in the right place at the right time. Other observers assert that some types of non-containerized cargo could also be used for smuggling a bomb.[89] The manager of port security at the Port Authority of New York and New Jersey states that their biggest concern is roll-on/roll-off cargo (ships that carry automobiles, trucks, and other vehicles).[90] Non-containerized cargo is more plentiful. By tonnage, containers carry only 11% of U.S. overseas waterborne trade[91] and container ships account for about one in every three U.S. port calls.[92] Other types of cargo also face less security screening.[93] Relatively low-value cargo might be targeted if terrorists perceive it receives less attention from U.S. Coast Guard and customs officials. For instance, a federal official familiar with New York harbor, pointing to a scrap metal terminal in Jersey City, stated the following to a reporter, "If I wanted to bring an atomic bomb into the port, I'd do it through that scrap operation."[94]

The Government Accountability Office (GAO) investigated the potential for maritime terrorists to use weapons of mass destruction (WMDs) in 2005. In its report, the GAO states that

> An extensive body of work on this subject by the Federal Bureau of Investigation and academic, think tank, and business organizations concluded that while the likelihood of such use of containers is considered low, the movement of oceangoing containerized cargo is vulnerable to some form of terrorist action. Such action, including attempts to smuggle either fully assembled weapons of mass destruction or their individual components, could lead to widespread death and damage.[95]

Liquefied Natural Gas (LNG) Tanker Attacks

Potential terrorist attacks on LNG tankers in U.S. waters have been a key concern of policy makers in ports with LNG facilities because such attacks could cause catastrophic fires in port and nearby populated areas. The Coast Guard's FY2006 budget specifically requested funding for "additional boat crews and screening personnel at key LNG hubs."[96] To date, no LNG tanker or land-based LNG facility in the world has been attacked by terrorists. However, similar natural gas and oil assets have been favored terror targets internationally. The attack on the *Limburg*, although an oil tanker, is often cited as an indication of LNG tanker vulnerability. The Department of Homeland Security (DHS) specifically included LNG tankers among a list of potential terrorist targets in a security alert late in 2003.[97] The DHS also reported that "in early 2001 there was some suspicion of possible associations between stowaways on Algerian flagged LNG tankers arriving in Boston and persons connected with the so-called 'Millennium Plot'" to bomb targets in the United States. While these suspicions could not be proved, DHS stated that "the risks associated with LNG shipments are real, and they can never be entirely eliminated."[98] A 2004 report by Sandia National Laboratories concluded that potential terrorist attacks on LNG tankers, could be considered "credible and possible."[99] The Sandia report identified LNG tankers as vulnerable to ramming, pre-placed explosives, insider takeover, hijacking, or external terrorist actions (such as a *Limburg*-type, missile or airplane attack).[100] Former Bush Administration counter-terrorism advisor Richard Clarke has asserted that terrorists have both the desire and capability to attack LNG shipping with the intention of harming the general population.[101]

Although they acknowledge the security information put forth by federal agencies, many experts believe that concern about threats to LNG tankers is overstated.[102] In 2003, the head of one university research consortium remarked, for example, "from all the information we have . . . we don't see LNG as likely or credible terrorist targets."[103] Industry representatives argue that deliberately causing an LNG catastrophe to injure people might be possible in theory, but would be extremely difficult to accomplish. Likewise, the Federal Energy Regulatory Commission (FERC) and other experts believe that LNG facilities are relatively secure compared to other hazardous chemical infrastructures which receives less public attention. In a December 2004 report, the FERC stated that

> for a new LNG terminal proposal . . . the perceived threat of a terrorist attack may be considered as highly probable to the local population. However, at the national level, potential terrorist targets are plentiful. . . . Many of these pose a similar or greater hazard to that of LNG.[104]

The FERC also remarked, however, that "unlike accidental causes, historical experience provides little guidance in estimating the probability of a terrorist attack on an LNG vessel or onshore storage facility."[105] Former Director of Central Intelligence, James Woolsey, has stated his belief that a terrorist attack on an LNG tanker in U.S. waters would be unlikely because its potential impacts would not be great enough compared to other potential targets.[106] LNG terminal operators which have conducted proprietary assessments of potential terrorist attacks against LNG tankers, have expressed similar views.[107] In a September, 2006, evaluation of a proposed LNG terminal in Long Island Sound, the USCG states that "there are currently no specific, credible threats against" the proposed LNG facility or tankers serving the facility.[108] The evaluation also notes, however, that the threat environment is dynamic and that some threats may be unknown.[109]

Passenger Ferry Attacks

Congressional policy makers frequently cite passenger ferries as a key maritime security concern. For example, in 2005, one Member of Congress stated that "there is a serious security gap in our ferry systems and we need to ensure that passengers on our nation's waterways are protected."[110] A RAND study in 2006 argued that attacks on passenger ferries in the United States might be highly attractive to terrorists because such attacks are easy to execute, may kill many people, would likely draw significant media attention and could demonstrate a terrorist group's salience and vibrancy.[111] One U.S. Coast Guard risk analyst reportedly has stated that "in terms of the probability of something happening, the likelihood of it succeeding and the consequences of it occurring, ferries come out at the very high end."[112] Such attacks have occurred overseas. As noted earlier in this report, terrorists linked to Al Qaeda attacked and sank the Philippine vessel *Superferry 14* in 2004.

In a 2006 report, the U.S. Department of Justice (DOJ) identified a ferry bombing as among the most likely types of maritime terror attacks.[113] The DOJ report reached this conclusion based largely on the number of suspicious incidents reported at marine facilities in the Seattle area and at other U.S. ports. However, officials in the Seattle office of the Federal Bureau of Investigation (FBI) reportedly suggested at the time that the DOJ's high ranking of the passenger ferry threat might be due to more aggressive reporting of suspicious incidents in that region than elsewhere in the country.[114] Seattle FBI officials also reportedly stated that they had never been able to tie a specific suspicious incident to a terrorist group or terrorist plan.[115] Thus, while there appears to be a logical case why ferries may be a key type of terrorist target, questions remain about actual terrorist activities related to ferries.

Overall Likelihood of Maritime Terrorism

The prior discussion illustrates the uncertainty surrounding some of the maritime terrorism scenarios of greatest concern to U.S. maritime security officials. Questions about the likelihood of these specific, high priority scenarios beg the larger question of how likely is *any* maritime terrorism attack against the United States. Some experts suggest that some such attack, in one form or another, is almost inevitable. For example, one senior U.S. military officer has reportedly asserted that "it's just a matter of time until the terrorists try to use a . . . maritime attack against us."[116] Security analysts also point to known terrorist plots to attack U.S. maritime targets, such as those passing the Straits of Gibraltar, as evidence that global terrorist groups continue to plan maritime terrorism activities. Information from captured Al Qaeda member Abd al Rahman al Nashiri reportedly included plans for attacks on a wide range of Western maritime targets, including military vessels, oil tankers, and cruise ships.[117]

Other analysts believe future maritime attacks against the United States are relatively unlikely, especially in U.S. waters. Notwithstanding specific acts of terrorism in the past, such as the *Cole* bombing, they note that fewer than 1% of all global terrorist attacks since 1997 have involved maritime targets.[118] Furthermore, international terrorists have attacked no maritime targets in U.S. territory since the anti-Castro attacks in 1976 despite their demonstrated ability to do so overseas.[119] Analysts also argue that U.S. ports and waterways are increasingly well-protected against terrorists due to the ongoing security activities of the U.S. Coast Guard, U.S. Customs and Border Protection (CBP), provisions of the Maritime Transportation Security Act (P.L. 107-295), protections added using DHS port security grants, and other U.S. maritime security measures.[120] Classification issues may also influence differing perceptions of maritime terrorism risk since piracy unrelated to terrorism is common in Southeast Asia and may be conflated with terrorism in maritime security statistics.[121]

A key consideration in assessing the general likelihood of a maritime attack against the United States is the inherent operational difficulty in mounting such attacks, especially compared to land attacks which may alternatively satisfy terrorist objectives. One U.S. naval analyst has identified a number of specific challenges for terrorists in the maritime environment:

- Maritime targets are relatively more scarce than land targets;
- Surveillance at sea offers less cover and concealment than surveillance on land;
- Tides, currents, wind, sea state, visibility, and proximity to land must all be factored into a maritime terror operation;
- Maritime terror operations may require skills that are not quickly or easily acquired such as special training in navigation, coastal piloting, and ship handling;
- Testing weapons and practicing attack techniques, hallmarks of Al Qaeda's typically meticulous preparation, are harder and more difficult to conceal at sea than on land;

- The generally singular nature of maritime targets, the low probability of damage and casualties secondary to the intended target, and the problems associated with filming attacks at sea for terrorist publicity may also reduce the desirability of maritime targets.[122]

Given these challenges, it remains an open question how likely maritime attacks against the United States may be. In terms of the scenario framework in this report, although a successful attack on U.S. maritime targets would likely satisfy certain objectives of known international perpetrators such as Al Qaeda, tactical uncertainties and security deterrents may lead terrorist planners to turn their attention elsewhere. It bears repeating, however, that maritime terror attacks against the U.S. have occurred and there is evidence they have been planned for the future, despite the operational challenges. The same naval analyst cited above calls for continued vigilance:

> Rather than develop a false sense of security based on the belief that inherent difficulties will limit maritime terrorism . . . caution is warranted in light of Al Qaeda's adaptability, ingenuity, tenacity, and audacity. Successful development and application of maritime tactics, techniques, and procedures has already occurred within the terrorist community.[123]

It appears, therefore, that while maritime terrorist attacks against the United States may be more difficult to execute and, consequently, less likely to occur than other types of attacks, they remain a significant possibility and warrant continued policy attention.

The key challenge in determining the overall likelihood of a terrorist attack on a U.S. port is reducing uncertainty about specific types of attacks and potential attackers. Because historical terrorist activity is not necessarily a reliable predictor of future activity, scenarios derived from attacks like that on the U.S.S *Cole* may not help prepare for actual future attacks. Furthermore, information about the ongoing motivations, capabilities, and plans of terrorist groups is limited and typically not in the public domain. Terrorist intelligence gathered by U.S. and foreign agencies may reduce this uncertainty, but is unlikely to eliminate it. Faced with this uncertainty, decision makers are to some extent forced to rely upon their own best judgment to reach conclusions about the likelihood of maritime terrorist attacks.

Policy Issues for Congress

Maritime terrorist threats to the United States are varied, and so are the nation's efforts to combat them. As Congress continues its oversight of ongoing U.S. maritime security activities, it may focus on issues related to the consistency of maritime terrorism scenario assessment, intelligence gathering, and responding to new intelligence.

Consistency of Terrorism Scenario Assessment

Development and assessment of maritime terrorism scenarios is a key element of federal port security exercises, grant administration, and legislative oversight. It appears, however, that these three dimensions of the nation's maritime security strategy emphasize terrorism scenarios in different ways. Port security exercises (conducted under a number of independent programs) address the broadest range of terrorism scenarios, with no obvious focus on any particular scenario. The DHS port security grant program currently emphasizes a subset of these scenarios—IED attacks on ferries and cruise ships in major ports, for example. Federal legislators appear to focus oversight on a different subset of scenarios, notably WMD's aboard container vessels and attacks on LNG tankers. As this report states, there is a logical basis underlying the scenario priorities established for exercises, grants, and oversight. Nonetheless, if these activities are intended to derive from a uniform federal maritime security strategy the question arises to what degree these activities are complementary or inconsistent.

If port officials, grant administrators, and legislators disagree on what types of attack scenarios are of greatest priority, either because their security assessments are inconsistent, or because they lack sufficient intelligence about terrorist threats, port security resources may be deployed inefficiently. For example, sharply increasing security against specific types of maritime attacks in specific locations may have limited benefits for overall port security if other significant vulnerabilities are not addressed as a result. A key question is whether policymakers are too focused on a narrow spectrum of the threat. A former Federal Maritime Commissioner has stated that "it [is] fair to say there has been little to no emphasis on non-containerized cargo in the political arena," while in contrast, "'virtually everyone' in the industry thinks non-containerized cargo is in 'many respects a more vulnerable path.'"[124] While concern, in this case, for container security may not be misplaced, there are other forms of cargo that terrorists could exploit just as effectively.

Intelligence Gathering

Because intelligence about terrorist capabilities and activities is a key factor in terrorism scenario assessment, Congress may act to ensure that the responsible U.S. intelligence agencies work to improve their intelligence gathering and reduce terrorism scenario uncertainty. As a Department of Defense official has reportedly remarked,

> We have the operational capabilities to defeat any of these threats . . . if we see the threat approaching . . ..The most important thing we can do is to dramatically improve our overseas intelligence collection, with a specific orientation toward the maritime threat.[125]

Better intelligence may also help ensure that various federal maritime security activities are more closely aligned. The Government Accountability Office (GAO) evaluated in December 2005 the port risk assessment practices of the U.S. Coast Guard, the Office for Domestic Preparedness, and the Information Analysis and Infrastructure Protection Directorate—all agencies within the Department of Homeland Security. The GAO report concluded:

> Each component faces many challenges in making further progress . . . For example, obtaining better quality data from intelligence agencies would help DHS components estimate the relative likelihood of various types of threats—a key element of assessing risks. In the longer term, progress will depend increasingly on how well risk management is coordinated across agencies, because current approaches in many ways are neither consistent nor comparable.[126]

Responding to New Intelligence

Given the dynamic nature of the terrorist threat, Congress may consider whether federal funding mechanisms for anti-terrorism measures are flexible enough to respond to new threat intelligence. Between the time Congress decides on the allocation of security grants among the various transportation modes in the annual appropriations process and the time that those grants are actually awarded can be almost a year. Within this time frame, new intelligence may indicate that security resources be reallocated to respond to a different threat. A related oversight issue for Congress is the capability of the U.S. Coast Guard and CBP to shift staff and resources as new threat information becomes available. For instance, the U.S. Coast Guard has developed Maritime Safety and Security Teams consisting of about 75 personnel that are designed to provide a rapid surge capacity at any port as the need arises. CBP may have more difficulty in shifting resources because, in addition to operating in seaports, it operates in airports and at land border crossings and not all of its inspection equipment is easily adaptable across these three environments.

Public information suggests that the threat of maritime terrorism is significant, and can take myriad forms, but that different dimensions of the nation's maritime security activities prioritize these activities in different ways. As oversight of the federal role in maritime security continues, Congress may raise questions concerning the relationship among these activities, and the implications of differing terrorism scenario priorities among them. Improved gathering and sharing of maritime terrorism intelligence may enhance consistency across various U.S. maritime security activities and increase the efficient deployment of maritime security resources.

In addition to these issues, Congress may assess how the various elements of U.S. maritime security fit together in the nation's overall strategy to protect the public from terrorist attacks. For example, bulk quantities of hazardous chemicals are found in marine vessels, in rail and highway tankers, and in chemical facilities on land. Terrorists may seek to exploit such chemicals in any of these sectors. Balancing the nation's homeland security resources across the maritime and non-maritime sectors is a policy challenge because specific sectors may fall under different homeland security authorities and regulations. Uncertainty about terrorist capabilities and activities complicates this problem by making it difficult to compare terrorist attack scenarios across sectors. Without such a comprehensive perspective on terrorist threats, security analysts may have difficulty identifying which assets to protect and how well to protect them with the limited security resources available. Reviewing how these security priorities and activities fit together to achieve common goals could be an oversight challenge for Congress.

Endnotes

[1] U.S. Dept. of Homeland Security (DHS) and U.S. Dept. of Defense (DOD). *The National Strategy for Maritime Security*. Sept. 2005. p. 2.

[2] "Ships as Terrorist Targets." *American Shipper*. November, 2002. p. 59; The *Limburg*, under French registry, was attacked on October 6, 2002 in the Gulf of Aden while carrying approximately 400,000 barrels of crude oil from Iran to Malaysia.

[3] For more information see CRS Report RL33383, *Terminal Operators and Their Role in U.S. Port and Maritime Security*, by John Frittelli and Jennifer E. Lake.

[4] Information in this report is based solely on publicly available information. In this report, attacks on the United States are broadly defined to include attacks on U.S. maritime assets (globally), military allies, and commercial partners if motivated by their relationship with the United States.

[5] National Memorial Institute for the Prevention of Terrorism (MIPT). Terrorism Incident Database. Incident profiles. July 20, 2006. [http://www.tkb.org/Home.jsp].

[6] Council on Foreign Relations. "Backgrounder: Abu Sayyaf Group." Nov. 2005. [http://www.cfr.org/publication/9235/].

[7] MIPT. July 20, 2006.

[8] U.S. Dept. of State. *Country Reports on Terrorism*. p. 13. April 28, 2006.

[9] For further discussion, see Enders, Walter and Sandler, Todd. *The Political Economy of Terrorism*. Cambridge University Press. Chap. 1. Nov. 2005; Lutz, James M. and Lutz, Brenda J. "Terrorism as Economic Warfare." *Global Economy Journal*. Vol. 6. No. 2. 2006; U.S. Army, Training and Doctrine Command. *A Military Guide to Terrorism in the Twenty-First Century*. Oct. 12, 2004. pp. 6.3-6.5.

[10] U.S. Army Corps of Engineers. *Waterborne Transportation Lines of the United States, Calendar Year 2004, Volume 1—National Summaries*. Tab. 4 and Fig. 14. Dec. 15, 2005.

[11] Carter, Mike. "Why Feds Believe Terrorists are Probing Ferry System." *Seattle Times*. Oct. 12, 2004.

[12] Hodges, James. "An Exercise in Disaster: Preparing for the Worst" *Daily Press*. Newport News, VA. Aug. 19, 2005.

[13] Vieth, Warren. "Owners of Oil Tankers Jittery." *Los Angeles Times*. Nov. 25, 2003. p. 1.

[14] U.S. Dept. of State. "Yemen's Economy Suffering Due to October Terrorist Attack." Nov. 8, 2002. [http://usinfo.state.gov/is/Archive/2004/Apr/01-745388.html]

[15] Hendawi, Hamza. "Yemen Acknowledges Terror Attack." Associated Press. Oct. 17, 2002.

[16] Purvis, Michael. "Bridge Out: Forces Plan for Terrorist Attack." *Sault Star.* Sault Sainte Marie, Ontario. May 4, 2005.

[17] Frey, Bruno S. and Rohner, Dominik. "Blood and Ink The Common-Interest-Game Between Terrorists and the Media." Center for Research in Economics, Management, and the Arts. Basel, Switzerland. Working Paper No. 2006-8. p. 18.

[18] American Association of Port Authorities. "U.S. Public Port Facts." Internet page. Alexandria, VA. July 18, 2006. [http://www.aapa-ports.org/industryinfo/portfact.htm]

[19] U.S. Maritime Administration. "U.S. Waterborne Trade by Trading Partners, 1997-2005." Online database. July 18, 2006. [http://www.iwr.usace.army.mil/ndc/usforeign/index.htm]

[20] Sawer, Patrick. "Terror Plot to Blow Up Navy Warships is Foiled." *The Evening Standard.* London. June 11, 2002. p.4.

[21] Raymond, Catherine Z. "The Threat of Maritime Terrorism in the Malacca Straits." *Terrorism Monitor.* Vol. 4 . No. 3. Feb. 9, 2006. p. 8.

[22] Organization for Economic Cooperation and Development (OECD). *Security in Maritime Transport: Risk Factors and Economic Impact.* July 2003. p. 14.

[23] Caldwell, Stephen L., U.S. Government Accountability Office. Statement at the House Committee on Government Reform, Subcommittee on Government Management, Finance, and Accountability hearing on "Securing Our Ports: Information Sharing is Key to Effective Maritime Security." July 10, 2006.

[24] Homeland Security Council. *Planning Scenarios: Executive Summaries.* July 2004. p. 6-1.

[25] DHS and DOD. Sept. 2005. p.4.

[26] "FBI Warns of Maritime Terror Threat." *The Journal of Commerce Online.* Jun. 28, 2004.

[27] See, for example: Murphy, Martin. op. cit.

[28] Dress, Caroline and Ang, Edgar. "U.S. at Risk from Boats Packed with Explosives." Reuters. June 1, 2006.

[29] Murphy, Martin. Feb. 1, 2006.

[30] For more information on PortSTEP, see the TSA's program brief, an electronic copy of which is available at [http://www.tsa.gov/interweb/assetlibrary/program_brief.pdf].

[31] Transportation Security Administration (TSA), PortSTEP program office. Personal communication. Dec. 20, 2006 and "PortSTEP Program Initiated." Press release. Aug. 18, 2005; Daniel, Mac. "Terror Preparedness Put to Test." *Boston Globe.* Sept. 20, 2005.

[32] U.S. Coast Guard, Area Maritime Security Training and Exercise Program (AMSTEP) Program Office. Personal communication. Jan. 4, 2007.

[33] Tully, Tasha, U.S. Coast Guard, 7th Distrist. "Tampa Bay Agencies Test Security Plans." *Coastline.* [https://www.piersystem.com/go/doc/586/136318]; Karl, Richard C., Director Superfund Division, U.S. Environmental Protection Agency, Region 5. "Reports of Significant Developments and Activities Ending on September 8, 2006." Memorandum. Sept. 18, 2006. [http:// www.epa.gov/regi on5superfund/significant _actions/2006/060908.pdf];

[34] Hanewich, Steve, Cpt., U.S. Coast Guard. "Coast Guard Plan of Action and Milestones: Natural Disaster Preparedness 2006." Slide presentation. Dec. 20, 2006. p. 15. [http://www.scaa-spill.org/noflash/meetings_events/2006meeting_presentation.html]

[35] Chawkins, Steve. "Agencies Get a Taste of Terrorism in Action." *Los Angeles Times.* Nov. 6, 2003.

[36] O'Sullivan, Mike. "Five-Day Exercise Simulates Coordinated Terror Attacks." *Voice of America.* August 5, 2004.

[37] Shukovsky, Paul. "Terrorism Simulation Exercises Set Today." *Seattle Post-Intelligencer.* May 23, 2006.

[38] Shear, Michael D. "Va. Terror Drills Set Up Worst-Case Scenarios." *Washington Post*. p. B01. Aug. 3, 2004.

[39] California Maritime Academy. "'Terrorists' Attack Training Ship *Golden Bear*." Press release. Oct. 29, 2004.

[40] Booz Allen Hamilton. *Port Security War Game: Implications for U.S. Supply Chains*. 2003.

[41] Dorsey, Jack. "Coast Guard, Navy, FBI to Team up for Security Exercise." *Virginian-Pilot*. June 12, 2006; U.S. Coast Guard (USCG). "Coast Guard Atlantic Area, Navy Second Fleet, FBI Participate in Maritime Homeland Security Exercise." Press release. Jun. 12, 2006.

[42] Nelson, Tim. "Is That a Speargun, or Are You Just Glad to See Me?" *City Hall Scoop*. Internet blog. July 22, 2005. [http://blogs.twincities.com/city_hall_scoop/2005/07]

[43] Pinto, C. Ariel. and Talley, Wayne K. "The Security Incident Cycle of Ports."Old Dominion Univ., Maritime Institute. Working paper. Norfolk, VA. July 2006.

[44] Purvis, Michael. May 4, 2005.

[45] Pyle, Richard. "Agencies Analyze Responses to Nightmare Scenario at U.S. Ports." Associated Press. June 7, 2006.

[46] Fuentes, Gidget. "Training Drills Test Threat Response at California Ports." *Navy Times*. June 13, 2005.

[47] Daniel, Mac. "Drill Will be Gauge of Terror Readiness." *Boston Globe*. Aug. 29, 2006.

[48] Baxter, Edward. "Thai Forces Board Button in Maritime Security Exercise." U.S. Military Sealift Command. Press release. May 22, 2006.

[49] "Navy Takes in Pacific Exercise." Associated Press. June 07, 2006.

[50] "Anti-Weapons Marine Exercise to Target 'Japanese' Vessel." Agence France-Presse. Sept. 09, 2003.

[51] Transportation Security Admin. (TSA). "PortSTEP: Mission and Goals." Web page. Aug. 1, 2006. [http://www.tsa.gov/what_we_do/layers/portstep/editorial_with_table_0060.shtm]

[52] U.S. Coast Guard (USCG). "Guidelines for Port Security Committees, and Port Security Plans Required for U.S. Ports." Navigation and Vessel Inspection Circular No. 902. Sept. 30, 2002. p.13.

[53] According to a PortSTEP official, the USCG did rank U.S. ports based on risk, but the selection of ports for the program was based on broader criteria, including port diversity.

[54] This figure includes $75 million in port security grants awarded under the DHS's Urban Area Security Initiative in FY2003.

[55] Transportation Security Administration (TSA). Port Security Grant Program Awards, Round 2. June 12, 2003. Available at [http://www.aapa-ports.org/govrelations/attachA.doc]

[56] Dept. of Homeland Security, Office of Inspector General. *Review of the Port Security Grant Program*. OIG-05-10 Jan. 2005. p. 17.

[57] Ibid.

[58] Dept. of Homeland Security. "FY2005 Port Security Grant Program." Fact sheet. May 13, 2005.

[59] Dept. of Homeland Security, Office of Inspector General. *Follow Up Review of the Port Security Grant Program*. OIG-06-24 Feb. 2006 (Revised). p. 5.

[60] Dept. of Homeland Security. "FY2006 Port Security Grant Program." Fact sheet. July 7, 2006. p. 1.

[61] Ibid, p. 2.

[62] Edmonson, R.G. "Coast Guard: Risk-Assessment Tools Aid Consistency." *Pacific Shipper.* Oct. 27, 2006. Numerical ratings from the MSRAM program reportedly accounted for 25% of port security grant applicants' overall application score in round six.

[63] Rooney, Beth. Manager of Port Security, Port Authority of NY and NJ. Statement before the House Government Reform Committee, Government Management Finance and Accountability Subcommittee. July 10, 2006.

[64] For more information see CRS Report RL33583, *Homeland Security Grants: Evolution of Program Guidance and Grant Allocation Methods*, by Shawn Reese.

[65] U.S. Office of Homeland Security. *National Strategy for Homeland Security.* July 16, 2002.

[66] Greenberg, Michael D., Chalk, Pete, Willis, Henry H., Khilko, Ivan. and Ortiz, David S.; *Maritime Terrorism: Risk and Liability.* RAND Center for Terrorism Risk Management Policy. 2006. p. xxi.

[67] Executive Office of the President. *The National Strategy for Maritime Security.* September 20, 2005. p. 4.

[68] Allison, Graham. Remarks on "CNN Presents: Nuclear Terror." *CNN Presents.* Broadcast transcript. Sept. 12, 2004. [http://transcripts.cnn.com/TRANSCRIPTS/0409/12/cp.00.html]

[69] Gorman, Siobhan and Sydney J. Freedberg, Jr. "Early Warning." *The National Journal.* June 11, 2005.

[70] For further analysis on this topic, see CRS Report RS21293, *Terrorist Nuclear Attacks on Seaports: Threat and Response*, by Jonathan Medalia.

[71] Hegland, Corine and Webb, Greg. "The Threat," *National Journal.* April 15, 2005. [http://nationaljournal.com/members/news/2005/04/0415nj1.htm#]; Senator Richard G. Lugar. "The Lugar Survey on Proliferation Threats and Responses." June 2005. p. 6. [http://lugar.senate.gov/reports/NPSurvey.pdf]

[72] Bunn, Matthew and Weir, Anthony. *Securing the Bomb 2006.* John F. Kennedy School of Government Harvard University. Commissioned by the Nuclear Threat Initiative. July 2006. p. 29.

[73] Collins, Graham P. "Kim's Big Fizzle: The Physics Behind A Nuclear Dud." *Scientific American.* Jan. 2007.

[74] Department of Homeland Security (DHS). Remarks by Secretary of Homeland Security Michael Chertoff at George Mason University. Fairfax, VA. April 26, 2006.

[75] de Rugy, Veronique. "Is Port Security Spending Making Us Safer?" American Enterprise Institute. Working Paper #115. Sept. 7, 2005. p. 8.

[76] For further information on dirty bombs, see CRS Report RS21528, *Terrorist 'Dirty Bombs': A Brief Primer,* by Jonathan Medalia.

[77] Ibid. Booz Allen Hamilton. 2003. p. 1.

[78] Senator Richard G. Lugar. "The Lugar Survey on Proliferation Threats and Responses." June 2005. p. 6. [http://lugar.senate.gov/reports/NPSurvey.pdf]

[79] Government Accountability Office (GAO). *Nuclear Nonproliferation: U.S. and International Assistance Efforts to Control Sealed Radioactive Sources Need Strengthening.* GAO-03-638. May 16, 2003. p. 65.

[80] Mayer, Josh. "Al Qaeda Feared to Have Dirty Bombs." *Los Angeles Times.* Feb. 8, 2003. p. 1.

[81] Gilbert, Gary. Senior V.P., Hutchison Port Holdings. Statement before the Senate Homeland Security and Governmental Affairs Committee, Permanent Investigations Subcommittee. March 30, 2006.

[82] Singer, S. Fred., Hoover Institution, Stanford Univ. "Nuclear Terrorism: Facts and Fantasies." Washington Times. (Commentary). April 5, 2002.

[83] *"Dirty Bomb" Fact Sheet.* Center for International Security and Cooperation, Stanford University. Oct. 2006. [http://iis-db.stanford.edu/pubs/20769/dirty_bomb_facts.pdf]

[84] Burgess, Mark. "Pascal's New Wager: The Dirty Bomb Threat Heightens." Center for Defense Information. Washington. Feb. 4, 2003. [http://www.cdi.org /terrorism/dirty-bomb.cfm]

[85] Sterngold, James. "Assessing the Risk of Nuclear Terrorism" *San Francisco Chronicle.* April 18, 2004.; Dotinga, Randy. "After the Beep, Exit the Premises." *Wired News.* May 6, 2004. [http://www.wired.com/news/technology/1,63328-0.html]

[86] Taylor, Guy. "Padilla Case Mum on 'Dirty Bomb'." *Washington Times.* Nov. 24, 2005. p. A03.

[87] Burgess, Mark. Feb. 4, 2003.

[88] See, for example, Hon. Edward J. Markey. "Rep. Markey Urges Scanning for Nuclear Devices in Container Ships Before They Arrive at U.S. Ports." Press release. Sept. 28, 2006; Office of Senator Patty Murray. "Cargo Security: Floor Remarks by Senator Patty Murray Introducing the GreenLane Bill for Senate Consideration." Press release. Sept. 7, 2006.

[89] For an analysis of smuggling a nuclear weapon in an oil tanker, see CRS Report RS21997, *Port and Maritime Security: Potential for Terrorist Nuclear Attack Using Oil Tankers,* by Jonathan Medalia.

[90] Ibid.

[91] U.S. Department of Transportation (DOT). *An Assessment of the U.S. Marine Transportation System.* Report to Congress. Sept. 1999.

[92] U.S. Maritime Administration (MARAD). *Vessel Calls at U.S. and World Ports 2005.* April 2006. p. 1.

[93] Stables, Eleanor. "For Better Cargo Security, Government Needs to Think 'Outside the Box,' Experts Say." *CQ Homeland Security.* Oct. 1, 2006.

[94] Finnegan, William. "Watching the Waterfront." *The New Yorker.* June 19, 2006. p. 63.

[95] Government Accountability Office (GAO). *Cargo Security: Partnership Program Grants Importers Reduced Scrutiny With Limited Assurance of Improved Security.* GAO-05-404. March, 2005. p. 7.

[96] Dept. of Homeland Security (DHS). *Budget-in-Brief, Fiscal Year 2006.* [https://www.dhs.gov/xlibrary/assets/Budget_BIB-FY2006.pdf]

[97] Office of Congressman Edward J. Markey. Personal communication with staff. Jan. 5, 2004.

[98] Turner, Pamela J., Assistant Secretary for Legislative Affairs, Department of Homeland Security (DHS). Letter to U.S. Representative Edward Markey. April 15, 2004. p. 1.

[99] Sandia National Laboratories (SNL). *Guidance on Risk Analysis and Safety Implications of a Large Liquefied Natural Gas (LNG) Spill Over Water.* SAND2004-6258. Albuquerque, NM. Dec. 2004. pp. 49-50.

[100] SNL. Dec. 2004. pp. 61-62.

[101] Clarke, Richard A., et al. *LNG Facilities in Urban Areas.* Good Harbor Consulting, LLC. Prepared for the Rhode Island Office of Attorney General. GHC-RI-0505A. May 2005.

[102] McLaughlin, J. "LNG is Nowhere Near as Dangerous as People Are Making it Out to Be." *Lloyd's List.* Feb. 8, 2005. p5.

[103] Behr, Peter. "Higher Gas Price Sets Stage for LNG." *Washington Post.* July 5, 2003. p. D10.

[104] Federal Energy Regulatory Commission (FERC). *Vista del Sol LNG Terminal Project, Draft Environmental Impact Statement.* FERC/EIS-0176D. Dec. 2004. p. 4-162.

[105] FERC. FERC/EIS-0176D. Dec. 2004. p4-162. Notwithstanding this assertion, in its subsequent draft review of the Long Beach LNG terminal proposal, the FERC states that "the historical probability of a successful terrorist event would be less than seven chances in a million per year . . ." See FERC. Oct. 7, 2005. p. ES-14.

[106] Woolsey, James. Remarks before the National Commission on Energy LNG Forum, Washington, D.C., June 21, 2006.

[107] Grant, Richard, President, Distrigas. Testimony before the Senate Committee on Energy and Natural Resources, Subcommittee on Energy hearing on "The Future of Liquefied Natural Gas: Siting and Safety." Feb. 15, 2005.

[108] U.S. Coast Guard. *U.S. Coast Guard Captain of the Port Long Island Sound Waterways Suitability Report for the Proposed Broadwater Liquefied Natural Gas Facility.* Sept. 21, 2006. p. 146.

[109] Ibid.

[110] Congressman Frank Pallone, Jr. "Pallone Calls for Increased Funding for Ferry Security." Press release. July 15, 2005.

[111] Greenberg, M.D. et al. 2006. p. 95.

[112] Lipton, Eric. "Trying to Keep the Nation's Ferries Safe from Terrorists." *New York Times.* March 19, 2005.

[113] U.S. Dept. of Justice, Office of the Inspector General. *The Federal Bureau of Investigation's Efforts to Protect the Nation's Seaports.* Audit Report 06-26. March 2006. p. 52.

[114] Shukovsky, Paul and Barber, Mike. "Ferries a Top Terror Target, FBI Cautions." *Seattle Post-Intelligencer.* April 21, 2006. p. A1.

[115] Ibid.

[116] Gen. Ralph Eberhart, U.S. Northern Command, as quoted in "Militants Eyeing Seaborne Attack, U.S. General Says." Reuters. Aug. 25, 2004.

[117] Köknar, Ali M. "Maritime Terrorism: a New Challenge for NATO." *Energy Security.* Institute for the Analysis of Global Security (IAGS). Jan. 24, 2005.

[118] National Memorial Institute for the Prevention of Terrorism (MIPT). Terrorist incident reports. July 20, 2006. [http://www.tkb.org/IncidentTargetModule.jsp]

[119] MIPT. July 20, 2006.

[120] For further discussion, see CRS Report RL31733, *Port and Maritime Security: Background and Issues for Congress,* by John F. Frittelli.

[121] Valencia, Mark J. and Young, Adam J. "Conflation of Piracy and Terrorism in Southeast Asia: Rectitude and Utility." *Contemporary Southeast Asia.* Vol. 25. No. 2. Aug. 2003. pp. 269-283.

[122] Captain James Pelkofski, U.S. Navy. "Before the Storm: Al Qaeda's Coming Maritime Campaign." *Proceedings.* U.S. Naval Institute. Vol. 132. No. 12. Dec. 2005. [http://www.usni.org/proceedings/Articles05/Pro12Pelkofski.html]

[123] Ibid.

[124] Robert Quartel, as quoted in Stables, Elanor. "For Better Cargo Security, Government Needs to Think 'Outside the Box,' Experts Say." *CQ Homeland Security.* Oct. 1, 2006.

[125] McHale, Paul F., Asst. Sec. of Defense for Homeland Defense quoted in Pyle, R. "Agencies Analyze Responses to Nightmare Scenario at U.S. Ports." Associated Press. June 7, 2006.

[126] Government Accountability Office. *Risk Management: Further Refinements Needed to Assess Risks and Prioritize Protective Measures at Ports and Other Critical Infrastructure.* GAO-06-91. Dec. 15, 2005.

DOCUMENT NO. 5

HOMELAND SECURITY: COAST GUARD OPERATIONS—BACKGROUND AND ISSUES FOR CONGRESS

CRS Report
RS21125

April 13, 2007

Ronald O'Rourke
Specialist in National Defense
Foreign Affairs, Defense, and Trade Division
Congressional Research Service

Summary

The Coast Guard is the lead federal agency for maritime homeland security For FY2008, the Coast Guard is requesting a total of about $4.5 billion, or a bit more than half its total proposed budget, for the five missions defined in The Homeland Security Act of 2002 (P.L. 107-296) as the Coast Guard's homeland security missions The Coast Guard's homeland security operations pose several potential issues for Congress This report will be updated as events warrant.

Background

The Coast Guard's Role in Homeland Security The Coast Guard, which is a part of the Department of Homeland Security (DHS), is the lead federal agency for maritime homeland security Section 888(a)(2) of The Homeland Security Act of 2002 (P.L. 107-296 of November 25, 2002), which established DHS, specifies five homeland security missions for the Coast Guard: (1) ports, waterways, and coastal security, (2) drug interdiction, (3) migrant interdiction, (4) defense readiness, and (5) other law enforcement.[1] The Coast Guard, in its own budget materials, excludes drug interdiction and other law enforcement from its definition of its homeland security missions.[2]

Under the Ports and Waterways Safety Act of 1972 (P.L 92-340) and the Maritime Transportation Security Act (MTSA) of 2002 (P.L 107-295 of November 25, 2002), the Coast Guard has responsibility to protect vessels and harbors from subversive acts With regard to port security, the Coast Guard is responsible for evaluating, boarding, and inspecting commercial ships approaching U.S. waters, countering terrorist threats in U.S. ports, and helping protect U.S. Navy ships in U.S. ports A Coast Guard officer in each port area is the Captain of the Port (COTP), who is the lead federal official for security and safety of vessels and waterways in that area.[3]

Homeland Security Missions In The Coast Guard Budget. Table 1 below shows FY2005-FY2008 funding for the Coast Guard's five statutorily defined homeland security missions As shown in the table, the Coast Guard for FY2008 is requesting a total of about $4.5 billion, or a bit more than half its total proposed budget, for these five missions. The Coast Guard states that in FY2006, it met it performance targets for two of its five statutorily defined homeland security missions (ports, waterways, and coastal security, and other law enforcement) and did not meet them for two others (defense readiness and migrant interdiction). Performance regarding the fifth mission (drug interdiction) was to be determined as of February 2007.[4]

Table 1. FY2005-FY2008 Funding for Homeland Security Missions

(homeland security missions as defined in Section 888(a)(2) of Homeland Security Act of 2002 [P.L 107-296]; totals may not add due to rounding)

	PWCS[a]	Drug interdiction[b]	Migrant interdiction	Defense readiness	Other law enforcement[b]	Total
Funding (millions of dollars, rounded to nearest million)						
FY05	1,625	1,017	549	613	95	3,899
FY06	1,718	1,437	574	550	122	4,402
FY07	1,840	1,349	515	664	161	4,529
FY08	1,928	1,293	521	627	131	4,500
% of total Coast Guard budget						
FY05	21.0	13.2	7.1	7.9	1.2	50.4
FY06	19.8	16.6	6.6	6.3	1.4	50.7
FY07	21.3	15.6	6.0	7.7	1.9	52.5
FY08	22.1	14.8	6.0	7.2	1.5	51.6

Source: Prepared by CRS using data from U.S. Department of Homeland Security, *U.S. Coast Guard [FY]2008 Budget in Brief and Performance Report,* Washington, 2007 (February 2007); Table 5 on p 19, and (for FY2005) the analogous document for the FY2007 budget. Figures may not add due to rounding.

[a] Ports, waterways, and coastal security.

[b] The Coast Guard excludes drug interdiction and other law enforcement from its definition of its homeland security missions.

Issues for Congress

Potential issues for Congress concerning the Coast Guard's homeland security operations include, among others, the following:

- the sufficiency of Coast Guard funding, assets, and personnel levels for performing both homeland and non-homeland security missions;
- the division of the Coast Guard's budget between homeland security and non-homeland security missions;
- whether the Coast Guard is achieving sufficient interoperability and coordination with other DHS, federal, state, and local authorities involved in the maritime aspects of homeland security, including coordination of operations and coordination and sharing of intelligence;
- monitoring compliance with the facility and vessel security plans that the Coast Guard has reviewed and approved;
- how the Coast guard assesses security risks to various ports and prioritizes these risks for allocating port-security funding;
- completing foreign port security assessments;
- implementing a long-range vessel-tracking system required by MTSA;
- implementing Automatic Identification System (AIS);
- inland waterway security; and
- response plans for maritime security incidents.

Performance of Homeland non-Homeland Security Missions. A December 2006 report from the DHS Inspector General on major DHS management challenges stated:

> To implement the Maritime Transportation Security Act of 2002 in a timely and effective manner, USCG must balance the resources devoted to the performance of homeland and non-homeland security missions; improve the performance of its homeland security missions; maintain and re-capitalize USCG's Deepwater fleet of aircraft, cutters, and small boats; restore the readiness of small boat stations to perform their search and rescue missions; and increase the number and quality of resource hours devoted to non-homeland security missions. For example, while overall resource hours devoted to USCG's homeland security missions grew steadily from FY 2001 through FY 2005, USCG continues to experience difficulty meeting its performance goals for homeland security missions.[5]

A July 2006 report from the DHS Inspector General on Coast Guard mission performance in FY2005 stated:

> Since FY 2001, more [Coast Guard] resource hours have been dedicated to homeland security missions than for non-homeland security missions. However, after an initial drop in FY 2002, non-homeland security resource hours have increased every period, and have now returned to within 3% of

> baseline levels . . . The Coast Guard has been more successful in meeting goals for its traditional non-homeland security missions, meeting 22 of 28 goals (79%) where measurable goals and results existed, but still leaving room for improved performance. Not including the Ports, Waterways, and Coastal Security mission, by far the largest user of resource hours of any Coast Guard mission, the Coast Guard achieved only 26% of its homeland security goals (5 of 19) . . . Growth in total resource hours has leveled off Since resource hours are based on the limited and finite number of available assets, the Coast Guard will be unable to increase total resource hours without the acquisition of additional aircraft, cutters, and boats Consequently, the Coast Guard has a limited ability to respond to an extended crisis, and therefore must divert resources normally dedicated to other missions To improve performance within their overall constraints, the Coast Guard must ensure that a comprehensive and fully defined performance management system is implemented, and that experienced and trained personnel are available to satisfy increased workload demands.[6]

In March 2005, the Government Accountability Office (GAO) testified that:

> The Maritime Transportation Security Act of 2002 charged the Coast Guard with many maritime homeland security responsibilities, such as assessing port vulnerabilities and ensuring that vessels and port facilities have adequate security plans, and the Coast Guard has worked hard to meet these requirements GAO's reviews of these efforts have disclosed some areas for attention as well, such as developing ways to ensure that security plans are carried out with vigilance The Coast Guard has taken steps to deal with some of these areas, but opportunities for improvement remain.[7]

Prototype Port Security System and AIS. A December 30, 2007, press article on a prototype port security system in Miami called Project Hawkeye and the AIS states in part:

> A Coast Guard plan to combat terrorism by creating the maritime equivalent of an air traffic control system in the coastal waters here, a test for a nationwide effort, has fallen far short of expectations.
>
> The Coast Guard installed long-range surveillance cameras, coastal radar and devices that automatically identify approaching vessels to help search out possible threats.
>
> But the radar, it turns out, confuses waves with boats The cameras cover just a sliver of the harbor and coasts. And only a small fraction of vessels can be identified automatically.
>
> Officials acknowledge the limited progress that the Department of Homeland Security and the Coast Guard have made toward creating a viable defense here in Miami or at harbors nationwide against a maritime attack, despite the billions of dollars invested since 2001. . . .

> Miami was selected to serve as a laboratory for the Maritime Domain Awareness project. . . .
>
> The surveillance effort in Miami, known as Project Hawkeye, was intended to search out vessels that might present a threat, allowing the Coast Guard to try to foil an impending attack.
>
> Using radar, the Coast Guard would track boats larger than 25 feet within 12 miles of shore Smaller vessels—as little as a Jet Ski—would be tracked with infrared cameras up to five miles offshore. The surveillance would cover an area from Fort Lauderdale to the Florida Keys.
>
> To identify which vessels among the thousands might pose a danger, the Coast Guard would rely on sophisticated software that would assemble and analyze all this data. Under the plan, Coast Guard officials would be alerted when boats entered restricted waters, loitered in a vulnerable spot or displayed an unusual course or speed.
>
> The cameras have at times proved helpful, allowing the Coast Guard to investigate how a ship went aground or to monitor security contractors at the cruise ship terminal, to make sure they are doing their job, said Capt. Liam Slein, deputy commander of the Miami sector.
>
> But the cameras, it turns out, are not powerful enough or installed widely enough to track small boats approaching the many inlets in the Miami area. The radar system is so unreliable—mistaking waves for boats, splitting large ships in two or becoming confused by rain—Coast Guard staff personnel have been told not to waste much time looking at it.
>
> And technology the Coast Guard has required for large ships and wants installed on commercial fishing vessels, devices that automatically identify an approaching ship's name, location and course, has also provoked concerns.
>
> The Automated Identification System, as it is known, was first developed as a collision avoidance measure, not a security system, and was not made tamperproof. A captain or crew wanting to hide or disguise their location could simply turn the system off, or enter data that transmitted false information about the vessel's whereabouts and identity. . . .
>
> Most critically, the software system intended to make sense of all the collected data has not yet been installed in Miami. That means that very little of what the cameras are filming or the radar is tracking is ever used or even watched. The data is of such limited value that at least for now, the Coast Guard has assigned only volunteers to deal with it. . . .
>
> A surveillance system similar to the one in Miami is supposed to be installed at as many as 35 ports. But given the challenges here, and the unwillingness of Congress to finance the still-unproven effort, the Coast Guard has delayed expanding the effort to other ports until at least 2014.[8]

Vessel Tracking System A March 31, 2007, press article about a private-sector vessel tracking system called the Automated Vessel Tracking System states in part:

> The Automated Secure Vessel Tracking System has proven itself to businesses around the world It gave real-time information to oil companies as

Hurricane Katrina raged in 2005, helping them follow oil platforms that had been torn from their moorings It has tracked ships in distress far out to sea.

But the system is getting more attention these days because of who isn't using it: the Coast Guard Juneau is one of the few Coast Guard district headquarters that subscribes to the system.

Congress ordered the Coast Guard to begin testing by Sunday a system that would track all ships approaching U.S. ports The Coast Guard says a system will be in place, but critics are concerned that it will prove to be insufficient.

The Coast Guard and Maritime Transportation Act of 2006 says the Coast Guard, part of the Department of Homeland Security, must begin a three-year pilot program of a system capable of tracking 2,000 ships at once "to aid maritime security and response to maritime emergencies." . . .

Some lawmakers are trying to convince the Coast Guard that the answer already exists in the maritime industry's vessel tracking system. . . .

The Coast Guard has been relying primarily on a radio-based tracking system Its new system is expected to use satellite technology, but not immediately and then only on a limited basis, Schumer said.

The system being pushed by [Senator] Schumer, [Representative] Sanchez and other members of Congress, however, has been used to monitor ship movement for the last five years by a coalition of nonprofit maritime organizations.

The system relies on emergency beacons that already are fixtures on most commercial vessels A software program "pings" the ship via satellite and retrieves data such as the name of the vessel, its owner, its latitude and longitude, its speed and its course It can also track a ship's route across the ocean, allowing observers to know whether the ship stopped and met another vessel at sea or diverted to a port that wasn't on its usual route. . . .

The tracking system was created in 1999 by a small family-run company called Yukon Fuel Co in Anchorage to keep tabs on its tugs and barges as they supplied fuel and freight to isolated Alaskan villages, fishing camps and mining sites. The software proved so popular that the family sold Yukon and formed Secure Asset Reporting Services Inc to market the system, said Clayton Shelver, the company's chief executive. . . .

The Coast Guard isn't the only player that still needs convincing. Most major shipping companies haven't signed on either. So far, only Taiwan-based Evergreen Marine Corp has agreed to test it.[9]

Endnotes

[1] Section 888(a)(1) defines the Coast Guard's non-homeland security missions as (1) marine safety, (2) search and rescue, (3) aids to navigation, (4) living marine resources (fisheries law enforcement), (5) marine environmental protection, and (6) ice operations.

[2] See, for example, U.S. Department of Homeland Security, *U.S. Coast Guard [FY]2008 Budget in Brief and Performance Report,* Washington, 2007 (February 2007) Table 5 on p. 19.

[3] For more on port security, see CRS Report RL33383, *Terminal Operators and Their Role in U.S. Port and Maritime Security*, by John Frittelli and Jennifer E. Lake; CRS Report RL33787, *Maritime Security: Potential Terrorist Attacks and Protection Priorities*, by Paul W. Parfomak and John Frittelli, and CRS Report RL31733, *Port and Maritime Security: Background and Issues for Congress*, by John F. Frittelli.

[4] U.S. Department of Homeland Security, U.S. Coast Guard [FY]2008 Budget in Brief and Performance Report Washington, 2007 (February 2007); Table 5 on p. 19 Subsequent pages discuss FY2006 performance of each of these missions in greater detail.

[5] U.S. Department of Homeland Security, Office of Inspector General, *Major Management Challenges Facing the Department of Homeland Security (Excerpts from the FY 2006 DHS Performance and Accountability Report)*, December 2006 (OIG-07-12) p. 21.

[6] U.S. Department of Homeland Security, Office of Inspector General, *Annual Review of Mission Performance, Untied States Coast Guard (FY 2005)*, July 2006 (OIG-06-50) p. 1.

[7] Government Accountability Office, *COAST GUARD[:] Observations on Agency Priorities in Fiscal Year 2006 Budget Request*, GAO-05-364T, Mar 17, 2005.

[8] Eric Lipton, "Security Effort by Coast Guard Is Falling Short," *New York Times*, Dec 30, 2006.

THREATS AND PREPAREDNESS

DOCUMENT NO. 6

TRANSPORTATION SECURITY: DHS EFFORTS TO ELIMINATE REDUNDANT BACKGROUND CHECK INVESTIGATIONS

GAO Report
(GAO-07-756)

April 26, 2007

Highlights

Why GAO Did This Study

Since 9/11, the federal government has taken steps to ensure that transportation workers are screened to ensure that they do not pose a security risk. However, the number of DHS background check programs has raised concerns that such workers may be subject to redundant background check programs. The Security and Accountability for Every Port Act of 2006 required GAO to conduct a study of those DHS background check programs similar to the one required of truck drivers to obtain a hazardous material endorsement (HME). For this study, GAO examined DHS background check programs to identify (1) potential redundancies and inconsistencies, if any, connected with these programs, and (2) actions, if any, DHS is taking or planning to coordinate its background check programs. To address these objectives, GAO examined selected background check programs, interviewed DHS officials and private stakeholders, and reviewed relevant documents.

What GAO Recommends

GAO recommends that DHS ensure that its coordination plan (1) includes implementation steps, time frames, and budget requirements, (2) discusses potential costs/benefits of program standardization, and (3) explore options for coordinating and aligning background checks within DHS and other federal agencies DHS generally agreed with GAO's findings and recommendations.

What GAO Found

The six programs GAO reviewed—HME, Transportation Worker Identification Credential, Merchant Mariner Document, Free and Secure Trade, Secure Identification Display Areas, and Air Cargo—are conducted independently of one another and collect similar information and use similar background check processes. Also, each program operates separate enrollment facilities to collect background information and does not share it with the other programs. In some cases, GAO found variations in the fees applicants are charged, as well as differences in disqualifying offenses and renewal requirements between the programs. Redundant background checks will affect program costs to workers and the government, for example through inefficient use of existing facilities. However, DHS does not keep track of the number of those workers who, needing multiple credentials, are subjected to multiple background check programs. Thus, DHS is not able to determine either potential costs associated with redundant checks or potential benefits to be derived from eliminating redundant checks by aligning the background check requirements to make the programs more consistent.

Several DHS components are in the initial stages of initiatives to consolidate, coordinate, and align background check programs, thereby potentially reducing redundancies among these programs. For example, in January 2007, TSA determined that the background checks required for an HME, Free and Secure Trade card, and Merchant Mariner Document issued during certain periods satisfy the background check requirement for a Transportation Worker Identification Credential. In addition, the Screening Coordination Office (SCO) was established in July 2006, in part, to coordinate DHS screening programs. In December 2006, SCO issued a report identifying common problems, challenges, and needed improvements in the credentialing programs and processes across the department. The SCO awarded a contract in April 2007 that will provide the methodology and support for developing an implementation plan to include common design and comparability standards and related milestones to coordinate DHS screening and credentialing programs. At the time of GAO's review, DHS did not have a plan with budget requirements or implementation steps, and related milestones for consolidating, coordinating, and aligning its screening programs. Prior GAO work has shown that it is essential to establish long-term action-oriented implementation goals and a time frame with milestone dates to track an organization's progress toward its goals and that uncoordinated program efforts can exceed budget requirements. Further, other federal agencies have background check programs as well. A governmentwide examination of such programs is beyond the scope of GAO's mandate; however, redundancies and inefficiencies may exist in the background check programs that GAO did not examine Because DHS is responsible for a large number of background check programs, the department might be best positioned to explore—with other federal agencies—possible options to coordinate and align background check programs governmentwide.

Abbreviations

ATSA	Aviation and Transportation Security Act
CBP	Customs and Border Protection
CDL	Commercial driver's license
DHS	Department of Homeland Security
DOT	Department of Transportation
FAA	Federal Aviation Administration
FAST	Free and Secure Trade
FBI	Federal Bureau of Investigation
HME	Hazardous Materials Endorsement
HSPD	Homeland Security Presidential Directive
MMC	Merchant Mariner Credential
MMD	Merchant Mariner Document
MML	Merchant Mariner License
MTSA	Maritime Transportation Security Act
SAFETEA-LU	Safe, Accountable, Flexible, Efficient Transportation Act: A Legacy for Users
SCO	Screening Coordination Office
SIDA	Security Identification Display Areas
STCW	International Convention on Standards of Training, Certification and Watchkeeping for Seafarers
TSA	Transportation Security Administration
TWIC	Transportation Worker Identification Credential

Congressional Committees

Since the terrorist attacks on September 11, 2001, the federal government has taken steps to ensure that transportation workers, particularly those that transport hazardous materials or have access to secure areas, are properly screened to ensure they do not pose a security risk. For example, the USA PATRIOT Act in October 2001 prohibited states from issuing hazardous material endorsements (HME) for a commercial driver's license (CDL) without a federally conducted, fingerprint-based applicant background check. In November 2002, the Maritime Transportation Security Act required the Department of Homeland Security (DHS) to conduct background checks on and issue credentials to merchant mariners and certain workers at seaports. The DHS background check programs prompted by these and other legal requirements have raised questions as to whether transportation workers may be subject to multiple background check programs with different standards and credentialing systems.

The Security and Accountability for Every Port Act of 2006 (SAFE Port Act)[1] required GAO to conduct a study of the DHS background check programs that are similar to those required of truck drivers to obtain an HME. The act required us to (1) identify any redundancies and inefficiencies in connection with such programs, and (2) recommend ways of eliminating any redundancies and inefficiencies To fulfill this requirement, we examined—in consultation with committee staff—DHS background record check programs with requirements that are similar to the HME-related background check to identify:

- potential redundancies and inconsistencies, if any, in connection with these background check programs, and
- actions, if any, DHS is taking or planning to coordinate its background check programs.

DHS components are in the preliminary stages of implementing several initiatives, that may consolidate, coordinate, and harmonize[2] such background check programs. Because it is too early to determine the effectiveness of these initiatives, we did not make specific recommendations to eliminate any redundancies and inefficiencies specific to the DHS background check programs examined.

To identify programs with background check requirements similar to those for the HME program, we examined the various programs' background check requirements and held discussions with Transportation Security Administration (TSA), Coast Guard, Customs and Border Protection (CBP), and DHS Screening Coordination Office (SCO) officials. On the basis of this information and as agreed with committee offices, we compared the HME program to the following five DHS programs:

- Transportation Worker Identification Credential (TWIC) for credentialed merchant mariners and personnel requiring unescorted access to secure areas at maritime facilities and vessels;
- Coast Guard's Merchant Mariner Document (MMD) for mariners on merchant vessels, which serves as a qualification and identity document;
- Customs and Border Protection's Free and Secure Trade (FAST), a voluntary program for commercial drivers to receive expedited border processing;
- Security Identification Display Areas (SIDA) badges for aviation workers who have unescorted access to an airport's secure areas; and
- Air Cargo security threat assessment for certain individuals with unescorted access to air cargo.

To identify any redundancies and inconsistencies, we examined the background check requirements and interviewed DHS and private stakeholders representing trucking, rail, and aviation transportation workers to help identify any gaps or overlaps in their coverage. We also spoke with the Federal Bureau of Investigation (FBI) and the Department of Transportation (DOT) concerning their roles in the background check programs. Further, we reviewed relevant laws—such as the USA PATRIOT Act, the Aviation and Transportation Security Act, and the Maritime Transportation Security Act—and agency actions, such as the TSA and Coast Guard rulemakings. We discussed with TSA's Transportation Threat Assessment and Credentialing Office the data collection methods and process that transportation workers may undergo We did not (1) evaluate the effectiveness of the background check programs and (2) include other potential DHS programs or any other federal agencies that also have background check programs.

To identify how redundancies and inefficiencies might be eliminated, we identified actions that DHS has taken or is planning to take to coordinate its background check programs by reviewing reports completed by the TSA, SCO, and Coast Guard, as well as relevant TSA regulations. We used prior GAO work on performance management to evaluate DHS efforts to minimize redundancies and inefficiencies in its background check programs.

In April 2007, we briefed your offices on the results of our work. This report conveys the information provided during those discussions in appendix I.

We performed our work from November 2006 through April 2007 in accordance with generally accepted government auditing standards.

DHS Actions to Reduce Redundancies in Background Check Programs

The six programs we reviewed for this report are conducted independently; that is, they collect similar information and use similar background check processes. Also, each program operates separate enrollment facilities to collect information and does not share background information with the other programs. In some instances, we found variations in the fees applicants are charged as well as differences in disqualifying offenses and renewal requirements between the programs DHS does not keep track of the number of those workers who, needing multiple credentials, are subjected to multiple background check programs. As a result, DHS is not in a position to determine the costs/benefits associated with reducing the number of redundant background checks.

At the time of our review, DHS did not have a plan that included the development of a common set of design and comparability standards, implementation steps, budget requirements, or related milestones for consolidating, coordinating, and aligning DHS screening programs. As our prior work has shown,[3] linking costs with performance data and budgetary deliberations prompts agencies to reassess their performance goals and strategies. In July 2006, DHS created SCO to coordinate DHS background check programs. The SCO was established, in part, to coordinate DHS screening programs, but the SCO is in the early stages of developing its plans to coordinate DHS's screening programs. In December 2006, SCO issued a report identifying common problems, challenges, and needed improvements in the credentialing programs and processes across the department. The office awarded a contract in April 2007 that will provide the methodology and support for developing an implementation plan to include common design and comparability standards and related milestones to coordinate DHS screening and credentialing programs. Prior GAO work has shown that long-term action-oriented goals and a timeline with milestones are necessary to track an organization's progress toward its goals.[4]

DHS components have also taken steps to reduce redundancies. For example, in January 2007, TSA determined that the background checks required for an HME, FAST card, and MMD (issued between Feb 3, 2003, and Mar 26, 2007) satisfy the background check requirement for a TWIC. Further, the TWIC and HME background check requirements were designed to closely resemble each other to reduce redundancy. Meanwhile, the Coast Guard plans to consolidate four credentials and require that pertinent information previously submitted by an applicant at a Coast Guard Regional Examination Center be submitted to TSA through the TWIC enrollment process and be shared with the Coast Guard by TSA. Other federal agencies such as the Departments of Defense and Energy also have background check programs. A governmentwide examination of such programs is beyond the scope of our mandate; however, the existence of redundancies and inefficiencies in the programs that we did examine may not be unique. Homeland Security Presidential Directive 11 (HSPD-11) on comprehensive terrorist-related screening procedures directs DHS to coordinate with other federal agencies to develop a strategy for developing coordinated terrorist screening procedures and capabilities.

Conclusions

Recent TSA and Coast Guard initiatives to harmonize background check programs are useful first steps. However, because workers are potentially subject to redundant information requests if they apply for more than one background check, duplication of efforts may continue until DHS further develops common standards for its background check programs.

The costs and benefits that can ultimately be derived by harmonizing background check programs will be determined in part by the number of individuals currently subject to multiple background check programs, as the costs of fees and inconvenience to workers and costs to government from inefficient use of facilities may be reduced by eliminating redundant checks. As our prior work has shown,[5] agencies can use performance information to make decisions that affect future strategies, planning and budgeting, identifying priorities, and allocating resources. Without knowing the potential costs/benefits associated with the number of redundant background checks that would be eliminated through harmonization, DHS lacks the performance information that would allow its program managers to compare their program results with goals and thus determine where to target program resources to improve performance.

Coordinating federal background check programs is a cross-cutting, governmentwide issue. Other federal agencies also have background check programs. Although these programs are outside the scope of this study, the existence of multiple programs highlights the importance of interagency coordination to ensure the most efficient use of resources. As a result of its current and planned initiatives, DHS should be in a position to support the needed coordination, in accordance with HSPD-11.

Recommendations for Executive Action

To help prevent redundancies and inefficiencies, we recommend that the Secretary of Homeland Security take the following three actions:

- Ensure that the plan being developed by DHS for coordinating its background check programs include, at a minimum, the steps the agency will take to align its screening and credentialing activities and include specific time frames and budget requirements for implementation. In addition, the plan should describe how and when DHS will establish and apply a common set of design and comparability standards for DHS's background check programs.
- Ensure that the plan being developed by DHS for coordinating its background check programs include, at a minimum, a discussion of the potential costs/benefits associated with the number of redundant background checks that would be eliminated through harmonization.
- Because of DHS's responsibility for a large number of background check programs, explore with other federal agencies options for harmonizing background check programs within DHS and other federal agencies.

Agency Comments and Our Evaluation

We provided a draft of this report to DHS, FBI, and DOT for review and comment. On April 20, 2007, we received technical comments on the draft report, which we incorporated where appropriate DHS, FBI, and DOT generally agreed with our findings and recommendations DHS component agencies provided technical comments on our draft report, which we have incorporated where appropriate.

We are sending copies to DHS, FBI, and DOT and other interested congressional committees We will also make copies available to others upon request In addition, the report will be available at no charge on GAO's Web site at http://www.gao.gov.

If you or your staff has any further questions about this report, please contact me at (202)-512-2757 or goldenkoffr@gao.gov. Contact points for our Offices of Congressional Relations and Public Affairs may be found on the last page of this report. Key contributors to this report are listed in appendix III.

Robert N. Goldenkoff
Acting Director, Homeland Security and Justice Issues

List of Committees

The Honorable Robert C. Byrd
Chairman
The Honorable Thad Cochran
Ranking Minority Member
Committee on Appropriations
United States Senate

The Honorable Frank R. Lautenberg
Chairman
The Honorable Gordon H. Smith
Ranking Minority Member
Subcommittee on Surface Transportation and Merchant Marine, Infrastructure, Safety and Security
Committee on Commerce, Science and Transportation
United States Senate

The Honorable Joseph I. Lieberman,
Chairman
The Honorable Susan M. Collins
Ranking Minority Member
Committee on Homeland Security and Governmental Affairs
United States Senate

The Honorable David R. Obey
Chairman
The Honorable Jerry Lewis
Ranking Minority Member
Committee on Appropriations
House of Representatives

The Honorable Bennie G. Thompson
Chairman
The Honorable Peter T. King
Ranking Minority Member
Committee on Homeland Security
House of Representatives

The Honorable Elijah E. Cummings
Chairman
The Honorable Steven C. LaTourette
Ranking Minority Member
Subcommittee on Coast Guard and Maritime Transportation
Committee on Transportation and Infrastructure
House of Representatives

The Honorable Charles B. Rangel
Chairman
The Honorable Jim McCrery
Ranking Minority Member
Committee on Ways and Means
House of Representatives

Endnotes

[1] Pub L No 109-347, § 105 (2006).

[2] The term harmonize is used to describe efforts to increase efficiency and reduce redundancies by aligning the background check requirements to make the programs more consistent.

[3] GAO, *Managing for Results: Enhancing Agency Use of Performance Information for Management Decision Making*, GAO-05-927 (Washington, D.C.: September 2005).

[4] GAO, *Highlights of a GAO Forum: Mergers and Transformation: Lessons Learned For a Department of Homeland Security and Other Federal Agencies*, GAO-03-293SP (Washington, D.C.: November 2002).

[5] GAO, *Managing for Results: Enhancing Agency Use of Performance Information for Management Decision Making*, GAO-05-927 (Washington, D.C.: September 2005).

Appendix I:
Briefing for Interested Committees and Subcommittees

Transportation Security:
DHS Efforts to Eliminate Redundant
Background Check Investigations

Briefing Prepared for Staff of:

- Subcommittee on Surface Transportation and Merchant Marine, Infrastructure, Safety and Security, Committee on Commerce, Science, and Transportation, U.S. Senate
- Committee on Homeland Security and Governmental Affairs, U.S. Senate
- Subcommittee on Coast Guard and Maritime Transportation, Committee on Transportation and Infrastructure, U.S. House of Representatives
- Committee on Homeland Security, U.S. House of Representatives

Overview

- Objectives, Scope, and Methodology
- Summary
- Background
- DHS Background Check Programs
- Efforts to Streamline Background Check Programs
- Conclusions
- Recommendations
- Appendixes

Objectives Scope, and Methodology

Objectives

- This study responds to a mandate in the Security and Accountability for Every Port Act of 2006 (SAFE Port Act), Pub L No 109-347, Section 105, which requires GAO to examine DHS background check programs that are similar to those that require truck drivers to obtain a hazardous materials endorsement (HME) for their commercial driver's licenses (CDL) The Act required us to:
  - identify any redundancies and inefficiencies in connection with such programs, and
  - recommend ways of eliminating any redundancies and inefficiencies.
- In conducting our study and in consultation with committee staff, we examined DHS background record check programs with requirements that are similar to the HME related background check to identify:

- potential redundancies and inconsistencies, if any, in connection with these background check programs, and
- actions, if any, DHS is taking or planning to coordinate its background check programs.

DHS components are in the initial stages of a number of initiatives intended to consolidate, coordinate, and harmonize* such background check programs. Because it is too early to determine the effectiveness of these initiatives, we are not making specific recommendations to eliminate redundancies and inefficiencies in the DHS background check programs examined.

* The term "harmonize" is used to describe efforts to increase efficiency and reduce redundancies by aligning the background check requirements to make the programs more consistent.

Scope and Methodology

In order to identify programs with background check requirements similar to those for the HME program, we examined various programs' background check requirements and held discussions with Transportation Security Administration (TSA), Coast Guard, Customs and Border Protection (CBP), and Screening and Coordination Office (SCO) officials. We also consulted with committee staff, who confirmed that their primary interest was in the HME, Transportation Worker Identification Credential (TWIC), and merchant mariner document programs, and agreed to examine, in addition to the HME program, the following five programs:

- **Transportation Worker Identification Credential (TWIC)**—a tamper-resistant biometric credential for credentialed merchant mariners and personnel requiring unescorted access to secure areas at maritime facilities and vessels.
- **Merchant Mariner Document (MMD)**—required for mariners who serve on merchant vessels of at least 100 gross tons and serves as a qualification and identity document, specifying each rating for which the holder is qualified.
- **Free and Secure Trade (FAST)**—a voluntary program for commercial drivers as part of a border accord Initiative between the United States, Mexico, and Canada to allow known low-risk participants to receive expedited border processing.
- **Security Identification Display Areas (SIDA)**—a security threat assessment for aviation workers who hold airport badges and have unescorted access to airport secure areas.
- **Air Cargo** requires a security threat assessment for individuals with unescorted access to air cargo who are employees or agents of certain aircraft operators, foreign air carriers, or indirect air carriers

In conducting our study, we:

- Reviewed relevant laws, strategies, directives, plans, and agency guidance to determine the objective and scope of the programs and DHS plans to implement the programs.
- Interviewed DHS officials responsible for managing the programs to determine how the programs are implemented and who is subject to the programs' requirements.
- Reviewed which industries were subject to the programs, type of information collected, fees, and the data bases used.
- Used prior GAO work on performance management as criteria to evaluate DHS coordination and planning efforts to minimize redundancies and inefficiencies in its background check programs.
- In accordance with the SAFE Port Act, the scope of the study was limited to DHS background check programs for transportation workers with special privileges or unescorted access to controlled locations (such as secure areas at ports and airports) and did not include other potential DHS programs or any other federal agencies that also have background check programs, such as agencies within the Department of Defense, U.S. Postal Service, or the Department of Energy.
- The study did not evaluate the effectiveness of the background check programs.
- We conducted our work between November 2006 and April 2007 in accordance with generally accepted government auditing standards.

Summary

- The six programs we examined collect similar information and use similar background check processes.
- Each background check program operates separate enrollment facilities for collecting biometric and biographic information.
- In some instances, we found variations among the DHS background programs we reviewed.
- DHS does not keep track by individual background check program of the number of workers who are subjected to multiple background check programs for each of DHS's background check programs.
- In July 2006, DHS announced the creation of the Screening Coordination Office (SCO) within the Office of the Secretary to coordinate DHS programs.
- In December 2006, SCO issued a report identifying common problems, challenges, and areas where DHS can improve credentialing programs and processes Department wide.

- The SCO is developing a plan for coordinating background check programs and common design and comparability standards for these programs.
- In January 2007, the Transportation Security Administration (TSA) announced standards to determine if a background check conducted by another government agency or by TSA is comparable to two of its background check programs, TWIC or HME, the application of which could help minimize duplication and inefficiencies.
- TSA's HME and TWIC background check requirements were designed to closely resemble each other to reduce redundancy.
- The Coast Guard plans to consolidate four credentials including the Merchant Mariner Document and require pertinent information previously submitted by an applicant at a Coast Guard Regional Exam Center be submitted to TSA through the TWIC enrollment process and be shared with the Coast Guard by TSA.

Background

Background Check Programs Exist in Multiple Federal Agencies

Coordinating federal background check programs is a cross-cutting, government wide issue. Other federal agencies also have background check programs, such as agencies within the Departments of Defense and Energy. Although these programs are outside the scope of this study, the existence of multiple programs highlights the importance of interagency coordination to ensure the most efficient use of resources.

Various Laws, Directives, and Studies Have Called for Increased Coordination

As GAO has reported in the past, uncoordinated program efforts can waste scarce funds, confuse and frustrate program customers, and limit the overall effectiveness of the federal effort.

In July 2004, the **9/11 Commission** reported that having too many different biometric standards, travel facilitation systems, credentialing systems, and screening requirements:

- Hampers the development of information crucial for stopping terrorists from entering the country,
- Is expensive, and
- Is inefficient.

The **9/11 Commission** further reported that:

- A coordinating body should raise standards, facilitate information-sharing, and survey systems for potential problems,

- The President should direct DHS to lead the effort to design a comprehensive screening system, addressing common problems and setting common standards with system-wide goals in mind, and
- Only presidential leadership can develop government wide concepts and standards.

Homeland Security Presidential Directive 11 (HSPD-11) (August 2004), announced a new U.S. policy to "implement a coordinated and comprehensive approach to terrorist-related screening—in immigration, law enforcement, intelligence, counterintelligence, and protection of the border, transportation systems, and critical infrastructure—that supports homeland security, at home and abroad."

In November 2005, as required by the Safe, Accountable, Flexible, Efficient Transportation Equity Act: A Legacy for Users (SAFETEA-LU) (Pub L No 109-59, August 2005), TSA issued a report on the implementation of fingerprint-based background checks TSA acknowledged the potential for duplication in assessments among individuals who fall within the populations of multiple TSA programs and the related need to develop policies and/or regulations on comparability The report stated that:

- TSA intended to establish a baseline "standard" of comparison for determining comparability.
- TSA could develop either a single or graduated standard of comparability that other federal agencies would be required to meet.
- When comparing TSA vetting and credentialing programs, similar requirements could be grouped together to develop thresholds of comparability under which multiple TSA programs would fall.

How the Hazardous Materials Endorsement Program Is Conducted

Hazardous Materials Endorsement (HME)—authorizes an individual to transport hazardous materials (Hazmat) for commerce HME must be indicated on an individual's CDL.

TSA determines that an individual poses a security threat if he or she:

- Is not a U.S. citizen, lawful permanent resident, refugee, alien granted asylum, or alien with a specified status or work authorization.
- Is wanted or under indictment for certain felonies.
- Has been convicted, or found not guilty by reason of insanity, of certain permanent disqualifying felonies.
- Has been convicted, or found not guilty by reason of insanity, of certain interim disqualifying crimes within the preceding seven years, or released from incarceration within the preceding five years after being convicted of an interim disqualifying crime.

- Has been adjudicated as lacking mental capacity or has been involuntarily committed to a mental institution.
- Is considered to pose a security threat based on review of pertinent intelligence, criminal, and immigration databases.

Overview of HME Background Check Process

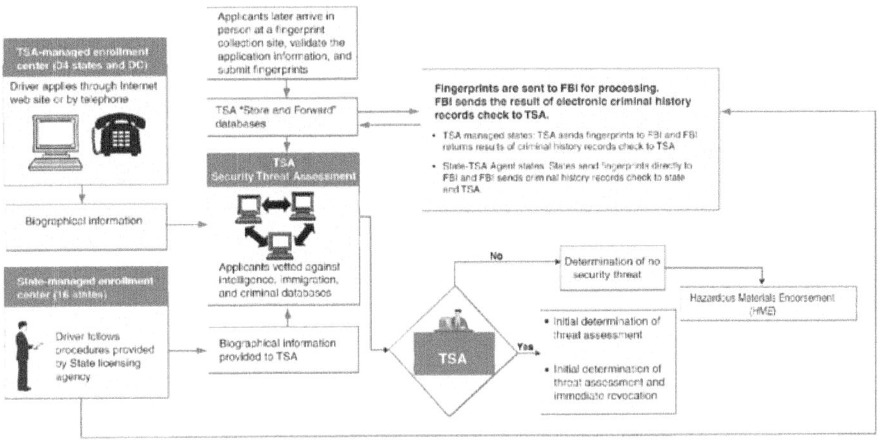

Source: GAO analysis of TSA provided information

Objective 1—Background Check Program Comparison: Frequency and Content

Program	Enrollment frequency	What's checked (A) criminal offenses, (B) immigration status, (C) mental capacity, (D) nexus to terrorism, (E) drug use	How checked (1) fingerprint-based criminal history check, (2) name-based biographic check*, (3) drug test, (4) national driver registry, (5) interview
HME	**5 years**	**A, B, C, D**	**1, 2**
TWIC	5 years	A, B, C, D	1, 2
MMD	5 years	A, B, C, D, E	1, 2, 3, 4
FAST	5 years	A, B, D	1, 2, 5
SIDA	Once, if continuously employed	A, B, D	1, 2
Air Cargo	Once, if continuously employed	B, D	2

*TSA checks a list of all individuals who have completed a TSA background check against databases that are updated regularly.

Source: GAO based on review of DHS provided program information

Profile of Each Program

Program	Agency	Sector	Number of Enrollment Centers	Number of Workers	Cost to Applicant
HME	**TSA**	**Trucking** (Hazmat)	**189 TSA managed** (fingerprint and application) **366 State managed** (fingerprint) **887 State managed** (application)	**2.7 million**	**$94** (TSA managed) **$58 - $138** (State managed)*
TWIC	TSA	All, except aviation	130+	750,000	$105.25 – $137.25
MMD	Coast Guard	Maritime	17	210,000	$45 – $140*****
FAST	CBP	Trucking	17	78,862	$50
SIDA	TSA	Aviation, trucking****	Not applicable**	2 million	$29***
Air Cargo	TSA	Aviation, trucking	Not applicable**	51,625	$28

*16 states manage the collection of HME background information.

** Enrollment is conducted by airport, aircraft operator, or air carrier.

***Airport and aircraft operators may charge additional fees.

****The number of truck drivers that apply for a SIDA is limited and does not occur often, according to TSA.

*****The Coast Guard does not charge a fee for the background check MMD cost to applicant includes evaluation of medical fitness and professional qualifications.

Source: GAO analysis of DHS provided information

Programs Determined Comparable by TSA

Program	Other Background Check Programs That Meet Program Requirements
HME	**TWIC, FAST**
TWIC	HME, FAST, or MMD or Merchant Mariner License (issued during certain periods)
MMD	None
FAST	None
SIDA	None
Air Cargo	SIDA, HME, TWIC, FAST

In the future, TSA may determine other background checks may be substituted for the for TWIC and HME background checks in order to satisfy the TWIC and HME related background check requirements.

Source: GAO analysis based on review of DHS provided program information

Redundancy

For the six programs we reviewed, we found several instances in which DHS component agencies:

- Use the same or similar background check process already completed on an individual by another program.
- **Possible Effect**: Workers are potentially subject to redundant information requests if they apply for more than one background check, although TSA and the Coast Guard have taken actions to reduce the redundancies For example, TSA and the Coast Guard plan to share background check information for the TWIC and MMD programs.

Each background check program operates separate enrollment facilities for collecting biometric and biographic information.

Possible Effect: DHS may incur additional start-up and development costs.

Possible Effect: Workers may have to enroll at a facility with less convenient location and hours than a comparable one in a different program.

Redundancy Examples

Program	Redundancy
HME	**An individual who has submitted fingerprints for the HME program and is later subject to another background check program with a criminal history records check would have to submit an additional set of fingerprints, pursuant to Public Law 105-251.**
TWIC	If an HME, MMD, or FAST cardholder applies for a TWIC background check, he or she will pay a reduced fee. To date, TSA has not worked out a process to reduce fees for an HME applicant who has completed a TWIC background check. FAST is managed by CBP and is not a TSA program; as a result, TSA cannot reduce those fees. Therefore, an individual may be subject to multiple background check fees. Individuals who satisfied an HME background check must still provide a biometric (fingerprint) if applying for a TWIC credential.
MMD	An individual that has already undergone a background check in connection with another program has to undergo a separate background check for an MMD.
FAST	A driver that has already undergone a background check in connection with another program has to undergo a separate background check for FAST.
SIDA	SIDA holders may be required to undergo another background check if they go to a different airport. An individual applying for a SIDA who already underwent an HME, TWIC, MMD, or FAST background check will need to provide fingerprints and similar biographical information for the SIDA background check.
Air Cargo	An individual subject to an Air Cargo background check who has already undergone an MMD background check will need to provide similar biographical information for the Air Cargo background check.

Source: GAO analysis based on review of DHS provided program information

Variations

In some instances, we found variations among the DHS background programs we reviewed, including:

- Disparity in the fees transportation workers are charged for the programs*
- Varying use of comparability standards; TSA has comparability standards, but CBP and the Coast Guard do not
- Different collection methods

- Different disqualifying offenses**
- Different look- back periods**
- Different renewal requirements
- Different appeal processes**
- Different adjudicating authorities

*Variations in fee levels result from the agency paying for a portion of the background check (FAST and SIDA) or all of the related expenses (MMD), whereas for others, the agency covers the entire cost of the background check through fees (TWIC, HME, Air Cargo), according to DHS officials In addition, inconsistencies in fees also results from differences in services provided For example, TSA charges a fee to produce a credential in the TWIC program but does not provide applicants with a credential for the SIDA and air cargo security programs.

**DHS officials attributed some of the variations—differences in disqualifying offenses (SIDA) and look back periods (SIDA), and appeal processes (TWIC)—to statutory requirements.

Variation Examples

Program	Variation
HME	**Fees for non-TSA agent states vary from TSA agent states.**
TWIC	At the time of our review, TSA has not worked out a process to reduce fees for an HME applicant who has completed a TWIC related background check. Therefore, an individual may be subject to greater background check fees.
MMD	TSA determined that TWIC, MMD, FAST, and HME are comparable programs. However, the Coast Guard does not accept other background checks in lieu of an MMD background check.
FAST	The FAST background check has no fixed time limit for crimes involving violence, weapons, narcotics, or customs and immigration offenses. Other felonies have a 10 year limit. In comparison, HME and TWIC have a 7 year limit from a conviction and a 5 year limit from release from incarceration for considering interim disqualifying crimes, Coast Guard looks at varying assessment periods based on the offense for the MMD program, SIDA has a 10-year limit from conviction for considering disqualifying crimes, and Air Cargo does not include disqualifying crimes. The FAST program does not have a waiver/appeal process.
SIDA	Unlike the HME, TWIC, and MMD background check programs in which the component agency serves as the adjudicator, the airport operator or aircraft operator serves as the adjudicator for the Criminal History Records Check results for SIDA.
Air Cargo	Unlike the HME, TWIC, MMD, and FAST programs, that require applicants to submit biographical information every 5 years, the air cargo program only requires applicants to submit biographical information once, as long as they are continuously employed. In contrast to some other programs in which the agency collects biographical information, aircraft operators and air carriers collect biographical information for Air Cargo background checks.

Source: GAO analysis based on review of DHS-provided program information

Objective 2—DHS Actions Taken/Planned:

Screening Coordination Office (SCO)

- In response to HSPD 11, Secretary Chertoff established the **Screening Coordination Office (SCO)** at DHS on July 31, 2006 The SCO reports to the Deputy Secretary.
- SCO **goals** include:
  - Identifying opportunities to harmonize and enhance screening and credentialing processes across DHS "people screening" programs;
  - Developing metrics for evaluating and improving screening processes and credentialing; and

- Conducting a review of DHS credentialing programs from a business process perspective and establishing common capabilities.

- Among other duties, the SCO is responsible for coordinating background checks that are conducted on individuals to ensure that DHS's background check programs are not duplicative, according to SCO officials.

SCO Background Check Program Initiatives

In December 2006, SCO issued a report identifying common problems, challenges, and areas where DHS can improve credentialing programs and processes department wide. As part of the report, SCO:

- developed an inventory comparing and contrasting 28 traveler/transportation worker credentials and their supporting background checks.
- identified common business processes shared by 28 programs.
- The SCO awarded a contract in April 2007 to develop a methodology to coordinate credentialing programs and to serve as support for SCO's data collection and analysis efforts This will provide the basis for developing an implementation plan and related milestones for coordinating DHS screening and credentialing programs.
- Our prior work has shown that interim goals and measures can be used to show progress or contribution to intended results Long-term action oriented goals and a timeline with milestone dates are necessary to track the organization's progress towards its interim and long-term goals.
- In addition, an agency's planning efforts should consider and discuss efforts to coordinate its programs with other internal and external federal programs performing related activities and provide evidence of such coordination.
- The SCO is focusing on reducing unnecessary redundancies However, at this point they do not know the extent of unnecessary background checks With this information SCO would be in a position to understand the extent of redundancy, the number of workers that are affected and the related potential cost implications for both the federal government and transportation workers.

TSA Background Check Program Initiatives

- In January 2007, TSA determined that the background checks required for an HME, FAST card, and MMD (issued between Feb 3, 2003 and March 26, 2007) satisfy the background check requirement for a TWIC Thus, a TWIC applicant who has already undergone a background check in association with the HME, FAST, or MMD program does not have to undergo an additional background check and pays a reduced fee to obtain a TWIC.
- TSA's HME and TWIC background check requirements were designed to closely resemble each other to eliminate or minimize duplication.

- TSA also promulgated a list of factors that TSA will consider to determine whether other background checks satisfy the TWIC background check requirement. The factors are:
  - The minimum standards used for the background check,
  - The frequency of the background check,
  - The date of the most recent background check, and
  - Whether the background check includes biometric identification and a biometric credential.
- TSA determined that the background checks required for a SIDA ID, TWIC, HME, and FAST satisfy the background check requirement for the Air Cargo security program. Thus, an aircraft or air carrier employee or agent who is seeking unescorted access to air cargo and already has a SIDA ID, TWIC, HME, or FAST credential does not have to undergo the Air Cargo background check.
- TSA used the statutory look back periods and appeal/waiver requirements in MTSA for TWIC when developing the hazmat rule, so that when TSA issued the final TWIC rule, HME and TWIC could be harmonized.
- TSA began conducting "perpetual vetting" in 2006, reducing the effect of inconsistencies relating to renewal requirements. Perpetual vetting allows TSA to compare a list of all individuals who have completed a background check with databases that are updated regularly, so that TSA can identify individuals who have successfully completed the background check, but who later appear in a database indicating the individual might be a threat, according to TSA officials.

Coast Guard Background Check Program Initiatives

- In May 2006, the Coast Guard issued a notice of proposed rulemaking that would:
  - Consolidate four documents including the **Merchant Mariner Document (MMD)** into one—**Merchant Mariner Credential (MMC)**.
  - Require pertinent information previously submitted by an applicant at a Coast Guard Regional Exam Center be submitted by the applicant to TSA through the TWIC enrollment process and be shared with the Coast Guard by TSA.
  - Move all identity verification and security-vetting processes from the Coast Guard to TSA The Coast Guard would continue to conduct a safety review.
  - Result in the MMC process being completed by mail.
  - Potentially reduce mariner travel costs and time required to obtain a credential because the Coast Guard expects there to be more TWIC enrollment centers than Coast Guard's Regional Examination Centers.

Conclusions

- For the programs we reviewed, we found instances of redundancies in each of the programs' use of the same or similar background check process already completed on an individual by another program. In addition, the HME, TWIC, MMD, and FAST programs operate separate enrollment facilities for collecting biometric and biographic information.
- Redundancies may result in workers having to provide redundant information if they apply for more than one background check. In addition, DHS may incur additional start up and development costs because the HME, TWIC, MMD, and FAST programs operate their own facilities.
- DHS components have several initiatives underway to minimize the redundancies and inefficiencies of the background check programs for determining if an individual is a low risk to transportation security.
  - The SCO was established, in part, to coordinate DHS screening programs, but the SCO is in the early stages of developing its plans to coordinate DHS's screening programs. As our prior work has shown, federal programs contributing to the same or similar results should be closely coordinated to ensure that goals are consistent and, as appropriate, program efforts are mutually reinforcing. Uncoordinated program efforts can waste scarce funds, confuse and frustrate program customers, and limit the overall effectiveness of the federal effort.
  - Recent TSA and Coast Guard initiatives to harmonize background check programs are useful steps. However, duplication of efforts may continue until DHS develops further common standards for its background check programs. As our prior work has shown, interagency coordination is often hindered by incompatible procedures, processes, data, and computer systems.
  - In addition, as our prior work has shown, intermediate goals and measures, such as outputs or intermediate outcomes, can be used to show progress or contributions to intended results. For instance, when it may take years before an agency sees the results of its programs, intermediate goals and measures can provide information on interim results. It is essential to establish long- term action-oriented implementation goals and a timeline with milestone dates to track the organization's progress towards its intermediate and long-term transformation goals.
  - The number of redundant background checks will affect background check program costs. As we have previously reported, linking cost with performance information infuses performance concerns into planning and budgetary deliberations, prompting agencies to reassess their performance goals and strategies and to more clearly understand the cost of performance.

- Coordinating federal background check programs is a cross-cutting, government wide issue. Other federal agencies also have background check programs, such as agencies within the departments of Defense and Energy. Although these programs are outside the scope of this study, the existence of multiple programs highlights the importance of interagency coordination to ensure the most efficient use of resources. As the 9/11 Commission reported, having too many different biometric standards, travel facilitation systems, credentialing systems, and screening requirements is expensive and inefficient.

Recommendations

- To help prevent redundancies and inefficiencies, we recommend that the Secretary of Homeland Security take the following three actions:
  - Ensure that the plan being developed by SCO for coordinating its background check programs include, at a minimum, the steps the agency will take to align its screening and credentialing activities and include specific time frames and budget requirements for implementation. In addition, the plan should describe how and when DHS will establish and apply a common set of design and comparability standards for DHS's background check programs.
  - Ensure that the plan being developed by DHS for coordinating its background check programs include, at a minimum, a discussion of the potential costs/benefits associated with the number of redundant background checks that would be eliminated through harmonization.
  - Because of DHS's responsibility for a large number of background check programs, explore with other federal agencies possible means to achieve harmonization and reduction of redundancies between background check programs within DHS and other agencies.

Appendix II: GAO Contact and Staff Acknowledgments

GAO Contact

Robert N. Goldenkoff, (202)-512-2757, goldenkoffr@gao.gov

Staff Acknowledgments

In addition to the person named above, Robert E. White, Assistant Director; Richard Ascarate; Nikki Clowers; Cindy Gilbert; David Hooper; Tracey King; Gary Malavenda; Jean Orland; and Meg Ullengren made key contributions to this report.

DOCUMENT NO. 7

FIRST RESPONDERS: MUCH WORK REMAINS TO IMPROVE COMMUNICATIONS INTEROPERABILITY

GAO Report (GAO-07-301)

April 2, 2007

Highlights

Why GAO Did This Study

As the first to respond to natural disasters, domestic terrorism, and other emergencies, public safety agencies rely on timely communications across multiple disciplines and jurisdictions. It is vital to the safety and effectiveness of first responders that their electronic communications systems enable them to communicate with whomever they need to, when they need to, and when they are authorized to do so. GAO was asked to determine, among other things, (1) the extent to which Department of Homeland Security (DHS) funding and technical assistance has helped to improve interoperable communications in selected states and (2) the progress that has been made in the development and implementation of interoperable communications standards. To address these objectives, GAO reviewed grant information, documentation of selected states' and localities' interoperability projects, and standards documents.

What GAO Recommends

GAO is making recommendations to DHS, which include assessing how states' grant requests support statewide communications plans and modifying its guidance on acquiring interoperable equipment. DHS disagreed with the latter recommendation, but GAO believes that it is important to provide more flexibility until completed subsets of standards have been fully defined. DHS agreed or deferred comment on all others. www.gao. gov/cgi-bin/getrpt?GAO-07-301.

What GAO Found

According to DHS, $2.15 billion in grant funding was awarded to states and localities from 2003 through 2005 for communications interoperability enhancements. This funding, along with technical assistance, has helped to make improvements on a variety of specific interoperability projects. However, states that GAO reviewed (see table below) had generally not used strategic plans to guide investments toward broadly improving interoperability. Further, no national plan was in place to coordinate investments across states. To its credit, DHS has required states to implement a statewide plan by the end of 2007, and DHS has recently been required to implement a National Emergency Communications Plan. However, no process has been established for ensuring that states' grant requests are consistent with their statewide plans. Until DHS takes a more strategic approach to improving interoperable communications—such as including in its decision making an assessment of how grant requests align with statewide communications plans—progress by states and localities improving interoperability is likely to be impeded.

Until recently, the private-sector coordinating body responsible for developing Project 25 standards—a suite of national standards intended to enable interoperability among the communications products of different vendors—has made little progress. Although one of the eight major subsets of standards was defined in the project's first 4 years (from 1989 to 1993), from 1993 through 2005, no additional standards were completed that could be used to develop Project 25 products. Specifications for three additional subsets of standards were defined over the past 2 years. However, ambiguities in the published standards have led to incompatibilities among products made by different vendors, and no compliance testing has been conducted to determine if these products are interoperable. Nevertheless, DHS has strongly encouraged state and local agencies to use grant funding to purchase Project 25 radios, which are substantially more expensive than non-Project 25 radios. As a result, states and local agencies have purchased fewer, more expensive radios that still may not be interoperable and thus may provide few added benefits. Until DHS modifies its grant guidance to provide more flexibility in purchasing communications equipment, states and localities are likely to continue to purchase expensive equipment that provides them with minimal additional benefits.

DHS Grant Funding to Improve Interoperability in Selected States

State	Grants from 2003 through 2005
New York	$145.5 million
Kentucky	$50 million
Oregon	$53.4 million
Florida	$55.7 million

Source: GAO analysis of DHS data

Abbreviations

COPS	Community Oriented Policing Services
DHS	Department of Homeland Security
FBI	Federal Bureau of Investigation
GHz	Gigahertz
ICTAP	Interoperable Communications Technical Assistance Program
IP	Internet Protocol
IWN	Integrated Wireless Network
kHz	kilohertz
MHz	megahertz
NIST	National Institute of Standards and Technology
OEC	Office of Emergency Communications
TIA	Telecommunications Industry Association
TICP	Tactical Interoperable Communications Plan
UASI	Urban Area Security Initiative
UHF	ultra high frequency
VHF	very high frequency
VoIP	Voice over Internet Protocol

The Honorable William Lacy Clay
Chairman
Subcommittee on Information Policy, Census, and National Archives
Committee on Oversight and Government Reform
House of Representatives

The Honorable Dennis J. Kucinich
Chairman
Subcommittee on Domestic Policy
Committee on Oversight and Government Reform
House of Representatives

Emergency "first responders"—personnel such as firefighters, police officers, and ambulance services who are the first to arrive at the scene of an emergency—are supported by a variety of public safety agencies, including 911 call center staff and other local, state, and federal authorities. Timely communications, often via wireless radios, are vital to the effectiveness and safety of first responders and their supporting agencies, as well as the safety of the public at large. Communications interoperability—also referred to as compatibility or connectivity—refers to the capability of different electronic communications systems to readily connect with each other and thus enable timely communications.

Facilitating interoperability has been a policy concern of public safety officials for many years. Toward that end, two major Department of Homeland Security (DHS) efforts under way to improve interoperable public safety communications are: (1) grant funding and technical assistance provided by the Office of Grants and Training to high-risk regions at the state and local level for on-site support as they work to improve their interoperability and (2) the SAFECOM program, intended to strengthen interoperable public safety communications at all levels of government. The program is intended to provide research, development, testing and evaluation, guidance, tools, and templates on communications-related issues. In addition, DHS supports Project 25, a joint initiative by government and commercial organizations to develop a set of national standards for vendors to use when designing radio communications equipment for first responders.

You asked us to assess the extent to which DHS has made progress in improving interoperable communications for first responders. Specifically, our objectives were to determine (1) the extent to which DHS funding and technical assistance have helped to improve interoperable communications in selected states, (2) the progress the SAFECOM program has made in improving interoperable communications, and (3) the progress that has been made in the development and implementation of interoperable communications standards.

To address our objectives, we conducted case studies of four states (Florida, Kentucky, New York, and Oregon) and 11 selected localities within those states. We used a number of factors to select states, including those that had received relatively large amounts of DHS funding, as well as those that routinely face natural disasters. The localities we selected included (1) large, high-risk urban areas, referred to as Urban Area Security Initiative (UASI) regions, which received the most funding from DHS within our selected states, (2) the non-UASI counties that received the largest amount of DHS funding within these states, and (3) the counties and cities where the state capitals are located.[1] To assess each state's use of DHS grants and technical assistance to improve interoperability and to identify common issues among states, we analyzed documentation obtained from state and local officials, such as grant allocation information and communications interoperability plans. To determine the progress SAFECOM has made in improving interoperable communications, we analyzed program management documentation (such as program goals, initiatives, and performance measures) and interviewed state and local officials regarding their use of SAFECOM tools and guidance. To determine the status of the development and implementation of interoperable communications standards, we obtained and analyzed documentation from DHS, the National Institute of Standards and Technology (NIST), and the four states. We performed our work from April 2006 to February 2007 in accordance with generally accepted government auditing standards. Further details of our objectives, scope, and methodology are provided in appendix I.

Results in Brief

According to DHS, $2.15 billion in grant funding was awarded to states and localities from fiscal year 2003 through fiscal year 2005 for communications interoperability enhancements. This funding, along with technical assistance, has helped to make improvements on a variety of specific interoperability projects. However, in the states we reviewed, strategic planning has generally not been used to guide investments and provide assistance to improve communications interoperability on a broader level. Specifically, not all states had plans in place to guide their investments toward long-term interoperability gains; no national plan was in place to coordinate investments across states; and while UASI officials stated that the technical assistance offered to them had been helpful, DHS curtailed full-scale exercises, limiting their value in measuring progress. Further, although DHS has required states to implement statewide plans by the end of 2007, no process has been established for ensuring that states' grant requests are consistent with their statewide plans. Until DHS takes a more strategic approach to improving interoperable communications—such as including in its decision making an assessment of how grant requests align with statewide communications plans—and until more rigorous exercises are conducted, progress by states and localities in improving interoperability is likely to be impeded.

The SAFECOM program has made limited progress in improving communications interoperability at all levels of government; however, the program has not addressed interoperability with federal agencies, a critical element to interoperable communications required by the Intelligence Reform and Terrorism Prevention Act of 2004.[2] The SAFECOM program has focused on helping states and localities improve interoperable communications by developing tools and guidance for their use. However, based on our review of four states and selected localities, SAFECOM's progress in achieving its goals of helping these states and localities improve interoperable communications has been limited. Officials from the states and localities we reviewed often found that the tools and planning assistance provided by the program were not helpful, or they were unaware of what assistance the program had to offer. The program's limited effectiveness can be linked to poor program management practices, including the lack of a plan for improving interoperability across all levels of government and inadequate performance measures that would provide feedback to better attune tools and assistance with public safety needs. Until SAFECOM adopts these key management practices, its progress is likely to remain limited.

Until recently, little progress had been made in developing Project 25 standards—a suite of national standards that are intended to enable interoperability among the communications products of different vendors. Although one of the eight major subsets of standards was defined in the project's first 4 years (from 1989 to 1993), from 1993 through 2005, no additional standards were completed that could be used by a vendor to develop elements of a Project 25 system. To its credit, over the past 2 years, the private-sector coordinating body responsible for Project 25 has defined specifications for three additional subsets of standards. However, ambiguities in the published standards have led to incompatibilities among products made by different vendors, and no compliance testing has been conducted to ensure vendors' products are interoperable. Nevertheless, DHS has strongly encouraged state and local agencies to use grant funding to purchase Project 25 radios, which are substantially more expensive than non-Project 25 radios. As a result, states and local agencies have purchased fewer, more expensive radios, which still may not be interoperable and thus may provide them with minimal additional benefits. Until DHS modifies its grant guidance to provide more flexibility in purchasing communications equipment, states and localities are likely to continue to purchase expensive equipment that provides them with minimal additional benefits.

We are making recommendations to DHS to enhance the effectiveness of the department's efforts to improve interoperable communications, including assessing how states' grant requests support their statewide communications plans as a factor in the grant allocation process, implementing a program plan and establishing performance measures to assess the effectiveness and usefulness of SAFECOM tools, and modifying guidance to states and localities regarding acquisition of communications equipment to allow a more flexible approach until completed subsets of standards have been fully defined, and products have been certified compliant.

We received written comments from the Deputy Secretary of Commerce and the director of the DHS liaison office for GAO and the Office of the Inspector General. Letters from these agencies are reprinted in appendixes III and IV. Commerce provided updated information and technical comments, which we have incorporated, where appropriate.

In its response to our five recommendations, DHS agreed with two, stated that it would defer commenting on two, and disagreed with one recommendation.

DHS agreed with the intent of our recommendation that it develop and implement a program plan and stated that it is currently working to develop such a plan. DHS also agreed with our recommendation to develop quantifiable performance measures for the program.

DHS disagreed with our recommendation on modifying grant guidance to provide more flexibility in purchasing communications equipment until standards for completed interfaces have been fully defined, stating that the recommendation would require SAFECOM to amend its interoperability grant guidance until after the entire Project 25 suite of standards is complete, and would undermine the final remaining negotiations between the public safety community and equipment manufacturers. We agree that not all interfaces need to be fully defined before agencies can begin acquiring Project 25 products; thus we have clarified the recommendation to reflect this. However, we are not recommending that the public safety community be prohibited from acquiring Project 25 equipment, and thus we do not believe negotiations with equipment manufacturers would be undermined.

DHS also provided technical comments that we incorporated as appropriate.

Background

Public safety agencies include the nation's first responders (such as firefighters, police officers, and ambulance services), 911 call center staff, and a number of local, state, federal, and regional authorities. Communications, often through wireless land mobile radios, are vital to these agencies' effectiveness and to the safety of their members and the public. Wireless technology requires radio frequency capacity in order to function, and existing wireless technology is designed to work within specified frequency ranges.

Interoperability in the context of public safety communications systems refers to the ability of first responders to communicate with whomever they need to (including personnel from a variety of agencies and jurisdictions), when they need to, and when they are authorized to do so. It is important to note that the goal of being able to communicate when necessary and authorized is not the same as being able to communicate with any other individual at any time—a capability that could overwhelm the communications infrastructure and would likely impede effective communication and response time.

Different first responder groups each have different professional practices, public safety missions, emergency response procedures, communication protocols, and radio frequencies. These differences have created a variety of obstacles to effective interoperable communications among first responders. Thus, facilitating interoperable communications has been a policy concern of public safety officials for many years.

Land Mobile Radio System Technology

Land mobile radio systems are the primary means of communications among public safety personnel. These systems typically consist of handheld portable radios, mobile radios, base stations, and repeaters. Handheld portable radios are typically carried by public safety personnel and tend to have a limited transmission range. Mobile radios are often located in vehicles and use the vehicle's power supply and a larger antenna, providing a greater transmission range than handheld portable radios. Base station radios are located in fixed positions, such as public service access points or dispatch centers, and tend to have the most powerful transmitters. A network is required to connect the different base stations to the same communications system. Repeaters are used to increase the effective communications range of handheld portable radios, mobile radios, and base station radios by retransmitting received radio signals. Figure 1 below illustrates the basic components of a land mobile radio system.

Figure 1: Basic Components of a Land Mobile Radio Communication System

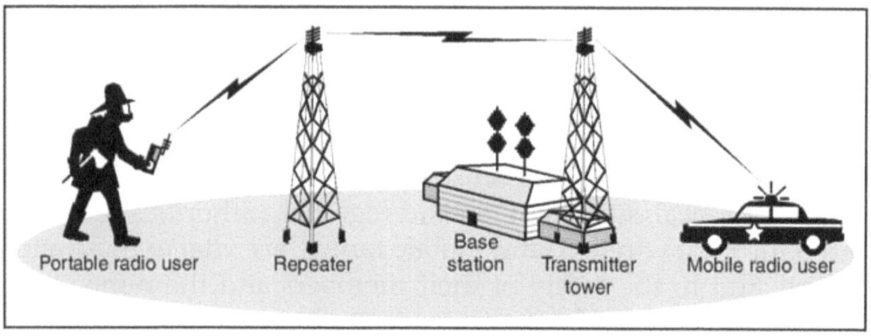

Sources: GAO and DHS

The transmissions between the elements of a land mobile radio system consist of electromagnetic waves that propagate along designated frequencies of the radio spectrum. Each communications link uniquely occupies a specific frequency or set of frequencies for as long as information is being transmitted. The radio spectrum is a fixed, limited resource that is shared among government and nongovernment entities for many uses in addition to public safety communications, such as television broadcasting, AM/FM radio, and aeronautical radio navigation. Most public safety agencies use their allocated frequencies for voice communications but are increasingly using their portion of the spectrum to support more advanced technologies, such as data, imagery, and video transmissions. The specific frequency bands allocated to public safety agencies are shown in figure 2.

Figure 2: Public Safety Agency Radio Frequency Bands and Their Location on the Radio Spectrum

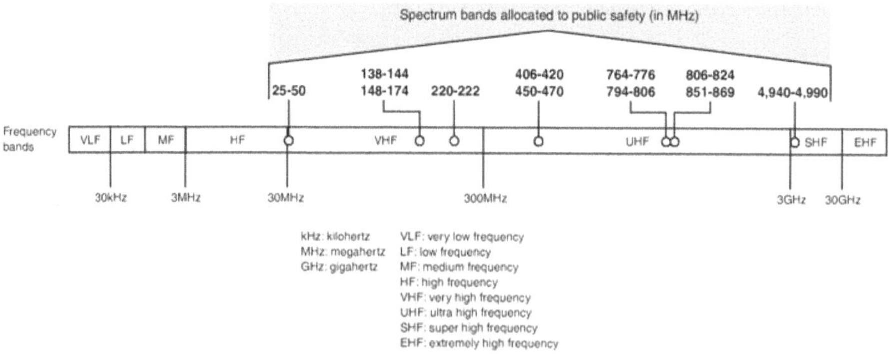

Sources: GAO and DHS

Major frequency ranges that are used for public safety communications include the very high frequency (VHF) range and the ultra high frequency (UHF) range. VHF signals travel farther than UHF signals and thus are useful in suburban and rural areas. However, they generally cannot penetrate building walls very well. In contrast, UHF signals are more appropriate for denser urban areas as they penetrate buildings more easily, and it is less critical that the signals be able to propagate for long distances. The frequencies used by federal agencies are managed by the National Telecommunications and Information Administration, while the Federal Communications Commission manages state and local government frequencies.

Radio systems are classified as either conventional or "trunked." Conventional radio systems have dedicated frequencies—also referred to as channels—assigned to individual groups of users. When a user makes a call, other members of the group cannot use the channel until the call is over. In contrast, trunked systems allocate pools of channels for use by multiple individuals. When a call is made by a user on a trunked system, an available channel is automatically selected from the pool of channels, leaving the remaining channels available for others. While trunked systems are more complex and require more infrastructure than conventional systems, they allow for more efficient use of communication channels, reducing congestion.

Lack of Interoperable Communications Has Long Hindered Emergency Response

In order to effectively respond to emergencies such as natural disasters and domestic terrorism, public safety agencies need the ability to communicate with their counterparts in other disciplines and jurisdictions. However, the wireless communications systems used by many police officers, firefighters, emergency medical personnel, and other public safety agencies do not provide such capability. For example, emergency agencies responding to events such as the bombing of the federal building in Oklahoma City and the attacks of September 11, 2001, experienced difficulties in trying to communicate with each other. The 9/11 Commission concluded that communications interoperability problems contributed to the large number of firefighter fatalities that occurred at the World Trade Center.[3]

Historically, first responder communications interoperability has been significantly hampered by different and incompatible radio systems. Different technologies and configurations, including proprietary designs, by different manufacturers have limited the interoperability of public safety wireless communications systems. These systems have also operated on different frequencies of the radio spectrum. In particular, public safety agencies have been assigned frequencies in new bands over time as available frequencies became congested, and as new technologies made higher frequencies available for use. Existing radios are unable to transmit and receive in all of the public safety frequencies, often making communications between first responders from different jurisdictions difficult. Additionally, as we have previously reported,[4] there is a need for better frequency planning and coordination. Further, public safety agencies have historically planned and acquired communications systems without concern for interoperability, often resulting in multiple, technically incompatible systems in operation throughout any given local jurisdiction.

A variety of technical approaches have been adopted to help improve interoperable communications, including the following:

- *Swapping radios:* Agencies maintain a cache of extra radios that they can distribute during an emergency to other first responders whose radios are not interoperable with their own. The advantage of this solution is that it does not require that all existing radios be replaced, an important consideration when funds to buy new equipment are limited. However, this approach requires significant logistical support and careful management to implement successfully.
- *Patching:* Two or more incompatible radio systems are connected to a central switchboard-like system that translates a signal sent from one connected system so that it can be received by any of the other connected systems. The principal advantage of this solution is that agencies can continue to use existing systems that would otherwise be incompatible. A major disadvantage is that patching requires twice as much spectrum because a patched transmission occupies separate channels on each connected system.
- *Shared channels or mutual aid channels:* Agencies agree to set aside a specific channel or channels for connecting to other incompatible systems. This approach provides direct interoperable communications and only occupies one channel per conversation. However, it can cause congestion since these channels require dedicated frequencies and thus have limited capacity.
- *Shared systems:* The use of a single or common radio system—typically a trunked system—to provide service to most agencies within a region. Shared systems are the most robust form of interoperability and do not require dedicated channels. While this approach produces optimal performance, it can be very expensive, because it generally requires purchasing all new radios and transmission equipment. Technologies that can help implement shared systems include the following:
- *Internet Protocol based systems:* Using the Voice over Internet Protocol,[5] advanced communications systems can offer the flexibility to transmit voice conversations over a data network such as the Internet or a private network.
- *Software-defined radios:* These are intended to allow interoperability among agencies using different frequency bands, different operational

modes (digital or analog), proprietary systems from different manufacturers, or different modulations (such as AM or FM). However, software-defined radios are still being developed and are not yet available for use by public safety agencies.

However, interoperability cannot be achieved solely by implementing technical solutions. Coordination among different agencies and governmental entities is also critical. Response to an emergency may involve all levels of government and many different disciplines, such as law enforcement organizations, fire departments, emergency medical services, transportation, natural resources, and public utility sectors. Each of these agencies is likely to have its own policies, procedures, and communications protocols when responding to an incident. A simplistic example is the word "fire," which to a firefighter means that something is burning but to a police officer is a command to shoot a weapon. Resolving such cultural and procedural differences can be challenging.

Further, the extent to which interoperable communications are needed among different agencies, disciplines, and levels of government (federal, state, local, and tribal) varies based on the size, significance, and duration of an emergency event. Increasing degrees of interoperability may be needed for (1) routine day-to-day coordination between a few agencies in a local area, (2) extended operations involving agencies from multiple jurisdictions working on a larger problem (such as the 2002 sniper attacks in the Washington, D.C., metropolitan area), and (3) a major, large-scale event that requires response from a range of local, state, and federal agencies and disciplines (such as major wildfires, hurricanes, or the terrorist attacks of September 11, 2001).

In 2004,[6] we reported that a fundamental barrier to successfully addressing interoperable communications problems for public safety was the lack of effective, collaborative, interdisciplinary, and intergovernmental planning. We recommended that DHS take a number of actions to address this barrier, such as determining the current status of interoperable communications across the nation and encouraging states to establish comprehensive statewide interoperability plans and certify the alignment of their grant applications with their statewide plans. DHS has taken steps to address these recommendations. For example, it recently completed a national survey of first responders to determine the current status of their interoperability capabilities, and it has required states to develop statewide communications plans by the end of 2007.

Programs Aimed at Improving Interoperable Communications

SAFECOM is a DHS program intended to strengthen interoperable public safety communications at all levels of government. The program provides research, development, testing and evaluation, guidance, tools, and templates on communications-related issues. We previously reported[7] that changes in leadership delayed progress during the initial years of the

SAFECOM program and that the program suffered from a lack of leadership and focus.

Since 2004, SAFECOM has spent $20.4 million developing several tools and providing assistance to help guide states and localities as they work to improve the interoperability of their communication systems. Table 1 outlines several tools and guidance that SAFECOM had developed as of July 2006. The program continues to develop additional tools.

Table 1: Description of SAFECOM Guidance and Tools

Guidance or tool	Description
Statement of Requirements	This document is intended to define and identify the range of future requirements for voice and data communications to enable interoperability. It provides definitions of a variety of interoperable communication subjects, such as public safety communication needs, public safety roles and functions, and the levels of operability and interoperability for each major public safety discipline.
Public Safety Architecture Framework	This framework is intended to provide a methodology to plan and develop the migration from current public safety architectures to the interoperable systems outlined in the Statement of Requirements.
Interoperability Continuum	The Interoperability Continuum provides a graphical depiction of five critical success factors for achieving interoperability that SAFECOM developed based on feedback from first responders. This tool is intended to provide a framework that emergency response agencies can use to baseline their planning and implementation of interoperability solutions.
RapidCom	RapidCom provided assistance to 10 high-threat urban areas, including New York City, Miami, and Los Angeles, to help improve incident-level communications interoperability capabilities in those locations. RapidCom was intended to help incident commanders communicate with each other and their command centers in a timely manner by helping them to establish objectives, identify solutions, and take steps toward implementation.
Regional Communications Interoperability Pilot projects	SAFECOM officials worked with public safety officials at all levels of government in Nevada and Kentucky to help them develop both short-term and long-term goals aimed at improving interoperability within their states.
Statewide Communication Interoperability Planning Methodology	The methodology describes a step-by-step process for developing a locally driven statewide strategic plan for enhancing communications interoperability.
Grant Guidance	SAFECOM's grant guidance is intended to provide consistent criteria for agencies to use when purchasing equipment with federal funds.

Source: GAO based on DHS data

We previously recommended that in order to enhance the ability of SAFECOM to improve communications among emergency personnel from federal, state, local, and tribal agencies, SAFECOM officials should complete written agreements with the project's identified stakeholders (including federal agencies and organizations representing state and local governments) that define the responsibilities and resource commitments that each of those organizations will assume and include specific provisions that measure program performance.[8] Since we made our recommendation, SAFECOM program officials have established a governance charter for the program, which outlines the roles, relationships, and operating guidelines for participating stakeholders.

The Office of Grants and Training, which is scheduled to become part of the Federal Emergency Management Agency, is a separate entity within DHS that is responsible for, among other things, providing grants and technical assistance to states and localities to help them improve their interoperable communications. Grants and Training provides funding to states and requires that at least 80 percent of grant funding provided to states through the Homeland Security Grant Program be passed to localities. Grants and Training also provides additional funding to address the unique planning, equipment, training, and exercise needs of UASI areas.[9]

DHS uses a partly risk-based approach to allocate grant funds. State agencies submit proposals to DHS which form the basis for its risk-based decisions. During the most recent grant allocation process in 2006 for the Homeland Security Grant Program, each state and territory received a portion of its grant funding through a base allocation. The remainder of funds was allocated based on an analysis of risk and need. In fiscal year 2006, the UASI funds were allocated based on risk and effectiveness. DHS estimated the relative risk of successful terrorist attacks on selected urban areas, considering threat, vulnerability, and consequences for both asset-based and geographic factors. On the basis of this analysis, it ranked the UASI areas and identified 35 urban areas as eligible to apply for UASI funding. In addition, the 11 urban areas that received funding previously, but were not identified as UASI areas in 2006, have been extended eligibility for funding for one additional year. DHS also used a peer review process to assess the effectiveness of each of the 35 urban areas' proposed investments using the grant funds.

Grants and Training has also established a monitoring program in which preparedness officers validate that grant funds are being administered legally and in accordance with the guidance provided to grantees. Preparedness officers work with the states to help address areas of concern, needs, and priorities. The monitoring program is also intended to provide a general assessment of where states and localities are in protecting their citizens. In addition, in efforts to control the use of awards, DHS officials have developed an Approved Equipment List that provides information on allowable equipment expenditures.

Further, Grants and Training established the Interoperable Communications Technical Assistance Program, which has provided guidance and technical assistance to the UASI areas. While the program focuses mostly on providing guidance and assistance to these specific areas, assistance is also provided to non-UASI areas. Table 2 provides a list of the assistance and guidance offered by Grants and Training.

Table 2: Office of Grants and Training Guidance and Technical Assistance

Guidance or technical assistance	Description
Tactical Interoperable Communications Plan (TICP) guidance	Each UASI area receiving DHS funds must develop a plan to achieve tactical interoperable communications across its separate jurisdictions. The TICP guidance provides an outline of key elements that should be covered in the plan, such as a governance structure and interoperability equipment in the region.
TICP exercise guidance	Each UASI area receiving DHS funds must validate the effectiveness of their communication plan by conducting a full-scale exercise. ICTAP provided supporting material, such as an evaluator handbook.
Interoperable Communications Technical Assistance Program (ICTAP)	An ICTAP technical assistance team works on-site with the UASI areas' communications representatives to identify gaps in existing communications infrastructure and to translate operational requirements into technical requirements that can be used to design an interoperable system.
UASI scorecard	Grants and Training, in consultation with SAFECOM and the Wireless Management Office, has developed scorecards that assess the maturity of tactical interoperable communications capabilities in the UASI areas. The goal of the scorecard effort is to provide an assessment of each urban/metropolitan area and to provide recommendations on how to best improve tactical interoperable communications. DHS released the scorecards to the UASI areas in January 2007.

Source: GAO based on DHS data

Another grant program focused on interoperable communications is the Department of Justice's Community Oriented Policing Services (COPS) Interoperable Communications Grant program. The program awards technology grants to law enforcement agencies for interoperable communications and information sharing. While the program used to have a larger role in providing grant funding to states and localities, its scope and budget was significantly reduced in 2006 in an effort to eliminate overlap with DHS's grant program.

More recently, the 2007 DHS Appropriations Act[10] transferred many SAFECOM program responsibilities to a new Office of Emergency Communications (OEC). This new office, which is not yet operational, is to take over the Interoperable Communications Technical Assistance Program from Grants and Training and the Integrated Wireless Network project, which is intended to create a consolidated federal wireless communications service for federal public safety agencies. This new office is tasked with improving overall emergency communications for first responders, as well as improving interoperability. In addition to the OEC, the Office for Interoperability and Compatibility within the Science and Technology Directorate will continue to house the remaining elements of SAFECOM related to research, development, testing and evaluation, and standards.

Project 25 Was Established to Address First Responder Interoperability Standards

In 1989, the Association of Public Safety Communications Officials, the National Association of State Telecommunications Directors, and selected federal agencies established Project 25 to develop open standards for vendors to use when designing land mobile radio communications equipment. Project 25 has the following four primary objectives:

- enable effective inter- and intra-agency communications,
- improve radio spectrum efficiency,
- focus equipment and capabilities on public safety needs, and
- leverage an open architecture to promote competition across land mobile radio vendors.

Project 25 standards are intended to be a suite of national standards, based upon public safety user requirements, which define operable and interoperable communications equipment for first responders. When complete, this suite of standards is intended to allow for specifications to be written for interfaces between the various components of a land mobile radio system. The Association of Public Safety Communications Officials, the National Association of State Telecommunications Directors, and federal agency representatives, work with the Telecommunications Industry Association (TIA)—an American National Standards Institute-accredited[11] standards development organization—to develop and maintain the standards.

DHS Assistance Has Helped on Specific Interoperability Projects, but a More Strategic Approach Is Needed

According to DHS, $2.15 billion in grant funding was awarded to states and localities from fiscal year 2003 through fiscal year 2005 for communications interoperability enhancements. This funding, along with technical assistance, has helped to make improvements on a variety of specific interoperability projects. However, in the states we reviewed, strategic planning has generally not been used to guide investments and provide assistance to improve communications interoperability on a broader level. Specifically, not all states had plans in place to guide their investments toward long-term interoperability gains; no national plan was in place to coordinate investments across states; and while UASI officials stated that the technical assistance offered to them had been helpful, DHS curtailed full-scale exercises, limiting their value in measuring progress. Further, although DHS has required states to implement statewide plans by the end of 2007, no process has been established for ensuring that states' grant requests are consistent with their statewide plans. Until DHS takes a more strategic approach to improving interoperable communications—such as including in its decision making an assessment of how grant requests align with statewide communications plans—and until more rigorous exercises are conducted, progress by states and localities in improving interoperability is likely to be impeded.

DHS Funding Has Helped Make Improvements on Specific Interoperability Projects in Selected States

One of the main purposes of the DHS grants program is to provide financial assistance to states and localities to help them fund projects to develop and implement interoperable communications systems. In addition, as previously mentioned, the Interoperable Communications Technical Assistance Program is intended to provide on-site assistance to UASI areas to, among other things, assist with developing tactical interoperability plans, planning exercises, assessing communication gaps, and designing interoperable systems.

The four states we reviewed received assistance from DHS, which helped make improvements on specific interoperability projects.

- *Florida:* Florida has spent $36.5 million in DHS funds to develop a system called the Florida Interoperability Network, which establishes network connections between federal, state, and local dispatch centers across Florida and provides mutual aid channels throughout the state. As a result, the level of interoperability across the state has improved significantly. First responders in 64 of Florida's 67 counties are now able to have their communications patched to each other as needed via the network. Previously, they had no such infrastructure for achieving interoperability. However, officials from localities in Florida raised questions about the long-term sustainability of the network. Each connected jurisdiction must pay the ongoing costs of their connection to the Florida Interoperability Network, and smaller jurisdictions are likely to find this unaffordable. Further, Florida officials remarked that training across the state is still incomplete. Additionally, in the Miami UASI region, a majority of the Urban Area Security Initiative funding for interoperable communications has been used to acquire communications equipment, such as radios, and interoperability solutions, such as devices that interconnect first responders on disparate radios, to make improvements in Miami City and in Miami-Dade County. However, limited UASI funding had been dedicated to making interoperability improvements in other localities in the Miami UASI, such as Monroe and Broward Counties.

- *Kentucky:* Kentucky used a portion of its DHS funding to expand the use of mutual aid interoperability radio channels that allow agencies on different communication systems throughout Kentucky to tune to a dedicated, shared frequency to communicate. Prior to this initiative, first responders operating on different frequencies were unable to communicate. Currently, approximately 34 percent of applicable agencies have signed a memorandum of understanding to commit to using the mutual aid channels in accordance to standardized procedures. However, mutual aid channels have limited capacity, and Kentucky has yet to implement a long-term solution for a statewide voice communications system that will allow federal, state, and local first responders to communicate directly as needed. Kentucky has also used DHS funding to implement a statewide wireless data communications system. The system provides functionality such as statewide records management, real-time crime coverage and data collection, and instant messaging. First responders use mobile data terminals to communicate with each other and, in many cases, retrieve information from agency databases. Kentucky's mobile data network currently has coverage across approximately 95 percent of the state's primary and secondary road systems. Such capabilities were not available to Kentucky's first responders prior to this initiative. In the Louisville UASI, local officials have utilized DHS funding to implement patching mechanisms to connect different communication systems throughout the region. However, according to officials, communications channels are frequently congested because of the amount of patching that needs to be done to connect responders.
- *New York:* In New York, DHS funding is generally being utilized by localities to address local interoperability issues within their counties and with neighboring counties. For example, Albany County is acquiring a new interoperable system that connects first responders on many disparate systems within Albany County and neighboring counties. Prior to this system, there was no single voice system or network that would al-

low incident commanders and first responders to be able to communicate directly. However, the local solutions do not always incorporate state and federal systems. For example, the state is using state funds to develop and implement a separate and incompatible statewide network called the Statewide Wireless Network, which localities are not required to join. Albany County, for example, has no immediate plans to connect their new system to the statewide system because of uncertainties about the expense and the expected benefits for the county. In the New York City UASI, local officials have used a portion of DHS funding to implement a citywide mobile wireless network. This system is intended to provide first responders throughout the city with high-speed data access to support large file transfers, including accessing federal and state anticrime and antiterrorism databases, fingerprints, mug shots, city maps, and full-motion streaming video.

- *Oregon:* Oregon, in accordance with DHS guidance, has dedicated most of its DHS funding to local projects that improve interoperability in specific regions. For example, Jackson and Josephine Counties are jointly implementing an interoperable communications system. Previously, first responders in these two neighboring counties relied on indirect means for establishing interoperable communications, such as radio channels, patching mechanisms, and a mobile command vehicle equipped with a cache of radios in different frequencies and a patching device that could be deployed as needed. However, this new system does not include federal or state first responders. In addition, limited DHS funding has been utilized for developing plans for the development of the Oregon Wireless Interoperability Network. This system is intended to replace state agencies' deteriorating systems with a new system. It is also intended to connect local agencies that continue to use their existing systems to other local agencies that they do not already have interoperability with. To date, the development of this system has not been initiated. In the Portland UASI, DHS funding was used to install repeaters in Columbia County to enhance interoperability with the other four counties in the urban area. However, while it has improved the interoperability, not all Columbia County first responders are able to utilize this solution. Therefore, the UASI funding was also used to purchase a supply of reserve radios— referred to as a cache—that can be shared.

Table 3 shows the amount of DHS funding states and localities have received and examples of what the money has been used for.

Table 3: Examples of Uses of DHS Funding for Interoperable Communications

Location	Examples of purchases	Total DHS grants[a] for interoperable communications from fiscal years 2003 to 2005[b]
State of New York	A communication vehicle with equipment to enable interoperable communications at the scene of an incident such as extra radios and patching devices.	$74.9 million[c]
	Studies of initial interoperability projects for Onondaga County.	
	Emergency Services Interoperability Radio System project, which provides interoperability among the county and surrounding counties, as well as radios and a patching system for Albany County.	
New York City UASI	Portions of the citywide-Mobile Wireless Network, communications enhancements for the New York City Fire Department Operations Center, and local area network installation for the police department.	$70.6 million[d]
Kentucky	Installation of infrastructure across the state to facilitate the use of interoperability radio channels.	$39.5 million
	Computer-aided dispatch consolidation efforts and upgrades to dispatch infrastructure for Montgomery County.	
	Development of a mobile data system for Franklin County.	
Louisville UASI	Mobile radios, training costs, accessories for radio equipment, and equipment used for patching communications.	$10.5 million[e f]
Oregon	Development of plans for the Oregon Wireless Interoperability Network, radios, mobile data terminals, and devices that interconnect first responders on disparate systems.	$45.9 million

Location	Examples of purchases	**Total DHS grants**[a] for interoperable communications from fiscal years 2003 to 2005[b]
	Hospital communication upgrades, base station equipment, and radios.	
	Development of a system that connects Jackson County to Josephine County.	
	Developing a communications plan for Marion County.	
Portland UASI	Radios, communication equipment for emergency operations center, mobile data terminals, and repeaters.	$7.5 million
Florida	The Florida Interoperability Network, which establishes network connections between federal, state, and local dispatch centers across Florida and provides mutual aid channels throughout the state.	$44 million[g]
	Emergency Deployable Interoperable Communications Systems, which are mobile systems that can be deployed to a specific response area to patch multiple disparate communications systems together.	
	Mutual Aid Radio Communications units, which are stand-alone mobile interoperable communications networks and self-contain the infrastructure to set up a communications system in the absence of an operable system.	
Miami UASI	Radios, back-up radio system, cache of radios, a mobile emergency operations center, and devices that interconnect first responders on disparate radio systems.	$11.7 million

Source: GAO analysis of DHS, state, and locality data

Note: These amounts include DHS funding from fiscal year 2003 through fiscal year 2005, as the complete 2006 figures were not available at the time of our review.

[a] Allocations of DHS grant funding to interoperable communications are determined by each state and reported by each state to DHS.

[b] DHS's grant funding figures for interoperable communications includes funding from each of the relevant grant programs within the Office of Grants and Training, including the State Homeland Security Program and the UASI program.

[c] The $74.9 million includes all other DHS funding that was awarded to New York, including the Buffalo UASI, with the exception of the $70.6 million that was awarded to the New York City UASI.

[d] For fiscal year 2003, New York did not designate separate Interoperable Communications funding for the state and urban area.

[e] From 2003 through 2005, Louisville was a designated UASI area. In 2006 DHS reduced the number of UASI areas; as a result, Louisville is no longer a designated UASI area. However, it received funding from the UASI program in 2006 to help it sustain ongoing projects.

[f] For fiscal year 2003, Kentucky did not designate separate Interoperable Communications funding for the state and urban area.

[g] The $44 million includes all other DHS funding that was awarded to Florida, including the Tampa and Jacksonville UASI areas, with the exception of the $11.7 million that was awarded to the Miami UASI.

A Lack of Statewide Plans Has Contributed to Limited Strategic Use of DHS Funding

According to SAFECOM guidance, interoperability cannot be solved by any one entity alone and, therefore, an effective and interoperable communications system requires a clear and compelling statewide strategy focused on increasing public safety effectiveness and coordination across all related organizations. A statewide interoperability plan is essential for outlining such a strategy. Such a plan should establish long-term objectives but also include short-term solutions that help incrementally achieve sustainable solutions to the long-term objectives. Thus, establishing long-term plans helps ensure that near-term solutions are consistent with the end goal.

The narrow and specific use of DHS funding in the states we reviewed can be traced in part to the lack of statewide plans; interoperability investments by individual localities have not been coordinated toward achieving a broader goal for the state. For example, Kentucky, which has received grant funding totaling approximately $50 million since fiscal year 2003 according to DHS, has not yet developed a statewide communications plan, although in January 2007, officials stated that they had begun developing a plan. While Kentucky has recently begun working to assess how best to address statewide needs, to date, grant reviewers at the state level who are in charge of disbursing DHS grant money to localities have had limited means for determining whether funding requests for equipment and training were compatible with statewide interoperability goals. For example, evaluators were required to assess aspects of request proposals such as whether they fully addressed the measurable objectives expected for a new wireless communication system and whether they addressed how the applicant agency would communicate with other public safety and/or public service organizations at the local, state, and federal levels. However, the available criteria do not provide the evaluators with an overall statewide strategy that the evaluators could use to assess whether the localities' proposal is aligned to it. As a result, the equipment and activities that localities have purchased have tended to address short-term voice communication solutions for local interoperability problems while long-term, statewide solutions have not been addressed. However, as previously stated, Kentucky has developed a data communications network to supplement gaps in its voice communications.

Similarly, New York does not yet have a statewide communications plan and, therefore, does not utilize DHS grant funding in support of such a plan. While state officials recommend that localities invest in interoperable communications, they provide no additional guidance to localities to ensure that local investments are consistent with statewide goals. As a result, localities have generally used the funding to address local interoperability issues within their counties and neighboring counties, with little regard for state and federal systems. For example, while New York is currently in the process of deploying the Statewide Wireless Network for $2 billion, localities are not required to participate, and local interest in the statewide system has been limited. As a result, localities are continuing to develop their own interoperability solutions that do not incorporate the network. Among localities we reviewed, Onondaga County is implementing its own $33 million interoperable communications system independently of the network, and Albany County, likewise, is currently developing a $1.7 million interoperability system that does not incorporate the Statewide Wireless Network. Officials stated that once the network's pilot period is complete they will decide whether to participate in the network.

In accordance with a previous recommendation, DHS has required grant recipients to develop and adopt a statewide communications plan by the end of 2007. Additionally, the 2007 DHS Appropriations Act states that DHS may restrict funding to a state if it does not submit a statewide interoperable communication plan.[12] However, despite our other previous recommendation that DHS should require that states certify that grant applications be consistent with statewide plans,[13] no process has yet been established for ensuring that states' grant requests are consistent with their statewide plans and long-term objectives for improving interoperability. Grants and Training officials are considering instituting such a process but they do not have specific plans to do so.

Because of the lack of coordination, state and local governments are investing significant resources, including DHS grant funds, in developing independent interoperability solutions that do not always support each others' needs. Until the DHS-mandated statewide communications plans are in place, and processes have been established for ensuring that each state's grant request is consistent with its statewide plan and longer-term interoperability goals, progress by states and localities in improving interoperability is likely to be impeded.

The Lack of a National Plan Has Also Contributed to Limited Strategic Use of DHS Funding

In addition to statewide plans, an overarching national plan is critical to coordinating interoperability spending, especially where federal first responders are involved. According to the Public Safety Wireless Advisory Committee,[14] improving interoperable communications across the nation will require a national plan that includes all levels of government and defines operational policies and procedures and the proper use of national communications resources. In responding to large-scale events—such as wildfires, hurricanes, or terrorist attacks—state and local government first responders require interoperable communications with federal agencies.

To date, however, interoperability investments have tended to be isolated and piecemeal, in part because they have not been guided by a comprehensive national plan. For example, officials stated that Oregon and its bordering states—Washington, California, and Idaho—are each working independently to try to implement and meet federal communication requirements and improve interoperability.

In a large-scale emergency, where first responders may need to coordinate with agencies from other states and a variety of federal agencies, the lack of national-level planning can result in substantial interoperability problems. During Hurricane Katrina, for example, Florida first responders spent half a day trying to contact their counterparts in Louisiana and Mississippi in an effort to share communications equipment. If these states coordinated prior to the catastrophe, it is likely that less time and energy would have been wasted.

The lack of a national strategy has also left state officials uncertain about whether they are taking appropriate steps to plan for interoperability. For example, Oregon officials indicated they are uncertain whether the approach they are taking is the best way to solve their interoperability problems.

The 2007 DHS Appropriations Act[15] requires DHS to develop a National Emergency Communications Plan by March 2008. Among other things, the plan is to identify necessary emergency communications capabilities for first responders and government officials, identify obstacles to interoperable communications, provide both short-term and long-term solutions to those obstacles, and establish goals and time frames for the deployment of emergency communications systems based on new and existing equipment across the United States.

Technical Assistance Has Been Helpful, but Exercises Curtailed by DHS Have Had Limited Strategic Value

According to state and local officials, the Interoperable Communications Technical Assistance Program has been beneficial to each of the four UASI areas we visited. For example, according to Miami officials, the program provided extensive support in the development of the tactical interoperable communications plan for the Miami area. Technical assistance representatives held meetings with each of the Miami area public safety agencies to compile a regional communications equipment inventory. Similarly, according to Louisville officials, the Interoperable Communications Technical Assistance Program held a 2-day workshop on developing the tactical interoperable communications plan for the Louisville area. Officials stated that this workshop represented the first time that all relevant communications officials and emergency responders were involved in a collaborative effort.

Guidance for the 2006 Homeland Security Grant Program required each of the high-risk UASI areas to plan and conduct a full-scale exercise to validate the effectiveness of their tactical interoperable communications plans. Full-scale exercises are the most complex type of exercises, involving multiple agencies and jurisdictions in testing plans, policies, and procedures. They are intended to be conducted in a real-time, stressful environment that closely mirrors real events. DHS required the exercises as a way to measure the progress each UASI has made in improving interoperability and developed "scorecards" to capture the results of the exercise.

However, while DHS provided extensive assistance to the urban areas in developing their tactical interoperability communications plans, it curtailed the exercises that were intended to validate the robustness and completeness of each plan. Due to the complexity of these exercises, the UASI areas were originally allotted 12 months to plan and execute robust, full-scale exercises; DHS subsequently reduced this to 5 months. DHS officials indicated that they accelerated the deadline so that they could use the results as inputs into the interoperability scorecards that they published in January 2007. To compensate for the reduced time frame, DHS reduced the requirements of the full-scale exercise, advising the UASI areas to limit the scope and size of their activities.

In reducing the scope of their exercises, the UASI areas had to reduce the extent to which they tested the robustness and effectiveness of their interoperability plans. For example, of the four UASI areas we visited, Portland, Miami, and New York City each reduced the scope of their exercise so they could meet DHS's accelerated deadline. For example, Portland had to significantly reduce the number of participants from each of the counties participating in the exercise. According to Portland officials, their exercise was not realistic for responding to a real-world incident. Likewise, New York City officials stated that they would have executed a higher quality exercise if DHS had not reduced the time frame. Moreover, according to the 2007 grant guidance, the UASI areas are not required to conduct any additional exercises to further validate their plans.

Without robust exercises to validate tactical interoperability communications plans, the UASI areas can only have limited confidence in the plans' effectiveness, and thus the value of DHS's efforts may continue to be limited. Similarly, the constraints placed on the exercises means that DHS's scorecards of each of the UASI areas are based on questionable data.

SAFECOM Program Has Made Limited Progress in Assisting All Levels of Government to Achieve Interoperability

Although initiated in 2001, the SAFECOM program has made limited progress in improving communications interoperability at all levels of government. The program has not addressed state and local interoperability with federal agencies, a critical element to interoperable communications that is required by the Intelligence Reform and Terrorism Prevention Act of 2004. Further, while the program has focused on helping states and localities improve interoperable communications by developing tools and guidance for their use, SAFECOM's progress in this area has been limited in the selected states. Specifically, officials from selected states and localities often found that the tools and planning assistance provided by the program were not helpful, or they were unaware of what assistance the program had to offer. The program's limited effectiveness can be linked to poor program management practices, including the lack of a plan for improving interoperability across all levels of government and inadequate performance measures that would provide feedback to better attune tools and assistance with first responder needs. Until SAFECOM adopts these key management practices, its progress is likely to remain limited.

SAFECOM Was Established to Improve Interoperable Communications at All Levels of Government

When SAFECOM was established in 2001, as one of the Office of Management and Budget's 25 electronic government initiatives[16] under the management of the Department of the Treasury, its goals were to (1) achieve federal-to-federal interoperability throughout the nation, (2) achieve federal to state/local interoperability, and (3) achieve state/local interoperability throughout the nation. Like the other e-government initiatives, the program was expected to achieve its goals within 18 to 24 months. As we reported in 2004, these are challenging tasks that will take many years to fully accomplish, and the program had made very limited progress at the time of our review.[17]

Since 2001, the management and goals of the program have changed several times. Most recently, in 2003, the SAFECOM program was transferred to the Office of Interoperability and Compatibility within the Directorate of Science and Technology in DHS. Its goals included increasing interoperable communications capacity of local, tribal, and state public safety agencies, and increasing the number of states that have initiated or completed statewide plans.[18] Program officials now estimate that a minimum level of interoperability will not occur until 2008, and it is unknown when full interoperability will occur.

In addition, the Intelligence Reform and Terrorism Prevention Act of 2004 required DHS to establish a program to enhance public safety interoperable communications at all levels of government, including federal, as well as state and local governments.[19] SAFECOM has been designated as the program responsible for carrying out this requirement.

SAFECOM Has Not Taken Action to Address Interoperability with Federal First Responders

While SAFECOM is required to improve interoperable communications at all levels of government, the objectives that the program has been working toward do not include improving interoperability between federal agencies and state and local agencies. For example, when conducting their baseline national survey of first responders to determine the current level of interoperability, program officials included state and local officials, but not federal officials. The survey included an extensive list of questions in which respondents were asked to rate interoperability (1) with other disciplines, (2) with other jurisdictions, and (3) between state and local governments. Respondents were also asked at the end of the survey to list federal agencies they interoperate with; however, no effort was made to gauge the level of interoperability with the federal government, as had been done for other disciplines and jurisdictions and between state and local governments.

As a result, SAFECOM has not addressed a variety of problems involving interoperability between federal and state and local agencies. According to first responders, these difficulties arise when trying to establish interoperable communication between federal and state and local agencies:

- *Uncoordinated interoperability investments.* The Departments of Justice, Homeland Security, and Treasury are developing the Integrated Wireless Network (IWN) to create a consolidated federal wireless communications service for federal public safety and law enforcement agencies. The level of interoperability that state and local first responders will have with federal first responders on this network is unknown.
- *Frequency incompatibilities.* The National Telecommunications and Information Administration, which manages frequencies used by federal agencies, and the Federal Communications Commission, which manages frequencies used by state and local governments, have established conflicting time frames for when federal agencies and state and local agencies need to implement narrowband systems.[20] Further, according to an Associate Chief of DHS's Office of Border Patrol, when federal communications networks are configured to narrowband, federal agencies could have difficulty interoperating with local wideband systems unless

special radios are procured that can operate both on the wideband and narrowband systems.

- *Use of encryption.* Federal agencies, such as the Federal Bureau of Investigation (FBI), use encryption[21] to secure their radio communications. Encryption can be vitally important in preserving the safety and security of their officers. However, they have not developed procedures for sharing the keys to decrypt the communication with state or local first responders in order to be able to communicate with them.
- *Unclear coordination procedures.* There is uncertainty within the first responder community regarding the allowable level of coordination and collaboration between federal agencies and state and local agencies. For example, while the National Telecommunications and Information Administration eliminated its requirement that state and local officials obtain written permission to use federal frequencies in May 2006, FBI officials that we interviewed were unaware that they were allowed to share their frequencies without written permission.

In lieu of having communications systems that enable direct interoperability between federal first responders and state and local first responders, first responders have resorted to alternative means of communicating. For example, state or local agencies may loan radios to federal first responders or physically pair a federal first responder with a state or local responder so they can share information and relay it back to their agencies. While approaches such as these may be effective in certain situations, they reflect a general lack of planning for communications interoperability. In many cases, using "work-arounds" such as these could reduce the efficiency and effectiveness of the overall public safety response to an incident.

SAFECOM officials stated that the program's focus has been on state and local agencies because they consider them to be a higher priority. Further, while they stated that it would be possible for federal agencies to make use of some of the planning tools being developed primarily for state and local agencies, SAFECOM has not developed any tools that directly address interoperability with federal agencies. However, interoperability with federal first responders remains an important element in achieving nationwide interoperability and is part of SAFECOM's tasking under the Intelligence Reform and Terrorism Prevention Act of 2004. Until a federal coordinating entity such as SAFECOM makes a concerted effort to promote federal interoperability with other governmental entities, overall progress in improving communications interoperability will remain limited.

SAFECOM Tools and Assistance Have Had Limited Impact on State and Local Agencies

In addition to supporting development of the Project 25 suite of interoperability standards (discussed in a later section of this report),

SAFECOM's activities have focused primarily on providing planning tools to state and local governments. However, based on our review of four states and selected localities, SAFECOM's progress in achieving its goals of helping these states and localities improve interoperable communications has been limited.

Several state and local officials did not find the tools and guidance useful. For example, of the 10 locations[22] we visited that were aware of the tools and guidance, 6 had not used the programs' Statement of Requirements or its Public Safety Architecture Framework. Additionally, 3 of the 4 states we reviewed had not used its Statewide Communication Interoperability Planning Methodology to develop a statewide communication plan. Further, officials from 4 of the 15 jurisdictions we reviewed were unaware that the SAFECOM program existed or that it provided interoperability guidance.

SAFECOM's Interoperability Continuum was the most widely used and recognized of its tools. Seven of the 15 states and localities we visited indicated that they used the continuum to assess their interoperability status and plan improvements. Another initiative that had a significant impact was the Regional Communications Interoperability Pilot. Officials from Kentucky—one of the two states that participated in the pilot—indicated that the pilot was very helpful in facilitating communications planning by identifying relevant stakeholders and bringing those stakeholders together for extended discussions about interoperability. And in Nevada, this program resulted in documentation of suggested near-term and long-term goals for improving interoperability.

However, the SAFECOM tools that were not widely used represent a significant investment of resources by DHS. For example, program officials said that they spent $9.2 million developing the Statement of Requirements and $2.7 million developing the Public Safety Architecture Framework.

State and local officials provided the following reasons for the limited utilization of SAFECOM tools:

- The tools and guidance are too abstract and do not provide practical implementation guidance on specific issues. For instance, the Statement of Requirements focuses on functional requirements based on textbook definitions of a variety of interoperable communication subjects, such as public safety communication needs, public safety roles and functions, and the levels of operability and interoperability for each major public safety discipline. SAFECOM officials indicated that the Statement of Requirements was meant to be a forward-looking document unconstrained by the limitations of current technology. However, states and localities must work to improve interoperability with technology that is currently available, and the Statement of Requirements does not describe specific technologies, infrastructure, or business models that state and local agencies can refer to when making key decisions regarding improvements to their communication systems. Additionally, neither the Statement of Requirements nor the Public Safety Architecture Framework identifies specific actions a state or local agency can take to make improvements.

- The documents are lengthy and hard to use as reference tools. For example, the two published volumes of the Public Safety Architecture Framework are approximately 270 pages combined and contain complex information about topics such as the elements and subelements of communication systems and their relationships to each other and to the environment. Officials indicated that they do not have the time to examine and analyze long reports that they believed contained limited useful information. According to SAFECOM officials, they plan to address this concern by publishing a third volume to guide public safety agency officials through the process of developing a communications system architecture. However, even with additional guidance, the framework will remain lengthy and complex.
- Awareness of SAFECOM and its tools has not reached all state and local agencies. Program officials indicated that they take steps to try to reach out to the broad first responder community, such as by publishing articles in major police and fire periodicals, presenting at events covering communications interoperability, and publishing a quarterly newsletter on interoperability issues called Interoperability Today. However, despite these efforts, several localities that we visited were completely unfamiliar with the program and/or the assistance it provides.

Figure 3 identifies which of SAFECOM's tools, guidance, or other assistance were used by officials at the locations we visited.

Figure 3: Use of SAFECOM Tools, Guidance, and Assistance, by Location

	Florida	Lee County, FL	Miami UASI, FL	Kentucky	Montgomery County, KY	Louisville UASI, KY	New York	Albany County, NY	Onondaga County, NY	NYC UASI, NY	Oregon	Marion County, OR	Jackson County, OR	Portland UASI, OR
Tools applicable to all regions														
Statement of Requirements			X	X			X							X
Public Safety Architecture Framework			X				X							
Interoperability Continuum	X		X			X	X			X	X			X
Statewide Communication Interoperability Planning Methodology				X										X
Tools applicable to UASI areas														
RapidCom			X							X				

Source: GAO analysis of SAFECOM data

Note: We visited 15 locations; however, Franklin County, Kentucky, did not indicate which tools they use.

Recently, SAFECOM has focused more on specific implementation issues, creating tools such as a writing guide for developing memorandums of understanding that could be used to establish agreements on the sharing of communication systems across agencies and jurisdictions. Officials have also developed a guide for writing standard operating procedures, which could be used to prepare written guidelines for incident response. Because these tools were still new, we did not receive assessments of them from state and local officials.

Lack of Program Plan and Performance Measures Has Contributed to SAFECOM's Limited Impact

One factor contributing to the limited impact that SAFECOM has had on improving communications interoperability is that its activities have not been guided by a program plan. A program plan is a critical tool to ensure a program meets its goals and responsibilities. Such a tool is used to align planned activities with program goals and objectives, as well as define how progress in meeting the goals will be measured, compared, and validated. For example, a program plan could be a useful tool for ensuring that key program goals—such as promoting interoperability across all levels of government including federal responders—are being addressed. In addition, a program plan would provide the structure to help plan tools and guidance that would address the greatest needs. Further, a program plan could be used to delineate performance measures, which are essential to determining the effectiveness of a program and for identifying the areas of a program that need additional attention.

Rather than using a program plan to guide their activities, SAFECOM officials stated that they develop tools and guidance based on a list of suggestions obtained from first responders. The SAFECOM Executive Committee—a steering group comprised of public safety officials from across the country—prioritizes the list of suggestions, but this prioritization has not been used to develop a plan. Instead, program officials have made ad hoc decisions regarding which suggestions to implement based on executive committee input, as well as the difficulty of implementation. While this approach incorporates a degree of prioritization from first responders, it does not provide the structure and traceability of a program plan.

Program officials have established six performance measures[23] to assess progress, including the percentage of fire, emergency medical services, and law enforcement organizations that have established informal interoperability agreements with other public safety organizations; the percentage of public safety agencies that report using interoperability to some degree in their operations; the percentage of states that have completed statewide interoperability plans; the percentage of grant programs for public safety communications that include SAFECOM guidance; and the amount of reduction in the cycle time for national interoperability standards development. However, several key aspects of the program are not being measured. For example, one of the program's goals is to increase the development and adoption of standards. However, the only associated performance measure is reduction in the cycle time for national interoperability standards development—not the extent to which adoption of standards has increased or whether interoperability is being facilitated. Also, in assessing the growth of interoperable communications capacity at local, tribal, and state public safety agencies, SAFECOM's measures—the percentage of states that have established informal interoperability agreements with other public safety organizations and the percentage of public safety agencies that report using interoperability to some degree in their operations—addresses only two of the five areas that SAFECOM has defined as key to improving interoperability (it does not assess improvements made in governance, technology, or training). Moreover, none of the program's measures assess the extent to which the first responder community finds the tools and assistance helpful or the effectiveness of program outreach initiatives. Consequently, measures of the effectiveness of the program and areas for improvement are not being collected and are not driving improvements in the program, contributing to its limited impact. According to SAFECOM officials, by mid-2007, they plan to establish a measure to assess customer satisfaction.

Until DHS develops and implements a program plan that includes goals focusing on improving interoperability among all levels of government, establishes performances measures that determine if key aspects of the SAFECOM program are being achieved, and assesses the extent to which the first responder community finds the tools and assistance helpful, the impact of its efforts to improve interoperable communications among federal, state, and local agencies will likely remain limited.

Recent Progress Has Been Made in Developing Interoperability Standards, but Early Implementation Has Had Unsatisfactory Results

Until recently, little progress had been made in developing Project 25 standards—a suite of national standards that are intended to enable interoperability among the communications products of different vendors. Although one of the eight major subsets of standards was defined in the project's first 4 years (from 1989 to 1993), from 1993 through 2005, no additional standards were completed that could be used by a vendor to develop elements of a Project 25 compliant system. To its credit, over the past 2 years, the private-sector coordinating body responsible for Project 25 has defined specifications for three additional subsets of standards. However, ambiguities in the published standards have led to incompatibilities among products made by different vendors, and no compliance testing has been conducted to ensure vendors' products are interoperable. Nevertheless, DHS has strongly encouraged state and local agencies to use grant funding to purchase Project 25 radios, which are substantially more expensive than non-Project 25 radios. As a result, states and local agencies have purchased fewer, more expensive radios, which still may not be interoperable and thus may provide them with minimal additional benefits. Until DHS modifies its grant guidance to provide more flexibility in purchasing communications equipment, states and localities that purchase Project 25 equipment cannot be assured that their investments are likely to result in meaningful gains in interoperability.

Until Recently, Progress in Developing Interoperability Standards Had Been Slow

Initial development of Project 25 began over 15 years ago. It took 4 years, from 1989 to 1993, to develop the standards that comprised the first of eight interfaces, known as the common air interface. The common air interface is one of the most critical elements of Project 25, and, therefore, efforts to develop standards for this interface were initiated first. However, from 1993 through 2005, no additional standards were developed that could be used by a vendor to develop additional elements of a Project 25 compliant system.

Concerned about the slow development of Project 25 standards, the conference committee on the Consolidated Appropriations Act for fiscal year 2005,[24] encouraged NIST and the Department of Justice to work with SAFECOM to consider the issuance of interim standards for interoperable communication systems. According to NIST officials, they, along with their federal partners, have established a process for developing interim standards and plan to institute it if progress in the development of Project 25 standards is not sufficiently accelerated. Industry representatives and public safety practitioners responded to these events by increasing the pace and scope of their standards development activities. As a result of their efforts, in the past 2 years, significant progress has been made in defining three additional critical interfaces: the fixed station subsystem interface, the console subsystem interface, and the inter-RF subsystem interface. NIST officials indicated that the focus has been on these interfaces because they will add significant functionality to the overall set of Project 25 standards.

Table 4 shows the progress that has been made on each of the eight Project 25 interfaces as of August 2006. Figure 4 shows the relationships among these interfaces.

Table 4: Status of Project 25 Interfaces

Interface	Description	Status	NIST projection for product availability[a]
Common air interface	Defines the wireless access between mobile and portable radios and between the portable and mobile radios and the fixed or base station radios.	This interface is considered the most mature of the eight interfaces; however, parts of it are currently being revised to clarify ambiguities. A full set of product compliance tests is not yet available.	Currently available.
Subscriber data peripheral interface	Characterizes the signaling for data transfer that must take place between radios and the data devices connected to the radios.	The interface is being redeveloped to align with other interfaces. In addition, there are no tests currently in place for this interface to test product compliance.	Limited availability of products that contain proprietary components.
Fixed station subsystem interface	Describes the signaling and messages between the radio frequency subsystem and the fixed/base station subsystem and between the console subsystem and the fixed/base station subsystem.	The initial version of standards has been developed for this interface; however, more work remains before this interface will be completed, such as developing compliance testing standards.	2007
Console subsystem interface	Defines the signaling between the radio frequency subsystem and the console subsystem.	The initial version of the standards is in the final stages of completion and is expected to be published in early 2007. Compliance testing standards are under development.	2007-2008
Network management interface	Allows administrators to control and monitor the network fault management and network performance management.	The interface is being redeveloped to align with other interfaces. In addition, there are no standards currently in place for this interface to test products for compliance.	To be determined.

Interface	Description	Status	NIST projection for product availability[a]
Data network interface	Describes the radio frequency subsystem's connections to computers, data networks, external data sources, etc.	The interface is being redeveloped to align with other interfaces. In addition, there are no standards currently in place for this interface to test products for Project 25 compliance.	Limited availability of products that contain proprietary components.
Telephone interconnect interface	Allows users to connect through the public switched telephone network using their radios rather than cellular phones.	Standards have been developed for the interface; however, work remains before this interface will be completed, such as developing compliance testing standards.	To be determined.
Inter-RF subsystem interface	Allows users in one system to communicate with users in another system.	The initial version of this standard was published in mid 2006. Compliance testing standards are under development.	2007

Source: GAO analysis of NIST and TIA data

[a] This information is based on NIST's working knowledge of Project 25 product lines. NIST has not performed a worldwide inventory of Project 25 products.

Figure 4: Project 25 Interfaces

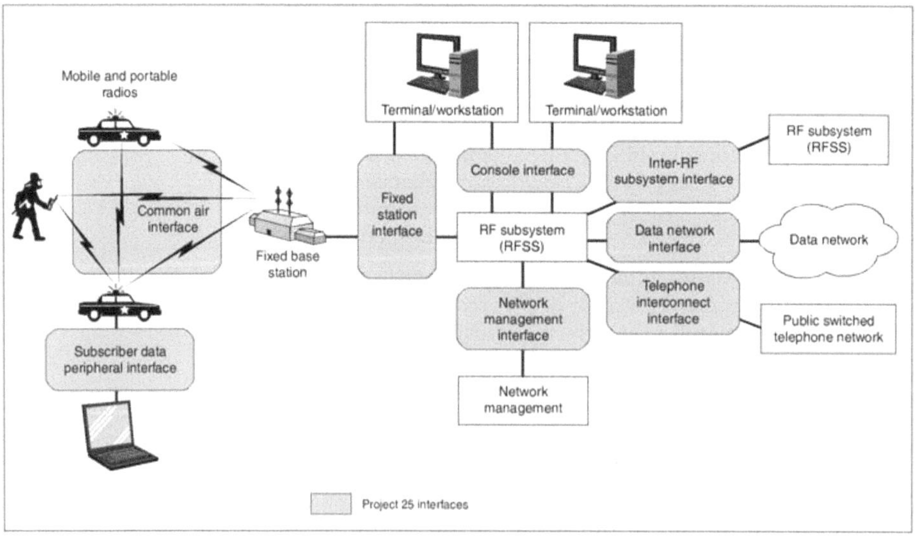

Sources: GAO analysis of TIA and NIST data

Implementation of Systems Based on Incomplete Project 25 Standards Has Been Problematic

There are a number of obstacles hindering effective implementation of first responder communications systems based on Project 25 standards:

- *Standards are incomplete or not well-defined:* NIST officials have stated that key standards that have been defined for several of the eight interfaces have not been adequately specified, allowing vendors to develop products based on inconsistent interpretations. For example, Project 25 manufacturers have determined that the specifications for the conventional and trunked mode operations of the common air interface—which is considered to be the most mature of the eight interfaces—were vague and led to inconsistent interpretations. More specifically, between 2003 and 2005, NIST conducted interoperability tests on the conventional operations mode of six different manufacturers' radios and found that none of them passed all aspects of the tests. In addition, according to NIST officials, in 2005, a manufacturer conducted interoperability tests on the trunked operations mode of three manufacturers' radios and also found that none of them passed the tests. More recently, in 2006, a manufacturer conducting interoperability tests found improvements in the consistency of other manufacturers' interpretations. However, according to NIST officials, ambiguities still need to be resolved in this interface. Additionally, many options available on radios are not specified in the standards, allowing vendors to address these capabilities with unique or proprietary technologies, which can cause interoperability problems. As a result, while recent tests have shown improvements, vendors have developed incompatible, proprietary products rather than interoperable, standards-based products.
- *Lack of compliance testing has limited product interoperability:* According to NIST officials, formal peer-review testing is necessary to ensure compliance with standards and interoperability among products. We have previously reported[25] that independent testing and evaluation of commercial products and accreditation of the laboratories that perform the test and evaluations can give agencies increased assurance that the products will perform as vendors claim. However, since 1995, Project 25 radios have been marketed to and purchased by federal, state, and local agencies without any formal compliance testing to validate vendors' claims of compliance with the Project 25 standards. As a result, recent testing has shown that products labeled "Project 25 compliant" do not necessarily interoperate.
- *State and local agencies do not know how to select Project 25 products:* With no formal compliance testing for Project 25 products, state and local agencies have limited means to determine if the products they purchase are compliant with the standards. Therefore, in absence of any other information, agencies have relied on information provided by vendors. Further, vendor

products have many different levels of functionality, and agency officials may not understand their specific needs well enough to purchase equipment tailored to their specific requirements that does not include costly functionality that they do not need. However, comparative information about product functionality and typical first responder requirements is not currently in a centralized location, making it difficult for officials to be able to judge which products are most appropriate for their agency's needs. For example, according to one manufacturer, public works agencies and schools would likely need radios with less functionality, while firefighters would likely need a midrange radio with more features, and a command center or federal law enforcement agency might need the most expensive radios with the greatest number of features. Because of the complexity of product options, agencies may not always be making well-informed decisions on the purchase of radios.

- *Complete Project 25 systems can be prohibitively expensive:* Project 25 radios are significantly more expensive than conventional analog radios, and while state and local agencies are paying two to three times more for Project 25 radios, they are not always able to take advantage of the intended interoperability benefits because they cannot afford to procure complete systems. Project 25 radios for first responders can range in price from about $1,000 to about $5,000. Most Project 25 radios used by first responders cost around $2,500. According to officials, a conventional analog radio suitable for first responder work generally costs about two to three times less than Project 25 radios. Benefits of using Project 25 radios, such as interoperability among multiple vendors' equipment, cannot be fully realized until a complete Project 25 system (base stations, repeaters, and radios) is implemented. Fully replacing an existing radio system with a Project 25 system is very expensive. For example, Arlington County, Virginia—a relatively small county—is acquiring and implementing a full Project 25 environment for $16.8 million. Many localities do not have the funding to make such a large investment.

Nevertheless, since 2003, DHS has strongly encouraged state and local agencies to use grant funding from the agency to purchase Project 25 compliant equipment. DHS grant guidance—which was developed by SAFECOM—states that all new voice system purchases should be compatible with the Project 25 suite of standards to ensure that equipment or systems are capable of interoperating with other public safety land mobile equipment or systems. If a grant applicant is interested in purchasing non-Project 25 compliant equipment, the applicant must demonstrate in its application that the system or equipment being proposed will lead to enhanced interoperability.

While states and localities have purchased Project 25 radios at the direction of DHS, there is little indication that these radios have enhanced interoperability. Most jurisdictions we visited were not using the Project 25 capabilities, such as interoperating with different vendors' radios, since they had not fully replaced their existing radio communications infrastructure with a complete Project 25 system. Specifically, of the 11 localities we visited, 8 were buying Project 25 radios and, of these, 7 were not using the Project 25 capabilities of the radios. Thus, as a result of the DHS requirement to buy Project 25 equipment, agencies have purchased fewer, more expensive radios with little or no additional benefit to date.

Table 5 shows a sample of spending by localities on Project 25 radios and their use of the Project 25 capabilities.

Table 5: Sample Project 25 Radio Purchases

Locality	Number of Project 25 radios purchased	Average Price per radio	Amount spent on Project 25 radios	Using Project 25 capabilities
Lee County, Florida	2,056	$4,305,850	$2,094	No
Albany County, New York	91	$120,879	$1,328	No
Louisville, Kentucky	52	$234,099	$4,502	Yes
Jackson County, Oregon	169	$571,338	$3,380	No

Source: GAO analysis of localities' data

Note: This table represents Project 25 radio purchases for which data was available and, therefore, may not include all Project 25 radio purchases by these localities.

Efforts Are Underway to Mitigate Project 25 Problems

To address the lack of well-defined standards, users and manufacturers have been revising the standards for the conventional and trunked mode operations of the common air interface to clarify ambiguities. To address the issue of a lack of formal compliance testing, SAFECOM, NIST, and the Project 25 steering committee, began developing a peer compliance assessment program for Project 25 products in April 2005. This compliance assessment program is to use various vendors' approved laboratories[26] to test Project 25 systems through a set of agreed-upon tests that will validate that the systems from various vendors can successfully interoperate and meet conformance and performance requirements. According to NIST, the vendors will be expected to conduct the tests in compliance with a handbook on general testing procedures and requirements, which NIST is preparing to publish. The assessment program is to be implemented in three phases, as described in Table 6.

Table 6: Development Schedule for Project 25 Compliance Assessment Program

Stage	Description	Status
Stage I	NIST is to develop a formal laboratory approval process for manufacturers to conduct compliance testing and a process handbook. Conduct initial common air interface testing. NIST and its partners will develop an automated test software suite to facilitate Project 25 performance testing, which will be made available for use by test laboratories and manufacturers. Subscriber units and base stations will also be evaluated for performance.	NIST is working to finalize the formal laboratory approval process, and the process handbook. Parts of the trunked interoperability test standard for the common air interface are complete. Informal testing is expected to begin by March 2007. Formal testing is expected to being by mid-2007. The automated test software suite to facilitate Project 25 common air interface performance testing is expected to be available by early 2007. Other aspects of the trunked mode for the common air interface are being revised and, therefore, these aspects will not be tested until such revisions are made.
Stage II	Test procedures will be developed and executed that will demonstrate the interoperability of Project 25 radios in both trunked and conventional modes of operation.	Development and completion of remaining test procedures for the common air interface are contingent upon completion of revisions to parts of this interface. The conventional mode interoperability test standard is expected to be available in mid-2007.
Stage III	Development of test procedures for the other critical Project 25 interfaces.	Conformance test procedures are currently being developed for the inter-RF subsystem interface and the fixed station subsystem interface. Performance test procedures are currently being developed for the inter-RF subsystem interface and the console subsystem interface. In addition, the interoperability test standards for the inter-RF subsystem interface are in the initial stages of development.

Source: GAO analysis of NIST data

Additionally, SAFECOM has issued guidance to supplement the 2007 DHS grant guidance stating that, beginning in fiscal year 2007, grant recipients purchasing Project 25 equipment must obtain documented evidence from the manufacturer that the equipment has been tested and passed all available compliance assessment test procedures for performance, conformance, and interoperability. The guidance also specifies the aspects of Project 25 equipment that are available for testing and that should be tested before a public safety agency acquires the equipment. However, as of January 2007, only limited aspects of the common air interface had been defined fully enough to conduct interoperability tests. Further, NIST's testing procedures handbook was not yet complete and thus vendors were unable to conduct testing. According to NIST officials, it has not been determined when the full set of conformance, performance, and interoperability tests for the common air interface will be available.

NIST and SAFECOM are also working on ways to help agencies make informed decisions when purchasing Project 25 radios to help them acquire features that are Project 25 compliant. Specifically, NIST and SAFECOM have developed a decision tree to help guide officials in selecting the appropriate Project 25 capabilities. NIST has also helped to develop a new process for posting test results online so that potential buyers can have ready access to this information.

While efforts are under way to address several of these issues, others remain. Specifically, DHS continues to strongly encourage state and local agencies to purchase Project 25 compliant equipment even though compliance testing is not yet available. Without flexibility to address their needs with equipment that is the most effective, economical, and meets defined interoperability requirements aligned with a statewide plan, states and localities that purchase Project 25 equipment cannot be assured that their investments are likely to result in meaningful gains in interoperability.

Conclusions

DHS grants, along with its technical assistance, have helped to make improvements on a variety of specific interoperability projects. However, in selected states, strategic planning has generally not been used to guide investments or provide assistance to improve communications interoperability across all levels of government. Specifically, not all states had plans in place to guide their investments toward long-term interoperability gains; no national plan was in place to coordinate investments across states; and while UASI officials stated that the technical assistance offered to them had been helpful, DHS curtailed full-scale exercises, limiting their value in measuring progress. Until DHS takes a more strategic approach to improving interoperable communications, such as including in its decision making an assessment of how grant requests align with statewide communications plans, and conducts a thorough assessment to identify strategies to mitigate obstacles between federal agencies and state and local agencies, states and localities are likely to make limited progress in improving interoperability. Additionally, until DHS plans another round of full-scale exercises that provide UASI areas with sufficient planning time, the robustness and effectiveness of UASI plans will be limited.

The SAFECOM program has had a limited impact on improving communications interoperability among federal, state, and local agencies. The program's limited effectiveness can be linked to poor program management practices, such as the lack of a plan for improving interoperability across all levels of government, and inadequate performance measures to fully gauge the effectiveness of its tools and assistance. The recent establishment of the OEC creates an opportunity for DHS to improve program management practices among formerly separate component organizations, including SAFECOM. Without a program plan for SAFECOM and other OEC interoperability programs that specifically addresses improvements to interoperable communications from federal to state and local agencies, and includes measures to assess the usefulness of its efforts, the effectiveness of the program is likely to remain limited.

While development of a comprehensive suite of standards such as Project 25 is critical to achieving interoperability among different manufacturers' products, such a suite is not yet fully developed. Further, ambiguities in published standards have led to incompatibilities among products made by different vendors and, to date, no compliance testing has been conducted to ensure that vendors' products interoperate. Nevertheless, DHS has strongly encouraged state and local agencies to use grant funding to purchase Project 25 compliant equipment. Until DHS modifies its grant guidance to give states and localities the flexibility to address their communications equipment needs effectively, economically, and in a way that meets interoperability requirements as defined in their statewide plans, states and local agencies are likely to continue to purchase expensive equipment that provides them with minimal additional benefits.

Recommendations for Executive Action

To better ensure that progress is made in improving interoperable communications among federal, state, and local first responders, we recommend that the Secretary of Homeland Security take the following five actions:

- assess how states' grant requests support their statewide communications plans and include the assessment as a factor in making DHS grant allocation decisions;
- plan for new full-scale exercises for UASI areas that provides local officials with sufficient time to develop and implement exercises to validate the robustness and effectiveness of their tactical interoperable communications plans;
- develop and implement a program plan for SAFECOM and other OEC interoperability programs that includes goals focused on improving interoperability among all levels of government;
- include in the program plan for SAFECOM and other OEC interoperability programs quantifiable performance measures that can be used to determine the extent to which each of the goals have been accomplished and that can be used to assess the effectiveness and usefulness of SAFECOM tools, assistance, and outreach, and make improvements based on the feedback; and

- modify grant guidance to provide more flexibility in purchasing communications equipment until standards for completed interfaces have been fully defined and products have been certified compliant.

Agency Comments and Our Evaluation

We received written comments from the Deputy Secretary of Commerce and the Director of the DHS liaison office for GAO and the Office of the Inspector General. Letters from these agencies are reprinted in appendixes III and IV. Commerce provided updated information and technical comments to help ensure the information in the report is accurately perceived. We have incorporated these comments as appropriate.

In its response to our five recommendations, DHS agreed with two, stated that it would defer commenting on two, and disagreed with one recommendation.

Regarding our recommendation that DHS develop and implement a program plan for SAFECOM and other Office of Emergency Communications (OEC) interoperability programs that includes goals focused on improving interoperability among all levels of government, the Director indicated that DHS agrees with the intent of the recommendation and stated that the department is currently working to develop a program plan.

However, DHS raised concern about the perceived implication that no action had been taken. It stated that SAFECOM has always had goals for improving interoperability among local, state, tribal, and federal emergency response agencies. Our review showed that while the program has had broad goals that include federal, as well as state and local agencies, its specific program goals and activities have not focused on improving interoperable communications between federal and other agencies. For example, one of the program's goals is to increase interoperable communications capacity of local, tribal, and state public safety agencies, not federal agencies. Thus, it will be important for DHS to develop and implement a program plan that includes goals focusing on improving interoperability among all levels of government.

DHS agreed with our recommendation to include quantifiable performance measures in the program plan for SAFECOM and other OEC interoperability programs. DHS indicated that it intends to establish such measures by the third quarter of 2007.

DHS stated that it is deferring comments on two recommendations: (1) assess how states' grant requests support their statewide communications plans and (2) plan for a new full-scale exercise for UASI areas to validate their interoperable communications plans.

DHS disagreed with our recommendation that it modify grant guidance to provide more flexibility in purchasing communications equipment until standards for completed interfaces have been fully defined and products have been certified compliant with all aspects of the standards. The Director stated that the recommendation would require SAFECOM to amend its interoperability grant guidance until after the entire Project 25 suite of standards is complete and could undermine remaining negotiations between the public safety community and equipment manufacturers. We agree that development of a comprehensive suite of standards such as Project 25 is critical to achieving interoperability among different manufacturers' products. We also agree that not all interfaces need to be fully defined before agencies can begin acquiring Project 25 products; thus we have clarified the recommendation to reflect this. However, we are not recommending that the public safety community be prohibited from acquiring Project 25 equipment, and thus we do not believe negotiations with equipment manufacturers would be undermined. Until critical interfaces are better defined and products have been certified compliant, DHS should allow state and local agencies the flexibility to purchase whatever products they can obtain that offer the best value and performance for their needs.

DHS also stated that it estimates that the Project 25 standards will be complete within the next 18 to 24 months, and stated that fiscal year 2007 grant funding will be spent by local public safety agencies not in fiscal year 2007 but in subsequent years. We have modified the discussion of this issue in the report to reflect this information. However, as previously stated, much additional work remains to be accomplished.

Additionally, DHS stated that our report should include other major programs that focus on interoperability among federal responders, such as the newly created Office of Emergency Communications within DHS, the Integrated Wireless Network, the Interoperable Communications Technical Assistance Program, and the Federal Partnership for Interoperable Communications. However, our report does discuss the first three of these. The primary purpose of the Federal Partnership for Interoperable Communications is to serve as a coordinating body to address technical and operational activities within the federal wireless community; it has limited applicability to state and local interoperability.

Finally, DHS raised concern with our view that SAFECOM had mistakenly made local, tribal, and state emergency responders its highest priority. DHS stated that when SAFECOM was established as one of the electronic government initiatives, it was placed within the government-to-government portfolio. According to DHS, state and local government agencies are the primary customers of this portfolio. However, according to OMB, the goal of the government-to-government portfolio is to forge new partnerships among all levels of government, not just state and local. Additionally, as we have previously stated, when SAFECOM was initially established, one of its major goals was to achieve federal to state/local interoperability. However, it is no longer a goal for SAFECOM. DHS also stated that since 90 percent of the public safety infrastructure is owned, operated, and maintained by local jurisdictions, state and local interoperability is a higher priority. However, our review has shown that in major incidents such as a terrorist attack, a major hurricane, or wildland fire, federal, state, and local first responders will need to interoperate in order to respond effectively to the incident. Therefore, interoperability with federal first responders should be included as a key element in the department's strategy for improving interoperable communications throughout the nation.

DHS also provided technical comments, which we have incorporated as appropriate.

We are sending copies of this report to the Secretaries of Homeland Security and Commerce and other interested congressional committees and subcommittees. We also will make copies available to others upon request. In addition, the report will be available at no charge on the GAO Web site at http://www.gao.gov.

Should you or your staff have any questions on matters discussed in this report, please contact me at (202) 512-6240 or by e-mail at koontzl@gao.gov. Contact points for our Offices of Congressional Relations and Public Affairs may be found on the last page of this report. Key contributors to this report are listed in appendix V.

Linda D. Koontz Director,
Information Management Issues

Keith A. Rhodes
Chief Technologist
Director, Center for Technology and Engineering

William O. Jenkins, Jr.
Director, Homeland Security and Justice Issues

Endnotes

1 We were unable to meet with local officials from Florida's state capital region.

2 Intelligence Reform and Terrorism Prevention Act of 2004, P.L. 108-458, section 7303, 118 Stat. 3638, 3843-44, Dec. 17, 2004.

3 National Commission on Terrorist Attacks Upon the United States, *The 9/11 Commission Report* (Washington, D.C: 2004), 322-3.

4 For more information on the need for better frequency planning and coordination, see GAO, *Homeland Security: Federal Leadership and Intergovernmental Cooperation Required to Achieve First Responder Interoperable Communications*, GAO-04-740 (Washington, D.C.: July 20, 2004).

5 Voice over Internet Protocol, also called VoIP, is the routing of voice conversations over the Internet or any other Internet Protocol network.

6 GAO-04-740.

7 GAO, *Project SAFECOM: Key Cross-Agency Emergency Communications Effort Requires Stronger Collaboration*, GAO-04-494 (Washington, D.C.: Apr. 16, 2004).

8 GAO-04-494.

9 Each year the number of urban areas designated as a UASI area changes. In 2005, DHS designated 43 UASI areas, and in 2006 DHS reduced the number of UASI areas to 35 (11 areas that had previously participated in the program but did not fall within in the top 35 urban areas in the 2006 risk analysis were eligible to apply for UASI funding for one additional

grant cycle to help sustain ongoing projects). In 2007, 45 areas were designated as UASI areas.

[10] Department of Homeland Security Appropriations Act, 2007, P.L. 109-295, Title VI, Subtitle D, section 671, 120 Stat. 1355, 1433-35, Oct. 4, 2006 (enacting new section 1801 of the Homeland Security Act of 2002, 6 U.S.C. 571).

[11] The American National Standards Institute coordinates and oversees the development and use of voluntary standards in the United States and participates in accrediting programs that assess conformance to standards.

[12] Department of Homeland Security Appropriations Act, 2007, P.L. 109-295, Title VI, Subtitle D, section 671, 120 Stat. 1355, 1438 Oct. 4, 2006 (enacting new section 1804 of the Homeland Security Act of 2002, 6 U.S.C. 574).

[13] GAO-04-740.

[14] The committee was established by the Federal Communications Commission and the National Telecommunications and Information Administration to evaluate the wireless communications needs of federal, state, and local public safety agencies.

[15] Department of Homeland Security Appropriations Act, 2007, P.L. 109-295, Title VI, Subtitle D, section 671, 120 Stat. 1355, 1435-36, Oct. 4, 2006 (enacting new section 1802 of the Homeland Security Act of 2002, 6 U.S.C. 572).

[16] The 25 e-government initiatives were established by the Office of Management and Budget to simplify and unify agency work processes and information flows, provide one-stop services to citizens, and enable information to be collected on line once and reused, rather than being collected many times.

[17] GAO-04-494.

[18] The program also had a goal of increasing the development and adoption of standards. Standards development is discussed in a separate section below.

[19] Intelligence Reform and Terrorism Prevention Act of 2004, P.L. 108-458, section 7303, 118 Stat. 3638, 3843-44, Dec. 17, 2004.

[20] Narrowband refers to the method of gaining more channels (and hence more capacity) by splitting channels into channels that are narrower in bandwidth.

[21] Encryption is the process of transforming ordinary data (commonly referred to as plaintext) into code form (ciphertext) using a special value known as a key and a mathematical process called an algorithm. Cryptographic algorithms are designed to produce ciphertext that is unintelligible to unauthorized users. Decryption of ciphertext is possible by using the proper key.

[22] We visited 15 locations. However, Franklin County, Kentucky, did not indicate which tools they use, and 4 localities were unfamiliar with the SAFECOM's Statement of Requirements and its Public Safety Architecture Framework.

[23] SAFECOM officials have recently added a sixth performance measure that is intended to measure "percent of federal agencies aligning to the SAFECOM program," however the measure does not reflect federal agency alignment to the SAFECOM program. Instead, it attempts to measure federal agencies' compliance with Project 25 standards.

[24] H.R. Rep. No. 108-792, 108th Cong., 2d Sess. (2004) at 755.

[25] GAO, *Information Assurance: National Partnership Offers Benefits, but Faces Considerable Challenges*, GAO-06-392 (Washington, D.C.: Mar. 24, 2006). 26 NIST is developing a process for determining manufacturers' laboratories as being "approved."

Appendix I: Objectives, Scope, and Methodology

Our objectives were to determine (1) the extent to which the Department of Homeland Security (DHS) funding and technical assistance have helped to improve interoperable communications in selected states, (2) the progress the SAFECOM program has made in improving interoperable communications, and (3) the progress that has been made in the development and implementation of interoperable communications standards.

To determine the extent to which DHS funding and technical assistance helped to improve interoperable communication in these states, we reviewed documentation and interviewed state and local officials from selected states.

We selected four states as case studies, using the following criteria:

- All of the states must have received at least an average amount of funding from fiscal year 2003 through fiscal year 2005.
- One of the states must have received over $100 million of grant funding for interoperable communications from DHS.
- One of the states must have received assistance from SAFECOM in applying the Statewide Communications Interoperability Planning Methodology.
- One of the states must have had an Urban Area Security Initiative (UASI) area involved in DHS's RapidCom program.
- One of the states must border another country.
- At least one of the states must be one of the top 10 states that regularly faces wildland fires.
- At least one of the states must be one of the top states that regularly faces other large natural disasters, such as hurricanes or earthquakes.

We selected localities from each state to visit, which included (1) the UASI region which received the most funding from DHS, (2) the non-UASI county that received the largest amount of DHS funding, and (3) the county and city where the state capital is located.[1] From each of these states and localities, we obtained and reviewed documentation such as grant funding amounts, Tactical Interoperability Communication Plans, exercise reports, and communication system documentation. We also met with interoperability committee members and first responders. Additionally, we obtained and analyzed documentation from, and met with DHS officials who are responsible for monitoring the use of DHS funds in each of these states.

To determine the progress SAFECOM has made in improving interoperable communications, we reviewed SAFECOM documentation such as its Statewide Communication Interoperability Planning Methodology, Public Safety Architecture Framework, and Statement of Requirements. We also analyzed program management documentation (such as program goals, initiatives, and performance measures), interviewed SAFECOM officials to discuss the progress of the program, and interviewed state and local officials to determine their use of SAFECOM tools and guidance. To obtain Federal Bureau of Investigation (FBI) information, we relied on interviews conducted by another GAO team.

To determine progress in developing and implementing interoperable communications standards, we obtained and reviewed documentation from National Institute of Standards and Technology (NIST) officials on standards development such as status updates and recent testimonies. Additionally, we reviewed documentation from states and localities to determine the extent to which they are implementing Project 25 products and spending on Project 25 products. We also met with officials from NIST and representatives from communications equipment manufactures.

Because our objectives were focused on DHS efforts to improve interoperable communications, we neither assessed programs in other agencies, such as the Federal Communications Commission or the National Telecommunications and Information Administration, nor reviewed issues related to spectrum allocation.[2]

We performed our work in the Washington, D.C., metropolitan area; Tallahassee, Fort Myers, and Miami, Florida; Louisville, Frankfort, and Mount Sterling, Kentucky; Albany, Syracuse, and Brooklyn, New York; and Beaverton, Salem, and Medford, Oregon, from April 2006 to February 2007, in accordance with generally accepted government auditing standards.

Endnotes

[1] We were unable to meet with local officials from Florida's state capital region.

[2] GAO-04-740.

Appendix II:
First Responder Communications Systems within Selected States

There is wide variation in the frequencies (i.e., very high frequency (VHF) and ultra high frequency (UHF)) and radio technologies (i.e., digital, analog, conventional, and trunked) that are used among federal, state, and local agencies within each of the four states we reviewed. A summary of communications systems and interoperability initiatives in each of these four states follows.

Florida

There are over 150 radio systems in use within the state of Florida. To improve interoperability among these systems, Florida officials have developed several centralized solutions that are used throughout the state at all levels of government. Localities maintain their existing communications systems, relying on

Florida's statewide systems only when they need to interoperate with another agency or jurisdiction. According to DHS, Florida has received approximately $55.7[1] million in DHS funding from fiscal year 2003 through fiscal year 2005 to improve interoperable communications.

Governance

Florida's centralized approach entails making funding decisions through a body (the Domestic Security Oversight Council) supported by a hierarchy of communications-related committees that includes local representation from each of the seven regions in the state. According to state officials, for the statewide interoperability solutions, Florida does not allocate DHS funding to local agencies; it takes on the responsibility of centrally purchasing equipment to ensure that all agencies and jurisdictions have equipment that is compatible. UASI grants are awarded directly to the UASI areas; therefore, Florida does not centrally manage those funds.

State Approach

To improve the interoperability among the 150 disparate communications systems throughout the state, Florida officials have developed the following several statewide solutions:

- In 2003, the Domestic Security Oversight Council and its supporting communication committees determined that it would not be economically feasible to replace all existing systems in the state with one new system. It therefore decided to develop a "backbone" system that could connect with each of the existing systems. This system, referred to as the Florida Interoperability Network, establishes network connections between federal, state, and local dispatch centers across the state (see fig. 5). It enables dispatchers to connect first responders on disparate radio systems and frequencies to allow them to directly communicate with one another. Existing independent systems are maintained. According to state officials, as of January 2007, first responders in 64 of Florida's 67 counties are able to have their communications patched to each other as needed via the network.

Figure 5: Illustration of Florida's Interoperability Network

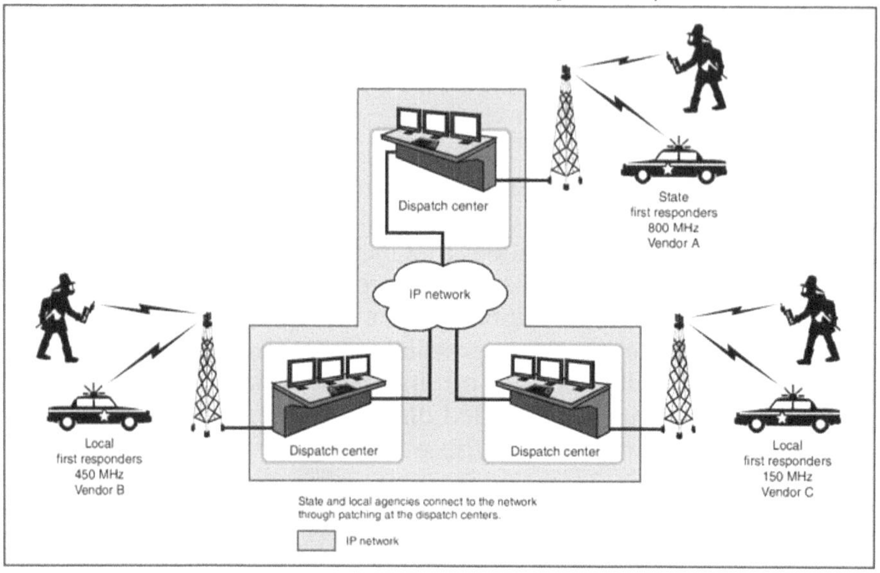

Source: GAO analysis based on Florida data

Legend
IP=Internet Protocol

- As part of the Florida Interoperability Network, Florida officials are also working to establish additional mutual aid channels that are intended to provide radio service to first responders outside the range of their agency's local system or when they need to communicate with users not on their local systems. These channels are intended to expand geographic coverage to ensure that, wherever they go, Florida's first responders have radio communication capability. To this end, officials are adding 428 tower sites to the existing 93 sites across the state.
- Florida also acquired and implemented a radio communications system to serve law enforcement units of state agencies and to serve local public safety agencies through a mutual aid channel. The Statewide Law Enforcement Radio System provides state law enforcement officers with a shared digital, trunked radio system that serves over 6,500 users with 14,000 radios in patrol cars, boats, motorcycles, and aircraft.
- Florida's first federally funded project was the Emergency Deployable Interoperable Communications Systems. These are mobile systems that can be deployed to a specific response area to patch together disparate communications systems. According to state officials, these systems are generally used in one of the following situations: (1) to tie different radio systems together in an area that is not connected to the Florida Interoperability Network, (2) to connect different radio systems together if the network becomes inoperable, or (3) to tie disparate radios together when assisting in an

out-of-state incident, such as Hurricane Katrina. Nine of these systems were purchased and deployed throughout the state.

- Florida has seven Mutual Aid Radio Communications units in the state, and officials are building an additional unit. The units are stand-alone mobile interoperable communications networks. Unlike Emergency Deployable Interoperable Communications Systems, Mutual Aid Radio Communications units include a cache of radios that can be distributed to first responders, a tower, and a mobile repeater system, so no patching needs to be done. These units are used when the local communications systems become inoperable, such as when a hurricane destroys the local communications infrastructure. The units provide temporary infrastructure for a response area to maintain communication during an incident.

Local Approach

Florida localities vary in their approaches and the level of interoperability within their regions. They utilize the statewide solutions to supplement their existing systems. For example, the 35 to 40 different radio systems throughout the Miami UASI area have limited direct interoperability. The Miami region relies on patching mechanisms, including the Florida Interoperability Network, to provide interoperable communications when needed. In contrast, according to officials, government agencies within Lee County, with the exception of the school board, utilize the same communications systems and, therefore, are all directly interoperable. The level of interoperability with surrounding counties varies. When they need to communicate with neighboring jurisdictions or state first responders, they utilize the interoperability network.

Kentucky

While Kentucky first responders coordinate interoperability primarily by sharing frequencies and establishing patches, the state is establishing mutual aid channels to better enable responders on different frequencies to communicate through patches. According to DHS, from fiscal year 2003 through fiscal year 2005, Kentucky received $50 million from DHS for interoperable communications.

Governance

Kentucky's governance structure for interoperable communications is organized centrally at the state level through the Kentucky Wireless Interoperability Executive Committee. To ensure that the committee has an awareness of initiatives across the state, all state agencies and local government entities must present project plans for primary wireless public safety voice or data communications systems for review and recommendation by the committee, even if no state or federal funding is used for the system. While the committee only has the authority to decline or approve projects funded with state or federal dollars, a large majority of local projects are financed through state or federal funding.

State Approach

Kentucky's strategy to improve interoperable communications in the near term is to utilize statewide mutual aid channels that allow agencies on different communication systems to tune into a dedicated frequency shared among one or more public safety agencies. Kentucky also plans to implement communications bridges to patch different systems together.

The mutual aid approach requires the deployment of three channels, one for each frequency band that Kentucky public safety agencies currently use. Currently, approximately 34 percent of applicable agencies have signed a memorandum of understanding to commit to using the mutual aid channels. Other agencies that have not yet signed a memorandum are also utilizing the channels.

Kentucky officials are also in the process of implementing a console-to-console bridge solution that will allow dispatchers to patch users on one frequency to users on another frequency (see fig. 6). For example, a first responder using a lower frequency who needs to talk to a first responder using a higher frequency would contact the Kentucky State Police dispatch center to request a patch. The dispatcher would then use a patching mechanism to patch the two channels so that the responders could talk directly to each other. The solution is operational in two of the three frequency bands and is nearing completion in the third.

Figure 6: Console-to-Console Bridge Solution

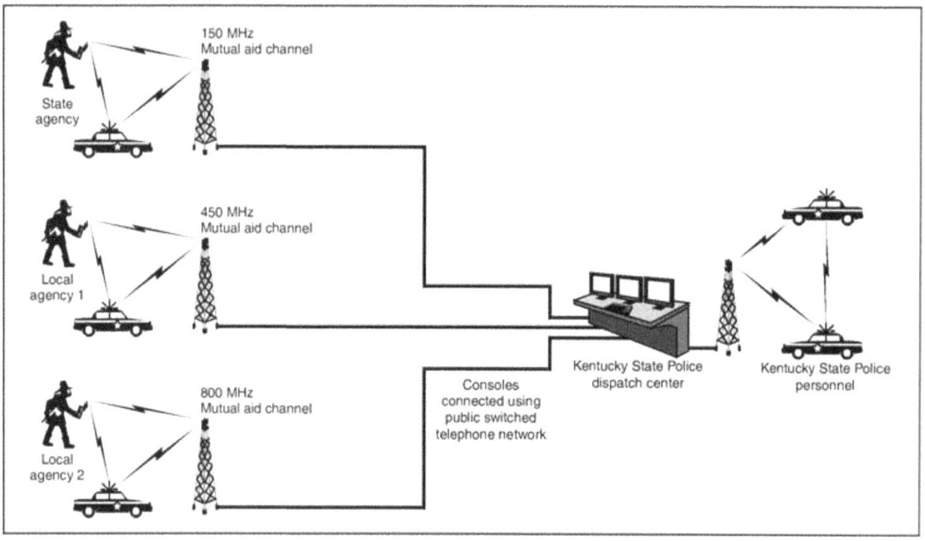

Source: GAO analysis based on Kentucky data

To supplement voice communications interoperability, Kentucky has implemented a wireless data communications interoperability solution as well. This solution provides functionality such as records management, real-time crime coverage, real-time data collection, and instant messaging. The system consists of approximately 165 base stations throughout the state to supply continuous wireless coverage in most regions. First responders use mobile data terminals to communicate with each other and, in many cases, retrieve information from their agency's database. Kentucky's mobile data network currently has coverage across approximately 95 percent of the state's primary and secondary road systems.

In the long term, the state officials intend to build a statewide public safety communications and interoperability infrastructure. They are in the process of completing a statewide baseline communications study as an initial step in the planning phase. No further specific initiatives and milestones have yet been identified for this project.

Local Approach

Interoperability is typically coordinated at the city and county levels. In the jurisdictions we visited, interoperability solutions included planning in advance to program other frequencies into radios, establishing patches through disparate communication systems through a dispatch center, and swapping radios.

In Louisville, Kentucky, both UHF and VHF systems are in use and, when necessary, connected through patching mechanisms. Many responders carry both a UHF and VHF radio in their vehicles. For major incidents, a mobile vehicle with a repeater system can be deployed to connect first responders. In addition, since 2000, Louisville has been utilizing a wireless data communications interoperability solution that includes 550 first responders in the Louisville metropolitan area.

All local agencies within Franklin County use VHF systems; first responders program each others' channels into their radios. Frankfort and Franklin County use mutual aid channels when needed. First responders have difficulty connecting to the Kentucky State Police, as that agency recently switched to a digital, trunked communications system. Currently, to connect to the state police, Frankfort and Franklin police contact a dispatch center and request a patch to Kentucky State Police.

Montgomery County agencies use both UHF and VHF systems. First responders within the county and in neighboring counties typically program each others' channels into their radios. Communication with state agencies varies, for example, fire and EMS agencies in Montgomery County cannot communicate with their state counterparts at present, whereas local police can communicate with the state police through mutual aid channels, or in instances in which they have interoperable radios.

New York

New York is currently in the process of implementing a statewide system that will connect all state agencies and offer connection services to local agencies. This initiative is being funded by the state. Localities continue to develop and maintain their own communication systems and interoperability solutions. According to

DHS, from fiscal year 2003 through fiscal year 2005, New York State has received $145.5 million in grant funding for interoperable communications.

Governance

New York has established a Statewide Interoperability Executive Committee that is currently working to establish a state interoperability plan. In addition, there are several different groups throughout New York that are involved with interoperability at the state and local level. According to state officials, the governance structure limits the state's ability to mandate requirements to local governments; therefore, individual counties and cities determine their own interoperability requirements and have their own governance structure in place for interoperable communications. The state, however, determines priority investments and the localities must spend grant money on these priority investments. Interoperable communications was a priority investment for both grants for fiscal year 2006.

State Approach

The state is currently in the process of deploying a Statewide Wireless Network intended to provide an integrated mobile radio communications network that links all state agencies and would be available to connect participating local agencies (see fig. 7). It will be a digital, trunked radio system with both voice and data capabilities and will be used in day-to-day operations, as well as large scale emergency situations. The network is to interconnect radio sites across the state through a "backbone network" based on Internet Protocol (IP). The network is to operate on the 700 and 800 MHz frequencies, as well as VHF frequencies in geographically challenging terrain, such as the Adirondack and Catskill Mountains. Users operating on other frequencies and with less advanced technology can be connected to the network through a gateway.

Figure 7: The New York Statewide Wireless Network

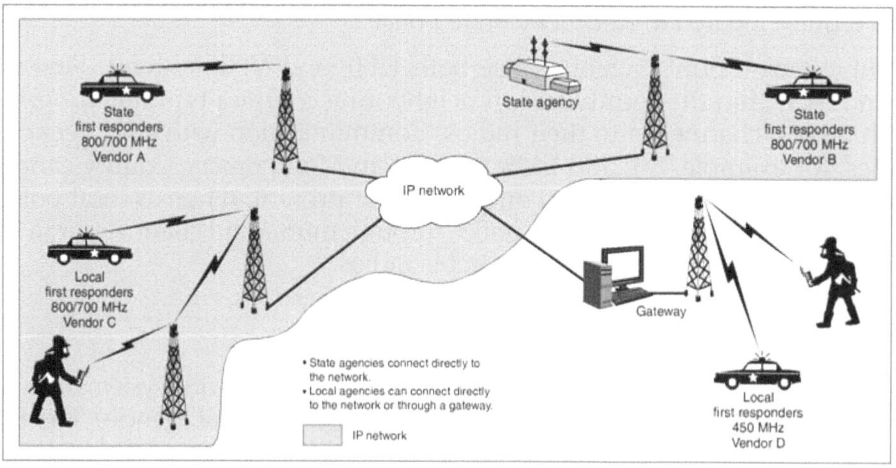

Source: GAO analysis based on New York data

State agencies are required to be a part of the Statewide Wireless Network, but local agencies may join on a volunteer basis. As previously mentioned, according to state officials, they are limited in their ability to require local agencies to utilize the network. Local agencies will have the following three different interoperability options:

- *Full system partnership:* the state will provide the base infrastructure such as radio towers, and the agency will purchase IP-addressable, digital, trunked radios, as well as any additional repeaters to operate on the network.
- *Interface/gateway partnership:* allows local agencies to maintain their own separate network and provides a connecting gateway between a local agency's dispatch console and the network.
- *Shared communication system infrastructure:* states and localities both use the same towers for their separate systems, but there is no mechanism for patching communications between the state and local systems.

New York is implementing the Statewide Wireless Network in several phases and expects full implementation to be completed in September 2010.

Even though joining this state network is free, localities need to buy digital, trunked, and IP-addressable radios to participate directly, and additional infrastructure such as repeaters to get complete coverage in urban areas and buildings.

Local Approach

Throughout the state of New York, many different communications systems exist. Each area has developed its own methods aimed at improving interoperability. Additionally, localities generally do not include the Statewide Wireless Network as part of their local approach to improving interoperable communications. As of December 2006, one agency in New York City and only 7 of the 62 counties in New York have partnered with the network to be full system users. Twenty-five counties have agreed to connect through a gateway.

In the New York City UASI area, the police department maintains six channels for citywide interoperability. Any agency can use these channels by signing a memorandum of understanding and ensuring that they meet the necessary technical requirements. Additional interoperability strategies used by the New York City UASI include using a federal interoperability channel and utilizing and deploying mobile patching devices to connect disparate systems at an incident site. In addition, New York City is working to develop the City-wide Mobile Wireless Network, which is intended to provide police and fire first responders with high-speed data access to support large file transfers, including federal and state anticrime and antiterrorism databases, fingerprints, and maps. Further, the city has implemented a regional wide-area interoperability system that is New York City's primary interoperability network for first responders in the city. It is currently being expanded to include first responders in Nassau, Suffolk, and Westchester Counties, and parts of New Jersey.

Agencies in Albany County typically interoperate by programming the frequencies of other agencies into their radios, including agencies in neighboring counties. The county also has a patching mechanism that can connect different radio networks during an emergency. To improve its interoperability and connect the county to neighboring counties, Albany County is currently in the process of developing a countywide system.

This system will use gateways to connect existing systems that operate on different frequency bands and allow all public safety responders within the county to communicate with any other responder in Albany County regardless of the radio system or technology used. Albany is also currently developing a fiber optic system that will connect all 12 Public Safety Access Points in the county.

Onondaga County relies on dispatchers to connect first responders. All dispatching for Onondaga County is centralized at the county's 911 call center. To improve its interoperability, Onondaga County is currently working to implement a countywide digital system that will connect all county agencies.

Oregon

Oregon is currently in the process of planning a statewide system to connect all state agencies and provide a means for local agencies to be patched to users on the statewide system. Localities continue to develop and maintain their own communication systems and interoperability solutions. According to DHS, Oregon has received $53.4 million from fiscal year 2003 through fiscal year 2005 in grant funding to improve interoperable communications.

Governance

Oregon has a State Interoperability Executive Council to centrally manage Oregon's interoperable communications. This body is composed of state and local representatives. This committee requires that each county prepare a communications plan. Additionally, the committee is in the process of developing a statewide interoperable communications plan that incorporates all the county plans.

State Approach

Most state agencies are currently using VHF and UHF analog, conventional radio systems, which are in some cases 30 years old and in need of major repairs and upgrades. Oregon state agencies experience significant coverage gaps in their existing communications systems due to a lack of transmission towers. Additionally, these state systems are not always interoperable with federal or local systems.

In the absence of shared radio systems among federal, state, and local first responder agencies, Oregon's state agencies use various alternative approaches to establish interoperable communications with agencies they work with on a regular basis, such as using a dispatcher or patching devices to establish connections between disparate radio systems, and lending radios to first responders from other agencies.

Due to the deteriorating status of the Oregon's state agencies' communication systems, State Interoperability Executive Council officials have been working with contractors to develop a concept for a new state system. The Oregon Wireless Interoperability Network is to be a Project 25, trunked, digital radio network that will rely on an IP interface to interoperate with state agencies' subsystems. Plans for the interoperability network are to allow the majority of state agencies to operate on a unified trunked system while supporting conventional operations where and when required. These officials plan to issue a contract to a vendor by October 2007 and implement the first phase of the network by October 2009.

The Oregon Wireless Interoperability Network is intended to be the primary system for state agencies; local agencies will be expected to maintain their existing systems as their primary systems and use the network as their secondary system. A patching mechanism would be established to allow local agencies to be connected to state agencies, as well as allow them to be connected to other local agencies that they do not already have interoperability. Figure 8 is a depiction of the interoperability network concept as currently envisioned.

Figure 8: Oregon Wireless Interoperability Network System Overview

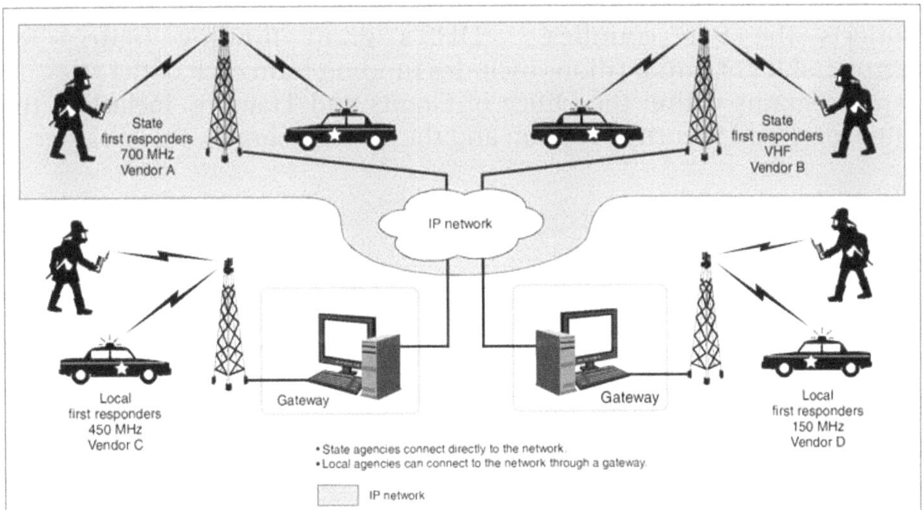

Source: GAO analysis based on Oregon data

Local Approach

Local agencies use a wide range of radio frequencies and communication technologies and have various strategies and solutions to improving interoperability. In particular, Marion County uses analog UHF and VHF systems; and trunked, as well as conventional radios. Officials stated that they have limited interoperability with state and federal agencies and that they, therefore, maintain a cache of 30 radios available to share, when needed. Additionally, they can use a mobile command unit that can be deployed to any area and contains another cache of radios.

In the Portland UASI, four of the five counties use 800 MHz, analog, trunked radio systems that provide direct interoperability among those four counties. The fifth county is on a separate VHF system. They have installed equipment to improve the interoperability with this fifth county. Additionally, to provide interoperability with the fifth county and other agencies outside the UASI area, the officials use mechanisms such as a mobile trailer to patch calls and loan radios from its cache of radios.

Jackson County agencies generally use conventional, VHF, analog radio systems. Officials indicated that although two of the cities within the county are digitally capable, their first responders use the analog mode due to the fact that many of their neighboring jurisdictions do not have digital radios. In order to interoperate with jurisdictions on different systems, they use common radio channels, patching mechanisms, as well as a mobile command vehicle that is equipped with a cache of radios in different frequencies and a patching device. In addition, Jackson County and Josephine County are developing a communications system that connects the two counties. [1] DHS's grant funding figures for interoperable communications includes funding from each of the relevant grant programs within the Office of Grants and Training, including the State Homeland Security Program and the UASI program.

Appendix III:
Comments from the Department of Commerce

THE DEPUTY SECRETARY OF COMMERCE
Washington, D.C. 20230

March 15, 2007

Ms. Linda Koontz
Director
Information Management Issues
U.S. Government Accountability Office
Washington, D.C. 20548

Dear Ms. Koontz:

Thank you for providing a copy of the GAO's draft report entitled "FIRST RESPONDERS: Much Work Remains to Improve Communications Interoperability" (GAO-07-301).

I commend you on the comprehensive nature of your report. The Department of Commerce takes its role in improving the technology that supports all first responders very seriously. In light of this, I enclose comments that will assist you in clearly interpreting the information provided by the National Institute of Standards and Technology and the National Telecommunication and Information Administration. These comments include specific concerns that could lead to an inaccurate perception of the current state of interoperability.

Again, thank you for the opportunity to review the draft report. I applaud your efforts to improve programs supporting our Nation's first responders.

Sincerely,

David A. Sampson

Enclosure

Appendix IV:
Comments from the Department of Homeland Security

U.S. Department of Homeland Security
Washington, DC 20528

Homeland Security

March 22, 2007

Ms. Linda D. Koontz
Director, Information Management Issues
U.S. Government Accountability Office
441 G Street, NW
Washington, DC 20548

Dear Ms. Koontz:

RE: Draft Report GAO-07-301, First Responders: Much Work Remains to Improve Communications Interoperability (GAO Job Code 310756)

The Department of Homeland Security (DHS) appreciates the opportunity to review and comment on the draft report referenced above. The Government Accountability Office (GAO) makes five recommendations. We agree with two recommendations, disagree with one recommendation, and will take two others under advisement.

We agree that a great deal of work remains before our Nation's emergency responders have seamless communications interoperability. However, there are several areas in the report that need to be corrected in order to provide an accurate picture of the current state of efforts to improve interoperability. We have provided specific lengthy comments with examples about inaccurate statements in the draft report as technical comments under separate cover and they are incorporated by reference. We highlight some of the comments herein.

GAO recommends that the Secretary of Homeland Security (1) assess how states' grant requests support their statewide communications plans and include the assessment as a factor in making DHS grant allocation decisions and (2) plan for a new full-scale exercise for UASI [Urban Area Security Initiative] areas that provides local officials with sufficient time to develop and implement exercises to validate the robustness and effectiveness of their tactical interoperable communications plans.

We will take these recommendations under advisement. Officials in what is now known as our Preparedness Directorate will comment on these recommendations when we provide a sixty day response to the recommendations following issuance of your report. Aspects of communications interoperability will transfer at the end of the month to the National Protection and Programs Directorate (NPPD) [now called the Preparedness Directorate]. Other changes at the Department include standing up the Office of Emergency Communication within NPPD's Cyber Security and Telecommunications. Programmatic elements of SAFECOM will be included in the Office of Emergency Communications.

GAO also recommends that DHS develop and implement a program plan for SAFECOM and other Office of Emergency Communications (OEC) interoperability programs that include goals focused on improving interoperability among all levels of government. We agree with the intent of the recommendation and have been addressing it. We disagree with the implication that action has not been taken. The program plan for SAFECOM is in development as the program transitions from Science and Technology's Office for Interoperability and Compatibility to the Office of Emergency Communications.

SAFECOM has always had goals for improving interoperability among local, state, tribal, and Federal emergency response agencies. SAFECOM, with support from OMB, adopted a strategy based on user needs and driven from the bottom-up to meet its mission as an E-Government project. Our technical comments include a list of SAFECOM metrics/goals.

SAFECOM heavily relies on input from local, state, and Federal emergency response practitioners. It has developed forums where practitioners can define and implement interoperable solutions, including its Executive Committee and Emergency Response Council. Among the Federal participants on these working groups are representatives from the Department of Justice, the Department of Agriculture, the Department of Energy, the Department of Interior, the Department of Defense, the Department of Commerce, the Department of Health and Human Services, the Environmental Protection Agency, the Federal Communications Commission, as well as multiple other offices within DHS. In addition, the Federal Partnership for Interoperable Communications (FPIC) seeks to improve interoperability at the Federal level. All FPIC member agencies have aligned to the SAFECOM program. Alignment is defined as being in compliance with the P25 standards, a suite of eight standards for the manufacturing of interoperable, digital, two-way wireless communications products.

In your fourth recommendation, you state that the DHS include in the program plan for SAFECOM and other OEC interoperability programs quantifiable performance measures that can be used to determine the extent to which each of the goals have been accomplished, and that can be used to assess the effectiveness and usefulness of SAFECOM tools, assistance, and outreach, and make improvements based on the feedback.

We agree with the recommendation. In addition to the current performance measures that SAFECOM reports to OMB, DHS agrees that it is important to establish performance measures that can be used to determine the extent to which each of the SAFECOM goals have been accomplished. To this end, DHS officials intend to establish quantifiable performance measures that can be used to determine the extent of accomplishment. The goals should be established by the third quarter of 2007.

We agree that it is important to not only produce tools that aid the emergency response community in achieving greater interoperability, but also to evaluate the efficacy of those tools. Once finalized and implemented, the performance measures will provide feedback that will influence the development of future tools in order to better serve the program's mission and accomplish its goals. Performance measures and methods of collecting data will be consistent with DHS and Federal regulations. Further, they will be based on best practices from the public and private sectors on measuring the efficacy of free publications.

Fifth, and finally, GAO recommends that the Secretary modify grant guidance to provide more flexibility in purchasing communications equipment until standards for completed interfaces have been fully defined and products have been certified compliant with all aspects of the standards. The recommendation suggests that grant guidance requirements related to Project 25 (P25) standards be diluted or expunged until P25 standards are complete. We disagree with the recommendation as it would require that SAFECOM amend its interoperability grant guidance by removing language that encourages grant recipients to purchase P25-compliant equipment until after the entire P25 suite of standards is complete. P25 represents the foundation for near-term communications interoperability and can be completed in the next 18 months if all parties are committed.

The recommendation discounts tremendous recent progress with P25, and could undermine the final remaining negotiations between the public safety community and equipment manufacturers. Our Science and Technology Directorate's Command, Control and Interoperability Division officials know from the National Interoperability Baseline Survey that 40 percent of agencies intend to procure new systems within the next five years. Muting the P25 language would remove all incentives for manufacturers to participate in completing the P25 standards. It would also ensure that tens of thousands of communities would invest Federal "interoperability" funds in proprietary systems that will never be interoperable. Indeed, one of the most frequent requests by public safety officials is for standards and comprehensive guidance.

The GAO draft report also implies that FY 2007 Homeland Security grant dollars received by applicants will be spent by local public safety agencies in FY 2007, but that is unlikely. States typically receive grant funds by the end of the fiscal year for which funding has been appropriated. This means these funds will be allocated to localities and drive requests for proposals through FY 2009. Therefore, the grant guidance serves as additional pressure on the P25 standard stakeholders to complete the standard in the next 18 to 24 months. However, even if the P25 committee fails to reach its final goal in the 18-to-24 month timeframe, new P25 features are being manufactured as they are ratified, which continually increases the capacity for interoperability among users.

GAO maintains that compliance assessment cannot begin until P25 standards development is complete. However, fully completed standards are not required for initial compliance assessments. In fact, the existing compliance assessment criteria was modeled after a highly successful compliance assessment effort conducted by the Army which resulted in manufacturers re-tooling their equipment to be as interoperable as promised. Standards development and compliance assessment have been successfully moving in parallel with each other, each influencing and refining the other for the benefit of all parties involved. More importantly, technology will continue to evolve, requiring continuous updating of the standards. Waiting for a "final" standard would prohibit any standards from ever being applied.

In addition, there are two particular areas of concern in the draft report that we urge GAO to address before the report is finalized and submitted to Congress:

1. The need to include information on several additional agencies and programs charged with improving Federal interoperability.
2. The need to clarify SAFECOM's strategy of addressing the interoperable communications needs of local, tribal, and state interoperability ahead of Federal responders.

The GAO report examined some communications interoperability programs, omitting critical activities being conducted by other major programs, particularly other programs focused on interoperability among Federal responders. These agencies include the newly created Office of Emergency Communications within DHS; the Integrated Wireless Network; the Interoperable Communications Technical Assistance Program; and the Federal Partnership for Interoperable Communications. A complete list of agencies involved with interoperable communications is included in our technical comments.

Under law, SAFECOM has a role in Federal interoperable communications and is meeting its requirement in three ways:

1. SAFECOM guidance to states requires the integration of Federal responders into their statewide interoperable communications plans.
2. SAFECOM's Executive Committee and Emergency Response Council includes representatives from the Department of Justice, the Department of Agriculture, the Department of Energy, the Department of Interior, the Department of Defense, the Department of Commerce, the Department of Health and Human Services, the Environmental Protection Agency, the Federal Communications Commission, as well as multiple offices within the Department of Homeland Security.
3. SAFECOM is a member and a regular participant in the FPIC. The FPIC consists of 44 Federal entities representing more than 200 participants. The report appears to recommend that SAFECOM should create or maintain a redundant functionality to compete with FPIC activities. SAFECOM does not believe that creating more interoperability programs will result in more interoperability.

By examining these other entities and the significant work they have accomplished, your report could offer a more complete picture of Federal efforts to improve interoperability.

The second major issue is GAO's view that SAFECOM has mistakenly made local, tribal, and state emergency responders its highest priority. In 2001 the President created the SAFECOM program under the Government to Government (G2G) customer segment as part of the Presidential E-Government strategy. State and local governments were the primary customer of the G2G customer segment, and are therefore SAFECOM's primary focus. SAFECOM also maintains that since ninety percent of the public safety infrastructure is owned, operated, and maintained by local jurisdictions, the Federal Government can have the greatest impact working with local, tribal, and state emergency responders, and by integrating those efforts with Federal plans—not by making local and state interoperability secondary to Federal requirements.

In every incident, it is a virtual certainty that a local, tribal, or state emergency responder will be the first to arrive on the scene. If interoperability does not occur at that level, then no amount of Federal interoperability will be able to compensate. Federal responders will be there to act primarily as support when possible. For this reason, SAFECOM continues to maintain that its prioritization of local, tribal, and state emergency responders is the most appropriate course of action. The draft report gives the impression that SAFECOM is targeting the wrong population despite its Presidential E-government mandate.

Sincerely,

Steven D Pecinovsky

Steven Pecinovsky
Director
Departmental GAO/OIG Liaison Office

Appendix V: GAO Contact and Staff Acknowledgments

GAO Contact

Linda Koontz, (202) 512-6240, koontzl@gao.gov

Staff Acknowledgments

In addition to the individual named above, John de Ferrari, Assistant Director; Neil Doherty; Richard Hung; Tom Mills; Shannin O'Neill; Karen Talley; Amos Tevelow; and Jayne Wilson made major contributions to this report.

DOCUMENT NO. 8

RADICALIZATION, INFORMATION SHARING AND COMMUNITY OUTREACH: PROTECTING THE HOMELAND FROM HOMEGROWN TERROR

Hearing Before the Subcommittee on Intelligence, Information Sharing, and Terrorism Risk Assessment

April 5, 2007

Statement of Congresswoman Jane Harman Subcommittee Chairwoman

Twenty months ago, police in Torrance disrupted the first known prison-based terrorist cell in the U.S. that was planning devastating attacks in the Los Angeles area.

Those arrested were Americans and one permanent resident.

The allegations against them, if true, present a chilling account of the threat we face from home grown terrorism.

Among other things, they are charged with having planned attacks on synagogues on Jewish holidays—in order to maximize the number of deaths—and on U.S. military bases and recruitment centers.

To fund their terror campaign, the defendants allegedly robbed 11 gas stations in and around Torrance. That's where the Torrance Police Department came in.

But for the hard work of some local officers—whose efforts led to the discovery of maps and other evidence that unraveled the plot—many, many lives could have been lost.

Those Torrance Police Department officers worked with LAPD and FBI partners to share information and build a case in a way that would have been almost unimaginable before 9/11.

I want to commend them all for that great service—to Torrance, to California, and to their country.

We're holding this field hearing on radicalization to learn more about the home grown" terror threat to our nation.

Let me be clear: when we talk about radicalization and "home grown" terrorists, we're not talking about people from any particular ethnic, political, or religious group.

On the contrary, we're talking about ideologically-driven violence, whether by a white, U.S. Bronze Star honoree named Timothy McVeigh; or in Belgium, a female Catholic convert to Islam who traveled to Iraq and blew herself up; or in the UK, third generation Britons of Pakistani descent who killed their countrymen on buses and trains.

Last fall, Dame Eliza Manningham Buller—the Director of Britain's MI5—revealed for the first time the seriousness of the home grown terrorism threat in her country.

She stated that MI5 and local police in the UK are currently investigating some 200 separate terrorist networks that include over 1600 individuals who are actively planning attacks both domestically and overseas.And those are just the ones she knows about.

When I met with her in my Washington office, I reminded her that what happened here in Torrance shows that the threat is also emerging on this side of the Atlantic.

But focusing our efforts against any particular group of people would be futile. The Washington Post recently reported that police in Western Europe are arresting significant numbers of women, teenagers, white-skinned suspects and people baptized as Christians"—people who until now were not on the radar screen as radicals prone to violence.

In fact, the demographics of those being arrested are so diverse that many European officials say that they have given up trying to predict who is most likely to become a terrorist. Age, sex, ethnicity, education and economic status simply have become more and more irrelevant.

The same is true here. How do we explain why Adam Gadahn, a 17-year -old Jewish kid from Santa Ana became a radical, moved to Pakistan, now works as Osama Bin Laden's spokesman, and is under indictment here for treason?

We simply need a better understanding of what's going on.

That's why I'm very pleased to be joined by the distinguished witnesses on our two panels this morning.

On the first, we'll hear from LAPD Chief William Bratton, Torrance Police Chief John Neu, and Special Agent in-Charge Janice Fedarcyk from the FBI's Los Angeles office.

They will be talking with us about the Torrance arrests, what home grown terrorism is, and what we might do about it.

We'll then hear from Sireen Sawaf from the Muslim Public Affairs Council who serves as a representative on the FBI's Multi Cultural Advisory Committee and David Gersten from DHS.

Both will share their own thoughts about home grown terrorism and how engagement with minority communities can help prevent it.

And finally, an old friend, author, and consultant on terrorism, Brian Jenkins of the RAND Corporation, will put our subjects in perspective.

I'm joined today by some of my Committee colleagues—Ranking Member Dave Reichert of Washington, Norm Dicks of Washington, Ed Perlmutter of Colorado, and Dan Lungren of California.

Welcome again to you all

Statement of John J. Neu
Chief of Police
Torrance Police Department

Needless to say, since the terrorist attacks of September 11, 2001, the role and responsibility of local law enforcement as first responders to terrorist activity have changed. Our mission demands that we make every effort possible to detect and prevent terrorist activity right here in our own communities. The new paradigm for local law enforcement is prevention, but the awareness, knowledge, skills and abilities of these officers must be enhanced in order to effectively thwart terrorist plots before they manifest as attacks.

The most significant trend that has been identified over the past several years is the rise of the "homegrown" threat, which has been publicized extensively in the media. The possibility of a "homegrown" terrorist attack against Los Angeles, New York, Chicago or any other American city is real and is worsening with time as the radicalization process unfolds. The fuel that ignites this inside threat is a significant challenge for law enforcement agencies across the United States.

In July of 2005, officers from my department arrested two suspects for robbing a local gas station. As the investigation continued to unfold, the officers came face-to-face with a direct act of domestic terrorism. An Islamic extremist group based here in California and known as "Assembly of Authentic Islam" (JIS) was uncovered. This group, operating primarily in state prisons without apparent connections or direction from outside the United States, committed several armed robberies throughout Southern California, including the one in Torrance. The robberies were committed with the goal of financing attacks against the enemies of Islam, including the United States government and supporters of Israel.

The investigation brought charges against Kevin James, Lavar Washington, Gregory Patterson, and Hammad Samana. The indictment alleges that James, while in prison in Sacramento, recruited fellow prison inmates to join JIS and preached the duty of members was to target for violent attack any enemies of Islam, or "infidels," including the United States government and Jewish and non-Jewish supporters of Israel. James allegedly distributed a document in prison that justified the killing of "infidels," and made members take an oath not to talk about the existence of JIS. He also allegedly sought to establish groups or "cells" of JIS members outside of prison to carry out violent attacks against "perceived infidels," including the United States government, the government of Israel and Jewish people.

Washington, also an inmate at the Sacramento prison, joined JIS in November 2004 and was paroled at the end of the month. In December 2004, James allegedly instructed Washington to recruit five people to train in covert operations, acquire firearms with silencers, and find contacts with explosives expertise or learn to make bombs that could be activated from a distance.

The indictment alleges that beginning in December 2004, Washington, Patterson and Samana targeted and conducted Internet research on and surveillance of United States military facilities, which included recruitment centers and military bases in the Los Angeles area, as part of their plot to kill United States military personnel. In July 2005, Patterson and Samana allegedly used computers to research military targets in the Los Angeles area, while Samana drafted a document listing Israeli and United States targets in Los Angeles. In addition to the United States military targets, the coconspirators specifically targeted Israeli and Jewish facilities in the Los Angeles area, including the Israeli Consulate, El Al (the national airline of Israel) and synagogues. They also allegedly engaged in firearms and physical training in preparation for attacks.

According to the indictment, the defendants purchased weapons or otherwise tried to acquire weapons in furtherance of their terrorist conspiracy, and made efforts to raise money by robbing gas stations. The indictment alleges that eleven times beginning May 30, 2005, the defendants, armed with shotguns, robbed or attempted to rob gas stations in several cities and towns in Southern California, including Los Angeles, Torrance, Playa del Ray, Bellflower, Pico Rivera, Walnut, Orange, Playa Vista and Fullerton. The indictment alleges that during the gas station robbery spree, Patterson updated James on the progress of the planned war of terrorism against the United States government.

The JIS case is a prime example of the powerful radical influence which poses a serious threat from within. Our greatest weapon against terrorism is unity. That unity is built upon information sharing and coordination of law enforcement at every level and the intelligence communities. The JIS case involved approximately 500 law enforcement officers from the federal, state and local levels. It has been described by some in our community as a model case of information sharing and investigation. The Los Angeles Police Department provided over 100 officers to this investigation alone.

The criminal investigation into the alleged terrorist conspiracy was lead by the FBI's Long Beach Joint Terrorism Task Force, whose participating agencies include the Los Angeles Police Department; U.S. Immigration and Customs Enforcement; the Torrance Police Department; the Los Angeles County Sheriff's Department; the Long Beach Police Department; the Bureau of Alcohol, Tobacco, Firearms and Explosives; U.S. Immigration and Customs Enforcement; the Los Angeles Port Police; U.S. Customs and Border Protection; the U.S. Coast Guard Investigative Service; the Defense Criminal Investigative Service; and the U.S. Environmental Protection Agency. The JIS case is a prime example of how far local law enforcement has come in our collaborative efforts in fighting domestic terrorism that involved radical homegrown terrorists.

Local law enforcement is, in fact, uniquely positioned to identify terrorist activity right here in our own communities. As displayed in the JIS case, local law enforcement's relationship with federal law enforcement has improved immensely. A major portion of this success is directly related to the training of our line level officers in regards to domestic terrorism. A specific focus on threat identification training paid dividends across the board during the JIS investigation. The vertical sharing of intelligence information, coupled with communication and coordination throughout the investigation, proved to be invaluable to all of the agencies involved.

Information Needs of Local Law Enforcement Relating to Islamic Radicalization

Local law enforcement plays a critical role in the identification and disruption of radicalized Islamic groups. Our personnel are on the streets of our community everyday interacting, observing, and maintaining the public safety. Our Community Based Policing model, Focus Based Policing, has proven to be successful mainly because of our steadfast relationships with the people we protect. Since the attacks of nine-eleven, local law enforcement has utilized these policing models to address our homeland security needs and specifically the radicalized Islamic extremist threat. We do, however, require better awareness in some critical areas such as:

- Understanding the threat of terrorism to our community and infrastructure
  - –Homegrown terror (JIS)
- Cultural awareness of the Muslim community we serve and equal knowledge of the very small percentage of Muslims that would be vulnerable to the radical ideologies
- What factors lead to radicalized beliefs and what are the trip wires or clues in the community that local law enforcement would encounter?
- Where could recruitment and radicalization occur in our community?
- Identification of material support efforts for terror and criminal organizations
- Gaining a better understanding of combating Fourth Generation Warfare
  - –Terrorism is a tactic of Fourth Generation Warfare

Our partners in the FBI and the region are facilitating the training and awareness through unprecedented lateral networking.

Our Well Established Relationship with the FBI

Our professional relationship with the Federal Bureau of Investigation has been well established for over twenty years. Our investigators from the

Crimes Persons, Narcotics, and Crime Impact Sections of our organization work hand in hand with FBI personnel on very successful regional investigations. Our organizations have synergized and we have gained from each others strengths. We consistently enjoy a seamless commingling of resources, training, and expertise with our FBI partners.

Our participation in the FBI Joint Terrorism Task Force was a natural progression of our professional relationship. We, as an organization, recognize the regional challenge to security and we meet the challenge without hesitation. Our investigators are contributors and team players within the task force initiative. The success of the JTTF initiative weighs heavily on local law enforcement participation. We understand our role and are prepared to endure the challenge. We recognize the value of the "Task Force" approach to investigations, and our National Security is paramount in our thoughts during this trying time in our history.

Our FBI partners, the Los Angeles Police Department, the Los Angeles Sheriff's Department, and other law enforcement agencies have embraced this spirit of cooperation. We truly witnessed this selfless commitment during the JIS investigation. This investigation tasked over 500 personnel and the Los Angeles Police Department alone contributed over 100 officers. This ability to force multiply was critical to the rapid dismantling of this dangerous threat and we are very appreciative to "our big brothers" in the region.

With the creation of the Los Angeles Joint Regional Intelligence Center (LA JRIC), the "fusion" of information sharing has really evolved. The centralized facility has truly encouraged both vertical and, more importantly, lateral information sharing. The initiative has spurred the growth of other Terror Early Warning Groups (TEW) and Terror Liaison Officer working groups within the region. These groups apply proven networking techniques; mentor one another, track crime trends, and train on terror related topics. The LA JRIC also provides terror reporting fusion procedures, predictive analysis relating to crime and terrorism, investigative support and training. All are critical components to enhancing line level officers' awareness.

Our Community Outreach Efforts

To address our community's safety, we have followed our successful Focus Based Policing model to reach out to the public and business sectors. We have modified the "focus" to include trip wires for terror related activities. We have identified areas within our jurisdiction such as the Del Amo Fashion Center, our many public and private schools, petrochemical facilities, Exxon Mobil Refinery, and secured our relationships and resources to maximize security efforts. This, too, has been a collaborated effort involving DHS, FBI, and local law enforcement. We are constantly reinforcing our methods and training to equal the threat and maintain the safety our community.

Focus Based Policing for Counterterrorism

- Building ties and relationships with the community
- Understanding socio-cultural, political, and religious issues
- Understanding terrorist indicators and behaviors
- Empowering the community

Engage the Community

- Town hall meeting and outreach programs
- School awareness programs and counter terror trained School Resource Officers
- Business contacts and critical infrastructure monitoring
- Deployment of Terror Liaison Officers

In closing, the Torrance Police Department has experienced "homegrown" terrorism firsthand. Our federal, state, and local partners were invaluable in uncovering and dismantling a very real threat to our region from JIS. Our success in this case was due to a professional, established, aggressive approach to investigating criminal activity, and the established partnership with the FBI Joint Terrorism Task Force. I would like to thank the committee for allowing me to participate in this hearing.

Thank you.

Statement of William J. Bratton
Chief of Police
Los Angeles Police Department

Chairwoman Harman, Ranking Member Reichert and members of the committee, thank you for holding this hearing on the pressing issue of Radicalization.

The Los Angeles Police Department (LAPD) and the City of Los Angeles have forged successful relationships with our local, state, and federal partners to begin examining and responding to the growing threat posed by radicalization. However, we need continued support for our efforts across a number of areas of concern. Today, I will address three issues of interest to this committee:

- First, the growing threat of Muslim radicalization in the United States, specifically here in the Los Angeles area, and the challenges posed to local, state, and federal authorities.
- Second, the connection between prison radicalization and the potential of homegrown Islamist terrorism.
- Third, the role that a congressionally funded National Counter Terrorism Academy (NCTA) serving state and local law enforcement would have in countering the these threats.

Beginning in May of 2005, four radical Muslim suspects—armed with shotguns—went on a significant crime spree that by itself would have been noteworthy. Eleven times they robbed or attempted to rob gas stations in the cities of Los Angeles, Torrance, Playa Del Rey, Bellflower, Pico Rivera, Walnut, Orange, Playa Vista, and Fullerton.

In investigating the crimes, the experienced detectives of the Torrance Police Department focused on the basics of any investigation: evidence, witnesses, and modus operandi. A lucky break occurred when a cell phone belonging to one of the suspects was recovered. When a search was conducted of the suspect's apartment the detective also observed disturbing evidence. This evidence included body armor, knives, and other evidence of the crime.

However, when the detective noticed jihad-related literature and the addresses of potential "targets" the detective fell back on his previous training as a Terrorism Liaison Officer (TLO) and recognized this as a pre-incident indicator to a terrorist attack. As a TLO, this detective had received minimal formalized terrorism training—in comparison to the routine training received by bona fide counter-terrorism professionals. Yet this training was sufficient enough to arm the Torrance detective with usable information.

To most detectives this "disturbing evidence" would have appeared as inconsequential to the robbery charge. Some of it, political or philosophical in nature, would have appeared as mere ramblings during a routine search. Directions, maps, and other non-overtly criminal articles would usually be brushed aside as miscellaneous. To the trained observer, however, the evidence clearly pointed to only one possibility—homegrown terrorism.

It was at the Los Angeles Joint Terrorism Task Force (JTTF) where LAPD task force officers—tenured detectives—and FBI special agents worked together diligently and tirelessly. As a result of this extraordinary teamwork, not only were the suspects apprehended but a larger and greater conspiracy was uncovered.

Experienced local detectives and federal agents conducted textbook interrogations of the suspects revealing a surprising fact. The cell of robbers and alleged terrorists were further along in their conspiracy than anyone knew or expected. These homegrown terrorists had already conducted surveillance of military recruitment stations, the Israeli consulate, El-Al airlines, and prominent synagogues. According to the federal indictment against the JIS members, they had selected attack periods "to maximize the number of casualties."

Further investigation revealed that this group was aligned with a California prison group known as Jamiyyat Ul Islam Is Saheeh (JIS), which translates to "Assembly of Authentic Islam." JIS practiced a radical form of Islam that was neither authentic nor peaceful. An inmate, Kevin Lamar James, founded this radical group in 1997 at California's notorious Folsom Prison. James, a Los Angeles-based gang member serving time for robbery, directed his followers "to target for violent attack any enemies of Islam or 'infidels,' including the United States government and Jewish and non-Jewish supporters of Israel."[1]

Hiding behind the guise of religious freedom, James' JIS used assumed protections such as the freedom of religion to advance its beliefs and pressure new recruits and converts into a hate-based cult. It affiliated itself with Al Qaeda's philosophies and targeting array *("The ruling to kill the Americans and their allies—civilians and military—is an individual duty for every Muslim who can do it in any country in which it is possible to do it.")*[2]

James has much in common with Ahmed Ressam, Richard Reid, Abu Musab al Zarqawi, and Jose Padilla. All were street thugs radicalized while behind bars. All were first encountered by local law enforcement before they were radicalized. And all plotted to kill Americans.

The tentacles of JIS reached beyond the prison's walls. A released member was able to recruit two otherwise law-abiding residents into a terrorist cell. He convinced them to rob and eventually commit terrorist acts for JIS. He also indoctrinated them into the radical philosophy of hate.

In this case, "Islamist" radicals were taken into custody, preventing terrorism at home. It was demonstrated that formal education in the subject matter of terrorist tradecraft, together with modern intelligence-led policing strategies and proven investigative techniques, could be used successfully to counter and prevent terrorism.

The successful approach taken by all participating agencies involved in the Torrance case is no accident. Rather, it was the result of the dedication, training, and expertise of the officers involved. More, however, can be done to locate and stop other attacks. We need to educate all of local law enforcement about counter-terrorism techniques and investigations. In this respect, as a region, as a state, and as a nation, in the Torrance Case we dodged a bullet.

Whether the motivation is religious fundamentalism, anti-government sentiment, or the disaffected loner, radicalized groups or individuals are increasingly perpetrating terrorism. A substantial attack upon U.S. soil is increasingly likely. The answer rests with prevention.

The nation's 12,000 FBI Special Agents are indeed some of the best investigators in the world, and the training they receive sets the benchmark for law enforcement. Despite their talents and abilities, the workload of most special agents is overwhelming and their enforcement scope is limited. However, over 700,000 local law enforcement officers in the U.S. are already on the front lines, fighting crime and gathering critical information on a daily basis.

Providing these 700,000 front-line officers standardized counter-terrorism training will transform these first responders into a coordinated collection and prevention asset. Such an approach can be a true force multiplier.

The only way to prevent radicalization is to end the conditions that foster it. When efforts at prevention are unsuccessful or impractical, a fully trained and seamlessly integrated public safety force is required to recognize pre-incident indicators and develop interdiction, disruption, or arrest strategies.

Furthermore, we must cultivate a working relationship with all religious groups in our region, and gain their trust. It is these congregations that will provide the needed intelligence of disaffected membership. However, a suspicious and frightened religious community will react to knee-jerk outreach efforts as dubious or disingenuous.

We have initiated a partnership with the Center for Policing Terrorism (CPT), which is part of the Manhattan Institute, a think tank in New York City. My working relationship with the Institute dates back to my days as the Commissioner of New York Police Department, where the Institute provided some of the intellectual force behind our crime reduction strategies and assisted in their dissemination. Similarly, the CPT leverages world-class intellectuals to help the LAPD and other departments tackle our most pressing counter-terrorism challenges smarter, faster, and cheaper.

As a result, it is the recommendation of the CPT that the LAPD partner with an existing school of higher education and our federal partners to create a National Counter Terrorism Academy (NCTA) in Los Angeles. The purpose of the NCTA would be to lead the way in ushering in a new era of policing strategy: Intelligence-Led Policing (ILP). Recognized as a national way forward, ILP is an all-crimes approach to enforcement that will revolutionize law enforcement. ILP richly integrates existing strategies and technologies into a coherent "game-plan" approach in allocating resources efficiently. Currently, without a national strategy, or a place where police executives can learn how to implement ILP, it is sitting on the shelf unused.

Setting national standards for training in the field of counter-terrorism would be the first step in pursuing a coordinated approach to intelligence gathering and analysis. Currently, unlike intelligence training, information technology systems and first responder training courses must be certified and approved as interoperable. As proposed by the LEAP Strategy report,[3] such an effort would be needed to train police officers at every level in a unified, scientific, and constitutionally-responsible manner. The NCTA would both seek out current and professional programs and curriculum and develop its own where gaps exist. By establishing a professional academic approach, the NCTA would be a first of its kind to forward ILP strategies for local police agencies and their partners who are going to be essential in transitioning national and international homeland security efforts into homeland security initiatives.

Public-private partnerships such as that exemplified by the Los Angeles Police Department and the Manhattan Institute build tangible results. For example, we have sought the advice of CPT and other private and public partners in developing our fundamental approach to building good community relations with faith-based groups in our City. I am proud to report that LAPD works extraordinarily hard at developing strong ties with the people of Los Angeles. In building effective relationships with those groups that the current terrorist operative is likely to exploit, we are learning that it is best to concentrate on shared goals such as public safety and quality of life issues. With the trust and mutual respect between police and citizen that such collaboration fosters, we are erecting the strongest of defenses against terrorism.

As with any new educational effort the basics are needed—a brick and mortar facility, and educational infrastructure, computers, networks, and other information technology. A core curriculum aimed at every level of law enforcement, one that is tailored to the students' needs, must be developed and quickly implemented.

Madam Chairwoman and members of the Subcommittee, thank you for inviting me to speak today on this important subject. I am happy to answer any questions you may have.

Endnotes

1 Kevin Lamar James.

2 Jihad Against Jews and Crusaders, World Islamic Front Statement, 23 February 1998.

3 Law Enforcement Assistance and Partnership Strategy—Improving Information Sharing Between the Intelligence Community and State, Local, and Tribal Law Enforcement.

Statement of Janice Fedarcyk
Special Agent in Charge (SAC)
Counterterrorism Division
FBI's Los Angeles Field Office

Chairman Harman, Ranking Member Reichert, and members of the Subcommittee, I want to thank you for this opportunity to speak to you on the topic of Islamic radicalization in the United States, and the Federal Bureau of Investigation's (FBI) efforts to address this emerging threat with our other federal, state, and local partners. I would like to emphasize before I begin that the issue is not Islam itself, but how the religious ideology is used by violent extremists to inspire and justify their actions. The FBI does not investigate members of any religion for their religious beliefs, but rather focuses on investigating activities that may harm the United States.

Successes in the war on terrorism and the arrests of many key Al Qaeda leaders have diminished the ability of the group to attack the United States (U.S.) Homeland. At the same time, a broader Sunni extremist movement has evolved from being run entirely by Al Qaeda central, to a broader movement. This is demonstrated by the 2004 Madrid bombings, the July 2005 London bombings, and recent disruptions in the U.S., United Kingdom, Canada, Bosnia, Denmark and elsewhere.

That said, Al Qaeda's core remains committed to attacking the United States and continues to demonstrate its ability to adapt its tactics to circumvent security measures and reconstitute its ranks.

Al Qaeda is also attempting to broaden its appeal to English-speaking Western Muslims by disseminating violent Islamic extremist propaganda via media outlets and the Internet.

Although the most dangerous instances of radicalization have so far been overseas, the Islamic radicalization of U.S. persons, whether foreign-born or native, is of increasing concern. Key to the success of stopping the spread of radicalization is identifying patterns and trends in the early stages.

The FBI characterizes homegrown Islamic extremists as U.S. persons who may appear to be assimilated, but, to some degree, have become radicalized in their support for Islamic jihad. They often see themselves as devout Muslims and reject the cultural values, beliefs, and environment of the United States. Let me make it clear that the FBI is not interested in these people because they have rejected American culture and adopted a strict, devout view of Islam. We are interested in them when and where there are reasonable indications that they may provide support for, or directly commit, a terrorist attack inside the United States because of their radicalized view of Islam. The threat from homegrown Islamic extremists is likely smaller in scale than that posed by overseas terrorist groups such as Al Qaeda, but is potentially larger in psychological impact. Several recent cases illustrate the nature of the issue.

- Since August 2005 the FBI, other federal agencies, and our foreign partners have dismantled a global network of extremists who are operating independently of any known terrorist organization. Several individuals affiliated with this network were arrested for providing material support in connection with the plotting of a terrorist attack in the United States.
- The apparent increase of cases involving homegrown Islamic extremists may represent an increased sensitivity of law enforcement to activities not previously regarded as terrorism, but we cannot rule out the possibility that the homegrown phenomenon could be growing.

The FBI has identified certain venues, such as prisons and the internet, that present opportunities for the proselytizing of radical Islam.

The European and American experience shows that prisons are venues where extremists can be radicalized and recruited among the inmate population. Prison radicalization primarily occurs through anti-U.S. sermons provided by contract, volunteer, or staff imams, radicalized inmates who gain religious influence, and extremist media. Ideologies that radicalized inmates appear most often to embrace include the Salafi form of Sunni Islam (including revisionist versions commonly known as "prison Islam") and an extremist view of Shia Islam similar to that of the Government of Iran and Lebanese Hezbollah.

Most cases of prison radicalization appear to be carried out by domestic Islamic extremist groups with few or no direct foreign connections, like the Sunni Islamic extremist group in California, the Jam'iyyat Ul-Islam Is-Saheeh (JIS), identified in July 2005. Although the Committee is familiar with this case, I regret that I am unable to elaborate publicly on it at this time due to pending legal proceedings, and the FBI's responsibility to ensure the defendants in this case receive a fair and impartial trial. I would like to emphasize, however, that not all prison radicalization is Islamic in nature. Domestic groups such as white supremacists also recruit in prisons.

In response to this possible threat, the FBI and the Bureau of Prisons (BOP) have been actively engaged in efforts to detect, deter, and interdict efforts by terrorist and extremist groups to radicalize or recruit in U.S. prisons since February 2003. As a result of the JIS case here in Los Angeles, the FBI organized a Prison Radicalization Working Group which is comprised of more than 15 federal, state, and local agencies, and over 30 task force officers. As part of these efforts, we have identified "best practices" for correctional institutions to combat the spread of radicalization.

The Internet is also a venue for the radicalization of young, computer-savvy Westerners—both male and female—who identify with an Islamic extremist ideology. An older generation of supporters and sympathizers of violent

Islamic extremism, in the post-9/11 environment of increased law enforcement scrutiny, has migrated their radicalization, recruitment, and material support activities online. Radicalization via the Internet is participatory, and individuals are actively engaged in exchanging extremist propaganda and rhetoric online which may facilitate the violent Islamic extremist cause. These online activities further their indoctrination, create links between extremists located around the world, and may serve as a springboard for future terrorist activities.

Overseas experience can also be a significant element in facilitating the transition from one who has a proclivity to be radicalized, and who may espouse radicalized rhetoric, to one who is willing and ready to act on those radicalized beliefs. Although radicalization can occur without overseas travel, the foreign experience appears to provide the networking that makes it possible for interested individuals to train for and participate in operational activity. The experience may vary from religious or language instruction, to basic paramilitary training.

- We assess that the overseas experiences of John Walker Lindh[1] played a pivotal role in his involvement with the Taliban. Once overseas, he was directed by radicalized individuals to attend extremist universities, and ultimately training camps in Pakistan and Afghanistan.

The FBI approaches the radicalization issue on two levels:

- We are attempting to understand the dynamics of individual and organizational radicalization to identify early indicators as to whether individuals or groups are demonstrating the potential for violence.
- We are engaged in extensive outreach to Muslim communities to dispel misconceptions that may foster extremism.

With respect to the latter point, I would like to spend some time discussing the Los Angeles Field Office's efforts over the years to develop and foster a positive working relationship with our Muslim, Arab, Armenian, Sikh, and Coptic communities.

In September 2003, the Los Angeles Field Office (LAFO) initiated the formation of the Muslim, Arab, Armenian, Sikh, and Coptic Ombudsman Program per a directive by Director Mueller.

It was decided that a council should be formed through which information, ideas, and concerns could be shared between the FBI and said communities. The inaugural meeting of the Committee was hosted by LAFO on May 17, 2004. Since that date, the Committee has met on the third Monday of each month to address issues and concerns ranging from the FBI's Counter Terrorism and Counter Intelligence missions, the Patriot Act, and interviews of individuals within Arab, Armenian, Muslim, and Sikh communities, as well as guest presentations by other agencies. The Committee has grown to 35 members, and is continuing to grow to include, among others, four members from college Muslim student organizations. As a result of the interactions between the FBI and the Committee members, LAFO has participated in a number of town hall meetings and community functions at which an FBI presence is requested, as well as media events hosted by Muslim community organizations. Members of the Multi-Cultural Advisory Committee have also provided information to the FBI which has resulted in investigations of potential radical extremists living among their communities. In the spirit of partnership and sharing information, Committee members have hosted a number of events for FBI personnel to broaden their cultural and religious understanding of the various aspects of the Arab, Armenian, Muslim, Sikh, and Coptic communities in the greater Los Angeles area. LAFO maintains daily contact with the Committee members via telephone, e-mail, and in person meetings.

With respect to collaborations that have been forged among law enforcement and other public safety sectors, the FBI and its law enforcement partners have been working together for a number of years to address terrorism related matters. In 1984, in order to coordinate counterterrorism threats and responses associated with the Summer Olympic Games event which took place in Los Angeles, the FBI initiated a working group with the Los Angeles Police Department and Los Angeles County Sheriffs Department. This led to the formation of the Los Angeles Joint Terrorism Task Force (JTTF) in 1986.

Today, the Los Angeles JTTF program has expanded to include the Long Beach JTTF, the Orange County JTTF, and the Inland Empire JTTF, which coordinate their investigations through the Los Angeles JTTF, and ultimately with the National JTTF. The combined resources of the various formalized and ad-hoc JTTF groups in the greater Los Angeles territory includes more than 260 full-time task force investigators, consisting of approximately 150 FBI Special Agents, and 110 other federal, state, and local task force agents/officers. The following is a listing of the various local, state, and federal agencies who participate on the JTTF's in LAFO's territory:

Local Agencies:

Los Angeles Police Department

Los Angeles County Sheriffs Department

Beverly Hills Police Department

Long Beach Police Department

Los Angeles International Airport Police Department

Los Angeles City Fire Department

Los Angeles County District Attorney's Office,
Bureau of Investigations

Torrance Police Department

Los Angeles Port Police
Redondo Beach Police Department
Orange County Sheriff's Department
Orange County District Attorney's Office
Ventura County Sheriff's Department
Santa Ana Police Department
Anaheim Police Department
Cypress Police Department
Garden Grove Police Department
Irvine Police Department
San Bernardino Police Department
San Bernardino Sheriff's Department
Riverside Sheriff's Department Banning Police Department
Barstow Police Department
Beaumont Police Department
BNSF Railroad Police Department
Chino Police Department
Colton Police Department
Corona Police Department
Fontana Police Department
Hemet Police Department
Indio Police Department
Montclair Police Department
Murrieta Police Department
Ontario Police Department
Ontario Airport Police Department
Palm Springs Police Department
Redlands Police Department
Riverside Police Department
UC Riverside Police Department
Upland Police Department
Buena Park Police Department

State Agencies:

California Highway Patrol

California Department of Justice (CATIC)

California Army National Guard

California Department of Motor Vehicles

Federal Agencies:

United States Secret Service

U.S. Immigration and Customs Enforcement

Department of State Diplomatic Security Service

United States Army

Air Force Office of Special Investigations

Department of Treasury, Internal Revenue Service

Bureau of Alcohol, Tobacco, Firearms, and Explosives

U.S. Postal Inspection Service

Naval Criminal Investigative Service

Defense Criminal Investigative Service

Central Intelligence Agency

Drug Enforcement Administration

Federal Air Marshals

U.S. Coast Guard

Environmental Protection Agency

U.S. Customs and Border Protection

Transportation Security Administration

Department of Defense

U.S. Bureau of Prisons

Amtrak Rail Police

In addition to the long standing JTTF program, the Los Angeles FBI has also developed a number of information sharing programs and initiatives to ensure that our partners are fully aware of intelligence and threat information developed by the FBI and other agencies.

As part of the transformation undertaken by the FBI since September 11, 2001, we have developed and directed the implementation of the Field Intelligence Group (FIG) program, which serves as the mechanism by which the Field Divisions evaluate threats. The FIG is utilized by the FBI to evaluate regional and local perspectives on a variety of issues, to include the receipt of and action on integrated investigative and intelligence requirements. FIGs further provide the intelligence link to the JTTFs, Fusion Centers, FBIHQ and the Intelligence Community at large. FIGs, which have been established in all 56 Field Offices since October 2003, consist of Intelligence Analysts, Special Agents, Language Analysts, and Special Surveillance Groups. FIG personnel have been embedded in more than twenty-five Fusion Centers and/or Multi-Agency Intelligence Centers (MAICs) around the country.

Among the fundamental post September 11th changes, sharing intelligence is now the paramount objective. We have developed an FBI intelligence presence within the intelligence and law enforcement communities by sharing Intelligence Information Reports (IIRs), Intelligence Assessments (IAs), Intelligence Bulletins (IBs), and related intelligence information on platforms routinely used by our law enforcement and Intelligence Community partners, including JWICS, SIPRNet and Law Enforcement Online (LEO), as well as on the FBI Intranet. This effort has resulted in more than 7,400 IIRs, 150 IBs, and 100 IAs that have been posted on all listed platforms; in addition, over 400 Current Intelligence Reports have also been produced, of which over 50 have been shared with the intelligence community through NCTC Online. We are also using our internal, closed network to provide FBI employees with access to raw, current and finished intelligence products. Additionally, we utilize unclassified, but law enforcement sensitive portals, such as Law Enforcement Online (LEO) and The Intelligence and Terrorism Alert Network (TITAN), to disseminate products to officers on the street relative to both terrorism and criminal matters on which we have developed analysis.

Regarding the Fusion Centers and/or Multi-Agency Intelligence Centers, Los Angeles established a Joint Regional Intelligence Center (JRIC) in which federal, state, and local resources were commingled in order to produce an integrated multi-agency intelligence processing center. The Los Angeles JRIC is a groundbreaking cooperative which fully integrates intelligence intake, vetting, analysis/fusion, and synthesis from a multitude of law enforcement and public safety agencies. The JRIC also disseminates developed intelligence, provides analytical case support, analyzes trends, and provides tailored analytical products to end users. The JRIC was founded by the FBI, the United States Attorney's Office for the Central District of California, the California Governor's Office of Homeland Security, the Los Angeles Sheriff's Department (LASD), and the Los Angeles Police Department (LAPD). Other agencies who participate in the JRIC provide analysts to staff the facility, and the JRIC's services are available to all law enforcement agencies throughout our seven county region. The partnerships formed in the JRIC allow the facility to be a central contact point for law enforcement and public safety intelligence, and provides for a smoother flow of leads and intelligence to prevent duplication, fragmentation, and circular reporting.

Chairwoman Harman, Ranking Member Reichert, and members of the Subcommittee, there has been a lot of discussion and speculation about the effectiveness of the FBI and its partners to combat terrorism, and the manner in which information is processed and shared to ensure the prevention of terrorist attacks on American soil. The FBI has made significant improvements in the past six years to ensure we are pooling our federal, state, and local resources accordingly, and working as one team to address potential threats to our homeland. In my 25 years working as a law enforcement officer, I have never experienced the level of collegial partnerships between law enforcement and public safety agencies as I have here in Los Angeles. We fully appreciate and understand the tasking that the American people expect of us, and we are standing shoulder to shoulder with our partners to accomplish this mission.

Thank you for the opportunity to come before you today and share the work the FBI and our federal, state, and local partners are doing to address terror threats to our country. I am happy to answer any questions.

Statement of Larry A. Mead
Deputy Sheriff
Los Angeles County Sheriff's Department

Madam Chairman, ranking member and members of the committee, thank you for the opportunity to speak to you on the issue of "Prison Radicalization."

The subject of "Prison Radicalization" reaches far beyond the walls of the California Department of Corrections and Rehabilitation (CDCR), county jails and juvenile facilities throughout the State of California. It has local, national and international implications. The effort to impact "homegrown" terrorism in prisons, jails and society is a monumental task which requires the cooperation of local, state and federal agencies and the community at large. My testimony will focus on the local gang culture and it's effects on the Los Angeles County Jail regarding radicalization and our Department's cooperation with federal, state and local agencies to share information thereby preventing, disrupting or mitigating a terrorist attack.

Within our custody operations division, our gang intelligence unit, Operation Safe Jails (OSJ), which originated in 1985, analyzes gang trends, conduct gang interviews, classifies and maintains gang files in an ongoing effort to prevent attacks on both staff and our inmate population. Over the years OSJ has evolved into an extremely critical asset for unit commanders and executives throughout the Department. OSJ's primary responsibility is gang intelligence. In addition, the unit assists local, state and federal agencies with ongoing investigations. In an effort to improve communications, a sergeant attends briefings and meetings with the Los Angeles area Joint Terrorism Task Force (JTTF), Terrorism Early Warning group (TEW), the Joint Regional Information Center (JRIC), the California Department of Corrections Gang Task Force and other regional gang meetings. These relationships have resulted in high quality products that are provided to decision makers covering a variety of terror-related subjects.

With an average daily population of 19,000 plus inmates, the Los Angeles County jail system is seen as a possible location where prison radicalization can sew it roots. Since late 1995, several OSJ gang intelligence deputies were designated Terrorism Liaison Officers (TLO's) who report on radical activities to the Department's Terrorism Early Warning group. This has expanded to other local state and federal agencies. Their activities were heightened by the July, 2005, discovery of the radical prison group, Jam'iyyat Ul-Islam Is-Sheeh (JIS) or the "Authentic Assembly of Islam," at Folsom State Prison, near Sacramento, California. Since then, analysis shows that radicalization and recruitment in U.S. prisons is still an ongoing concern. Prison radicalization primarily occurs through anti-U.S. sermons provided by contract, volunteer's, staff imams, radicalized inmates who gain religious influence, or extremist media. Ideologies that radicalized inmates appear most often to embrace, include or are influenced by the Salafi form of Sunni Islam (including revisionist versions commonly known as "prison Islam") and an extremist view of Shia Islam similar to that of the government of Iran and Lebanese Hizballah.

Jail Radicalization Initiatives in Los Angeles County

- Two deputies working full time on the radicalization issue within the Los Angeles County Jail System
- LASD participates on the Jail Radicalization Working group with FBI, LAPD, CDC
- Ongoing integration effort with Jail Investigations Unit, Operation Safe Jails, Classification Unit and the Joint Regional Intelligence Center
- Ongoing interaction with religious leaders (more than 100) who conduct services at all Los Angeles County jail facilities
- Continued outreach for better communication between local, state and federal custodial facilities regarding the transfer and travel of "problem inmates"
- Participation with George Washington University on the study of issues related to radicalization

Religious Leader Verification Process

– Application
– Copy of Ordination
– Support Letter from sponsoring church
– Background by Inmate Services Unit
– Orientation program
– Random monitoring by Inmate Services Unit
– Random monitoring by Chapel Deputies

Sheriff Baca's Statement:

> The effort to impact radicalization and "homegrown" terrorism in mainstream society is an inherently difficult task, especially without the cooperation and partnership of the local Muslim community. Muslim-American organizations have been working on various ways of supporting and participating in the security needs of America, as well as people of all nations. Sheriff Leroy D. Baca, of the Los Angeles County Sheriff's Department, has taken the lead to formalize this endeavor by forming a national organization known as the Muslim-American Homeland Security Congress (MAHSC). This is a non-political, non-governmental, non-religious, and non-profit organization. Through partnerships, cooperation and assistance with national and local elected officials, law enforcement, civic and

inter-faith groups, the Muslim-American Homeland Security Congress will educate, reach out to the disenfranchised, and communicate to all Americans the goals and purpose of the organization.

Mission

The Muslim-American Homeland Security Congress shall foster education & understanding, organization & empowerment, along with Communication & Cooperation with the American public to protect and defend the United States of America and all people through the prevention of terrorism and any acts of prejudice.

Operation Safe Jails gang intelligence deputies are continuously monitoring our inmate population for radical activity. The Imams who conduct religious service go through a thorough background check and their teachings are not associated with the radicalized form of Islam. Inmates who attempt to spread radical Islam are monitored and reported to the appropriate agencies. We have identified several inmates who had radical correspondence, drawings of airplanes flying into the World Trade Center, e-mail addresses to radical websites, and in one disturbing instance, we interviewed a foreign national who provided information regarding a safe house radical mosque where large sums of U.S. Currency is counted and forwarded to a Middle Eastern country for dissemination. There is no doubt that "Prison Radicalization," is an ongoing problem. We all need to continue our focus on this growing phenomena and add additional resources to combat this growing trend or run the risk of another similar situation such as the JIS incident which occurred at Folsom State Prison in July, 2005.

Statement of Ms. Sireen Sawaf
Director, Southern California Government Relations
Muslim Public Affairs Council

Chairwoman Harman and distinguished members of the Subcommittee, thank you for the opportunity to testify before you today. It is a privilege to testify before you today on behalf of the Muslim Public Affairs Council to discuss the phenomenon of radicalization and some of the work the Muslim American community has done alongside law enforcement to counter this threat and enhance our nations security.

First and foremost, radicalization must be seen as a socio-political set of behaviors and is not simply a law enforcement problem. If not understood, mishandled, or even exacerbated, the emotions and political persuasions of the people we are trying to help, in this case Muslim American youth, will be further alienated and marginalized from the mainstream, and hence a sense of ghettoization will take place in various communities. We cannot afford to continue with language that imposes suspicion on Muslim American youth, whereby they are guilty before proven innocent, and then spend millions of dollars on studies and programs to engage them. The key to countering extremism and radicalization, therefore, is understanding and partnering with the Muslim American community, as we are one of the most underutilized but irreplaceable assets in protecting the homeland. When extremists use Islam to justify acts of terrorism, the only group that can counter bad theology with accurate theology is the Muslim American leadership. We are best equipped to detect criminal activity and distinguish it from cultural norms (such as prayer in airport terminals), and we are most qualified to win the hearts and minds of the Muslim world. It takes leadership and insight to recognize the critical role American Muslims play in protecting this country; hence I commend this Subcommittee for including our much-needed perspective in this solution-seeking effort.

It is important to note that one of the key factors in preventing another 9/11 from happening is the patriotism of the Muslim American community in openly rejecting Al Qaeda as a legitimate group within Islamic discourse. Through counter-terrorism policy papers and public pronouncements against terrorism, such as the Fatwa (legal opinion) of Muslim American scholars, Muslim Americans have separated legitimate Islamic discourse and activity from violent radicalism using religion as a vehicle for mobilization. We recommend that policy-makers and opinion-shapers should apply the same practice. Otherwise, we afford Al Qaeda the only source of legitimacy, the veneer of Islam.

As we collectively strive to analyze the reality and possibility of "homegrown terrorism" in the West, the bombings in London, Madrid and the recently foiled plots in Canada have fueled public anxiety and the concerns of public officials. In order to effectively counter homegrown terrorism in the

U.S., particularly the potential for radicalization of Muslim youth, it is necessary to understand the roots of that extremism and the key factors that may cause one to cross the line from rhetoric to violence.

The Muslim Public Affairs Council has just completed the first substantive American Muslim position paper addressing radicalization that contributes to preventing this phenomenon from taking root in U.S. soil by 1) framing the issues related to the radicalization of Muslim youth in the West while considering the realities on the ground, and 2) providing recommendations to Muslim American institutions, government and the media to engage young Muslims in a healthy partnership of respect and equality and subsequently reduce the possibility of radicalization by enhancing integration. For the purpose of today's hearing, I will highlight key parts of this paper entitled, "Effectively Countering Extremism and Supporting Muslim American Youth." The Muslim Public Affairs Council is offering an opportunity to all staff and members of this distinguished committee a briefing on this Muslim Youth paper in Washington, DC, at a time of your convenience.

Radicalization and Key Factors

The radicalization of young Western Muslims, while on the minds of many, is void of thoughtful analyses that explain core dynamics within Western societies and how they uniquely affect youth within extremely diverse Muslim communities. Only when we delve into the key issues of identity, social and political alienation, the definition of a moderate, and Islamophobia as a root cause of radicalization can we understand and prevent radicalization from taking root in the U.S.

First and foremost, when defining radicalization, government agencies across the board must articulate a clear distinction between healthy challenging of the status quo in current affairs with the expression of radical rhetoric, and the willingness to use, support or facilitate violence as a means for change. Until today, the public officials striving to understand and prevent violence have yet to effectively articulate this distinction to the public, particularly the Muslim American community, which has increased the gap of community distrust and suspicion of government officials.

Moreover, when law enforcement or anti-academic freedom groups (e.g., Campus Watch) engage in what some have called "thought policing", many young Muslim Americans feel alienated. To criticize the lack of free expression in the Muslim world while discouraging the same in the U.S. is perceived to be hypocritical or at least incongruent. As a result Muslim American youth can end up resisting or distrusting mainstream political and civic participation leaving them vulnerable to fringe radical groups.

Identity

We at MPAC believe that an accurate evaluation of the state of the Muslim American community must be built upon an assessment of the health and vibrancy of the Muslim American Identity. Since the early 1980's, MPAC and its affiliate institutions have focused resources and efforts on building a community of Muslims in America that are forward-looking and contributing components of American pluralism. This and similar Muslim American experiences across the nation aim to build communities that are organic to the global community of Muslims and also at "home" in the American project.

A recent Gallup poll discussed in our position paper on youth that accounted statistically for the opinions of 1 billion Muslims and their opinions of the West presented data challenging those who argue a "clash of civilizations" analysis to explain present concerns around extremism and terrorism. The study's findings further challenge the notion that religiosity and radicalism are two sides of the same coin of terrorism. The inability to realize that religion is an answer to radicalization, that only a good and authentic theology can overcome a zealous and fraudulent one, has led us down a slippery slope of conflating religious conservatism for radicalism or extremism.

While rejecting the simplistic "clash of civilizations" theory, as realities on the ground including the adoption of the Muslim American Identity have proven false, it is important to recognize the sense of marginalization many youth feel and the importance of reaffirming the contributory role Muslim American youth play in our nations pluralism.

Social and Political Alienation

It is important to note that the factors that increase the wedge of identity, such as alienation and marginalization of Muslims, vary in the United States and in Europe. MPAC's position paper on youth brings to light the different factors contributing to the more successful integration of Muslim Americans into American pluralism, such as the demographic and structural differences between the U.S. and Europe.

As of today, we have not seen a terrorist group forming amongst youth here in the U.S. In fact, the Muslim American community at large has rejected any militancy within the mainstream community and there is no indication that any Al Qaeda-like movement has gained traction in America.

In recent decades, however, some Muslim groups drew young people into communities that attempted to live self-sufficiently from the broader society surrounding them with the intent of living a Puritan life. Throughout the course of American history, the idea of "separating" as a race or a religion from the larger society has been viewed repeatedly as an option for the disenfranchised or a desire by immigrant communities to maintain ones identity. It is important to emphasize that in the U.S. experience, none of these social manifestations represented a terrorist threat but were an expression of marginalization, even frustration with current foreign and domestic policies of the U.S. government.

Moderates vs. Extremists

Much of the global conversation about Islam and Muslims is focused on labeling the different camps of Muslims from a perspective completely out of touch with the realities on the ground. Since our inception in 1988, MPAC has proposed that moderation, particularly of Muslims, cannot be gauged by the political ideas and ideologies that one holds, but rather by ones understanding of moderation as defined by the Qur'an and the tradition of the Prophet. If acquiescence to or active support of American global interest were the test, then characters such as Saddam Hussein and Usama bin Laden would each have qualified at different junctures in their careers.

MPAC's position paper details the distinction between a moderate and a radical, the problems that arise when we invoke rhetoric and terminology, such as Islamic Radicalization, and the key to marginalizing the extremists. Suffice it to say, the litmus tests for moderation, rather, revolve around topics such as the role of women in the public square and in leadership roles within Muslim institutions, the impermissibility of the use of violence as a means for political change, the acceptance of disparate segments of the Muslim American community, the rights of non-Muslims in Muslim-majority societies and the role of critical thinking in building the character of a Muslim. When it comes to the topic of reform, it is the sole role of Muslim Americans to lead this discourse within arenas of authentic and well-grounded sources of Islam.

Islamophobia: A Root Cause of Radicalization

We at MPAC have consistently argued through publications such as our Counterproductive Counterterrorism policy paper and other avenues that much of the hate disguised in counterterrorism is counterproductive, and the anti-Islamic rhetoric will eventually result in impeding our national security and ability to defend the homeland.

Too frequently, communities that are excluded from conversations tend to use that exclusion as an excuse to withdraw from any discussion on religious reform and civic engagement. Since the 1980's, MPAC has advocated for civic and political engagement as the key tools for the inclusion of Muslim Americans and the consequent prevention of extremism. Our position paper on youth lists recommendations for Universities, American Muslim institutions, the media, and government to quell the potential for radicalization in the U.S. Here, it is important to highlight some of the relationships MPAC has built with government officials, particularly law enforcement.

Muslim Community-Law Enforcement Relations

MPAC has been heavily involved in counter-terrorism and outreach efforts in cooperation with national and local law enforcement agencies as well as the equally important efforts of counter-extremism in the Muslim American community with a focus on youth. We have also been engaged with European Muslim communities and governments in numerous arenas on both sides of the Atlantic as well as in Muslim-majority countries in an effort to assess the environments that produce such extremism. Recognizing the importance of engaging young people in planning for the future as a central theme to constructive religious, social and political work, MPAC is committed to building a future generation of leaders.

Since the early 1990's, MPAC has worked closely with federal agencies such as the FBI, and has contributed to enhancing our nations security by providing analysis and a unique perspective through direct communication with key officials and thoughtful mediums, such as MPAC's 1999 Counterterrorism Policy Paper. Following 911, many of these relationships have become institutionalized and formalized to some degree, and have expanded to include leadership from other 911-impacted communities on the local and national levels. MPAC currently participates in regular meetings with state and local law enforcement, and on a local and national level, the Department of Homeland Security and the Federal Bureau of Investigations. The partnership model in Los Angeles I wish to elaborate on is the FBI-initiated Multi-Cultural Advisory Committee (MCAC).

As the Government Relations Director of Southern California for the Muslim Public Affairs Council, it is my responsibility to enhance civic engagement amongst the Muslim American community and to ensure that the concerns of the community are being addressed by the appropriate government agencies responsible for those concerns, which is what lead to my participation in MCAC since it's inception.

I must start by commending the FBI for being among the first government agencies to recognize the importance of engaging with and outreaching to the community following the horrific attacks of 911. In response to the increasing concerns of American Muslim, Arab, Sikh, South Asian, Coptic Christian, Bahai and Iranian communities in the post-911 era, the FBI initiated the creation of the Multi-Cultural Advisory Committee in 2004. MCAC's mission of creating "an environment to facilitate dialogue and enhance the relationship between the FBI and the Community, which is based upon mutual respect, understanding, and the protection of Constitutional rights and civil liberties" is necessary in ensuring communities become part of the solution. Creating and strengthening a two-way line of communication with the government has provided the opportunity for community leaders to raise concerns about policies and procedures and regain confidence in the government when concerns are resolved given their due attention, encouraging the use of community expertise towards problem-solving.

While most of what I will share will apply to other communities, I will be addressing the concerns of the Muslim American community. Upon its inception, establishing a strong relationship with the FBI and the grassroots Muslim American community was burdened with external factors such as cultural baggage, particularly cultural distrust due to previous experiences within the indigenous African American Muslim community, and suspicion of law enforcement by first and second-generation Muslims due to experiences in ones country of origin, where police were an extension of an oppressive regime. Muslim leadership and the FBI have continued to jointly craft solutions to these challenges such as providing constructive feedback on watch lists for the purpose of enhancing efficacy and avoiding wrongful inclusion of innocent people; increasing direct communication between the FBI and community members to ensure the sharing of accurate information and citizens have direct access to their public servants; and providing cultural sensitivity trainings to law enforcement designed to increase sensitivity toward the community. These efforts have been successful in breaking down the communication barrier, and they must continue, as the road ahead is a long one.

Unfortunately, several internal factors have and continue to inhibit the relationship to some degree, much of which are due to the bureaucracy in the FBI rather than the lack of desire for engagement by the community. The names of innocent citizens landing on watchlists, controversy around high profile cases, the use of informants, the use of foreign intelligence in the prosecution of domestic cases, and the conflation of every criminal activity by Muslims that makes it's way to public media as terrorism are just a few issues that drive a wedge between the FBI and the Muslim American community. The perception of the community has become one where they believe they are viewed as suspect rather than partner in the War on Terror, and that their civil liberties are "justifiably" sacrificed upon the decisions of federal agents. So the task of building the level of communication, trust and confidence with the Muslim American community has become much more challenging. It is the responsibility of the FBI to provide clarity in the midst of confusion, and of the community to ensure accurate information surpasses the rumors that can cause fear and alienation. Here, I'd like to highlight an example of a success.

Following a series of politically controversial events held by Muslim students at the University of California, Irvine, Pat Rose, the head of the FBI's Orange County Al Qaeda squad was quoted as saying her agency was looking for and electronically monitoring potential terrorists in Orange County.

Rose also said that the FBI is aware of large numbers of Muslims at UCI and USC, and was "quite surprised" that "there are a lot of individuals of interest right here in Orange County." The publication and timing of this quote caused an uproar in Muslim youth and the Orange County Muslim community, as they understood these comments to suggest that the FBI was monitoring student groups, possibly due to organizing unpopular but nevertheless legal political events on campus. In efforts to nip this rumor in the bud, FBI Assistant Director in Charge of the Los Angeles field office, Stephen Tidwell, clarified these remarks at an emergency town hall meeting of youth, parents and other community members in Irvine in June 2006, and in a written statement in July 2006. While some were skeptical of Tidwell's clarification, this swift response by the FBI should serve as an example to the importance of disseminating accurate information about FBI operations and answering to the legitimate grievances of community members.

Many challenges remain ahead, and despite the deficiencies in partnerships that currently exist, the MCAC model is an example of how to create and maintain partnership, understanding, information sharing, and bridge building between government officials and community members. The responsibility to maintain a successful partnership falls on both parties. For instance, government public pronouncements about criminal activity should avoid the conflated use of terrorism terminology that implicates Islam and motivations sourced in Muslim culture and Islamic tradition. Moreover, when cases that are championed as terrorism-related are resolved with no relation to issues related to Islam or the American Muslim community, law enforcement should clearly and loudly inform the public. In tandem, community members should continue to engage their public officials, and ensure decision-makers and public servants are addressing their concerns, while we continue to collectively think of innovative ways to participate in the protection of the country and the principles upon which it was founded. Tensions that will challenge the partnership will certainly arise, but we must patiently persevere to create and maintain positive, constructive relations as we find each other on the frontlines of protecting this nation. Sincere partnership based on accurate and responsible communication sharing, the recognition of the critical role the community plays in enhancing our nations security, and collective problem solving is a key tool in preventing radicalization from taking root in our soil. I thank you for the opportunity to testify today, and I welcome your questions.

Statement of Brian Michael Jenkins[1]
Senior Advisor
RAND Corporation

Building an Army of Believers: Jihadist Radicalization and Recruitment[2]

Madame Chair: I appreciate the opportunity to be here today where you have experienced homegrown terror firsthand to discuss the issues of radicalization and how to protect the homeland. Although the United States and its allies have achieved undeniable success in degrading the operational capabilities of jihadist terrorists worldwide, they have had less success in reducing the radicalization and recruitment that support the jihadist enterprise.

Nearly five years after 9/11, a 2006 National Intelligence Estimate concluded that "activists identifying themselves as jihadists . . . are increasing in both number and geographic dispersion." As a consequence, "the operational threat from self-radicalized cells will grow in importance to U.S. counterterrorism efforts, particularly abroad, but also in the Homeland."[3] In testimony before the Senate, FBI Director Robert Mueller indicated concern about extremist recruitment in prisons, schools, and universities "inside the United States."[4] In March of this year, Charles Allen, Assistant Secretary of Homeland Security, concurred that "radicalization will continue to expand within the United States over the long term."[5]

Recently, we have begun to focus more attention on what I refer to in my book as the "front end" of the jihadist cycle.[6] Growing concern has produced a growing volume of literature on the topic.[7] My testimony today will simply highlight a few areas for further discussion:

- Building an army of believers—how the jihadists recruit
- Radicalization and recruitment in the United States
- How we might impede radicalization and recruitment, and
- Guiding principles for any actions we might consider.

These comments derive from my own study of terrorism over the years, and from a large body of research done by my colleagues at the RAND Corporation.[8]

Building an Army of Believers

More than a military contest, the jihadist campaign is above all a missionary enterprise. Jihadist terrorist operations are intended to attract attention, demonstrate capability, and harm the jihadists' enemies, but they are also aimed at galvanizing the Muslim community and, above all, inciting and attracting recruits to the cause. Recruiting is not merely meant to fill operational needs. It is an end in itself: It aims at creating a new mindset.

At one time, Al Qaeda dispatched recruiters, but the jihadists never created a central recruiting organization. Instead, they relied upon a loose network of like-minded extremists who constantly proselytized on behalf of jihad. Recruiting was always diffused, localized, and informal.

Self-radicalization was often the norm, even before the worldwide crackdown on Al Qaeda and its jihadist allies forced them to decentralize and disperse. Those who arrived at jihadist training camps were already radicalized. At the camps, they bonded through shared beliefs and hardships, underwent advanced training, gained combat experience, and were selected by Al Qaeda's planners for specific terrorist operations.

There is a distinction between radicalization and recruitment. Radicalization comprises internalizing a set of beliefs, a militant mindset that embraces violent jihad as the paramount test of one's conviction. It is the mental prerequisite to recruitment. Recruitment is turning others or transforming oneself into a weapon of jihad. It means joining a terrorist organization or bonding with like-minded individuals to form an autonomous terrorist cell. It means going operational, seeking out the means and preparing for an actual terrorist operation—the ultimate step in jihad.

Worldwide, radicalization and recruiting vary from country to country. In some places, such as the Philippines, Indonesia, Pakistan, and Chechnya, potential recruits are already members of a locally dominant culture and may be involved in an on-going conflict that seeks independence, autonomy, or nationwide adherence to a fundamentalist interpretation of Islam. They draw on local tradition and, in some cases, family histories of resistance. The local population is sympathetic to their cause, although it may not always support their actions.[9]

In the core Arab countries, where potential jihadists may share the basic beliefs of the dominant national culture or a fundamentalist subculture, they confront hostility and oppression from the central political authorities and therefore must go abroad or operate underground.

The situation in the West is still different, and there are further differences between recruiting in Europe, where there are large and largely unassimilated Muslim immigrant populations, and recruiting in the United States, a nation with a long tradition of assimilating immigrants. Potential jihadist recruits in Western countries are part of a marginalized immigrant subculture or are themselves cut off even from family and friends within that community. The more vulnerable are those who are at a stage of life where they are seeking an identity, while looking for approval and validation. They are searching for causes that can be religiously and culturally justified, that provide them a way to identify who they are, and that provide a clear call for action.

The jihadist agenda is action-oriented, claims to be religiously justified, and appeals to this relatively young, action-oriented population. Self-radicalization begins the day that an individual seeks out jihadist websites. In the real world they seek support among local jihadist mentors and like-minded fanatics. This is the group that currently poses the biggest danger to the West.

Jihadists recruit one person at a time. The message from the global jihad is aimed directly at the individual. It argues that the Islamic community faces assault from aggressive infidels and their apostate allies; it is threatened by military attack, cultural corruption, social disintegration, and substandard zeal. The antidote to these threats is jihad, not as a spiritual quest, but as an armed defense. This is a religious obligation incumbent upon all true believers.

Al Qaeda's brand of jihad offers a comprehensive and uncomplicated solution—the possibility of adventure, a "legitimate" outlet for aggression, the lure of clandestinity, pride, camaraderie, an elixir to cure all ills, an antidote to anxiety, an achievable goal, a seemingly noble cause, a sense of direction and meaning in life, and the eventual promise of earthly pleasures in the hereafter. It is a message that is especially attractive to angry young men and frustrated, compliant individuals.

Becoming a jihadist is a gradual, multi-step process that can take months, even years, although since 9/11 the pace has accelerated. The journey may begin in a mosque where a radical Imam preaches, in informal congregations and prayer groups—some of which are clandestine—in schools, in prisons, on the Internet.

The process starts with incitement—a message that commands and legitimizes violent jihad—and it combines self-selection and persuasion by jihadist recruiters. Volunteers are recruited into a universe of belief, not a single destination. Eager acolytes may coalesce into an autonomous cell, as did the original Hamburg group that later carried out the 9/11 attack, or they may join an existing local group. Individuals may be moved along to training camps or be persuaded by jihadist exhortation to act on their own.

Becoming a jihadist may involve a series of invitations and proofs of commitment; it may also involve training abroad. Proceeding to the next step, ultimately to act, is always an individual decision. Volunteers move on by self-selection. There may be powerful peer pressure, but there is no coercion. Submission is voluntary. Not all recruits complete the journey. Commitment is constantly calibrated and re-recalibrated. Some drop out along the way. A component of our counter-recruiting strategy must be to always offer a safe way back from the edge.

Jihadist recruiting emphasizes various themes: Honor, dignity, and duty versus humiliation, shame, and guilt. Fighting is God's mandate, a religious duty—paradise is guaranteed to those who join jihad. Jihad provides an opportunity to demonstrate commitment, courage, prowess as a warrior, and although it is not explicit in the recruiting, jihad is a license for violence. At the very least, it provides vicarious participation in war through martial arts, paintball battles, reconnaissance of potential targets, and endless discussion of fantasy terrorist plans.

Short of preparing for a specific attack, it is hard to define the exact point at which one becomes a jihadist: Internalization of jihadist ideology? Bonding with brothers at a jihadist retreat? Downloading jihadist literature or bomb-making instructions from the Internet? Fantasizing about terrorist operations? Reconnoitering potential targets? Going to Pakistan? Signing a contract to pray for the jihadists, collect money, or support operations? Taking an oath of loyalty to Osama bin Laden? The legal definition is broad.

Personal problems also play a role. Recruits often come from dysfunctional families, have experienced disruptive relocations, suffer identity crises, face uncertain futures, feel alienation; many are in trouble with authorities. Some of the problems are typical of the age group, and some come with immigration. Many recruits in the West are second- or third-generation immigrants. Others display the zeal typical of new converts. But jihadists also include sons of well-off families, people with promising careers, and individuals who are seemingly well-adjusted. There is no single psychological profile and no obvious indicator to permit targeted intervention.

While the jihadist message is widely and increasingly disseminated, the actual connection with the jihadist enterprise, outside of Middle Eastern and Asian madrassahs, appears random, depending on personal acquaintance, finding a radical mosque, or being spotted by a recruiter. That, in turn, suggests that the numbers are driven not merely by the appeal of the jihadist narrative, but also by the number of "retail outlets" where recruiters can meet potential recruits.

The recruiting process, therefore, seems to be not very efficient—the yield is low. However, only a few converts suffice to carry out terrorist operations. Nevertheless, this suggests that reducing the number of suspected recruiting venues would seriously impede jihadist recruiting.

Radicalization and Recruiting in the United States

Neither imported nor homegrown terrorism is new in the United States. Many immigrant groups have brought the quarrels of their homeland with them. Anti-Castro Cubans, Croatian separatists, Puerto Rican separatists, Armenian extremists, Taiwanese separatists, earlier cohorts of Islamist extremists have all carried on terrorist campaigns on U.S. soil, along with domestic ethnic groups, right-wing extremists, and ideologically driven fanatics.

A homegrown conspiracy (albeit with foreign assistance) was responsible for the 1993 bombing of the World Trade Center. Another homegrown conspiracy carried out the devastating 1995 bombing in Oklahoma City. The

United States, over the years, has successfully suppressed these groups through domestic intelligence collection and law enforcement.

However, Europe faces different problems. With a population of 350 million, Europe is home to between 30 and 50 million Muslims—estimates vary. By 2025, one-third of all children born in Europe will be of the Muslim faith. In contrast, the United States, with a population of 300 million, has approximately 4.7 million Muslims, most of them native Americans. Of the 3.5 million Arab-Americans in the United States, fewer than 25 percent are Muslim.

Large numbers of poor immigrants enter Europe legally and illegally from the Maghreb and Middle East, and assimilation is a problem. America, in contrast, is a distant destination for the Arab and Muslim masses; its recent Muslim immigrants tend to be better educated, better off, and more easily integrated. As a nation of immigrants, America does not demand cultural assimilation as a prerequisite to citizenship, and accented English is no barrier to achievement. These are inherent national strengths.

Since 9/11, U.S. authorities have uncovered a number of alleged individual terrorists and terrorist rings, including clusters in Lackawanna, Northern Virginia, Portland, New York City, and Lodi and Torrance, California. In all, several dozen persons have been convicted of providing material support to a terrorist organization, a crime that U.S. courts have interpreted broadly, or related crimes. Others, without demonstrable connections to terrorism, have been expelled for immigration offenses.

Most of those arrested have been young men of Middle Eastern or South Asian descent. They include both native and naturalized citizens, although almost all are citizens. Most were Muslims by birth, although some are converts. Most of them have been middle-class, with educations ranging from less than high school to postgraduate degrees. They represent diverse professions, and some are veterans of military service.

The Lackawanna, Northern Virginia, and Portland groups began to radicalize before 9/11, while the individuals in New York City, Lodi, and Torrance were more recent arrivals in the jihadist universe. The Northern Virginia and Portland groups planned to join jihadist groups abroad; those in New York City, Lodi, and Torrance contemplated action in the United States; the Lackawanna group had no apparent operational plans.

These arrests, along with intelligence operations, indicate that radicalization and recruiting are taking place in the United States, but there is no evidence of a significant cohort of terrorist operatives. We therefore worry most about terrorist attacks by very small conspiracies or individuals, which nonetheless could be equivalent to the London subway bombings or the 1995 Oklahoma City bombing.

This suggests that efforts should be made to enhance the intelligence capabilities of local police, who through community policing, routine criminal investigations, or dedicated intelligence operations may be best positioned to uncover future terrorist plots.

Of these, continued intelligence operations are the most important. Radicalization makes little noise. It occurs in an area protected by the First and Fourth Amendments. It takes place over a long period of time. It therefore does not lend itself to a traditional criminal investigations approach.

Impeding Radicalization and Recruitment

How might we best impede radicalization and recruiting? Let me suggest several possible angles of approach. These are not recommendations; they are options aimed at provoking further discussion, and each raises a number of questions.

Blocking The Message. Is exhortation to violence free speech protected by the First Amendment, or does it fall into the category of conduct that can be legally prohibited? Can Internet content be controlled? European governments argue that it can be. Clearly, the Internet is a new battlefield in the jihadist campaign, and the U.S. Army is reportedly preparing an assault on jihadist websites.[10]

But does the United States need a new information service to wage an information war? A new United States Information Agency? If so, where should it be located within our government?

How can anti-jihadist messages be facilitated? Would distributing such messages violate rules against domestic propaganda? Current law does allow messages against drugs, drunk driving, smoking, domestic abuse, dropping out of school, and publicizing the identity of wanted gang leaders. Can we do the same with jihad?

Removing the Inciters. Should the United States, like the United Kingdom, seek to expel foreign-born clerics who incite hatred and violence? Should institutions that host those exhorting violence lose their tax-free status and face other restrictions? Can foreign contributions be blocked when they clearly support radicalization?

Are inciters legitimate targets of intelligence efforts? Should messages of hate and their authors be publicly exposed? How can alternative role models be publicized?

Focusing on Recruiting Venues. Recruiting for jihad takes place both inside and outside of identified radical mosques and other known venues. These "retail outlets" can be identified and monitored. Surveillance, real and imagined, of recruiting venues can inform authorities of possible terrorist plots and may discourage recruiting.

The 2004 Herald Square Case in New York City is a good example of the methods, patience, and persistence that are needed to identify, understand, and thwart a jihadist recruitment that would have resulted in a terrorist attack. In fact, the New York Police Department has developed a very sophisticated understanding of the radicalization process and, in my view, has made some of the greatest strides in addressing it.[11] Prisons are another recruiting venue that could be better controlled.

Dissuading Potential Recruits. Can the community offer attractive alternatives to potential recruits—national and community service, education and technical training, sports, etc.? Can at least some imprisoned jihadists be rehabilitated to counter the recruiting message? Imprisoned terrorists in Italy were offered reduced sentences in return for renunciations of violence and cooperation with the authorities. Current programs to rehabilitate imprisoned jihadists in Singapore and Yemen may also provide valuable experience.

Enlisting The Broader Community. Can we implement educational programs at mosques and community centers, as Singapore is also doing, to expose the nature of jihadist ideology?

The absence of significant terrorist attacks or even advanced terrorist plots in the United States since 9/11 is good news that cannot be entirely explained by increased intelligence and heightened security. It suggests that America's Muslim population may be less susceptible than the Muslim population in Europe, if not entirely immune to jihadist ideology; indeed, there appear to be countervailing voices within the American Muslim community. Conversely it may merely indicate that the American Muslim population has not yet been exposed to the degree, variety, of radicalization as that of its European counterparts. This "success," or temporary reprieve, whatever its explanation, suggests in turn that we move cautiously to fix what may not be broken while realizing that the threat from radicalization continues to grow.

Some Guiding Principles

Society's purpose in this area is twofold: to deter vulnerable individuals from recruitment into destructive paths and to protect society itself against destruction—this may require preemptive intervention before manifest criminal behavior occurs.

However, the first principle must be to do no greater harm, to avoid misguided policies, needless hassles that only create enemies. A more permissive intelligence environment, society's demand to intervene before terrorist attacks occur will inevitably result in occasional errors. These should not be the basis for dismantling intelligence efforts or imposing unreasonable controls: Errors should produce prompt apologies. Systematic abuse should be punished.

Rules may be altered, but rules must prevail—assertions of extraordinary wartime authority or extrajudicial measures are unacceptable and dangerous. Domestic intelligence, surveillance, the rendering safe of dangerous ideologies are delicate undertakings that, as we already have seen, can slide into despotic behavior.

A nation of immigrants, America has been successful at integrating new arrivals without specific policies beyond guaranteeing equal opportunity and fairness to all, so long as they obey its laws. This success makes one wary of government programs aimed at specific ethic or émigré communities.

We owe immigrants nothing more than freedom, freedom from exploitation, freedom for prejudice, tolerance of different cultures and customs, and fair access to opportunity. In return, immigrants are not asked to abandon their faith or customs. They are required only to abide by the same laws and rules that govern our behavior.

Proposed measures must fit the magnitude of the threat. Isolated terrorist attacks can always occur, as they have in the past and almost certainly will in the future, but at present there is no significant jihadist underground in this country. Good domestic intelligence can discourage overreaction as well as contribute to deterrence.

Faith alone should cast no shadow of suspicion, but religion should provide no shield for subversion—society need not be shy about attacking hatred and exhortation to violence even when they are cloaked as religious belief. Protecting the freedom of religion may require enforced tolerance—that is, attacking exhortations to violence—in order to protect the freedom of all.

Incitement to violence, especially when there is an expectation that it will lead to action, is not protected by the First Amendment.

A sensible response requires a broad understanding of community structure and dynamics—innocent enterprises may at times be the subjects of official inquiry, if only to dismiss them from further scrutiny; intelligence activities should not imply suspicion.

Intervention measures should not isolate, alienate, stigmatize, or antagonize the communities in which recruiters look for quarry.

It is important to keep lines of communication open at all levels of government. This is community policing in its broadest sense, but the collection of intelligence and initiatives aimed at maintaining dialogue among communities and faiths are best handled at the local community level.

Whatever we do must be done with strict oversight and a sense of proportion to the threat. We should not, by our very efforts to protect society against terrorism, destroy what may be our best defense—a free and tolerant society.

Endnotes

[1] The opinions and conclusions expressed in this testimony are the author's alone and should not be interpreted as representing those of RAND or any of the sponsors of its research. This product is part of the RAND Corporation testimony series. RAND testimonies record testimony presented by RAND associates to federal, state, or local legislative committees; government-appointed commissions and panels; and private review and oversight bodies. The RAND Corporation is a nonprofit research organization providing objective analysis and effective solutions that address the challenges facing the public and private sectors around the world. RAND's publications do not necessarily reflect the opinions of its research clients and sponsors.

[2] This testimony is available for free download at http://www.rand.org/pubs/testimonies/CT278.

[3] U.S. Government, Declassified Key Judgments of the National Intelligence Estimate "Trends in Global Terrorism: Implications for the United States." April 2006.

[4] Testimony of Robert S. Mueller, III, Director, Federal Bureau of Investigation Before the Senate Committee on Intelligence, February 16, 2005.

[5] Testimony of Charles E. Allen, Assistant Secretary, Intelligence and Analysis, Chief Intelligence Officer, Department of Homeland Security Before the Senate Committee on Homeland Security and Governmental Affairs, March 7, 2007.

[6] Brian Michael Jenkins, *Unconquerable Nation: Knowing Our Enemy, Strengthening Ourselves,* Santa Monica: RAND Corporation, 2006. See specifically pp. 123-132.

[7] Edwin Bakker, *Jihadists in Europe—Their Characteristics and the Circumstances in which They Joined the Jihad: An Exploratory Study,* Clingendael: Netherlands Institute of International Relations, 2006. Paul K. Davis and Brian Michael Jenkins, *Deterrence and Influence in Counterterrorism: A Component of the War*

[8] See for example, Scott Gerwehr and Sara Daly, "Al-Qaida: Terrorist Selection and Recruitment," in David G. Kamien (ed.), *The McGraw-Hill Homeland Security Handbook,* New York: McGraw-Hill, 2005, pp. 73-89; William Rosenau, "Al Qaeda Recruitment in the United States: A Preliminary Assessment," *MIPT Yearbook 2004.* Oklahoma City: Memorial Institute for the Prevention of Terrorism, 2004, pp.23-31. See also Kim Cragin and Sara Daly, *The Dynamic Terrorist Threat: An Assessment of Group Motivations and Capabilities in a Changing World,* Santa Monica, California: RAND Corporation, MG-246-AF, and Angel Rabasa, et al, *The Muslim World After 9/11,* Santa Monica, CA: RAND Corporation, 2004.

[9] For an informative discussion of the different routes to radicalization, see Matenia Sirseloudi and Peter Waldman, "Where Does the Radicalization Lead? Radical Community, Radical Networks and Radical Subcultures," forthcoming.

[10] Jim Michaels, "Military Readies Internet Assault: Terrorist Activity Expands on Web," *USA Today,* March 28, 2007.

[11] An insightful analysis of radicalization and recruitment is provided by Arvin Bhatt and Mitchell Silber in "Radicalization in the West and the Homegrown Threat," forthcoming.

Statement of David D. Gersten
Director, Civil Rights and Civil Liberties Programs
United States Department of Homeland Security

Introduction

Chairwoman Harman, Ranking Member Reichert, and distinguished Members of the Subcommittee: Thank you for providing me the opportunity to testify today. It is a privilege to testify alongside other dedicated public servants and community leaders. I hope that our testimonies today will demonstrate how closely our offices are working together to tackle the issues you are considering. In seeking to counter the phenomenon of radicalization, it is critical that our country better understand and engage Muslim communities, both in America and around the world. Though there is no magic formula, we believe that engaging key communities and promoting civic participation can help prevent the isolation and alienation that many believe are necessary precursors for radicalization. I look forward to working with this Committee to tackle this complex issue.

Mission of the Office for Civil Rights and Civil Liberties

In accordance with 6 U.S.C. § 345, the mission of the Office for Civil Rights and Civil Liberties is to assist the dedicated men and women of the Department of Homeland Security to enhance the security of our country while also preserving our freedoms and our way of life. In essence, we provide advice to our colleagues on issues at the intersection of homeland security and civil rights and civil liberties. We work on issues as wide ranging as: developing redress mechanisms related to watch lists; integrating people with disabilities into the emergency management system; ensuring appropriate conditions of detention for immigrant detainees; reviewing how the Department's use of technology and its approach to information sharing impacts civil liberties; adopting equal employment opportunities policies to create a model federal agency; and, ensuring that information technology is accessible to people with disabilities.

Since its inception, the Office for Civil Rights and Civil Liberties has worked to help the Department establish and cement positive relationships with a variety of ethnic and religious communities, and the organizations that represent them. We have worked with Catholic and Protestant organizations concerned with immigration law and policy, with Sikh Americans concerned about various screening policies, with the leaders of the Amish community regarding identification issues, and with Jewish community groups on a wide variety of issues.

Today, I want to specifically address the Department's work with American Arab and Muslim communities, but it is important to remember that the work I describe is part of a broader effort to ensure that all communities in this country are active participants in the homeland security effort.

Engagement with American Arab and Muslim Communities

When the Department of Homeland Security's Officer for Civil Rights and Civil Liberties, Daniel Sutherland, launched the work of our Office in April 2003, he quickly realized that many of the issues facing us would be those affecting Americans of Arab descent and those of the Muslim faith. There was an opportunity to do much more than solve specific isolated problems. These communities want to have two-way communication with the government—certainly they want to be able to raise complaints about various situations or policies, but they also want to be invited to roll up their sleeves and help find solutions.

Therefore, the Department has embarked on a project to develop, cultivate, and maintain partnerships with key leaders of the American Arab, Muslim, Sikh, and South Asian communities. We believe that a critical element of our strategy for securing this country is to build a level of communication, trust, and confidence that is unprecedented in our nation's history. We believe that we will be a much safer country if we better connect the government to these strong communities; if we learn to improve our work through listening to their concerns and ideas; if we convince more young people from these communities to join public service; if we receive their help in educating us about the challenges we face; and, if we receive help from key leaders in explaining our security mission to their constituents.

We will have a greater impact in all of these efforts if our State and local authorities create similar models of engagement on their own accord. Just as the Federal government shares information and intelligence needed to save lives and protect our communities, we must also share best practices and experiences in community engagement and invite our non-federal government partners to participate in our dialogue with these communities. When appropriate, we should offer materials and facilitate training for our local partners to empower and advise them. Likewise, we should always be open to learning from them.

Infrastructure

We have invested a great deal of time in developing an infrastructure for success.

For example, we now know many key leaders of the American Arab and Muslim communities. We have solid lines of communication with community activists, renowned scholars, and business leaders; we have established good links with professional and social organizations; and we have constructive and frank interactions with many of the leading civil rights organizations. In short, we have cemented positive relationships with key figures and civil society institutions in these communities.

We now know many of the concerns of these communities. We know that these include: aviation watch lists; immigration processing; encounters at the border; investigative methods; detention and removal; and, of course, foreign policy. We know that government works best when it is not intrusive and it is encouraging to note that socio-economic indicators point to widespread achievement and assimilation among American Arab and Muslim communities. While most of their concerns are recent and related to post-9/11 security efforts, we in government are now better able to appreciate and welcome faith-based viewpoints as a result of our investment of time engaging on immediate concerns.

We also have some understanding of the level of trust and cooperation between representatives of these communities and State and local authorities.

Finally, we now have a better understanding of what the government wants and needs from American Arab and Muslim communities, and what these communities want from the government.

Engagement

Based on this infrastructure, we have been very active in trying to engage with these communities. This applies, as well, to our colleagues at the Department of Justice, FBI, Treasury, and others, who have all made concerted efforts in this regard. Of course, as with all outreach efforts, the government must be careful to choose constructive people to partner with, and, by the same token, community members are careful to meet with government officials who they believe will be reliable partners.

Much of our Office's work has involved bringing leadership to the interagency engagement effort. Together with our partners in other agencies, we have worked hard to ensure that national organizations have access to leaders here in Washington. Within the past several months, national community leaders have had substantive meetings with the Secretary of Homeland Security, the Attorney General, the Director of the FBI, the Secretary of Treasury and others. Our Office has arranged for local officials to participate with us in engaging these communities, most recently hosting Los Angeles Deputy Mayor for Homeland Security & Public Safety Arif Alikhan at our regular L.A. roundtable which I will describe further in a moment. These are not simply occasional meetings, but are becoming part of the structure of our work. For example, several senior leaders of our Department have met with community leaders in both formal and informal settings over the past several months. Moreover, the Assistant Attorney General for Civil Rights at the Justice Department hosts regular meetings between government agencies, including the Departments of Homeland Security, State, Treasury, Education and Transportation, and national civil rights organizations.

This engagement takes place across the country. The Office for Civil Rights and Civil Liberties now actively leads or participates in regularly scheduled meetings with leaders from these communities in cities such as Houston, Chicago, and Buffalo. Since October, I have led the meeting here in Los Angeles. In Detroit, the U.S. Attorney has asked Daniel Sutherland to chair the regular meeting there, referred to as "BRIDGES." In all of these venues, the local leaders of the DHS component agencies participate, usually along with the U.S. Attorneys' offices and the FBI. These meetings typically include two to three dozen people around a table in a conference room, at either a government agency or a community center. The meetings typically begin with a substantive presentation by the government on an issue of concern, such as redress for watch list misidentifications. Then, old business is discussed—government agencies are asked to provide updated information on issues that have been raised in previous meetings. Finally, the communities present new issues to discuss with the agencies. As you can see, the meetings provide an opportunity for the communities to learn information about significant new government projects, as well as to raise specific issues of concern in a format that emphasizes accountability for answers.

Building capacity

Our Office is also working hard to build the capacity of our workforce to address the new challenges that face us. Through a project we call "Civil Liberties University," we have developed training that provides new skills and competencies for our front-line officers and their State and local partners.

For example, we have just released an intensive training DVD for Department personnel who interact with Arab Americans, Muslim Americans, and people from the broader Arab and Muslim world. The training includes insights from four national and international experts—an Assistant U.S. Attorney who is Muslim, a member of the National Security Council who is Muslim, an internationally renowned scholar of Islamic studies, and a civil rights attorney who advocates on issues of concern to Arab American and Muslim American communities. As with many of the materials we produce, our Federal and non-Federal partners have also found this training module on Arab and Muslim cultures useful. Last month our Office made available this DVD to nearly 600 fusion center directors and local, State, tribal, and Federal law enforcement officers within intelligence units attending the National Fusion Center Conference in Florida.

This training program has been applauded by the communities who believe that they will be treated with more dignity and professionalism if front-line officers understand their cultures, traditions, and values; and, by our colleagues in the Department who believe that such training will help them do their jobs more efficiently and effectively.

We have also produced educational materials with guidance to Department personnel on how to screen and, if necessary, search individuals who wear common Muslim and Sikh head coverings; training on how to screen those of the Sikh faith who carry a *kirpan*, or ceremonial religious dagger; and a tutorial on the Department's policy prohibiting racial profiling.

This type of training is truly a win-win situation: our workforce and state and local partners win by acquiring new skills that they need to better carry out their jobs; and, we all win because American Arab and Muslim communities gain confidence that their insights and contributions are welcomed in the homeland security effort.

Incident Management Team

If there is another terrorist attack on the United States, American Arab, Muslim, and South Asian communities would likely be at center stage. These communities may be a focus of investigative activity, rightly or wrongly, and quite possibly could be victims of racist retaliation. These communities could also be important keys to calming tensions throughout the Nation, assisting law enforcement in locating the perpetrators and serving as public spokespersons in the media. Therefore, it is critical that the U.S.

Government be in contact with leaders from these communities in the hours and days after an incident.

As a result, we have established an "Incident Management Team" that will connect government officials with key leaders of these communities in the event of another attack on our country.

This Incident Management Team is made up of key government agencies, as well as approximately two dozen community leaders that we have come to know well.

Government participants include several components within the Department, including the Office of Public Affairs, Office of Strategic Planning, and the Office of Intelligence & Analysis (I&A). We are joined by the Justice Department's Civil Rights Division, the FBI, the State Department, and the Department of the Treasury. Daniel Sutherland serves as the chair and activates the team and reaches out to incident specific participants.

Community participants include scholars, community activists from several cities, and representatives of national organizations. Depending on the incident, State and local authorities responsible for community outreach may also be contacted and asked to participate. These meetings are meant to afford both Federal and non-Federal participants with real-time sharing of information and common messages needed in the aftermath of an attack.

On the morning of the announcement of the London arrests this past August, our office convened this Incident Management Team. Representatives from Transportation Security Administration, I&A, and the British embassy all provided briefings to the community leaders on the events from the last several hours. While no classified or sensitive material was provided, the briefings were very substantive and gave these leaders concrete information they could share with their communities. There was a question and answer session for the briefers, and then the community leaders shared reactions to the events. The call was valuable for the community leaders, because they received key and timely information, and it led to tangible results. Several organizations issued press releases, which assured their communities that the government was engaging actively with them, again illustrating that there is no need to feel isolated from the homeland security effort.

In addition to building bridges with community leaders, we have also developed strong relationships across the government. The working relationships among Federal agencies on these issues are extremely strong. We work on a daily basis with colleagues from State, Justice, FBI, Treasury, the National Counterterrorism Center (NCTC), and the National Security Council.

We have also developed strong relationships with allied governments. We work particularly closely with our colleagues in the United Kingdom, but also regularly meet with representatives of the Canadian and Australian governments, and others as well—such as colleagues from Denmark and the Netherlands.

Next Steps

Again, our goal is to develop, cultivate and maintain partnerships with key leaders of the American Arab, Muslim, Sikh, and South Asian communities. We have laid a strong infrastructure, and we have taken a number of important steps in the early phases of this project. We have seen enough progress to know that we can reach this goal, in the relatively near future, if there is a continuing strong and sustained commitment from all.

Let me highlight four steps that we believe need to be taken at this time: First, we must deepen the engagement; we must take all of this activity to the next level. Leaders from all branches of government need to take steps to engage with these communities; meet them, learn about them, and open lines of communication.

Government leaders also need to make public statements that impact opinion and drive current debates in ways that increase our citizens' desire to get involved in public life and public policy, and that decrease the natural tendency toward isolation from government.

For example, in the days after the August 2006 arrests of the bomb plotters in London, Secretary Chertoff made the following remarks to an audience here in Los Angeles:

> Given recent events, I think it's good to reinforce the message that America values its rich diversity. Muslims in America have long been part of the fabric of our nation. The actions of a few extremists cannot serve as a reflection on the many people who have made valuable contributions to our society. Right here in Los Angeles we work with several Muslim American leaders who are helping us to better secure our country. Muslim Americans, like all Americans are united in our resolve to live in safety and security."

We need to ensure that a wide range of senior government leaders make statements such as these.

We also need to connect with young people from these communities. We need to find innovative new strategies to improve communication with young people from these ethnic and religious communities.

Second, we must institutionalize the engagement effort for success over the long term. At the Department of Homeland Security, we have established the Department's Radicalization and Engagement Working Group. We have also established the Incident Management Team and our colleagues at I&A have established a unit focused on radicalization issues. But we need to redouble our efforts to ensure that all of the component agencies are equipped to play a significant role in reducing isolation and therefore radicalization.

The work that we are trying to do is also taking place at our sister agencies—Justice, State, Treasury, NCTC, and others—and, at a vital level, by the State and local authorities who interact where members of these communities live. We need to ensure that State and local governments are equipped with resources to reach out and connect with these communities, all the while, helping them comply with civil rights and civil liberties protections.

Third, we must continue to address policy issues of concern. In preparing for our community meetings, we remind ourselves that the meetings will be seen as useless if concrete results are not visible. We have found that these communities have provided a great deal of constructive criticism—that is, they have identified problems we need to address and, in some cases, made excellent recommendations for solutions as well. To be credible, the government must continue to address issues of concern and report back to the communities when progress is made.

Finally, we must challenge the communities to get involved. To achieve our mission, we need help from every part of America. We know that these communities are anxious to roll up their sleeves and get involved. It is important at this time that we say loudly and clearly: "We need your help and we welcome you to the table." Specifically, we need community leaders to convince more of their young people to consider public service as a career. One of our priorities as a government has to be to get young people from American Arab and Muslim families to join government service.

We desperately need their language skills, but we also need their cultural insights. We need to challenge community leaders to extol the virtues of public service, whether it is as a candidate for political office, as an FBI agent, a soldier, an accountant, a lawyer, or an IT specialist—we need more people from this community to see government service as a place they can build a successful career.

We also need to challenge these communities to help us increase the integration and assimilation of new immigrants, particularly those from the Arab and Muslim worlds.

We need to ensure that these new immigrants become comfortable with their children's schools, get plugged into places of worship where they can build friendships, learn to speak English, and become familiar with their local government. This is a job that local communities are best poised to accomplish.

We need to challenge community leaders to spread understanding of our security mission. There are times when we must deport someone who has come to our country illegally; we need community leaders to calm community tensions and explain the role that Homeland Security officers must play. There are times when someone is questioned at an airport or border port of entry; we need community leaders to explain that in many cases, these are important features of the landscape we have post 9/11. We do not need community leaders to become our spokespeople; but we do need them to help build a level of understanding regarding these issues, which will help people respond to the latest headlines most successfully.

We also need to challenge community leaders to influence Muslim perspectives in other parts of the world. For example, Muslim communities in Europe are much less integrated, successful, and prosperous than American Arab and Muslim communities.

We need to challenge community leaders here to communicate with communities in Europe, to convince them Muslims can successfully integrate into secular democracies while maintaining their religion, and fully participate in those countries. From decades of experience, Muslims in America know that the environments created by democracies such as ours give them freedom to choose the way they want to worship, raise their families, get an education, relate to their government, start a business, and become prosperous in their professions. Muslims in Europe need to be convinced of these principles, and American Arab and Muslim leaders can play a significant role.

In all of these areas, community leaders are already stepping up to the plate. For example, many Arab and Muslim community leaders have traveled internationally and talked about the issues of the day. As a government, we simply need to recognize the efforts that have already been made, and then step up our support and encouragement for even more significant efforts in all of these areas.

Conclusion

In conclusion, we recognize that this will not be an easy task. This will be a path with many peaks and valleys. There are constant pressures that seek to pull us apart; we must resist those. We have to make sure that those who believe in cementing positive relationships are the voices that shape opinions, and that these are the people who are influencing the debate. Thank you for the opportunity to testify today, and I welcome your questions.

Statement of John M. Vanyur
Assistant Director
Correctional Programs Division
Federal Bureau of Prisons

The Bureau of Prisons (BOP) is pleased to submit this statement for the record regarding the efforts our agency is taking to ensure we are preventing the recruitment of terrorists and extremists in Federal prisons.

The BOP is responsible for the custody and care of approximately 195,500 inmates confined in 114 Federal prisons and facilities operated by private companies, State and local governments. Our mission is to protect society by confining offenders in the controlled environments of prisons and community-based facilities that are safe, humane, cost-efficient, and appropriately secure; and to provide work and other self-improvement opportunities to assist offenders in becoming law-abiding citizens.

The BOP is committed to ensuring that Federal prisoners are not radicalized or recruited for terrorist causes. The support that has been provided by the FBI, the agencies represented on the National Joint Terrorism Task Force (NJTTF), other components of the Department of Justice, and many other members of the law enforcement and intelligence communities has been invaluable to our efforts in this area.

We understand the importance of controlling and preventing the recruitment of inmates into terrorist activities and organizations. We also acknowledge that this is an evolving issue, especially as it relates to the relationships between terrorism, certain radical or extremist ideologies, and the penchant of those who adhere to these ideologies to recruit others to their positions. The BOP's efforts at preventing radicalization focus on:

(1) managing and monitoring inmates who could attempt to radicalize other inmates

(2) screening religious service providers to avoid hiring or contracting with anyone who could radicalize inmates, and

(3) providing programs to help inmates become less vulnerable to attempts at radicalization.

We know that some inmates may be particularly vulnerable to radical recruitment and we must guard against the spread of terrorism and extremist ideologies. Our practices in institution security and inmate management are geared toward the prevention of any violence, criminal behavior, disruptive behavior, or other threats to institution security or public safety, which includes the radicalization of inmates.

Over the last several years, our agency has taken a number of significant measures, and we are actively engaged in several ongoing initiatives to ensure that inmates in Federal prison are not recruited to support radical organizations or terrorist groups. For example, we have eliminated most institution-based inmate organizations with community ties to control the influence that outside entities have on Federal inmates. We also have enhanced our information and monitoring systems, intelligence gathering and sharing capabilities, and identification and management of disruptive inmates.

For over a decade, we have been managing inmates with ties to terrorism by confining them in more secure conditions and closely monitoring their communications. We have established a strategy that focuses on the appropriate levels of containment to ensure that inmates with terrorist ties do not have the opportunity to radicalize or recruit other inmates.

We define terrorist inmates as those having been convicted of, charged with, associated with, or linked to terrorist activities or belonging to organizations that planned and/or executed violent and destructive acts against the U.S. Government and/or privately owned American corporations.

All inmates determined to have terrorist ties are clearly identified and tracked in our information systems. The most dangerous terrorists are confined under the most restrictive conditions allowed in our most secure facility, the Administrative Maximum United States Penitentiary (ADX) in Florence, Colorado. We have also transferred a number of terrorist inmates to the Federal Correctional Complex in Terre Haute, Indiana, to consolidate them at one facility and increase the monitoring and management of these inmates.

We monitor, record, and translate if necessary, all telephone communications (except attorney-client conversations) involving inmates with terrorist ties. We then share any relevant information with the FBI, the NJTTF, and other agencies.

We also monitor all of the general mail delivered to or sent from terrorist inmates. Mail is not delivered to or sent from terrorist inmates until it is read, and if necessary, translated and/or analyzed for intelligence purposes. If suspicious content is found, the correspondence is referred to the FBI for analysis before being processed any further. In addition, we have eliminated outgoing "special mail" drop boxes.[1] Inmates must deliver outgoing special mail directly to a staff member for further processing. All outgoing special mail is subject to scanning by electronic means such as x-ray, metal detector, or ion spectrometry equipment.

We recently established a Counter-terrorism Unit in Martinsburg, West Virginia. One of the responsibilities of that Unit is to process inmate correspondence that requires language translation and content analysis. The Unit will improve our ability to monitor correspondence and analyze it for potential terrorism-related intelligence. The Unit also oversees telephone monitoring systemwide and has implemented mechanisms to ensure phone calls by terrorist inmates are being monitored.

In addition, an FBI special agent and an FBI intelligence analyst are assigned to assist ADX Florence with communication and intelligence matters.

We have worked diligently, particularly since 9/11, to enhance our intelligence gathering and sharing capabilities in order to ensure a seamless flow of intelligence information between our agency and other law enforcement and counter-terrorism agencies.

We have two individuals (one employee and one contractor) detailed to the NJTTF to facilitate our involvement on this task force and to coordinate the exchange of intelligence related to corrections. These two members of the NJTTF manage the Correctional Intelligence Initiative (CII), a nationwide NJTTF special project involving correctional agencies at the Federal, State, territorial, tribal, and local levels, designed to detect, deter, and disrupt the radicalization and recruiting of inmates. This initiative involves training of correctional administrators by each local JTTF; exchanging of intelligence; communicating best practices to local JTTFs in order to detect, deter, and disrupt radicalization; and coordinating of liaison and intelligence-sharing activities between local JTTFs and corrections agencies.

Most importantly, through the CII, intelligence regarding any attempts by inmates, religious providers, or others to radicalize any segment of the population is gathered and shared, and interdiction action is taken by the appropriate correctional authority.

In addition, we have established intelligence officers at the majority of our metropolitan detention centers under a Joint Intelligence Sharing Initiative. These intelligence staff members gather and share intelligence information with the FBI and with our Central Office intelligence operations. This staff also coordinate with the local JTTF and act as full JTTF members in some cases. All BOP facilities are required to coordinate with their local JTTFs on matters with a connection to terrorism.

In addition to managing and monitoring inmates who could attempt to radicalize other inmates, we help inmates become less vulnerable to any such attempts.

Experts have identified the societal marginalization of inmates as a key factor in their becoming radicalized. Our agency provides inmates with a broad variety of programs that are proven to assist in the development of key skills, thereby minimizing the likelihood of the inmates being marginalized.

The programs we provide include work in prison industries and other institution jobs, vocational training, education, substance abuse treatment, religious programs, and other skills-building and pro-social values programs.

Moreover, we are very aware of the important role religious programs play in preparing inmates to reintegrate successfully into society following release from prison. Religious programs and chaplaincy services are provided to the approximately 30 faiths represented within the Federal prison population. Within the constraints of security, we provide worship services, study of scripture and sacred writings, and religious workshops; and we make accommodations to facilitate observances of holy days. Full-time civil service chaplains in the BOP lead worship services and provide pastoral care and spiritual guidance to inmates, and chaplains oversee the breadth of religious programs and monitor the accommodations provided by contract spiritual leaders and community volunteers. The overwhelming majority of inmates participate in religious programs in a positive, healthy, and productive way.

We screen all of our civil service staff, volunteers, and contractors to avoid hiring or contracting with anyone who would pose a threat to institution security. Every BOP civil service chaplain must meet all the requirements for employment as a Federal law enforcement officer, including a field investigation, criminal background check, reference check, drug screening, and pre-employment suitability interviews and screenings. In addition, chaplains must meet requirements unique to their employment and the scope of their duties. Like all BOP employees, chaplains are strictly prohibited from using their position to condone, support, or encourage violence or other inappropriate behavior.

Our religious contractors and volunteers are also subject to a variety of security requirements prior to being granted access to an institution, including criminal background checks, law enforcement agency checks to verify places of residence and employment, a fingerprint check, information from employment over the previous 5 years, and drug testing.

The BOP continues to work closely with the FBI and the NJTTF with regard to the screening of contract service providers. Information on contractors and volunteers (whether the contractor or volunteer is being considered to help provide religious services or not) is checked against databases supported by the FBI. Moreover, over the last 4 years, we have enhanced supervision of programs and activities in our chapels.

We also have increased the training of our staff in the areas of counter-terrorism and recognition of potential radicalization. All BOP staff receive basic correctional skills training at the beginning of their career, and on an annual basis, BOP employees receive additional training that addresses current security and inmate management issues. Since 2004, our agency has included a training segment titled "Terrorism Management and Response" in Annual Training for all BOP staff. In addition, Religious Services personnel present a segment during Annual Training that emphasizes an awareness of discriminatory language, behaviors, rhetoric, and speech that could indicate the presence of radical ideology in the inmate population.

In 2003, we distributed a Terrorism Training for Law Enforcement CD, developed by the Bureau of Justice Assistance, to all of our facilities. We are in the process of distributing the updated 2006 version of the Terrorism Training for Law Enforcement CD to all institutions. Among the activities of our Martinsburg Counter-terrorism Unit are the production and distribution of intelligence-related documents to BOP staff and the development and provision of counter-terrorism training programs for BOP staff.

Every BOP facility has one or more Special Investigative Supervisors/Special Investigative Agents who serve as the focal point in our agency's efforts to manage all security threat groups, including terrorists. This staff helps identify and track members and associates, monitor mail and telephone communications, provide enhanced supervision of identified security threat group members, and share intelligence on the activities of any security threat group. Special Investigative Agents serve as a liaison to the FBI, the U.S. Marshals Service, and the U.S. Secret Service regarding the activities of security threat group members and the investigation of criminal activity in BOP facilities.

In 2004 and 2005, Special Investigative Supervisors and Special Investigative Agents from every BOP institution received specialized training in the control and management of terrorist inmates. In December 2006, twenty BOP intelligence staff participated in a 32-hour intelligence gathering and analysis training course provided by the FBI. Two additional classes are planned for over 45 special investigative supervisors and special investigative agents in June and August of this year.

BOP chaplains receive specialized training to ensure they have the necessary information about each religion to oversee and manage religious services and programs effectively. Our agency has prepared a comprehensive technical reference manual that describes appropriate religious services procedures and behaviors. The manual is available for use by any staff member overseeing a religious service or activity. Thirty chaplains recently participated in mandatory training designed to enhance their awareness and knowledge about identifiers of radical religious groups. The training will be repeated each year until all BOP chaplains have attended.

I hope the information provided in this statement will be beneficial to the Subcommittee in its investigation of efforts underway to prevent radicalization in America's prisons.

Endnotes

[1] Special mail is privileged communication between an inmate and his or her attorney or government officials. Federal regulations prohibit the BOP from monitoring the content of special mail (28 CFR 540.18).

DOCUMENT NO. 9

"WELCOME TO AMERICA?": PROMOTING TRAVEL TO AMERICA: AN EXAMINATION OF ECONOMIC AND SECURITY CONCERNS

Hearing Before the
Committee on Foreign Affairs
Subcommittee on International Organizations,
Human Rights, and Oversight

March 20, 2007

Statement of Geoff Freeman
Executive Director
Discover America Partnership

Let me first thank Chairman Delahunt, Ranking Member Rohrabacher and members of the Subcommittee for holding today's hearing and taking a critical look at America's broken travel system. My name is Geoff Freeman, and I am the executive director of the Discover America Partnership. The Partnership was launched last year by some of America's foremost business leaders to highlight the unique role that travel can play in bolstering America's economy, security and public diplomacy efforts.

Our country is in the midst of a complex travel crisis that is having an enormous impact on our economy. At a time when the number of travelers worldwide is at an all time high, the number of overseas travelers visiting the U.S. remains well below pre-9/11 levels. In 2000 the U.S. market share of the $6 trillion worldwide travel market stood at 7.5 percent; by 2006 that share had dropped to 6.1 percent. The result is a loss of nearly 60 million visitors over five years, $94 billion in spending nearly $16 billion in tax revenue and approximately 194,000 jobs according to the Travel Industry Association.

In total numbers, the U.S. has experienced a 17 percent decline in overseas visitors since 9/11. In 2000, the U.S. welcomed approximately 25 million Canadians and Mexicans and approximately 25 million overseas visitors. In 2006, the U.S. returned to 50 million visitors, but the make-up was far different: approximately 30 million Canadians and Mexicans, but only 20 million overseas visitors. Overseas visitors tend to stay longer, spend more and can play a critical role in strengthening America's image around the globe by engaging in people-to-people diplomacy.

Declining visitation to the U.S. is not limited to tourists. All forms of travel—business, student and medical—have witnessed a decline. From 2004 to 2005, for example, business travel to the U.S. fell 10 percent according to the World Travel Market. Over this same time period, business travel to Europe increased by eight percent.

Six countries—the UK, Japan, South Korea, Germany, France and Australia—represent the top source markets for long-distance travelers to the U.S. Between 2000 and 2005, fewer people came to the U.S. from the UK, Japan, Germany and France. While we did see a 6.5 percent increase in arrivals from South Korea, the UK experienced an 18.9 percent increase in travel from Korea; Canada experienced a 34.5 percent increase; Australia a 56.3 percent increase; Russia a 58.7 percent increase and Turkey a 451.2 percent increase in arrivals from South Korea. Similarly, the U.S. experienced a 3.5 percent increase in arrivals from Australia, but Canada experienced a 15.8 percent increase; the UK saw a 17.7 percent increase; Japan a 44.5 percent increase; Hong Kong a 49.1 percent increase; and Vietnam a 324.2 percent increase. So while the U.S. did experience modest increases in arrivals from two of our top six top source markets between 2000 and 2005, it's painfully clear that other countries are winning the highly competitive fight for the world's travelers.

The ripple effect of this downturn in travel is significant economically—the potential loss in spending, employment, payroll and tax receipts—as well as diplomatically—fewer opportunities to compete for hearts and minds around the world.

The Discover America Partnership believes that travel is a critical component of America's economic security, but we also believe that travel is a critical component of our national security and public diplomacy efforts.

Last November, the Partnership commissioned RT Strategies, a prominent, bipartisan polling firm, to conduct a survey of more than 2,000 international travelers. The study sought to gauge travelers' perceptions of the U.S. visa and entry process, and how opinions of America differ between those who have visited our country and those who have not. The results, which have been covered extensively by media around the world, were significant.

Among the study's key findings:

The U.S. entry process is considered the "world's worst" by travelers

- Travelers rate America's entry process as the "world's worst" by greater than a 2:1 margin over the next-worst destination area.
- The U.S. ranks with Africa and the Middle East when it comes to traveler-friendly paperwork and officials.
- 54 percent of international travelers say that immigration officials are "rude."
- Travelers to the U.S. are more afraid of U.S. government officials (70%) than the threat of terrorism or crime (54%).
- Two-thirds of travelers surveyed fear they will be detained at the border because of a simple mistake or misstatement.
- Reports of bad treatment at the point of entry have as much an impact on America's image as news reports in the foreign media or comments made by foreign government officials.

By deterring visitors, the U.S. is missing an enormous diplomatic and economic opportunity

- Those with experience visiting America are 74 percent more likely to have an extremely favorable opinion of the country versus those who have not visited recently.
- 63 percent of travelers feel more favorable towards the U.S. as a result of their visit.
- 61 percent agree that, once a person visits the U.S., they become friendlier towards the country and its policies.
- Negative attitudes about U.S. treatment of visitors are having a much larger effect on keeping travelers away from the U.S. than negative attitudes about U.S. policies in the world.
- Nearly nine in 10 travelers tell their friends, relatives about their travel experiences most or all of the time.

Minor changes in the U.S. treatment of foreign business and leisure travelers would yield substantial gains

- In every destination criteria but the point of entry experience, international travelers rank America in the top three. Travelers *want* to come to the U.S.
- Travelers are willing to wait an average of 46.5 days to get a visa to visit the U.S–15 days beyond U.S. State Department standards, but far less than current wait times in many countries.
- Travelers' expectations include clear communications, respect and courteous treatment.

Anecdotal evidence uncovered in focus groups, media reports and conversations as well as empirical evidence support the findings from our survey. From companies like Exxon-Mobile that are looking to hold major meetings in other countries because they can not get their own workers back in to the U.S., to universities that have seen dramatic declines in applications from international students, to other countries being chosen over the U.S. to host major international sporting events—such as a Pan American games coming up this summer that would have contributed $1-$2 billion in economic activity for the city of San Antonio—America is no longer a destination of choice. Whether perceptions are based in truth or not they have a way of becoming reality. The reality today is that travelers are choosing other destinations—largely because of the U.S. entry experience. We must do something to reverse this trend.

Security is America's Number One priority. However, the Discover America Partnership does not believe that inefficiencies should be mistaken for security. Long lines, inadequate use of technology and poor treatment of visitors does nothing to make America more secure.

To that end, in our *Blueprint to Discover America* the Partnership recently issued a three-point plan to strengthen America's security and fix our country's travel crisis. Our plan calls on government to:

1. Create a 21st century visa system;
2. Modernize and secure our ports of entry; and
3. Change global perceptions of America through coordinated communications.

There are several key points about our plan that must be understood.

- First, we strongly believe that travel and security are not mutually exclusive, and at no point do we recommend a loosening of security measures. In fact, we call for a *strengthening* of America's security, but we insist that it be done with the right resources, new technologies and a focus on travelers as an opportunity.
- Second, we recommend common-sense solutions, not revolutionary changes. Fixing America's travel system requires that we hire appropriately, engage the private sector and learn from our peers around the world.
- Finally, we think that a relatively modest investment—$300 million according to our plan—will have extraordinary results. If the United States gains one share point of global travel (about 10 million new visitors), we can create 190,000 new jobs, $17 billion in new spending and nearly $3 billion in tax revenue. Not only are those number significant to our economy, but 10 million new visitors represent enormous public diplomacy potential and would help fund new security programs thus making our country even more secure.

America is at a travel crossroads and how we respond as a nation will be hugely determinative of our standing in the world and of international support for U.S. policies in the future. International travel to the U.S. is the greatest public diplomacy tool we have and declining overseas travel only serves to weaken our diplomacy efforts.

Chairman Delahunt and Ranking Member Rohrabacher, it is time that we fix a flawed travel system and take advantage of this incredible vehicle for economic security, national security and public diplomacy. On behalf of the CEOs who make up the Discover America Partnership, we stand ready to help in this effort.

Again, thank you for the opportunity to testify before you today. I would be happy to answer any questions that you may have.

Statement of Charles L. Merin
President
Travel Business Roundtable

Good afternoon. I am Chuck Merin, President of the Travel Business Roundtable. I am speaking here today on behalf of TBR, an organization comprised of some 70 corporate and association CEOs whose mission it is to educate policymakers about the importance of travel and tourism to the nation's economic, social and diplomatic well being. I am also here on behalf of TBR's strategic partner, the Travel Industry Association (TIA), which represents roughly 1,600 travel and tourism companies across the country. Together, TBR and TIA encompass every sector of this diverse industry.

Chairman Delahunt, Ranking Member Rohrabacher and Members of the Subcommittee, thank you for inviting me to discuss the unique relevance of travel and tourism to this subcommittee's ongoing public diplomacy review. At its core, the travel industry represents an opportunity to bring people of different cultures and backgrounds face-to-face—to visit, to do business, to study, to receive medical treatment and to learn more about America and Americans.

Ranking Member Rohrabacher, I greatly appreciate what you said in the first in this series of hearings. You told a story about how President Reagan advised you that when delivering a message, it must be directed not only to a U.S. audience but also to the wider world. We could not agree with you more. At a time when America's image continues to decline, what and how we communicate is closely scrutinized around the globe. We have found that people-to-people communication provided through the travel experience not only helps boost our economy but also helps convey a more positive image of America and its people.

An Economic Generator

In 2006, the travel and tourism industry generated $703 billion in expenditures, directly employed 7.5 million Americans and accounted for $171 billion in direct travel-generated payroll. Our industry creates jobs and careers; we fulfill important social policy goals, such as moving people from welfare to work; and we contribute more than $105 billion in tax revenue for local, state and federal governments that support essential services.

Travel and tourism is a nonpartisan issue and it flourishes in all 50 states and all 435 Congressional districts.

The industry is one of the largest exports for the U.S. and the single largest services sector export, accounting for 27 percent of all services exports. Directly and indirectly, international travel to the U. S. generates $1.3 trillion, and we are one of very few industries that creates a multi-billion dollar trade surplus. That surplus declined to $7.4 billion in 2005, after a peak in 1996 of $26.3 billion.

The Post 9/11 World

The 9/11 tragedy had a huge impact on our industry. International travel and tourism expenditures fell 19 percent, and 340,000 American jobs were lost between 2000 and 2002. For many lawmakers, it was the first time they understood the very real economic and social impact of travel and tourism on communities throughout America. Not only were planes not flying and hotels at low occupancies, but Broadway theatres, restaurants and shopping malls were also impacted. Just as no other industry was more immediately affected by 9/11, so it is that no American industry has the potential to do more to positively address the ignorance and contempt which fuels such heinous acts.

The impact of 9/11 on the nation's travel and tourism economy has been significant. A recent study by TIA estimated a total loss of 58 million visitors; 194,000 jobs; $25.9 billion in payroll; $94 billion in spending; and $15.6 billion in taxes to federal, state and local governments since that tragedy. That dollars-and-cents loss is quantifiable; the squandered opportunity to present America to the world in a more positive light is not.

The U.S. is steadily losing its share of the lucrative international travel market. International travelers offer economic opportunity: they stay longer and spend much more than their domestic counterparts. For instance, last year New York City welcomed a record 44 million visitors. Only 18 percent of those were international travelers, but they were responsible for approximately 45 percent of all visitor spending. More importantly, international travelers represent the opportunity to win the hearts and minds of people around the world. When travelers don't come here, they learn about America and Americans through headlines rather than personal experiences. What the Discover America Partnership has found is that when international visitors actually visit the U.S., they are 74 percent more likely to have a favorable opinion about us.

Nations, much like individuals, are often defined by perceptions. Emotion and intuition usually drive perception rather than rational, analytical thoughts. According to noted pollster Frank Lutz, eighty percent of life is emotion and only 20 percent is intellect. He remarked, "I can change how you think, but how you feel is something deeper and stronger." As each of you has learned by experience throughout your political careers, perception is reality for many people. The perception of this country is that of a Fortress America, unable or unwilling to courteously invite legitimate travelers to participate in the American experience.

Unfortunately, in terms of inbound travel, the U.S. now ranks third behind France and Spain, and China is close behind. Worldwide travel continues to increase at record rates, but America's piece of the ever-growing pie is shrinking. In 1992, the U.S. had 9 percent of the world market share; today we have 6 percent. That represents a 35 percent decrease. The Commerce Department reports that inbound travel to the U.S. has rebounded to pre-9/11. These numbers are misleading, however. Were it not for significant increases in inbound travel from Mexico and Canada, travel from overseas markets has actually decreased 17 percent.

As I mentioned before, we are not just referencing the leisure travel market. Business travel to the U. S. declined 10 percent between 2004 and 2005 while the number of business travelers to Europe grew by 8 percent over the same period. A study by the Foreign Business Trade Council found that U.S. business lost $30 billion between 2002 and 2004, citing U.S. visa policy as the major deterrent to traveling here. Major conferences and sporting events have been canceled or scheduled for other destinations, costing our country billions of dollars. For example, San Antonio lost out to Rio de Janeiro as the host of the 2007 Pan-American games, in large part because of real and perceived visa and entry-exit difficulties. In addition the United States Olympic Committee has stated that the U.S. will never host another Olympic games until we change the way we treat travelers attempting to come to our country.

NAFSA, the Association of International Educators, has told us that while the State Department is reporting all-time high numbers of visa applications issued to students, student travel to the U.S. has not resurged. In a March 9 column in the Washington Post, David Ignatius wrote about the challenge in this way:

> When people think about American power in the world, they usually list the country's forbidding arsenal of bombers, aircraft carriers and troops. Yet America's greatest strategic asset these days might not be its guns but its universities . . .
>
> Pentagon officials are always bragging about their "smart bombs," which sometimes go wide of the target. American education is a smart bomb that actually works. When we think about the foreign outreach efforts by university presidents and dozens of others, we should recognize that they are a national security asset- making the world safer, as well as wiser.

The same is true for international travelers seeking medical treatment in the United States. I recently spoke with Ardell Brede, the mayor of Rochester, Minnesota, and he informed me that international patients seeking medical treatment at the Mayo Clinic have begun seeking treatment in other countries because of our visa and entry policies. The impact is not only devastating to the Mayo Clinic, but also to the surrounding community—the hotels, the rental car companies, the restaurants and shopping malls that support the city.

As the industry most immediately affected by the spectre of terrorism, we strongly support any and all initiatives that intelligently and respectfully improve our nation's security. We believe that economic prosperity and homeland security are not mutually exclusive, and in the fullest sense, actually complement one another. Two examples of well-intended but poorly implemented policy come to mind as examples of what not to do.

The industry supported the implementation of both biometric passport technologies and WHTI as part of the effort to better protect Americans from those who would seek to do us harm. However, we never thought that both initiatives would be implemented as poorly as they were. When America promulgates biometric standards for the world by deadlines certain that we ourselves cannot meet, that reinforces the worst imagery about American policy. When our good neighbor to the north, Canada, America's largest trading partner and biggest international arrivals market, feels that we have failed to work cooperatively to implement the new policy, then once again perception becomes reality. Biometrics and WHTI implementation are powerful reminders that "how" we execute homeland security policies is every bit as important as "what" we implement.

Overcoming Obstacles

Numerous surveys of an increasingly hostile world indicate that our country and our industry face a grave problem. What we have been doing over the past few months is offering to be part of the solution.

Our industry has repeatedly offered to provide hospitality training to the State Department and its consular service, and to DHS and its Customs and Border Protection and TSA personnel. Our offer isn't to teach them how to do their jobs, but rather how to execute those jobs in a more hospitable and respectful fashion. Recent meetings with the Foreign Service Training Institute suggest that State is willing to embrace this offer.

My friend and colleague, Geoff Freeman, will speak to this in much greater detail. I'd like to emphasize that what makes travel unique is that it remains the industry of dreams. Travel evokes positive feelings in people and creates a more positive prism through which to experience a country and its people. In this case, America and its people are the most effective mediums for reaching a hostile and wary world.

Fareed Zakaria recently wrote his February 26, 2007 column in Newsweek magazine about "How Homeland Security harms U.S. image and economy." Zakaria wrote:

> This is more than a dollars-and-cents issue. America as a place has often been the great antidote to U.S. foreign policy. When American actions across t he world have seemed harsh, misguided or unfair, America itself has always been open, welcoming and tolerant. I remember visiting the United States as a kid from India in the 1970s, at a time when as a country, India was officially anti-American. The reality of the America that I experienced was a powerful refutation of the propaganda and caricatures of its

> enemies. But today, through inattention, stupidity and bureaucratic cowardice, the caricature is becoming a reality.

Dick Martin, author of a fabulous new book entitled *Rebuilding Brand America* made the point clearly when he wrote:

> Those who believe America's declining reputation can be restored through a more forceful explanation of its foreign policies are fishing in trees. Doing a better job of explaining itself is certainly part of the answer, but it fails to address the core of the problem. America's declining reputation has less to do with what people think of America than how they feel about it.

Recognizing the New Realities

We live in a market-driven era. Companies, communities and even countries are all brands in the sense that they evoke emotions and loyalties. America's brand has been compromised around the world, but its companies and its people are still held in high regard. The federal government, by word and by deed, cannot single-handedly restore that brand. It can, however, do what federal governments are supposed to do: defend the country and promote economic opportunity.

The absence of a Cabinet-level position and the determination to use travel as a national economic engine sets our country apart from the world in disadvantageous ways. When countries around the world spend millions of dollars to establish and promote their national travel brand, they highlight their nation, not the companies that comprise the industry. Nations from France to Fiji understand the power of these tools in a global economy; the United States has yet to fully embrace its potential.

Dysfunctional visa and entry-exit policies that intimidate and alienate legitimate international travelers help no one, and need to be addressed by the Congress and the Administration. And while this relates to outbound U.S. travel, we are compelled to point out that dysfunctionalities in the U.S. government do not end there. With several years to prepare, even our own State Department is struggling to meet demand for U.S. passports as a result of the Western Hemisphere Travel Initiative (WHTI) requirement. Congress has provided State additional resources, but obviously much better planning is needed because U.S. travelers are now waiting ten weeks to get a passport and this is threatening to ruin business and leisure trips abroad.

In a global economy, economic opportunity is truly a two-way street. McKinsey & Company recently predicted that almost one billion new consumers will enter the global marketplace as incomes worldwide grow over the next decade. America's decreasing share of a burgeoning international travel market portends ominous trends lines for the world economy of the future.

Travel and tourism uniquely evokes those qualities that much of the world still associates with what it is to be an American: tolerance, liberty, opportunity and dreams. We need to remind the world that the American dream still lives and that their opportunity to participate first-hand in the American experience remains an open opportunity.

John Stuart Mill long-ago wrote something that powerfully makes this point. He wrote:

> The economic advantages of commerce are surpassed in importance by those of its effects, which are intellectual and moral. It is hardly possible to overstate the value of placing human beings in contact with persons dissimilar to themselves and with modes of thought and action unlike those with which they are familiar.

Travel and tourism does just that, while simultaneously creating jobs and powerful economic growth across our nation. Travel and tourism remains the leading edge of the service economy that defines America and the world. Its role as a catalyst for human, economic, societal and cultural growth is remarkable. Isn't it time for the federal government to harness that energy and creativity in a partnership that enriches America at home and abroad?

Thank you for the opportunity to appear before you today. I would be delighted to answer any questions you might have about my presentation.

Statement of Peter Gadiel
President
9/11 Families for a Secure America

Thank you for the chance to speak on behalf of 9/11 Families for a Secure America, a group comprised exclusively of relatives of those murdered in the September 11th attacks and of victims of violent crimes committed by illegal aliens.

My members and I paid a terrible price for the open borders espoused by the travel industry, which profits from our government's failure to properly screen the millions of aliens who enter our country each year. So I will not mince words: The policies that the travel industry successfully lobbied for led directly to the admission of the terrorists of September 11 and thus to the murders of 3,000 Americans.

The culture of "open the doors and let everyone in" which, prior to 9/11 pervaded the State Department's Consular Service, was exposed in the 9/11 Commission staff monograph entitled *9/11 and Terrorist Travel*. This report showed how travel industry lobbying had instilled this "open doors" mindset in consular officers whose job was purportedly to screen potential visitors to the USA. It detailed how State Department officials were grossly negligent in creating the "Visa Express Program," the set of lax procedures which permitted the 9/11 terrorists to enter our country. And what term did the 9/11 staff use to describe Visa Express? They called it a "virtual Visa Waiver Program." And they made clear that this virtual Visa Waiver Program came about as a result of travel industry lobbying.[1]

The 9/11 Commission monograph proved beyond doubt the need to tighten and enforce visa requirements for *all* foreign visitors, yet today the citizens of 27 countries can visit the U.S. without first obtaining a visa. Among those countries are France and Great Britain, homelands of Zacarias Moussaoui, the so-called 20th 9/11 hijacker, and shoe bomber Richard Reid. But 27 visa waiver countries is not enough for the travel industry that today lobbies for more countries to be exempted from the screening process, which a visa application is supposed to entail. They continue to put profits over the safety of their fellow Americans.

It is fascinating that Mr. Freeman's group, on its website, alleges that one of its primary motives is to increase foreign support for the war on terror. It claims that promoting travel to America "may" result in nations viewing the U.S. more favorably and that parallel with this improved view will come more support for our anti-terrorism efforts. But the website names Spain as a country where support for the war on terror has been declining and India as a country where it has been increasing. Yet Spain is in the Visa Waiver Program , so its citizens don't need visas to visit the U.S. while India is not a Visa Waiver nation and its citizens must get them. Thus, Mr. Freeman's own website suggests that looser standards for foreign visitors contribute to a *decline* in other nations' support for the war on terror rather than the other way around.

Let us not be fooled by industry claims that amount to saying "golly, we're only doing this only for the good of our country." The real motive is profit. The GAO reaffirmed this fact last July in a report on the Visa Waiver Program saying "The program was designed to boost international business and tourism." In other words, its purpose is to increase profits.[2]

The travel industry has not been content with undermining the process for issuing visas. Consider the following direct quotes from the 9/11 Commission Monograph resulting from interviews with customs agents at Ports of Entry: "The travel industry... airlines in particular—loudly insisted on efficient passenger processing. Most inspectors said that their supervisors would monitor processing times and "remind" inspectors to keep within 45 seconds for each passenger ... if processing times were not kept to a minimum, a supervisor would threaten to send the inspector back to training ... immigration inspectors were graded on how fast airline passengers were processed. ... Driving this emphasis on speed was a 1990 congressional guideline that limited the total amount of time for a visitor to disembark from a plane and be processed through immigration inspection to 45 minutes, regardless of the number of passengers on the flight. ... The effect of this guideline was that inspectors ... had between 30 seconds and one minute to decide whether a visitor was admissible. ... "[3]

Lawrence Tisch, Chairman of both the giant Loew's Hotel Corporation and of the Travel Business Roundtable states in the Roundtable's website that increased profits is that group's reason for being. But Mr. Tisch also resorts to the pretense that tourism is a solution to our problems, saying that when people from other nations visit the U.S. "they interact with the American people and that goes to dispel growing myths overseas." It appears that Mr. Tisch doesn't care that the open borders he helped to bring about led to an "interaction" of Mohammed Atta and 18 other terrorists on four aircraft on 9/11/01 which resulted in the murder of my son.

The groups represented by the other two witnesses have boards of directors that are filled with the heads of huge corporations, so powerful that officials of the State Department and many other Administration officials have promised support on this and other issues. According to a September 2006 issue of the National Journal, Secretary of Commerce Gutierrez has become, in effect the travel industry's chief lobbyist. If only the average citizen of this country had such a powerful voice in this Administration.

Last July's GAO report listed the many ways in which Visa Waiver substantially increases the threat of terrorism. Two examples: Visa officers at U.S. embassies have time to interview applicants, in their own language and they have country -specific knowledge. But the Visa Waiver Program transfers the entire burden of screening visitors to inspectors at ports of entry who have less than a minute to make a decision, are probably unable to converse with the person before him in Urdu or Farsi, and have none of the other advantages available to American personnel stationed in the travelers' countries of origin. Putting the entire burden of screening on POE inspectors is a system designed to fail, with catastrophic results.

The GAO report also noted that stolen blank passports from Visa Waiver countries are used by aliens from non Visa Waiver nations to evade the visa requirement. It added that several unnamed Visa Waiver countries failed to report thefts of blank passports. In one case, a theft of 300 blanks was not reported for 9 years after the theft. Thus it was impossible for the American officials to know that these passports were not perfectly legitimate.

Nevertheless, DHS permits these nations to remain in the Visa Waiver Program.[4]

GAO's list of the dangers is far too long for my oral testimony, but it is enough to say that many of these are inherent in the nature of the program and even if sufficient funds were guaranteed for the foreseeable future and even if the bureaucracies assigned to police the program were always highly motivated and competent (two questionable propositions) the program would still present a danger to the American people. The threat can be summarized briefly in one phrase: Maussaoui and Richard Reid.

Earlier, I mentioned Secretary of Commerce Gutierrez's role as lobbyist for the tourism industry. He is perfectly suited to this Administration. Shortly after 9/11 President Bush stood atop the ruins of the WTC. Because I have never received any remains of my son, that is the only tomb my son will ever know, and Mr. Bush announced to America, "I hear you." But since that time he has shamelessly and consistently refused to secure our borders in order to increase corporate profits. Members of Congress, you have the power to thwart wealthy corporate interests and act on behalf of the "little guy" who would like not to see a loved one go off to work in the morning only to see him or her die in the hell of a crashing airplane or burning skyscraper.

I close with the following thought: The first time I had the opportunity to speak for 9/11 families on Capital Hill, I said that the main obstacles to securing our borders were the Congress and the White House, and I predicted that sooner or later the great mass of our citizens would come to understand this. I say with confidence that this process of recognition is now well advanced. So, if you expand the VWP, when a future Moussaoui or Shoe Bomber succeeds in committing mass murder, Americans will understand that he was allowed to enter the USA without proper screening because people in Congress voted to allow him to do so. How many members of Congress will want to face the voters having to admit that they cast a vote that brought this about?

Again, thank you for the opportunity to be heard.

Endnotes

[1] 9/11 and Terrorist Travel Staff Report of the National Commission on Terrorist Attacks Upon the United States, Washington, D. C. 2004 PP 4-32, 43-44, 111, 119-120. See also U.S. Department of State, Office of Inspector General, Review of Non-immigrant Visa Issuance Policy and Procedure, Memorandum Report ISP-I-03-26. December 2002: Office of Inspector General stated that "Until the events of September 11, the visa process was seldom considered a major element of national security. This was so despite the fact that after the first attack on the World Trade Center [in 1993] Congress mandated" that visa applicants' names be run through various terrorist watch lists.

[2] GAO Report 06-854 July 2006: Border Security: Stronger Actions Needed to Assess and Mitigate Risks of the Visa Waiver Program.

[3] 9/11 Commission Monograph 9/11 and Terrorist Travel pp 135-136.

[4] Ibid.

Statement of Senator Daniel K. Inouye

Encouraging international travelers to visit the United States is both economically and diplomatically beneficial to our country. As we know from experience in Hawaii, attracting visitors to the United States requires a great deal of investment in marketing and promotion. Travel and tourism is Hawaii's number one industry and the State actively markets to residents in countries around the world, including Japan, Australia, the United Kingdom, and Germany.

Most states, however, do not find it economical to devote large resources to international advertising. That is unfortunate given the many natural and cultural treasures this country has to share. Travelers around the world would be willing and eager to spend more time visiting America if they knew what we have to offer.

In 2006, international receipts for travel-related tourism spending reached $107.4 billion. Travel and tourism exports accounted for seven percent of all U.S. exports and 26 percent of services exports last year. The travel industry is a driving force for the U.S. economy and its potential has barely been tapped.

As an added benefit, tourism greatly advances international goodwill. Studies have shown that, after visiting the United States and interacting with Americans, 74 percent of visitors have a more favorable opinion of our country.

This does not surprise me because, with all due respect to the State Department, Americans in their natural environment are among the best diplomats in the world.

In recent years, however, the international reputation of the United States has suffered. America became a less desirable destination for international travelers as a result of the September 11th terrorist attacks.

In addition, in the wake of the attack, the Administration tightened visa application and border entry procedures. Addressing national security is of paramount importance and we must protect our nation from terrorists. But some of the changes had the unintended consequence of deterring legitimate international travelers from coming to America.

I was pleased that Secretaries Rice and Chertoff initiated the Rice-Chertoff Joint Vision in January 2006 to establish new procedures designed to facilitate travel without compromising security.

Despite good efforts of both agencies, many in the travel and tourism industry continue to express concerns about the efficiency of the visa application process and the perception that the U.S. entry process is unnecessarily antagonistic.

I am interested in hearing from the witnesses on the status of implementing the Joint Vision and their thoughts on the recommendations of groups such as the Discover America Partnership and the U.S. Travel and Tourism Advisory Board.

Statement of Senator Byron L. Dorgan

Today's hearing is the second in a series of travel promotion hearings designed to examine how the United States can remain competitive internationally in the travel industry. Generating approximately 8.3 million jobs, the U.S. travel industry both serves as a major employer and constitutes an indispensable part of our economy. According to the Department of Commerce in 2006, international tourism spending in the United States comprised $107.4 billion. Despite these seemingly impressive numbers, the country has seen a decrease in market share of international travelers. In order to preserve this vital sector of our economy, we must work with expediency to reverse the decline.

In the first travel promotions hearing, we heard from the private sector the problems that the travel and tourism industry face today. The Discover America Partnership pointed to a complex visa application process, an intimidating and often bewildering experience for travelers at ports of entry, and a tarnished reputation around the world as factors that undermine international travelers' desire or ability to visit our great country. In addition, the Partnership advocated for the creation of a nationally coordinated travel promotion initiative. An initiative that would both highlight destinations throughout America and inform international travelers about how best to navigate the U.S. visa and entry process.

While in the past few years, the Commerce Department worked on limited promotions to Japan and the United Kingdom, the Department has lacked the resources to conduct a comprehensive and coordinated effort. I believe that a more aggressive approach is warranted. Since September 11th, the United States' market share of international travelers has significantly decreased. The Commerce Department working in concert with industry experts should work to rebuild America's place in the travel market.

In doing so, we need not compromise our national security. We can strengthen security at our borders without closing our doors to friendly travelers. In addition, creating a more welcoming climate for new arrivals would be a boon to diplomacy.

Travelers overwhelmingly leave this country with a better impression of America and its people. They take this goodwill back to their native land and raise the esteem of the United States overseas.

In fairness to our federal agencies, the Department of State and the Department of Homeland Security have not only recognized the need to improve the entry process via technological efficiency, but they have also created a framework for facilitating international tourism while maintaining national security. They have begun to implement the goals established in the Rice-Chertoff Joint Vision in a thoughtful way, but I believe that more work can be done.

Today we will hear testimony from two panels of witnesses in considering how to attract more international visitors without jeopardizing our safety. The first panel consists of government representatives from the Departments of Commerce, State, and Homeland Security. The second panel consists of industry leaders from Hawaii, North Dakota, Alaska, and South Carolina. We will hear about their respective experiences in attracting visitors to their states and about how the federal government could better serve them.

Based on the testimony we hear today and what we heard in the first hearing, I plan to introduce legislation to reinvigorate America's tourism industry.

Statement of Robert Jacksta
Executive Director of Traveler Security and Facilitation, Office of Field Operations U.S. Customs and Border Protection

Good morning Chairman Dorgan, Senator DeMint, and distinguished Members of the Subcommittee. I am pleased to be here today to discuss how the Department of Homeland Security (DHS) is moving forward on programs that will facilitate travel but still provide the level of security required to protect the United States. This is an enormous challenge. We have over 7,000 miles of shared borders with Canada and Mexico and 326 official ports of entry, and each day Customs and Border Protection (CBP) officers must inspect more than 1.2 million passengers and pedestrians. Last year alone, CBP welcomed over 423 million travelers through our ports of entry. During fiscal year 2006, CBP processed a record 87 million passengers arriving from abroad by air, the second consecutive fiscal year the number of such passengers has exceeded pre-9/11 levels.

As America's frontline border agency, CBP employs highly trained and professional personnel, resources, and law enforcement authorities to discharge our priority mission of preventing terrorists and terrorist weapons from entering the United States. CBP has made great strides toward securing America's borders while facilitating legitimate trade and travel and ensuring the vitality of our economy.

As part of our layered approach to border security, CBP operates several "trusted traveler" programs, including the Secure Electronic Network for Travelers Rapid Inspection (SENTRI), Free and Secure Trade (FAST), and NEXUS programs. These bi-national programs facilitate the crossing of low-risk frequent travelers and commercial truck drivers at the land borders through exclusive, dedicated lanes. To enroll in these programs, travelers must provide proof of citizenship; a Border Crossing Card (BCC) or other visa, if required; and other identity documentation, such as a driver's license or ID card. An intensive background check against law enforcement databases and terrorist databases is required and includes fingerprint checks and a personal interview with a CBP officer. Approximately 225,000 SENTRI, NEXUS, and FAST cards have been issued. SENTRI is now operational at the nine largest Southwest border crossings, and as of November 1, 2006, the Global Online Enrollment System (GOES) is available for SENTRI applicants. With GOES, SENTRI applicants may register and input their applications at a single location, the Williston Centralized Vetting Center. This centralized location will help facilitate increased accuracy and quicker processing time of SENTRI applications

In December 2006, enrollment in the NEXUS Air, Highway, and Marine programs was harmonized. As of February 2007, 119,861 members are now "in for one, in for all" and can cross the border using any of the three modes of transportation (air, land, and sea) at participating locations. These programs are implemented in partnership with the governments of Canada and Mexico, and many citizens of these countries currently participate in the programs.

The standardization of travel documents is a critical next step to securing our Nation's borders and increasing the facilitation of legitimate travelers. Currently, there are thousands of different documents a traveler can present to CBP officers when attempting to enter the United States, creating a tremendous potential for fraud. In fiscal year 2006 alone, over 209,000 individuals were apprehended at the ports of entry trying to cross the border with fraudulent claims of citizenship or false documents. The Western Hemisphere Travel Initiative (WHTI) is a joint effort by DHS and the Department of State to address this security vulnerability and increase traveler facilitation.

The initial phase of WHTI went into effect January 23, 2007, obligating all air travelers, regardless of age, to present a passport, NEXUS Air Card, or Merchant Mariner Card for entry to the United States. The implementation of the air portion of WHTI was highly successful, with documentary compliance rates nearing 99.9% and no interruption to air transportation. This high level of compliance was due to the holistic and collaborative planning approach taken by DHS and the Department of State, starting well before the new rules went into effect. An aggressive public outreach campaign aimed at increasing awareness of the new documentary requirements was a critical first step, as was working closely with private industry and air carriers from the planning stages through implementation, in enforcing the new rules in a flexible and reasonable manner.

As early as January 1, 2008, U.S. citizens traveling between the United States and Canada, Mexico, Central and South America, the Caribbean, and Bermuda by land or sea will be required to present a valid passport or other WHTI-compliant documents, as determined by DHS. As with the air portion of the WHTI requirement, we are taking a holistic and collaborative approach to implementing these new requirements. As an example, DHS recently announced its intent to propose, as part of the forthcoming Notice of Proposed Rulemaking (NPRM) on WHTI, significant flexibility regarding travel documents required for U.S. and Canadian children. This proposal, which will be subject to public comment as part of the WHTI NPRM process, would allow U.S. and Canadian citizens, ages 15 and younger and with parental consent, to cross the border at land and sea ports with a certified copy of their birth certificate as an alternative to a passport or other WHTI-compliant identity card. U.S. and Canadian citizen children, ages 16 through 18, traveling with public or private school groups, religious groups, social or cultural organizations, or teams associated with youth athletics organizations would also be able to enter, under adult supervision, with a certified copy of their birth certificate. This proposal does not affect the documentary requirements for air travel within the Western Hemisphere, as I have outlined earlier.

In partnership with the private sector and State and local governments, DHS has introduced a pilot "Model Airport" program to ensure a more welcoming environment for foreign visitors. The pilot projects at the Houston Intercontinental Airport and Washington Dulles International Airport feature customized video messages for the public with practical information about the entry process, improved screening and efficient movement of people through the border entry process, and assistance for foreign travelers once they have been admitted to the United States. The Model Airport program is progressing as scheduled. By March 23, 2007, CBP will complete the customized video providing practical information about the entry process to arriving international travelers. Broadcast systems explaining the entry process to travelers while they are in the Federal Inspection Services (FIS) area will be installed and operational at the Houston Intercontinental Airport by April 2, 2007, and at the Washington Dulles International Airport by April 17, 2007. The directional signage and banners to guide travelers through the entry process have already been installed in the FIS area of both airports. New brochures explaining the inspection process to the public are being printed and will be made available in April 2007.

The Model Ports concept document is complete and has been distributed to stakeholders. The Performance Measurements Committee, tasked with identifying recommendations to improve the international passenger arrivals process has met and is analyzing the collected data. CBP entry documents are currently being reviewed to determine the feasibility of document consolidation. In addition, CBP is in the process of reviewing the current professionalism initiative for enhancement measures, and Disney has expressed its desire to participate in the process. CBP is currently scheduled to meet with Disney executives on March 29, 2007, to discuss CBP's current professionalism initiative process and conduct a walk-through to evaluate the CBP process in the FIS at the Orlando International Airport.

The "Blueprint to Discover America Partnership" has been reviewed by CBP, and we are in agreement with its three main goals: a faster and more secure visa system, more rapid processing of passengers at airports, and the creation of a more welcoming environment for international passengers. The Rice-Chertoff Initiative, the DHS/State Department "Secure Borders, Open Doors" Initiative, the US-VISIT Program, and the Commerce Department's Travel and Tourism Advisory Board (TTAB) have all focused on these same goals to improve the international traveler experience. Through various government initiatives, such as requiring e-passports for Visa Waiver Program (VWP) travelers, setting up Model Airports, and developing a "single portal" for transmission of passenger information, we are going a long way towards improving the air passenger experience. We support the fundamental objectives in the "Blueprint" to speed passengers through airports, to expedite visa processing and enhance security, and to make the travel experience more enjoyable. We will continue to work collaboratively and expeditiously towards meeting these goals.

The DHS Travel Redress Inquiry Program (DHS TRIP) is a single point of contact for individuals who have inquiries or seek resolution of difficulties experienced during their travel screening at transportation hubs—like airports and train stations—or while crossing U.S. borders. Difficulties such as denied or delayed airline boarding, denied or delayed entry or exit at a port of entry or border checkpoint, or continuous referral to additional (secondary) screening can be addressed through DHS TRIP. Travelers who have been repeatedly identified for additional screening can file an inquiry to have erroneous information corrected in DHS systems. Information provided by travelers is used solely to process their request for redress, and safeguards are in place to protect the privacy of any personal information provided.

An effort similar to DHS TRIP is the Primary Lookout Over-Ride (PLOR), a systems upgrade created in February 2006 that benefits antiterrorism security measures as well as international travelers by alleviating additional screening procedures for individuals with the same, or similar, biographical information as watch-listed individuals. This system upgrade allows CBP officers at ports of entry to eliminate the need for secondary inspections on subsequent trips in cases where travelers' names, birthdates, or other biographical information match those of high-risk individuals. This is only done once the CBP officer has verified that a particular individual is not the person of interest. It is important to note that PLOR does not involve the collection of any new data, does not create new databases or lists, and does not require any action on the part of the traveler. To date, this process has resulted in over 17,000 additional inspections being avoided—a significant savings in both processing times and operational costs.

CBP collects biometrics on almost all non-U.S. citizens at the primary inspection area in our air and sea ports and at the secondary inspection in our land ports. Through the US-VISIT system, CBP checks individuals against a fingerprint-based watchlist of known or suspected terrorists, wants and warrants, immigration violations, and other criminal history information and verifies whether a person is the same one previously encountered by DHS and/or the Department of State. The US-VISIT Program has substantially added to CBP's screening capabilities, enhancing our ability to process travelers in a timely and secure fashion. US-VISIT's transition to a full ten-fingerprint collection system is paramount to further strengthening and expanding our screening capabilities.

The Immigration Advisory Program (IAP) extends our zone of security outward by screening overseas passengers before they board aircraft destined for the United States. IAP teams identify high-risk and terrorist watch-listed passengers using the Automated Targeting System and use that information to advise airlines whether passengers should not be boarded on a flight to the United States. Since IAP became operational, 1,500 passengers have been prevented from boarding planes bound for the United States. Of those, nine were prevented from boarding flights due to security concerns—four were on the Transportation Security Administration (TSA) No-Fly list, and five were the subject of TIDE records with sufficient derogatory information to support a refusal of admission. TIDE is the comprehensive terrorist database. In addition, 88 passengers attempting to travel with fraudulent documents were stopped, and 1,403 that were otherwise improperly documented were also intercepted. To date, IAP has saved CBP $2.26 million in processing costs and the airlines $2.21 million in fines.

The Carrier Liaison Program (CLP) was developed to enhance border security by helping commercial carriers to become more effective in identifying improperly documented passengers destined for the United States. The primary method for accomplishing this mission is by providing technical assistance and training to carrier staff. Technical assistance includes publication and distribution of information guides and document fraud summaries and alerts. In addition, CBP is developing the 24/7 Carrier Response Center phone line to provide real-time entry requirements and document validity advice to carrier staff worldwide. The U.S. Immigration and Customs Enforcement (ICE) Forensic Document Laboratory (FDL) supports the CLP in multiple ways and provides FDL Document Alerts to the CLP for distribution to airline personnel. The CLP provides training on U.S. entry requirements, passenger assessment, fraudulent document detection, and imposter identification using state-of-the-art document examination material, equipment, and training tools. Training is delivered at U.S. ports of entry and at airports abroad by experienced CLP officers and is customized to meet the needs of specific carriers or locations based on performance analysis or emergent circumstances. CLP officers also assist carriers to develop and implement strategies to reduce travel document abuse. To date in FY 2007, CBP has completed 31 training sessions—17 overseas and 14 at U.S. ports of entry—and over 1,900 airline personnel and document screeners have been trained. CBP has scheduled training at over 40 overseas locations and 30 U.S. ports of entry this fiscal year. For FY 2008, CBP anticipates training sessions at over 50 overseas locations and 30 U.S. ports of entry.

In January 2005, CBP created the Fraudulent Document Analysis Unit (FDAU) to collect documents, provide ports with analysis of document trends and intelligence information, and target persons being smuggled into the United States using fraudulent documents.

Between January and December 2005, the FDAU received 40,875 fraudulent documents confiscated at ports of entry and mail facilities. Working with the FDAU, CBP expects the seizure of fraudulent documents to increase.

The Advance Passenger Information System (APIS) was developed in 1988 in cooperation with the airline industry as a voluntary program. This program established a system for the electronic transmission of passenger and crew biographical data by commercial carriers. Commercial carriers and the international community recognize APIS as a standard for passenger information processing and enhanced security. APIS information is a critical tool that allows CBP to target high-risk travelers while facilitating the progress of legitimate travelers through the entry and clearance process.

On April 7, 2005, the APIS Final Rule (AFR) was published in the Federal Register, requiring the submission of manifest information by all commercial air and sea carriers arriving into or departing from the United States. Additionally, the AFR established the required data elements and timelines for manifest submissions. Pursuant to the Intelligence Reform and Terrorism Prevention Act (IRTPA) of 2004, the CBP Pre-Departure Notice of Proposed Rulemaking (NPRM) was published in the Federal Register on July 14, 2006. The NPRM proposed that commercial carriers transmit APIS manifest data prior to departure from, and arrivals to, the United States. The NPRM offered two options: carriers could continue to use the current manifest transmission format for submission, or carriers could start using APIS Quick Query (AQQ), where a single APIS message would be submitted as passengers check in. As part of the DHS commitment to establishing a common reporting process for carriers submitting traveler information, CBP has been working with TSA to align the CBP Pre-Departure requirements with the Secure Flight program. The APIS Pre-Departure Final Rule is undergoing final DHS and CBP review prior to submission to the Office of Management and Budget (OMB).

As reflected in the *National Strategy for Pandemic Influenza*, the goals of the federal government's preparedness and response to a potential pandemic are to stop, slow, or otherwise limit the spread of the pandemic to the United States; limit the domestic spread of a pandemic, and mitigate disease, suffering and death; and to sustain our infrastructure and mitigate the impact to our economy and the functioning of society. CBP must be prepared to maintain essential services, mitigate against the introduction, spread, and consequences of a pandemic, and protect our workforce and the public. CBP is working with our DHS partner agencies, as well as the Centers for Disease Control and Prevention (CDC), to develop effective and appropriate entry/exit procedures and travel restrictions during a pandemic.

CBP officers are committed to the highest standards of professional conduct. We want to assist the millions of legitimate travelers who pose little or no threat in gaining proper entry into the United States, both safely and efficiently. As part of this effort, CBP recently implemented a campaign to educate travelers. Here are some of the best pieces of advice CBP can provide to travelers to help them have a safe, efficient and enjoyable trip abroad:

First, travelers should be sure to declare everything they bring in from abroad, even if the item is bought it in a duty-free shop. All passengers arriving on a plane must complete a CBP declaration form. This declaration prevents the unintentional introduction of prohibited items, such as fruits and food products that could introduce devastating diseases and pests into the United States and severely damage U.S. agriculture. If items purchased abroad are intended for personal use or as gifts, they are eligible for duty exemptions. If they are intended for resale, they are not. If any duty is owed, a CBP officer will assist you in paying that duty.

Second, travelers need to be aware that every food product, fruit, and vegetable must be declared to a CBP officer and must be presented for inspection. Many travelers look forward to bringing home special food items from abroad. However, it is important to "know before you go" which items can and cannot be brought into the United States from abroad. It is important to remember that the rules and regulations are in place to protect the American economy, plant and animal wildlife, and the health of the American people.

Mr. Chairman, Members of the Subcommittee, I have outlined a broad array of initiatives today that, with your assistance, will help DHS continue to protect America from terrorist threats while fulfilling our other important traditional missions. But our work is not complete. With the continued support of the Congress, DHS will succeed in meeting the challenges posed by the ongoing terrorist threat and the need to facilitate ever-increasing numbers of legitimate shipments and travelers.

Thank you again for this opportunity to testify. I will be happy to answer any questions you may have.

Statement of Alfonso Martinez-Fonts, Jr.
Assistant Secretary, Private Sector
Department of Homeland Security

Good Morning, Chairman Dorgan, Senator DeMint and Members of the Subcommittee. Thank you for inviting me to be here today to join my colleague Mr. Robert Jacksta in representing the Department of Homeland Security (DHS) and to discuss the efforts of the Department to facilitate travel and tourism policy for the United States. The DHS Private Sector Office was given in the Intelligence Reform and Terrorism Prevention Act of 2004 the very important responsibility of working with, and consulting with, the travel and tourism industry. As a result, significant effort of our office goes towards this goal. This is in addition to the overall mission of our office, which is to provide America's private sector with a direct line of communication to DHS, utilize information received from the private sector, and promote Departmental policies to the private sector.

I first would like to emphasize that we have established and maintained very strong relationships with the industry's largest associations, including the Travel Industry Association of America, Travel Business Roundtable, and the World Travel and Tourism Council. We have also reached out to and worked well with other sector-specific organizations, including, but not limited to, the American Bus Association, the National Restaurant Association, the International Council of Cruise Lines, NAFSA: the Association of International Educators, the American Hotel and Lodging Association, and the Air Transport Association. We also work with individual companies, including Disney Parks and Resorts and Marriott Hotel. As a result of these relationships, we have learned private sector best practices and have encouraged their use by the U.S. government.

As you may know, the Rice-Chertoff Joint Vision, which is commonly referred to as the Rice-Chertoff Initiative (RCI), was announced in January of 2006 by the Secretaries of State and Homeland Security in order to focus efforts on the important need to facilitate travel while ensuring the security of the nation. Secretary Chertoff has tasked my office with coordinating progress on the objectives laid out in the RCI. The Private Sector Office has played an integral role in forming and coordinating a successful network to make this happen. This network has three levels: 1) coordination within DHS; 2) inter-agency approach, facilitating communication among multiple Departments of the U.S. government; and 3) linkages to the private sector.

Let us start by discussing the first level of coordination within DHS. Over the past year, we have worked with all DHS components that affect travel and tourism. This includes U.S. Customs and Border Protection, the Transportation Security Administration, the Privacy Office, the Office for Civil Rights and Civil Liberties, U.S. Immigration and Customs Enforcement,

U.S. Citizenship and Immigration Services, US-VISIT, as well as my own Directorate, the Policy Office. The Policy Office sets DHS policy. As you may know, DHS sets the visa policy which the Department of State then executes—an example of a close and productive working relationship between the agencies.

This leads me to point out the second level of the network: coordination among DHS and other governmental agencies. When Secretary Rice and Secretary Chertoff announced their joint vision, it was the continuation of a very productive relationship between the Departments. We at the Private Sector Office have collaborated closely with Department of State's Bureau of Consular Affairs, to meet the goals outlined by the initiative. One example of streamlined coordination between the Departments is the extension from 90 days to 120 days of the amount of time before the start of classes that international students can apply for a visa. This extension was approved by both DHS and State and is currently being implemented by the Department of State at U.S. Consulates around the world and communicated on the Department's website. This ruling makes studying in the United States more convenient and attractive to international students.

In addition to collaborating with State, the network includes a strong partnership with the Department of Commerce. This includes participation with the Tourism Policy Council, led by Secretary Gutierrez and comprised of 17 agencies and offices of the federal government.

This network also is not complete without involvement by the private sector, including the airlines, amusement parks, hotels, universities, hospitals, and trade associations. It is at this level where the Private Sector Office lends value by exchanging useful information advocating private sector interest when policies such as the Western Hemisphere Travel Initiative (WHTI) are being drafted. Our Office also helps to incorporate best practices. Government agencies must coordinate better not only amongst themselves, but with private industry as well. A system for promoting cooperation between the government and the private sector to promote travel to the United States is a recommendation laid out by the travel and tourism industry. We recognize the value of public-private partnerships.

One example of a system where all three levels come together is the creation and implementation of the Secure Borders Open Doors Advisory Committee (SBODAC), an advisory board to the RCI, formed under the auspices of the Homeland Security Advisory Council (HSAC) in coordination with the Department of State. The SBODAC represents a broad spectrum of private sector partners impacted by RCI and its programs and completes one of the 13 RCI objectives. Secretaries Rice and Chertoff selected the members of the Committee including leaders from academia, business, hospitals, media, and the travel and tourism industry.

The first meeting of the SBODAC was held on December 6, 2006, and focused on Model Ports of Entry and One Stop Redress. Present at the meeting were representatives from private industry in addition to officials from the Departments of State, Homeland Security, Commerce, and Education. The SBODAC has since formed four working groups to address various components of RCI: 1) public diplomacy and international outreach; 2) visa policy and processing; 3) critical success factors and metrics; and 4) ports of entry. These working groups are meeting throughout the month of March of this year with colleagues from DHS and the Department of State to start putting forth recommendations with the goal of achieving a balance between security and economic prosperity.

Another example of this third level of the network is DHS' work with the Department of Commerce's Travel and Tourism Advisory Board, headed by Mr. Jay Rasulo of Disney Parks and Resorts, whom I know testified before you on January 31 of this year. Our Office joined the Department of State in presenting a six-month RCI Progress Report to the TTAB at their July 2006 meeting in Chicago. In other meetings with the TTAB, we have reported on the status of the Western Hemisphere Travel Initiative and heard the concerns and recommendations of the board.

One recent example of this is our work with U.S. Customs and Border Protection to incorporate the participation of the Travel Industry Association, Disney Parks and Resorts, and Universal Parks and Resorts into a task force that will form recommendations to improve the entry process.

Another example of collaborative work we've done with private industry is collaboration during the air roll-out of the Western Hemisphere Travel Initiative. In the months before the roll-out, DHS worked with our travel and tourism stakeholders, including the airlines, hotels, travel distribution channels (such as Expedia and Orbitz), to ensure that travelers were aware of the new passport requirements far in advance of the deadline. Success was demonstrated by the numbers, as 94% of Americans that entered the U.S. by air had passports the week before implementation and 99% of travelers had passports by the second day after implementation of the air rule. We will continue our collaboration with the travel and tourism industry with the land and sea rollout.

While we have had the pleasure of helping to form the network of players for RCI, we are also pleased to witness the progress that others have made on the initiative. In addition to the SBODAC, DHS and the Department of State are on a path to meet all 13 of the RCI objectives. Today I especially want to highlight the efforts of my colleague, Mr. Robert Jacksta, in leading DHS full speed ahead on RCI's first objective in creating our two model ports at Washington Dulles International Airport and Houston Bush-Intercontinental Airport, with new signage already up and more progress on recommendations already on the way. I would also like to highlight the success of DHS' first one-stop travel screening redress program, known as DHS

Traveler Redress Inquiry Program (TRIP). The system satisfies another of RCI's objectives and has begun receiving redress requests as of February 20, 2007.

While we are pleased with the successes of the past year, we are also aware of the continuing need to evaluate and improve on our efforts. At the Private Sector Office, we understand the importance of this industry to our nation and are continuously assisting DHS in finding the right balance between economic vitality and national security. We are cognizant of the need for our government and private sector partners to work closely in order to facilitate travel in a safe and secure manner and demonstrate the greatness of this nation to international visitors. As the industry's research has pointed out, traveling to the United States makes visitors 74% more likely to feel extremely favorable about our country. The Blueprint to Discover America lays out some policy recommendations, which I would welcome the opportunity to address for you during the question and answer session. Many of these recommendations are consistent with current government programs which have been underway since the inception of RCI.

I close today by emphasizing that completion of the objectives of RCI requires successful work and coordination within agencies, between agencies, and through public-private partnerships. We are using this three-tiered network to reach our goals. Thank you Chairman Dorgan, Ranking Member DeMint, and Members of the Subcommittee for providing me the opportunity to update you about our efforts. I look forward to your questions.

Statement of Stephen A. Edson
Deputy Assistant Secretary for Visa Services
Department of State

Chairman Dorgan, Ranking Member DeMint, distinguished members of the Subcommittee:

I appreciate this opportunity to discuss how the Bureau of Consular Affairs is facilitating the travel of legitimate international visitors to the United States while vigilantly protecting U.S. border security for the benefit of Americans and our foreign visitors.

Secretary of State Condoleezza Rice identified these objectives as part of the mission of the Department of State to the Senate Foreign Relations Committee on February 8, 2007, when she said, "The State Department mission extends to defending our borders and protecting our homeland. We must strive to remain a welcoming nation for tourists, students and businesspeople, while at the same time increasing our security against terrorists and criminals who would exploit our open society to do us harm."

Together with our colleagues in the Departments of Homeland Security and Commerce, we strive constantly to strike the right balance between protecting America's borders and preserving America's welcome to international visitors and our fundamental openness to the world, which is the source of our strength and sense of ourselves.

Secure Borders, Open Doors

The context for all our efforts with regard to visa procedures continues to be September 11, 2001. On that terrible day, when so many Americans and citizens from 90 other nations lost their lives in New York, Pennsylvania, and Virginia, we saw the lengths to which some would go to exploit our open society to do us harm. I think that all people of good will can appreciate that we had to act swiftly and decisively in the aftermath of 9/11 to address our nation's border security needs.

Since 9/11 the Department of State has instituted numerous changes to the way U.S. visas are processed. Some of these changes were instituted by law, others through the interagency process. Together, they legitimately aim to improve the security and integrity of the visa process for the benefit of both U.S. citizens and our international visitors.

As we have implemented these changes to strengthen U.S. border security through the visa process, we have worked tirelessly to ensure that our visa process remains the beginning of a positive welcome to legitimate travelers. Security is, and must be, our primary concern, but welcoming international visitors is also a matter of national security. Foreign visitors accounted for $107.4 billion in spending and other economic activity in the United States in 2006, according to Department of Commerce figures. International students contribute an additional $13.5 billion each year to the institutions that they attend and the surrounding communities where they live and study.

Beyond the financial benefits that are clearly good for our nation, we need to remain the welcoming country that the United States has traditionally been because of the intangible benefits of such a posture. It is essential that we provide visitors with a positive experience because that experience has incalculable influence in shaping impressions and opinions of our nation and our people. The best advertisement for America is America.

Our policy of increasing the national security of the United States while welcoming international visitors is captured by the phrase "Secure Borders and Open Doors." These objectives are by no means mutually exclusive; in fact, they are mutually reinforcing. We can, and must, achieve both. Meeting these two objectives presents us with management, resource, security, and public diplomacy challenges. We are proceeding aggressively yet deliberately, in order to get the balance right.

Implementing the Rice-Chertoff Joint Vision

In January 2006, the Secretaries of State and Homeland Security launched the "Rice-Chertoff Joint Vision: Secure Borders and Open Doors in the Information Age" as a commitment to striking that balance. This initiative aims to improve:

- The efficiency, predictability, and transparency of the visa process;
- The security of U.S. passports and other travel documents; and
- The U.S. government's ability to screen visa applicants and travelers who arrive at our borders.

Our efforts to implement the goals and spirit of the Joint Vision began long before the formal launch of this plan. Over the past year we have made significant progress in advancing these objectives. Let me take this opportunity to highlight some recent achievements.

Improvements to the Visa Process

We have made changes that enhance the efficiency, predictability, and transparency of the visa process and thereby facilitate international travel.

We introduced an electronic visa application form, or EVAF, and mandated its use at consulates worldwide in November 2006. EVAF use reduces data entry errors, eliminates duplicative data entry, and increases the number of applicants whom consular staff can interview daily.

We introduced an Internet-based visa appointment system. All consular posts have placed appointment wait times online on our website at travel.state.gov, so that visa applicants have more information to plan their travel.

Since 2001 we have created 570 new consular positions at posts worldwide to handle visa demand.

Visa processing delays have been cut dramatically:

- By fully automating the process and streamlining information sharing with other agencies, we have drastically reduced to two weeks in most cases the amount of time it takes to process security clearances. We are constantly working with our interagency partners to reduce this time frame while still meeting our legal obligations in this area.
- We have also established a process for individuals or their legal representatives to inquire through our public inquiries division about the status of clearance requests.

We have responded to suggestions from the business and academic communities and established mechanisms to assist student and business travelers, thus improving the welcome America provides to these key sectors:

- All posts have established mechanisms to expedite visa appointments for legitimate business travelers, students, and international exchange visitors. We do not want students to miss the start dates for their planned study, or legitimate business travelers to have to forego a business meeting, because they could not get an appointment.
- A Business Visa Center (BVC) located in the Visa Office explains the visa process to U. S. companies, convention organizers, and others who invite employees or current or prospective business clients to the United States. The BVC handled almost 2,800 requests from American businesses for information and assistance in cases involving over 139,000 business travelers in 2006.
- Many posts have imaginative programs—often organized in conjunction with local branches of the American Chamber of Commerce (AmCham)—to facilitate business and tourist travel. For example, Consulate General Shanghai's Corporate Visa Program (CVP) with AmCham Shanghai lessens the interview wait time for business applicants—most interviews take place within a week after application materials have been submitted—and establishes effective communication channels between AmCham and the Consulate General. Shanghai processed over 9,600 visas for nearly 500 CVP member companies through its program last year.

These efforts have produced results. We have "turned the corner," and our metrics are positive across the board. Non-immigrant visa issuances in FY 2006 rose 8 percent over the previous year, with business/tourist visa issuances increasing by 12 percent. We issued an all-time high of 591,000 student and exchange visitor visas in FY 2006. We have seen increases from every region in the world, but the numbers for some of our key business and travel markets are especially marked. For example, business/tourist visa issuance is up 12 percent for Indian citizens, 16 percent for Chinese, 13 percent for Koreans, and 70 percent for Brazilians.

We have put the structures in place to ensure that the visa process is not the daunting ordeal that it is sometimes portrayed to be. Visa applications are up 5 percent worldwide. The growth in demand is explosive in some markets—for example, 17 percent in China and 30 percent in Brazil. Clearly, travelers still seek to come to the United States, and we are helping them get here while still ensuring national security.

Secure Travel Documents

As part of the promotion of secure travel documents, the first phase of the Western Hemisphere Travel Initiative (WHTI)—that all travelers arriving in the United States by air present a passport or other approved document—went into effect on January 23. The overwhelming majority of arrivals from destinations that previously did not require a passport did in fact present a passport. DHS facilitated entry for the handful that did not. U.S. Customs and Border Protection (CBP) reports 99 percent compliance with the passport requirement. This smooth transition was the result of aggressive outreach by the travel industry, foreign countries affected by WHTI legislation, and the Departments of State and Homeland Security, and is an excellent example of how government and the private sector can work together to facilitate international travel.

The Department of State began issuing diplomatic e-passports on December 30, 2005, and official e-passports in April 2006. We began issuing e-passports to the public on August 14, 2006. All our domestic passport agencies have been fully converted to issue e-passports. Conversion of the two remaining mega-centers is forthcoming, pending sufficient blank e-passport inventory.

We are also aggressively moving forward with the Department of Homeland Security on a "Model Ports of Entry" concept. Our goal is to ensure that international visitors' positive experience continues from the time they make a visa appointment to the time they pick up their bags at baggage claim.

While it does not directly relate to the Rice-Chertoff Joint Initiative, I want to take this opportunity to say a few words about the unprecedented demand by American citizens for U.S. passports. Applications received for the first five months of Fiscal Year (FY) 2007 are 44 percent higher than for the same period last year. Two key factors are driving this increase. January through April is typically the peak passport demand period, as travelers prepare for spring and summer holidays. In addition, the WHTI requirements created a surge in demand which began in November 2006.

We see this higher demand as a positive development. Currently, 74 million Americans—approximately one-quarter of the population—are documented with a U.S. passport. As more of our fellow citizens obtain these secure documents, the more secure and efficient our nation's borders will be. The Department of State is committed to ensuring that Americans will have passports when they need to travel.

In anticipation of this high demand for passports, the Department of State hired more than 250 additional passport adjudicators in the past year and will hire an additional 86 this year. This month alone, 49 new passport adjudicators began work. The National Passport Center (NPC) is operating 24 hours a day in three shifts per day; all 16 passport agencies are working overtime to get passports out to applicants as quickly as possible. In April, the Department of State will increase its passport issuance infrastructure with the opening of a "mega-processing" center in Hot Springs, Arkansas, which will have the capacity to produce as many as 10 million passport books annually.

Future Enhancements to the Visa Process

The Department of Commerce figures show that we experienced the highest number of international arrivals in 2006 since 2000 and project that 2007 international visitor levels, at 52.9 million, will surpass the 2000 record. Those figures are good news, and we welcome them. Yet we are still not satisfied. To continue to meet the demand for visas, to continue to keep our national welcome mat out, and to continue to facilitate legitimate international travel, we want to introduce additional enhancements.

We plan to introduce several changes over the next two years. Many of these innovations—on which we have been working for many months—parallel suggestions made by the U. S. Travel and Tourism Advisory Board (TTAB), the Discover America Partnership, and others. Please allow me to describe these changes in detail.

Reducing Visa Appointment Wait Times

For those travelers who require a visa, the wait to get an appointment can impact short-term travel plans. Despite the explosive demand I described earlier, nearly 90 percent of our 219 visa-issuing posts currently have average wait times of 30 days or less, and at a large majority the wait time is less than one week.

Many of the overall changes we've already introduced to streamline the visa process have helped to keep down wait times. We are employing customized solutions to tackle situations in particular countries with persistent and unacceptably high appointment wait times. In October 2006, for example, we sent a team of experienced current and retired officers on temporary duty to India to help the consulates there process a backlog of appointment requests, reducing wait times from over 100 days to less than 10. Since that effort, appointment wait times have begun to gradually increase again. We view this as a positive sign, indicating that visa applicants who might have in the past been deterred by the appointment wait time are now choosing to apply for visas. A fresh wave of temporary duty support is currently in India assisting posts to manage the continued heavy workload.

"Surges" such as we employed in India can be useful in tackling short-term situations, and we may use them in other places. They aren't a viable long-term solution in places with structurally high visa demand. We need to consider and implement other approaches.

Aligning Consular Assets to Meet Demand

We must ensure that we have our consular assets appropriately deployed where we need them, so that we can provide consistent, timely, quality consular services to our clientele.

After careful analysis of detailed workload figures submitted by posts, and considering other factors that impact workload and productivity, such as the fraud environment and physical plant, we have concluded that consular sections in several regions are understaffed to meet current and anticipated workload, while posts in other regions are overstaffed.

To correct the imbalance, the Bureau of Consular Affairs plans to transfer approximately 30 consular positions from overstaffed to understaffed posts and create 22 additional positions. Most of these will be entry-level positions, although some mid-level positions will be included as well. There will be gains and losses at posts in all bureaus, but we anticipate net gains at certain posts in Asia and the Western Hemisphere—places like India, China, Brazil, and Mexico. Most of the transfers will come from European posts.

We have begun this repositioning exercise and expect it to continue over the coming two to three years, in order to provide time to create the positions and identify suitable officers, ensure there is adequate space to accommodate new personnel, and minimize the disruption to posts that are identified for position transfers.

We will open additional consular facilities in key countries. The Department of State has obtained funding to open a fifth consulate in Hyderabad, in southern India. A team led by Under Secretary for Management Henrietta Fore was in Hyderabad earlier this month to inspect the proposed site. We hope to be able to open a consulate in Hyderabad, to include the provision of visa services, in FY 2008.

Technological Improvements

The Bureau of Consular Affairs exploits advanced technologies to automate consular processes wherever possible. This promotes security and efficiency by reducing or eliminating data entry, printing, shipping, storage, and filing burdens on our posts worldwide. Our strategy for meeting our visa demand challenges includes exploring how technology can provide consular officers with the information to make more rapid and accurate decisions and to collapse the distance between the consular officer and the traveler.

Building on the successful and widespread use of the EVAF, we anticipate moving to an entirely paperless, electronic visa application process by the end of 2007.

Current law and regulations require the incorporation of biometrics in all U.S. visas and the State Department meets this requirement by collecting two fingerprint scans from each visa applicant. The prints are verified against interagency databases to screen for terrorists and others who may be ineligible for a visa. Two fingerprint scans provide a limited amount of data, and our experience is that they yield a large number of "false positive" results, which can delay the visa process and inconvenience legitimate travelers. Ten fingerprints provide a greater number of data points and much more accurate responses, allowing us to more broadly screen individuals to better verify identity and ensure that the individual does not pose a risk to security prior to travel to the United States. We are piloting the collection of ten fingerprints at five posts (London, San Salvador, Riyadh, Dhahran, and Asuncion) and plan to deploy this technology at every post by the end of 2007.

We are also exploring other technological developments, such as remote data collection and visa adjudication and interviews via digital videoconference. Pilot tests of remote data collection at several locations in the field (UK, Germany, Japan, and Samoa) demonstrated that the technology is not yet fully mature. We must address technical issues concerning data transmission and security, as well as legal issues, before we are able to incorporate remote adjudication into a workable visa system.

Similarly, although we have successfully tested interviews via digital videoconference between London and Belfast, there are considerable technical and security issues to resolve before we can consider wider application of this technology—including, for example, ensuring that the video image on the screen and the fingerprint data sent in remotely belong to the same applicant. We will continue to explore the possibilities of this and other technologies for our ability to provide remote visa services and for improving visa services overall.

In February 2007 the Bureau of Consular Affairs established a worldwide customer service standard by which every non-immigrant visa applicant at any post should be scheduled for an appointment within 30 days. The customer service standard for students and U.S.-interest business visas is 15 days or less. In addition, all applicants who are found eligible for a visa and who do not require additional security-related processing should expect the visa to be issued within three days of the interview.

As I previously noted, we already meet these standards at the majority of our posts. Our goal is that by the end of 2008, 100 per cent of posts will be able to meet this 30-day appointment benchmark.

To achieve this goal, posts have been instructed to conscientiously update appointment wait times. The Bureau of Consular Affairs will continue to monitor appointment wait times closely. We will work with posts that approach or exceed the benchmark to refine internal management practices and devise solutions, and we will consider the use of temporary duty assistance when warranted.

Public Diplomacy: Dispelling Misperceptions

Despite the initiatives we have taken, despite the U.S. visa issuance and demand numbers, and despite the international visitor figures, there is still the perception in some quarters that the visa process discourages travelers from seeking to come to the United States. In some cases, that perception is borne of the small number of cases where travelers encounter real difficulties. In many cases, however, it is fueled by stories in the media which rely on outdated statistics or anecdotes that do not reflect current realities. I regret this very much, particularly given what has been done by my colleagues at the Department of State and at embassies and consulates overseas.

We need to dispel misperceptions. We have been doing so with an aggressive public outreach campaign. Assistant Secretary of State for Consular Affairs Maura Harty has spoken to a number of business audiences over the past two years, and she takes every opportunity to reach out to international audiences during her official travel overseas. Most recently, she addressed the Istanbul Chamber of Commerce on March 5, and in February she spoke to the American Chambers of Commerce in Shanghai, Guangzhou, and Macau regarding our efforts to facilitate legitimate tourist and business travel to the United States. She has published letters to the Editor on the same subject which have appeared in outlets such as *The Economist* and the *New York Times*. We raise this important issue at every opportunity during our extensive domestic outreach program. Ambassadors and other officials lead our outreach efforts overseas, speaking to business and student groups and placing op-ed articles in local newspapers to encourage travelers to consider travel and study in the United States.

We have also consulted closely with the travel community over the past three years to take their concerns into account and solicit suggestions on how we can improve the visa process without compromising national security. A "Secure Borders, Open Doors" Advisory Committee, composed of government and travel community representatives and established under the Rice-Chertoff Joint Vision, held an inaugural meeting on December 6, 2006, to devise strategies to get our message out to legitimate travelers: America wants you and we welcome you.

Mr. Chairman, our efforts to facilitate legitimate travel to the United States while protecting the security of this nation will continue. Improving America's welcome for foreign visitors, and countering lingering misperceptions about that welcome, will require joint efforts by both government and private stakeholders. We look forward to working with business groups and our partner agencies toward that goal. In the meantime, we will ensure that our welcome begins with an efficient, accessible, and secure visa process.

Statement of Jamie Estrada
Deputy Assistant Secretary for Manufacturing
Department of Commerce

Chairman Dorgan, Ranking Member DeMint, and distinguished Members of the Subcommittee, thank you for the invitation to appear today to update you on the status of the United States travel and tourism industry. I would also like to take this opportunity to thank you for your support of this important sector of our economy.

The travel and tourism industry in the United States is strong and continues to be the most lucrative travel and tourism industry in the world. I am pleased to report that international visitors to the United States set a new record level of spending in 2006. While we are enjoying record levels of revenues, it is also noteworthy that sectors such as hotels and lodging and restaurants are achieving new levels of profitability.

Although the industry is making significant progress, the United States faces its share of challenges due to the impact of 9/11, uncertainties in the airline industry, and increased competition from emerging destinations. We are working to address these issues collaboratively with our colleagues at the Departments of State and Homeland Security and with the private sector.

Tourism and the U.S. Economy

I would like to begin by sharing with you the good news before discussing existing challenges.

The travel and tourism industry is a major contributor to our nation's gross domestic product (GDP). Travel and tourism represent 2.6 percent of GDP and generated more than $1 trillion of sales in 2006 alone.[1]

The travel and tourism industry is one of America's largest employers, with more than 8 million Americans employed. It is important to highlight that over 90 percent of the U.S. travel and tourism industry is classified as small and medium-sized businesses.[2]

The travel and tourism sector has been a substantial contributor to our positive balance of trade in services. The United States has enjoyed a continuous surplus in travel since 1989. A surplus occurs when international visitors spend more in this country than we do when traveling abroad. In 2006, the United States exported more than $107 billion in travel and tourism-related goods and services and posted its 18th consecutive annual trade surplus in travel. In fact, travel and tourism generate over one fourth of total U.S. services exports, according to the Bureau of Economic Analysis.

Key sector indicators are largely positive. According to Price Waterhouse Coopers, in 2006 lodging industry profit levels have returned to the previous record level of $22.5 billion. In addition, data from the Bureau of Economic Analysis indicate total restaurant sales were less affected by 9/11 relative to other travel and tourism sectors and have steadily increased 15 percent in real terms between 2000 and 2005.

Recent Trends and Challenges

Following the events of September 11, 2001, U.S. travel and tourism receipts and international visitor levels both sharply declined. Receipts declined roughly 22 percent from the peak in 2000 to a trough in 2003. As the accompanying chart indicates, travel and tourism receipts in 2006, at $107.8 billion, are five percent over the record set in 2000. At the same time, our 2007 international visitor levels are projected to surpass the 2000 record, reaching 52.9 million. This clearly demonstrates the industry's resiliency as we move forward.

The United States is first in the world with respect to travel receipts, with nearly double the value of receipts generated by France, even though they lead the world in visitation. While receipts provide a critical measure to gauge the industry's strength, it is true that global market share of visitors to the United States has fallen since its peak in 1992. However, global market share of visitors alone does not give an accurate measure of performance. In fact, eight out of the world's top ten markets have lost market share of global visitors. This is due to the reality of considerably more competitors in the global arena for travelers today than in 1992. In addition, much of global growth in visitors is due to short trips. For example, while France and Spain are the world's number one and two markets for numbers of international visitors, much of their leading positions are attributable to intra-regional travel (i.e., people from Spain visiting France and vice versa). Therefore, concerns about declining market share should be put in perspective. In summary, multiple yardsticks are necessary to accurately assess the performance of travel and tourism as an export value.

While the U.S. travel and tourism industry is strong and growing, in recent years it has had to wrestle with various challenges in a post-9/11 environment.

I would now like to focus on how we are responding.

The development of new security processes has challenged both government and the private sector to achieve the right balance of security while continuing to welcome visitors and facilitate their entry into the United States. Secretary Gutierrez requested that the Department of Commerce's Travel and Tourism Advisory Board (TTAB) make recommendations on how the federal government can support the travel and tourism industry's efforts to compete for international travelers. The TTAB is a private sector advisory board comprised of 15 industry leaders, representing various sectors of the industry. These recommendations have been referred to the Tourism Policy Council (TPC), which is led by the Secretary of Commerce and made up of 17 federal agencies engaged in travel and tourism issues and policies. The TPC is currently engaged in a review of these recommendations and member agencies are actively moving forward on implementing a number of them. I am pleased to report that many of the issues covered by the TTAB's recommendations were already being addressed by the Departments of Homeland Security and State. We believe that this cooperation indicates that government and industry are largely in agreement on the way to move forward.

Safety and Security

At the Department of Commerce, we believe that the safety and security of Americans and those who visit our nation are paramount. The events of 9/11 demonstrated that our nation must migrate to a new generation of travel security processes in order to protect our citizens and guests. This requires the development of new and secure travel documents and ways of matching individual travelers to those documents in order to verify entry and departure, as well as screening procedures to ensure that air travel to and from the United States is safe.

This is no small undertaking, and requires the development of new technologies and new work processes and collaboration and communication with other nations, the travel industry and consumers. Government and industry share a vision that upon completion of this effort our system will in fact result in the United States being one of the most accessible and safest nations for people to visit. Such a system is good for our economy, good for our national security, and good for our public diplomacy.

We have worked with the Departments of Homeland Security and State to provide industry perspectives in the development and implementation of some of these measures and see progress being made toward this goal. Allow me to briefly review a few examples in this regard.

The Departments of State and Homeland Security are collaborating with the travel and tourism industry and the Department of Commerce on model ports of entry projects at the Houston International Airport and the Washington Dulles International Airport. The goal of this initiative is to ensure a more welcoming environment for international visitors through improved entry procedures and passenger assistance measures.

Another challenge is implementation of the next phase of the Western Hemisphere Travel Initiative (WHTI), which requires that all tourist travelers, including U.S. citizens, traveling to and from Canada, Mexico, the Caribbean, and Bermuda have a passport, or other acceptable documents, to enter or re-enter the United States by land or sea. The Administration will make every effort to ensure that implementation and communication of the land and sea requirements will be as successful in facilitating travel into the United States as were the implementation and communication of the requirements for travel by air. Implementation of the requirements for air has not inhibited travel to the United States from within the Western Hemisphere.

We will continue to work with our colleagues at the Departments of Homeland Security and State to facilitate input from business and industry, provide statistical analysis, and assist the efforts of those agencies to communicate the new requirements to industry and the traveling public.

Visas

The United States welcomes legitimate travelers from all regions. More than 68 percent of our international travelers not from Mexico and Canada come to the United States from Visa Waiver Program (VWP) countries and 60 percent of all our receipts (exports) come from VWP countries.[3] The VWP enables nationals of 27 countries to travel to the United States for tourism or business for stays of 90 days or less without requiring them to obtain a visa, and is an important program for the health of the U.S. travel and tourism industry.

For citizens of non-VWP countries, a visa is necessary for entry to the United States. We must ensure that our visa policy excludes those who would do our country harm, but at the same time, the policy should ensure that to the extent possible, legitimate travelers are permitted entry. In the transition to the next generation of travel security processes, we are challenged to meet the demand for visas as quickly as both the government and the private sector would like. The Department of State has taken a number of steps to improve the transparency, efficiency and predictability of the visa process. These efforts have included adding new consular positions, investing in automating outdated systems, and finding new ways to streamline the visa process while maintaining all necessary security measures.

In November 2006, President Bush announced his intention to work with Congress to reform the VWP. It is in our interest to ensure that countries across the globe join us in implementing travel security processes that ensure the safety and security of travelers to the United States and protect our national security interests. Reforming the VWP and extending it to countries that demonstrate a commitment to security will facilitate travel to our country while maintaining the safety and security of our people.

Tourism Export Expansion

The Department of Commerce identifies U.S. export opportunities and eliminates barriers to entry into those markets. The Department is currently working to identify key travel and tourism markets and facilitate access to markets with significant growth potential, such as China and India.

Travel and Tourism Promotion

U.S. Commercial Service

Staff in the Department's Commercial Service, who work in 108 offices in the United States and in more than 80 countries worldwide, helps to increase U.S. travel exports.

This effort is effectively delivered through the Commercial Service's Travel and Tourism Team, which has a total of 125 (74 international and 51 domestic) travel and tourism industry sector specialists. The Team also has partnerships with other U.S. Government agencies such as the Department of State, the National Park Service, and the Department of Homeland Security.

In some countries, the Team coordinates with the local Visit USA Committee. These Committees are primarily comprised of local travel agencies, tour operators, marketing companies and representatives of U.S. companies selling travel to the United States (e.g., airlines, destinations, hoteliers, attractions, etc.). The Team is instrumental in providing a variety of market entry services to the Visit USA Committees, including seminars, trade show support, and opportunities for the travel and tourism industry to gain exposure with local media.

The Commercial Service officers work to match U.S. suppliers with international buyers. They do this by assisting U.S. businesses with trade shows (over 200 in the past three years), travel missions, familiarization tours, and other marketing venues to sell U.S. travel products and services. In 2006, the Team participated in 79 travel and tourism events. Since 2005, the Commercial Service has posted over 735 export successes, accounting for over $61 million dollars in the travel and tourism sector. As an example, the Las Vegas Convention and Visitors Authority (LVCVA) worked with Commercial Service officers on trade missions to Brazil and China to sell Las Vegas as a destination for trade shows. The LVCVA reports that since the trade missions an additional 3,000 Brazilian and Chinese visitors have visited the Las Vegas area, equating to approximately $4,515,000 of revenue.[4]

Department of Commerce International Tourism Promotion Program

In 2005, Congress provided the Department of Commerce with $9.6 million to conduct an international tourism promotion campaign to market the United States as a travel destination. The program was implemented for a second year in the United Kingdom. In addition, a pilot program was implemented in Japan in the fall of 2006. A third-party research study by Longwoods International indicated that the initial campaign in the United Kingdom returned $117 in spending on travel to and within the U.S. for every $1 of advertising expenditures. Japan is on track to show positive results as well.

Congress further allocated $3.948 million for international tourism promotion. The TTAB recommended that these funds be used to provide a grant or cooperative agreement to develop a web portal for the nation's top five source markets. In March 2007, a $3.9 million cooperative agreement was awarded to the Travel Industry Association for this purpose.

The promotion campaigns in the United Kingdom and Japan demonstrate that marketing the United States as a travel destination can be effective. We encourage the U.S. travel and tourism industry to consider the results of these programs as it makes its own marketing plans.

Facilitation of Chinese Group Leisure Travel to the United States

Trends reveal that there is significant potential for growth of Chinese tourism to the United States. In fact, Chinese visitation to the United States increased 19 percent last year compared to 2005. However, Chinese policies restrict group leisure travel to destinations, such as the United States, that do not have a bi-lateral agreement with China. Traditional agreements of this kind are not in keeping with U.S. laws or open market principles. We are working through the Strategic Economic Dialogue and through the U.S.-China Joint Commission on Commerce and Trade to open this market through a commercial agreement tailored to the United States which would comply with all of our laws. The Department of State, through the TourTrack program, has demonstrated how the U.S. might facilitate visas for legitimate travelers who wish to engage in group leisure travel to the United States, should the Chinese government eliminate its market restrictions on this type of travel.

Brazil Dialogue

The Department of Commerce is engaged in a series of commercial dialogues with Brazil, including discussions on travel and tourism. Brazil is becoming an outbound travel market again, due to the increased strength of its economy. We are working to support the Departments of State and Homeland Security in exploring such possible policy changes as extending visa length from five years to ten years on a reciprocal basis. Such an agreement would ease pressures on visa issuance, reduce costs for individuals and families to come to the United States, and facilitate market access.

Air Linkages

Air service is key to tourism growth. The liberalization of air services between countries generates significant additional opportunities for airlines, consumers, travel and tourism, and other industries. To date, the U.S. Government has initiated and completed over 70 Open Skies bilateral agreements with foreign countries. In addition, more liberalized (but not yet 'Open Skies' per se) agreements are in place with China and Japan. An Open Skies agreement with the EU was initialed on March 2, 2007. Under the agreement, key gains for the United States will include greater access to London's Heathrow airport, cargo rights in the UK, and Open Skies treatment for new EU Member States. We are hopeful that a final agreement can be achieved.

Forecast

Now let us look toward the future—what we believe will be a bright future for the U.S. travel and tourism industry. The Department of Commerce forecasts a record number of travelers will come to the United States in 2007. This will mark a full recovery since the attacks of 9/11, surpassing the previous peak in 2000. In addition, we forecast a 21% increase in travelers over the next five years, reaching 61.6 million visitors by 2011. Overseas markets, especially South America and Asia, will significantly contribute to this projected growth. Chart 3 (Charts 1 and 2 have been omitted) includes 2011 projections for the top ten markets. We feel confident that the travel and tourism sectors are on track to deliver increasingly strong performances for years to come.

Conclusion

The travel and tourism industry in the United States leads the world in market share of global travel revenues and is well on its way to enjoying record levels of visitors. We are on track for full recovery since 9/11 and project continued growth in international travel for the next five years. Since the last quarter in 2003, both arrivals and receipts have been on the rise.

We believe that the appropriate role for government is to create a positive business climate by promoting supportive policy within our own government and working with other governments to remove market impediments and build bridges to new markets. We are working with our colleagues at the Department of Homeland Security and the Department of State to evaluate and respond to industry concerns and evaluate industry recommendations. I am pleased to report that the majority of industry concerns have previously been identified and are being addressed, largely through the *Rice-Chertoff Joint Vision: Secure Borders and Open Doors*. This document, issued in January 2006, outlines next steps on issues such as Model Ports of Entry, Improved Visa Processing, and Improved Exit Systems.

At the Department of Commerce, we are working to open new markets and improve market access in countries like China and Brazil. We are reviewing additional growth markets to identify and remove barriers to entry. In this way, we will create the most competitive business climate for the private sector to continue to reach record highs.

Chart 3
Top Origin Markets for International Travelers to the United States (2006 and 2011 projected)

	Origin of Visitors	2006 (000s)	2011p (000s)	2011p/2006 (% change)
	International Total	51,061	61,556	21%
1	Canada	15,993	19,106	19%
2	Mexico	13,400	15,699	17%
3	United Kingdom	4,176	5,213	25%
4	Japan	3,673	4,661	27%
5	Germany	1,386	1,707	23%
6	France	790	923	17%
7	South Korea	758	958	26%
8	Australia	603	746	24%
9	Italy	533	653	23%
10	Brazil	525	672	28%

p=projected

Source: U.S. Department of Commerce, Office of Travel and Tourism Industries

Endnotes

[1] U.S. Department of Commerce, Travel and Tourism Satellite Accounts.

[2] U.S. Chamber of Commerce.

[3] U.S. Department of Commerce, Office of Travel and Tourism Industries.

[4] Las Vegas Convention and Visitors Authority.

Statement of Rex Johnson
President and CEO
Hawaii Tourism Authority

Good morning, Mr. Chairman and members of the Committee. I am Rex Johnson, President and CEO of the Hawaii Tourism Authority (HTA), the official tourism agency for the State of Hawaii. It has been my pleasure to serve Hawaii in this capacity for the past three years.

For your information, I am also a member of the U.S. Travel and Tourism Advisory Board (USTTAB), which serves in an advisory capacity to the Secretary of Commerce. In addition, I serve as secretary of the Western States Tourism Policy Council (WSTPC), a consortium of 13 western state tourism offices, that work together to support public policies that enhance the positive impact of tourism on the American West.

On behalf of the State of Hawaii and the twelve other WSTPC member state tourism offices, I am pleased to be here today to provide testimony on opportunities to enhance and promote international travel to the United States. To clarify, my testimony will be composed of three parts.

HTA's Efforts to promote travel to Hawaii

First, is the Hawaii Tourism Authority's (HTA) efforts to promote travel to Hawaii. To begin, I would like to state the importance of tourism to Hawaii. Since 1976, tourism has been Hawaii's number one industry. As the chief generator of employment in Hawaii, tourism currently provides about one in every four jobs in the State in direct travel-industry jobs or in indirect employment. Hawaii's travel and tourism industry also produces $12.4 billion, or approximately 23 percent of the State's Gross State Product, and contributes $1.3 billion tax dollars to the state and county government, or 23.2 percent of total state and county tax revenues.

From a marketing perspective, the HTA spends approximately $50 million annually in marketing programs designed to support a healthy tourism economy. The programs support advertising, promotion, public relations, trade relations and other marketing efforts in our major market areas of North America, Japan, Other Asia (excluding Japan), Europe and Oceania. Our efforts cover a variety of markets, including meetings, conventions and incentive travel in the business sector; weddings and honeymoons, leisure travel, cultural tourism, and other markets related to vacation travel. While Hawaii tourism in total generates $12 billion in visitor spending annually, international visitors contribute about $4 billion of this amount and account for approximately 32 percent of visitor arrivals.

Unfortunately, the condition of Hawaii's international tourism markets has weakened over the years, due in many respects to the issues outlined in the USTTAB white paper which I will talk about shortly and in the blueprint that has been developed by the Discover America Partnership. Travel to Hawaii from some international markets has fallen by 50 percent from their peak periods. These markets are strategically important to Hawaii because they provide a stability and diversity to our visitor industry base and support other sectors of our economy such as retail and entertainment.

Federal efforts that would aid state tourism

That brings me to my second point and that is, what the federal government can do to assist state tourism. For one, maintaining and expanding the Visa Waiver Program (VWP) is central to keeping the U.S. competitive for inbound international travel. Currently, more than two-thirds of all overseas travelers enter the U.S. under the VWP. Easing international travel into the United States would provide a significant benefit for Hawaii tourism. The expense and difficulty in obtaining visas has had a negative effect on markets such as Korea, and Taiwan, which have declined with the imposition of stricter travel policies. In this regard, we particularly commend the Senate for recently approving the recommendations of the leaders of this committee and other Senators and adding provisions to the 9/11 Commission Act, which will strengthen and expand the visa waiver program. We will be urging the House of Representatives to concur with these Senate provisions.

Additionally, the negative experience of international visitors going through our security systems is a deterrent for some to travel to the U.S. According to a June 2006 survey of international travel agents, 77 percent believe the U.S. is more difficult to visit than other destinations. A recent survey by the Discover America Partnership revealed that international travelers believe that the U.S. has the "world's worst" entry process. This perception creates a significant disadvantage for the U.S. in its efforts to compete for world travelers. However, with more efficient access to our country and hospitality training for our security professionals, travel to the U.S. will definitely be easier to promote.

Recommendations made by USTTAB and the Discover America Partnership

Since 1992, America's share of the world travel market has fallen 35 percent, despite a healthy boom elsewhere. The price tag for this loss is staggering—about $300 billion in revenue over the last 15 years. In particular, since 2001, the U.S. has experienced a 17 percent decline in overseas inbound travel. In comparison, between 2004 and 2005, the U. S., witnessed a 10 percent decline in business travel while Europe experienced an 8 percent increase. As pointed out in the Discover America Partnership Blueprint, travelers from America's top source countries are either declining significantly or failing to keep pace with sizeable increases in travel to other destinations. The gravity of the situation is more significant in light of a U.S. dollar that is 30 percent cheaper than it was five years ago.

Please note, reports that say international travel to the U.S. is increasing are misleading. When you remove Canada and Mexico, and look solely at overseas travel, the number of visitors is declining—and it is doing so precipitously. According to figures from the Department of Commerce, in 2006 inbound travel declined from each of America's top 5 markets.

There are many reasons for this decline, including the increased and enhanced travel restrictions related to understandable homeland security concerns, as well as greater competition from destinations abroad for the international traveler. Another reason is the fact that the U.S. is one of the only industrialized nations in the world that lacks a nationally-coordinated program to compete for world travelers. Today, nearly every industrialized country in the world, with the exception of the U.S., has a nationally-coordinated program designed to promote its destination to international travelers.

For example, Australia spends $113 million dollars a year communicating and promoting itself to travelers, while Canada spends $58 million. In comparison, the Travel Industry Association (TIA) estimates that all the combined states together spend about $25 million, but notes that many of the allocations are small. It is imperative that the U.S. implement its own nationally-coordinated public-private marketing campaign in order to be competitive with other countries in the dynamic new world market.

A promotional program of this type could explain our travel policies to world travelers, highlight improvements in the process and invite millions more to enjoy the unique American experience every year.

And that brings me to my final point—the need for the U.S. to develop a national tourism strategy to compete for a greater share of the growing travel and tourism market. That's the intent behind the U.S. Travel and Tourism Advisory Board recommendations and the Discover America Partnership Blueprint. Together, these documents provide well-founded proposals to improve international travel to the United States that we fully endorse. The HTA, along with other state tourism offices and organizations, are especially supportive of a promotional program to establish a national image for the United States as a visitor-friendly destination, while supporting improvements to security and entry formalities that ease the ability of visitors to enter our country.

Without the benefit of a program establishing a national brand to promote visitation to the United States, some of our uncoordinated spending on international marketing is dedicated to diverse branding programs that, in other countries, would be initiated and focused by a national ministry of tourism. If we had the support of a national promotional program as envisioned by the U.S. Travel and Tourism Advisory Board and the Discover

America Partnership Blueprint, our efforts would be much more effective, since the national program would create a "visit USA" brand and a better selling environment.

Importantly, the development of a national strategy as outlined above would be immensely productive for all states, including Hawaii. As an example, the programs that would originate from this strategy could include creating a brand for America that is not just friendly and welcoming, but is also consistent with Hawaii's "aloha spirit".

I would be remiss in not also emphasizing that another benefit of a nationally coordinated marketing program for international tourism would be to enhance the image of the United States around the world. Nothing will more contribute to a positive view of our nation among the world's citizens than the personal experience of visiting here, meeting face to face with our wonderfully hospitable and welcoming citizens and experiencing American culture and values first-hand. At a time when our nation's international image has fallen to unprecedented levels, tourism could dramatically help reverse those attitudes.

Conclusion

In closing, I would like to thank you for the opportunity to speak with you today. On behalf of the HTA and my colleagues in the travel and tourism industry, we look forward to working with you, the federal government and others in support of the 9/11 Commission Act and other legislation that will enhance the competitiveness of our nation in the global tourism market and help improve our international position.

Statement of David Borlaug
President
Lewis & Clark Fort Mandan Foundation

Thank you, Chairman Dorgan and members of the subcommittee for inviting me here today. It is an honor to represent the Lewis & Clark Fort Mandan Foundation and the State of North Dakota at this important hearing.

Let me say at the outset that I join with other members of the travel industry in heartily endorsing the recommendations of the Discover America Partnership and the USTTA, which have been lobbying for the return of a centralized, government-endorsed promotional entity to provide leadership in attracting international visitors to the United States.

The specific recommendations of the Discover America proposal, in particular, are well thought-out, prudent and will result in a very effective organization dedicated to promoting travel to our country. It is my fervent hope that these recommendations will be given serious consideration in the Congress. Thank you for thoughtfully considering these proposals.

North Dakota, in spite of a tourism marketing budget that ranks among the lowest in the nation, has been promoting itself to the international market for the past 15 years. With our limited resources, we have focused on Scandinavian countries in particular and as a result, North Dakota is now among the top five destinations for all Norwegian air travel.

Two weeks ago, North Dakota joined with our neighbors Montana, Wyoming and South Dakota, spending a week promoting the four state region to the travel industry of Denmark and Sweden. One of the ways that we are showcasing our region is comparing our geographic size, nearly 2½ times the size of Germany, with our low combined population— barley larger than Copenhagen.

This is what those Scandinavian visitors want to hear, that we offer a land of beauty with National Parks and other tourist destinations unspoiled by the traffic and crowds to which they are accustomed. What they are seeking, and what we offer in North Dakota and the other prairie and mountain states is THE REAL AMERICA.

Statistically, after foreign visitors have come to New York City, Disney World, Las Vegas or any of our other leading attractions, they are eager to see another side of our country. A land that spreads out in front of them on the blue highway with a vastness that takes their breath away. A land with more than terrific scenery, but incredible stories to tell. In North Dakota, we call it LEGENDARY. With Lewis and Clark, Sacagawea, General Custer, Sitting Bull and Theodore Roosevelt among our cast of legendary historic figures, you can see the attraction we offer foreign visitors, who are fascinated by the American West—the Real America.

When you make the decision to create a new centralized entity to promote international travel, please include in its charter that it promotes ALL of the United States, not just those metropolitan areas which appear to have the greatest appeal. We ALL have something to offer those visitors, each in our own unique way.

Not long ago, our Lewis & Clark Fort Mandan Foundation, which operates the North Dakota Lewis & Clark Interpretive Center and the reconstructed Fort Mandan, the Expeditions' winter home of 1804-05, hosted travel writers from Norway, Sweden, Denmark, Germany and France, all within a 10-day period. These nations' travelers are hungry for information about our special part of America, and writers and photographers keep coming back, because they just can't drink it all in during one visit.

My non-profit foundation cannot afford international marketing on our own. We rely on our state tourism division, which has a total budget of only $4 million a year. However, we have made the most of our limited resources, and by joining with a coordinated, national effort, we know that we can attract more and more visitors here.

I was asked what specific areas the federal government may assist our efforts. Let me give you one request. The effectiveness of any marketing campaign is built upon good, solid research. We must know what our best target market is, to maximize the utilization of resources. States need to better understand the habits and intentions of international travelers once they arrive on our shores.

For years, our industry has been asking Homeland Security for data which will tell us where foreign travelers are headed after they have entered the key ports of entry. This information is gathered, but not made available to the states. If we could simply get this information, where people are going after they have entered our gateways airports, this would be extremely valuable in knowing where to target our messages. We are not asking to compromise national security. We are not asking for names and addresses. This is not about telemarketing. We just want the total numbers, by region. This seems a reasonable request for our industry to make, and one that I hope will be agreed upon soon.

Thank you again for inviting me here today, and for your commitment to America's travel industry.

Statement of Ron Peck
President and Chief Operating Officer
Alaska Travel Industry Association

Chairman, Vice Chair and Senate Commerce Committee, my name is Ron Peck. I am President and Chief Operating Officer of the Alaska Travel Industry Association. I have served in this capacity for 4.5 years. I have been employed in the visitor industry for almost 30 years. ATIA is a broad based coalition of over 1,000 visitor related businesses. We represent large and small companies including B&Bs, fishing lodges, cruise companies, airlines, and day tour operators.

We are a trade association acting as an advocate on land use, planning, and assessment issues. ATIA is not a government agency. We are a non-profit service organization. Our other main mission is promote Alaska as a premier travel destination nationally and internationally. We do this on behalf of the state of Alaska through an annual contract.

Prior to 2000, three distinct organizations did advocacy work, and the destination marketing for Alaska. Two of those agencies were government entities and one was a trade association. Overlap and inefficiencies existed. Funding for destination marketing fluctuated drastically, declining from a high of $15M in 1990 to $7M by 2000.

A new, unique and creative plan that involved both private and public sector involvement was implemented. Essentially the three organizations were dissolved. The state reduced the Dept. of Tourism to an office and totally eliminated the second government agency. The former trade association also dissolved.

The idea was to consolidate, be more efficient increase effectiveness. We believe that ATIA has done just that with this unique private / public partnership. We are also pleased with the level of private sector involvement. Thirty-five marketing experts volunteer from the private sector to create and develop the annual marketing plan that is then approved by the SOA and implemented by ATIA staff. Again, the unique part of this relationship is that we have actually reduced government staffing levels, and increased the private sector involvement at no cost to the SOA.

Funding for the program is done on a 50%/50% match basis, with the state contributing up to $5M, which allows for a Core Marketing program of $10M. Because of recent additional specific taxes on the visitor industry in Alaska, the funding model may need to change but the excellent working relationship between the public and private sector will continue.

The success of our concept is proven and other states such as Washington have studied the ATIA model and they are considering implementing changes to their destination marketing efforts.

Addressing International Travel—We as an industry fully understand the importance of keeping our country, our borders and our citizens safe from terror and violence. From the Alaska visitor industry perspective almost 250,000 (15%) of Alaska's of 2006 summer visitors were International arrivals with the major countries of origin being Canada, UK, German-speaking Europe, Australia, Japan and Korea. international visitors are an integral part of the traveler mix to Alaska. We as an industry need to work diligently to make our great country as inviting and visitor friendly as possible. Some specific suggestions for your consideration:

- Continue to work toward simplifying the Visa application and approval process. From first hand experience I have been made aware of the exhaustive and exasperating processes and steps that are involved in obtaining a visa.
- Expand the Visa Waiver Program—and consider including a larger number of countries such as South Korea.
- Improve Customs and Border processes by hiring the additional 200 officers in the recently passed legislation by the Senate. Thanks to vice chair Stevens and Senator Inouye for their efforts in this regard. I believe that this specific action will help alleviate perceptions that we are not a welcoming country to our international guests.
- Consider developing an International Registered Traveler Program. Other countries have developed IRT programs that work to ensure security by focusing attention on lesser known travelers. A good example for Alaska is with Japan and the business traveler volume for commercial fishing related business between Japan and Alaska.
- Establish a public-private partnership focusing on global promotion tasked to market the U.S. as an great place to visit. We should also focus on communicating effectively to clearly explain U.S. policies as well as marketing the U.S. as a destination. One useful communication media specific vehicle of communicating that I believe should continue enhanced is the internet. In four short years with continued refinement and improvement, our TravelAlaska.com site has more than doubled in the number of unique visitors. It has definitely enhanced our ability to sell Alaska to our visitors. I believe that the web can do likewise for our future international visitors.

Similar to Alaska's model that blends the marketing promotion expertise and flexibility of the private sector with oversight from the government, such an effort could change misconceptions of the U.S., and bring more international visitors to America. Thanks to the Senate Commerce committee for this opportunity to present some of Alaska's visitor experiences.

Statement of Chad Prosser
Director, South Carolina Department of Parks, Recreation and Tourism

Good Morning Mr. Chairman and members of the committee. I appreciate the opportunity to appear before you today to discuss how the federal government might aid the states in growing America's tourism industry. I am the Director of the South Carolina Department of Parks, Recreation and Tourism. Because of South Carolina's coastline, freshwater lakes, mountains, and extraordinary culture, tourism is the state's largest export. Tourism contributes more than $16 billion annually to South Carolina's economy, accounts for 11 percent of the state's employment and generates over $1.1 billion in yearly state and local tax revenue.

South Carolina is not alone in the prominent role that tourism plays in our state's economy. For many states, tourism ranks as one of the top three industries. Worldwide, tourism is the fourth-largest export industry after chemicals, automobiles and fuel. It is the largest service export, making up more than a 30% of world service exports and accounting for one out of every ten jobs around the globe. More importantly, tourism continues to grow steadily. Over a span of 25 years from 1975 to 2000, tourism grew by 4.6% per year compared with overall GDP growth worldwide of 3.6%. Tourism is a growing and healthy industry, but while the industry has continued to grow worldwide, visitation to the United States by overseas travelers has dropped 17 percent since 2001. This is particularly troubling given that outbound travel from many of our key overseas markets has increased, and the value of the dollar has decreased, effectively putting the United States "on sale" as a travel destination. For instance, outbound international travel from Europe grew by 3.2% last year. But travel from the United Kingdom to the United States declined by more than 3.7% from 2005 to 2006. The numbers are even worse for Germany, which is the second-largest overseas market for South Carolina after the United Kingdom. From 2000 to 2005 travel from Germany was down more than 20 percent. It is clear that not only is the United States not reaping the benefits of a growing international travel and tourism market, we are losing ground to emerging destinations and other competitors.

How, then, do we explain this loss of trade in the context of increasing international travel and a cheap dollar, factors which should contribute to growth? Data from a 2006 survey of non-U.S., international travelers conducted for the Discover America Partnership show that it is neither the product nor the people of the United States that deter international travel. Interestingly, this survey shows that 72 percent of international visitors describe their time here as "great" once they get beyond the airport experience.

According to the Discover America Partnership survey, the reasons we are losing ground in the international travel market are related to the lack of an inviting message to let potential visitors know that they are welcome in the United States, along with the confusing, difficult and sometimes hostile entry process. The survey shows that most visitors are more concerned about being detained or treated rudely by U.S. immigration officials than they are about the threat of crime or terrorism. They fear that they will be detained for hours because of a simple mistake or misstatement at a U.S. airport. They also perceive that the United States makes little effort to attract visitors and that the U.S. government does not want their travel business. I can tell you anecdotally from my own discussions with international tour operators and direct experience with international visitors that these are the primary deterrents keeping legitimate visitors away from our country.

Visualize a local restaurant. Now, let's assume that this restaurant does not advertise that it is open for business and it has no signage to indicate its location to potential customers. This restaurant also requires reservations, but has no one available to answer the phone when you call so it's difficult to book a reservation. Additionally, when by chance customers come to the restaurant, the maitre d' is rude and questions why the customers have come to his restaurant. This restaurant might have the best food in town, and it might even offer great service once you get past the reception desk, but with all of the obstacles on the front end it's unlikely to have much business. This is the situation in which the United States finds itself today as a travel destination. In a world of choices we cannot afford unnecessary obstacles that hinder our ability to compete.

So what is the solution? Here in our own country when travelers cross state borders they are greeted by state Welcome Centers. But when international visitors arrive at our airports, they are met by long lines leading to immigration desks. Of course immigration processing is necessary and security must remain of paramount importance; however, there are tools and techniques that Customs and Border Patrol agents could borrow from travel professionals to make the reception experience less unpleasant. Small improvements in process, appearance and customer service training could make a positive difference in the minds of visitors. Picture frontline immigration officers wearing a welcoming logo on their uniforms instead of a badge. Wouldn't that help visitors to feel more welcomed? Would it remind the agents that part of their job is to treat visitors courteously? I'm certainly not suggesting that our Customs and Border Patrol agents become travel counselors handing out brochures and giving directions. But the job of ensuring that our borders are secure can be done with the same welcoming attitude and professionalism that is displayed daily by those who work in our state Welcome Centers.

The Senate 9/11 Bill and the Rice-Chertoff Initiative are positive steps. Congress should continue its efforts to make the entry process more welcoming and efficient while closely monitoring how these initiatives are implemented on the front lines.

In addition to making it easier for legitimate visitors to enter our country, America must work deliberately to communicate that we are open for business and that we welcome international travelers. Sharing with an international audience the things that make this country special serves both the economic and diplomatic interests of our country. I support the recommendations of both the Discover America Partnership and the U.S. Travel and Tourism Advisory Board to reestablish a nationally coordinated umbrella marketing program to enhance our national image and to ensure that American businesses can fully participate in the growing market for international tourism.

Some have asked why a nationally coordinated marketing campaign cannot be launched without the participation of the federal government. It's a natural question. I'm often asked the same question with regard to South Carolina's umbrella marketing campaign. The answer is simple. The tourism industry, while it is a large industry in the aggregate, is made up of mostly small businesses. It's highly fragmented. In fact, while you often see the CEO's of major airlines or multinational hotel groups representing the industry, nationwide 90 percent of tourism businesses are small and medium-sized, according to the U.S. Chamber of Commerce.

In South Carolina half of the tourism industry is comprised of small businesses. Because the tourism economy touches so many dissimilar enterprises, ranging from small inns and restaurants to gas stations and farms that give tours to visitors to supplement their income, it is very difficult to coordinate these businesses for the purposes of a mass cooperative marketing effort. In fact, it would not make economic sense for these businesses to contribute to a national or international marketing campaign. It's a great challenge even at the local level to coordinate the activities of these small businesses. Even among the large corporations or the state tourism organizations, there are not enough resources or common strategic interests to coordinate an umbrella marketing effort for the United States. South Carolina is a member of Travel South USA, which is the oldest multi-state tourism marketing cooperative in the country. But even with the combined strengths of the twelve states that comprise Travel South, we are only able to focus on a portion of one international market, Canada, with mostly publicity and promotional efforts supplemented with a small amount of advertising limited to the Greater Toronto area. When thousands of diverse small businesses are involved, only government can effectively represent their collective interests on a national or international scale. It's a role that my department plays at the state level, and a role that the federal government should play at the national level.

A fascinating parallel can be drawn to the U.S. Small Business Administration. Why does this agency exist? According to the SBA website, it exists to, among other things, "preserve free competitive enterprise and to maintain and strengthen the overall economy of our nation . . . building America's future and helping the United States compete in today's global marketplace." These are the exact reasons that the federal government should be involved in a nationally coordinated international marketing effort. Such an effort would allow the tourism industry as a collection of small businesses to combine their strengths in order to compete in the international marketplace. No single business or trade association alone can accomplish this without the coordination of the federal government. Small businesses are the backbone of America and they are the majority of the tourism industry. These businesses can compete for international travelers, but they need federal cooperation to create a brand for America in the international marketplace.

The predecessor agencies of the SBA were formed to respond to the special needs of small businesses following the Great Depression and World War II. During the Korean War, Congress created another organization to handle small business concerns. Do we not find ourselves in a similar predicament now in a post-9/11 world? I'm not suggesting that the structure of a nationally coordinated tourism campaign mirror the scope of the SBA. However, we do need national coordination in our effort to counter the challenges that we face in today's global market for tourists.

I'm not here to tell you that the sky is falling. In fact, South Carolina tourism is growing. Even our international visitation has seen modest growth over the last five years. In 2005, the last year for which data are available, South Carolina hosted more than 173,000 overseas visitors. As a state, two years ago we doubled our budget for international marketing. This increase was part of a strategic shift to attract more high-value visitors. International visitors are a particularly attractive market because of their long stays and high spending levels. South Carolina, however, is a second-tier market for most international visitors. We are a destination where international visitors come once they have visited New York City or the Florida theme parks. We have products such as golf, beaches and cultural experiences that are a very attractive to international visitors. But it is a real challenge for us alone to get that word out in a crowded global marketplace.

Imagine how a small state like South Carolina could benefit if the United States once again had a nationally coordinated marketing effort to drive travel here and to let the international consumer know about the diversity of product available in our country.

It is important to realize that by supporting a nationally coordinated marketing program you are not subsidizing the marketing budgets of large corporations in the travel industry. Instead, you are leveling the playing field for thousands of small businesses so that they can combine their strengths in order to compete in a global market for tourists. The tourism industry can survive without assistance from Washington. We have proved that over the last decade since the closure of the United States Travel and Tourism Administration. But the industry cannot thrive and reach its full potential without the federal government lending a hand to do for the industry what it cannot do for itself. The tourism industry must participate in any national effort; however, the impetus for the program can only come from our government. Upon closer examination, the U.S. tourism industry is not big business, it is a large industry made up of predominantly small businesses. Therefore, assistance to tourism is assistance to American small business.

Unlike many mature industries, we have only scraped the surface of the potential for the U. S. tourism. The right to travel freely and safely has become a hallmark of American life and a cornerstone of our economy. Sharing that part of American culture with the world not only supports our diplomatic efforts abroad, but also works to strengthen economic prosperity at home.

Mr. Chairman, thank you again for the opportunity to share my thoughts with you today. I would be happy to respond to any questions that you might have.

DOCUMENT NO. 10

THE DEPARTMENT OF HOMELAND SECURITY'S RISK ASSESSMENT METHODOLOGY: EVOLUTION, ISSUES, AND OPTIONS FOR CONGRESS

CRS Report
RL33858

February 2, 2007

Todd Masse
Specialist in Domestic Intelligence and Counterterrorism
Domestic Social Policy Division
Congressional Research Service

Siobhan O'Neil
Analyst in Domestic Security and Intelligence
Domestic Social Policy Division
Congressional Research Service

John Rollins
Specialist in Terrorism and International Crime
Foreign Affairs, Defense, and Trade Division
Congressional Research Service

Summary

As early as his Senate confirmation hearing, Department of Homeland Security (DHS) Secretary Michael Chertoff advocated a risk-based approach to homeland security. Secretary Chertoff has stated "DHS must base its work on priorities driven by risk" and, increasingly, risk assessment and subsequent risk mitigation have influenced all of the department's efforts intended to enhance our nation's ability to prevent, respond to, and recover from future terrorist attacks and natural disasters. While the practice of risk analysis may be advanced in the insurance and financial industries, it is relatively less developed in the homeland security field. Although there are numerous reasons that account for this dynamic, two primary reasons include (1) the dynamic nature of terrorism and ability of terrorists to adapt to successful countermeasures, and (2) the lack of a rich historical database of terrorist attacks, which necessitates a reliance on intelligence and terrorist experts for probabilistic assessments of types of terrorist attacks against critical assets and/or regions. This report begins with an overview of the evolution of risk assessment methodologies from the Department of Justice in FY2002 to DHS in FY2007, and then discusses the discipline of risk management and risk assessment as applied to Homeland Security Grant Program (HSGP).

Terrorism risk analysis and assessment do not exist in a vacuum. Risk is analyzed and assessed as a means to mitigate or "buy down" risk over time by developing certain capabilities across the country. At DHS, the State Homeland Security Grant Program is the primary tool the agency has to influence the behavior of State and local partners to take actions that reduce what both parties agree are the risks of a terrorist attack and to respond effectively to such an attack, or other catastrophe. Regardless of the complexity of the risk assessment methodology, due to the inherent uncertainties associated with assessing risk in a dynamic counterterrorism context, some level of flexibility in managing risk may be necessary. Empirical data on historical terrorist attacks in the United States may, therefore, continue to play an important role in resource allocation to reduce risk.

This report presents several risk assessment and related grant program options for congressional consideration: (1) maintain the status quo in the inextricably linked areas of risk assessment and grant allocation, (2) draft a national impact assessment to understand return on investment of the approximately $12 billion of HSGP spent by FY2008, (3) enhance the transparency of the risk allocation methodology to state and local governments, and (4) develop a comprehensive and long-term strategy for managing, assessing and mitigating risk. To achieve these goals, the department could opt to consider procedural or organizational changes. Possible approaches are discussed in the report's final section. This report may be updated.

Introduction

As early as his Senate confirmation hearing, Homeland Security Secretary Michael Chertoff advocated a risk-based approach to homeland security. Under Secretary Chertoff's direction, the use of risk assessment has become pervasive throughout DHS. Increasingly, risk assessment and subsequent risk mitigation efforts influence many aspects of the department's work intended to enhance our nation's ability to prevent, respond to, and recover from future terrorist attacks and natural disasters. Indeed, Secretary Chertoff has stated "DHS must base its work on priorities driven by risk."[1]

The purpose of this report is to analyze how DHS assesses risk.[2] In the absence of sound risk assessment methods, the prioritization of homeland security activities at the federal, state, and local level is problematic. If DHS is to "prevent terrorist attacks within the United States,"[3] one of its primary statutory missions, it needs to assess risk in an accurate manner. However, risk assessment does not occur in a vacuum; the end goal is to reduce and mitigate risk. All of DHS's employees work to reduce risk, respond to a terrorist attack or natural disaster should one occur, and/or protect the country by preventing dangerous materials or individuals from crossing U.S. borders. The primary tool DHS has to "buy down" or minimize risk and to influence the behavior of State and local public safety and law enforcement officials who collectively represent substantial "force multipliers" is the Homeland Security Grant Program. Others have written extensively about DHS grant programs and the allocation of such programs across the country.[4] The purpose of this report is not to re-construct grant program research, but to examine the concept of DHS risk assessment itself and how the evolution of risk assessment flows through the DHS grant programs. The report has three sections (1) the evolution of risk assessment from the Department of Justice in FY2002 to DHS in FY2007, (2) fundamental questions about risk analysis as applied to homeland security, and (3) possible options for Congress. It will examine strategic questions about risk, and how risk is defined and distinguishable from other terms, such as vulnerability. Finally, the report will discuss a possible range of approaches for Congress with respect to DHS risk assessment practices, DHS's organization to assess risk, and the implementation of risk mitigation efforts using the DHS grant tool.

Given the focus of this report, an analysis of the DHS's risk assessment methodology through the lens of the homeland security grant process, some background information on the grant process is necessary. As previously stated, the risk assessment process cannot be examined in isolation. Rather, the context of the homeland security grant program is discussed to illuminate the homeland security risk assessment methodology and its implementation throughout various homeland security initiatives. This report may be updated.

Background

In FY2004, the allocation of homeland security grant monies inspired debate in states across the country. One often-reported anecdote noted that Wyoming's FY2004 State Homeland Security Grant Program (SHSG) award was $14,360,000, while New York and California received $78,827,000 and $133,964,000, respectively.[5] On its face, it seemed intuitive that New York and California would receive more money than Wyoming. But when examined in light of 2004 census bureau estimates, it appears that Wyoming received approximately $28.34 in SHSG funding per capita while New York and California received $4.10 and $3.73 per capita, respectively.[6] The rationale behind the disbursement of funds seemed counterintuitive to many, especially given the recent attacks and continued plots against locations in New York and California, to include the 1993 World Trade Center Bombing, the 1994 Blind Sheikh plot, the Millennium plot against Los Angeles International Airport (LAX), and the September 11th attacks, amongst others. Numerous interested stakeholders at all levels of government sought to learn more about the homeland security grant allocation methodology and process.

Figure 1 below provides a time line to track major milestone events in the evolution of risk assessment in a homeland security context.

Figure 1. Tracking Time Line

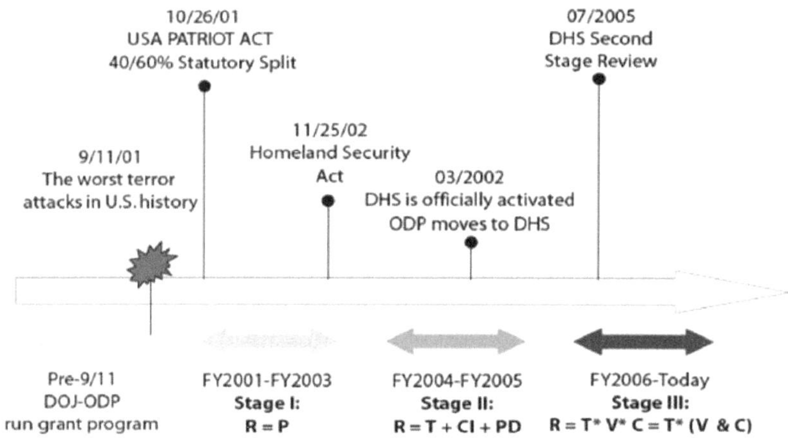

Source: CRS presentation of significant events and current law

Risk experts appear to agree that all communities have some level of risk from terrorism. Yet, homeland security officials acknowledge that it is impossible to protect every target and harden every community to the extent that they become impervious to future attacks. It seems clear that it is necessary, from a national perspective, to identify the areas and entities across the country most at risk and to work to reduce that risk. What is less clear is the best way to evaluate *relative* homeland security risk, and establish an acceptable level of risk while attempting to close the most dramatic gaps between risk and capabilities. What follows is a chronological overview of the DHS risk assessment methodology examined through the prism of the Homeland Security Grant Program.

Evolution of the DHS Risk Assessment Methodology

The federal government's approach to distributing funds to State/local governments to enhance the latter's ability to prepare for and respond to terrorist acts has evolved in the last six years. It is important to understand the genesis of this grant program and the reactions to each stage of its development in order to better comprehend the current methodology. The evolution of the grant program and the risk methodologies it employs has occurred against the backdrop of the transformation of the nation's understanding of 'homeland security' itself. Borne out of the September 11 attacks, the term 'homeland security' and the department designed to enhance it, were initially solely terrorism-focused. With time, and other catastrophic incidents, the focus of the department expanded to include a range of potentially destabilizing, non-terrorism threats, such as natural disasters. This evolution in mission has significant ramifications for the calculation of the threat aspect of the risk formulas utilized to allocate some of the homeland security grant funds, as will become evident in the following section's overview of grant allocation and related risk methodologies.

Over the years, there have been numerous criticisms from various groups[7] over how risk is assessed and, as a result, DHS grants are allocated. Following the FY2004 homeland security grant allocation process, the 9/11 Commission (hereafter Commission) weighed in on the funding controversy when it issued the following recommendation in its final report, published in late July 2004:

> Homeland security assistance should be based strictly on an assessment of risks and vulnerabilities. Now, in 2004, Washington, D.C., and New York City are certainly at the top of any such list. We understand the contention that every state and city needs to have some minimum infrastructure for emergency response. But federal homeland security assistance should not remain a program for general revenue sharing. It should supplement state and local resources based on the risks or vulnerabilities that merit additional support. Congress should not use this money as a pork barrel.[8]

The Commission report asks a second question: "Can useful criteria to measure risk and vulnerability be developed that assess all the many variables?"[9] The Commission lists a variety of factors that should be considered in the assessment of "threats and vulnerabilities" to include "population, population density, vulnerability, and the presence of critical infrastructure within each state."[10] The Commission suggests that the federal government should then require each State that receives such funds to provide an "analysis based on the same criteria to justify the distribution of funds [with]in that State."[11] The Commission understood that the "benchmarks" chosen to evaluate a site's threat and vulnerability ". . . will be imperfect and subjective; [but] they will continually evolve."[12]

Given the criticisms associated with the DHS risk assessment methods, a look at congressional interest in risk assessment as it relates to the homeland security grant programs may be instructive.

Risk Assessment-Related Legislative Activity[13]

Concurrent with the Commission's critique and internal efforts within DHS to move to a more risk-based approach, Members of Congress put forth a series of bills and amendments to the Homeland Security Act that sought to reform the criteria for distributing homeland security grant funds. Each effort sought to remedy the perceived issues associated with the homeland security risk assessment process. Some suggested the creation of new oversight or coordination bodies. Most importantly, for purposes of this report, each bill and amendment proposed changes to reduce guaranteed allotments and enhance the percentage of funding allocated based on risk. To varying detail, each legislative initiative suggested definitions or approaches to evaluate risk with regards to homeland security. The Appendix provides additional information on the legislative initiatives referenced in this section.

Understanding the criticisms of the DHS risk assessment process and the proposed congressional remedies, an analysis of how the various stages of risk assessment have evolved over time may be useful.

Risk Assessment: Stages of Development

There have been at least three stages in the evolution of risk assessment methodology as it pertains to homeland security. These stages and unique developments within each era are summarized below.

Stage I: R=P. This period covers from FY2001, when the Department of Justice (DOJ) had primary responsibility for assessing risk, to FY2002-FY2003, when this responsibility was transferred to DHS. This first stage of risk assessment could be characterized as early stage developmental. During this period, risk was generally assessed and measured according to population numbers. In short, risk ®) was equated to population (P).

Stage II: R=T+CI+PD. This period covers from FY2004 to FY2005. During this period, the importance of critical infrastructure, population density[14] and a number of other variables was included in the assessment of risk. However, the formula for risk remained additive and "risk-like," as probabilities were not an essential element of the risk assessment process. Risk was assessed as the sum of threat (T), critical infrastructure (CI), and population density (PD).

Stage III: R=T*V*C=T*(V&C). This period covers from FY2006 to today, a time when probability of particular events was systematically introduced into the formula. As will be discussed more in-depth below, FY2006 also marked another important departure from the previous risk assessment methodology: For the first time, when calculating risk, DHS chose to examine both risk to assets and geographic areas. With the swearing in of Michael Chertoff as Secretary of the DHS in February 2005, the department underwent both organizational and strategy-related changes. Concurrent with DHS's reorganization, Secretary Chertoff announced that a new risk-based methodology would dictate department al activities and all future federal funds would be distributed accordingly.[15] This new approach to allocating the remaining funds required an assessment of risk using a formula that considers the threat to a target/area, multiplied by vulnerability (V) of the target/area, multiplied by consequence ©) of an attack on that target/area. As a result, the risk assessment formula became R=T*V*C. Variables were no longer additive, but were multiplied, implying weighting of variables and some assessment of the likelihood that certain events would occur.

The Current Process

FY2007. The FY2007 Homeland Security Grant Guidance describes the DHS approach to risk assessment as:

> Risk will be evaluated at the Federal level using a risk analysis model developed by DHS in conjunction with other Federal entities. Risk is defined as the product of three principal variables:
>
> - **Threat (T)**—the likelihood of an attack occurring
> - **Vulnerability and Consequence (V&C)**—the relative exposure and expected impact of an attack [16]

Although DHS continues to discuss its risk methodology in terms of the R=T*V*C formula, it appears as if the department is treating vulnerability (V) and consequence ©) as an amalgamated, single variable as depicted in **Figure 2**. As mentioned above, due to difficulties associated with differentiating vulnerability values across areas and states, according to DHS it has, in effect, assigned a value of one to vulnerability. As a result, while three variables may formally remain in the formula, in effect only two exist for FY2007. In addition, significant changes to the underlying elements of each variable were made for the FY2007 process.[17]

While the FY2007 HSGP Guidance[18] does not provide additional detail as to the specifics of the risk methodology, a separate document, the FY2007 DHS *Grant Programs Overview*, accompanying the Guidance sent to state homeland security leaders does provide greater transparency into how risk is assessed. In the *FY2007 DHS Grant Programs Overview*, the weighting of each variable is provided and includes a description of the underlying data-sets supporting the calculation for each variable. As demonstrated in **Figure 2** the vulnerability[19] and consequence variables of the risk methodology now include the sub-elements of population index (comprising 40% of the risk methodology), a national infrastructure index (15%), an economic index (20%), and a nation security index (5%).

Figure 2. FY2007 Risk Formula

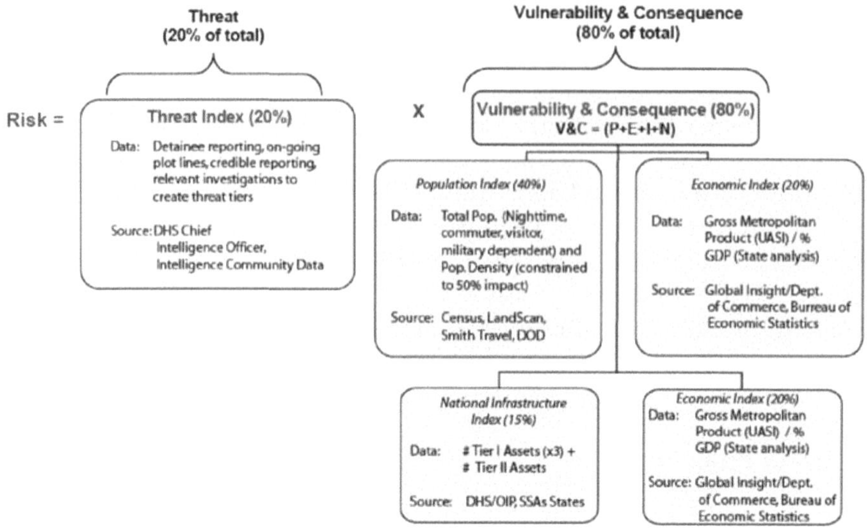

Source: CRS presentation of DHS FY2007 Risk Formula

In FY2007, DHS's manner for determining threat (20% of the risk methodology) underwent a significant change in how intelligence and investigative information was analyzed. DHS's Office of Intelligence and Analysis for the first time undertook an historical analysis of threats to the representative UASI cities that spanned from the attacks of September 11, 2001, to the release of the FY2007 Homeland Security Grant Guidance. Prior to FY2007, in supporting the Homeland Security Grant effort, DHS evaluated threats to cities for the preceding year only and did not consider historical threat trends. For FY2007, DHS also initiated an effort whereby the cities deemed most at risk were placed in four tiers based on assessed level of threat.

It should be noted that DHS's efforts to evaluate and analyze threats only consider federal government intelligence and investigative information. To date, State and local intelligence and investigative information are not systematically considered in DHS's assessment of threats to a given locality. It could be argued that the establishment of the State and local fusion centers may assist in ensuring relevant State and local threat information[20] is considered in future federal government risk analysis efforts.

The Current State. The evolution of the DHS risk assessment process and formula, as summarized in **Table 1**, continues to spark additional questions and some concerns in the following areas: the transparency of the risk assessment process; the implications of an evolving risk formula; minimum grant allotments; and the responsibility for buying down risk.

Transparency. The additional information provided by the department in FY2007 should allow applicants of DHS grant funds to have a better understanding of the types of information contained in the underlying data-sets and how each is assessed and weighted during the risk assessment process. While this transparency in the methodology may satisfy some grant process critics, others remain concerned with the formula's effectiveness in meeting the needs of those most at risk.[21]

Risk Formula Evolution. With the adoption of R=T*V*C, many see FY2006 as the first significant change to DHS's risk assessment methodology. Some observers could express concern that continued changes to the methodology will not allow the United States to establish a baseline of risks to the nation, thus jeopardizing any attempts to spot current trends or forecast future security concerns. Others might view the changes to the methodology as steps toward improving the risk assessment process and suggest that as DHS's understanding of risk evolves and its access to data increases, the associated methodology will stabilize and provide a sound foundation from which to make analytic and grant decisions.

Guaranteed Minimums. Some homeland security observers suggest that future congressional or executive branch changes to DHS's risk-based formula should include the elimination of the disbursement of guaranteed funding minimums to all states and municipalities.[22] Noting that HSGP grants "enhance States, territories, and Urban Areas ability to prevent, protect against, respond to, and recover from terrorist attacks, major disasters, and other emergencies,"[23] others may argue that the continuation of a minimal level of funds to all states might be beneficial in shoring up vulnerabilities or buying equipment that can equally respond to man-made and natural threats to a jurisdiction, citizens, property, or government functions. Other commentators may maintain that disbursing a significant portion of the funds without regard to the risk level of a given locality will continue to impair the prevention, preparedness, and response capabilities of those cities deemed highest at risk.

Responsibility for Reducing Risk and Federal Grant Levels. Since its inception, DHS's risk-based formula for distributing funds to state and local communities has been a source of frustration for members of the federal, state, and local governments[24] and those who assess post-9/11 counterterrorism program implementation efforts.[25] Some homeland security observers suggest that it is unrealistic to expect grant levels to continue to increase as U.S. budget concerns weigh on future appropriations. Others might note that as at-risk jurisdictions continue to shore up previously known vulnerabilities they will require less federal funding due to a lowering of their risk profile.

Table 1 below provides a cursory overview of the evolution of the DHS grant and risk assessment formula from FY2001 through FY2007.

Table 1. Evolution of DHS Grant and Risk Assessment Formula

Agency—Period	Funding Proportion & Related Risk Assessment Formulas	
DOJ—Pre-9/11	Risk Allocation—Risk ®) = Population (P) (Defense Against Weapons of Mass Destruction Act of 1996, P.L. 104-201).	
DOJ—Post-9/11	Funding Proportion—(USA PATRIOT Act of 2001, P.L. 107-56) 40% Statutorily Mandated (.75% per state, Puerto Rico and Wash., D.C. + .25% per U.S. territory). The remaining 60% allocated by Risk—the assessment of which is statutorily unspecified. R=P. Funding formula, not to be confused with risk assessment formula used to determine the aforementioned 60% of the homeland security grants.	
DOJ/DHS—FY2002 &FY2003	40% Statutorily Mandated	60% allocated by Risk R = P
DHS—FY2004	40% Statutorily Mandated	60% allocated by Risk R = T+CI+PD[a]
Weighting of DHS—FY2004 Risk Formula	Threat (T) = Intelligence Community credible threats & FBI/ICE Field Investigations (weighted 3) Critical Infrastructure(CI) = (weighted 6) Population (P) = population/population density (weighted 9)[b]	
DHS—FY2005	40% Statutorily Mandated	60% allocated by Risk R = T+V[c]
Weighting of DHS—FY2005 Risk Formula	Threat (T) = Intelligence Community credible threats (2) & FBI/ICE Field Investigations (2) (weighted 4) Critical Infrastructure(CI) = (weighted 6) Population (P) = population/population density (weighted 9) *Additional factor = Mutual Aid Agreements (weighted 1)	
DHS—FY2006	40% Statutorily Mandated	60% allocated by Risk R = T*V*C. First year in which probability was systematically included in risk assessment.
Weighting of DHS—FY2006 Risk Formula	Risk is calculated for both geographic areas and assets. While both calculations include T, V, and C factors, they have distinct subcategories. *Geographic* *Threat (T)*—(IC reports, FBI investigations, ICE investigations, suspicious incidents, I-94 visitors from countries of interest, total # of visitors from such countries with state as destination) *Vulnerability (V)*—(total # international visitors, miles of international border, miles of designated WIPP route) *Consequence ©)* —(human health, economic, strategic mission, and psychological—as well as numerous subsets of each) *Asset* *Threat (T)* (strategic intent, 'chatter,' attractiveness of target, capabilities) *Vulnerability (V)* (value assigned by DHS) *Consequence* ©) (human health, economic, strategic mission, and psychological) It is not clear how each factor and sub-factor were weighted.[d]	

Agency—Period	Funding Proportion & Related Risk Assessment Formulas	
DHS—FY2007	40% Statutorily Mandated	60% allocated by Risk R = T*(V&C)[e]
Weighting of DHS—FY2007 Risk Formula	*Threat (T)* = detainee reporting, on-going plot lines, Intelligence Community credible threats & FBI/ICE field investigations (weighted 20%) *Vulnerability (V) & Consequence ©)* = (weighted 80%—the sum of the following factors: *Population Index*—total population (nighttime, commuter, visitor, and military dependent) and population density—constrained to 50% impact (weighted 40%) *Economic Index* (gross metropolitan product for UASI or %GDP for states (weighted 20%) *National Infrastructure Index (# Tier 1 Assets (X3)* = # Tier II Assets) (weighted 15%) *National Security Index* (presence of military bases + # of defense industrial base sites + international border crossings) (weighted 5%)[f]	

Source: CRS presentation of DOJ and DHS Risk Assessment Formula

a. This was the first year DHS considered several sub-categories of data when calculating risk: current threat estimates (T), critical infrastructure (CI) assets within an urban area, and population density (PD)-related information.

b. The P calculation appears to have initially focused on population, but later incorporated population density information.

c. In FY2005, DHS added four more streams of data into the risk calculation. These seven categories of information have been represented in various forms and to various degrees in the subsequent formulas. See *DHS Risk Fiscal Year 2005 Homeland Security Grant Program: Program Guidelines and Application Kit,* p.1. What remains unclear is how the two variables (T and V) interact. Based on available information and discussions with DHS Officials, the relationship between T and V is assumed to be additive, as DHS did not move to a probabilistic risk formula until FY2006.

d. It is clear that both the geographic and asset-based risk assessment scores were utilized to determine the total area/state risk score. U.S. Department of Homeland Security, "Overview of the FY2006 DHS Risk Analysis Methodology," 1-2. However, how those scores translated into grant allotments is uncertain.

e. According to a DHS representative, due to the difficulties associated with differentiating levels of vulnerabilities across communities, DHS has effectively assigned a value of one to the vulnerability variable for each city and area. As a result, while DHS continues to use the FY2006 risk assessment formula of R=T*V*C, and state that risk is the product of three variables, in effect, the formula is R=T*C, and risk is the product of two variables.

f. Risk continues to be calculated for both geographic areas and assets, but it is unclear how the aforementioned weighting changes affect each calculation, and how the two scores are used to determine grant allocation. U.S. DHS, "FY2007 DHS Grant Programs: Program Overview," p. 15.

To inform the ongoing congressional debate on risk assessment as it flows through the DHS grant program, the following section provides an assessment of some of the policy questions associated with risk assessment in a homeland security context.

Risk Assessment[26] and Resource Allocation—Macro Questions

The overview of the evolution of the risk assessment methodology as it pertains to homeland security grant allocations highlights a number of questions at the macro level, such as how to best measure risk, that might be considered before contemplating questions of allocation. As mentioned above, the Commission recommended that the allocation of grants should be based on risk *and* (emphasis added) vulnerability. Vulnerability is but one of three elements of risk, as defined by DHS.[27] In recent Senate testimony, former Congressman and Vice Chair of the 9/11 Commission Lee Hamilton suggested that experience serve as a guide for risk assessment and resource allocation. Mr. Hamilton noted three elements worthy of consideration when allocating homeland security spending: (1) historical and empirical data on what has been attacked not only within the United States but overseas—Washington, DC; New York City, New York; Madrid, Spain; and London, England—all large cities; (2) Al Qaeda statements—according to Mr. Hamilton—"... So far as we know they (Al Qaeda) continue to target symbols of American power"; and (3) the best available intelligence.[28] While this approach is reasonable and based on sound logic, some might argue that broader questions and a more anticipatory approach may need to be considered to arrive at some credible and predictive value for future risk.

According to a recent RAND study, the following three questions might be addressed by policymakers before resource allocation decisions are made:

- Should resources be allocated based on risk, risk reduction, or some other basis?
- How can terrorism risk be estimated?
- What are the tolerable levels of risk?[29]

Another fundamental question in this area is "what is the risk to" and "from what sources does the risk originate?" Is the risk to people, infrastructure, the economy, or all of the above? Is the source of risk acts of terrorism, or the broader "all-hazards" approach, where the interests lie in responding to "incidents of national significance," as defined in the *National Response Plan*? Does DHS, as suggested by the department's Inspector General, "need to continue refining its risk-based approach to award first responder grants that ensure the areas and assets that represent the greatest vulnerability to the public are as secure as possible?"[30]

With respect to the threat element of the risk equation, to what extent is unique data collected by state and local officials being incorporated into the threat element of risk? State and local law enforcement and public safety personnel provide substantial amounts of data to DHS and other federal entities with the understanding that the information will be used, in part, to assess threat. Yet, according to a DHS official, the methodology for incorporating that data are under-developed and, as a result, the data is not currently incorporated into threat assessment at the federal level in any systematic and meaningful manner.[31] It may be possible that the emergence and proliferation of state, local, and regional intelligence fusion centers could become a funnel through which such state and local data could be aggregated and provided to the federal government in a manner that would allow it to contribute to threat assessment, an element of the risk equation that is weighted at 20% in FY2007.

The answers to these questions can have a fundamental impact on how grants are allocated. While the risk management process may be similar whether the source of risk is a hurricane or a terrorist attack, arguably, the inputs provided into the risk assessment model will be far different. DHS guidance shows that both the UASI and LETPP Programs are largely designed to provide state and local governments with funds to prepare and protect against as well as respond to and recover from acts of terrorism.[32] While this purpose also exists in the SHSP, it has the additional purpose of supporting the implementation of the National Preparedness Goal. The other two grants currently under the Homeland Security Grant Program umbrella, the Metropolitan Medical Response System (MMRS) and the Citizen Corps Program (CCP), are almost completely focused on preparedness for post-event response. Consistent with a need to ensure all phases of a catastrophe are considered and program objectives are clearly defined, the DHS Inspector General found that "the department must incorporate sound risk management principles and methodologies to successfully prepare for, respond to, recover from, and mitigate acts of terrorism and natural disasters."[33] In short, while DHS's risk assessment methodology is largely geared toward countering terrorism, the results of the assessment, along with other factors, such as effectiveness, are used for purposes which go beyond terrorism.

Once the fundamental questions of "risk to" and "risk from what" are answered, it is necessary to form a methodology to measure relative risk and to draft and implement a strategy to reduce it. To this end and from an economic efficiency perspective, it could be argued that the optimal manner in which homeland security grants might be allocated would be according to a comparative analysis of how historical homeland security grants have actually reduced risk. From September 11, 2001, through FY2008, approximately $12 billion will have been provided to state and local governments by DHS to prepare for and respond to terrorist attacks and other disasters.[34] A central question that may be asked is what has been the rate of return, as defined by identifiable and empirical risk reductions, on this $12 billion investment? It does not appear, however, that there is an established methodology to engage in such analyses, nor are the data sets necessary for such analyses well-developed. According to one DHS official, while the department is planning to assess the impact of DHS grants on risk reduction in FY2008, it has been somewhat constrained by resources and the absence of a methodology to conduct such an assessment.[35] As a result, some might argue, the next best method to allocating resources is to assess, measure and rank relative risk. This is, in essence, the approach currently being used by DHS.

Risk Management & Assessment: Complex Activities

The concept of risk—how to define, assess, and manage it—is relatively complex. According to DHS, ". . . Risk is classically represented as the product of a probability of a particular outcome and the results of that outcome."[36] As mentioned above, it was not until FY2006 that DHS moved from a risk-like or additive approach to assessing risk to one that is guided by more classically defined or probabilistic methods of assessing risk. As will be expanded upon below, DHS differentiates between two different, but complementary types of risk: asset-based risk and geographic-based risk. Because DHS is assessing risk as a means to allocate resources to buy down risk, it is imperative, according to DHS, that its risk calculations be relative. That is, ". . . Because of the dynamic nature of temporal valuations in the many elements that figure into risk, an absolute value, even if it could be calculated, would be meaningful for a very limited time."[37] Moreover, DHS differentiates between risk analysis and risk management. According to the Society for Risk Analysis:

> Risk analysis is broadly defined to include risk assessment, risk characterization, risk communication, risk management, and policy relating to risk, in the context of risks of concern to individuals, to public and private sector organizations, and to society at a local, regional, national, or global level. Risk analysis seeks to inform, not to dictate, the complex and difficult choices among possible measures to mitigate risks.[38]

Risk *management* is a continual process or cycle in which risks are identified, measured and evaluated; countermeasures are then designed, implemented and monitored to see how they perform, with a continual feedback loop for decision-maker input to improve countermeasures and consider tradeoffs between risk acceptance and avoidance.[39] Risk *assessment* pertains to the quantification or measurement of identified risk and probabilistic assessment that certain risks will manifest themselves.[40] According the Government Accountability Office (GAO), risk assessment is:

> the process of qualitatively or quantitatively determining the probability of an adverse event and the severity of its impact on an asset. It is a function of threat, vulnerability and consequence. A risk assessment may include scenarios in which two or more risks interact to create greater or lesser impact. A risk assessment provides the basis for the rank ordering of risks and for establishing priorities for countermeasures.[41]

The practice of risk management is well-developed within the insurance, engineering, finance, and political risk industries. It is clear, however, that risk management remains relatively immature in its application to the homeland security field. Some might that argue the implementation of risk assessment and management in the homeland security and counter-terrorism fields may be more complex than in its industrial application where the primary objective is to protect against financial loss. Financial loss is, of course, one element of assessing and mitigating risk in a homeland security context, but of equal if not more importance are threats to human health and strategic national missions, among other factors. According to DHS, the following issues must be taken into consideration in the assessment of risk in the homeland security context:

- *Historical Data.* In the insurance or financial sectors, the assessment of risk benefits from a rich and voluminous set of data which can be mined for patterns of historical behavior. While there are various governmental and non-governmental databases on terrorism, these data sources are relatively less robust. As a result, the subjective judgment of intelligence and terrorism experts become relatively more important in the projection of likely threat scenarios directed against categories of assets and/or geographic areas.
- *Risk "Inheritance."* Because grant candidates include states and Urban Areas, and individual assets exist in both spaces, risk can be "inherited" from one candidate to another. For example, the risk score for a port will be "inherited" by the city and state in which that port is located. As such, according to DHS, it utilizes various mathematical techniques, including weighting, normalization and order of computation to control for such unique factors.[42]

There are numerous other complicating factors associated with assessing risk in the homeland security context.[43] Notwithstanding a common framework for assessing risk at an aggregate level, one of the central problems is that risks need to be defined at a micro level—for example, the risk to a certain asset or geographic area, given terrorist capabilities and intentions—to be very useful.[44] At least with respect to assessing risk from terrorism, the nature of the risk is dynamic, as terrorists continually monitor successful countermeasures and adapt their targets, tactics, and modes of operation to surmount the countermeasures. Moreover, as alluded to above, a related problem is the absence of a definitive answer to the question of "how much risk is acceptable?" Secretary Chertoff has been open and frank in discussing the department's risk-based approach—that is—the fact that the country has to accept some level of risk, as it is not feasible to protect against every real or perceived risk. Yet that level of acceptable risk, the threshold over which federal resources will be dedicated to managing risk, is not yet defined.[45] In short, the successful risk reduction measures of today, may not necessarily be as successful in the near-to-medium term.

As will be outlined below, even if there is agreement on the central elements of risk, these elements are not necessarily independent of one another, thus requiring a sophisticated understanding of how each of the elements or variables of risk are interdependent.[46] Stochastic and sensitivity tests for each variable and regression between variables may be of some utility in understanding how strong the relationships between variables are.[47] For FY2007, as mentioned above, DHS has in effect assigned a value of one to vulnerability. While understandable at some level, this essentially eviscerates any interplay between vulnerability and consequence by having the effect of weighting the consequences of such an attack at 80%. It could be argued that if the vulnerability of a particular asset is exceedingly low, regardless of how grave the consequence, the risk to the asset may also be very low and, therefore, allocating relatively scarce homeland security resources to such an asset may be inefficient and ineffective.

Insofar as measuring risk is concerned, it could be argued that it is essential to identify the primary drivers of risk and collect the most appropriate data to quantify those risks. Collecting and measuring data that is readily available, but not central to risk yields quantifiable risk scores, yet some could argue that the results would be indefensible and relatively meaningless. If data which drive risk are not currently being collected, perhaps in the short-term such data deficiencies might be clearly recognized and controlled for in calculating risk. Reducing a variable value to zero or one based on the difficulty of collecting appropriate data to measure that variable should only be used as a temporary, stop-gap technique, as invariably such practices result in inaccurate risk assessments. Moreover, the level of confidence decision-makers have in data collected to assess risk is important. Resource allocation could be based, for example, *solely* on population figures, a statistic for which high confidence data exists. However, detriments of such a system are that population, *in and of itself*, may not necessarily be a terrorist target. If the population is not particularly dense, or exists in an area of marginal national economic impact or exists in an area where there are few critical national infrastructure assets, the population may not necessarily be a target for various terrorist groups.

There may be a balance to be struck between a risk assessment methodology that is too simple and one that is too complex. The question is what is the appropriate balance, and how a consistent methodology can be applied to a dynamic set of terrorist threats. Some homeland security observers might argue that the development of a long-term risk assessment strategy implemented by a strong DHS or broader government risk assessment analytic center that has as its sole mission the study of risk—its inputs and assessment of risk reduction results—may prove highly useful to help achieve this balance.[48] Regardless of the complexity of the risk assessment methodology, due to the inherent uncertainties associated with assessing risk in a dynamic counterterrorism context, some level of flexibility in managing risk may be necessary. Empirical data based on historical terrorist attacks in the United States may, therefore, continue to play an important role in resource allocation designed to buy down risk. Some might argue that such an approach constitutes a "rearview mirror" or reactive perspective. Others might argue that unless and until reliable intelligence can demonstrate otherwise, historical attack patterns, informed by the best available current and strategic intelligence, will remain an essential risk assessment indicator.

Risk Assessment: Some Critical Drivers and Perspectives

Numerous factors drive risk and are essential to understanding risk assessment and management. This section will provide some basic definitions common to the risk assessment and management field. Although they are often used interchangeably, the terms associated with risk assessment have unique, though related, meanings. The most recent data available is included in the *FY2007 Homeland Security Grant Program—Grant Guidelines and Application Kit*, in which it is stated that:

> Risk will be evaluated at the Federal level using a risk analysis model developed by DHS in conjunction with other Federal entities. Risk is defined as the *product* of three principal variables: (1) Threat, or the likelihood of a type of attack occurring, (2) Vulnerability, or the relative exposure of an attack and (3) Consequence, or expected impact of an attack.[49]

As alluded to above, DHS also differentiates between the following two types of risk, the attributes of which are depicted in **Figures 3 and 4** below:

- *Asset-Based Risk*". . . employs strategic threat estimates from the Intelligence Community of an adversary's intent and capability to attack different types (e.g. chemical plants, stadiums, commercial airports) using different methods of attack. The vulnerability of each asset type to each attack method is analyzed to yield the form of attack most likely to be successful."[50]
- *Geographically-Based Risk*". . . considers general characteristics associated with a geographic area independent of the assets that exist within that area. This type of risk evaluates reported threats (credible and less credible), law enforcement activity (FBI and ICE terrorism case data and suspicious incidents). . . . Vulnerability factors considered include international border, number of international visitors and port channel length. The consequences of an attack on that area are then estimated to include human health. . . economic . . . strategic mission . . . and psychological impacts."[51]

Figure 3. Asset-Based Risk Analysis Attributes

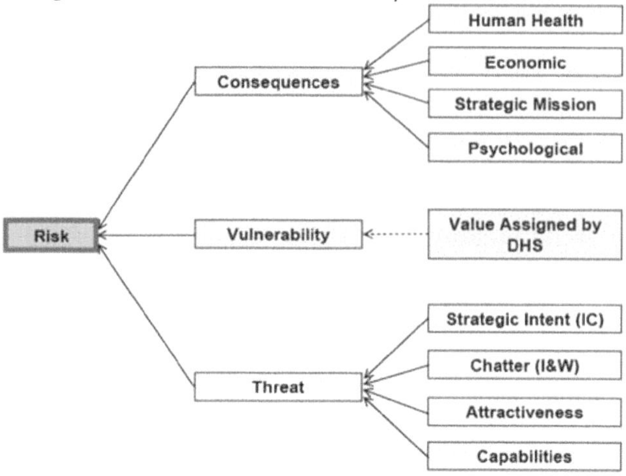

Source: CRS presentation of DHS risk analysis attributes.

Figure 4. State Geographic Risk Analysis Attributes

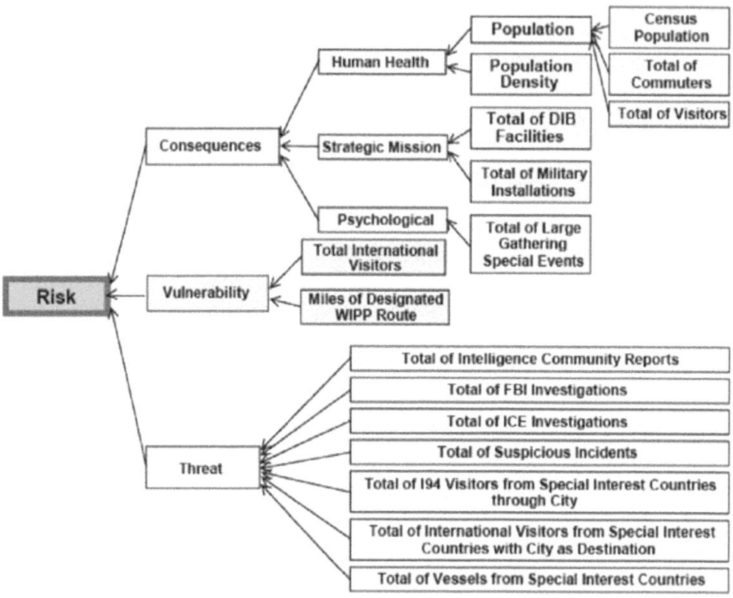

Source: CRS presentation of DHS risk analysis attributes

In short, as alluded to above, the DHS formula for assessing risk, whether it is asset-based or geographic-based, is: *Risk = Threat*Vulnerability*Consequence*, otherwise expressed as,

$$R=T*V*C$$

This formula is central not only to the allocation of DHS grant programs, but to all of the department's activities, as Secretary Chertoff has stated.[52] It is important to define these variables for a number of reasons:

- Without a common understanding of the lexicon, it is difficult to assess risk at the strategic and tactical levels.
- In order to gather the appropriate data which serves as an input to the risk assessment process, state and local agencies must understand how DHS is defining the elements of risk.
- In the absence of an understanding of each of these elements individually, it becomes increasingly difficult to comprehend how they are inter-related and inter-dependent.

There are numerous DHS elements, including the U.S. Coast Guard, Office for Domestic Preparedness and the Homeland Infrastructure Threat and Risk Analysis Center (HITRAC), among others, that are responsible for risk analysis and management.[53] An example of how one component defines and practices risk assessment is instructive. HITRAC is the entity within DHS that is tasked with combining intelligence threat data as assessed and accessed by the DHS Office of Intelligence and Analysis with infrastructure vulnerabilities. According to a HITRAC Representative:

> While inherently the most subjective component of the risk equation, threat of enemy attack is derived from study of enemy intent and capability. Intent of this adversary is assessed after study of all available information about they want to accomplish by attacking the United States. We work with our partners in the intelligence community to understand as much as we are able about the terrorists' goals, plans, and desires. We match what we know about the intentions of the adversary with information we have about what the enemy is capable of accomplishing. For this part of the equation we rely both on what we see the enemy discussing, recruiting and training for as well as lessons learned from overseas attacks. . . .[54]

This is just one example of how a single entity within DHS is approaching risk and specifically defining its components. It should be noted that although DHS headquarters has adopted a particular risk methodology, it is unclear how pervasive that approach has become outside headquarters, specifically within agencies brought under the department in 2004.

Given the evolution of DHS's risk assessment methodology and associated complexities translating risk assessments into well-targeted allocations of HSGP funds to buy down risk, there are a number of possible approaches for Congress to consider in this area.

Possible Approaches for Congress

More than natural disasters, assessing risk emanating from manmade actions is an extremely difficult task. Methodological tension is created when attempting to apply a quantitative formula to human-driven activities that require subjective assessments of enemy capabilities and intentions. Were a truly effective risk assessment tool to be created to help decision-makers manage risk, it would have to recognize that "management of risk is not elimination of risk."[55] Whether focused on an "all-hazards" or counter-terrorism approach, tools that attempt to quantify risk will always be inexact. However, sound data, a well thought-out formula, and consistent application of the methodology are important when attempting to measure terrorism risk to the U.S. and systematically buy down the risk to a particular location or asset. Such clarity and consistency are particularly important as the funds granted based on the DHS's risk methodology are the primary tools the federal government has to influence the behavior of state and local partners who will be the first on the scene of a terrorist attack and will be responsible for returning the community to pre-incident conditions. Congress has a number of apparent options concerning DHS's risk methodology efforts, including the following:

Maintaining Status Quo. Congress may wish to maintain the current policy and practices associated with DHS's existing risk assessment methodologies, and their affect on HSGP allocations. Some might argue that in the absence of measures to assess historical effectiveness of DHS grant programs, changing formulas and methodologies may be premature. Others might argue that with more than $12 billion worth of investment aimed at risk reduction and preparedness, state and local governments should have achieved a level of preparedness and capability that can allow room for negotiation on financial burden-sharing with the federal government for those programs deemed worthy of future support.

National Impact Assessment. By FY2008, more than $12 billion will have been provided to states, localities, and regions to buy down risk and enhance preparedness and capabilities to prevent a terrorist attack or to respond to such an attack or natural disaster should one occur. While audits have been conducted to determine how allocated funds have been spent, a national assessment of how much risk has been reduced as a result of such expenditures has not been undertaken. How much has risk been bought down? What investments have yielded the highest rate of return? What is the risk profile of each grant recipient moving forward? How are their existing capabilities measured against extant risk? What capabilities gaps exist, and how can resources best be targeted to address those gaps? There are at least two possible precursors to the drafting of such an impact assessment: (1) a defensible methodology that can (a) reasonably define and measure risk, (b) provide a means for measuring how developing capabilities are reducing that risk, and ©) illustrate how to identify specific capability gaps which might serve as an input for future allocation of homeland security grants; and (2) articulation of this methodology, including the data necessary to conduct such an assessment, to grant recipients. With the results of such an assessment, federal, state, local, and regional authorities might arguably be in a better position to understand the most effective and efficient way to target relatively scarce homeland security resources.

Further Enhance Transparency. While safeguarding the intelligence, law enforcement, and other sensitive information weighted and analyzed through DHS's risk methodology, disclosure of the mathematical equation used to determine threat, vulnerability, and consequence may allow all applicants and stakeholders to understand and have a basis to confirm or challenge the results prior to funds being allocated. It could be argued that providing this level of detail regarding the methodology and underlying equation may allow those who would seek to attack U.S. facilities to reverse-engineer the formula, thus increasing the probability of a successful terrorist attack. Others might maintain that allowing the risk formula equations to be revealed would encourage state and municipalities to manipulate the data provided to DHS, thus increasing their chances of receiving additional funding without a sufficient risk-based justification. Homeland security observers could counter these arguments by suggesting that though there may be the potential for those wishing to take advantage of the transparency of the system, the positives include possible increases in information sharing between DHS and state and local governments due to an understanding of how data is used and as such result in increased confidence in the other entity. Some could argue more transparency would allow DHS to more confidently allocate resources, as enhanced transparency may reduce the surprised outcries that seem to arise with each cycle's award announcements. This argument is based on the assumption that grant applicants that are comfortable with the risk assessment process and familiar with the data streams used to calculate risk. As a result, the applicants may be less likely to be surprised by their jurisdiction's ranking and awards.

Development of a Risk Strategy Both Within DHS and Throughout All Government Agencies. Since the establishment of DHS in March of 2003, the department's risk formula has evolved. Though it could be argued that these changes are indicative of a maturing organization and process, it is possible that the lack of a coherent, long-term, overarching risk strategy, which forms the foundation of departmental activities, could have negative repercussions for buying down risk. Without a clearly articulated risk methodology based on fundamentals intrinsic to risk, yet adaptive to changing threats, a baseline understanding of the nation's risk profile may never be achieved and the department's risk assessment process could potentially be vulnerable to budget fluctuations and political influence. This is especially important given the apparent division of risk assessment responsibilities throughout various offices and directorates within the department.

Arguments can be made that such an overarching risk philosophy needs to be adopted throughout the federal government. In a December 2005 report on homeland security risk management, GAO concluded that

> for the results of a risk management system to be meaningful and useful, all related agencies should be using similar methods. If agencies' methods are

> not compatible, then comparisons between agencies become difficult and sector or national risk assessments becomes less reliable. In our earlier work, we concluded that a structured, systematic approach to risk management offers the best assurance that activities designed to protect the homeland and combat the effects of terrorism will produce the most effective and efficient results.[56]

A cohesive risk strategy and agreement on core terms amongst disparate agencies is desirable because many aspects of the risk assessment process are dependent on functions performed by agencies outside the department.[57] However, the necessity of common definitions and standards goes beyond the federal government. As states and localities continue to provide information to be included in the risk assessment process, to include, information on critical infrastructure sites within their respective jurisdictions and, eventually, investigative information, the rationale for attempting to develop national-wide risk assessment strategy at all levels of government becomes stronger.

Appointment of a DHS Risk Assessment Manager (RAM). With regards to DHS's risk assessment efforts, the department might potentially create a Risk Assessment Manager (RAM) position charged with better integrating the various elements working on aspects of the risk assessment process. In addition, the RAM might be assigned the responsibility of creating and subsequently implementing a department-wide strategic risk strategy. Such a position could be in an advisory capacity to the Secretary or entail operational and oversight functions of a permanent DHS Risk Assessment Center (see below). The creation of a RAM within DHS responsible for coordinating all inter-departmental risk methodology activities would provide Congress, other federal government agencies, and state and local homeland security leaders with a single person accountable for explaining the complexities of future risk management strategy efforts and a specific office to receive suggestions regarding improving current processes. The RAM could also serve in a liaison capacity to ensure external agencies are familiar with DHS's approach to risk and facilitate agreement on key terms and processes amongst other agencies.

Creation of a DHS Risk Advisory Board (RAB). As previously stated, Secretary Chertoff has made it clear that risk assessment underlies all elements of the department's operations. Risk management and assessment are disciplines which are relatively well-developed across the private sector. Moreover, within the U.S. government, there are numerous experts on risk assessment. To ensure that the Secretary is getting the best possible advice as to how DHS should continue to refine its risk management activities, a formal board of senior- level risk management professionals might be established to advise the Secretary. While not having program management responsibilities, the Risk Advisory Board (RAB) might advise the Secretary on the best risk management practices across industry and government. It could also lead the DHS effort, with substantial input from a potential Risk

Assessment Center (see below), to draft a long-term risk management strategy.

Creation of a Permanent Risk Assessment Center (RAC). While the proposed RAB would operate on a strategic level, it could be beneficial for DHS to examine its current efforts to apply risk strategy to its various programs and initiatives. Risk is central to DHS's operations. DHS may not necessarily have the appropriate resources dedicated full-time to (1) pro-actively assess the dynamic drivers of risk, (2) lead the collection of the right types of data to assess risk, and (3) develop a methodology to analyze how effectively past homeland security grant investments have "bought down" risk. These tasks are relatively complex and, it could be argued, require the formation of a group of professional methodologists whose sole function is risk assessment. While elements of this capability may exist now within the Preparedness Directorate, no single group has this sole responsibility. For example, HITRAC is charged largely with mapping vulnerabilities to threats, which is an essential function unto itself.

There are several potential benefits offered by a risk center: First, a permanent center would likely help DHS to think strategically about the current risk assessment process. Second, continued attention to this issue and sufficient time to address it would probably allow DHS to create more effective assessment tools and use those multiple tools in tandem to analyze various risk areas. Third, the risk center would potentially allow DHS to draw on the existing expertise and resources of all the offices and divisions within DHS, as well as external entities, such as other Intelligence Community agencies.

Implement 9/11 Commission Recommendation. As mentioned above, the 9/11 Commission recommended that ". . . homeland security assistance should be based strictly on an assessment of risks and vulnerabilities. . . But federal homeland security assistance should not remain a program for general revenue sharing. It should supplement state and local resources based on the risks or vulnerabilities that merit additional support."[58] Some homeland security observers could interpret this literally to mean that after six years and $12 billion of homeland security investments, most states should be at some minimal level of security and capability. Therefore, some might argue, the time may be appropriate to revisit the USA PATRIOT Act formula which results in 40% of the total DHS grant funding being allocated based on formula which is not based primarily on risk. Others might argue that until a methodology is developed to ascertain how prior years' grant allocations have decreased each state's risk levels, it may be premature to alter the formula. Questions that might be addressed when considering this options include

- What duration did Congress originally intend when it created the DOJ and now DHS homeland security grants?

- What measures are in place to ensure that state and local governments are spending resources in a manner that is consistent with congressional intent?
- To what extent, if at all, has congressional oversight yielded any indications that state and local governments have come to view homeland security grants as entitlements?
- Has DHS or Congress entered into discussions with state and local governments about sustainable burden-sharing arrangements with respect to state and local programs assessed as being worthy of continued financial support?

Treat Terrorism Prevention Grants Uniquely. Secretary Chertoff recently stated that one of the unique areas in which the DHS can add value is in the area of prevention. He stated, ". . . obviously, when it comes to terrorism, our best solution is a solution that prevents a terrorist act before it actually comes about. And a critical element in that is our early warning system, which is intelligence. . . ."[59] Notwithstanding this statement, a review of aggregate budget data for homeland security expenditures suggests that less than 1% of what the U.S. government spends on homeland security is dedicated to intelligence and warning, an essential element in the prevention component of homeland security.[60] While there are many similarities in the response capability, whether the response be to a successful terrorist attack or natural disaster, terrorist acts can be prevented, natural disasters cannot. Information related to meteorology is different from intelligence related to national security. The threat element of the risk reduction formula is what differentiates terrorism from all other hazards. As mentioned throughout this report, terrorist threats are dynamic and evolve over time; some might argue the risk assessment methodology and attendant grant allocation process should be as agile as the adversary against which its resources are directed. DHS currently has an *Intelligence Enterprise Strategic Plan,* and the FY2007 grant application kit provides guidance for state, local and regional intelligence fusion centers. Yet, the linkages between these two documents and the grant process, some would argue, is tenuous. One of the Homeland Security Presidential Directive (HSPD)-8 derived "Universal Tasks" is prevention. Drawing upon the *National Strategy for Combating Terrorism,* Congress may ultimately consider recommending that DHS provide a specific and articulable strategy and approach to terrorism prevention, which would include a focus on how the grant allocation process is tailored to fully leverage intelligence across levels of government to *prevent* terrorist acts.

Appendix.
Legislative Activity on DHS Risk Formula for Grants

	S. 1013 Homeland Security FORWARD Funding Act of 2005 109th Congress	**S. 21 Homeland Security Grant Enhancement Act of 2005 109th Congress**	**H.R. 1544 Faster and Smarter Funding for First Responders Act of 2005 109th Congress**	**H.R. 1 Implementing the 9/11 Commission Recommendations Act of 2007 110th Congress**	**S. 4 Improving America's Security by Implementing Unfinished Recommendations of the 9/11 Commission Act of 2007 110th Congress**
Statutory Minimum Allocations	50 States, DC, & Puerto Rico (PR)[a] = 0.25% of the SHSGP monies, while the four U.S. territories receive 0.08% of the SHSGP funding. No other grants are mentioned in this section. TOTAL GUARANTEED = 13.32% of SHSGP allotment *Includes: SHSGP, UASI, LETTP, and CCP.	50 States & DC = the greater of either (1) 0.55% of all appropriated funds, or (2) the state's sliding scale baseline allocation[b] multiplied by 28.62% of the total amount appropriated for the Threat-Based Homeland Security Grant Program. PR = 0.35%, and the four U.S. territories = 0.055%. TOTAL GUARANTEED= 28.62% based on option (1), option 2 was not calculated *Includes: SHSGP, UASI, and LETTP.	Most States[c] & DC and PR will receive 0.25% for covered grants, however states that qualify as having "additional high-risk qualifying criteria" will receive 0.45%. Four U.S. territories will receive 0.08% and directly eligible tribes would receive 0.08%. TOTAL GUARANTEED= between 13.32%—23.72% plus whatever percentage is awarded to directly eligible tribes. *Includes: SHSGP, UASI, LETTP, and CCP	50 States, DC, & PR[d] are insured to receive no less than 0.25% and those that have an approved plan and meet at least one of the "additional high risk criteria"[e] will receive no less than 0.45% of the funds available for covered grants for that fiscal year. The four U.S. territories will receive no less than 0.08%. TOTAL GUARANTEED= between 13.32%—23.72% *Includes: SHSGP, UASI, and	SHORT TITLE. This act may be cited as the `Improving America's Security by Implementing Unfinished Recommendations of the 9/11 Commission Act of 2007'. SEC. 2. SENSE OF CONGRESS. It is the sense of Congress that Congress should enact, and the President should sign, legislation to make the United States more secure by implementing unfinished recommendations of the 9/11 Commission to fight the war on terror more effectively and to improve homeland security.

	S. 1013 Homeland Security FORWARD Funding Act of 2005 109th Congress	S. 21 Homeland Security Grant Enhancement Act of 2005 109th Congress	H.R. 1544 Faster and Smarter Funding for First Responders Act of 2005 109th Congress	H.R. 1 Implementing the 9/11 Commission Recommendations Act of 2007 110th Congress	S. 4 Improving America's Security by Implementing Unfinished Recommendations of the 9/11 Commission Act of 2007 110th Congress
Risk Funding	The bill creates a Homeland Security Grants Board to allocate the remaining funds based on an annual prioritized "risk- based ranking," which is based on the degree to which the monies would enhance essential capabilities to lessen the threat, vulnerability, and consequences of attack.[f]	The bill does not stipulate how the remaining funding would be allocated.	The bill contains almost the exact language as S. 1013 with regards to a similar Board to allocate the remaining funds based on a "risk-based ranking" and prioritizing terrorist threats.	The bill directs the Secretary of Homeland Security to "evaluate and annually prioritize all pending applications for covered grants. . . based upon the most current risk assessment available. . . "	

Source: CRS presentation of select legislation in the 109th and 110th Congress

a. There is a requirement for states to have a security plan in order to qualify for the automatic grant allocation minimum- "Each State that has an approved State homeland security plan receives no less than 0.25 percent of the funds available of the State Homeland Security Grant Program."

b. The sliding scale defined in Section 1801, "represents each states's weighted share (where weighting is done based on a combination of population and population density) of the pot of money (28.62%) that results from adding together the 0.55% minimum distribution to each state, plus the amounts allocated for the District of Columbia and the remaining territories." Homeland Security Grant Enhancement Act of 2005, report of the U.S. Senate Committee on Homeland Security and Governmental Affairs to accompany S. 21, S.Rept. 109-071.

c. There is a similar requirement for states to have a security plan in order to qualify for the automatic grant allocation minimum in S. 1013 and S. 21.

d. H.R. 1 states "each of the States, other than Virgin Islands, American Samoa, Guam and the Northern Mariana Islands. . . "

e. "Additional high-risk qualifying criteria consists of—(A) having a significant international land border; or (B) adjoining a body of water within North America through which an international boundary line extends." H.R. 1, Implementing the 9/11 Commission Recommendations Act of 2007, Sec. 2004-6.

f. S. 1013, Sec. 1802, A, I, May 12, 2005.

Endnotes

[1] U.S. Department of Homeland Security, "Homeland Security Secretary Michael Chertoff Announces Six-Point Agenda for Department of Homeland Security," Press Release, July 13, 2005, Office of the Press Secretary, available at [http://www.dhs.gov/xnews/releases/press_release_0703.shtm], accessed Jan. 26, 2007.

[2] DHS is primarily concerned with assessment of terrorism risk. As a result, a terrorism risk assessment model is currently being used by the department to allocate resources for purposes which include, but also go beyond terrorism prevention, such as preparation and response to natural disasters.

[3] See P.L. 107-296, Sec 101, codified at 6 U.S.C. §111.

[4] A non-exhaustive list of these reports and articles includes CRS Report RL33583, *Homeland Security Grants, Evolution of Program Guidance and Grant Allocation Methods*, Aug. 7, 2006, by Shawn Reese; CRS Report RL33241, *FY2006 Homeland Security Grant Distribution Formulas: Issues for the 109th Congress*, Jan. 20, 2006, by Shawn Reese; The Heritage Foundation, *DHS 2.0: Rethinking the Department of Homeland Security*, Dec. 13, 2004, by James J. Carafano and David Heyman; Michael E. O'Hanlon et. al, The Brookings Institution, *Protecting the Homeland 2006/2007*; Michael E. O'Hanlon, "Homeland Security Funding: Urban Area Grant Maze," *Washington Times*, June 29, 2006; Council on Foreign Relations, *Backgrounder: Risk-Based Homeland Security Spending*, Feb. 8, 2006, by Eben Kaplan.

[5] Department of Homeland Security, "FY2004 Homeland Security Grant Program," Department of Homeland Security Office of Grants and Training website, available at [http://www.dhs.gov], accessed on Dec.1, 2006, p. 7.

[6] Comparison made using Department of Homeland Security's "FY 2004 Homeland Security Grant Program," and 2004 U.S. population estimates from U.S. census data.

[7] For the past several grant cycles, many States and local leaders have expressed frustration and disappointment with DHS's risk assessment process and the related distribution of grant funds. Much of the disappointment with respect to FY2006 grants was the result of the first post-9/11 decline in funds provided to state and local communities. For FY2006, the total amount allocated for homeland security grants was $1.7 billion, (DHS, "DHS Announces $1.7 Billion in Homeland Security Grants: Grants will build States' and Urban Areas' Preparedness," May 31, 2006) a significant decrease from $2.5 billion in FY2005 (DHS, "Homeland Security Grants FY2005," Updated December 3, 2004, Office of Grants and Training). Another source of frustration was a perceived lack of transparency regarding the risk assessment process, especially with regard to the sources of information used and the weighting of the formula's variables and underlying data sub-elements. Furthermore, the continued shift towards a risk-based approach may have caused consternation amongst some jurisdictions due to the inference that future grant funding may be threatened. Spurred on by congressional pressure, the department has continued to move toward a methodology that is more heavily risk-based.

[8] National Commission of Terrorist Attacks Upon the United States, *The 9/11 Commission Report: Final Report of the National Commission of Terrorist Attacks Upon the United States*, Authorized Edition (New York: WW Norton and Company, 2004), p. 396.

[9] Ibid.

[10] Ibid.

[11] Ibid.

[12] Ibid.

[13] The intent of this section and the appendix is to provide a snapshot of recent historical and current legislative activity with respect to risk assessment. This section is not provided with intent to track this legislation over time and, as such, will not be continually updated.

[14] It should be noted that population density numbers can be misleading. Cities define geographic boundaries differently which may lead to municipalities with similar populations having very different density ratios. While population density is often a good indicator of individuals that may be affected by a terrorist attack, such a criteria may not be useful for cities where the citizens are located far away from the center of the municipality.

[15] Secretary Michael Chertoff U.S. Department of Homeland Security Second Stage Review Remarks, July 13, 2005, available at [http://www.dhs.gov/xnews/speeches/speech_0255.shtm], accessed Jan. 26, 2007. "We must make tough choices about how to invest finite human and financial capital to attain the optimal state of preparedness. To do this we will focus preparedness on objective measures of risk and performance. Our risk analysis is based on these three variables: threat, vulnerability, and consequences. These variables are not equal. For example, some infrastructure is quite vulnerable, but the consequences of an attack are relatively small; other infrastructure may be much less vulnerable, but the consequences of a successful attack are very high, even catastrophic."

[16] U.S. Department of Homeland Security, "FY2007 Homeland Security Grant Program: Program Guidance and Application Kit," Office of Grants and Training website, available at [http://www.ojp.usdoj.gov/odp/docs/fy07_hsgp_guidance.pdf], p.8, accessed Jan. 29, 2007.

[17] Though not the focus of the report, it is important to demonstrate how the evolution of the risk methodology has supported the significant changes included in the FY2007 Guidance. Two significant changes are contained in the FY2007 Guidance directly related to DHS's risk methodology evolution: the dividing of the Urban Area Security Initiative jurisdictions into two tiers with the six municipalities in tier one receiving 55% of the total allocation and the department's establishment of a pilot program to allow the six highest risk UASI cities authorized to use up to 25% of the awarded funds to support the personnel costs associated with counterterrorism operations.

[18] U.S. Department of Homeland Security, FY2007 Homeland Security Grant Program, Program Guidance and Application Kit, Office of Grants and Training website, available at [http://www.ojp.usdoj.gov/odp/docs/fy07_hsgp_guidance.pdf], accessed Jan. 29, 2007.

[19] As mentioned above, for FY2007, vulnerability has been assigned a value of one. In effect, then, consequence is weighted at 80%.

[20] It has recently been reported that ". . . homeland security officials are opposed to letting representatives of State and local governments serve on. . . ," the Interagency Threat Assessment Coordination Group (ITACG). See Siobhan Gorman, "Out of the Loop on Terror Threats: Homeland Security Excludes, State, Local Officials from Group that Shares Data," *Baltimore Sun,* Feb. 2, 2007. The ITACG was recommended in the *Information Sharing Environment (ISE) Implementation Plan*, published in Nov. 2006, by the Program Manager of the Information Sharing Environment, a group located within the Office of the Director of National Intelligence. According to the *ISE Implementation Plan* (p.29), ". . . A primary purpose of the ITACG will be to ensure that classified and unclassified intelligence produced by Federal organizations. . . is fused, validated, deconflicted, and approved for dissemination in a concise and, where appropriate, unclassified format." It was reported that DHS officials stated that the department has ". . . always sought ways to incorporate State and local officials by assigning them to offices within the Department, such as its intelligence office and its operations center." Homeland security officials reportedly stated that the presence of

State and local officials at the ITACG would create ". . . unnecessary confusion at a unit whose main role is merely to package information."

[21] According to New York City Mayor Michael Bloomberg, "The freedoms and opportunities that New York symbolizes mean that we remain a prime—if not the prime -target for Al Qaeda and other terrorist groups. . . . Yet, time and time again our appeals for fully risk-based funding have been ignored." Testimony before the Senate Homeland Security and Governmental Affairs Committee, Jan. 9, 2007.

[22] Ibid.

[23] Homeland Security Grant Program, Department of Homeland Security. Available at [http://www.ojp.usdoj.gov/odp/newsreleases/HSGP_effectiveness_analysis.pdf], accessed Jan. 26, 2007.

[24] "Mayors, lawmakers press for more urban security funds," *Government Executive*, June 21, 2006, available at [http://www.govexec.com/story_page.cfm?articleid=34377&ref =rellink], accessed Jan. 26, 2007.

[25] National Commission on Terrorism Attacks Upon the United States (9/11 Commission), Recommendation 12.4 Protect Against and prepare for terrorist Attacks, p. 396. Available at [http://www.9-11commission.gov/report/911Report.pdf], accessed Jan. 26, 2007.

[26] From a DHS perspective, risk assessment pertains solely to assessing the risk associated with terrorist attacks, not necessarily natural disasters.

[27] It should be noted that quite often the terms risk, vulnerability, consequence, and threat are erroneously used interchangeably, as will be further discussed below.

[28] "Ensuring Full Implementation of the 9/11 Commission's Recommendations," a hearing of the Senate Homeland Security and Governmental Affairs Committee, Jan. 9, 2007.

[29] See Henry H. Willis, *Guiding Resource Allocations Based on Terrorism Risk* (A RAND Working Paper), March 2006.

[30] DHS Office of Inspector General, *Major Management Challenges Facing the Department of Homeland Security*, Dec. 2006, p. 8.

[31] Interview with DHS Official, Jan. 9, 2007.

[32] DHS *FY2007: Homeland Security Grant Program: Program Guidance and Application Kit*, Jan. 2007, pp. 1-2 and A1-A4.

[33] Ibid., p. 8.

[34] DHS, "DHS Announces $1.7 Billion in Homeland Security Grants," press release, May 31, 2006.

[35] Interview with DHS Official, Jan. 9, 2007.

[36] DHS, Directorate of Preparedness, Risk Management Division, and DHS Office of Grants and Training, *Risk Analysis for Fiscal Year 2006 Homeland Security Grants*, p. 4.

[37] Ibid., p. 2. For the relatively parochial purpose of allocating homeland security grant resources, absolute risk may be of marginal utility. However, the absolute risk to a certain critical asset or infrastructure may be highly relevant to state, local and private sector officials. For example, risk management analyses have been conducted on the terrorist threat to liquified natural gas (LNG) terminals in the United States. See Richard A. Clarke, *LNG Facilities in Urban Areas: A Security Risk Management Analysis for Attorney General Patrick Lynch Rhode Island*, May 2005. See also Carl Southwell, Center for Risk and Economic Analysis of Terrorism Events, University of Southern California, *An Analysis of the Risks of a Terrorist Attack on LNG Receiving Facilities in the United States, Nov. 9, 2005.* Because the risk analysis is conducted for one set of assets, Clarke, et.al. use numerous variables including intent, capabilities, vulnerabilities, consequences and recovery to assess security risk. These variables are, of course, relevant to assessing relative risk as well. However, in order to assess the at-

tractiveness of LNG terminals as a target, Clarke uses the U.S. military—Special Operations Force's CARVER target selection model. CARVER stands for criticality, accessibility, recuperability, vulnerability, effect and recognizability (See Field Manual 34-36 *Special Operation Forces Intelligence and Electronics Warfare Operation*, Sept. 30, 1991). The aforementioned Rhode Island LNG report states (p.76) that ". . . Since we are aware that al Qaeda has adopted much of U.S. Army doctrine for use in its training camps, it is fair to assume the principals in the CARVER matrix apply to their targeting." With its highly tactical focus on specific assets and characteristics of those assets, this model may have limited utility for the relative homeland security risk assessments.

[38] Society for Risk Analysis. Available at [http://www.SRA.org], accessed Jan. 26, 2007.

[39] This definition is derived from (1) Yacov's definition of risk management (see Yacov V. Haimes *Risk Modeling, Assessment, and Management* (2nd) (John Wiley & Sons, 2004), p.57-58) and (2) *Risk Management: Further Refinements Needed to Assess Risks and Prioritize Protective Measures at Ports and Other Critical Infrastructure*, (GAO 06-91), Dec. 2005, p. 111.

[40] See Yacov V. Haimes *Risk Modeling, Assessment, and Management* (2nd) (John Wiley & Sons, 2004), p.57-58.

[41] See *Risk Management: Further Refinements Needed to Assess Risks and Prioritize Protective Measures at Ports and Other Critical Infrastructure*, (GAO 06-91), Dec. 2005, p. 111.

[42] DHS, *Risk Analysis for Fiscal Year 2006 Homeland Security Grants*, pp. 8-12.

[43] See Henry H. Willis, Andrew R. Morral, Terrence K. Kelly, Jamison Jo Medby, *Estimating Terrorism Risk*, RAND Center for Terrorism Risk Management Policy (2005). See also *Managing Terrorism Risk in 2004*, Risk Management Solutions, Inc., Newark, CA.

[44] If risk is equal to threat*vulnerability*consequence, by mathematical principle if any value on the right side of the equation is assessed to be zero, risk is also zero. For example, because the vulnerability of a bridge to a chemical attack is zero, the risk to bridges from chemical attacks is also zero.

[45] Some would argue that given the statutory formula in the USA PATRIOT Act (P.L. 107-56, §1014, codified at 42 U.S.C., §3711) stipulating that .75 percent of the total amount of grants shall be allocated to each state (plus the District of Columbia and Puerto Rico), and .25 % for the territories of Guam, American Samoa, Northern Mariana Islands, and the Virgin Islands, the risk threshold is minimal, as this formula assumes that all states experience some level of risk and receive funding as a result. As will be discussed in the options section of this report, whether this funding was intended to be perpetual, or to bring all states up to a minimal level of security and capability, and then allow the states to assume financial responsibility for continued operations and maintenance of established security programs and activities, may be an issue for the 110th Congress. In FY2006, this .75% formula equates to 40% of the total $1.7 billion homeland security grant appropriation.

[46] Yacov Y. Haimes, founding director of the Center for Risk Management of Engineering Systems at the University of Virginia argues "Quantitative risk assessment and management cannot be conducted on an ad hoc basis or by addressing selective sources of risk." This engineering or systems based approach may be one of the areas where there is a commonality between an engineering approach to risk management and a homeland security approach, as terrorist threats, infrastructure vulnerabilities and the consequences associated with a successful attack are also inter-related. See Yacov V. Haimes *Risk Modeling, Assessment, and Management* (2nd) (John Wiley & Sons, 2004), p.18.

[47] Bayesian probability represents the degree of belief that an event will occur, and has been used by some in assessing the probabilities of a successful terrorist attack against a target. In Bayesian analysis, investigators assess the current state of knowledge regarding the issue of interest, gather new data to address remaining questions, and then update and refine their understanding to incorporate both new and old data. See [http://www.bayesian.org/], accessed Jan. 26, 2007.

[48] In a related organizational development, the Homeland Security Advisory Council recently recommended that DHS establish an Office of Net Assessments to ". . . provide the Secretary with comprehensive analysis of future threats and U.S. capabilities to meet those threats." Ostensibly, this office would also work with the Director of National Intelligence to develop a comprehensive National Intelligence Estimate to address threats to the homeland. See *Homeland Security Advisory Council, Future of Terrorism Task Force*, Jan 11, 2007, p.7. Any such office would apparently work closely with a potential risk assessment center, particularly with respect to assessment of terrorist threats and the means to combat such threats using, among other tools, the homeland security grants.

[49] *FY2007 Homeland Security Grant Program—Grant Guidelines and Application Kit.*, p.8.

[50] DHS, *Overview of the FY2006 DHS Risk Analysis Methodology*, p.1.

[51] Ibid.

[52] On Nov. 28, 2006, Secretary Chertoff stated "I'm going to repeat something I've said a lot in the almost two years I've been on this job, which is the core principle that animates what we do at DHS and this is risk management. It is a recognition of the fact that management of risk is not elimination of risk. There is no elimination of risk in life. . . ." Keynote Address by Secretary of Homeland Security Michael Chertoff to the 2006 Grants & Training National Conference.

[53] See General Accountability Office, *Risk Management: Further Refinements Needed to Assess Risks and Prioritize Protective Measures at Ports and Other Critical Infrastructures*, GAO-06-91, Dec. 2005. GAO reviewed the risk practices of these three DHS elements and concluded, in part, that "progress in risk management is affected by organizational maturity and the complexity of the risk management task."

[54] See testimony of Melissa Smislova, Acting Director HITRAC, before the House Homeland Security Committee, Subcommittee on Intelligence, Information Sharing and Terrorism Risk Assessment, Nov. 17, 2005. How subjective data are treated; the extent of expert input into a strategic, dynamic, and continual risk assessment process; the continually updated weighting of various factors; and the presence of *both* intent and opportunity are all critical elements of the risk assessment process. Whether HITRAC has the appropriate mix of personnel, resources, and singularity of focus on risk assessment methods to serve as a potential, permanent DHS entity to continually refine and implement a dynamic risk assessment model is an open question.

[55] Michael Chertoff, DHS Secretary, Keynote Address by Secretary of Homeland Security Michael Chertoff to the 2006 Grants & Training National Conference, Nov. 28, 2006. Available at [http://www.dhs.gov/xnews/speeches/sp_1164738645429.shtm], accessed Jan. 26, 2007.

[56] U.S. Government Accountability Office (GAO), Risk Management: Further Refinements Needed to Assess Risks and Prioritize Protective Measures at Ports and Other Critical Infrastructure,"GAO-06-91, Dec. 2005, available at [http://www.gao.gov/new.items/ d0691.pdf], accessed Jan. 26, 2007.

[57] A hypothetical example is provided by examining the FY2007 risk formula weights. This year's formula assigns a 20% weight to the Threat (T) variable. Threat is determined using a variety of data points, to include detainee reporting, on-going plot lines, credible threat reporting, and investigations. The investigations portion of the threat variable is comprised of terrorism investigations-related information provided by the FBI and Immigration and Customs Enforcement (ICE). Hypothetically, if the FBI and ICE did not operate using the same conception of what constitutes a terrorist threat and/or utilized alternate metrics to determine source credibility and determine corroboration, the output of DHS's risk assessment could be skewed. This is just one of many potential unintended negative consequences that can occur if federal agencies involved in aspects of the risk management process are not operating using the same definitions.

[58] National Commission of Terrorist Attacks Upon the United States, *The 9/11 Commission Report: Final Report of the National Commission of Terrorist Attacks Upon the United States*, Authorized Edition (New York: WW Norton and Company, 2004), p. 396.

[59] Keynote Address by Secretary of Homeland Security Michael Chertoff to the 2006 Grants & Training National Conference, Nov. 28, 2006.

[60] See Office of Management and Budget, *Analytical Perspectives: Budget of the United States Government Fiscal Year 2007*, Table 3-2, p. 33. Intelligence and warning is one of six critical mission areas outlined in the *National Strategy for Homeland Security*. There is at least one caveat to these figures. While the figures for the intelligence and warning include those reported by the Departments of Defense and Justice and the Intelligence Community Management Account, other Intelligence Community funds dedicated to the homeland security intelligence and warning function might not be captured in the OMB data.

DOCUMENT NO. 11

CURRENT AND PROJECTED NATIONAL SECURITY THREATS

Hearing Before the Senate Select Committee on Intelligence

January 11, 2007

Statement of Senator John D. Rockefeller IV Committee Chairman

Today the Senate Select Committee on Intelligence embarks on an ambitious agenda of hearings and committee reviews that will restore meaningful congressional oversight of the activities of the United States Intelligence Community.

It is fitting that the Committee's first hearing of 2007 is on the worldwide threat. It is important that not only the Congress but the American people understand the threats facing our country both inside our borders and abroad. This is why the Committee is conducting today's hearing in open session.

I am extremely concerned that misguided policies of the Administration have increased the threats facing our Nation and hampered our ability to isolate and defeat Al Qaeda and other terrorists that seek to strike against the United States.

I believe our actions in Iraq have placed our Nation more at risk to terrorist attack than before the invasion. Based on the findings of the Committee's Iraq investigation, I have concluded that the Administration promoted non-existent links between Iraq and Al Qaeda in an effort to sell a war that was fundamentally about regime change, not about an imminent threat to America.

The sobering consequences of our actions are well-known. Over 3,000 Americans have died in Iraq, many thousands more gravely wounded. Our military and intelligence efforts in fighting and capturing the Taliban and Al Qaeda in Afghanistan were diverted at a critical juncture to support the invasion of Iraq. Now these agents of extremism and violence have reestablished themselves in a safehaven that threatens not only America but also the governments in Kabul and Islamabad.

Al Qaeda and foreign jihadists have used our occupation as an opportunity to strike against Americans and as a propaganda tool to spread its influence in Iraq and the region. I also believe this portrayal of our actions in Iraq has fueled the spread of the terrorist message and increased the number of terrorist cells in other parts of world, such as Asia and Europe.

The ongoing war in Iraq has demanded enormous funding and personnel resources which has strained our efforts in the global war on terrorism.

I have seen nothing in my service on the Intelligence Committee, or in any other forum, that suggests sending an additional 21,500 American troops to Iraq will bring about greater security on the ground or lead to a more successful outcome.

There is little reason to believe that the diplomatic, political and economic objectives will be any more successful with 153,000 troops than with the current 132,000 troops. And that's really the crux of the President's new strategy—more troops.

It is an approach that tinkers at the margins of a grave and deteriorating situation. It is not grounded in the realities we face in Iraq and in the region, and it is an unacceptable gamble with additional soldiers' lives.

The President must understand that even as Congress continues to support and fund the brave work of the servicemen and women who are now serving in Iraq, we will push back on an ill-conceived plan to put more soldiers in harms way.

I am also troubled by what I see as an Administration counter-terrorism policy which, in certain respects, may be complicating if not worsening our ability to win the war on terrorism.

To be specific, I have serious misgivings about the soundness and the effectiveness of the CIA's secret detention program and the NSA's warrantless surveillance program, both publicly acknowledged by the President.

I am concerned that the very existence of a separate CIA prison program established to interrogate high value detainees under a different set of rules than those outlined in the Army Field Manual and repudiated by the FBI has undermined our moral standing in the eyes of the world.

How many millions of moderate Arabs and Muslims around the world, having seen the photos of Abu Ghraib, heard stories about abuses at Guantanamo, and who are now aware that the CIA operates a secret prison, believe that America tortures detainees?

How does this perception help foster extremism around the world and how do we weigh this fact, combined with the lasting damage done to America's image, against the putative intelligence benefits of operating a separate CIA program in lieu of single Pentagon program that is subjected to greater scrutiny?

With respect to the NSA surveillance program, I believe the Administration's policy has unnecessarily alienated an essential ally in combating the terrorist threat: the United States Congress.

In the aftermath of 9/11, our Nation stood unified to defeat the terrorists. The Administration's decision to go it alone and work outside the legal parameters of the Foreign Intelligence Surveillance Act was a serious miscalculation and undercut the strength of our unity of purpose.

This approach also created serious doubts in the minds of Americans—whose support is essential in any successful war effort—as to how far the Administration would go in unilaterally carrying out secret programs seeking to identify potential terrorists inside our borders.

The Administration has still not convincingly demonstrated to me that the end justifies the means—in other words, that the NSA program has produced the sort of unique, timely and actionable intelligence to justify the surveillance of American phone calls and email messages without a court warrant.

As we hear from our witnesses today, I hope they can address these concerns about the effectiveness of our counter-terrorism programs and whether the situation in Iraq has worsened the threats facing America's security.

In the coming weeks and months, the Committee will receive testimony from intelligence officials and outside witnesses on critical questions at the heart of our national security policies.

Next week, the Committee will hold a closed hearing on Iraq's regional neighbors and their influence on the war, including, in light of the Iraq Study Group recommendations, the Intelligence Community's assessment on the receptivity of Syria, Iran, and other nations to a regional diplomatic initiative and the consequences of changes in the U.S. military presence in Iraq.

The Committee will then turn its attention to an examination of current, emerging, and future terrorist safehavens. Our focus will be not only on current operations, such as in Somalia, to deny terrorists sanctuary where they can plot and carry out attacks but also on the soundness and foresight of our counterterrorism policy to identify those places where the terrorists virulent message of violence may take root and preemptively prevent its spread.

In two weeks, the Committee will hold a pair of open hearings on the state of Intelligence Community reform two years after the passage of landmark legislation establishing an empowered Director of National Intelligence to manage and coordinate our intelligence programs.

At the first hearing we will receive testimony from Director Negroponte on what has been accomplished in this two-year period, what work remains unfinished, and what changes to the reform law should be considered by the Committee. We also will examine whether the recently established National Counterterrorism and Counterproliferation Centers are realizing the vision behind their creation.

The focus of our second open hearing will be on the intelligence activities of the Federal Bureau of Investigation and the Department of Homeland Security. We will be interested in evaluating the pace of transformation at the FBI and the effectiveness of newly-created Joint Terrorist Task Forces and state and local fusion centers in carrying out counter-terrorism investigations that do not run afoul of privacy rights and civil liberties.

We will have outside witnesses at each reform hearing to hear informed perspectives of those not in the Administration, including witnesses representing state and local law enforcement and homeland security agencies.

The Committee's workload will continue to be heavy beyond January. In addition to a number of closed hearings on developments in Afghanistan, Pakistan, Iran, and North Korea, the Committee will hold monthly hearings on the situation in Iraq, including a hearing on the Intelligence Community's new Iraq National Intelligence Estimate once it is completed.

Our first act of committee business will be to re-pass the Fiscal Year 2007 intelligence authorization bill the Committee unanimously reported out last May but which never received Senate approval.

We must also complete the Committee's two-and-a-half year investigation of prewar intelligence on Iraq in a prompt but thorough and objective manner. We should have, and could have, completed this effort long ago.

There is other important unfinished business before the Committee in the area of counterterrorism.

For four years, the Administration kept the very existence of the National Security Agency's warrantless surveillance program and the Central Intelligence Agency's detention, interrogation and rendition program from the full membership of this Committee.

Through the over-restriction of member and Committee staff access to the NSA and CIA programs and the denial of requested documents, the White House has prevented the Committee from completely understanding the programs and thoroughly evaluating their legal soundness and operational effectiveness.

The Administration can no longer stonewall the Committee's legitimate requests with respect to these two programs. It needs to understand the fundamental precept that congressional oversight is a constructive and necessary part of governance. Our Committee stands ready to work with the Administration to fashion responsible legislation in these and other areas, but we cannot responsibly do so as long as we are deprived critical information we need to do our job.

Before introducing the witnesses, I now turn to Vice Chairman Bond for his opening remarks.

Statement of John D. Negroponte
Director of National Intelligence (DNI)

Chairman Rockefeller, Vice-Chairman Bond, Members of the Committee, thank you for the invitation to offer my assessment of threats to our nation.

I am pleased to be accompanied by General Michael Hayden, Director of CIA, Lt. General Michael Maples, Director of DIA, Mr. Robert Mueller, Director of the FBI, and Mr. Randall Fort, Assistant Secretary of State for Intelligence and Research.

Introduction

The judgments I will offer the Committee are based on the efforts of thousands of patriotic, highly skilled professionals, many of whom serve in harm's way. I am proud to lead the world's best Intelligence Community and pleased to report that it is even better than it was last year as a result of reforms mandated by the President and the Congress. These reforms promote better information sharing, the highest standards of analytic rigor, the most innovative techniques of acquiring information, and a stronger sense of community across our sixteen agencies.

We know that the nation requires more from our Intelligence Community than ever before because America confronts a greater diversity of threats and challenges than ever before. Globalization, the defining characteristic of our age, mandates global intelligence coverage. Globalization is not a "threat" in and of itself; it has more positive than negative characteristics. But globalization does facilitate the terrorist threat, heightens the danger of WMD proliferation, and contributes to regional instability and reconfigurations of power and influence—especially through competition for energy. Globalization also exposes the United States to mounting counterintelligence challenges. Our comparative advantage in some areas of technical intelligence, where we have been dominant in the past, is being eroded. Several nonstate actors, including international terrorist groups, conduct intelligence activities as effectively as capable state intelligence services. A significant number of states also conduct economic espionage. China and Russia's foreign intelligence services are among the most aggressive in collecting against sensitive and protected U.S. targets.

This array of challenges to our national security is shaped by dramatic advances in telecommunications, technology, new centers of economic growth, and the consequences of crises within traditional cultures.

As a result of these and other challenges exacerbated by globalization, many nation states are unable to provide good governance and sustain the rule of law within their borders. This enables non-state actors and hostile states to assault these fundamental building blocks of international order, creating failed states, proxy states, terrorist safehavens, and ungoverned regions that endanger the international community and its citizens. More to the point, it threatens our national security and support for freedom and democracy, notably in Iraq and Afghanistan, where our troops and those of our allies are helping to defend freely elected governments and sovereign peoples against determined insurgents and terrorists.

Terrorism

Terrorist threats to the Homeland, to our national security interests, and to our allies remain the pre-eminent challenge to the Intelligence Community, operationally and analytically. Working closely with our international partners, we have scored remarkable successes and disrupted terrorist plots aimed at murdering thousands of U.S. and allied citizens. Despite these successes, we must maintain maximum vigilance, flexibility, and operational aggressiveness to counter the constant evolution and adaptive capability of our enemies. To support these efforts, we must understand the enemy, his intentions, and his capabilities. Much of what we have learned this past year underscores the judgments that I shared with the Committee last year, but we now have a deeper understanding of the enemy we face.

Al Qaeda is the terrorist organization that poses the greatest threat to U.S. interests, including to the Homeland. We have captured or killed numerous senior Al Qaeda operatives, but we also have seen that Al Qaeda's core elements are resilient. They continue to plot attacks against our Homeland and other targets with the objective of inflicting mass casualties. And they continue to maintain active connections and relationships that radiate outward from their leaders' secure hideout in Pakistan to affiliates throughout the Middle East, northern Africa, and Europe.

Use of a conventional explosive continues to be the most probable Al Qaeda attack scenario. The thwarted UK aviation plot last summer and the other major threat reports that we have been tracking all involve conventional bombs. Nevertheless, we receive reports indicating that Al Qaeda and other groups are attempting to acquire chemical, biological, radiological, and nuclear weapons or materials.

In addition to Al Qaeda, its networks and affiliates, I mention the terrorist threat from Hezbollah, which is backed by Iran and Syria. As a result of last summer's hostilities, Hezbollah's self-confidence and hostility toward the U.S. as a supporter of Israel could cause the group to increase its contingency planning against U.S. interests.

We know from experience since 9/11 that countering terrorism depends on unprecedented levels of international cooperation. Our successes so far against Al Qaeda and other jihadists—and our ability to prevent attacks abroad and at home—have been aided considerably by the cooperation of foreign governments, among them Iraq, the UK, Saudi Arabia, Turkey, Pakistan, Afghanistan, and many others. They, too, are targets of terror. As illustrated by Al Qaeda's plots in the U.K., Kurdish separatist attacks in Turkey, and the recent airport bombing in Spain, terror is a worldwide scourge.

It is important to note our shared successes, with a focus, not on taking credit, but on demonstrating results. I will highlight four major accomplishments.

- We eliminated Al Qaeda in Iraq's murderous leader, Abu Musab al'Zarqawi.
- Also in Iraq, we have severely damaged Ansar al Sunna's leadership and operational capacity.
- In the UK, as noted earlier, a plot to perpetrate the worst terrorist slaughter of innocent civilians since 9/11 was thwarted.
- And in Pakistan Abd al-Rahman al-Muhajir and Abu Bakr al-Suri, two of Al Qaeda's top bomb makers were killed last April.

Again, I emphasize that we, the United States, do not and could not accomplish our counterterrorism mission unilaterally. Our role varies from situation to situation. What does not vary is our requirement for good intelligence and committed partners, which we have in all parts of the world—because terrorists have killed far more non-Americans than Americans and far more Muslims than non-Muslims.

Iraq, Afghanistan, and Pakistan

The two countries where the United States military is engaged in combat—Iraq and Afghanistan—face challenges that are significantly exacerbated by terrorism but not exclusively attributable to it. And Pakistan, despite its ongoing efforts, continues to face terrorism's many challenges, while that country also raises other concerns for us.

In Iraq, sectarian divisions are widening but the multiparty government of Nuri al-Maliki continues to seek ways to bridge the divisions and restore commitment to a unified country. The effort to build a "moderate front" of major parties from the country's three ethno-sectarian groups has underscored moderates' interest in bridging the gaps between Iraq's communities by appealing to non-violent actors. Iraqi security forces have become more numerous and more capable since my last threat briefing. Six division headquarters, 30 brigades, and more than 90 battalions have taken the lead in their operational areas, have battled insurgents on their own, and have stood up to the militias in some cases.

Despite these positive developments, Iraq is at a precarious juncture. Communal violence—accelerated by AQI's attack on the Samarra mosque in February 2006—and scant common ground between Shias, Sunnis, and Kurds have polarized politics. Prime Minister Maliki's national reconciliation agenda is still at its initial stages. The various parties have not yet shown the ability to compromise effectively on the thorny issues of de-Ba'thification, constitutional reform, federalism, and central versus regional control over hydrocarbon revenues. Provision of essential public services is inadequate; oil output remains below pre-war levels; hours of electrical power available have declined and remain far below demand; and inflationary pressures have grown since last year.

With political reconciliation stalled, Iraqis increasingly resort to violence. The struggle among and within Iraqi communities over national identity and the distribution of power has eclipsed attacks by Iraqis against the Coalition Forces as the greatest impediment to Iraq's future as a peaceful, democratic, and unified state.

Prospects for increasing stability in Iraq over the next year will depend on how several issues evolve:

- Foremost is the ability of the Iraqi government to establish and nurture effective national institutions that are based on national rather than religious or ethnic interests; and within this context, the willingness of the security forces to pursue extremist elements of all kinds.
- The extent to which the Shia feel sufficiently secure in their political position: despite their recent electoral victories and overall political ascendancy, the Shia at present remain deeply insecure about their hold on power. This insecurity is manifested in the Shia's refusal to make real concessions to the Sunnis on a range of issues, such as easing of de-Ba'athification and clamping down on radical Shia militias.
- The extent to which Arab Sunnis develop trust and participate in the new political order: now, many remain unwilling to accept their minority status, continue to resist violently this new political order, and distrust the Shia-led government and its commitment to their security.
- The extent to divisions *within* the Shia and the Sunni are addressed: profound intra-group divisions among the Shia and Sunnis complicate the situation, because no single leader can speak for or exert control over these groups.
- The extent to which extremists—most notably Al Qaeda in Iraq (AQI)—are suppressed: these groups continue to conduct high-profile, often mass casualty attacks that are effective accelerants for the self-sustaining inter-sectarian struggle between Shia and Sunnis.
- And lastly, the extent to which Iraq's neighbors can be persuaded to stop the flow of militants and munitions across their borders: Iran's lethal support for select groups of Iraqi Shia militants clearly exacerbates the conflict in Iraq, as does Syria's continued provision of safehaven for expatriate Iraqi Ba'thists and less-than-adequate measures to stop the flow of foreign jihadists into Iraq.

Indeed, our friends in the region are concerned about the consequences of growing instability in Iraq. Many are increasingly apprehensive about ethno-sectarian strife spilling out of Iraq and infecting their minority populations and all in the region are nervous about the growing role of radical Islamists.

As in Iraq, 2007 will be a pivotal year for Afghanistan. The ability of the Karzai government, NATO, and the United States to arrest—if not reverse—the resurgence of the Taliban will determine the country's future. The insurgency probably does not directly threaten the government, but it is deterring economic development and undermining popular support for President Karzai.

Afghan leaders also face critical challenges in building central and provincial government capacity and in confronting pervasive drug cultivation and trafficking. Neither task will be easy. The country faces a chronic shortage of resources and of qualified and motivated government officials at the national and local level. Further, the drug trade contributes to endemic corruption at all levels of government, undercutting public confidence. A dangerous nexus exists between drugs and the insurgents and warlords who derive funds from cultivation and trafficking.

Many of our most important interests intersect in Pakistan, where the Taliban and Al Qaeda maintain critical sanctuaries. As I noted earlier, Pakistan is our partner in the war on terror and has captured several Al Qaeda leaders. However, it is also a major source of Islamic extremism.

Eliminating the safehaven that the Taliban and other extremists have found in Pakistan's tribal areas is not sufficient to end the insurgency in Afghanistan but it is necessary. We recognize that aggressive military action, however, has been costly for Pakistani security forces and appreciate concerns over the potential for sparking tribal rebellion and a backlash by sympathetic Islamic political parties. There is widespread opposition among these parties to the U.S. military presence in Afghanistan and Iraq. With elections expected later this year, the situation will become even more challenging—for President Musharraf and for the U.S.

Proliferation: States of Key Concern

After terrorism, the ongoing efforts of nation-states and terrorists to develop and/or acquire dangerous weapons and delivery systems constitute the second major threat to the safety of our nation, our deployed troops, and our friends.

The time when only a few states had access to the most dangerous technologies has been over for many years. Dual-use technologies circulate easily in our globalized economy, as do the scientific personnel who design and use them. As a consequence, it is more difficult for us to track efforts to acquire, for nefarious purposes, these widely available components and production technologies.

Iran and North Korea are the states of most concern to us because their regimes disregard international opprobrium, flout UN Security Council restrictions on their nuclear programs, pervert the legitimate purposes of governance, and ignore the needs and rights of their citizens. The United States' concerns about Iran are shared by many nations, including Iran's neighbors. We assess that Tehran is determined to develop nuclear weapons—despite its international obligations and international pressure. It is continuing to pursue uranium enrichment and has shown more interest in protracting negotiations than reaching an acceptable diplomatic solution. This is a grave concern to the other countries in the region whose security would be threatened by Iranian nuclear weapons. Any such development could prompt dangerous and destabilizing countermoves in a volatile region that is, because of its energy reserves, critical to the global economy.

North Korea's threat to international security is also grave. Last year I highlighted that point. In the intervening twelve months, Pyongyang substantiated our concerns. In July it flight-tested missiles and in October it tested a nuclear device. We remain concerned it could proliferate these weapons abroad. Indeed, it already has sold ballistic missiles to several Middle Eastern countries. By pressing forward with its nuclear weapon and missile programs, North Korea threatens to destabilize a region that has known several great power conflicts over the last one hundred years and now comprises some of the world's largest economies. Other northeast Asian states might decide to pursue nuclear weapons if their governments perceive increased regional threats as North Korea's nuclear program proceeds.

The advent of more nuclear powers in northeast Asia or the Middle East could unravel the global nonproliferation regime. We are watching several states for signs of nuclear weapons aspirations, in part because of reporting of past contact with A. Q. Khan and his network when it was active. We also are concerned about rogue or criminal elements willing to supply materials and technology—alone or with a network—without their government's knowledge.

Regional Conflicts, Instability, and Reconfigurations of Power and Influence

As I said at the outset of my statement, globalization is contributing to conflicts, instability, and reconfigurations of power and influence. These consequences of globalization manifest themselves most clearly at the regional level, although at times we can see the effects across regions. Again, the attempt by states or non-state actors to co-opt, dominate, turn into proxies, or destroy other nation states is our primary concern. This is the explicitly stated goal of Al Qaeda's leadership vis-á-vis Iraq and the Levant, and it is an accurate appraisal of the foreign policy aims of states like Iran. However they occur, violent conflicts in a given state—as we see in Africa today—can swiftly lead to massive humanitarian tragedies and, potentially, regional wars.

The Middle East—An Emboldened Iran

In the Middle East, Iran and its neighbors see a strategic shift: Iran's influence is rising in ways that go beyond the menace of its nuclear program. The fall of the Taliban and Saddam, increased oil revenues, HAMAS's electoral victory, and Hezbollah's perceived recent success in fighting against Israel all extend Iran's shadow in the region. Our Arab allies fear Iran's increasing influence, are concerned about worsening tensions between Shia and Sunni Islam, and face heightened domestic criticism for maintaining their decades-old strategic partnerships with Washington.

Iran's growing influence has coincided with a generational change in Tehran's leadership. Iranian President Ahmadi-Nejad's administration—staffed in large part by second-generation hardliners imbued with revolutionary ideology and deeply distrustful of the U.S.—has stepped up the use of more assertive and offensive tactics to achieve Iran's longstanding goals.

However, Ahmadi-Nejad's supporters suffered setbacks in the recent Assembly of Experts and local council elections. Moreover, ethnic tensions in Iran's Baloch, Kurdish, and, to a lesser extent, Arab and Azeri areas continue to fester, creating concern in Tehran about the potential for broader ethnic unrest to generate large-scale anti-regime activity. While record oil revenues and manageable debt suggest that Iran is capable, for now, of weathering shocks to the economy, inflationary pressures, exacerbated by Ahmadi-Nejad's expansionary fiscal and monetary policies, are harming Iran's consumer and investment climates and causing employment opportunities to decline.

Regarding Tehran's regional policies, Iran continues to be active in Iraq, seeking to influence political, economic, religious, and cultural developments to ensure a non-threatening, cooperative, and Shia-dominated regime to its west.

- Iran uses radio, television, and print media to influence Iraqi public opinion and help promote pro-Iranian individuals in the Iraqi government at all levels. It has offered financial and other support to its political allies in the United Iraqi Alliance, but its electoral impact appears to have been marginal, given the likelihood that Shia voters would have voted for the unified Shia ticket anyway.

Iranian conventional military power threatens Persian Gulf states and challenges U.S. interests. Iran is enhancing its ability to project its military power—primarily with ballistic missiles and naval power—with the goal of dominating the Gulf region and deterring potential adversaries. It seeks a capacity to disrupt the operations and reinforcement of U.S. forces based in the region—potentially intimidating regional allies into withholding support for U.S. policy—and raising the political, financial, and human costs to the U.S. and our allies of our presence in Iraq. Tehran views its growing inventory of ballistic missiles (it already has the largest inventory of these missiles in the Middle East), as an integral part of its strategy to deter—and if necessary retaliate against—forces in the region, including U.S. forces.

We assess that Iran regards its ability to conduct terrorist operations abroad as a key element of its national security strategy: it considers this capability as helping to safeguard the regime by deterring U.S. or Israeli attacks, distracting and weakening Israel, enhancing Iran's regional influence through intimidation, and helping to drive the U.S. from the region.

At the center of Iran's terrorism strategy is Lebanese Hezbollah, which relies on Tehran for a substantial portion of its annual budget, military equipment, and specialized training. Hezbollah is focused on its agenda in Lebanon and supporting anti-Israeli Palestinian terrorists, but, as I indicated earlier, it has in the past made contingency plans to conduct attacks against U.S. interests in the event it feels its survival—or that of Iran—is threatened.

Syria has strengthened ties with Iran and grown more confident about its regional policies, largely due to what it sees as vindication of its support to Hezbollah and HAMAS and its perceptions of its success in overcoming international attempts to isolate the regime. Damascus has failed to crack down consistently on militant infiltration into Iraq and continues to meddle in Lebanon. Lebanon remains in a politically dangerous situation as Damascus, Hezbollah, and other pro-Syrian groups attempt to topple the government of Prime Minister Siniora.

In the Palestinian territories, inter-factional violence, which has intensified in the Gaza Strip and the West Bank since the establishment of the HAMAS-led Palestinian Authority (PA) government in March, threatens to escalate further absent success in forming a national unity government. Talks have stalled over disputes about the political platform and control of key cabinet positions. HAMAS has continued to reject Quartet and Israeli demands for explicit recognition of Israel, renunciation of armed resistance to Israeli occupation, and acceptance of previous PLO and international agreements.

Turmoil in Major African States

In sub-Saharan Africa, the picture is mixed. We see the consolidation of democracy in some countries and the persistence of political crises and violent conflict in others. Many of Africa's past and present crises have occurred in countries run by entrenched regimes with little to no real democratic foundations and weak control of areas outside the capital. Sudan and Somalia are cases in point. Turmoil and conflict threaten large portions of the sub-Saharan region, stretching from the Horn of Africa in the east to Nigeria in the west.

The Darfur conflict is the world's fastest-growing humanitarian crisis, with more than 200,000 people killed, 2 million internally displaced and another 234,000 refugees in neighboring Chad. Internally divided rebel groups continue to fight against the government because the existing peace agreement fails to provide security and power sharing. The Sudanese military has been unable to force the rebels to sign the peace accord and, with assistance from local militia, is conducting a dry season campaign against civilian villages suspected of harboring the rebels.

Already facing the prospect that its southern region will choose to secede in a referendum scheduled for 2011, the Sudanese government fears that additional concessions to the Darfur rebels and the deployment of UN peacekeepers to the region would lead to further disintegration of Sudan. Chadian and Central African Republic (CAR) rebel groups have become entangled in the Darfur crisis, and the spillover of violence in the past ten months threatens to destabilize already weak regimes in both countries.

The rapid collapse of the Council of Islamic Courts and arrival in Mogadishu of the Transitional Federal Government (TFG) has altered the political dynamics in southern Somalia. The TFG faces many of the same obstacles that have kept any single group from establishing a viable government in Somalia since the country collapsed in 1991. Somali society is divided into numerous clans and sub-clans that are reluctant to see one group rise above the others. To win the confidence and support of the population and have any chance of restoring order, the TFG will need to be more inclusive and demonstrate effective governance. More turmoil could enable extremists to regain their footing absent mechanisms to replace the temporary Ethiopian presence with an internationally-supported Somali solution. Al Qaeda remains determined to exploit turmoil in Somalia.

Nigeria's fragile democratic transition is in danger of collapsing in the coming months. The government's institutional foundations are hollow from decades of neglect and corruption and will continue to make the country susceptible to recurring crises in the coming years. Abuja has been unable to stem rising lawlessness and insecurity in its oil-producing region, and the Nigerian population is increasingly demoralized from worsening living conditions in the face of much publicized improvements in the country's macroeconomic indicators. Major political unrest in Nigeria would threaten other countries in the region.

Latin America

Gradual consolidation of democracy remained the prevailing tendency in Latin America over the election-packed year that just concluded, despite the challenge to core democratic tenets in a few countries. Although some commentators spoke of a "lurch to the left" in the region, the election results point to no dominant ideological trend. Moderate leftists who promote macroeconomic stability, poverty alleviation, and the building of democratic institutions fared well, as did able right of center leaders. Indeed, the overall health of Latin American democracy is reflected in the results of a recent survey by a reputable Latin America polling organization: fifty-eight percent of the respondents said that democracy is the best system of government. This number is up five percentage points, compared to results from the same poll in 2005.

At the same time, individuals who are critical of free market economics and have friendly relations with Venezuela's President Chavez won the presidency in two of Latin America's poorest countries, Ecuador and Nicaragua—both after Evo Morales' victory in Bolivia in December 2005.

The strong showing of presidential candidates with leftist populist views in several other countries speaks to the growing impatience of national electorates with the failure of incumbent governments to improve the living standards of large elements of the population. Public dissatisfaction with the way democracy is working is especially troubling in the Andes, most notably in Ecuador and Peru.

Democracy is most at risk in Venezuela and Bolivia. In both countries, the elected presidents, Chavez and Morales, are taking advantage of their popularity to undercut the opposition and eliminate checks on their authority.

In Venezuela, Chavez reacted to his sweeping victory on 3 December by promising to deepen his self-described Bolivarian Revolution and to intensify the struggle against U.S. "imperialism." In recent days he has announced plans to prevent a leading opposition television station from continuing to broadcast and begun action to nationalize the country's main telecommunications enterprise and largest private electric power company. Chavez is among the most stridently anti-American leaders anywhere in the world, and will continue to try to undercut U.S. influence in Venezuela, in the rest of Latin America, and elsewhere internationally.

Chavez's effort to politicize the Venezuelan Armed Forces and to create a large and well-armed Territorial Guard and military reserves is another sign that he is breaking with the trend in the region toward more professional and apolitical militaries. His purchase of modern military equipment from Russia, including 24 SU-30 advanced fighter-bombers, and moves toward developing his own weapons production capability are increasingly worrisome to his neighbors. These weapons purchases could fuel an arms race in the region.

Fidel Castro's Cuba continues to be Venezuela's closest ally. Castro's apparent impending demise will deprive Chavez of a valued mentor and strategic adviser. The post-Castro transition in Cuba has begun. Key drivers in influencing events in post-Fidel Cuba will be how cohesive the governing elite will remain in the absence of Cuba's iconic leader, how astute Raul Castro proves to be as his brother's successor, and how much pressure the population will exert on the government in seeking economic and political reforms.

In Mexico, President Felipe Calderon of the ruling National Action Party (PAN) was inaugurated on 1 December after a razor-thin margin of victory over his closest opponent, leftist populist Andres Manuel Lopez Obrador of the Party of the Democratic Revolution (PRD). The July election illustrated the country's polarization along socioeconomic lines. The new government has initiated steps to address problems in northern Mexico that affect both Mexican and U.S. security concerns, including drug smuggling, human trafficking, and associated violence.

Crosscurrents in Asia

Northeast Asia

The rise of China and economic prosperity more generally—except for North Korea—are changing Northeast Asia in unprecedented ways. Trade and investment, driven by China's successful integration into the world economy through the World Trade Organization framework, is rapidly bringing the countries of this region closer together; but it still lacks mature, integrating security mechanisms, beyond the U.S. security treaties with Japan and South Korea.

In 2006, Chinese leaders increasingly moved to align Beijing's foreign policy with the needs of domestic development, identifying opportunities to strengthen economic growth, gain access to new sources of energy, and mitigate what they see as potential external threats to social stability. At one and the same time, China places a priority on positive relations with the United States while strengthening ties to the other major powers, especially the EU and Russia.

PRC leaders continue to emphasize development of friendly relations with the states on China's periphery to assure peaceful borders. In the past year, China achieved notable success in improving relations with Japan under newly elected Prime Minister Abe and prospects for cross-straits conflict with Taiwan diminished. In addition to establishing strong bilateral ties, Beijing actively engages with many multilateral organizations, including ASEAN.

Beijing continues its rapid rate of military modernization, initiated in 1999. We assess that China's aspirations for great power status, threat perceptions, and security strategy would drive this modernization effort even if the Taiwan problem were resolved. The Chinese are developing more capable long-range conventional strike systems and short- and medium-range ballistic missiles with terminally guided maneuverable warheads able to attack US carriers and airbases.

Maintaining domestic social stability remains one of Beijing's top priorities. Rural discontent, which has erupted in an increasing number of local demonstrations and riots, could undermine continued rapid economic growth if not addressed. Hu Jintao's "harmonious society" program is an attempt to address these concerns by enhancing environmental protection, social service, and rule of law, while strengthening the Communist Party's position. The 11th Five-Year Plan enacted in 2006 seeks to put economic growth on a more secure footing by attempting to address rural complaints and extending economic prosperity to more disadvantaged segments of Chinese society. Implementation of this program would require a major shift of resources to the countryside, greater accountability of provincial leaders to Beijing, and stronger efforts to root out local corruption.

Lastly, some aspects of China's financial system are unhealthy, with state-owned banks maintaining large balances of non-performing loans. We nevertheless see a low risk of severe financial crisis over the next five years; China is introducing market measures to the financial sector, and has massive foreign exchange reserves, current and capital account surpluses and low exposure to short-term foreign currency debt.

South Asia

We expect that India's growing confidence on the world stage as a result of its sustained high rates of economic growth will make New Delhi a more effective partner for the United States but also a more formidable interlocutor in areas of disagreement, particularly in the WTO.

New Delhi seeks to play a role in fostering democracy in the region, especially in Nepal and Bangladesh, and will continue to be a reliable ally against global terrorism, given the fact that India is a major target for jihadists in part because of the insurgency in Kashmir.

The three-year peace process between India and Pakistan has lessened tensions in the region and both sides appear committed to improving the bilateral relationship. New Delhi's threshold for responding militarily to terrorist attacks has apparently increased since the two countries last approached the brink of war in 2002. The Mumbai train bombings last year disrupted but ultimately did not derail the composite dialogue and a mechanism for exchanging information on terrorist attacks has been established. Yet, the prospect of renewed tensions between the two remains despite these improved relations, and we are mindful that Pakistan was a major source of nuclear proliferation until our efforts disrupted A.Q. Khan's network.

Nonetheless, New Delhi's concerns about Pakistan's tolerance, at a minimum, of terrorist attacks on Indian soil remains a dominant theme in relations, and risks derailing rapprochement. An attack on a high-profile target might lead New Delhi to take action to curtail militant capabilities in Pakistan or Pakistani Kashmir and punish Islamabad for its continued support to Pakistan-based militants. We remain concerned about the potential that such a conflict could escalate.

Although both New Delhi and Islamabad are fielding a more mature strategic nuclear capability, they do not appear to be engaged in a Cold War-style arms race based on a quest for numerical superiority.

For its part, as I noted previously, Pakistan is a frontline partner in the war on terror. Nevertheless, it remains a major source of Islamic extremism and the home for some top terrorist leaders. The prospect of renewed tensions with nuclear-armed India remains despite improved relations, and Pakistan had been a major source of nuclear proliferation until the disruption of the A.Q. Khan's network. Meanwhile, democracy has not been fully restored since the Army took power in 1999. With elections expected later this year, Musharraf continues to be criticized for remaining both the President and Chief of Army Staff, but there are no political leaders inside the country able to challenge his continued leadership. Musharraf s secular opponents are in disarray, and the main Islamic parties continue to suffer from internal divisions and an inability to expand their support base.

Eurasia in Flux

Fifteen years after the dissolution of the USSR, post-Soviet Eurasia remains in a state of flux—more so than even a year ago—but increasingly subject to Russian assertiveness.

Russia

As Russia moves toward a presidential election in March 2008, succession maneuvering has intensified and increasingly dominates Russian domestic and foreign policy. Against that backdrop, the last year has seen expanded Kremlin efforts to stifle political opposition and widen state control over strategic sectors of the economy. Those trends are likely to deepen as the succession draws closer.

Meanwhile, high energy prices and abundant oil and gas reserves continue to fan Kremlin aspirations for Russia to become an energy super-power. A flush economy and perceived policy successes at home and abroad have bolstered Russian confidence, enabled increased defense spending, and emboldened the Kremlin to pursue foreign policy goals that are not always consistent with those of Western institutions. Indeed, Russia is attempting to exploit the leverage that high energy prices has afforded it, increasingly using strong-arm tactics against neighboring countries.

Russian assertiveness will continue to inject elements of rivalry and antagonism into U.S. dealings with Moscow, particularly our interactions in the former Soviet Union, and will dampen our ability to cooperate with Russia on issues ranging from counterterrorism and nonproliferation to energy and democracy promotion in the Middle East. As the recent Litvinenko murder demonstrates, the steady accumulation of problems and irritants threatens to harm Russia's relations with the West more broadly.

Other Eurasian States and Balkans

Ukraine's political situation is also unsettled. The power struggle between President Yushchenko and recently re-installed Prime Minister Yanukovych continues to buffet Ukrainian politics and national policy.

- Ukraine's Orange Revolution brought lasting changes, including greater media freedom and a strengthened role for civil society. Improvements to the political process resulted in free and fair parliamentary elections in March 2006. However, Yanukovych's re-emergence after his party won that election increased cynicism in the region about the promise of "colored" revolutions, bolstered Russia's position in the region and leaves Georgia isolated as virtually the only former Soviet republic fully-committed to Euro-Atlantic integration.

The future development of the Caucasus is likely to be intertwined with what may happen outside the region in Kosovo. If Kosovo gains independence this year—as seems likely—Russia has signaled that it might respond by recognizing breakaway regions in Georgia, a risky step.

American interests in Central Asia also face increasing challenges. Of the five countries in the region, three—Kazakhstan, Tajikistan, and especially Uzbekistan—are authoritarian; another, Kyrgyzstan, is semi-authoritarian and increasingly fearful of losing control; and the last, Turkmenistan, is a dictatorship in the midst of a power struggle. All view our democratization agenda with suspicion. The repression, leadership stasis, and corruption that tend to characterize these regimes provide fertile soil for the development of radical Islamic sentiment and movements, and raise questions about the Central Asian states reliability as energy and counterterrorism partners.

- There is no guarantee that elite and societal turmoil across Central Asia will stay within the confines of existing autocratic systems. In the worst, but not implausible case, central authority in one or more of these states could evaporate as rival political factions, clans, or regions vie for power—opening the door to a dramatic expansion of terrorist and criminal activity along the lines of a failed state.

Energy Security and Competition for Supplies

Energy resources have long been a critical element of national security but globalization, unprecedented increases in demand, and the interactive effects of energy and other issues have both magnified and broadened the significance of developments in the global energy system. Oil prices have fallen by more than 25 percent since their peak last July and spare production capacity has grown to more than 2 million barrels per day. . Nevertheless we have entered a new era in which energy security has become an increasing priority not only for the U.S. and the West, but also rapidly developing economies like China and India that are becoming major energy consumers.

This means that developments in the energy arena, narrowly defined, have significant and often multiple consequences in other areas. For example, high and escalating demand for oil and gas fueled by five years of unusually robust world economic growth have resulted in higher prices and windfall profits for producers. Producer nations benefiting from higher prices, and the potential political, economic, and even military advantages include several countries that are hostile to U.S. interests.

Conclusion

Each of the national security challenges I have addressed today is affected by the accelerating change and transnational interplay that are the hallmarks of 21st century globalization. Globalization has transformed the way we communicate and conduct business, but it has also transformed the way we think about challenges and opportunities and in the way we define and confront our foes. Indeed, it is not too much of a stretch to say that events anywhere can—and often do—affect our interests and the security of our nation and our people. As a result, the Intelligence Community must maintain global coverage.

This does not mean that all places and problems are equally important. At any given point in time, we must and do accord greater attention to those that are most dangerous, most difficult, and most important to the policymakers, warfighters, and first responders who depend on information and insights from the Intelligence Community. The challenge we face is not catching up to globalization or getting ahead of globalization—it is recognizing the degree to which our national security is inextricably woven into the fabric of globalization.

In intelligence, our focus on the military, foreign, counterintelligence, and domestic dimensions of the threat must be all of a piece, seamlessly integrated to thwart attacks, prevent surprises, and provide policymakers with the time and insight they need to make decisions that will keep Americans safe. Thank you very much.

Statement of General Michael V. Hayden
Director, Central Intelligence Agency (CIA)

Thank you Mr. Chairman and members of the Committee.

The CIA is at the forefront of our nation's response to many of the challenges the DNI has just presented to the Committee. The men and women of the Central Intelligence Agency are indeed central to our nation's ability to detect, analyze, and warn of the risks and opportunities we face in an increasingly complex and fluid global environment.

Today, I will share with you briefly in open session—and more comprehensively in my classified Statement for the Record—some of the steps CIA is taking to build on our unique strengths and to help assure that the United States is able to meet the security challenges the DNI has described. This Strategic Intent—as I have discussed with the CIA workforce in recent weeks—is our roadmap to becoming a more effective organization in fulfilling our paramount mission: protecting the American people. Its central theme is integration—operating as a team within our Agency and with our Intelligence Community colleagues. We must combine our talents according to what the mission requires.

CIA must have world-class analysts who are experts in their fields and who employ rigorous analytic tradecraft in the assessments they provide policymakers—to include the U.S. Congress. We must have core collectors who are conversant in the languages and cultures of the countries in which they serve and who can collect decisive intelligence against the hardest targets from a variety of platforms. Our support specialists must have the agility and proficiency to facilitate our Agency's work anywhere in the world, often on short notice. And our science and technology officers must always give our operations an edge our adversaries cannot match. The American people expect nothing less from us.

Collection

As the National HUMINT manager, CIA is working to build an integrated national HUMINT service and working to enhance relationships with foreign intelligence services while also coordinating the Intelligence Community's relationships with foreign partners.

Our focus remains on collecting information that reveals the plans, intentions and capabilities of our adversaries and provides the basis for decision and action. It is crucial that we develop and deploy innovative ways to penetrate the toughest targets. From the perspective of CIA's collection, globalization is—as the DNI has stated—the defining characteristic of our age, requiring us to find new ways to collect key intelligence on the terrorist threat, emerging WMD proliferation, and volatile regional conflicts.

Counterterrorism

Waging a global, high-stakes war against Al Qaeda and other terrorists that threaten the United States remains a fundamental part of CIA's mission. We work on our own, with other U.S. Government agencies, and with foreign liaison partners to target terrorist leaders and cells, disrupt their plots, sever their financial and logistical links, and roil their safehavens.

- CIA's war on terror is coordinated and run from our Counterterrorism Center, or CTC, and carried out for the most part from our stations and bases overseas. CTC has both operational and analytic components, and the fusion of these two is key to success. CTC, moreover, works closely with the National Counterterrorism Center to assure protection of the homeland.

CIA's collection on terrorist targets—particularly human intelligence—has been steadily improving in both quantity and quality since 9/11.

- Access to information is a primary factor in an informant's value to us, and penetrating secretive terrorist organizations is among our greatest challenges.
- We have made significant strides in this regard—though I am extremely concerned about the damage done by rampant leaks in recent years. Besides setting back our efforts, leaks can and have led to grave consequences for our assets.

Terrorist plots and groups are not broken by single reports or sources, and no detainee knows everything about the compartmented activities of a group. Painstaking, all-source analysis is crucial to supporting and driving operations. The work of CTC has been crucial to identifying and targeting terrorists, vetting assets, and supporting overseas work.

WMD

CIA also dedicates significant resources to countering the threat posed by Weapons of Mass Destruction and associated delivery systems.

- We focus on North Korea and Iran, two states with WMD programs that threaten regional balances, U.S. interests, and international arms control mechanisms like the Nonproliferation Treaty.
- We focus on the WMD and missile programs of Russia and China, which are large enough to threaten U.S. survival if their political leaderships decided to reverse themselves and assume a hostile stance.
- We watch also for signs that other states or non-state actors may be taking early steps toward acquiring nuclear, biological, or chemical weapons.

- We also are trying to watch emerging technologies for any that might turn into the WMD of tomorrow.

Iraq and Afghanistan

In both Iraq and Afghanistan, we are working to gather critical information on terrorism, insurgency, stabilization, nation building, security issues, foreign relations, and infrastructure on both the strategic and tactical levels. A priority for our efforts is the collection of force protection intelligence to support the war fighting and counterterrorism activities of U.S. and partner forces.

In Iraq, the insurgency, sectarian violence and the role of external actors acting against Coalition goals—such as Iran and Syria—remain key features of the unstable security situation and a major focus of our collection. In Afghanistan we are working to counter Al Qaeda, Taliban, and other anti-coalition militants who threaten the stability of the Afghan state. We work closely with our military to enhance this collection in order to provide focused, significant intelligence to the policymaker.

- We maintain a very close relationship with the U.S. military on many levels, providing liaison officers dedicated to senior U.S. commanders as well as operating several working-level fusion cells to ensure all actionable intelligence is available immediately.

Open Source

To meet the challenge of global intelligence coverage that the DNI has outlined, the CIA is also playing a leading role in exploiting rapidly expanding open source information. As the executive agent for the DNI Open Source Center, CIA has elevated both the organizational status and visibility of the open source discipline, recognizing its unique and growing contributions to integrated collection and analysis within CIA and the Intelligence Community at large.

- The OSC collects from and analyzes a host of publicly available sources worldwide to alert against threats made against the United States and its citizens and to deliver the most reliable information possible to inform policymakers, warfighters, and all-source analysts throughout the government.

Analysis

Mr. Chairman, the ongoing successes of these collection and other efforts by the men and women of the CIA are also a foundation for our equally important analytic mission. Producing timely analysis that provides insight, warning and opportunity to the President and other decisionmakers is the foundation of CIA's analytic effort. As the DNI has made clear in his remarks today, we operate in an unstable and dangerous world where international terrorism, the rise of new powers, and the accelerating pace of economic and technological change are placing strains on the ability of states to govern and increasing the potential for strategic surprises.

- Our adversaries in the long war on terrorism are dispersed across the globe; they are resilient, ruthless, patient and committed to the mass murder of our citizens.
- The possession and proliferation of weapons of mass destruction threatens international stability and the safety of our homeland.
- The rise of China and India and the emergence of new economic "centers" will transform the geopolitical and economic landscape.
- Weak governments, lagging economies, and competition for energy resources will create crises in many regions.

The complexity and interdependence of these issues demands nothing less than the very best analysis. To achieve this we are pursuing a number of initiatives to continue to enhance analytic tradecraft, strengthen strategic analysis, and expand our analytic outreach.

We are making major investments in our analytic training. A 16-week course for all incoming analysts—the Career Analyst Program—has a dozen modules built around the analytic thinking process, including sessions on assumptions, framing questions, analytic tools, alternative analysis, and weighing information.

- The Sherman Kent School's 22-week Advanced Analyst Program is designed to meet the tradecraft needs of experienced analysts. Required courses focus on critical thinking, writing, briefing, and collection.

We have also established analytic tradecraft units in the analytic production offices to promote greater and consistent use of structured analytic techniques, including alternative analysis. We are developing a more consistent dialog about research programs with other IC members, with an eye toward some joint products that can draw on the comparative strengths of various IC members.

- These tradecraft cells, as well as the Red Cell, continue to produce alternative analytic papers designed to challenge conventional wisdom, lay out plausible alternative scenarios, and re-examine working assumptions. They work with analysts and with the Sherman Kent School to help ensure that stretching the analytic spectrum is a routine part of CIA's analytic work.

CIA's analysts also routinely engage academics and outside experts to critique and strengthen our analysis. Analysts organize conferences to address strategic trends, host academics and other expert speakers, and attend conferences and other events sponsored by academic associations and think tanks.

In November, CIA launched an innovative online presentation of its daily intelligence publication—the World Intelligence Review (WIRe). The WIRe online leverages the best of modern web technology to ease access to CIA's intelligence, provides links to related content, and allows users to "tag" items in whatever fashion best supports their needs.

Mr. Chairman and Members of the Committee, in closing, I would like to affirm that as we pursue our strategic goals and position ourselves to meet the threats outlined here today, we will remain true to our core values of service, integrity, and excellence. They are the constants that reflect the best of our Agency's unique history and accomplishments. These are the values that have served us well and will continue to guide us.

Thank you.

Statement of Randall M. Fort
Assistant Secretary of State for Intelligence and Research (INR)
Department of State

Thank you, Mr. Chairman and members of the Committee.

I am pleased to have the opportunity today to present the views of the State Department's Bureau of Intelligence and Research on current and projected threats to the United States. As Ambassador Negroponte has noted, the Intelligence Community is acutely aware of, and there is a broad IC consensus about, the dynamic nature of threats to U.S. interests. And INR generally shares the judgments presented by my IC colleagues.

Therefore, rather than revisit the assessments already stated, I would like to explain how INR, as the State Department's in-house intelligence unit, supports the Secretary of State and department principals by acting as what I would call an intelligence "force multiplier," identifying, assessing, and explaining the significance and relevance of threats that could jeopardize U.S. diplomatic and foreign policy interests.

As the DNI stated, it is essential that the IC has in-depth, comprehensive global coverage to identify and understand the threats we face. At the same time, the difficulties inherent in anticipating rapid and unexpected changes within global financial markets and the technology sector, for example, pose potential challenges to our defense and foreign policy establishments.

In recognition of the urgency of these new challenges, Secretary of State Rice has established "Transformational Diplomacy" as one of the engines of our foreign policy. The aim of this new approach is to re-fashion traditional diplomatic institutions and practices to serve new diplomatic purposes. Changing the world, not merely reporting on it, is the operative essence of Transformational Diplomacy.

- The Secretary's new initiative underscores the pivotal role diplomacy plays in anticipating, understanding and countering real and potential threats to vital U.S. interests. INR's mandate is to provide the timely, accurate and actionable intelligence analysis necessary to enable U.S. diplomacy to confront and address those threats and challenges, and we are uniquely placed to do so.
- It is critical that our diplomats receive intelligence and analytic support that both informs current operations and looks beyond the horizon at broader strategic dynamics, such as the effects of our democratization efforts—a key element in "Transformational Diplomacy"—on regional political stability. INR seeks to identify threats, challenges, and opportunities at an early stage to provide policymakers time to take appropriate action.

In sum, the complexities of the world in which we live have blurred traditionally discrete lines among security interests, development efforts, economic objectives, and other traditional areas of diplomatic and analytic endeavor. Consequently, INR, and the Department of State are repositioning resources to focus on and support Transformational Diplomacy.

For example, the Department aims both to increase U.S. diplomatic presence in more remote locations and prepare to react to a wide variety of humanitarian crises, including refugee flows, pandemics, and natural disasters. Naturally, INR must be ready to respond at a moment's notice and provide the intelligence support necessary to address those challenges.

Yet in an era of almost instant global awareness, the impact of our actions in one area can now be felt, or at least perceived, almost immediately elsewhere. Thus, analytical intelligence support is critical to an accurate understanding of the environment in which diplomatic initiatives are undertaken. INR is working within the Department and with our Embassies and smaller posts abroad to help policymakers both anticipate emergent crises and understand their long-term repercussions.

- INR's Humanitarian Information Unit (HIU), for example, shares broadly unclassified information via a web-based platform to facilitate coordination between U.S. government civilian and military resources and private sector humanitarian response groups. The HIU is an excellent example of an open source intelligence "force multiplier."

An informed understanding of the perceptions of U.S. policies and actions on the part of foreign publics and governments is prerequisite both to deciphering and comprehending the nature of the global environment, including potential and actual threats. Such knowledge is also critical to anticipating potential reactions to our policy initiatives and receptivity to offers of assistance generally and in crisis situations.

- To that end, INR conducts public opinion polling and focus group surveys throughout the world in order to gauge how U.S. policies are perceived, as well as how individuals in key countries perceive the role and behavior of their own governments. The sharper our understanding of the forces that drive those perceptions, the better prepared we will be to anticipate emergent threats.

The cross-cutting nature of the threats and challenges we face—especially from terrorism and weapons of mass destruction (WMD)—requires a fresh emphasis on understanding the intentions, and managing the behavior, of terror groups and related transnational actors. Regional cooperation is thus a key element of our counterterrorism strategy. Yet there are times when economic, political, and cultural barriers complicate or impede the cooperation we seek.

- Comprehensive, accurate intelligence analysis is needed to support policymakers in this regard, not only by identifying the threats, but also by ensuring a full understanding of the strengths, weaknesses, and perceptions of partners or potential partners so that policy is devised with the best information available.

Even as we seek to understand the terrorism threats faced by our allies, we must also remain vigilant to emerging trends, not only to identify threats, but to assist in identifying new potential partners and their strengths and weaknesses.

- INR prepares the annual all-source assessment of state sponsorship of terrorism that serves as the evidentiary base for the Secretary's determination regarding which states are publicly designated as state sponsors or as not-fully-cooperating with U.S. Government counterterrorism measures. The "State Sponsor's" list thereby becomes a useful diplomatic tool for building and maintaining the counterterrorism coalition.

The threat posed by "failed states" points to the critical intersections of diplomacy, democracy promotion, economic reconstruction, and military security. And INR analysts routinely monitor local and regional political dynamics, economic and financial developments, and shifts in military operations, doctrine and thinking. Deep analytic expertise is required to confidently tease apart and make sense of seemingly unrelated trends and anomalies in these areas, even if our policy colleagues might not wish to hear about them.

- To focus our perspectives and encourage analysts to look beyond immediately recognizable trends, INR publishes a quarterly report on "global hotspots" designed to alert the Secretary of State and other interested policymakers to potentially troublesome trends that we have detected.
- Our focus is on areas that may have received only limited policy attention, but where significant threats may emerge in the future. The aim is to identify areas where diplomatic action could make a difference, either by shifting the direction of a trend to forestall a threat from manifesting, or by enabling actions that could mitigate the impact of a crisis. In our first report published in early November 2006, the issues raised ranged from repercussions of electoral fallout in Mexico to concerns over political violence in Bangladesh and friction between Russia and Georgia. Policymakers were pleased with the product.

In conclusion, I believe INR's abiding challenge will be not only to maintain our vigilant watch over those threats that we know present a clear danger to U.S. interests; going forward, we must also strive to think, analyze and write strategically in order to identify the challenges and opportunities arising from the complex and dynamic global environment. Thank you very much.

Statement of Robert S. Mueller III
Director, Federal Bureau of Investigation (FBI)

In 2006, successes in the war on terrorism and the arrests of many key Al Qaeda leaders and operatives have diminished the ability of the group to attack the United States Homeland. At the same time, the growing Sunni extremist movement that al-Qa'ida successfully spearheaded has evolved from being directly led by al-Qa'ida, to a global jihadi movement that is able to conduct attacks independently.

As a result, the United States Homeland faces two very different threats from international terrorism—the attack planning that continues to emanate from core Al Qaeda overseas and the threat posed by homegrown, self radicalizing groups and individuals—inspired, but not led by Al Qaeda—who are already living in the U.S. While they share a similar ideology, these two groups pose vastly different threats due to their differences in intent and attack capability.

Al Qaeda

The United States has made significant headway in countering Al Qaeda's ability to execute attacks worldwide, including the U.S. homeland, but the group continues to pose the most serious international terrorism threat we face.

Despite the successes this year in depleting Al Qaeda's senior ranks and disrupting ongoing attack planning, the group has been able to rebuild itself and remain viable—finding new staging grounds for attacks, promoting from within, and using the skills and abilities of its seasoned veterans to continue its worldwide attack planning.

We assess Al Qaeda's strategy for conducting an attack inside the United States continues to include proven tactics and tradecraft with adaptations designed to address its losses and our enhanced security measures.

For example, we believe:

- Al Qaeda is still seeking to infiltrate operatives into the U.S. from overseas who have no known nexus to terrorism using both legal and possibly illegal methods of entry.
- We also believe, if it can, Al Qaeda will obtain and use some form of chemical, biological, radiological or nuclear (CBRN) material.
- Al Qaeda's choice of targets and attack methods will most likely continue to focus on economic targets, such as aviation, the energy sector and mass transit; soft targets such as large public gatherings and symbolic targets, such as monuments and Government buildings.

Throughout 2006, Al Qaeda made efforts to align itself with established regional terrorist groups, such as the **Salafist Group for Preaching and Com-**

bat or GSPC that may expand the scope of the threat to the Homeland. In addition, Al Qaeda is also finding it easy to attract individual members of these groups who align closer to Bin Ladin's ideology and crave a more global agenda. This strategy has been particularly successful in recruiting individuals from Pakistani and Kashmiri militant groups operating overseas as was evident in the recently disrupted Al Qaeda related airline plot out of the United Kingdom.

In a recent and rare public statement by the director of the British Security Service, Director Manningham-Buller outlined the terrorist threat the United Kingdom is currently facing and cited some sobering statistics that highlighted the continuing threat to U.S. and its allies.

- According to the BSS Director, the United Kingdom is tracking 1600 individuals who are part of at least 200 networks that are actively plotting terrorist attacks against British targets, as well as Western targets overseas. She added the United Kingdom is following at least 30 plots as of November 2006, many of which are linked to Al Qaeda in Pakistan and using British born foot soldiers living in the United Kingdom in its attack planning.

Due to the stark differences in the history, the population, and the immigrant assimilation in our two countries, it is difficult to directly compare our terrorism threat to theirs. While in general, the number of subjects we are monitoring is proportional to the number of subjects BSS is monitoring—based on gross national population—we see relatively fewer active "plots" involving physical attacks within the United States, less defined networks of extremists, and less developed attack planning compared to those described by the BSS Director.

It is also possible, however, that Al Qaeda's strategy for attacking the U.S. Homeland includes using the UK as a stepping stone for Al Qaeda operatives to enter the United States. We are working closely with our partners in the United Kingdom to counter this possible threat and to identify any U.S. connections to the UK networks currently being monitored.

Homegrown Threat

As I stated earlier, we face two different threats from international terrorism and when we look at the homegrown threat, in contrast to the threat from Al Qaeda, it is critical to be aware of the differences in intent and capability in order to understand and counter the threat. This year, we disrupted several unsophisticated, small scale attack plans that reflect the broader problem homegrown extremists pose.

- Last year, we disrupted a homegrown Sunni Islamic extremist group in California known as the **JIS, a.k.a. "Assembly of Authentic Islam,"** operating primarily in state prisons, without apparent connections or direction from outside the United States and no identifiable foreign nexus. Members of the JIS committed armed robberies in Los Angeles with the goal of financing terrorist attacks against the enemies of Islam, including the U.S. Government and supporters of Israel.

- This past summer, we arrested Narseal Batiste, the leader of a group with intentions to wage Jihad against the United States who were seeking to create their own army and government. Batiste also recognized his resource limitations, and sought to obtain material support or take direction from Al Qaeda. The group was composed mostly of U.S. persons, many of them born in the United States, and their intentions were to attack inside this country.
- Also in 2006, the FBI, along with other federal agencies and foreign partners, dismantled a global network of extremists operating primarily on the Internet and independently of any known terrorist organization. The leaders of this group, who were from Georgia, had long term goals of creating a large network of extremists in preparation for conducting attacks, possibly inside U.S.

The diversity of homegrown extremists and the direct knowledge they have of the United States makes the threat they pose potentially very serious. The radicalization of U.S. Muslim converts is of particular concern. While conversion to Islam, in itself, does not directly lead to radicalization, converts appear to be more vulnerable and likely to be placed in situations that put them in a position to be influenced by Islamic extremists.

Radicalization

In 2006, Al Qaeda and its sympathizers continued their attempts to make global jihad accessible to English-speaking Western Muslims by disseminating large amounts of violent Islamic extremist propaganda in English via media outlets and the Internet. Multiple Internet sites that are dedicated to the spread of radical Islamic propaganda, deftly exploited any and all terrorist and political events, including the war in Iraq.

Al-Sahab, Al Qaeda's official media component, released 48 videos last year, the most Al Qaeda ever released in one year. This acceleration in production is likely intended to mobilize the global jihad movement and demonstrate that Al Qaeda remains relevant and its main ideological driver.

The Internet has facilitated the radicalization process, particularly in the United States, by providing access to a broad and constant stream of extremist Islamic propaganda, as well as experienced and possibly well connected operators via web forums and chat rooms.

The Threat from other Terrorist Groups

While Al Qaeda, its affiliates and independent Islamic jihadist groups inspired by the global jihad remain the primary threat to the U.S. homeland, other groups, such as Iranian-supported Lebanese Hezbollah, warrant attention due to their ongoing fundraising, recruitment, procurement, and capability to launch terrorist attacks inside the U.S.

Shia Extremists

As seen in the summer 2006 conflict with Israel, Hezbollah has a well trained guerilla force that is proficient in military tactics and weaponry capable of striking U.S. interests. To date, Hezbollah has not conducted an attack within the U.S. homeland. Rather, U.S. Hezbollah associates and sympathizers primarily engage in a wide range of fundraising avenues in order to provide support to Hezbollah to include criminal activities such as money laundering, credit card, immigration, food stamp, and bank fraud, as well as narcotics trafficking.

- Our efforts to stem the flow of material and monetary support to Hezbollah over the past few years has led to numerous Federal indictments, including material support to a terrorist organization and federal racketeering charges, resulting in the arrest of suspected Hezbollah supporters and approximately 5 million dollars in property seizure and court ordered restitution.

Iran continues to present a particular concern due to its continued role as a state-sponsor of terrorism, its development of a nuclear program and commitment to promoting an Iranian-inspired extreme version of Shia Islam within the United States. Iran is known to support Iraqi Shia militia groups and terrorist groups such as Hezbollah and non-Shia Palestinian terrorist organizations.

Palestinian Terrorist Groups

Despite calls from Al Qaeda's Ayman Zawahiri to Palestinian terrorist groups to don the mantle of the global jihad, most Palestinian groups have maintained their longstanding policy of focusing their attacks on Israel. Additionally, the ongoing factional in-fighting between HAMAS and Fatah elements in the Palestinian territories has consumed the attention of most of the Palestinian organizations. The primary focus of U.S.-based Palestinian groups remains fundraising, propaganda for the Palestinian cause and proselytizing.

The FBI continues to make inroads into dismantling the U.S. financial infrastructures of these Palestinian terrorist organizations.

- On April 14, 2006, Sami al-Arian pled guilty to one count of conspiracy to support a designated foreign terrorist organization in violation of International Emergency Economic Powers Act and as part of the plea, admitted to material support of Palestine Islamic Jihad or PIJ.

The Threat Posed by Domestic Terrorist Groups

While much of the national attention is focused on the substantial threat posed by international terrorists to the Homeland, we must also contend with an ongoing threat posed by domestic terrorists based and operating strictly within the United States. Domestic terrorists, motivated by a number of political or social issues, continue to use violence and criminal activity to further their agendas.

Despite the fragmentation of white supremacist groups resulting from the deaths or the arrests of prominent leaders, violence from this element remains an ongoing threat to government targets, Jewish individuals and establishments, and non-white ethnic groups.

The militia/sovereign citizen movement similarly continues to present a threat to law enforcement and members of the judiciary. Members of these groups will continue to intimidate and sometimes threaten judges, prosecutors, and other officers of the court. Sporadic incidents resulting in direct clashes with law enforcement are possible and will most likely involve state and local law enforcement personnel, such as highway patrol officers and sheriff's deputies.

Some U.S.-based black separatist groups follow radical variants of Islam, and in some cases express solidarity with international terrorist groups. These groups could utilize black separatists to collect intelligence on U.S. targets or to identify radical elements within the African-American community who could act as surrogates on their behalf.

Animal rights extremism and eco-terrorism continue to pose a threat. Extremists within these movements generally operate in small, autonomous cells and employ strict operational security tactics making detection and infiltration difficult. These extremists utilize a variety of tactics including arson, vandalism, animal theft, and the use of explosive devices.

WMD Acquisition and Use by Terrorist Groups

Transnational and domestic terrorists and state sponsors of terrorism continue to demonstrate an interest in acquiring and using chemical, biological, radiological, and nuclear weapons or CBRN. CBRN weapons are advantageous for terrorists to use to cause mass casualties, mass panic, economic disruption, and summon U.S. government responses.

Few if any terrorist groups are likely to have the capability to produce complex biological or chemical agents needed for a mass casualty attack, but their capability will improve as they pursue enhancing their scientific knowledge base by recruiting scientists as some groups are doing. Currently, terrorist groups have access to simple chemical and biological agent recipes passed on at training camps or through the Internet and anarchist cookbook publications. Although a nuclear terrorist attack is the least likely to occur due to the required technical expertise and challenges associated with acquiring weapons usable material, the intent of terrorists to obtain this material is a continuing concern. The ability of a terrorist group to build and use a Radiological Dispersal Device (RDD) is well within the capability of extremists who already understand explosives if they are able to acquire radiological material.

To counter this threat, the FBI established the WMD Directorate in July 2006 to consolidate the FBI's WMD components. The Directorate integrates and links all the necessary intelligence, scientific, and operational components to detect and disrupt the acquisition of WMD capabilities and technologies for use against the U.S. homeland by terrorists and other adversaries.

WMD Proliferation and other Foreign Intelligence Threats

The U.S. government has identified 21 countries, of which Iran, North Korea, and China are of greatest concern, with the capability to either develop WMD systems or acquire export-controlled WMD and dual-use items and sensitive technologies. The FBI has leveraged its statutory authority in export matters with nexus for foreign counterintelligence activities and enhanced interagency cooperation and coordination to address this threat to U.S. national security.

From an operational perspective, FBI Headquarters, field agents, and their counterparts at DHS and the Department of Commerce have successfully conducted joint investigations that have led to arrests of individuals for violations of U.S. export laws and have produced intelligence in support of national intelligence collection requirements. The resulting intelligence has enabled the intelligence community to better understand the threat to national security from foreign government exploitation of international commerce in foreign targeting of WMD and other sensitive U.S. technologies and information.

While preventing another terrorist act on U.S. soil is the FBI's primary mission, protecting the United States from espionage and foreign intelligence operations is also of vital importance. Recent investigative successes highlight the fact that foreign governments continue to target the United States for sensitive and classified information and technology.

In 2006, the FBI arrested 20 individuals on espionage-related charges and disrupted foreign intelligence operations through *persona non grata* and other removal actions, and by objecting to visas for intelligence officers seeking entry into the United States.

- Espionage arrests include that of a Cuban-American university professor for acting as an agent of the Cuban Government. Though the professor had no direct access to classified U.S. information, one of his tasks was to spot and assess American students who may pursue a career in the U.S. Government.

Similarly, the arrests of a U.S. defense contractor and his co-conspirators for passing sensitive weapons technology to the People's Republic of China (PRC), confirm that foreign states are using non-traditional actors and methods to collect classified, sensitive, and commercially valuable proprietary information and technology. Other FBI investigations revealed trusted insiders compromising classified or sensitive information to a wide range of U.S. allies.

In 2006, the FBI identified a core group of top country threats demonstrating the intent, capability, and opportunity to target and collect information and technology in the United States using both traditional and non-traditional means.

Within this core group, two countries' targeting was both broad and deep—aimed at the United States' most sensitive technologies, such as those related to weapons of mass destruction (WMD), as well as others deemed critical to the U.S. national defense, and at the U.S. Government itself, in an attempt to penetrate organizations that set policy, collect intelligence, or protect against foreign adversaries.

While not posing as broad a threat as these two countries, the remaining top country threats engaged in activities inimical to U.S. interests, such as attempts to penetrate the U.S. Government or repeated efforts to collect sensitive or critical technologies, to include WMD. Given the United States' continuing dominance in world affairs, there is every expectation that we will continue to be targeted, by these and other countries. In response, the FBI must continue to refine and improve its foreign counterintelligence (FCI) program.

Since implementing its first National Counterintelligence Strategy in 2002, the FBI has improved its understanding of the threat. Through partnerships with other government agencies and the private and academic sectors, the FBI has not only corroborated long-standing assumptions concerning high-level foreign intelligence activities in the United States, but has detected far greater levels of activity than originally projected; stealing and compromising of classified and non-classified technologies are occurring at levels previously unknown. As a result, this year the FBI is updating its National Counterintelligence Strategy to reflect more advanced objectives and priorities. The focus of the 2007 Strategy will continue the shift from investigating activities after the fact to preventing foreign intelligence collectors from stealing our most sensitive and vital information and technologies in the first place.

Cyber Security Threats

Finally, the FBI is concerned by cyber security threats, which may come from a vast array of groups and individuals with different skills, motives, and targets. The nation's security, economy, and emergency services rely on the uninterrupted use of the Internet and telecommunications infrastructure to ensure continuity of government and military operations, financial services, transportation, and Supervisory Control and Data Acquisition (SCADA) systems such as water, power and fuel refinement, storage, and transportation.

Terrorists increasingly use the Internet to communicate, conduct operational planning, propagandize, recruit, train, store information, and obtain logistical and financial support. Foreign governments have the technical and financial resources to support advanced network exploitation, and to launch attacks on the information infrastructure and physical infrastructure. Criminal hackers can also pose a national security threat if recruited, knowingly or unknowingly, by foreign intelligence or terrorist organizations. In addition, cyber fraud activities pose a growing threat to our economy, a fundamental underpinning of our national security.

Computer networks may be targeted for a variety of reasons. In addition to the national security implications of stealing or altering military or intelligence data, a cyber attack might be launched to facilitate or amplify a physical attack, for example by disrupting critical emergency response services or denying access to health records. Finally, it is worth noting that computer networks—and our reliance upon them to enhance our national security—also remain vulnerable to physical damage by way of intentional attack or natural disaster.

Conclusion

Mr. Chairman, working closely with our partners in intelligence, law enforcement, military and diplomatic circles, the FBI's primary responsibility is to neutralize terrorist cells and operatives here in the United States and help dismantle terrorist networks worldwide. Although protecting the United States from terrorist attacks is our first priority, we remain committed to the defense of America against foreign intelligence threats as well as the enforcement of federal criminal laws, all while respecting and defending the Constitution.

Mr. Chairman, thank you for the opportunity to join my colleagues today to provide an update on our efforts to combat all threats against this nation. I look forward to working with this Committee as we continue these crucial efforts. I am happy to take any questions you might have.

Statement of Lieutenant General Michael D. Maples
Director, Defense Intelligence Agency (DIA)

Introduction

Good afternoon Chairman Rockefeller, Vice Chairman Bond, and members of the committee. Thank you for this opportunity to testify today and your continued support to the dedicated men and women of the Defense Intelligence Agency. Our nation faces a variety of complex national and transnational threats and challenges. My testimony will outline the state of the insurgencies in Iraq and Afghanistan, the current threat from global terrorism and proliferation of Weapons of Mass Destruction. Finally, I will discuss defense related developments in states and regions of concern and other transnational issues.

Conflict in Iraq

We have seen some recent developments that give hope for progress. These include efforts to address problems associated with de-Ba'athification and increased cooperation between Sunni Arab tribes and the government in al Anbar Province. Additionally, Prime Minister Maliki has made gestures to the Sunni minority such as offers to reinstall some Saddam-era military leaders and the issuance of arrest warrants for Ministry of Interior personnel accused of abuses. Some rogue elements from Muqtada al-Sadr's movement have also been expelled from his organization.

We note the continued development and increased capability of the Iraqi Security Forces (ISF) and police. The ISF will meet manning, training, and equipment milestones, improving unit capabilities. Nevertheless, the ISF will remain dependent on Coalition support. ISF units continue to struggle with militia influence and instilling discipline in their formations to gain legitimacy with the population.

Despite these positive developments, significant challenges to U.S. and Coalition Forces remain. Violence in Iraq, as measured over the past year, continued to increase in scope, complexity, and lethality. The Sunni Arab-based insurgency continues to gain strength and capacity despite progress in the political arena and positive developments in the ISF. The conflict remains a sectarian struggle for power and the right to define Iraq's future identity. Overall attacks averaged approximately 160 per day in December 2006, down from record high in October 2006 of approximately 180. The daily average of attacks against Iraqi Security Forces in December remained consistent with recent months averaging approximately 30 per day. Daily attacks on civilians in December also averaged approximately 30 per day, down from record highs in October. IED use increased in 2006 and was responsible for roughly 60% of Coalition casualties.

We have also noted a change in the character and dynamics of the conflict. The perception of unchecked violence is creating an atmosphere of fear, hardening sectarianism, empowering militias and vigilante groups, hastening a middle-class exodus, and shaking confidence in government and security forces. The sectarian violence, a weak central government, problems in providing basic services, and high unemployment are encouraging more Iraqis to turn toward sectarian groups, militias, and insurgents for basic needs, threatening the unity of Iraq. Moreover, robust criminal networks act as insurgent and terrorist force multipliers. Many Sunni Arabs, motivated by fear, financial incentive, perceptions of marginalization, and exclusion from Iraqi government and security institutions, act as insurgent sympathizers, capable of supporting the insurgency.

Since 2003, the fight to define post-Saddam Iraq has been primarily an intra-Arab conflict to determine how power and authority will be distributed. We note that conditions for the further deterioration of security and stability exist within this ongoing struggle. Although a significant breakdown of central authority has not occurred, Iraq has moved closer to this possibility because of weak governance, increasing security challenges, and the lack of a national compact.

Conflict in Iraq is in a self-sustaining and growing cycle in which violent acts increasingly generate retaliation. Insecurity rationalizes and justifies militias, in particular Shi'a militias and increases fears in the Sunni Arab community. The result is additional support, or at least acquiescence, to insurgents and terrorists such as AQI.

Shi'a militants, most notable Jaysh al-Mahdi, account for some of the increases in violence.

Baghdad is the center of the Shi'a and Sunni Arab conflict as both groups fight for territory and political influence. Sectarian attacks constitute most of the violence in mixed-ethnic areas in and around the capital, while Coalition Forces remain the primary target in the Shi'a South and Sunni West.

Iraqi Security Forces, particularly the Ministry of Interior forces, are infiltrated by members of the Supreme Council for Islamic Revolution in Iraq's Badr organization and Muqtada al-Sadr's Jaysh al-Mahdi. The Jaysh al-Mahdi often operates under the protection or approval of Iraqi Police. Many Sunnis view the ISF as a Shi'a led tool of oppression. Some Jaysh al-Mahdi cells may operate outside Sadr's direct guidance and conduct independent operations.

Attacks by terrorist groups account for only a fraction of insurgent violence, yet the high-profile nature of their operations and tactics have a disproportionate impact. Al Qaeda in Iraq (AQI) is the largest and most active of the Iraq-based terrorist groups. AQI's attacks against Iraqi government targets and Coalition Forces continue apace. AQI is one of the most visible perpetrators of anti-Shi'a attacks in Iraq and has capitalized on the current cycle of sectarian violence by increasing perceptions its operations are in defense of Sunni interests. Ansar al-Sunna, the second most prominent terrorist group in Iraq, also poses a threat to stability in Iraq and has longstanding ties to AQI and external Al Qaeda elements. Hard numbers for foreign fighters in the Iraq insurgency are unavailable. DIA judges less than 10% of insurgents are foreign fighters. The majority of these individuals are used as suicide bombers.

The building, training, and deploying of Iraqi Security Forces and police is progressing, although politicization of the security ministries remains a challenge. The ISF are meeting the manned, trained and equipped milestones, have improved unit capabilities, and are increasingly taking the lead in security operations. They remain generally dependent on Coalition support. We judge the Iraqi Security Forces are presently unable to stand alone against Sunni insurgents, Al Qaeda in Iraq and Shi'a militias. Moreover, the Iraqi Government has not yet effectively addressed core Sunni Arab grievances.

Iraqi government officials continue attempts to achieve national reconciliation, but attacks against civilians, a key driver of ethno-sectarian conflict, continue to increase. Political leaders' inability to resolve key issues such as federalism, de-Ba'athfication, amnesty for insurgents, and militia integration also contribute to continued Sunni Arab discontent, fueling support for terrorist and insurgent groups. Sectarian differences limit the effectiveness of government as groups maintain hard-line stances on contentious issues.

The Iraqi economy has experienced moderate growth despite the security situation, which continues to impede and increase overall costs of reconstruction. However, the inability to realize significant improvements in the oil and fuels sector and in electricity production and distribution creates drag on the economy while undermining the average Iraqi citizen's support for the central government and Coalition.

DIA judges that continued Coalition presence is the primary counter to a breakdown in central authority. Such a breakdown would have grave consequences for the people of Iraq, stability in the region, and U.S. strategic interests. No major political figure in Iraq has endorsed the notion of civil war or partition, and most political and religious leaders continue to restrain their communities. Moreover, DIA judges that most Iraqis recall a past in which sectarian identity did not have the significance it does today. Although leaders across the political spectrum who are participating in the government continue to talk and search for a positive way forward, the challenges to bringing stability and security with a cohesive, unified, and effective government remain significant.

Conflict in Afghanistan

The Taliban-led insurgency is a capable and resilient threat to stability in Afghanistan, particularly in the Pashtun south and east. Despite absorbing heavy combat losses in 2006, the insurgency strengthened its military capabilities and influence with its core base of rural Pashtuns. Overall attacks doubled in 2006 from the previous year. Suicide attacks quadrupled from 2005 levels and large-scale operations—those involving 50 or more fighters—increased significantly as well. A sustained international military and Afghan security presence in the volatile Pashtun south and east alongside credible civil administration is essential for solidifying central government control. Otherwise, the Afghan government may find itself in a stalemate with insurgents where it maintains control over cities and insurgents retain freedom of movement in the Pashtun dominated countryside.

Al Qaeda's strategic objectives—re-establishing the Islamic caliphate, unified by a common ideology rooted in a violent rejection of apostasy and characterized by fervent opposition to Western influence in traditionally Islamic countries—compel Al Qaeda's commitment to the Afghan jihad, help shape its strategy there, and help to recast Afghanistan as a critical battleground in a broader battle against the West and apostate regimes. In a July 2005 letter, Ayman al-Zawahiri framed the jihad in Afghanistan as a vanguard for ultimately establishing an Islamic state in the Levant, Egypt and neighboring states in the Arabian Peninsula and Iraq; multiple public statements by Zawahiri have since repeated this point.

The Afghan government is maintaining generally favorable and stable relations with most, but not all, of its neighbors. Afghanistan's relations with Pakistan are strained due to continued Taliban reliance on safe-haven in Pakistan.

In 2006, efforts by the government and provincial governors resulted in the greatest poppy eradication in four years. However, the Afghan drug trade remains a major source of revenue for insurgents and is a corrupting influence over government officials. Poppy cultivation will continue unless improved alternative livelihood programs, law enforcement, and judicial reform are implemented.

President Karzai's administration has been struggling to improve its performance and expand its presence. Although the Afghan government has established national-level political institutions by drafting a new constitution, holding a legitimate presidential election, and creating a democratically elected National Assembly, local governments receive limited resources from Kabul and struggle to provide effective governance. Additionally, the Afghan National Army and Police have been unable to effectively promote security, particularly in the volatile south and east. They remain hindered by a shortage of skilled personnel, tribal and ethnic rivalries, and corruption.

Nearly five years after the Taliban's fall, many Afghans expected the situation to be better by now and are beginning to blame President Karzai for the lack of greater progress. These unrealized expectations contributed to an erosion of support for his administration. Nevertheless, President Karzai is still the most powerful political figure in Afghanistan. President Karzai will need to secure successes in the months ahead to convince Afghans that his administration can counter and eventually defeat the Taliban. DIA assesses the Taliban led insurgency will remain a threat in 2007 and its attacks will increase this spring.

War on Terrorism

Al Qaeda and Sunni Extremists. Developments over the last year have highlighted the continuing threat posed by terrorism to the security of the United States. The United States and its allies achieved major successes against Al Qaeda and its associated movement, including the elimination or capture of key leaders and the disruption of major plots. These achievements unfortunately highlight the resiliency of these groups and resonance of their message. For example, in August 2006, British and Pakistani security disrupted an Al Qaeda cell, directed by Al Qaeda leadership in Pakistan that planned to bomb nearly a dozen U.S. airliners bound for the U.S. in mid-air. The group intended to smuggle liquid explosives aboard the aircraft and assemble and detonate the devices while the airliners were in mid-air. In June 2006, Canadian authorities detained 17 individuals who were planning a series of attacks in Ontario to include bombings, seizing Canadian Parliamentary buildings and a broadcast center, and taking hostages. Also, documents captured in a raid on an Al Qaeda in Iraq (AQI) safehouse in Iraq revealed AQI was planning terrorist operations in the U.S. The disrupted plots underscore both the accomplishments achieved in union with our partners in the War on Terrorism and the continuing danger posed by Al Qaeda. Despite being forced to decentralize its network, Al Qaeda retains the ability to organize complex, mass-casualty attacks and inspire others.

Al Qaeda remains the most dominant terrorist organization and the most significant threat to U.S. interests worldwide. In 2006, Al Qaeda remained a loose network, broadly defined by the strategic objective of re-establishing their version of an Islamic caliphate, and unified by a common ideology rooted in the violent rejection of Western influence, especially in traditionally Islamic countries. Al Qaeda has consistently recovered from losses of senior leadership. Despite the deaths and capture of key operatives, new but less experienced leaders step forward and remain committed to transnational terrorist operations, including in the United States. Additionally, Al Qaeda's increasing cooperation with like-minded groups has improved its ability to facilitate, support, and direct its objectives. For example, in his 2006 9/11 anniversary video, Zawahiri announced that the Algerian Group for Salafist Preaching and Combat formally aligned itself with Al Qaeda.

Al-Qaida senior leadership in Afghanistan and Pakistan remain under pressure from U.S. and our Global War on Terrorism partners' military and intelligence efforts, hindering their ability to direct global operations. The increased number of statements issued last year by Al Qaeda leadership, in particular Ayman al-Zawahiri, indicate the continuing strategic role Usama bin Ladin and al-Zawahiri seek to play despite their isolation. This rhetoric is designed primarily to provoke Arab and Islamic audiences to undertake militant activities, regardless of locale or affiliation, in order to broaden and deepen their perceived global struggle; it is also designed to maintain influence over that struggle, to maintain recruitment and morale, and to place local insurgencies into the context of the wider global struggle.

AQI is the largest and most deadly of the Iraq-based terrorist groups. It continues to target Iraqi government interests and Coalition Forces. AQI conducts the most provocative anti-Shi'a attacks in Iraq—a hallmark of its strategy since 2003. It has instigated cycles of sectarian violence by characterizing its operations as defending Sunni interests. Furthermore, AQI continues to pose a regional and global threat. Seized documents and interrogations reveal AQI's intent to continue external attack planning.

CBRN Terrorism. Some terrorist groups see employing chemical, biological, or radiological materials as low-cost, high-impact options for achieving their goals. Even an inefficient dissemination of these materials, or a hoax incident, could have a substantial psychological and economic impact. Reporting continues to indicate that non-state actors, specifically Al Qaeda, continue to pursue CBRN options. Usama bin Ladin has openly declared his interest in such materials since the 1990s. The recent press claim made by the Al Qaeda in Iraq leader asking for nuclear scientists to make 'germ' and 'dirty' weapons reinforces Al Qaeda's interest and desire to acquire CBRN materials. CBRN-related information is widely available, and if terrorists were to use unconventional materials in an attack, we believe they likely would use low-level biochemical agents such as ricin, botulinum toxin or toxic industrial chemicals such as cyanide. In addition to these low-level biochemical agents, Al Qaeda exhibited an interest in anthrax, mustard, and sarin prior to Operation ENDURING FREEDOM. We also judge that Al Qaeda and other terrorist groups have the capability and intent to develop and employ a radiological dispersal device. At this time, we do not believe that Al Qaeda has a nuclear weapon capability, although acquisition remains a goal; the acquisition of sufficient weapons usable nuclear material remains Al Qaeda's key obstacle to an improvised nuclear capability.

Other Terrorist Groups. Lebanese Hezbollah continues training Iraqi Shi'a militias. Hezbollah also continues to provide support to Palestinian terrorist elements to facilitate attacks in Israel. Iran's Islamic Revolutionary Guard Corps-Qods Force (IRGC-QF) has the lead for its transnational terrorist activities, in conjunction with Lebanese Hezbollah and Iran's Ministry of Intelligence and Security (MOIS).

The Revolutionary Armed Forces of Colombia (FARC) continues to view U.S. government and DoD personnel as legitimate targets in Latin America. The FARC has held three U.S. DoD contractors hostage since 2003. The possibility of the FARC targeting U.S. interests and persons will remain as long as we are directly involved in Colombian counter-drug and counter-terrorism efforts.

Islamic World. Favorable opinion of Sunni extremists is waning among Muslims worldwide. Muslim casualties in the 2005 Amman bombings accelerated the decline that began in response to Al Qaeda's attacks against Iraqi civilians. In a summer 2006 multi-country poll conducted by a U.S. NGO, approximately 25% of Jordanians expressed a lot or some confidence in Usama bin Ladin compared to 60% the year before. In Pakistan, approximately 38% of respondents stated they had some level of confidence in Usama bin Ladin, compared to 51% in May 2005.

Opinions of the West remain low in many Muslim countries. The caricatures of the Prophet Muhammad eroded the good will gleaned from U.S. relief efforts. Many Muslims believe the cartoons were deliberate insults and part of a Western besiegement of Islam. Muslim public opinion will continue to be sensitive to perceived affronts to Muslim values.

The Sunni-Shi'a divide remains largely a vehicle for Muslim power politics. Sunni and Shi'a governments will continue cooperation through their surrogates when presented with a common enemy, such as the coalition in Iraq or Israel. Where the sponsors' interests diverge—as with their spheres of influence in Iraq or on the African periphery of the Islamic world—conflict will increase as competition for influence stiffens.

Islamic extremist groups will continue to attempt to gain popular support by exploiting governments' shortcomings in governance, corruption, economic development, and provision of critical services.

Extremism in Europe remains more a secular issue than a religious one. Many within Europe's burgeoning Muslim population increasingly voice discontent through extremism and violence with Europe's integration attempts. Extremism throughout the West will continue to be spread primarily through radical clerics, the Internet, and in prisons.

Egypt. Egypt is generally supportive of U.S. goals and objectives. Most recently, President Mubarak's government has tried to mediate between HAMAS and Israel to secure the release of a captured Israeli soldier. Egypt's overall security environment is generally stable although susceptible to terrorist attacks as demonstrated by the April attacks on the Multinational Forces and Observers mission and on civilian targets in the Sinai Peninsula.

Other Persian Gulf States. Gulf Cooperation Council (GCC) states are stable, but leaders are concerned that instability in Iraq, the threat of terrorism, and a more aggressive Iran will directly affect them. Counterterrorism cooperation is improving, with pledges being made to increase regional effectiveness in the war on terrorism. There has also been progress in developing legal frameworks for the prosecution of terror planners and facilitators, although prosecution in the courts remains difficult. Despite GCC-wide acknowledgement of the Sunni extremist threat, two Sunni regimes with substantial Shi'a minorities—Saudi Arabia and Kuwait—and one with a Shi'a majority—Bahrain—have a fear of their Shi'a population's ability to threaten internal stability; a concern likely related to their fear of Iranian hegemony.

Pakistan. Pakistan's direct assistance has led to the eradication or capture of numerous Al Qaeda terrorists. A series of counterterrorism successes earlier this year—including the capture or death of several key operatives—delayed Al Qaeda attack planning and temporarily diminished leadership resources. Nevertheless, Pakistan's border with Afghanistan remains a haven for Al Qaeda's leadership and other extremists. In a September accord with the Pakistan government, North Waziristan tribes agreed to curtail attacks into Afghanistan, cease attacks on Pakistani forces and expel foreign fighters. However, the tribes have not abided by most terms of the agreement. Al Qaeda's network may exploit the agreement for increased freedom of movement and operation.

The Pakistan government remains at odds with Afghanistan over the Taliban's presence in Pakistan. Additionally, Pakistan-based militants' continued attacks against India undermine Pakistan's ability to make lasting peace with its neighbor.

Southeast Asia. Thailand continues to struggle with entrenched Muslim separatist unrest in its southern-most provinces. Approximately 400 individuals were killed in shootings, arson attacks, and bombings in 2006—approximately the same number as 2005—although we cannot confirm that all such incidents were insurgency related. The insurgency is home grown, although local Muslim extremists have sought to emphasize solidarity with "oppressed" Muslims worldwide in order to incite hatred against Thailand's Buddhist majority. The government, installed following the September coup, has adopted a conciliatory approach that it hopes will ease tensions, but the insurgency is a decentralized movement and many younger militants appear intent to continue the struggle.

Separatist unrest elsewhere in Southeast Asia has been largely contained, in part, through government reconciliation efforts. Indonesia continues to successfully advance last year's historic peace accord that ended the 29-year conflict in the Aceh province, with elections on 11 December. Sporadic separatist violence in Indonesia's Papua province poses no serious security threat. The Philippines also achieved success sustaining a ceasefire in its Muslim south with the Moro Islamic Liberation Front, although a risk of resumed fighting persists in the absence of an agreement. Elsewhere in the south, Philippine military operations since August have increased pressure on the terrorist Abu Sayyaf Group and Jemaah Islamiyah operatives on Jolo Island. These groups nonetheless are intent on continuing attacks, posing a persistent threat to American interests.

Weapons of Mass Destruction

NBC Weapons. After global terrorism, the proliferation of weapons of mass destruction (WMD) remains the most significant threat to our homeland, deployed forces, allies, and interests. Increased availability of information together with technical advances has the potential to allow many new countries to develop nuclear, biological, and chemical weapons. This is an area of increasing concern.

North Korea continues to develop its WMD capability. North Korea's October 2006 detonation of a nuclear device marked its first nuclear test and an attempt to win international recognition as a nuclear state after a decades-long program to develop these weapons. North Korea could have produced several nuclear weapons from plutonium produced at its Yongbyon facilities. Major uncertainties surround the conditions under which the North would entirely abandon its nuclear weapons capability or the likelihood of the North transferring nuclear weapons-related technology abroad. North Korea's resources include a biotechnical infrastructure that could support the production of various biological warfare agents. DIA believes North Korea has had a longstanding chemical weapons stockpile of nerve, blister, blood, and choking agents.

Iran also continues to develop its WMD capabilities. Although Iran claims its program is focused on producing commercial electric power, DIA assesses with high confidence Iran remains determined to develop nuclear weapons. In 2007, DIA expects further progress including completion of a nuclear reactor Fuel Manufacturing Plant and installation of additional centrifuges at Natanz. Iran has a growing biotechnology industry, significant pharmaceutical experience and the overall infrastructure that could be used to support a biological warfare program. DIA believes Iran is pursuing development of biological weapons. Iran has a large and growing commercial chemical industry that could be used to support a chemical agent mobilization capability.

DIA expects China's nuclear weapons stockpile to grow over the next ten years as new ballistic missile systems reach operational status. DIA also believes China has produced sufficient weapon-grade fissile material to meet its military nuclear weapons requirements for the immediate future. DIA believes China continues to maintain some elements of an offensive biological weapons program. China possesses a sufficiently advanced biotechnology infrastructure to allow it to develop and produce biological agents.

Russia maintains a full compliment of nuclear weapons. Although thousands of warheads have been dismantled, Russia relies on nuclear weapons as its primary means of deterrence and will continue to maintain and improve its forces and warheads. While we expect Russia to meet strategic nuclear warhead limits mandated by the 2002 Strategic Offensive Reduction Treaty (Moscow Treaty), we also believe they will continue to maintain a relatively large stockpile of non-strategic nuclear warheads. Russia's nuclear warhead and material security programs have improved. However, we continue to be concerned with the insider threat, terrorist attacks, and Russia's commitment to maintaining security improvements. We judge Russia also continues research and development that could support its chemical and biological warfare programs.

India and Pakistan are building larger stockpiles of fission weapons and are likely to work on advanced warhead and delivery system designs to increase the effectiveness of these weapons. Both nations have the infrastructure to support biological and some aspects of their chemical warfare programs.

Syria has pursued development of a strategic deterrent principally based on ballistic missile, chemical, and, to a limited extent, biological warfare programs, as a means of countering Israel's conventional force superiority. Syria's biotechnical infrastructure is capable of supporting limited biological agent development. DIA assesses Syria has a program to develop select biological agents. Syria has had a chemical weapons program for many years and already has a stockpile of the nerve agent sarin, which can be delivered by aircraft or ballistic missiles.

Ballistic Missiles. North Korea has an ambitious ballistic missile development program and has exported missiles and missile technology to other countries, including Iran and Pakistan. North Korea continues to develop the Taepo Dong 2, which could reach parts of the United States and is capable of carrying a nuclear payload. On 4–5 July 2006, North Korea conducted seven widely-published launches. The Taepo Dong 2 space launch vehicle / intercontinental ballistic missile was flight-tested for the first time and failed shortly after launch. Despite the failure of the Taepo Dong 2, North Korea successfully tested six theater ballistic missiles, demonstrating the capability to target U.S. forces and our allies in South Korea and Japan. North Korea is also developing a new intermediate-range ballistic missile and a new short-range, solid-propellant ballistic missile. Export of North Korea ballistic missiles will continue to be a concern.

Iran's ballistic missile forces continue to train extensively in highly publicized exercises. These exercises enable Iranian ballistic missile forces to hone wartime operations skills and new tactics. Iran continues its efforts to develop and acquire ballistic missiles capable of striking Israel and central Europe. It is fielding increased numbers of theater ballistic missile, and claimed it has incorporated anti-missile defense tactics and capabilities into its ballistic missile forces.

China continues to modernize and expand its ballistic missile forces to improve survivability and conventional war-fighting capabilities. It also continues to field an overwhelming number of conventional short-range ballistic missiles opposite Taiwan and is currently developing a number of new mobile conventional medium range systems.

Beyond increasing the capabilities of its theater ballistic missile force, China continues to develop and test three strategic long-range missile systems—the DF-31 and DF-31A road-mobile ICBMs and the JL-2 SLBM. China remains committed to developing conventional ballistic missiles capable of targeting U.S. and allied military assets in the region to deter intervention in a Taiwan crisis.

Russia remains committed to maintaining formidable strategic nuclear forces as a credible nuclear deterrent and symbol of great power status. Russia began fielding its new road-mobile SS-27 intercontinental ballistic missile in 2006 and fielding silo-based variants is ongoing.

Cruise Missiles. Advances in anti-ship cruise missiles, land-attack cruise missiles, and armed unmanned aerial vehicles will continue to threaten deployed U.S. forces and our allies. The number of systems achieving operational status, exports, and the sale of dual-use technology continues to fuel this threat. Advancements in anti-ship cruise missiles including the capability for land-attack will present a challenge in countering these missiles.

China's development of a Tomahawk-class ground-launched land-attack cruise missile continues and will enable it to execute strikes in the Asian theater. Iran continues to pursue development and production of improved anti-ship cruise missiles. During the conflict with Israel, Lebanese Hezbollah became the first non-state actor to launch an anti-ship cruise missile. In several unsuccessful attacks, Hezbollah also launched probable Iranian-supplied unmanned aerial vehicles; at least one was armed with explosives. Pakistan continues flight-testing indigenous land-attack cruise missiles. The Indian Navy has begun taking delivery of the ship-launched version of the Russian/Indian Brahmos supersonic anti-ship cruise missile.

Major Exporters. North Korea and entities in Russia and China continue to sell technologies applicable to WMD and missiles for revenue and diplomatic influence.

Russian entities continue to support missile programs and civil nuclear and biotechnology projects in other countries. Some of these projects can have weapons applications.

Chinese entities continue to supply key technologies to countries with WMD and missile programs, though it appears to be living up to its 1997 pledge to limit nuclear cooperation with Iran.

North Korea remains committed to selling missiles and related technologies. Although sales have declined to most customers due to its increasing international isolation, North Korea's relationship with Iran and Syria remain strong and of principal concern.

Non-governmental entities and individual entrepreneurs remain a concern. Past revelations regarding the A.Q. Khan nuclear proliferation network demonstrate how a complex network of suppliers with the requisite expertise and access to the technology, middlemen, and front companies can successfully circumvent international controls and support multiple nuclear weapons programs. Other examples of WMD-related supplier networks include those headed by Chinese national Q.C. Chen, which operated various supplier organizations over the past several years. Chen has been subjected to U.S. sanctions in violation of the Iran Non-Proliferation Act.

Other States and Regions Of Concern

North Korea. We judge North Korea's missile launches and nuclear test were in part intended to improve its bargaining position at Six-Party Talks. DIA expects North Korea to continue to seek relaxation of U.S. financial actions against its banking interests and eventual recognition as a nuclear power.

North Korean military forces continue to suffer the consequences of the North's economic decline. Nevertheless, they remain capable of initiating an attack on South Korea. Its large force provides the regime with an effective deterrent against the prosperous and modern South and the self-perceived option of employing threats to further North Korean national security goals.

No immediate prospect of regime collapse is evident. Kim Jong H continues to maintain tight control over the military, government, and communist party. North Korea's pervasive ideological indoctrination has helped foster extreme nationalism which contributes to the strength of the regime.

Levant Conflict. The Israel Defense Forces (IDF) damaged some of Hezbollah's arsenal and many of its buildings, but Hezbollah's leadership remains unscathed and probably has already replenished its weapons stockpiles with Iranian and Syrian assistance. Lebanon was compelled to deploy the Lebanese Armed Forces (LAF) to the south, though the LAF has not moved to disarm Hezbollah. Additionally, the Lebanese government has now been told it is accountable for what occurs on all Lebanese territory as a result of UN Security Council Resolution 1701.

Hezbollah leaders claimed victory and grew more assertive in their political demands as demonstrated by ongoing opposition demonstrations in Beirut. Hezbollah is currently focused on asserting political dominance in Lebanon. Iran and Syria remain committed to Hezbollah's survival. Israeli defense officials have publicly opined that due to the fluid situation the conflict could reignite during the summer of 2007.

Iran. Iran continues to push for a reduced U.S. military presence in the Persian Gulf and Central Asia and weakened ties between the U.S. and its key Arab allies. Iran does not expect to militarily defeat any U.S.-led coalition. Rather, it seems intent on imposing greater costs than western leaders and publics are willing to bear. As shown in its highly publicized Noble Prophet exercises, Iran intends to rely on asymmetric tactics, using its ballistic missiles, naval attacks in the restricted waters along its coast against U.S. forces, and possibly a strategic terror campaign to disrupt U.S. war plans. Iran has sought to improve its capabilities through equipment upgrades, procurement, and exercises. Iran may be in the process of receiving the SA-15 air defense system from Russia, adding to its short-range air defense capability. Iran may also eventually acquire other advanced defense systems. Anti-ship cruise missiles, a small boat fleet, sea mines, and submarines comprise Iran's efforts to contest access to the Persian Gulf.

Meanwhile, Iran is attempting to expand its own regional influence. Iran seeks to bring Iraq into its sphere of influence and is providing economic aid to both win Iraqi hearts and minds and to gain an economic foothold. Iran is assisting Iraq's infrastructure needs; it recently agreed to supply kerosene to Kurdish areas, and intends to build a gas pipeline and rail lines between the two countries. Iran is also suspected of providing lethal aid to Shi'a elements.

Iran probably is pursing a dual-track policy in Afghanistan of publicly promoting Afghan stability, while possibly supporting some insurgent groups. This approach reflects Iran's intent to maximize political influence, hedge against uncertainty in Afghanistan by building relationships with several groups, and maintain pressure on U.S. forces.

Iran also continues to support Hezbollah for countering Israeli and U.S. efforts in the region, especially after Hezbollah's perceived success against Israel during clashes in July 2006.

Syria. Syria continues to support and help arm Hezbollah to protect Syrian interests in Lebanon and provide leverage against Israel, which it continues to view as its greatest threat. Syrian interference in Lebanon is likely to continue, aimed at influencing Lebanon's policies on Hezbollah, Israel, and the UN investigation of the assassination of former Lebanese Prime Minister Hariri.

The Syrian leadership is trying to balance a complex mix of objectives in Iraq. These include preventing U.S. success in Iraq and encouraging our eventual withdrawal, while at the same time improving relations with the Baghdad government, supporting a unified Iraq, and avoiding a full-blown Iraqi civil war. Syria remains the primary insurgent gateway into Iraq due to corruption, smuggling networks, and cross-border tribal ties.

Syria continues to make minor improvements to its conventional forces. It did not make any major weapons acquisitions in 2006, continuing a trend begun in the mid-1990s. Instead, the Syrian military has focused its limited defense procurement dollars on low cost-high impact weapons such as anti-tank guided missiles, advanced tactical surface-to-air missiles like the SA-24, and upgrades to existing platforms. Syria also maintains an active chemical weapons program.

We judge the regime is generally stable with no cohesively organized opposition supported by a domestic constituency. The regime considers Islamic extremism its greatest internal threat.

China. The People's Republic of China (PRC) is in the midst of a more-than-decade-long military modernization program. The program's announced defense budget in 2006 was approximately $35 billion—a 14% increase from 2005—but we assess actual spending to be higher. PRC leaders remain focused on improving the quality of military personnel and developing or acquiring long-range, precision-strike missiles, modern fighter aircraft, a blue-water navy, and improved amphibious forces. China took delivery of the final three SS-N-27B-capable KILO-class submarines over the past year, completing its contract with Russia for eight of these submarines. China continued fielding its first indigenously built fourth-generation F-10 fighters. In addition, China remains focused on counterterrorism, domestic security, and maritime deployments, which hone its ability to respond to domestic instability and tensions in the East China or South China Seas.

China's strategic course appears to focus primarily on internal issues, and its foreign policy is driven by several related internal concerns: continuing economic development, maintaining communist party control, and safeguarding internal stability.

Recent PRC publications assert China's commitment to peaceful development. However, a major driver of Chinese foreign policy is the acquisition of adequate supplies of resources and materials for its development. China's energy demands, particularly petroleum, have risen sharply. China is the world's second largest consumer and third largest importer of oil, importing over 40 percent of its needs. China's continued search for energy may become a point of contention between itself and the West, potentially affecting its policy towards Iran, a key Chinese energy supplier.

Unification with Taiwan remains a long-term national goal. China's cross-strait policy through the Taiwan Presidential Elections in 2008 is to "prevent Taiwan independence." As long as Taiwan takes no further action toward independence, we judge China—assessing long-term military, economic, and diplomatic trends favors its interests—will not try to force unification. Also, recent political difficulties by Taiwan's President Chen Shui-bian probably reassured China's leaders over the course of its present policy.

China remains committed to resolving North Korea's nuclear issue through the Six-Party Talks. However, North Korea's provocative nuclear weapons test and multiple missile launches, including the Taepo Dong 2, most likely prompted China to be more discriminating in its support for the North, as indicated by its UN Security Council votes supporting international sanctions on the Kim Jong Il regime.

Russia. Presidential succession politics will preoccupy Russia over the next two years. As the end of President Putin's second term draws near in 2008, the battle for power and property will take increasing precedence over policymaking. We judge defense policy will not be a significant issue in the campaign and, whichever candidate is elected, it will not likely result in significant changes in Russian defense policy the first year in office.

Russian leaders view a strong military as a necessary component to return their country to great power status. They believe Russian strategic and non-strategic nuclear capabilities are key factors in deterring aggression. To meet future mission requirements, modernization initiatives are ongoing, with primary emphasis on the SS-27 ICBM and Bulava SLBM strategic systems. In the general purpose forces, training activity within units of the Permanently Ready Force (PRF), which form the backbone of Russia's conventional capability, is at their highest post-Soviet level. In 2006, Russian military participation in exercises with foreign militaries increased by over 50 percent over the 2005 level. No 2006 exercise rose to the significance of the 2005 Russo-Chinese exercise, although additional Russian naval exercises in the Black Sea and an increased number of air/ground exercises with Central Asian and European countries were notable. Modernizing the country's outdated equipment and planning conversion to all-contract manning remain significant challenges despite increased defense spending. Converting the PRF to an all-volunteer force is likely to take longer than planned, since Russia is having significant problems in both attracting new and retaining already-signed contractees. Dissatisfaction comes primarily from perceived low pay, hostile service conditions, inadequate housing, poor family support, and other unfulfilled government promises.

Russia has made progress in suppressing North Caucasus separatists by employing more effective counterinsurgency operations and co-opting insurgents to fight former compatriots. Although weakened, small insurgent groups continue attacks on Russian targets in the region.

Russia opposes closer integration of former Soviet countries with the West. It has been especially adamant that Georgia abandon its western-leanings and has condemned the Georgian government for its "anti-Russian" policies. Russia remains steadfast in its peacekeeping commitments in the Georgian separatist area of Abkhazia and South Ossetia, although its presence there is a source of contention between Russia and Georgia.

Russia opposes comprehensive sanctions on Iran, in part to protect its own economic interests with Iran. Russia continues to press Iran to cease uranium enrichment activities, if only temporarily, and tone down its inflammatory rhetoric.

Russia's primary focus on the North Korean nuclear issue is to prevent an escalation to war. It stresses the necessity of the Six-Party Talks to resolve the conflict in a peaceful way. Russia viewed North Korea's October 2006 nuclear test as a blow to the nonproliferation regime.

Latin America. Nearly a dozen presidential elections in 2006 produced winners ranging from pro-business center-right to market-friendly social democrats and radical populists. Venezuela's President Chavez hardly won re-election and is following his mentor, Cuban President Fidel Castro, and President Chavez's vision for the continent. Venezuela cooperates with Cuban projects abroad. Key to this ideology is President Chavez's agenda to neutralize U.S. influence throughout the hemisphere. Regional military spending is increasing, Venezuelan purchased weapons and services from Russia, Iran, and China. Since 2005, Venezuela signed contracts with Russia for 24 Su-30MK2 advanced fighter aircraft, 50 transport and attack helicopters, and 100,000 assault rifles. President Chavez found allies in the newly-elected presidents of Bolivia and, to a lesser extent, Ecuador, and Nicaragua.

Other center-left leaders in Latin America have found common ground with the U.S. on a variety of issues. Chile's President Bachelet is a model for the reformist left in Latin America. She promotes democratic institutions, supports free trade, and favors constructive engagement with the U.S. Peru's recently-elected President Garcia continues to publicly oppose President Chavez's Bolivarian vision. Brazil's President Lula has his own vision of regional solidarity and eschews President Chavez's strident rhetoric. Early indications suggest Nicaragua's president-elect Ortega will also follow a pragmatic approach to governing, including pursuing free trade agreements.

In Cuba, Raul Castro is firmly in control as Cuba's acting president and will likely maintain power and stability after Fidel Castro dies, at least for the short-term. Raul Castro has widespread respect and support among Cuban military leaders who will be crucial in permanent government succession.

Africa. While there has been progress towards democracy and the diplomatic resolution of conflict in much of Africa, such advances remain fragile. In Sudan, despite a peace agreement that ended a 21-year long civil war between the north and south, violence and human insecurity in Darfur, Sudan are the worst since 2003-2004. Sudan is pursuing a military solution, using Arab "Janjaweed" militias to attack rebels and civilians. The African Union Mission in Sudan (AMIS) lacks the capacity to contain the violence, but the Sudanese government continues to oppose converting AMIS into a

UN force. Since 2003, fighting has displaced over 2.2 million people, resulted in over 200,000 deaths, and contributed to instability in neighboring Chad and Central African Republic. Finally, statements from senior Al Qaeda leaders have advocated attacks against UN or NATO peacekeepers if deployed to Darfur, creating an additional threat to Western forces.

In Nigeria, upcoming presidential elections will test the strength of the fledgling democracy as the public prepares for the first civilian-to-civilian transfer of power since independence. The potential for violence remains high as candidates from the predominantly Muslim north and Christian south compete for office. Among the leading issues is administration of Nigeria's oil wealth. Violence over control and access to oil in the Niger Delta has resulted in the kidnapping of oil workers, destruction of oil facilities, and a 25% reduction in oil production over the past year. Nigerian security forces have been unable to secure the vast oil infrastructure from militant attacks. Some oil companies warn that continued violence may prompt them to curtail future operations.

In Somalia, Ethiopian forces and the Ethiopian-backed Somali Transitional Federal Government (TFG) forces have forced Council of Islamic Courts (CIC) radical Islamists from Mogadishu. CIC forces have fled south to Kismayo and Ras Kamboni on the Kenyan border with Ethiopian forces in pursuit. Ethiopia likely intends to eliminate as many of the radical Islamists and their camps as possible before withdrawing. The TFG remains dependent on Ethiopia for its existence. Meanwhile, multiple reports indicate the presence of foreign trainers in Somalia from Afghanistan, Pakistan, and the Arabian Peninsula. Al Qaeda is assessed to be assisting the radical Islamist elements of the CIC with leadership and training with hopes of establishing a future Taliban-like state.

Transnational Issues

Insurgencies. Insurgencies continue in other parts of the world. The only major insurgency in Latin America is the Revolutionary Armed Forces of Colombia (FARC). Its power and scope has waned under President Uribe's counterinsurgency efforts and that trend is expected to continue in 2007. Additionally, President Uribe may reach a peace agreement with the National Liberation Army (ELN), Colombia's second largest insurgent group. Colombia will also continue efforts to complete the complex paramilitary demobilization. In Sri Lanka, fighting between government forces and the Liberation Tigers of Tamil Eelam (LTTE) intensified since last summer. The situation is likely to remain unstable, marked by flare-ups of fighting and LTTE bombings and assassinations. Clashes between government and rebel forces in Eastern Chad continue. The looting of the UN humanitarian key supply point in Abeché during the most recent attacks has impeded international humanitarian efforts in eastern Chad. Recent government successes against rebels have diminished insurgent violence in eastern Chad and reduced the prospects of an imminent rebel attack toward N'djamena. Inter-tribal violence between black African and Arab tribes continues fueling tensions along the Chadian-Sudanese.

Global Defense Spending. Non-U.S. global defense spending grew in real terms by 2.5 percent in 2006, amounting to an estimated $738 billion. China ranked first with estimated spending of $80-115 billion. Russia was second at about $90 billion. The top ten countries account for almost two-thirds of total spending, or $480 billion. Of the top ten spenders, China and South Korea increased spending in real terms the most, by 9.6 percent and 9.9 percent respectively. Surging economies allowed Russian defense spending to grow an estimated 6.4 percent and Indian by 4.2 percent. Defense spending by oil exporters, Iran and Venezuela, grew 6.7 percent and 12.5 percent respectively. We judge these trends will continue in 2007.

China and India are major buyers of advanced weapons systems and military technology, with acquisitions for the past two years of $3.4 billion and almost $12 billion, respectively. When combined with joint doctrine, increased training, and supported by adequate logistics, these advanced systems have the ability to significantly improve military capabilities. Venezuela emerged as a major arms buyer with acquisitions valued at $4.3 billion for the past two years. Venezuela has turned to Russia for hi-tech weaponry, including multi-role fighters with advanced air-launched missiles. Pakistani and Iranian purchases also have grown in the past two years, with Pakistan signing arms contracts worth almost $3 billion and Iran almost $1.7 billion.

Russia and China are of particular note as proliferators of conventional weapons. Russia is a leading arms exporter, with major sales of advanced weapons and military-related technology to China, India, Iran, and Venezuela. Items include multi-role fighter aircraft, ground equipment, major surface combatants and submarines, advanced air defense systems, and sophisticated communication and radar systems. Chinese sales declined to approximately $500 million in 2006 after surging to over $2 billion in 2005. China is a leading supplier to Sub-Saharan Africa.

International Crime. Some terrorist organizations, primarily the FARC and the Taliban, derive income from opiates and stimulants in drug-producing regions, like Afghanistan, South America, and Asia. In addition to direct profits from drug sales and the distribution of opiates and narcotics, some groups, like the Taliban, derive income from taxation along the drug trafficking route. For the Revolutionary Armed Force of Columbia (FARC), the drug-trade is an integral source of revenue. Some South America based supporters of Lebanese Hezbollah are suspected of sending a portion of their profits from narcotics trade to the group in Lebanon.

Space and Space-Denial Capabilities. Russia and China continue to be the primary states of concern regarding military space and counter-space programs.

However, as the availability of space technology and services continues to increase, other nations already possessing capabilities in key areas will acquire military and commercial space-based assets. Increasing levels of international cooperation, along with the growing number of commercial space consortia, is allowing the proliferation of advanced satellite technologies and knowledge of space systems operations to become available to nations lacking a domestic space capability. These developments provide some countries new or more capable communications, reconnaissance, and targeting capabilities as most space systems have dual-use, military-civilian applications.

Several countries continue to develop capabilities that have the potential to threaten U.S. space assets, and some have already deployed systems with inherent anti-satellite capabilities, such as satellite-tracking laser range-finding devices and nuclear-armed ballistic missiles. A few countries are seeking improved space object tracking and kinetic or directed energy weapons capabilities. However, developing these technologies is financially taxing, and most countries assessed to be pursuing these capabilities are not expected to acquire them within the next few years. Other states and non-state entities are pursuing more limited and asymmetric approaches that do not require excessive financial resources or a high-tech industrial base. These efforts include denial and deception, electronic warfare or signal jamming, and ground segment physical attack.

Information Operations (IO). Information technology (IT) is integral to virtually all aspects of U.S. national and economic security. IT also is a truly global industry, and the U.S. is growing ever more dependent on foreign suppliers in order to maintain our political, military, and economic position. The increasing role of international companies and foreign individuals in information technologies and services used by U.S. critical infrastructures raises the specter of persistent, stealthy subversion, particularly by hostile foreign intelligence and military services with computer network operations (CNO) capabilities, but also by international terrorist or criminal organizations. The exclusion of foreign-origin products from sensitive networks or applications will become increasingly difficult to implement or verify.

Russia has the most highly developed, capable, and well-resourced IO capability among potential foreign adversaries. Russian foreign and military intelligence, as well as the Russian Security Service, have active offensive and defensive CNO programs. Assessed capabilities include insider recruitment, cryptology, viruses, software and hardware attacks, and remote penetration.

China has developed an apparent large scale CNO program, including military exercises to refine and implement concepts. China's robust presence in the global IT hardware and software supply chain enhances its technical expertise and IO capability. China is the number one IT hardware provider for U.S. consumers, accounting for 42 percent of U.S. IT hardware imports in 2005. As such, U.S. dependence on China for certain items critical to the U.S.

defense industry and the waning of U.S. global IT dominance are valid concerns that demand vigilance.

Public Health Security. The uncontrolled spread of disease remains a significant international health concern. A nation's inability to control or contain diseases within its borders can have a negative impact worldwide. Conversely, rapid and effective responses enhance international safety. Thailand recently limited the spread of the H5N1 avian influenza by rapidly controlling outbreaks among poultry. Indonesia's continued struggle to control H5N1 raises the risk for an international pandemic. H5N1 remains a serious threat, with approximately 110 human infections and 80 deaths in 2006. H5N1 is only one of many potential infectious threats.

Damage to industrial or hazardous material storage facilities during armed conflict also poses catastrophic health risks. During Hezbollah missile attacks in July 2006, Israel moved significant amounts of potentially hazardous materials from the Haifa area to prevent the potential release of toxic industrial chemicals. Trans-boundary environmental issues also pose health and security threats. In 2006, in Cote d'Ivoire, the illegal dumping of hazardous waste shipped from other countries resulted in 10 deaths and triggered mass demonstrations.

Underground Facilities. The rising importance of hardened or deeply buried facilities to potential adversarial nations and non-national organizations is becoming more apparent each year. Whether those nations and non-government organizations are classified as rogue, major, or emerging powers, or terrorist groups, their critical military, leadership and national security assets are increasingly protected by these facilities. The growth and sophistication of Hard and Deeply Buried Targets (HDBTs) is especially significant among countries whose support for terrorism and potential possession of WMD constitute threats to world peace and U.S. Security. Of concern is what these countries have learned from recent U.S. military successes over the last decade in the Balkans, Afghanistan and Iraq. Their new and modified facilities incorporate features that make them more survivable against known U.S. weapons. Moreover, these countries are exporting underground construction techniques, and construction equipment.

Conclusion

Our nation is engaged in a long war against terrorism and violent extremism. We are faced with a multitude of issues and events that affect our national security. The intelligence professionals of the Defense Intelligence Agency will continue to provide critical information to our warfighters, defense planners, and national security policy makers. In concert with our fellow Intelligence Community members and allies, we are supporting our Soldiers, Sailors, Airmen and Marines engaged in combating insurgents in Iraq and Afghanistan and terrorists globally. This effort remains our first priority. We are also focusing considerable resources to prevent or counter the proliferation of Weapons of Mass Destruction. Finally, we are carefully monitoring states of concern and other transnational issues.

Over the past few years, the Defense Intelligence Agency, like the rest of the Intelligence Community, has made major strides to improve our core business processes of intelligence collection, all-source analysis, and information management. With your support, the Defense Intelligence Agency has expanded our human and technical collection. Our human intelligence collectors are better trained, supported, and integrated with their Intelligence Community counterparts and our own military forces across the globe. In all-source analysis, we have increased the number of analysts with advanced and technical degrees. Those analysts are equipped with better information technology systems and more rigorously trained in the use of cutting edge analytic techniques. Improvements in our information management systems and procedures are critical to achieving the information sharing environment mandated by the Intelligence Reform and Terrorism Prevention Act. Today analysts, collectors, and our customers, to include national security policy makers, warfighters, the weapons acquisition community, law enforcement agencies, and our coalition partners, are better connected and have greater access to our information and all-source analysis. Much has been accomplished; however, more needs to be done. With your continued support, I am confident we will achieve greater levels of security for our citizens, our national interests, and those of our allies. Thank you.

DOCUMENT NO. 12

FOREIGN STUDENTS IN THE UNITED STATES: POLICIES AND LEGISLATION

CRS Report
RL31146

May 11, 2007

Chad C. Haddal
Analyst in Immigration Policy
Domestic Social Policy Division
Congressional Research Service

Summary

Five years after the September 11, 2001, terrorist attacks by foreign nationals—including several terrorists on students visas—the security concerns over foreign student visas are being weighed against competitiveness concerns. Potential foreign students, as well as all aliens, must satisfy Department of State (DOS) consular officers abroad and immigration inspectors upon entry to the United States that they are not ineligible for visas under the so-called "grounds for inadmissibility" of the Immigration and Nationality Act, which include security and terrorist concerns. The consular officers who process visa applicants are required to check the consolidated Terrorist Screening Database (TSDB) before issuing any visa. In part because of these security measures, student visa debates have expanded to include both security and market-based discussions.

Higher education institutions in the United States are concerned over their ability to attract the numbers and quality of foreign students, and whether the post-September 11 security measures impede the entry of potential students into the U.S. education system. The fields of science, technology, engineering and mathematics (STEM) increasingly rely on foreign students, and these fields hold a top priority with most research institutions. Furthermore, the U.S. economy has a high demand for the skill-sets produced in these fields of study, and the STEM students often provide a major link between the academic community and the labor market. Consequently many groups in higher education and the private sector are seeking to expand pathways for foreign students to emigrate.

All non-immigrant students are issued visas from one of three categories, and are monitored and tracked by the Department of Homeland Security (DHS). The three visa categories used by foreign students are F visas for academic study; M visas for vocational study; and J visas for cultural exchange. The numbers admitted have more than doubled over the past two decades. In FY1979, the total number of foreign student and cultural exchange visas issued by DOS consular officers was 224,030 and comprised 4% of all non-immigrant visas issued. In FY2005, DOS issued 565,790 visas to F, J, and M non-immigrants, making up 10.5% of all non-immigrant visas issued. The Student and Exchange Visitor Information System (SEVIS) aims to manage the tracking and monitoring of foreign students. Participation in the SEVIS program is now mandatory for all higher education institutions enrolling foreign students.

Issues related to foreign students continue to arise. Foreign student funding, as well as English-language competency, have raised concerns with some universities, advocacy groups, and other observers. Additionally, some recent legislation has focused on attracting foreign students in STEM fields. Legislation introduced in the House (H.R. 1645) and in the Senate (S. 1348) would create pathways to legal permanent residence for foreign students in the STEM fields of study. Although there are provisions in this legislation for undergraduate students, the emphasis has been on students obtaining advanced degrees. This report will be updated as warranted.

Background[1]

Since the Immigration Act of 1924, the United States has expressly permitted foreign students to study in U.S. institutions. Most foreign students are at least 18 years old and are enrolled in higher education programs. If they attend public high schools in the United States, the law requires that foreign students pay tuition, with some exceptions. It also bars the admission of foreign students for the purpose of attending public elementary schools. Although foreign students are also barred from receiving federal financial assistance, many are successful at gaining financial assistance from the colleges and universities they attend.[2]

Foreign students are generally considered to enrich cultural diversity of the educational experience for U.S. residents as well as enhance the reputation of U.S. universities as world-class institutions. Concerns have arisen in recent years that have caused Congress to take a new look at the Immigration and Nationality Act (INA) provisions that govern their admission. The September 11, 2001 terrorist attacks conducted by foreign nationals—including several terrorists on foreign student visas—raised a series of questions about foreign students in the United States, their rights and privileges, the extent to which the U.S. government monitors their presence in this country, and whether U.S. policy hampers the ability of domestic higher education institutions to attract foreign students.

Foreign Student Visas

There are three main avenues for students from other countries to temporarily come to the United States to study, and each involves admission as a non-immigrant. A non-immigrant is an alien legally in the United States for a *specific purpose* and a *temporary period* of time. There are more than 20 major non-immigrant visa categories, and they are commonly referred to by the letter that denotes their subsection in the law.[3] The three visa categories used by foreign students are F visas for academic study; M visas for vocational study; and J visas for cultural exchange.

F Visa

The most common visa for foreign students is the F-1 visa. It is tailored for international students pursuing a full-time academic education. The F-1 student is generally admitted as a non-immigrant for the period of the program of study, referred to as the duration of status.[4] The law requires that the student have a foreign residence that they have no intention of abandoning. Their spouses and children may accompany them as F-2 non-immigrants.

To obtain an F-1 visa, prospective students also must demonstrate that they have met several criteria:

- They must be accepted by a school that has been approved by the Attorney General.[5]
- They must document that they have sufficient funds or have made other arrangements to cover all of their expenses for 12 months.[6]
- They must demonstrate that they have the scholastic preparation to pursue a full course of study for the academic level to which they wish to be admitted and must have a sufficient knowledge of English (or have made arrangements with the school for special tutoring, or study in a language the student knows).

Once in the United States on an F visa, non-immigrants are generally barred from off-campus employment. Exceptions are for extreme financial hardship that arises after arriving in the United States and for employment with an international organization.[7] F students are permitted to engage in on-campus employment if the employment does not displace a U.S. resident. In addition, F students are permitted to work in practical training that relates to their degree program, such as paid research and teaching assistantships. An alien on an F visa who otherwise accepts employment violates the terms of the visa and is subject to removal and other penalties discussed later in this report.

J Visa

Foreign students are just one of many types of aliens who may enter the United States on a J-1 visa, sometimes referred to as the Fulbright program. Others admitted under this cultural exchange visa include scholars, professors, teachers, trainees, specialists, foreign medical graduates, international visitors, au pairs, and participants in student travel/work programs. Those seeking admission as a J-1 non-immigrant must be participating in a cultural exchange program that the U.S. Department of State's Bureau of Educational and Cultural Affairs (BECA)[8] has designated. They are admitted for the period of the program.[9] Their spouses and children may accompany them as J-2 non-immigrants.

Responsible officers of the sponsoring organizations must be U.S. citizens. The programs that wish to sponsor J visas also must satisfy the following criteria:

- be a bona fide educational and cultural exchange program, with clearly defined purposes and objectives;
- have at least five exchange visitors annually;
- provide cross-cultural activities;
- be reciprocal whenever possible;
- if not sponsored by the government, have a minimum stay for participants of at least three weeks (except for those designated as "short term" scholars);
- provide information verifying the sponsoring program's legal status, citizenship, accreditation, and licensing;
- show that they are financially stable, able to meet the financial commitments of the program, and have funds for the J non-immigrant's return airfare;
- ensure that the program is not to fill staff vacancies or adversely affect U.S. workers;
- assure that participants have accident insurance, including insurance for medical evacuations; and
- provide full details of the selection process, placement, evaluation, and supervision of participants.[10]

As with F visas, those seeking J visas must have a foreign residence they have no intention of abandoning. However, many of those with J visas have an additional foreign residency requirement in that they must return abroad for two years if they wish to adjust to any other non-immigrant status or to become a legal permanent resident in the United States. This foreign residency requirement applies to J non-immigrants who meet any of the three following conditions:

- An agency of the U.S. government or their home government financed in whole or in part—directly or indirectly—their participation in the program.
- The BECA designates their home country as clearly requiring the services or skills in the field they are pursuing.
- They are coming to the United States to receive graduate medical training.

There are very few exceptions to the foreign residency requirement for J visa holders who meet any of these criteria—even J visa holders who marry U.S. citizens are required to return home for two years.[11] Although many aliens with J-1 visas are permitted to work in the programs in which they are participating, the work restrictions for foreign students with a J-1 visa are similar to those for the F visa.

M Visa

Foreign students who wish to pursue a non-academic (e.g., vocational) course of study apply for an M visa. This visa is the least used of the foreign student visas. Much as the F students, those seeking an M visa must show that they have been accepted by an approved school, have the financial means to pay for tuition and expenses and otherwise support themselves for one year, and have the scholastic preparation and language skills appropriate for the course of study. Their spouses and children may accompany them as —2 non-immigrants. As with all of the student visa categories, they must have a foreign residence they have no intention of abandoning. Those with M visas are also barred from working in the United States, including in on-campus employment.

Duration of Status Visa

Although most non-immigrants are admitted with visas that have a precise expiration date, foreign postsecondary students are admitted for "duration of status," which lasts as long as they are full-time students or participating according to the terms of their exchange programs. It is difficult for DHS to know when foreign students have overstayed because the duration of status lacks a fixed termination date and schools, although required to report students who stop attending, have not been required until recently to systematically report data on the progress of the foreign student (see below).

For many years, a foreign student was admitted for only one year and had to renew his or her visa each subsequent year for as long as he or she was enrolled. The former-INS then issued regulations in 1978 and 1981 allowing for visa validity periods longer than one year. In regulations in 1983 and 1987 that were aimed at "eliminating burdensome paperwork," the same agency reduced the reporting requirements and established the "duration of status" policy that remains in practice currently.[12]

Processing, Screening, and Reporting

Agency Involvement

Non-immigrant foreign students are processed by four different federal agencies during their tenure as applicants to and foreign students at United States higher education institutions. The first U.S. institution involved is the Department of State (DOS), which conducts the applicant interviews and either grants or rejects the visa applications. Once a non-immigrant arrives at a United States port of entry, the individual receives an inspection by the Customs and Border Protection (CBP). The student's arrival is reported to the Immigration and Custom Enforcement (ICE) for entry in to the Student and Exchange Visitor Information System (SEVIS). After entry, the alien's academic institution is responsible for reporting information to the SEVIS database. The SEVIS information is then shared with DOS, CBP, and the U.S. Citizenship and Immigration Services (USCIS). The latter agency is responsible for adjudicating any adjustments in visa status the foreign students wishes to make.

Screening Procedures

Potential foreign students, as well as all aliens, must satisfy DOS's consular officers abroad and DHS inspectors upon entry to the United States that they are not ineligible for visas under the so-called "grounds for inadmissibility" of the INA. These criteria include security and terrorist concerns as well as health-related grounds and criminal history.[13] Some provisions may be waived/overcome in the cases of non-immigrants, refugees, and certain other aliens. To become a non-immigrant, aliens also must demonstrate that they are not "intending immigrants" (i.e., wanting to reside permanently in the United States).[14]

In terms of criminal, security and terrorist concerns, the consular officers who process visa applicants are required to check the consolidated Terrorist Screening Database (TSDB)[15] before issuing any visa; thus, the names of foreign students are run through various databases, as are those of all other non-immigrants seeking a visa to enter the United States. In FY2005, DOS identified 333 potential non-immigrants (i.e., foreign nationals coming temporarily) as inadmissible because of security or terrorist concerns.[16] In comparison, DOS identified 7,454 potential non-immigrants as inadmissible on criminal grounds in FY2005. It is not known how many, if any, of these potential non-immigrants were seeking to enter the United States on student visas.

The Immigration and Nationality Act of 1952 originally included a requirement that all visa applicants be fingerprinted, with waivers for A visa (diplomats) and G visa (representatives of international organizations) non-immigrants.[17] The statutory requirement for fingerprinting non-immigrants was repealed in 1986, but the Attorney General still has the discretionary authority to require fingerprints of aliens applying for non-immigrant visas "for the purposes of identification and investigation."[18]

Security Concerns

In 1995, the former-INS began a review of the admission and monitoring of foreign students. Impetus for the review came in part from former Federal Bureau of Investigation Director Louis Freeh who expressed concern that possible terrorists could use foreign student status as a way of entering the United States.[19] Those concerned with the security risks of the foreign student visa often pointed out that one of the men convicted in the 1993 World Trade Center terrorist bombing had entered the United States on a student visa, dropped out of school, and yet stayed in the country.

Former INS Commissioner Doris Meisner emphasized plans to automate a foreign student reporting and monitoring system when she testified before the Senate Committee on the Judiciary's Subcommittee on Immigration in 1995.[20] The former-INS had not been maintaining the addresses of foreign students, and reviews of the reporting system questioned the accuracy of the data.[21] The National Commission on Terrorism, a bi-partisan commission established by Congress, cited the vulnerability of the foreign student visa in its June 2000 report, which recommended, among other things, that the former-INS automated system to monitor foreign students be enhanced and expanded.[22] Reports that several of the terrorists involved in the September 11 attacks entered the United States on foreign student visas led many others to echo earlier calls for a better monitoring system.

Student and Exchange Visitor Information System (SEVIS)

When Congress enacted the Illegal Immigration Reform and Immigrant Responsibility Act (IIRIRA) of 1996, it added statutory language mandating that the Attorney General (now Secretary of Homeland Security), in consultation with the Secretaries of State and Education, develop by January 1, 1998, a program to collect data on F, J, and M non-immigrants from at least five countries. By 2003, the data collection requirement included all countries. This provision, §641 of IIRIRA, requires that DHS collect the following data elements:

- identity and address of the alien;
- non-immigrant classification of the alien, date of visa issuance, and any change or extension;

- academic status of the alien (e.g., full-time enrollment); and
- any disciplinary action taken by the school, college, or university as a result of a crime committed by the alien.

DHS is to collect the information electronically "where practical." According to §641 of IIRIRA, educational institutions are required to report this information to DHS as a condition of continued approval to enroll foreign students.[23]

From June 1997 to October 1999, the former-INS conducted the first pilot program known as the Coordinated Interagency Partnership Regulating International Students (CIPRIS) at 21 educational institutions in Georgia, Alabama, North Carolina, and South Carolina, at Atlanta's Hartsfield Airport, and at the former-INS Texas Service Center. In July 2001, the former-INS announced that the second phase of its foreign student monitoring system, referred to as the Student and Exchange Visitor Information System (SEVIS), would begin at 12 Boston area institutions.

According to published statistics, there are currently 8,803 SEVIS-approved schools and 915,531 current active international non-immigrant students, exchange visitors, and their dependants in SEVIS.[24]

Prior to September 11, 2001, some university officials argued they would be turned into an enforcement agent of the former-INS and expressed concern that the confidentiality of their student records would be compromised.[25] Although educational institutions stopped their calls to repeal §641 of IIRIRA after the terrorist attacks and now support a tracking system, many educational institutions across the country expressed frustration about these new reporting requirements. They argued that the SEVIS is burdensome and that DHS is not providing training to staff who must use SEVIS.[26] All continuing foreign students were required to be entered into SEVIS as of August 2003.[27]

Following the full implementation of SEVIS in 2003, there has not been much legislative activity on foreign student monitoring. Some believe that SEVIS has been left relatively unaltered due to high profile incidents have positively contributed to the SEVIS image with the general public. Notably, the data from SEVIS resulted in the detection of several instances of unaccounted alien students, including some as recent as the summer of 2006. In this high profile incident, 11 Egyptian student visa holders were admitted at U.S. ports of entry, but never reported to classes or to the appropriate SEVIS officials at Montana State University. University officials reported the absence to DHS, which was able to locate and apprehend all of the 11 students.[28] Incidents such as this one are generally accepted as indicators that SEVIS is working as intended.

At this time, most observers view the SEVIS system as adequate for monitoring students and alerting authorities to suspicious behavior or unlawful movement. Yet, concerns continue with respect to whether increased security is detracting from the United States' ability to attract the number and quality of foreign students that higher education proponents advocate. The fields of science, technology, engineering and mathematics (STEM) have become particularly dependent upon foreign students, and these fields hold a top priority with most research institutions. Furthermore, the U.S. economy has a high demand for the skill-sets produced in these fields of study, and the STEM students can provide a major link between the academic community and the labor market. Consequently, with security measures now implemented, many groups in higher education and the private sector are seeking to develop pathways to immigration for foreign students.

Trends and Characteristics

Foreign students have been coming to study in the United States for almost a century, and the numbers admitted have more than doubled over the past two decades. In FY1979, the total number of F and J visas issued by DOS consular officers was 224,030 and comprised 4% of all non-immigrant visas issued.[29] In FY1989, the number of F, M, and J visas had grown to 373,932, constituting 5% of all non-immigrant visas DOS issued. By FY2006, the most recent year data are available, DOS issued 642,097 visas to F, J, and M non-immigrants, and these categories made up 11% of all non-immigrant visas issued.[30] As **Figure 1** illustrates, J cultural exchange visitors lead all student visa categories with 340,055 visas issued in FY2006.[31] The F academic students followed with 294,637, and the M students trailed with 7,405 visas issued in FY2006.

Figure 1. F, J, and M Non-immigrant Visas Issued in FY2006

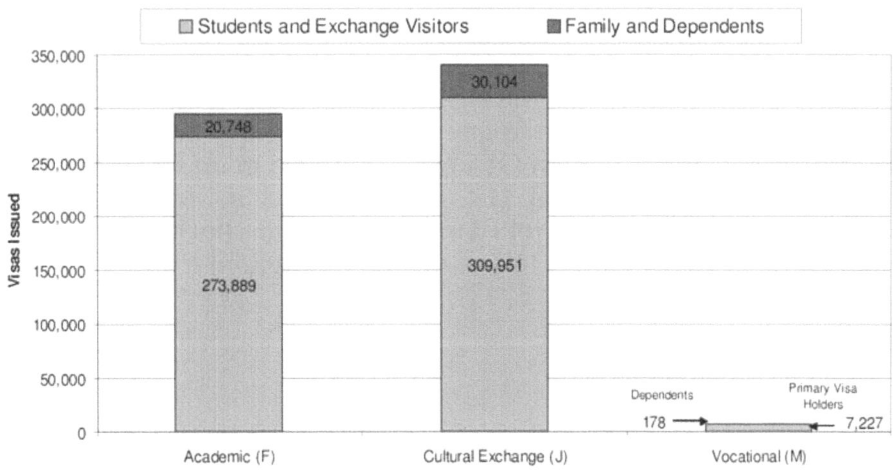

Source: CRS presentation of U.S. Department of State, Bureau of Consular Affairs, *Report of the Visa Office: 2006* data

Note: While Department of State data from the *Report of the Visa Office: 2006* on the program type of the J visa recipient are not available, the *Open Doors2006* survey by the Institute of

International Education reports that roughly 5% of foreign students are on J visas, but over half of international scholars are on J visas.

The largest sending region of the world for F and M student visas is Asia, as **Figure 2** depicts. The latest available data show Asia having 65% of the 301,985 visas issued to F and M non-immigrants in FY2006, representing 196,281 visas issued. Europe had the second largest portion with roughly 18%, or 55,349. North and South American countries had smaller portions, with 17,736 and 17,415, respectively, or approximately 6% each. Africa's share of F and M non-immigrant visas issued was 13,233 or roughly 4% of the total, while Oceania's 1,971 visas issued constituted approximately 1% of the total for F and J visas.

Figure 2. Region of Origin for F and M Non-immigrants, FY2006

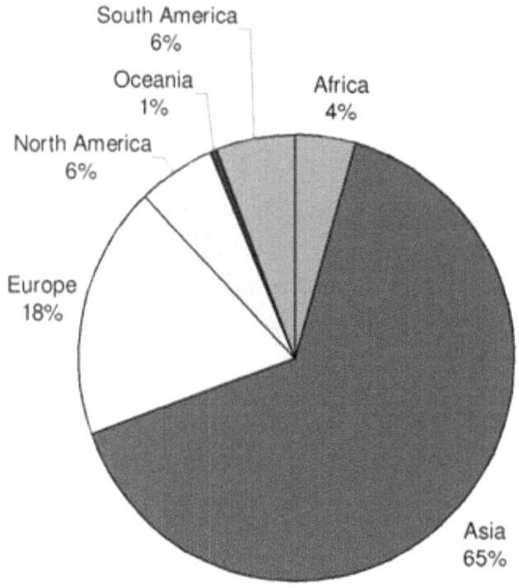

Source: CRS presentation of U.S. Department of State, Bureau of Consular Affairs, *Report of the Visa Office: 2006* data

According to International Educational Exchange's *Open Doors* survey of U.S. colleges and universities, the largest group (46%) of foreign students enrolled in 2005-2006 were in graduate degree programs.[32] As **Figure 3** presents, the second largest portion (31%) were enrolled in undergraduate degree programs. An additional 11% were enrolled in associate degree programs. Foreign students enrolled in other programs (including practical training programs) comprised 12% of the foreign student total.[33]

Figure 3. Academic Levels of Foreign Students, 2005-2006

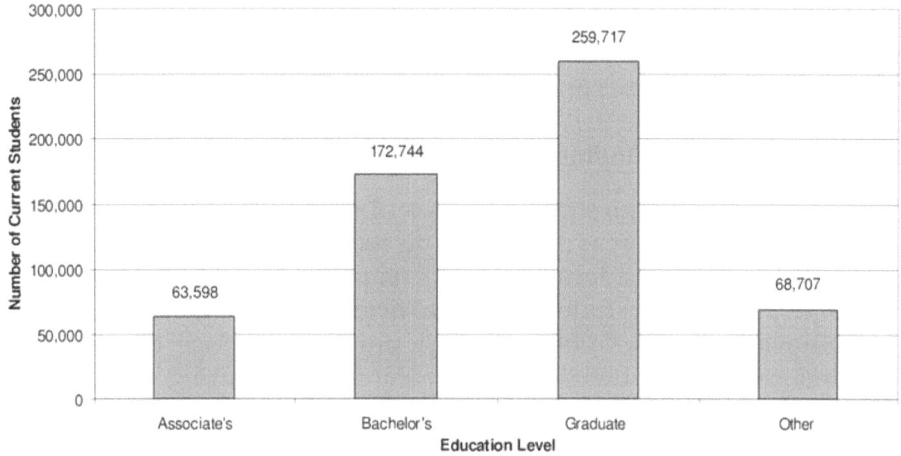

Source: CRS Presentation of data from the *Institute of International Education's Open Doors: Report on International Educational Exchange, 2006*

The fields of study undertaken by foreign students appear to be quite diverse, as **Figure 4** shows. The largest category is business and management, which is the field of study for 18% of foreign students. Engineering along with mathematics and computer sciences follow with 16% and 8%, respectively. The number of students participating in optional practical training has seen a marked increase in the last couple of years and currently accounts for 7% of foreign students' major study fields.[34]

Figure 4. Major Fields of Study for Foreign Students, 2005-2006

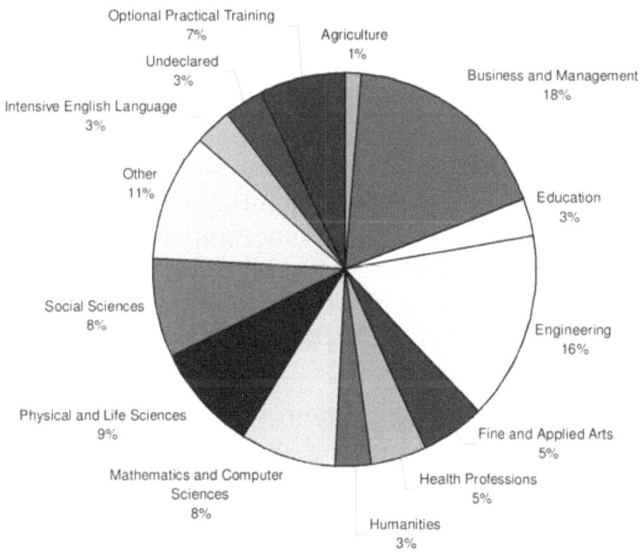

Source: CRS Presentation of data from the *Institute of International Education's Open Doors: Report on International Educational Exchange, 2006*

Current Issues

After dedicating the past five years to improving security and tracking measures for foreign students, universities are now gearing their efforts toward attracting foreign students in high-demand fields of study.

Foreign Students and Funding

A newly emerging foreign student focus is the targeting of students intending to specialize in the areas of STEM. This focus is part of a broader movement within higher education that emphasizes STEM-related skill development.[35] Foreign students in these fields of study represent a particularly attractive demographic for most universities since they provide skilled assistants and other forms of research labor during their time of study. Furthermore, undergraduate foreign students pay full tuition and are therefore an important source of revenues for many universities. This is highly relevant in discussions of STEM students, because foreign students constitute a significant portion of the overall STEM student population. For example, data from the National Science Foundation (NSF) show that in 2004, foreign students on non-immigrant visas accounted for 28.4% of all the doctorates in the sciences and 57.2% of all the doctorates in engineering.[36] Institute of International Education's (IIE) Open Doors data collection shows that STEM students accounted for 33.09% of foreign students in the 2005-2006 academic year.[37]

An ongoing point of contention for both STEM and non-STEM alike has been the availability of fellowships and teaching assistantship funding for foreign graduate students. Although these foreign graduate students are ineligible for direct aid from the government, most receive work-supported aid from the universities, where the funds stem from federally funded research grants to the university. This arrangement has been an ongoing source of controversy.[38] A 2004 study revealed that a greater percentage of financial support for doctoral students goes to non-U.S. citizens than to U.S. citizens. According to the survey, 85.5% of temporary visa doctoral recipients received some form of assistantship, traineeship, fellowship, or dissertation grant as their primary source of funding. By comparison, similar funding support was received by 75.9% of permanent visa holders, 61.6% of U.S. citizens, and 69% of all doctoral recipients.[39] Minority groups claim to be particularly disadvantaged

by the university support of foreign students.[40] Among ethnic groups, approximately 44% of African Americans and 48.3% of American Indians use their own resources to support their graduate studies, as compared with 32.8% of Caucasians, 32.7% of Hispanics, and 18.1% of Asian Americans.[41]

Foreign Students and Language Competence

Complaints have been levied against the support of foreign graduate students due to the lack of English competence.[42] Foreign students are required to take the Test of English as a Foreign Language (TOEFL) in order to demonstrate that they could effectively study and provide instruction in English. In Asian countries, such as China, cases of identity fraud have occurred at the test taking centers.[43] Students with lower levels of English competence have paid others to conduct the test in their place while falsely presenting themselves as the student seeking admission to a U.S. institution. Universities have had difficulty determining whether TOEFL scores are fraudulent until the student actually arrives in the United States. At this time, written offers of support have already been extended to the student and accepted. Although English-language competency persists as a problem for many programs, some university programs have reacted by not admitting any graduate students from countries with a history of fraudulent TOEFL scores, or requiring additional in-person interviews and making admission conditional upon successfully completing such interviews.[44]

New Pathways to Permanent Residence

Many employers in STEM-related fields find the hiring of U.S. trained alien graduates to be an enticing prospect because of the diminishing proportion of U.S. citizens to foreign nationals among STEM-trained graduates. For those students on F-category non-immigrant visas, a relationship with an employer can be built through the use of the optional training period. For up to 12 months after graduation, an F-visa student can serve as an intern for a United States firm without having to adjust his or her visa. Some firms find this option appealing because it can help bring in needed skills without being restricted to numerical limits or the same strict criteria as the H-1B visa for non-immigrant professional workers.[45]

For those students who pursue optional practical training with a U.S. employer, the training period becomes a valuable opportunity to develop a relationship with an employer that could eventually result in an employment-based petition for permanent residence. Any individual wishing to come to the United States as an employment-based legal permanent resident (LPR) must have the employer submit a petition on his/her behalf. Because of the diminishing proportion of U.S. citizens to foreign nationals among STEM-trained graduates, some employers have pushed for the lengthening of the optional practical training period, as well as the creation of direct pathways to LPR status for foreign students in U.S. higher education institutions.[46] Such proposals are reflected in some recent legislation.

Legislation in the 110th Congress

In the 110th Congress, student visa reform is included as a part of more comprehensive immigration reform in H.R. 1645, the Security Through Regularized Immigration and a Vibrant Economy Act of 2007 (STRIVE), as well as in S. 1348, (entitled "A Bill to Provide for Comprehensive Immigration Reform and for Other Purposes," which is a reintroduction of S. 2611 as passed by the Senate from the 109th Congress). Each of these bills would create a new F-1 visa category specifically designed for foreign students intending to pursue studies in a STEM-related field, while renumbering the old F visa categories.[47] Students obtaining a newly created F-1 non-immigrant visa would not need to demonstrate an intent of departing the United States upon completion of their studies.[48] Students in this category could also pursue optional practical training periods of up to 24 months after completing their degree. Furthermore, foreign students on F-class non-immigrant visas would be allowed to pursue off-campus work provided that the employer attempted to first hire a similarly qualified U.S. citizen for a period of 21 days prior to employment. Employers would be required to pay foreign students the higher of the average or prevailing wage in the field of employment. The act would also make provisions to preserve the visa status of foreign students and exchange visitors who resided within a district declared to have been affected by Hurricane Katrina or Hurricane Rita.

Alongside the addition of the new F-1 visa category, the STRIVE Act would also remove LPR numerical limits on foreign nationals who obtained a master's degree or higher at a U.S. accredited university. Furthermore, others exempted from the numerical limit on LPR status would be aliens who have earned a master's degree or higher in science, technology, engineering, or math (STEM) and have been working in a related field in the United States in a non-immigrant status during the three-year period preceding their application for an employment-based immigrant visa. These exemptions from LPR numerical limits would not only apply to current and future students, but would also apply to foreign degree recipients of U.S. universities who received their degree prior to the legislation.

With the exception of the provisions for off-campus employment and displaced students from natural disasters, the Securing Knowledge, Innovation and Leadership Act of 2007 (SKIL), or S. 1083, would provide the same visa reforms as those of the STRIVE Act. The bill would create a new F-1 visa category for STEM students and remove the same LPR numerical limits as those proposed to be removed through the STRIVE Act. The SKIL Act was previously included as part of the Comprehensive Immigration Reform Act of 2006 (S. 2611 as passed by the Senate) in the 109th Congress.[49] The SKIL Act is also contained within S. 1348.

Endnotes

[1] This report was originally authored by Ruth Ellen Wasem.

[2] T.B. Hoffer, V. Welch, Jr., K. Williams, M. Hess, K. Webber, B. Lisek, D. Loew, and I. Guzman-Barron, *Doctorate Recipients from United States Universities: Summary Report 2004* (Chicago: National Opinion Research Center, 2005). (The report gives the results of data collected in the Survey of Earned Doctorates, conducted for six federal agencies, NSF, NIH, USED, NEH, USDA, and NASA by NORC), p. 60.

[3] §101(a)(15) of INA.

[4] Those entering as secondary school students are only admitted for one year.

[5] Schools that wish to receive foreign students must file a petition with DHS district director. The particular supporting documents for the petition depend on the nature of the petitioning school. Once a school is approved, it can continue to receive foreign students without any time limits; however, the approval may be withdrawn if DHS discovers that the school has failed to comply with the law or regulations.

[6] F, J, and M students are barred from federal financial aid. See §484(a)(5) of the Higher Education Act of 1965, as amended.

[7] The Immigration Act of 1990 created an F-1 pilot employment program, but authority for this pilot off-campus work program expired Sept. 30, 1996.

[8] This bureau was formerly the United States Information Agency (USIA).

[9] As with secondary students entering with F-1 visas, J-1 students in secondary school programs are only admitted for up to one year.

[10] 22 CFR §514.

[11] INA §212(e) provides only a few exceptions, including cases of exceptional hardship to the spouse or child of a J-1 if that spouse or child is a U.S. citizen or permanent resident alien and in cases of persecution on the basis of race, religion, or political opinion if the alien returned home, and if it is in the national interest not to require the return.

[12] *Federal Register*, vol. 44, Nov. 22, 1978, p. 54620; *Federal Register*, vol. 46, Jan. 23, 1981, p. 7267; *Federal Register*, vol. 48, Apr. 5, 1983, p. 14575; and *Federal Register*, vol. 52, Apr. 22, 1987, p. 13223.

[13] §212(a) of INA lists the grounds for inadmissibility categories as: health-related grounds; criminal history; security and terrorist concerns; public charge (e.g., indigence); seeking to work without proper labor certification; illegal entrants and immigration law violations; lacking proper documents; ineligible for citizenship; and, aliens previously removed. For more information, see CRS Report RS20916, *Immigration and Naturalization Fundamentals*, by Ruth Ellen Wasem.

[14] For background and analysis of visa issuance policy and activities, see CRS Report RL31512, *Visa Issuances: Policy, Issues, and Legislation*, by Ruth Ellen Wasem.

[15] The TSDB is maintained by the Terrorist Screening Center (TSC), which is a multiagency collaborative effort administered by the Federal Bureau of Investigation (FBI). For more information, see CRS Report RL33645, *Terrorist Watchlist Checks and Air Passenger Prescreening*, by William J. Krouse and Bart Elias.

[16] The inadmissibility of members and supporters of foreign terrorist organizations can be waived under §212(d), which provides the Attorney General with that authority, if he deems that it is in the national interest to do so. Such waivers are usually granted at the request of the Secretary of State, with the concurrence of the Attorney General.

[17] Immigration and Nationality Act of 1952, P.L. 82-414.

[18] Immigration and Nationality Amendments of 1986, P.L. 99-653. See CRS Report RL31570, *Immigration: Alien Registration*, by Andorra Bruno.

[19] For a discussion of Mr. Freeh's memorandum, see *Interpreter Releases*, vol. 71, Dec. 19, 1994.

[20] U.S. Congress, Senate Committee on the Judiciary, *Examining Non-immigrant Immigration Issues*, hearing, 104th Cong., 1st sess., Sept. 28, 1995, S.Hrg. 104-814, Serial No. J-104-48 (Washington: GPO, 1995).

[21] There have long been record keeping requirements for schools with foreign students covering such information as name, address, country of citizenship, enrollment status, and field of study. The regulations were revised in 1983 so that schools no longer had to report changes in status directly to the former-INS. Since 1983, schools have had 3 business days to respond to requests for information about a foreign student. DHS can bar schools that did not meet record keeping requirements from enrolling foreign students. (8 CFR §214.3(g)(1))

[22] National Commission on Terrorism, *Countering the Changing Threat of International Terrorism*, June 5, 2000. For a discussion of this report, see CRS Report RS20598, *National Commission on Terrorism Report: Background and Issues for Congress*, by Raphael F. Perl.

[23] The law also required, as of Apr. 1, 1997, that the educational institutions collect a fee (not to exceed $100) from each of the foreign students to remit to the Attorney General to carry out the program. The 106th Congress amended this provision so that INS rather then the institutions would collect the fee (P.L. 106-396).

[24] U.S. Department of Homeland Security, Immigration and Customs Enforcement, *Student and Exchange Visitor Information System: General Summary Quarterly Report*, Feb. 20, 2006, p. 5, at [http://www.ice.gov/doclib/sevis/pdf/quarterly_report_dec06v4.pdf], visited May 8, 2007.

[25] *Interpreter Releases*, vol. 74, Mar. 17, 1997.

[26] Statement of Terry W. Hartle, American Council on Education, in U.S. Congress, House Committee on the Judiciary, Subcommittee on Immigration, Border Security, and Claims, hearing, *INS's Implementation of the Foreign Student Tracking Program*, Sept. 18, 2002, at [http://www.house.gov/judiciary/immigration.htm].

[27] *Federal Register*, vol. 67, no. 238, Dec. 11, 2002, pp. 76256-76280.

[28] U.S. Department of Homeland Security, Immigration and Customs Enforcement, *SEVIS Newsletter*, vol. 3 no. 3 (October 2006), p. 1.

[29] The M visa was not established until 1981 by P.L. 97-116.

[30] U.S. Department of State, Bureau of Consular Affairs, *Report of the Visa Office: 2006*.

[31] Although a large number of J visa holders are exchange students, a number are participants in work exchange programs and other non-academic programs.

[32] Koh Chin, Hey-Kyong, and Rajika Bhandari, *Open Doors 2006: Report on International Educational Exchange*, New York: Institute of International Education, 2006.

[33] Trade schools, such as flight schools, generally do not participate in this privately-conducted annual survey.

[34] For example, in 2005/06 there were 41,535 foreign students in optional practical training, while in 2004/05 there were 28,432 foreign students in these same programs (Koh Chin, Hey-Kyong, and Rajika Bhandari, *Open Doors 2006: Report on International Educational Exchange*, New York: Institute of International Education, 2006).

[35] For discussion on domestic STEM development, see CRS Report RL33434, *Science, Technology, Engineering, and Mathematics (STEM) Education Issues and Legislative Options*, by Jeffrey J. Kuenzi, Christine M. Matthews, and Bonnie F. Mangan.

[36] National Science Foundation, Division of Science Resources Statistics, *Science and Engineering Doctorate Awards: 2004*, NSF 06-308, Project Officer, Susan T. Hill (Arlington, VA, 2006), pp. 3-6, 66-67.

[37] *Open Doors 2005: Report on International Educational Exchange*, Hey-Kyung Koh Chin, ed. (New York: Institute of International Education, 2005).

[38] See for example House Subcommittee on Immigration and Claims, Impact of Immigration on Recent Immigrants and Black and Hispanic Citizens, 106th Cong., 1st Sess., Mar. 11, 1999, p.22, prepared statement of Julian R. Betts, Associate Professor, Department of Economics, University of California, San Diego.

[39] T.B. Hoffer, V. Welch, Jr., K. Williams, M. Hess, K. Webber, B. Lisek, D. Loew, and I. Guzman-Barron, *Doctorate Recipients from United States Universities: Summary Report 2004* (Chicago: National Opinion Research Center, 2005). (The report gives the results of data collected in the Survey of Earned Doctorates, conducted for six federal agencies, NSF, NIH, USED, NEH, USDA, and NASA by NORC), p. 60.

[40] See for example House Subcommittee on Immigration and Claims, Impact of Immigration on Recent Immigrants and Black and Hispanic Citizens, 106th Cong., 1st Sess., Mar. 11, 1999, p. 33, prepared statement of Frank L. Morris, former Dean, Morgan State University.

[41] *Doctorate Recipients from United States Universities: Summary Report 2004*, p. 60.

[42] Gravois, John, "Teach Impediment—When Students Can't Understand the Instructor, Who Is to Blame?," *The Chronicle of Higher Education*, vol. 51, Apr. 8, 2005, p. A10, and Bollag, Burton, "New Test of English as a Foreign Language Puts an Emphasis on Speaking," *The Chronicle of Higher Education*, vol. 52, Oct. 7, 2005, p. A49.

[43] Mooney, Paul. "Chinese Court Reduces Penalty for Pirating Exams." *The Chronicle of Higher Education*, Jan. 14, 2005, p.35.

[44] Bollag, Burton. "New Test of English as a Foreign Language Puts an Emphasis on Speaking," *The Chronicle of Higher Education*, vol. 52, Oct. 7, 2005, p. A49.

[45] There are many anecdotal accounts of foreign students using the optional practical training period as a means of creating the necessary employer relations for LPR petitions. While some policymakers consider this a natural and positive chain of events, others consider this "F-1 to H-1B to LPR" pathway an abuse of the temporary element of non-immigrant status and a way to circumvent U.S. worker protection laws. For more discussion of the H-1B non-immigrant visa, see CRS Report RL30498, *Immigration: Legislative Issues on Non-immigrant Professional Specialty (H-1B) Workers*, by Ruth Ellen Wasem.

[46] For example, see "Ease Immigration for Foreign Grad Students," *Minneapolis Star Tribune*, editorial, Nov. 28, 2005.

[47] This new category would not displace the other categories. Instead, the other F-visas would be renumbered such that the current F-1 would become an F-2, the current F-2 would become an F-3, and the current F-3 would become an F-4.

[48] Under current statute, in order for an applicant to qualify for an F visa, the applicant must appear to have no intention of abandoning his or her foreign residence to permanently migrate to the United States. (INA §101(a)(15)(F)).

[49] One provision that existed in S. 2611 as passed by the Senate that does not exist in the SKIL Act or STRIVE Act is a provision for exchange students. Under the Comprehensive Immigration Reform Act of 2006, a new J-STEM non-immigrant category would have been created for advanced students in higher education cultural exchange programs. In addition to not needing to demonstrate an intent to depart the United States at the conclusion of their visa duration, J-STEM visa holders would also not have been subject to the two year foreign residency requirement before adjusting to a new status, which current J-class visa holders are subject. (INA §212(e)).

DOCUMENT NO. 13

9/11 COMMISSION RECOMMENDATIONS: IMPLEMENTATION STATUS

CRS Report
RL33742

December 4, 2006

Richard F. Grimmett, Coordinator
Specialist in National Defense Foreign Affairs,
Defense, and Trade Division
Congressional Research Service

Summary

This report provides a review of the 9/11 Commission recommendations and the status of their implementation at the end of the 109th Congress. The discussions herein are organized on the basis of policy themes that are at the core of the 9/11 Commission's recommendations, rather than through a review of each numbered item set out in the Commission's final report. The analysis was produced by a large team of CRS Specialists, analysts, and attorneys who are responsible for the wide variety of policy areas covered by the 9/11 Commission in its work. The authors of the varied segments of this report are identified in footnotes. Each section of the report summarizes the pertinent elements of the 9/11 Commission's recommendation relevant to the section's policy theme. Then a review is made of responses made by the Congress to implement, in whole or in part, the given recommendation. Where appropriate, notice is taken of Executive branch actions regarding the policy matter. A detailed table of contents provides the reader with a guide to each of the policy themes discussed. Footnotes in each section of the report provide references to more detailed information on particular topics related to each policy theme.

This report will only be updated if circumstances warrant.

Introduction

This report provides a review of the 9/11 Commission recommendations and the status of their implementation at the end of the 109th Congress. It is intended to provide a structured road map to this end. The discussions herein are organized on the basis of policy themes that are at the core of the 9/11 Commission's recommendations, rather than a review of every numbered item set out in the Commission's final report. The analysis was produced by a large team of CRS Specialists, analysts, and attorneys who are responsible for the wide variety of policy areas covered by the 9/11 Commission in its work. The authors of the varied segments of this report are identified in footnotes. Each section of the report summarizes the pertinent elements of the 9/11 Commission's recommendations relevant to that section's policy theme. Then a review is made of responses made by the Congress to implement, in whole or in part, the given recommendation. Where appropriate, notice is taken of executive branch actions regarding the policy matter. A detailed table of contents provides the reader with a guide to each of the policy themes discussed. Footnotes in each section of the report provide references to more detailed information on particular topics related to each policy theme.

Strengthening the Intelligence Function[1]

Commission Concerns and Recommendations

The 9/11 Commission concluded that the organization of the U.S. Intelligence Community had contributed to a failure to develop a management strategy to counter Islamic terrorism. The Commission recommended a major reordering of the Intelligence Community to enable a single official to manage the entire national intelligence effort and oversee the agencies that contribute to it. The Commission also recommended the establishment of national intelligence centers, including a National Counterterrorism Center (NCTC), to correlate and analyze information from all sources on particular topics.

A principal recommendation of the Commission was the creation of the position of Director of National Intelligence (DNI), separate from the Director of the Central Intelligence Agency (CIA), who would have major statutory authorities over the Intelligence Community's 16 agencies, including the preparation of budgets, systems acquisition, and the setting of personnel policies and standards for information use throughout the Intelligence Community. The DNI would also be the principal intelligence advisor to the President and would prepare national intelligence estimates.

Congressional Responses

Congress responded to many of the recommendations of the 9/11 Commission by passing the Intelligence Reform and Terrorism Prevention Act of 2004 (P.L. 108-458), hailed by some as the most important intelligence legislation since the National Security Act of 1947. The Act established a DNI (along with a separate Director of the CIA) and provided him with additional authorities beyond those that the former Director of Central Intelligence (DCI) had over all intelligence agencies. The DNI possesses substantial authorities to prepare the national intelligence budget and the expenditure of funds appropriated for the national intelligence effort. The DNI also is charged with establishing priorities for collection and analysis; and managing intelligence centers composed of analysts from various intelligence and law enforcement agencies.

Questions involving the DCI's budgetary authorities were debated at length during consideration of the legislation. The management and oversight authorities proposed by the 9/11 Commission and reflected in some versions of intelligence reform legislation appeared to some Members as complicating, undermining, or replacing the authorities of the Secretary of Defense over intelligence agencies in the Defense Department (in particular, the National Security Agency, National Reconnaissance Office, and National Geospatial-Intelligence Agency, that are also integral components of DOD's warfighting capabilities). The agreement reflected in the final legislation provides the DNI with authority to "develop and determine an annual consolidated National Intelligence Program budget," along with authorities to manage appropriations, transfer or reprogram funds (within strict limitations), transfer a limited number of personnel annually, and establish common information technology standards. At the same time, the Act called for the President to issue guidelines to ensure that the authorities granted to the DNI are implemented "in a manner that respects and does not abrogate the statutory responsibilities" of other departments including DOD. Some observers have suggested that the legislation has not definitively resolved the question of the DNI's responsibilities for the Defense agencies in particular, and have argued that further legislative changes may be required and/or that an effective solution will depend on the ability of the DNI and the Secretary of Defense to work in close coordination.

To a large extent P.L. 108-458 adopted the recommendations of the 9/11 Commission regarding the organization of the Intelligence Community but it did not centralize management of the Intelligence Community to the extent that at least some on the 9/11 Commission would have preferred. As a result there remains a potential that the national intelligence agencies within the Department of Defense may be subject to conflicting guidance from the Secretary of Defense and the DNI. Thus far, however, there has been little public controversy regarding the budgets of intelligence agencies since the enactment of P.L. 108-458.

Intelligence Oversight: Congressional Options[2]

Commission Concerns and Recommendations

The 9/11 Commission stated that congressional oversight for intelligence and counter-terrorism is "dysfunctional." Commission members suggested two basic alternatives for strengthening and improving Congress's oversight of these policy domains. The two recommendations were: (1) to create either a joint committee on intelligence modeled after the former Joint Committee on Atomic Energy; or (2) establish a committee in each chamber that has the authority to both authorize and appropriate for intelligence agencies and activities. In addition, the commission suggested that an intelligence committee should have a subcommittee specifically dedicated to oversight; the panel should have subpoena authority; majority party representation on the panel should exceed the minority by only one member; a member from each of these panels—Armed Services, Judiciary, Foreign Affairs, and the Defense Appropriations Subcommittee—should serve on an intelligence committee; Members who serve on an intelligence committee should not be subject to term limits; the staff of an intelligence committee should be nonpartisan and serve the entire committee; and the size of an intelligence committee should range from seven to nine members.

Congressional Responses

The House and Senate did not create a joint intelligence committee, nor did either chamber consolidate authorizing and appropriating responsibility for the intelligence community in a single committee. On the other hand, the two chambers followed some but not all of the commission's other recommendations.

In the House, the Permanent Select Intelligence Committee for the 109th Congress has an oversight subcommittee, subpoena authority, and members who serve also on the Defense Appropriations Subcommittee and the Armed Services, Judiciary, and International Relations Committees. The House panel's ratio of majority to minority party members does not, however, track the commission's recommendation. The House Permanent Select Intelligence Committee's size is larger than nine; its members are subject to tenure limitations with exceptions for the chair and ranking minority member; and it has a partisan staff model.

In October 2004, the Senate adopted S.Res. 445, which made a number of changes affecting oversight of the intelligence community. Some of the recommendations in S.Res. 445 parallel the commission's ideas, while others are new proposals agreed to by the Senate. The ideas in S.Res. 445 that affect the Select Intelligence Committee, and which generally emulate the commission's proposals, are these: an oversight subcommittee; subpoena authority; a one-seat margin for the majority party; a two-seat representation on the panel from each of these committees: Appropriations, Armed Services, Foreign Relations, and Judiciary; moreover, Intelligence members are not subject to term limits. On the other hand, the Select Intelligence Committee employs a partisan staff model and its size is larger than nine members.

S.Res. 445 made a number of other changes affecting the Select Intelligence Committee. These include granting the Majority Leader formal authority to name the chairman, and the Minority Leader the vice chairman, of the panel; authorizing the chair and vice chair of the Intelligence panel to name, respectively, the chair and vice chair of any subcommittee; assigning to the panel jurisdiction over civilian nominations to advice-and-consent positions within the intelligence community; permitting each Intelligence member to appoint a staff aide to the committee (subject to appropriate security clearances); allocating committee staff resources between the parties on a 60/40 ratio, excluding staff designees appointed by individual Senators; expanding current requirements that the Intelligence Committee report periodically to the Senate on its findings and to require such reports quarterly; elevating the Select Intelligence Committee to a category "A" assignment status; obligating the panel to consult with the Majority Leader and Minority Leader about the disclosure of classified information given to the committee by the executive branch; and reducing what are called "on demand sequential referrals" from 30 days to 10 days.

S.Res. 445 recommended that the Committee on Appropriations "shall reorganize into 13 subcommittees as soon as possible after the convening of the 109th Congress." The Senate Committee on Appropriations did not establish its customary 13 subcommittees. Bicameral discussions at the start of the 109th Congress involving, among others, the majority party leaders and the respective House and Senate Appropriations chairs, led to a downsizing and reshuffling of Appropriations subcommittees and jurisdictions.

In mid-February 2005, the House panel established 10 subcommittees, eliminating three (District of Columbia, Legislative Branch, and VA-HUD). A few weeks later the Senate Appropriations Committee created 12 subcommittees. The panel retained its District of Columbia and Legislative Branch subcommittees, but, like the House, it eliminated its VA-HUD subcommittee and transferred its jurisdiction to other Appropriations subcommittees. One goal of revamping the organizational structure of the two Appropriations Committees is to minimize the need for end-of-year appropriations measures.

The recommendation in S.Res. 445 for an Appropriations Subcommittee on Intelligence was not acted upon by the Committee on Appropriations during the 109th Congress. The Resolution stated that the proposed Intelligence subcommittee "shall have jurisdiction over funding for intelligence matters, as determined by the Senate Committee on Appropriations." A Senate Appropriations member indicated that it would be difficult to create a subcommittee with a classified budget. The 9/11 Commission recommended public disclosure of the nation's budget for intelligence, which has not been agreed to by the Congress.[3]

Improving Transitions Between Administrations[4]

Commission Concerns and Recommendations

The *9/11 Commission Report*[5] included a general recommendation that appointments to key national security positions at the time of presidential transitions occur more quickly. The goal of the 9/11 Commission's recommended changes was to "minimize as much as possible the disruption of national security policymaking" and maintain national security continuity when a new President comes into office. The recommendation addressed the commission's concern about the length of time a new Administration takes to install key national security personnel. The commission noted, in particular, the abbreviated transition period resulting from the delayed resolution of the 2000 presidential race. The report stated, "Given that a presidential election in the United States brings wholesale change in personnel, this loss of time hampered the new administration in identifying, recruiting, clearing, and obtaining Senate confirmation of key appointees."[6] As a result, the commission reported, "the new administration did not have its deputy cabinet officers in place until the spring of 2001, and the critical subcabinet officials were not confirmed until the summer—if then. In other words, the new administration—like others before it—did not have its team on the job until at least six months after it took office."[7]

In line with its overall recommendation, the commission called for seven specific changes, six of which are related to presidential appointments and transitions. Two of these proposed changes are related to the national security clearance process during transitions. First, the commission recommended starting the security clearance process for prospective appointees to national security positions immediately after the presidential election. It also proposed that, prior to the election, each presidential candidate provide to the FBI "the names of selected members" of his or her prospective transition team to facilitate quicker security clearances following the election.

Three additional recommendations would modify the nomination and Senate consideration processes for certain national security positions. First, the report proposed that all nominations to positions on the "national security team"[8] be submitted to the Senate by the President-elect no later than the date of his or her inauguration. Furthermore, the commission called for the Senate to "adopt special rules requiring hearings and votes to confirm or reject national security nominees within 30 days of their submission." The final recommended change to the appointment process would be the elimination of advice and consent requirements for any "national security team" members below Level III of the Executive Schedule.

The commission also suggested that, beginning immediately after the election, the transition include a prompt and thorough written national security information exchange between the outgoing and incoming Administrations.

In addition to these six changes, the commission called for centralization of the security clearance process in one agency, including providing and maintaining security clearances and ensuring uniform standards.[9]

Congressional Responses

Enacted Provisions. The Intelligence Reform and Terrorism Prevention Act of 2004 (hereafter the "Intelligence Reform Act")[10] included several provisions that responded to commission concerns and recommendations. The legislation amended the Presidential Transition Act of 1963 to (1) recommend submission by the President-elect to the agency with national security clearance functions of the "names of candidates for high level national security positions through the level of undersecretary" of agencies and departments, as soon as possible after the presidential election; (2) require the responsible agency or agencies to carry out background investigations of these candidates for high-level national security positions "as expeditiously as possible . . . before the date of the inauguration"; and (3) authorize "relevant outgoing executive branch officials" to prepare a "detailed classified, compartmented summary . . . of specific operational threats to national security; major military or covert operations; and pending decisions on possible uses of military force," which would be provided to the President-elect and Vice President-elect as soon as possible after the general election.[11]

Just as the Intelligence Reform Act seeks to facilitate more rapid security clearances for top national security position candidates, it also does so for transition team members. It allows each major party presidential candidate to submit, before the general election, security clearance requests for "prospective transition team members who will have a need for access to classified information" in the course of their work. The law directs that resulting investigations and eligibility determinations be completed, as much as possible, by the day after the general election.[12]

The Intelligence Reform Act also expresses "the sense of the Senate" about a timetable for submission and consideration of high-level national security nominations during transitions. Under this timetable, nominations to such positions should be submitted by the President-elect to the Senate by Inauguration Day, and Senate consideration of all such nominations should be completed within 30 days of submission.[13] Because most presidential appointees are subject to a limited "vetting" process and not a full-scale security clearance investigation and adjudication, these changes may have a significant impact on the duration and difficulty of the confirmation process. A personnel security clearance investigation, for instance, is normally more exhaustive and longer than the usual "vetting" process for potential nominees. A background investigation for access to the highest clearance level—Top Secret with access to Sensitive Compartmented Information—may take a year. That is because the process requires a full field investigation, including interviews with former colleagues and employers, neighbors, friends, and acquaintances, along with checks of databases from law enforcement entities, financial services, and, to a degree, medical services.

The Intelligence Reform Act also made government-wide changes to the national security clearance process that are designed to consolidate and streamline this function. Concerns have long existed over the substantial backlog, delays, and time consumed in initial background investigations and subsequent re-investigations associated with gaining access to classified national security information. These problems have been exacerbated by the increased number of personnel requiring access to classified information and the growth of materials being classified or being classified at higher levels; both of these changes, in turn, have been driven by the expanding programs in national and homeland security. Other reasons for seeking improvements in the clearance process, especially the background investigations, are (1) the lack of reciprocity among agencies, so that one federal agency may not accept the findings of investigations previously conducted for another federal agency; and (2) questions about the capacity of existing agencies to handle the increased workload (or overload) in light of its size and recent growth.[14]

The Intelligence Reform Act required the President to designate a single executive entity to oversee and develop uniform standards and policies for access to classified information and to designate other investigative agencies, if appropriate, for national security and efficiency purposes.[15] The statute further stipulated that reciprocity should be the rule among agencies for clearances at the same level and the legislation established a national database to track clearances. The head of the entity charged with overseeing the process is to evaluate and report to Congress on the use of available technology in clearance investigations and adjudications, as well as to consult with Congress and adjudicative agencies in developing a plan, within five years, to reduce the length of the clearance process.

The first step along this new path was undertaken during the 109th Congress, with the Office of Personnel Management (OPM) designated as the lead agency in conducting security clearance background checks under the guidance and oversight of the Deputy Director of OMB. Certain deadlines and a reciprocity requirement among agencies have also been established to speed up the process and make it less costly and more efficient. Setting this in motion was an executive order issued by President George W. Bush, designed to strengthen and speed up processes to determine eligibility for access to classified national security information.[16] In the order, the President called upon the Director of the Office of Management and Budget (OMB) to develop the policy for meeting the following goals: "To the extent consistent with safeguarding the security of the United States and protecting classified national security information from unauthorized disclosure, agency functions relating to determining eligibility for access to classified national security information shall be appropriately uniform, centralized, efficient, effective, timely, and reciprocal."[17] The Intelligence Reform Act also contained appointment process-related provisions[18] that were not specifically recommended by the 9/11 Commission. These included provisions that (1) require a report from the Office of Government Ethics (OGE) regarding potential improvements to the financial disclosure process for executive branch employees;[19] (2) direct the Office of Personnel Management (OPM) to transmit an electronic record "on Presidentially appointed positions," with specified contents, to each major party presidential candidate soon after his or her nomination, and to make such a record available to any other presidential candidate after this; (3) direct each agency head to submit an advice and consent position reduction plan, with specified contents, to the President, the Senate Committee on Governmental Affairs (as of the 109th Congress, the Senate Committee on Homeland Security and Governmental Affairs), and the House Committee on Government Reform;[20] and (4) require the Director of OGE, in consultation with the Attorney General, to "conduct a comprehensive review of conflict of interest laws relating to Federal employment," with specified contents and recipients.[21]

Although the Intelligence Reform Act addressed each of the recommendations in this section of the *9/11 Report*, its provisions were generally not identical to the commission's recommended actions. For example, whereas the commission recommended that the "Senate should not require confirmation of [national security] executive appointees below Executive Level 3," the statute requires agencies to submit advice and consent position reduction plans to the President and congressional committees.

Related Potential Congressional Concerns for the 110th. The presidential transition process changes called for by the 9/11 Commission and provided for in the Intelligence Reform Act are arguably more critical to national security continuity at the time of a transition between Presidents than between the first and second terms of a two-term President. Nonetheless, some top-level national security positions changed hands at the beginning of the second George W. Bush Administration, and Congress may elect to conduct oversight, during the 110th Congress, on the implementation of the modifications to the presidential transition process. Congress might also elect to conduct oversight regarding provisions that would be implemented during the run-up to the 2008 presidential election.

Changes to the national security clearance process under the Intelligence Reform Act extend beyond the presidential transition and presidential appointment processes.

Some changes are designed to modernize the national security clearance process, by adding new formal requirements (e.g., for reciprocity among agencies) and by consolidating the process under a single entity, the Office of Personnel Management, with guidance and supervision under the Deputy Director of the Office of Management and Budget. The implementation of these and other new developments might become the subjects of congressional oversight, to determine whether the changes are proceeding as expected, whether their goals are being met, whether legislative intent is being followed, what the implementation costs are, and what other modifications might be necessary.

Several provisions of the law reflect ongoing concern among some Members of Congress about the length and complexity of the presidential appointment process. The last several Congresses have seen efforts to develop consensus, inter alia, on streamlining executive branch financial disclosure requirements; reducing the number of positions requiring Senate confirmation for appointment; and simplifying conflict of interest laws and decriminalizing conflict of interest. With the submission of reports to Congress concerning these topics, required by the Intelligence Reform Act, discussions regarding possible changes may be renewed during the 110th Congress.

Congress might elect to revisit provisions contained in earlier versions of the intelligence legislation that were not included in the enacted law. These include proposed changes to provisions of the Federal Vacancies Reform Act of 1998 that would make it easier for the President to make long-term temporary appointments to advice and consent positions during presidential transitions.[22]

Other appointments-related issues could be of interest in the 110th Congress. For example, it is possible that the Senate may attempt to change its floor procedures concerning nominations. In addition, issues related to recess appointments may come to the fore. At times, for instance, the President's use of his recess appointment power has been seen as circumventing the Senate confirmation process and has proven controversial.

Afghanistan and Terrorism[23]

Commission Concerns and Recommendations

The 9/11 Commission Report (p. 370) praised the U.S. efforts in Afghanistan to that date, but emphasized the need for a sustained, long-term commitment by the United States and the international community to Afghanistan's stability and security,[24] in order to prevent Afghanistan from "again becom[ing] a sanctuary for international crime and terrorism." The Commission was far-reaching in its recommendations, calling for greater peacekeeping participation by international forces, particularly NATO; stepped up counter-narcotics activities, disarmament of regional militias, and efforts to promote rule of law; and follow through on funding pledges with increased flexibility in allocating money for relief and reconstruction.[25]

Most of the recommendations had already formed major pillars of Administration policy on post-Taliban Afghanistan, and these efforts accelerated after the release of the 9/11 report. Key milestones in the U.S. stabilization effort were the October 9, 2004 presidential election, in which interim leader Hamid Karzai was elected, and the September 18, 2005 elections for a 249 seat lower house of parliament, and subsequent selections to a 102-seat upper house.

The Commission recommendation for increased NATO participation in Afghanistan peacekeeping has, by most accounts, been implemented. As of October 5, 2005, NATO now has overall control of peacekeeping operations throughout Afghanistan, including the volatile and violent south and east of the country. NATO's force in Afghanistan now numbers about 31,000, including about 11,250 U.S. forces. NATO countries run 13 of the 25 total "provincial reconstruction teams" (PRTs)—regional civilian-military enclaves intended to promote security and reconstruction.

The United States, Afghanistan, and the international community have also had significant success over the past few years in disarming regional militiamen—a "disarmament, demobilization, and reintegration program (DDR), run jointly by the United Nations, Japan, and the United States, resulted in the disarmament of 63,000 private militiamen by the June 2005 close-out of the program, according to U.S. and UN officials. A follow-on program, called Disarmament of Illegal Armed Groups (DIAG) is currently in the process of attempting to disband several hundred illegal militia groups around Afghanistan, although progress is said to be slow.

Counter-narcotics programs, on the other hand, have not been as successful. UN officials estimate that a record opium poppy crop was produced in Afghanistan during the 2005-2006 season that supplied 92% of the world's illicit opium and reversed a slight reduction that occurred from 2004-2005. U.S., Afghan, and international officials have cited the cultivation and trafficking as a serious strategic threat to U.S.-led efforts to stabilize and reconstruct Afghanistan.

Congressional Responses

The 108th and 109th Congresses have acted to implement at least some of the Commission's recommendations. The Intelligence Reform and Terrorism Prevention Act of 2004 (P.L. 108-458) contained a subtitle called "The Afghanistan Freedom Support Act Amendments of 2004." The subtitle mandated the appointment of a U.S. coordinator of policy on Afghanistan in order to streamline and instill greater flexibility and inter-agency cooperation in the administration of U.S. programs in Afghanistan. The subtitle also required additional Administration reports to Congress on progress in reconstruction. In addition, the subtitle contained "sense of Congress" provisions recommending more rapid disarmament of private militias; expansion of the NATO-led peacekeeping force; and new initiatives to combat narcotics trafficking. The subtitle did not specify dollar amounts for U.S. aid to Afghanistan for FY2005 and FY2006, authorizing instead "such sums as may be necessary for each of the fiscal years 2005 and 2006."

In appropriations legislation, the 108th and 109th Congresses have sought to address the need for reconstruction funds. For FY2005, a total of $4.3 billion was appropriated for programs in Afghanistan, from a regular foreign aid appropriation (P.L. 108-447) and a supplemental (P.L. 109-13). Of those funds, about $1.6 billion was earmarked to equip and train the Afghan National Army (ANA) and Afghan National Policy (ANP). Slightly less was appropriated for FY2006—a total of about $3.05 billion in a regular appropriation (P.L. 109-102) and a supplemental (P.L. 109-234). The FY2006 funds include a total of about $2 billion to train and equip the ANA and the ANP. As noted above, building up the ANA is a key recommendation of the September 11 Commission so that the central government can extend its writ and services throughout Afghanistan.

Future Considerations. For FY2007, some funding for Afghanistan awaits congressional action. The Administration requested $1.1 billion for civilian reconstruction programs, including counter-narcotics, and congressional action on these funds has not been completed to date, although both House and Senate versions fund roughly the total amounts requested. The FY2007 Defense appropriation (P.L. 109-289) provides $1.5 billion to train and equip the ANA and ANP and provides $100 million for Defense Department counter-narcotics support activities for Afghanistan. Some experts believe that the upsurge in Taliban opposition violence during 2006 is a product of popular frustration at the slow pace of reconstruction, particularly in southern Afghanistan, and several experts believe the remedy for this is accelerated reconstruction.

Pakistan and Terrorism[26]

Commission Concerns and Recommendations

The 9/11 Commission Report emphasizes that the mounting of large-scale international terrorist attacks appears to require sanctuaries in which terrorist groups can plan and operate with impunity. In addition to identifying Pakistan as a principal transit country for the 9/11 hijackers and naming the western regions of the country as one of six "actual or potential terrorist sanctuaries" worldwide, the report warns that Pakistan's "vast unpoliced regions" remain attractive to extremist groups. The first recommendation of the Commissioners is identification and prioritization of terrorist sanctuaries and the development of a realistic strategy for denying them to terrorists.

In its country-specific discussion, *The 9/11 Commission Report* further claims that—even after acknowledging problems in U.S.-Pakistan relations and President Musharraf's role in them—"Musharraf's government is the best hope for stability in Pakistan and Afghanistan." It recommends that the United States make a long-term commitment to provide comprehensive support for Islamabad so long as Pakistan itself is committed to combating extremism and to a policy of "enlightened moderation." Specifically, the Commission urges sustaining U.S. assistance to Pakistan at "current scale" with programs that extend from military aid to support for better education.[27] A November 2005 follow-on report by Commissioners gave a "C" grade to U.S. efforts to support Pakistan's anti-extremism policies and warned that the country "remains a sanctuary and training ground for terrorists."

The issue of a long-term U.S. commitment to supporting Pakistan is key for many analysts, as past experiences have engendered Pakistani skepticism regarding the strategic (as opposed to tactical) reliability of the United States as an ally. Many Bush Administration officials, Members of Congress, and independent analysts remain concerned about the continued existence in Pakistan of terrorist groups and their supporters, evidence that Pakistan has been the source of significant "onward" proliferation of nuclear weapons materials and technologies to third parties, and continuing human rights abuses, including perceived nondemocratic practices, by the military-dominated government in Islamabad.

Congressional Responses

In passing the Intelligence Reform and Terrorism Prevention Act of 2004 (P.L. 108-458), the 108th Congress broadly endorsed the Pakistan-specific 9/11 Commission recommendations. Section 7103 of the bill, entitled "United States Commitment to the Future of Pakistan," called for U.S. aid to Pakistan to be sustained at a minimum of FY2005 levels and required the President to report to Congress a description of a long-term U.S. strategy to engage with and support Pakistan. It further extended the President's authority to waive coup-related sanctions on Pakistan through FY2006, allowing continued U.S. military and economic assistance to Pakistan despite the 1999 overthrow of an elected government in Islamabad.

Foreign Assistance. In June 2003, President Bush vowed to work with Congress on establishing a five-year, $3 billion aid package for Pakistan. Annual installments of $600 million each began in FY2005 and are split evenly between military and economic aid. The Foreign Operations FY2005 Appropriations bill (P.L. 108-447) established a new base program of $300 million for military assistance for Pakistan. When additional funds for development assistance, law enforcement, and other programs are included, the aid allocation for FY2005 was about $688 million. Significant increases in economic support, along with relief funding in response to Pakistan's devastating October 2005 earthquake, may bring the FY2006 total to around $874 million. The Bush Administration's FY2007 request calls for another $739 million in aid to Pakistan, although the House Appropriations Committee (H.Rept. 109-486) recommended reducing that amount by $150 million (ostensibly for domestic budgetary reasons unrelated to Pakistan-U.S. relations). In S.Rept. 109-277, the Senate Appropriations Committee called for redirecting some of the requested FY2007 U.S. economic aid to Pakistan toward development and democracy promotion programs there (House and Senate committees have issued separate concerns about "the slow pace of the democratic development of Pakistan").

In the five years since September 2001, Pakistan has received nearly $1.5 billion in direct U.S. security-related assistance (Foreign Military Financing totaling $970 million plus about $516 million for other programs). Congress has taken no action to block major U.S. arms sales to Pakistan during this period, including the multi-billion dollar sale of F-16 combat aircraft currently in process.[28] Programs overseen by USAID in Pakistan include those aimed at strengthening that country's democratic institutions and civil society, reforming the education sector, alleviating poverty, improving health, and bolstering macroeconomic stability while stimulating economic growth. Such efforts have been funded with some $2 billion since September 2001 (Economic Support Funds of nearly $1.7 billion plus $288 million for other programs). Congress also has eased Islamabad's foreign debt burden by authorizing Pakistan to use $388 million in economic support to cancel about $1.5 billion in concessional debt to the U.S. government.

Coalition Support Funds. In addition to the foreign assistance discussed above, Congress has appropriated billions of dollars to reimburse Islamabad for its support of U.S.-led counterterrorism operations (Pakistan has since 2002 been undertaking military operations along its border with Afghanistan). As of December 2006, a total of $6.65 billion had been appropriated for FY2002-FY2007 Defense Department spending for coalition support payments to "Pakistan, Jordan, and other key cooperating nations." Pentagon documents indicate that disbursements to Islamabad—averaging about $66 million per month—account for the majority of these funds. This amount is roughly equal to one-fifth of Pakistan's total military expenditures. The Defense Department Appropriations Act, 2007 (P.L. 109-289) allows that up to $900 million in Pentagon funds be used for FY2007 reimbursements.

Saudi Arabia and Terrorism[29]

Commission Concerns and Recommendations

The September 11, 2001 attacks kindled criticism within the United States of alleged official Saudi involvement in terrorism or of Saudi laxity in acting against terrorist groups. Some critics believe that Saudi domestic and foreign policies have created a climate that may have contributed to terrorist acts by Islamic radicals. Critics, for example, have cited reports that the Saudi government permitted or encouraged fund raising by allegedly charitable institutions with links to Al Qaeda. Saudi leaders maintain that they are working to suppress terrorism, which they say is aimed even more at the Saudi regime than at the United States. The U.S. State Department acknowledges a more proactive Saudi stance against terrorist groups since terrorist attacks on Saudi Arabia in 2003.

In its July 2004 report, the 9/11 Commission described Saudi Arabia as having been "a problematic ally in combating Islamic extremism." The report took note of long-standing cooperative relations between the U.S. and Saudi governments and acknowledged the integral role of charitable donations in the Islamic religion. At the same time, the report noted a lack of oversight mechanisms to monitor charitable spending in Saudi Arabia, misunderstandings between the United States and Saudi Arabia at the popular level, and recent reform measures adopted by the Saudi Government. In its recommendations, the Commission states that the United States and Saudi Arabia must confront openly the problems in their relationship and "determine if they can build a relationship that both sides are prepared to publicly defend—a relationship about more than oil." The report went on to urge a "shared commitment" to political and economic reform" in Saudi Arabia and a "shared interest in greater tolerance and cultural respect," as a means of fighting violent extremists.[30] In late 2005, U.S. and Saudi officials initiated a "strategic dialogue" to expand cooperation in six key areas: counter-terrorism, military affairs, energy, business, education and human development, and consular affairs.

Congressional Responses

Provisions Enacted. Relevant sections of the Intelligence Reform and Terrorism Prevention Act of 2004 (P.L. 108-458) capture many of the concerns reflected in the 9/11 Commission report regarding Saudi Arabia. Section 7105(a) contains findings which review problems in the bilateral relationship but note improvements in counter-terrorism cooperation between the two countries since mid-2003. Section 7105(b) expresses the sense of Congress that "there should be a more robust dialogue between the people and Government of the United States and the people and Government of Saudi Arabia." Section 7120(b) required the President to submit to Congress within 180 days a strategy for collaboration with Saudi Arabia, as part of a larger report on U.S. government activities to implement the provisions of this act. The strategy paper was to include steps to institutionalize U.S.-Saudi relationships, intelligence and security cooperation, ways to increase Saudi contributions to peace and stability in the Middle East, political and economic reform, ways to promote tolerance and diversity in Saudi Arabia, and ways to diminish support from Saudi sources to extremist groups. The Administration transmitted the classified report to designated congressional committees on September 7, 2005.[31]

Though not directly addressed as an issue in the 9/11 Commission Report, some Members of Congress have criticized the U.S. military assistance program of $20-25,000 per year under the International Military Education and Training (IMET) program because of what they perceive to be the failure of Saudi authorities to suppress terrorist activity and incitement. House amendments to the Foreign Operations Appropriations Acts for FY2005 (incorporated as Division D of the FY2005 Consolidated Appropriations Act, P.L. 108-447, December 8, 2004) and FY2006 [P.L.109-102] banned U.S. aid to Saudi Arabia. However, Senate versions of both bills did not include such bans, and presidential national security waiver authority was included in the final versions of both pieces of legislation. President Bush exercised his waiver authority in FY2005, but did not issue a waiver for FY2006 funds because, according to State Department officials, FY2006 funds appropriated for use in Saudi Arabia were not obligated. On June 9, 2006, the House adopted H.Amdt. 997 to the Foreign Operations Appropriations Act for FY2007 (H.R. 5522) by 312-97 (Roll no. 244); the amendment prohibits U.S. assistance to Saudi Arabia and contains no presidential waiver provision. H.R. 5522 passed the House on June 9; the Senate has not passed its version as of November 20.

Related Options Also Considered. Congressional concerns continue during the 109th Congress over the role of Saudi Arabia in the war against terrorism, with particular emphasis on encouraging Saudi leaders to heighten their efforts against terrorist financing. H.R. 2037/S. 1171, the Saudi Arabia Accountability Act of 2005, is similar to the Saudi Arabia Accountability Act proposed but not enacted in the 108th Congress (H.R. 3643/S. 1888). Like the earlier bills, the 109th proposal would prohibit export or issuance of an export license to Saudi Arabia for any U.S. defense articles or defense services on the U.S. munitions list or dual use items and would restrict travel of Saudi diplomats in the United States. S. 12, the Targeting Terrorists More Effectively Act of 2005, introduced on January 24, 2005, contains sections on Saudi Arabia including:

- A statement of U.S. policy to work with the Saudi government to curtail terrorist financing through a variety of methods.
- Findings that Saudi Arabia has an uneven record in fighting terrorism, especially with regard to terrorist financing, support for radical *madrasas*

(schools), and lack of political outlets for its citizens; and that the Saudi government must undertake political and economic reforms.

- A requirement for the President to submit a report to designated congressional committees containing a long-term strategy for U.S.-Saudi engagement and for effective prevention of terrorist financing.[32]

H.R. 2037, S. 1171, and S. 12 remained in committee and had not passed as of November 30, 2006.

Terrorism: Its Global Dimensions[33] (Denying Sanctuary and Building a Coalition)

Commission Concerns and Recommendations

The 9/11 Commission Report emphasizes the global nature of the terrorist threat. It is portrayed as a threat that is motivated by religion. It is a threat consisting of a stateless network of terrorists. This threat with global dimensions is also characterized as a radical ideological movement in the Islamic world, inspired in part by Al Qaeda. The Commission advocates attacking terrorist organizations as a strategy and tactic for responding to the threat. It recommends that the United States identify and prioritize terrorist sanctuaries, working with allies, and developing a realistic strategy to keep terrorists insecure and on the run. As specific examples, it refers to Pakistan, Afghanistan, and Saudi Arabia, but also identifies broader regions: the Arabian Peninsula; Horn of Africa; Southeast Asia; West Africa; and European cities. The National Strategy for Combating Terrorism, released by the Bush Administration in September 2006, places strong emphasis on closing down terrorist sanctuaries.

A second Commission recommendation relating to the global dimensions of terrorism centers on turning a national strategy into a coalition strategy. To this end, the Commission recommends that the United States engage other nations in developing a comprehensive coalition strategy against Islamist terrorism. Included here are joint strategies for targeting terrorist travel and a common strategy to deal with sanctuaries.

The National Strategy for Combating Terrorism, released by the Bush Administration in September 2006, also places strong emphasis on promoting international cooperation in the global fight against terrorism.

Congressional Responses

Legislation Enacted. Many congressional decisions related to measures designed to respond to the global terrorist threat are expected to be manifested through the appropriations process. Title VII, of the Intelligence Reform and Terrorism Prevention Act of 2004, P.L. 108-458, section 7102, mirrors Commission recommendations by expressing a Sense of the Congress that it should be the policy of the United States to identify terrorist sanctuaries, work with allies, and develop a strategy to prevent terrorists from using foreign countries as sanctuaries. It also requires a report from the President to Congress on terrorist sanctuaries and what is being done to eliminate them. H.R. 4942, (109th Congress, Second Session), the Promoting Antiterrorism Capabilities through International Cooperation Act, would establish an office within DHS to promote international anti-terrorism cooperation.

Policy Concerns Not Addressed or Postponed. The issue of creating a coalition is arguably, a matter best suited for diplomats and not legislators. Notwithstanding, an office within DHS charged with promoting anti-terror cooperation could arguably do much to enhance such cooperation. However, the need for such cooperation, as envisioned by the 9/11 Commission, goes well beyond the jurisdictional domain of DHS. In this regard, creation of a joint congressional/executive branch commission to look at the overall issue of promoting international anti-terror cooperation—similar in structure to the National Commission on terrorism may warrant consideration.

Arguably also, physical sanctuaries are declining in overall importance to terrorist groups which are becoming increasingly decentralized both geographically and in terms of organizational hierarchy. This might warrant congressional consideration of the pro's and con's of including the issue of use by terrorists of virtual sanctuaries in any required reports to Congress on the issue of terrorist sanctuaries.

Islam and U.S. Policy[34]

Commission Concerns and Recommendations

Since the September 11, 2001, terrorist attacks, many experts have stated that the fight against terrorism cannot be won using force alone; it must be accompanied by long term policies that address development and reform issues in Arab and Muslim-majority countries and by a sophisticated public diplomacy effort that seeks to counter anti-American views commonly found in these countries. The 9/11 Commission Report's recommendations on tempering extremism in the Middle East and elsewhere echoed these sentiments. According to the report, "A comprehensive U.S. strategy to counter terrorism should include economic policies that encourage development, more open societies, and opportunities for people to improve the lives of their families and to enhance prospects for their children's future."

The 9/11 Commission Report also stressed that while U.S. public diplomacy, trade and cultural exchange, and international assistance programs are necessary, ultimately, it is our policies in the region that fuel anger and resentment. According to the report, "Right or wrong, it is simply a fact that American policy regarding the Israeli-Palestinian conflict and American actions in Iraq are dominant staples of popular commentary across the Arab and Muslim world." Increasingly, public debate over how best to win the "struggle of ideas"in the Arab and Muslim world has shifted away from the "means" (policy instruments) and toward the "ends" (overall direction of U.S. policy). Critics charge that U.S. efforts to highlight its outreach and assistance to Muslim societies has been overtaken by the negative Arab and Muslim reaction to alleged human rights abuses at Abu Ghraib, and Guantanamo Bay. Furthermore, many Arabs and Muslims feel that the United States continues to place its strategic regional interests above those of human rights and democracy by insufficiently protesting alleged abuses committed by friendly regional governments under the guise of the war on terror.

Congressional Responses

Due to the complexity and broad scope of directives laid out by the 9/11 Commission Report, it has been difficult for the U.S. government, including Congress, to address all of the various policy problems and solutions to the challenge of Islamic extremism. P.L.108-458, the Intelligence Reform and Terrorism Prevention Act of 2004, is one piece of legislation that addresses many of the 9/11 Commission Reports recommendations. However, P.L.108-458 only authorized the expansion of existing programs; it did not appropriate new funds. For example, P.L.108-458 authorized the following steps to expand U.S. public diplomacy efforts with the Muslim world and promote reform and democracy throughout the "broader Middle East:"

- (section 7112) authorized a substantial expansion of U.S. exchange, scholarship, and library programs that benefit people in the Muslim world.
- (section 7112) authorized the creation of a pilot program to make grants to United States-sponsored elementary and secondary schools in countries with predominantly Muslim populations for the purpose of providing full or partial merit-based scholarships to students from lower-income and middle-income families of such countries to attend such schools.
- (section 7113) authorized the establishment of an International Youth Opportunity Fund to provide financial assistance for the improvement of public education in the Middle East and other countries of strategic interest with predominantly Muslim populations.
- (section 7115) authorized the Middle East Partnership Initiative (MEPI), an economic assistance program designed to promote reform and democracy in the Arab world. MEPI, which Congress had not previously authorized, has received $284 million since its creation in FY2002.

For fiscal years 2005-2006 and possibly for fiscal year 2007, Congress has used the appropriations process to expand funding for various government sponsored activities such as cultural exchange, democracy promotion in the Arab world, international broadcasting in Arabic and Farsi, and development assistance for education and health. H.R. 5522, the FY2007 Foreign Operations Appropriations bill (passed the House but not the Senate), provides $75 million for MEPI, of which $9 million is for scholarship programs for students from countries with significant Muslim populations at not-for-profit institutions of basic and higher education in the Middle East. H.R. 5522 also recommends $20 million for the promotion of democracy in countries located outside the Middle East region with significant Muslim populations, such as Indonesia. The Senate version of H.R. 5522 also recommends $750,000 for the Center for Middle Eastern-Western Dialogue, an organization whose mission is to provide a forum for ongoing interaction and dialogue between citizens of the United States and Muslim-majority countries on key issues of mutual concern.

Policy Concerns Not Addressed

Radical Islam in Europe. Some critics assert that although poverty-reduction measures and the promotion of liberal reforms are desperately needed in many Arab and Muslim-majority countries, they are not a panacea and that many international terrorists, including some of Al Qaeda's top planners, were Western-educated and middle class residents of European countries. Some terrorism experts suggest that fundamentalist ideologies enjoy the most receptivity among Arab and Muslim migrant communities in Western countries, which face psychological dislocation and alienation in a new and unfamiliar environment.[35]

Islam in Politics. By calling for political reform and liberalization in the Muslim world, policymakers run the risk of empowering religious opposition parties that may seek to permanently enshrine Islamic religious law in a country's political and social system. Critics of U.S. foreign policy to combat extremism argue that based on their experience with Iran during its 1979 revolution and the subsequent influence of Islamist militant groups elsewhere in the region, the United States and other Western powers are wary of Islamist groups taking power (as Hamas did in 2006) and that Western support for secular autocratic regimes further enhances the credibility of opposition Islamist groups and some radical organizations. Political conditions vary across the Middle East and some Islamic groups are more moderate than others.

Terrorism: U.S. Policy Instruments[36]

Commission Concerns and Recommendations

The report of the 9/11 Commission underlined the importance for the United States of using the full range of policy instruments at its disposal to attack terrorists and their organizations and prevent the continued growth of Islamic terrorism. These policy instruments include not only intelligence, law enforcement, military force (treated elsewhere), but also diplomacy, bilateral support and economic assistance to front- line and failing states, support for democracy and good governance, international education and exchanges, and public diplomacy to engage the struggle of ideas and define and defend U.S. ideals and values (see below).

The Commission called on the United States to offer an example of moral leadership in the world, commit to treating people humanely, abide by the rule of law, and be generous and caring to its neighbors. It argued that the United States must stand for a better future in countries whose governments are repressive, even if they are friendly towards the United States.

Congressional Responses

The Intelligence Reform and Terrorism Prevention Act of 2004 (P.L. 108-458) addressed a number of themes in the 9/11 Commission Report. In Sec. 7101, Congress found that long-term success in the war on terrorism would require the use of all elements of national power, in addition to military action, intelligence, covert operations, law enforcement, and homeland defense, also including economic policy, foreign aid, and public diplomacy. The Act stated that the United States must give economic and diplomatic instruments as high a priority as military capabilities. This implied the need for increased funding for foreign affairs programs.

In Sec. 7115, it was the sense of Congress that U.S. strategy to counter terrorism should include economic policies that encourage development, open societies, and opportunities for people. The Act further states that U.S. policy should include lowering of trade barriers for poor countries, as well as promote economic reform and rule of law, especially in Muslim countries.

More concrete Congressional action related to these recommendations was not contained in P.L.108-458. The Administration's and Congress' response to these recommendations was reflected to some degree in subsequent foreign relations authorizations and the FY2006 and FY2007 State Department and Foreign Operations Appropriations legislation. While the FY2007 appropriations have not yet been enacted, both the President's request and the relevant bills in the House and Senate reflect some of the priorities contained in the recommendations. Funding for diplomacy and foreign aid have been more closely tied to strategic requirements of the war on terrorism. Foreign aid to the "front-line states" in the war has been increased. More generally, economic assistance has been directed to reducing poverty, creating jobs, and improving education as an antidote to terrorist recruitment in impoverished areas. Resources have also been increased for improving America's image through public diplomacy and international broadcasting, as well as for cultural and educational exchange programs. In the FY2007 appropriations the Administration has requested funding to implement its "transformational diplomacy" and "transformational development" initiatives, aimed at revamping U.S. diplomacy and foreign aid policy for the 21st Century.

Public Diplomacy, Education and Exchange Programs[37]

Commission Concerns and Recommendations. Noting that terrorism is a result of resentment by some Muslims because of American engagement in the Muslim world, the 9/11 Commission asserted that public diplomacy is a key tool in the war on terrorism in helping to change attitudes about America. The Commission recommended that the United States, through the use of public diplomacy, convey respect for human dignity, assist in providing education for their children, and offer hope for economic opportunity. The Commission recommended that America more aggressively promote its values and advertise the aid given by the citizens of the United States. The Commission specifically recommended increasing funding for such public diplomacy activities as international broadcasting, exchanges, and overseas library programs, targeting these activities toward the youth.

Congressional Response. The Intelligence Reform and Terrorism Prevention Act of 2004 (P.L. 108-458) contained several measures intended to increase U.S. government public diplomacy activities as recommended by the 9/11 Commission. Sense of Congress provisions affirmed that the U.S. government should offer an example of values and respect for human dignity and should work with other governments to provide human dignity, economic opportunity, and tolerance. Furthermore, the United States should promote the ideas of individual freedom, educational opportunity, political participation and tolerance for opposing points of view.

Other provisions:

- stated that it is United States policy to promote free media and journalistic integrity overseas through public diplomacy programs and required establishing a media network with grants provided to the National Endowment for Democracy (NED) and authorizes such sums as may be necessary to establish the media network.
- required the Secretary of State to make public diplomacy an integral component in U.S. foreign policy and coordinate public diplomacy activities with all agencies as well as the Broadcasting Board of Governors.
- urged the Secretary of State to recruit, hire, train and promote Foreign Service Officers with an emphasis on public diplomacy and foreign languages of Muslim populations.
- declared that the President and Secretary of State should use the weight of the United States to promote public diplomacy in multilateral organizations and shall provide public diplomacy training for Foreign and Civil

Service personnel who represent the United States in multilateral organizations.

For the Consolidated Appropriations Act of FY2005 (P.L. 108-447), conferees noted that alarming public opinion polls and media content continue to reveal profound anti-American sentiments and direct the Department of State to submit reports outlining the criteria for measuring performance of expanded public diplomacy efforts. This Act expanded funding for international information programs, cultural exchanges and international broadcasting, particularly in Muslim populations.

The 109th Congress made some gains in meeting the public diplomacy recommendations of the 9/11 Commission largely through the appropriations process. The Foreign Operations, Export Financing, and Related Programs Appropriation, FY2006 (P.L. 109-102) established a new account entitled Democracy Fund. This account is intended to increase effectiveness and oversight of programs that promote democracy, governance, human rights, independent media, and the rule of law globally. Within this new account amounting to $95 million for FY2006 is additional funding for the National Endowment for Democracy (NED), as well as other programs and countries.

Within the State Department appropriation for FY2006 (P.L. 109-108) Congress increased funding for already-established public diplomacy programs, including educational and cultural exchanges, international broadcasting, and regular appropriations for the NED. Additional funding for public diplomacy programs, specifically U.S. broadcasting into Iran, was included in the FY2006 supplemental (P.L. 109-234).

The 109th Congress also considered, but did not pass, Foreign Relations Authorization legislation (H.R. 2601/S. 600) which included measures to authorize grants be extended to the Middle East Broadcasting Networks (MBN), subject to specified limitations and restrictions, such as the Broadcasting Board of Governors (BBG) taking full responsibility for the direction taken by the MBN.

Terrorist Financing[38]

Commission Concerns and Recommendations

The report of the National Commission on Terrorist Attacks Upon the United States (the 9-11 Commission report) sought to refocus the policy debate concerning terrorist financing. The Commission recommended that the Bush Administration shift its focus from seizing terrorist funds to tracking terrorist financial networks in order to gain actionable counter-terrorism intelligence.[39] The Commission also emphasized terrorist organizations' increasing shift to informal methods of money transfer such as *hawala* or *hundi*.[40]

These recommendation have led to an ongoing discussion over the sources and methods used to collect financial intelligence. For example, Congress has investigated efforts by the Department of the Treasury to track international transfers of funds to and from terrorists by accessing information held by the Society for Worldwide Interbank Financial Telecommunication (SWIFT).[41] SWIFT is a Brussels-based entity that serves as a major hub for international communications among banks and other financial institutions.

Given the experience of the five years since 9/11, legislators and executive branch officials have determined that combating terrorist financing requires effective coordination of many different federal government activities including intelligence gathering, financial regulation, law enforcement, and building international coalitions. Improving the interagency coordination of U.S. counter-terrorist financing efforts remains one of the largest challenges for the U.S. government. According to a 2006 Government Accountability Office report, "the U.S. government lacks an integrated strategy to coordinate the delivery of counter-terrorism financing training and technical assistance to countries it deems vulnerable to terrorist financing."[42] The report recommends, among other things, that the Secretaries of State and the Treasury implement an integrated strategic plan and a Memorandum of Agreement for the delivery of training and technical assistance.

In an effort to focus U.S. counter-terrorist financing efforts, in March 2004, the Department of the Treasury created the Office of Terrorism and Financial Intelligence (TFI). TFI was designed to integrate several offices within Treasury: the Office of Terrorist Financing and Financial Crime (TF/FC), the Office of Foreign Assets Control (OFAC), the Financial Crimes Enforcement Network (FinCEN), the Office of Intelligence and Analysis (OIA), and the Treasury Executive Office for Asset Forfeiture (TEOAF). In addition to an Under Secretary, four new senior level positions were created: Assistant and Deputy Assistant Secretaries for Terrorist Financing and Assistant and Deputy Assistant Secretaries for Intelligence and Analysis.

Congressional Responses

Several sections of the Intelligence Reform and Terrorism Prevention Act of 2004 (PL 108-458) address terrorist financing. The Act made technical corrections to the International Money Laundering Abatement and Anti-Terrorist Financing Act, Title III of the *USA PATRIOT Act* (PL 107-56) (Sec. 6202); authorized the Treasury to produce currency, postage stamps, and other security documents for foreign governments subject to certain conditions (Sec. 6301); and reauthorized funds for the biannual money laundering and financial crimes strategy report, the most recent of which was released in 2003 (Sec. 6102).[43] As of November 2006, the expected 2005 national money laundering and financial crimes strategy report has not been released.

The Act authorized funding to improve FinCEN (Sec. 6101). The Act authorized $19 million for improvements related to FinCEN's telecommunications and analytic capacity and authorized $16.5 million for the development of FinCEN's Bank Secrecy Act (BSA) Direct program. In June 2004, Treasury established the BSA Direct Retrieval and Sharing program (BSA R&S). This program was designed to make it easier for law enforcement to access and analyze BSA data and to improve overall data management. Treasury had trouble implementing the BSA R&S program due to problems with its main contractor, Electronic Data Systems. On July 13, 2006, FinCEN halted the program.[44] Robert Werner, FinCEN Director, testified on September 12, 2006 that FinCEN is initiating a "re-planning effort" for the retrieval and sharing component of BSA Direct. No expected completion date has been announced.[45]

The Act required the Secretary of the Treasury to prescribe regulations requiring selected financial institutions to report to FinCEN certain cross-border electronic transmittals of funds (wire-transfers) (Sec. 6302). New regulations must be promulgated by December 2007. Treasury is currently determining the feasibility and impact of these additional reporting requirements.[46]

The Act required the President to submit to Congress a report evaluating and making recommendations on: (1) the effectiveness of efforts and methods to track terrorist financing; (2) ways to improve governmental cooperation; (3) ways to improve the performance of financial institutions; (4) the adequacy of agency coordination and ways to improve that coordination; and (5) recommendations for changes in law and additional resources required to improve this effort (Section 6303). This report was due in September 2005 and has not yet been submitted to Congress.[47]

The Act requires the Secretary of the Treasury to work with the International Monetary Fund (IMF) to combat terrorist financing and to testify before Congress on the status of implementation of international anti-money laundering and counter-terrorist financing standards by the IMF and other multilateral agencies (Sec. 7703). The IMF is actively involved in establishing anti-money laundering standards and continues to review the anti-money laundering frameworks of IMF member countries.[48]

The Secretary of the Treasury is also required to continue to convene the interagency United States Government Financial Action Task Force (FATF) working group to review and develop U.S. and international anti-money laundering standards (Sec. 7704).[49] The U.S. government is actively involved in FATF operations and has promoted the adoption of international anti-terrorist financing best practices through engagement with and support of a number of FATF-style regional bodies, such as the Middle East and North Africa (MENA) FATF. In March 2006, the Treasury Department established a U.S.-MENA Private Sector Dialogue. A similar dialogue with the Latin American financial community is underway and Treasury is planning to hold an anti-money laundering conference in Latin America in early 2007.[50]

U.S. Military Forces and the War on Terrorism[51]

Commission Concerns and Recommendations

Recommendation 32 of the 9/11 Commission Report states that "the lead responsibility for directing and executing paramilitary operations, whether clandestine or covert, should shift to the Defense Department. There it should be consolidated with the capabilities for training, direction, and execution of such operations already being developed in the Special Operations Command." (Page 415).

The 9-11 Commission's apparent concern appeared to be both performance and cost-based. The report states that the CIA did not sufficiently invest in developing a robust capability to conduct paramilitary operations with U.S. personnel prior to 9/11, and instead relied on improperly trained proxies (foreign personnel under contract) resulting in an unsatisfactory outcome. The report also states that the United States does not have the money or people to build "two separate capabilities for carrying out secret military operations," and suggests that we should "concentrate responsibility and necessary legal authorities in one entity."

Congressional Responses

Relevant Provisions Enacted by Congress. Section 1013 of P.L. 108-458 requires the National Intelligence Director, in consultation with the Secretary of Defense and the Director of the Central Intelligence Agency to develop joint procedures to improve the coordination and deconfliction in the planning, execution, and sustainment of operations involving DOD and the CIA. It also requires information exchange between the Secretary of Defense and Director CIA, so that senior operational officials have knowledge of the existence of all ongoing operations. When appropriate, it requires mutual agreement on tactical and strategic objectives.

Policy Concerns Not Addressed. P.L. 108-458 did not address the recommended shift of responsibility for paramilitary operations from the CIA to DOD. Some speculated that this particular issue was too complex and contentious to be included in intelligence reform legislation and that it required further study and analysis. Others suggested that there was no need to shift responsibilities, only to improve coordination and planning between the CIA and DOD which Section 1013 addresses.

Options Considered by the 109th Congress. The 109th Congress did not address this issue legislatively. On November 23, 2004, President Bush issued a letter requiring the Secretary of Defense and the Director of Central Intelligence to review matters relating to Recommendation 32 and submit their advice to him by February 23, 2005. This review directed the examination of all aspects including legal, funding, operational, and supporting infrastructure. A preliminary Pentagon study reportedly concluded that

DOD should not take over the paramilitary responsibility from the CIA.[52] In unclassified testimony to the Senate Select Committee on Intelligence in February 2005, the Director of the CIA testified that the CIA and DOD disagreed with the 9-11 Committee's recommendation.[53] In June of 2005 it was reported that the Secretary of Defense and the Director of the Central Intelligence Agency responded to the President, stating that "neither the CIA nor DOD endorses the commission's recommendation on shifting the paramilitary mission or operations."[54] The Administration apparently accepted DOD's and the CIA's recommendation and reportedly rejected the 9-11 Commission's recommendation to shift the responsibility for paramilitary operations to DOD.[55]

Weapons of Mass Destruction: Proliferation Security and Threat Reduction[56]

Commission Concerns and Recommendations

In view of intelligence assessments that Al Qaeda has been seeking to acquire weapons of mass destruction for several years, the 9/11 Commission concluded that WMD nonproliferation efforts should be expanded and provided additional resources. Specifically, the Commission recommended: (1) the development of an international legal regime "with universal jurisdiction" to interdict, capture, and prosecute those trafficking in WMD and related technology; (2) the expansion of the Proliferation Security Initiative (PSI) to include Russia, China, and all NATO countries; (3) the expansion of the Cooperative Threat Reduction (CTR) program and the provision of additional financial resources.

Congressional Responses

There has been no congressional initiative regarding the establishment of an international WMD anti-smuggling regime, aside from the continued full funding of the Proliferation Security Initiative (PSI).[57] The Administration has secured the passage of United Nations Resolution 1540 which requires member states to criminalize proliferation, establish export controls over WMD-related technology, and secure WMD-related materiel. The resolution does not provide for enforcement, nor address the establishment of any international anti-smuggling regime.

Members of the 109th Congress introduced several bills and resolutions that called for strengthening and expanding the PSI: S.Con.Res. 36, H.Con.Res. 133, S.Con.Res. 40, H.R. 422, H.R. 665, H.R. 5017/S. 3456, and S. 2566. None, however, was brought to the floor of either chamber. Geographic expansion remains a key issue—particularly how to engage China and India, as well as states in important regions like the Arabian Peninsula. The 110th Congress may consider how intelligence resources are handled.

Is intelligence sufficient and are there intelligence-sharing requirements with non-NATO allies? Also, how is PSI coordinated with other federal interdiction-related programs (e.g., export control assistance)? One potential complication for congressional oversight of PSI is the absence of a way to measure PSI's success, relative to past efforts.

The Cooperative Threat Reduction (CTR) program (also known as NunnLugar), which is administered by DOD's Threat Reduction Agency, continues to receive congressional funding support. In the FY2004 National Defense Authorization Act (P.L. 108-176, Sec. 1308), Congress authorized the Bush Administration to spend $50 million of unobligated funds from the Cooperative Threat Reduction Program in states outside the former Soviet Union. As of September 2006, the Administration had spent such funds only in Albania ($38.5 million) for the purpose of eliminating chemical weapons stockpiles.

The 109th Congress considered the following legislation that could restrict the provision of CTR assistance to some countries. The State Department's annual foreign operations appropriations bill, the Foreign Operations, Export Financing, and Related Programs Appropriations Act, includes provisions that prohibit assistance to certain countries. Section 507 of the FY2006 foreign operations appropriations bill (P.L.109-102) states that no funds will be "obligated or expended to finance directly any assistance or reparations to Cuba, Libya, North Korea, Iran, or Syria." The FY2007 bill passed in the House (H.R. 5522) and awaiting passage in the Senate includes the same provision. The Iran Freedom Support Act, introduced in both the House and the Senate (H.R. 282/S. 333), could make supplying CTR assistance to Iran more difficult. The Iran-Libya Sanction Act (P.L. 104- 172) has been extended through September 2011, pursuant to the Iran Freedom Support Act (P.L. 109-293). Sudan has been severely limited from receiving U.S. assistance since 1997 by a combination of executive order and U.S. law. These include Executive Order 13067, Section 520 of the Foreign Operations, Export Financing, and Related Programs Appropriations Act, 2006 (P.L. 109-102), the Comprehensive Peace in Sudan Act of 2004 (P.L. 108-497) and The Sudan Peace Act (P.L. 107-245). The 109th also considered legislation that could affect third party states, or any state that could potentially receive CTR assistance, to the extent such states are considered for these initiatives. For example, Section 542 of the FY2006 foreign operations bill (P.L.109-102) prohibited assistance to countries that provide lethal military equipment to State Sponsors of Terrorism. Other examples include P.L. 109-267 which extended the Iran-Libya Sanctions Act, the Iran Nonproliferation Amendments Act (P.L. 109-112), which added Syria to that Act, and the North Korea Nonproliferation Act of 2006 (S. 3728), which added North Korea to the Iran—Syria Nonproliferation Act.[58]

Border Security and Immigration[59]

Terrorist Travel

Commission Concerns and Recommendations. The 9/11 Commission issued several recommendations that directly pertain to immigration law and policy. These recommendations focused primarily on targeting terrorist travel through an intelligence and security strategy based on reliable identification systems and effective, integrated information-sharing, including the expansion and consolidation of the border-screening systems. More specifically, the 9/11 Commission concluded that targeting travel is at least as powerful a weapon against terrorists as targeting their money, and recommended that the United States combine intelligence, operations, and law enforcement in a strategy to intercept terrorists, find terrorist travel facilitators, and constrain terrorist mobility.

Congressional Response.[60] The Intelligence Reform and Terrorism Prevention Act (ITRPA) of 2004 (P.L. 108-458) included several provisions aimed at targeting terrorist travel. The Act calls for the accelerated deployment of the biometric entry and exit system to process or contain certain data on aliens and their physical characteristics (see discussion below).[61] It required an in-person consular interview of most applicants for non-immigrant visas between the ages of 14 and 79, and also required an alien applying for a non-immigrant visa to completely and accurately respond to any request for information contained in his or her application.[62] The Act also expanded the pre-inspection program that places U.S. immigration inspectors at foreign airports, increasing the number of foreign airports where travelers would be pre-inspected before departure to the United States. Moreover, it required individuals entering the United States (including U.S. citizens and visitors from Canada and other Western Hemisphere countries) to bear a passport or other documents sufficient to denote citizenship and identity.

The Act required improvements in technology and training to assist consular and immigration officers in detecting and combating terrorist travel. It (1) established the Human Smuggling and Trafficking Center, which included an interagency program devoted to countering terrorist travel; (2) required the Secretary of Homeland Security, in consultation with the Director of the National Counter Terrorism Center, to establish a program to oversee DHS's responsibilities with respect to terrorist travel; and (3) established a Visa and Passport Security Program within the Bureau of Diplomatic Security at the Department of State.

In the 109th Congress, the REAL ID Act of 2005 (P.L. 109-13, Division B), among other things, required DHS to: conduct a study on U.S. border security vulnerabilities; establish a pilot program to test ground surveillance technologies on the northern and southern borders to enhance U.S. border security; and implement a plan to improve communications systems and information-sharing between federal, state, local, and tribal agencies on matters relating to border security. DHS was also required to submit reports to Congress regarding its implementation of these requirements.[63] The Secure Fence Act (P.L. 109-367) required DHS to deploy double-layer fencing to 850 miles of the U.S. international border with Mexico.[64]

Terrorist Screening and Watch Lists[65]

Commission Concerns and Recommendations. The 9/11 Commission concluded that the U.S. intelligence and law enforcement community missed several vital opportunities to watch-list and screen several conspirators involved in the 9/11 terrorist attacks.[66] In addition, the Commission recommended that U.S. border security systems be integrated with other systems to expand the network of screening points to include the nation's transportation system and access to vital facilities.[67] Despite problems with high-profile misidentifications,[68] the Commission also recommended that the controversial "No-Fly" and "Automatic Selectee" lists maintained by the DHS's Transportation Security Administration be improved without delay.[69]

Congressional Response. In the Intelligence Reform and Terrorism Prevention Act of 2004 (P.L. 108-458), Congress included several watch list related airline passenger prescreening provisions that require that airline passengers, among others, be prescreened against the consolidated terrorist watch list database. Another provision requires the Administration to report to Congress on (1) the criteria used to place persons on terrorism-related watch lists, and (2) the privacy and civil liberty implications of the further use of the "No Fly" and "Automatic Selectee" lists. These and other aviation security provisions are described below under "Transportation Security."

Related Administrative Response. Under Homeland Security Presidential Directive 6 (HSPD-6),[70] the Bush Administration elevated and expanded terrorist identification and watch-list functions by establishing a consolidated terrorist watch list database.[71] Undergirding these screening processes is a consolidated Terrorist Screening Database (TSDB), which under HSPD-6 has been established and maintained by the Terrorist Screening Center (TSC) —a multi-agency effort administered by the Federal Bureau of Investigation (FBI). Among other things, the TSC provides support to:

- the Department of State's Bureau of Consular Affairs by issuing terrorism-related security advisory opinions for visa issuance purposes;
- the Department of Homeland Security's (DHS's) Customs and Border Protection in evaluating potential matches between terrorist lookout records and persons entering the United States at international ports of entry; and

- nearly 750,000 state and local law enforcement officers to whom limited TSDB lookout records have been made available through the National Crime Information Center.

In April 2006, the DHS Privacy Office issued a report assessing the impact of the "No Fly" and "Automatic Selectee" lists on privacy and civil liberties.[72] The report cited concerns about the quality of the information of those lists, as well as the underlying intelligence.[73] The report also noted allegations about profiling on the basis of race, religion, or national origin, but reported that it could not substantiate those allegations.[74]

In regard to the criteria used to place individuals on terrorist watch lists, it is unknown whether the Administration reported to Congress on this matter. Nevertheless, the Privacy Office report stressed that those criteria could not be made public without: (1) comprising intelligence and security, or (2) allowing persons wishing to avoid detection to subvert those lists.[75]

In addition, in late September 2006, the Government Accountability Office (GAO) released a report on efforts to reduce the adverse effects of terrorist watch list screening, outlining measures that DHS and the TSC had taken to reduce and alleviate misidentifications.[76] It also noted that while the total number of misidentifications is unknown, their frequency, which is estimated to be in the tens-of-thousands, remains a serious concern.[77]

Biometric Screening System and Data Systems Integration[78]

Commission Concerns and Recommendations. The 9/11 Commission called for the expeditious implementation of "a biometric entry-exit screening system, including a single system for speeding qualified travelers." With respects to biometrics, the 9/11 Commission noted the following: "Biometrics have been introduced into an antiquated computer environment" and that "replacement of these systems and improved biometric systems will be required." The 9/11 Commission also recommended the integration of the various border screening systems with the US-VISIT system, including frequent traveler programs such as NEXUS and the Secure Electronic Network for Travelers' Rapid Inspections (SENTRI).[79]

Congressional Responses.[80] In an effort to implement the 9/11 Commission recommendations, Congress passed the Intelligence Reform and Terrorism Prevention Act of 2004 (P.L.108-458). Previously, Congress passed legislation that mandated DHS to implement entry and exit controls and integrate immigration-related databases and data systems.

Congress first mandated that the former Immigration and Naturalization Service (INS) implement an automated entry and exit data system that would track the arrival and departure of every alien in §110 of the Illegal Immigration Reform and Immigrant Responsibility Act of 1996 (IIRIRA; P.L. 104-208).[81] Several provisions in the Enhanced Border Security and Visa Entry Reform Act (Border Security Act; P.L. 107-173) and the Intelligence Reform and Terrorism Prevention Act of 2004, however, required the immediate implementation of an automated entry and exit data system and called for enhancements in its development, including a requirement that biometric identifiers be used in all visas and other travel documents and that the entry and exit data system be interoperable with other law enforcement and national security databases. Congress, however, first required the entry and exit data system be interoperable with other law enforcement systems in the Uniting and Strengthening America by Providing Appropriate Tools Required to Intercept and Obstruct Terrorism Act (PATRIOT Act; P.L. 107-56). The PATRIOT Act was also the first time Congress required the development and certification of a technology standard that has the capacity to verify the identity of persons applying for a visa or seeking to enter the United States.

The Intelligence Reform and Terrorism Prevention Act of 2004 called for the Secretary of DHS (Secretary) to develop a plan to accelerate the full implementation of an automated biometric entry and exit data system and to submit a report to Congress on the plan by July 17, 2005. The Act required the entry and exit data system to collect "biometric *exit* data for all categories of individuals who are required to provide biometric entry data."

The Act also required the integration of all databases and data systems that process or contain information on aliens by December 2006. The Act required the integrated data system to be an interoperable component of the entry and exit data system. The Act further required the Secretary to fully implement the interoperable electronic data system as specified in the Border Security Act. In addition to the integration of the entry and exit data system with other databases and data systems, the Act required the Secretary to develop and implement a plan to expedite the processing of registered travelers through a single registered traveler program that can be integrated into the broader automated biometric entry and exit data system.

Standards for Identification Documents[82]

Commission Concerns and Recommendations. The 9/11 Commission recommended that standards should be set "for the issuance of birth certificates and sources of identification, such as drivers licenses." The 9/11 Commission noted that fraudulent documents are ". . . no longer just a problem of theft," and that ports of entry are "the last opportunity to ensure that people are who they are. . ." Additionally, the 9/11 Commission recommended the elimination of the "Western Hemisphere Exception," whereby U.S. citizens returning from countries in the Western Hemisphere, and some citizens from designated Western Hemisphere nations, are not required to show a passport when entering the United States (but they are required to demonstrate citizenship). In doing so, the 9/11 Commission advocated for ensuring that all individuals presenting themselves for entry into the United States present biometric passports or other identification allowing their identities to be securely verified.

Congressional Response. In the 108th Congress, the Intelligence Reform and Terrorism Prevention Act of 2004 (P.L. 108-458) required the establishment of new standards aimed at ensuring the integrity for federal use of birth certificates, state-issued driver's licenses and identification cards, and social security cards. States may receive grants to assist them in implementing the proposed birth certificate and driver's license standards.[83] In the 109th Congress, the REAL ID Act of 2005 (P.L. 109-13, Division B) addressed this issue more directly, and while the Act does not directly impose federal standards with respect to states' issuance of driver's licenses and personal identification cards, states nevertheless appear to need to adopt such standards and modify any conflicting laws or regulations in order for such documents to be recognized by federal agencies for official purposes.[84]

The Intelligence Reform and Terrorism Prevention Act of 2004 also addressed the "Western Hemisphere Exception" by requiring individuals entering the United States (including U.S. citizens and visitors from Canada and other Western Hemisphere countries) to bear a passport or other documents sufficient to denote citizenship and identity as of January 1, 2008. In the 109th Congress, the fiscal year (FY) 2007 DHS Appropriations Act (P.L. 109-295) extended this deadline to the earlier of two dates: June 1, 2009; or no later than three months after the Secretary of Homeland Security and the Secretary of State certify that a series of implementation requirements have been met.[85]

Other Immigration Concerns[86]

Commission Concerns. Reforming the enforcement of immigration law is an underlying theme of the recommendations made by the 9/11 Commission. The 9/11 Commission concluded that the key officials responsible for determining alien admissions (consular officers abroad and immigration inspectors in the United States) were not considered full partners in counterterrorism efforts prior to September 11, 2001, and as a result, opportunities to intercept the September 11 terrorists were missed.[87]

They further recommended that the U.S. border security system be integrated into a larger network of screening points that includes our transportation system and access to vital facilities, such as nuclear reactors. In addition, they maintained that the Department of Homeland Security, with proper support from Congress, should complete a biometric entry-exit screening system, including a single system for speeding qualified travelers, as quickly as possible. They also expressed the view that the U.S. government cannot meet its own obligations to the American people to prevent the entry of terrorists without a major effort to collaborate with other governments.[88]

Congressional Response. The Intelligence Reform and Terrorism Prevention Act of 2004 (P.L. 108-458) included many immigration-related provisions aimed at addressing broad immigration enforcement concerns raised by the 9/11 Commission. The major features of these immigration-related provisions are summarized below.[89]

Grounds for Alien Exclusion, Removal, and Relief from Removal. The Intelligence Reform and Terrorism Prevention Act made any alien deportable who has received military training from or on behalf of an organization that, at the time of training, was a designated terrorist organization. It also made the revocation of a non-immigrant visa by the State Department grounds for removal. The visa revocation, however, is reviewable in a removal proceeding in cases where visa revocation provides the sole ground for removal. The Act made inadmissible and deportable any alien who (1) has ordered, incited, assisted, or participated in conduct that would be considered genocide under U.S. law; (2) committed or participated in an act of torture or an extrajudicial killing; or (3) while serving as a foreign official, was responsible for or directly carried out, at any time, particularly severe violations of religious freedom. The Act also required the Government Accountability Office to conduct a study evaluating the degree that weaknesses in the current U.S. asylum system have been or could be exploited by aliens involved in terrorist-related activity.

Allocation of Additional Resources to Improve Enforcement. The Act authorized the Secretary of State to increase the number of consular officers by 150 per year from FY2006 through FY2009 above the number of such positions for which funds were allotted for the preceding fiscal year. It also increased the numbers of border patrol agents by not less than 2,000, in each year FY2006 through FY2010, and required a number of agents equaling at least 20% of each year's increase in agents to be assigned to the northern border. The Act also increased the number of ICE investigators by not less than 800 in each year FY2006 through FY2010, and required an increase in the number of beds available for immigration detention and removal operations by not less than 8,000 over the same period. Further, the Act established a pilot program to test advanced technologies to improve border security between ports of entry along the northern border of the United States. It also required the Secretary of Homeland Security to submit to the President and Congress a plan for the systematic surveillance of the southwest border of the United States by remotely piloted aircraft, and to implement such plan as a pilot program.

In the 109th Congress, the REAL ID Act required DHS to develop a pilot program to increase the use of ground-surveillance technologies, including video cameras, sensors, and motion-detection technology, to monitor the northern and southwestern borders. The Secure Fence Act (P.L. 109-367) required DHS to deploy double-layer fencing to 850 miles of the U.S. international border with Mexico.[90]

Penalties for Immigration-Related Fraud and Alien Smuggling. The Intelligence Reform and Terrorism Prevention Act increased criminal penalties for alien smuggling in certain circumstances and required the Secretary of Homeland Security to develop an outreach program in the United States and overseas to educate the public about the penalties for illegally bringing in and harboring aliens.

Transportation Security

Aviation Security[91]

Commission Concerns and Recommendations.[92] The 9/11 Commission expressed concerns over air cargo security, the security of general aviation aircraft, screening of airline passengers and baggage, and access controls at airports. The 9/11 Commission made several specific recommendations to address these concerns.

The 9/11 Commission recommended that improved passenger prescreening not be further delayed by the long-running argument about a successor to the existing computer assisted passenger prescreening (CAPPS) program run by the airlines.[93] The 9/11 Commission recommended that the Transportation Security Administration (TSA) take over the function of prescreening passenger names using the larger set of watchlists maintained by the federal government and that the airlines should be compelled to provide the data needed to test and implement this new prescreening system.

The 9/11 Commission also recommended that the TSA and the Congress give priority attention to improving checkpoint screening for detecting explosives on passengers. It recommended that the TSA also conduct a human factors study to examine screener performance, and establish objectives for screeners and screening checkpoints.

The Commission expressed continued concerns over the screening of checked baggage and cargo. It indicated that the TSA should expedite the installation of advanced in-line baggage screening systems that are integrated with airport baggage processing systems. The Commission noted that, because the aviation industry will derive substantial benefits from this deployment, it should pay a fair share of the associated costs, although the commission did not provide specifics regarding recommended allocation of contributions to pay for in-line explosive detection systems integration.

The Commission recommended that the TSA intensify efforts to identify, track, and screen potentially dangerous cargo in aviation as well as in maritime operations. Additionally, the Commission specifically recommended the deployment of at least one hardened cargo container on every passenger aircraft that also hauls cargo to carry any suspicious shipments.

In addition to these recommendations directly addressing aviation security, the 9/11 Commission also urged establishing risk-based priorities for protecting transportation assets in all modes. It recommended that the TSA select the most practical and cost effective approaches for defending transportation assets and formalize a plan for implementing, budgeting, and funding this effort. The 9/11 Commission noted that the plan should assign roles to federal, state, and local authorities, as well as to private stakeholders.

Congressional Response. The 108th Congress passed two major pieces of legislation containing numerous provisions pertaining to aviation security: Vision 100—Century of Aviation Reauthorization Act (P.L. 108-176) and the Intelligence Reform and Terrorism Prevention Act of 2004 (P.L. 108-458).

Vision 100—Century of Aviation Reauthorization Act. Before the 9/11 Commission had completed its report, several aviation security-related provisions were included in Vision 100—Century of Aviation Reauthorization Act (P.L. 108-176) which was enacted on December 12, 2003. Vision 100:

- established a redress process for pilots, mechanics or other licensed aviation professionals whose certification is denied, suspended, or revoked on the grounds that they pose a risk to aviation security. Vision 100 also requires the Federal Aviation Administration to provide a justification to Congress when establishing an Air Defense Identification Zone (ADIZ) around cities where pilots are required to use special communications and operating procedures to enable air traffic controllers to identify potential security threats.
- modified existing requirements for security training of airline flight and cabin crew members. Under these provisions, the airlines are responsible for providing mandatory basic training in security for crews, while the TSA was to develop and provide a voluntary advanced self-defense training program for crew members.
- required the Department of Homeland Security to study and report to Congress on the effectiveness of the aviation security system, including the air marshal program, hardening of cockpit doors, and security screening of passengers, checked baggage, and cargo. The report was to include recommendations, including legislative recommendations, for improving the effectiveness of aviation security.
- created the Aviation Security Capital Fund. The Act authorizes up to $500 million per year through FY2007 to be appropriated to this fund and requires that the first $250 million in aviation security fee collections be deposited in this fund each year through FY2007. The Act also provided the Under Secretary for Border and Transportation Security with the authority to issue grants to airports for projects to integrate baggage explosive detection systems with baggage conveyer systems; reconfigure terminal baggage areas as needed to install explosive detection systems; deploy

explosive detection systems behind the ticket counter, in baggage sorting areas, or in line with baggage handling systems; and for other aviation security-related capital improvement projects. Vision 100 set the federal share of costs for such projects at 90% for large and medium hub airports, and at 95% for all other airports and set guidelines for the allocation of Aviation Security Capital Fund monies for these projects. However, appropriations language (see, for example, P.L. 109-295) has limited the federal share to 75% for large and medium hubs, and 90% for all other airports.

- required the implementation of security programs for air charter operators who use aircraft weighing more than 12,500 pounds maximum takeoff weight.
- required the Government Accountability Office (GAO) to review the proposed CAPPS II passenger prescreening system and prevented the TSA from fully implementing this program until the Under Secretary for Border and Transportation Security certified that a variety of enumerated issues pertaining to civil liberties, privacy, data protection, system security, system performance, and system oversight had been adequately addressed. The TSA has since scrapped the CAPPS II program and is developing an alterative prescreening system called "Secure Flight."
- authorized flight crew members of all-cargo airlines to voluntarily participate in the Federal Flight Deck Officer Program that trains and deputizes armed pilots to guard aircraft cockpits against hostile attacks. Vision 100 also expanded the program to include other flight crew members, such as flight engineers, in addition to pilots.
- requires the promulgation of regulations to ensure the security of foreign and domestic aircraft repair stations. The Act also requires the TSA, in coordination with the FAA, to complete a security review and audit of foreign repair stations that work on air carrier aircraft and components.
- modified the background check requirements for foreign pilots seeking flight training in the United States. The Act transferred the duties of conducting these background checks from the Department of Justice to the DHS. The provisions require flight schools or instructors to provide notification and identification information for individuals seeking training in smaller aircraft, weighing less than 12,500 pounds, and require background checks be completed before training can be initiated in larger aircraft. The legislation authorizes fee collections to offset the costs of conducting these background checks.[94]

The Intelligence Reform and Terrorism Prevention Act of 2004. The Intelligence Reform and Terrorism Prevention Act (P.L. 108-458) contains numerous provisions related to aviation security, many directly addressing the concerns and recommendations of the 9/11 Commission. The Act:

- requires the Department of Homeland Security to develop, prepare, implement, and update as needed, a National Strategy for Transportation Security as well as modal-specific security plans including a plan for aviation security. The modal security plan for aviation is to include a threat matrix outlining each threat to the United States civil aviation system and the corresponding layers of security in place to address these threats and a plan for mitigation and reconstitution of the aviation system in the event of a terrorist attack.
- requires the TSA to issue guidance for the use of biometrics in airport access control systems and establish biometric credential and authentication procedures to identify law enforcement officers authorized to carry firearms aboard passenger aircraft. The Act authorizes $20 million, in addition to any other authorized amounts, for research and development of biometric technologies for aviation security. The Act also authorizes $1 million to establish a center of excellence in biometric technologies.
- required the TSA to begin system testing of an advanced passenger prescreening system by January 1, 2005. Although the Act does not provide a deadline for the completion of testing the prescreening system, it requires the TSA to begin to assume the role of passenger prescreening and checking passenger names against watch lists no later than 180 days after completing that testing. The Act requires the TSA to establish redress and remedy procedures for passengers who are delayed or denied boarding because of being falsely identified or targeted by the system, and requires the TSA to ensure that the number of such false positives is minimized. The Act also requires the TSA to establish an oversight board and implement safeguards to ensure the security and integrity of the system and address and resolve any privacy concerns. The Act also requires that the DHS prescreening of international flights to or from the United States be conducted prior to departure.
- requires that individuals seeking FAA certificates, such as pilots and mechanics, as well as individuals requesting unescorted access to airport secure areas and air operations areas be screened against the consolidated and integrated terrorist watch list. The Act also requires the TSA to establish a process where air charter and leasing companies can voluntarily submit information regarding prospective customers seeking to use aircraft weighing more than 12,500 pounds for prescreening.
- requires the Security Privacy Officer of the Department of Homeland Security to report on the impact of the automatic selectee and no fly lists on privacy and civil liberties and the Director of National Intelligence, in consultation with the Secretary of Homeland Security, the Secretary of State, and the Attorney General, to report on the criteria and standards applied in placing the names of individuals on the consolidated screening watch list.

- directs the DHS to give high priority to developing, testing, improving, and deploying airport checkpoint screening technologies to detect non-metallic, chemical, biological, and radiological weapons, and explosives on passenger and carry-on items and requires the DHS to create a strategic plan for the deployment and use of explosive detection equipment at airport screening checkpoints. The Act requires the TSA to initiate a pilot program to test advanced airport checkpoint screening systems at five or more airports by March 31, 2005 and authorizes $150 million per year in FY2005 and FY2006 to carry out this pilot. The Act also requires the TSA to carry out and report on a human factors study to better understand problems with screener performance and take such action as may be necessary to improve the job performance of airport screening personnel.
- requires the Federal Air Marshal Service to continue operational initiatives to protect the anonymity of Federal air marshals. The Act also provides for training law enforcement officers authorized to carry firearms on passenger aircraft in inflight counterterrorism and weapons handling procedures and in the identification of fraudulent identification documents such as passports and visas. The Act also encourages the President to pursue international agreements to allow the maximum deployment of Federal air marshals on international flights, and authorizes the DHS to provide air marshal training to foreign law enforcement personnel.
- authorizes the TSA to take necessary action to expedite the installation and use of in-line baggage screening equipment at airports. The Act further requires the TSA to establish a schedule to expedite this activity and study cost-sharing options among federal, state, and local governments, and the private sector for integrating in-line baggage screening systems. The Act increases the authorization for the aviation security capital fund by authorizing up to $400 million per year through FY2007, in addition to the initial $250 million deposited from aviation security fee collections set forth in Vision 100.
- directs the TSA to study the application of readily available wireless communication technologies to enable cabin crew members to discreetly notify the pilot in the case of a security breach or safety issue occurring in the cabin.
- requires the FAA to begin issuing tamper resistant pilot licences with a photograph of the bearer. The license is to be capable of accommodating a digital photograph, a biometric, or any other unique identifier considered necessary for identification purposes.
- requires the TSA to develop and report to Congress on standards for determining appropriate screener staffing levels at airports that provide necessary levels of security and keep passenger wait times to a minimum. The DHS is also to study the feasibility of integrating operations of the screening workforce and other aviation security-related DHS func-

tions to coordinate these activities and increase their efficiency and effectiveness. The Act also authorizes the expenditure of $100 million for research and development of improved explosive detection systems and directs the TSA to develop a plan and guidelines for implementing these systems.

- required the TSA to prohibit airline passengers from carrying butane lighters and any other objects considered by the TSA to be inappropriate carry-on items.
- directs the President to urgently pursue international treaties to limit the availability, transfer, and proliferation of Man-portable Air Defense Systems (MANPADS), such as shoulder-fired missiles, worldwide. The Act further directs the President to continue to pursue international arrangements for the destruction of excess, obsolete, and illicit MANPADS stockpiles worldwide. The Act requires the President to report on diplomatic efforts to address MANPADS non-proliferation and requires the Secretary of State to provide the Congress with annual briefings on the status of these efforts. The Act also requires the FAA to establish a process for expedited certification of airworthiness and safety for missile defense systems that can be mounted on commercial aircraft. The Act also requires the DHS to provide a report within one year assessing the vulnerability of aircraft to MANPADS attacks and plans for securing airports and aircraft from this threat.
- requires that a pilot program be established to evaluate the use of blast-resistant cargo containers. The Act authorizes $2 million to carry out this pilot program. The Act also authorizes $200 million each year through FY2007 for improved air cargo and airport security related to the transportation of cargo on both passenger aircraft and all-cargo aircraft, and $100 million per year through FY2007 for the research, development, and deployment of technologies to better identify, track, and screen air cargo. The Act establishes a grant program to encourage the development of advanced air cargo security technology. The Act also requires the TSA to issue a final rule regarding its proposed regulations for the security of cargo operations for both passenger and all-cargo aircraft. Finally, the Act requires the DHS, in coordination with the Department of Defense and the FAA, to report on the threats posed by international cargo shipments bound for the United States and provide an analysis of the potential for establishing secure facilities along established international aviation routes for the purposes of diverting and securing aircraft believed to pose a security threat.

In addition to the air-cargo security provisions in the Intelligence Reform and Terrorism Prevention Act of 2004, the Department of Homeland Security Appropriations Act, 2005 (P.L 108-334, Sec. 513) directs the DHS to research, develop, and procure certified systems to inspect and screen air cargo on passenger aircraft at the earliest date possible and amend security directives and procedures to, at a minimum, triple the percentage of cargo inspected on passenger aircraft.

Policy Concerns Not Addressed In Enacted Legislation. Since several major provisions pertaining to aviation security were enacted during the 108th Congress—many directly reflecting the concerns and recommendations of the 9/11 Commission—there are few policy concerns that have not been addressed to some degree. During the 109th Congress, aviation security legislation directly addressing 9/11 Commission findings and recommendations were not taken up. However, two areas where some may consider that policy concerns have not been adequately addressed through legislation include general aviation security and air cargo security procedures and oversight.

The 9/11 Commission made brief reference to concerns over the security of general aviation operations, however it did not make any formal recommendations to address this concern. During the 108th Congress, legislation on the security of general aviation operations focused on airport and airspace restrictions and examining ways to alleviate what some believed to be unnecessary constraints on certain operations. For example, a provision in Vision 100 required the DHS to develop and implement a security plan allowing general aviation flights to resume at Ronald Reagan Washington National Airport but set no timetable for carrying out this provision. The TSA has now implemented regulations allowing certain general aviation flights, adhering to extensive operational requirements, to operate to and from Ronald Reagan Washington National Airport. In appropriations language, however, temporary flight restrictions over stadiums and other venues during major outdoor sports events were kept in full force and made permanent. Arguably, the legislation pertaining to general aviation security enacted to date has been viewed by many as not being as cohesive and comprehensive as legislation addressing other aviation security concerns.

Some may also argue that comprehensive legislation pertaining to air cargo security operations and oversight and expansion of the known-shipper program have not been adequately addressed. Specifically, comprehensive measures that had been passed by the Senate in the 108th Congress (see S. 165, 108th Congress) were stripped from the final version of the Intelligence Reform and Terrorism Prevention Act of 2004 (P.L. 108-458) and replaced by language directing the TSA to issue final rulemaking addressing these issues. This was presumably done because the TSA's regulatory proposals largely reflected the intent of the proposed legislation. However, because Congress did not formally enact several of these specific provisions pertaining to air cargo security operations and oversight, the 110th Congress may be particularly interested in oversight of the TSA's implementation of its air cargo security rules and its air cargo strategic plan to ensure that they meet desired objectives.

Port and Maritime Security[95]

Commission Concerns and Recommendations. The 9/11 Commission was not as specific in making recommendations for non-aviation modes of transportation as it was for aviation.[96] However, one conclusion of the 9/11 Commission is that transportation security resources are not being "allocated to the greatest risks in a cost effective way. . . Opportunities to do harm are as great, or greater, in maritime or surface transportation [than in aviation]."[97] The 9/11 Commission also reported that deployment of scanning technologies designed to screen containers that can be transported by plane, ship, truck, or rail is still years away.[98]

Under "Strategies for Aviation and Transportation Security," the 9/11 Commission recommended that the federal government identify and evaluate the transportation assets that need to be protected, set risk-based priorities for defending them, select the most practical and cost-effective ways of doing so, and then develop a plan, budget, and funding to implement the effort. The Commission recommended that the plan assign roles and missions to the relevant authorities (federal, state, regional, and local) and to private stakeholders. The Commission further noted that perfection is unattainable but that terrorists should perceive that potential targets are defended in order to deter them. It also recommended that Congress set specific dates for the completion of these plans.

Congressional Response. Since September 11, 2001, Congress has enacted two major port and maritime security acts. The Maritime Transportation Security Act of 2002 (MTSA, P.L. 107-295), which was passed by Congress on November 25, 2002, requires ports and vessels to take certain security measures to safeguard their operations and puts the U.S. Coast Guard in charge of enforcing these security measures. The SAFE Ports Act (P.L. 109-347), which was passed by Congress on September 30, 2006, requires shippers to take certain security measures to safeguard their cargo from terrorist infiltration and puts U.S. Customs and Border Protection (CBP) in charge of ensuring compliance. Sections 70102 and 70103 of MTSA requires the DHS to prepare a National Maritime Transportation Security Plan and vulnerability assessments of individual marine facilities and vessels. However, these two sections of MTSA did not impose deadlines on DHS in carrying out the prescribed security planning activities. Section 4072 of IRTPA (P.L. 108-458) imposed a deadline of April 1, 2005 for completion of the National Maritime Transportation Security Plan and a deadline of December 31, 2004 for the completion of marine facility and vessel vulnerability assessments. The Administration completed its National Strategy for Maritime Security in September 2005[99] and completed a National Strategy for Transportation Security in August 2006.[100]

The Coast Guard and Maritime Transportation Act of 2004 (P.L. 108-293) was signed into law on August 9, 2004. Title VIII of the Act contains a number of provisions related to maritime security, many of which add specificity to provisions in MTSA. Among other things, the Act requires the DHS to submit a plan to Congress implementing a maritime intelligence system (section 803); it requires the DHS to submit a plan for a maritime security grant program, including recommendations on how funds should be allocated (section 804); it requires the DOT to investigate and examine sensors that are able to track marine containers throughout their supply chain and detect hazardous and radioactive materials within the containers (section 808); it requires the DHS to report on the costs of vessel and container inspections, and a plan for implementing secure systems of transportation, including the need for and feasibility to inspect and monitor intermodal shipping containers within the United States (section 809).

The SAFE Ports Act requires DHS to set up a pilot program at three overseas ports to test the feasibility of scanning all containers bound for the United States at those ports before they are loaded onto a ship. Currently, under the Container Security Initiative (CSI), which is operational at 50 overseas ports accounting for approximately 90% of transatlantic and transpacific containerized cargo, U.S. CBP reviews cargo manifest information at these 50 loading ports to target certain high-risk or unknown-risk containers for closer inspection.[101] At U.S. ports, CBP has thus far deployed 267 Radiation Portal Monitors (RPMs) to scan containers before they leave the port for their final inland U.S. destination.[102] By the end of 2006, CBP expects 75% of containers will be scanned by RPMs and has a goal of scanning 98% by the end of 2008.[103] The SAFE Ports Act authorizes the CSI program and requires DHS to scan all containers for radiation entering the 22 busiest U.S. ports by the end of 2007. In addition, the Act also authorizes the Domestic Nuclear Detection Office within DHS whose primary mission is to further advance and deploy nuclear detection technology. The SAFE Ports Act also modifies the port security grant program from awarding grants in a "fair and equitable" manner to awarding grants based solely on risk.

Surface Transportation Security[104]

Commission Concerns and Recommendations. The 9/11 Commission expressed concern that transportation security resources may not be allocated to the greatest risks in a cost-effective way. They noted the government did not have a strategic plan that analyzed assets, risks, and costs and benefits of security measures for the entire transportation system, nor was there a specific security plan for each transportation mode. The Commission recommended that such a strategic plan be prepared to: identify the assets that need protection; set risk-based priorities for defending them; select the most cost-effective ways of protecting those assets; then develop a plan, budget, and funding to implement this strategy, assigning roles and missions to federal, state, regional and local governments and private stakeholders.

Status of Implementation of the Recommendations. The 108th Congress passed the Intelligence Reform and Terrorism Prevention Act of 2004 (P.L. 108-458), which includes a provision directing the Department of Homeland Security to create a National Strategy for Transportation Security (NSTS). The Act directed that the NSTS should identify national transportation assets, set risk-based priorities for their protection, assign responsibilities for their protection, and recommend appropriate levels and sources of funding for these efforts. The Department of Homeland Security submitted the NSTS, in the form of a classified report, to Congress in the fall of 2005; an update was submitted in the summer of 2006. The initial version of the NSTS was criticized by the original 9/11 Commission members, acting as a private organization called the "9/11 Public Discourse Project," as lacking "the necessary detail to make it an effective management tool."[105] The Government Accountability Office has noted that the use of risk management in homeland security is relatively new, and that addressing risk across different types of infrastructure with multiple parties involved is highly complex.[106]

In June 2006, DHS issued a National Infrastructure Protection Plan (NIPP) which is to serve as a guide to using risk management principles for prioritizing protection efforts within infrastructure sectors (e.g., transportation) and across sectors.[107] The NIPP requires that sector-specific agencies submit plans to DHS by December 2006 identifying critical assets, evaluating the risk to them, and developing measures to protect them.

As for the recommendation that a plan, budget, and funding be provided to implement the NSTS which assigns roles and missions to federal, state, regional and local governments and private stakeholders, the NIPP calls for the sector plans to be developed by councils of federal, state, and regional and local government agencies involved in that sector, along with sector councils made up of private sector stakeholders. The government council for the transportation sector was formed in January 2006, but, alone among the seventeen infrastructure sectors, the transportation sector does not yet have a private sector council.[108]

Congress also began providing funding for grants to transit and rail agencies for security improvements in the annual Department of Homeland Security appropriations bill. Congress provided $150 million in FY2005 and FY2006 and $175 million in FY2007 for this program. As the NSTS had not been completed at the time the grants began, and the risk-based allocation process to implement the NSTS has not been developed, this grant program has operated independently of the NSTS. Several proposals have been introduced in Congress to authorize new multi-billion dollar grant programs to fund security improvements for passenger rail, freight rail, and public transit organizations.

Critical Infrastructure Security[109]

Commission Concerns and Recommendations

The 9/11 Commission expressed its concerns and recommendations regarding critical infrastructure security in three primary areas: transportation security, allocation of assistance to states and localities, and the adequacy of the government's plans, in general, to protect the nation's critical infrastructure. The Commission devoted most of its attention to the transportation infrastructure, and, in particular, aviation security; making relatively specific recommendations in specific areas (e.g., explosive detection). It also recommended that a date specific be set for the Department of Homeland Security to complete its security plans for all transportation modes, as called for in the Aviation and Transportation Security Act (P.L. 107-71). In regard to the allocation of federal assistance, the Commission recommended that the allocation to states and localities be based on an assessment of risks and vulnerabilities and no longer remain a "program for general revenue sharing." While much of the federal assistance to states and localities supports response capabilities, some is also devoted to the protection of critical infrastructure. In the background discussion for its final recommendation, the Commission stated that the Department of Homeland Security (DHS) should identify those elements of the nation's critical infrastructure (beyond just the transportation sector) that need protection and to develop plans to protect them. It recommended that the Department and its oversight committees should regularly assess the types of threats facing the nation's critical infrastructure to determine the adequacy of the government's plans to protect and respond to a terrorist attack on critical infrastructure across all relevant sectors. The rest of this discussion focuses on this last recommendation. A discussion of the first two areas can be found elsewhere in this report under Border and Transportation Security and Emergency Response and Preparedness. Also, a more detailed discussion of the Commission's recommendations related to critical infrastructure protection and the subsequent Congressional response in the Intelligence Reform and Terrorism Prevention Act (P.L. 108-458) is given in CRS Report RL32531, *Critical Infrastructure Protections: The 9/11 Commission Report and Congressional Response*, by John D. Moteff (archived, contact author for a copy).

Congressional Responses

Section 7306 of the Intelligence Reform and Terrorism Prevention Act (P.L. 108-458) incorporated similar language to that used by the Commission in its final recommendation. Like the Commission, it noted the responsibilities given the Department by the Homeland Security Act to: a) carry out vulnerability and risk assessments associated with specific threats against the nation's critical infrastructure; b) identify priority protective measures; and c) develop a comprehensive national plan for securing the nation's critical infrastructure. Section 7306 required the Secretary of Homeland Security to report to Congress, within 180 days after enactment (i.e., June 2005), on the progress being made by the Department in assessing the vulnerability and risk associated with the nation's critical infrastructure, and on the adequacy of the government's plans to protect that infrastructure and the readiness of the government to respond to threats. This reporting is to be done in conjunction with the reporting requirements of the Homeland Security Financial Accountability Act (P.L. 108-330). The Homeland Security Financial Accountability Act requires the Department to submit a Performance and Accountability report for each fiscal year. It also amended the requirements for the Future Years Homeland Security Program (i.e., a five year program and planning document required by the Homeland Security Act), which is to be submitted to Congress with, or about the same time as, the Department's annual budget request.

Vulnerability and risk assessments of critical infrastructures began shortly after the terrorist attacks of September 11, 2001. These were primarily conducted by owners/operators of the infrastructure themselves, to varying degrees, sometimes with the assistance of federal agencies, and using a variety of techniques and assumptions. Shortly after the Department of Homeland Security was established, the Department began identifying, on its own, certain critical infrastructure assets or sites as having a high-priority. The Department planned to assess the vulnerability of each of these assets or sites and to assist local law enforcement in developing Buffer Zone Protection Plans. DHS also made itself available to discuss protective strategies with the owners/operators of those sites, on a voluntary basis. DHS keeps the process by which it decides which assets are high-priority relatively secret, stating only that it is based on an initial assessment of vulnerability and the potential consequences associated with a possible attack. The sites or assets themselves are considered classified. However, its initial list of priority assets and sites was met with some criticism.[110]

To meet its responsibility to coordinate a national effort to protect the nation's critical infrastructure, the Department released its long-awaited National Infrastructure Protection Plan in June 2006. The Plan outlines a standardized process by which each critical infrastructure sector is to assess and integrate threat,[111] vulnerability, and consequences, to determine risks and to prioritize actions to reduce those risks. This is to form the basis for Sector Specific Plans for each critical infrastructure sector, which the National Plan expects to be completed by the end of 2006. DHS will use the same process to integrate the Sector Plans in a way that will allow it to identify national priorities, at some yet-to-be-determined date in the future.

The DHS appears to meet its reporting obligations under Section 7306 through its Department of Homeland Security's annual Performance Budget (which implements the current year of the Future Years Program) and the subsequent Performance and Accountability Report published some time after the end of each fiscal year. The Performance Budget and Performance and Accountability Report associate programs, performance measures, and resource allocations with the strategic goals and objectives as laid out in the Department's Strategic Plan. The Department's Strategic Plan, released February 2004, listed 7 goals and a number of objectives under each goal. A number of goals and objectives could be considered relevant to measuring the progress being made in assessing vulnerability and risk and touching upon the adequacy of plans to protect critical infrastructure and preparedness.

For example, in the FY2007 Performance Budget, the Infrastructure Protection Program (listed under Prevention, one of the 7 goals) has two relevant performance measures. One of the performance measures is the percent of high-priority critical infrastructure sites at which a vulnerability assessment has been conducted. The target for this measure in FY2005 was 10%, increasing to 25% for FY2007. According to the FY2007 Performance Budget, DHS stated that vulnerability assessments had been conducted at 14% of the sites. Percentages were not available for FY2006 or FY2007. The other performance measure was the percent of high-priority critical infrastructure sites at which a Buffer Zone Protection Plan had been implemented. The target in FY2005 was 70%. According to the Performance Budget, only 18% of the sites had implemented Buffer Zone Protection Plans. The target for this measure was reduced to 38% for FY2007. The Performance Budget did not mention the actual percentage of sites that had implemented plans after FY2005. Similarly, other programs support other goals and objectives associated with preparedness and anticipating future threats.

Numerous bills have been introduced that address infrastructure security within specific sectors. Some have made it into public law. However, none address the coordination of a national effort across all sectors that characterize the Commission's recommendation.

Emergency Preparedness and Response and the 9/11 Commission[112]

Commission Concerns and Recommendations

The 9/11 Commission report presented distinct descriptions of the emergency response actions taken in New York City and at the Pentagon after the attacks. The report described operational complications in Manhattan that did not occur in Virginia. The Commission found that deficiencies in planning and communications around the World Trade Center towers contributed to the deaths of police and fire officials as well as civilians. By comparison, the Commission concluded that emergency response at the Pentagon was "generally effective," largely because the responding agencies used a standard, formalized, incident command system and coordinated communications networks to marshal and coordinate multiple agencies.[113]

The primary emergency preparedness and response concerns identified by the Commission focused on three general deficiencies: the lack of standard command procedures, the lack of a standard communications protocol and standards, and insufficient emergency preparedness steps taken by the private sector. According to the Commission report, the adoption of standardized response procedures, public safety communications standards, and other warning system enhancements, as well as increased emergency preparedness activity in the private sector, would resolve these problems. Accordingly, the Commission recommended that Congress, the Executive Branch, state and local governments, and private sector entities take specified actions.[114]

Recommendations by the Commission regarding the development of standards may be categorized in four areas—(1) encouraging and facilitating the development of open architecture and voluntary standards for interoperable public safety communications and warning systems, (2) the resolution of liability concerns to expedite mutual aid efforts among the states, (3) adoption of a formalized and intergovernmental incident response command system, and (4) the consideration of private sector emergency preparedness standards in assessments of insurability and creditworthiness. Steps to be taken to resolve these gaps rested largely with administrative entities.

The Commission also recommended congressional action in two resource allocation areas—(1) the distribution of federal funding for first responders based on risks and vulnerabilities,[115] and (2) the reallocation of electromagnetic radio spectrum for public safety communications purposes.

Congressional Responses

The 108th Congress acted upon some of the concerns and recommendations of the Commission through enactment of the Intelligence Reform and Terrorism Prevention Act of 2004 (P.L. 108-458), hereafter the Intelligence Reform Act. While this legislation addressed some of the issues, Members of Congress left the two resource allocation issues unresolved, one of which (spectrum allocation) was addressed by the 109th Congress.

Enactments. The Commission's call for the development of standards resulted in the inclusion of several provisions in the Intelligence Reform Act. First, the statute addressed concerns about mutual aid agreements by authorizing federal, state and local officials in the National Capitol Region to enter into mutual aid agreements for emergency response.[116] Specifically, the Act authorizes District of Columbia officials to purchase liability and indemnification insurance or self insure against claims, provides that the laws of the emergency responders' "home" states prevail in litigation actions, and requires the establishment of a program to support emergency management compacts throughout the nation.

With regard to the spectrum allocation issue, the Homeland Security Act (P.L. 107-296) and the Intelligence Reform Act required that the Secretary of the Department of Homeland Security, in consultation with other Administration officials, establish a national strategy for public safety interoperable communications that includes voluntary consensus standards. The Intelligence Reform Act also required that the Secretary establish a program for interoperable communications in high risk urban areas and two pilot projects in high threat urban areas that might serve as national models. In other legislation (the Deficit Reduction Act, P.L. 109-171), Congress addressed the spectrum allocation issue by requiring that the public safety community be given suitable access by February 18, 2009.[117] This legislation also required that the Federal Communications Commission lead a study on spectrum needs for public safety and homeland security. The report was released December 2005; a key conclusion was that it was premature for the FCC to make specific recommendations to increase the amount of spectrum available for public safety.[118]

Despite these congressional actions, DHS has been criticized for insufficient response to the mandates for action expressed in the Intelligence Reform Act. Accordingly, the 109th Congress provided further direction in the "21st Century Emergency Communications Act of 2006" (Subtitle D, Title VI, of P.L. 109-295), by establishing an Office of Emergency Communications within DHS and requiring that the director of the office, among other responsibilities, assist the DHS Secretary in carrying out the program responsibilities required by the Intelligence Reform Act and working with officials of the National Communications System on the establishment of a national response capability.

The emergency preparedness and response concerns raised by the Commission about private sector preparedness standards and adoption of a standardized incident command system resulted in Sense of the Congress provisions in the Intelligence Reform Act that urged administrative action.

Policy Concerns Not Addressed. Neither the 108th nor the 109th Congresses reached agreement on how to best allocate first responder funding. The Intelligence Reform Act included a Sense of Congress provisions that called for action by the 109th Congress, but, as noted below, legislation was not enacted.

In addition to pressing forward with fundamental policy issues such as standards development and funding, the 110th Congress could explore DHS's response to recently enacted legislation, such as planning and coordination at the state and regional level for emergency communications. Legislation has also required assessments of emergency communications capabilities,[119] including an inventory used by federal departments and agencies that identifies radio frequencies.[120] The requirements for studies on spectrum needs, as stated in the Intelligence Reform and Terrorism Prevention Act, have apparently not met the expectations of the public safety community, which continues to put pressure on Congress for more substantive steps. The 110th Congress could, for example, find itself facing calls to reallocate for public safety use channels at 700 MHz that were designated for auction by the Deficit Reduction Act. There is also interest in creating a structure where spectrum could be shared between the private sector and public safety.

109th Congress Activity. No legislation in the 109th Congress was enacted that modified or altered the distribution method of federal homeland security assistance to states and localities. In the FY2006 and FY2007 DHS appropriations (P.L. 109-90 and P.L. 109-295), Congress continued to require DHS to allocate 0.75% of homeland security funding to states[121], with the remainder of total appropriations to be allocated at the discretion of DHS. In FY2006, DHS allocated the discretionary portions of homeland security grants on the basis of two factors: risk and effectiveness. DHS calculated two kinds of risk: *asset-based risk*, which uses threat values derived from the U.S. intelligence community's assessment of threats to specific critical infrastructure, and *geographic-based risk*, which uses values based on inherent risks associated with geographic areas, taking into account such factors as international borders, terrorism reports and investigations, and population density.[122]

Department of Defense and the 9/11 Commission[123]

Commission Concerns and Recommendations

Aside from ongoing anti-terrorist military operations (see **U.S. Military Forces and the War on Terrorism**), the 9/11 Commission's attention to the Department of Defense was limited to its recommendation that Congress should "regularly assess the strategies and planning" of the new Northern Command (NORTHCOM)which is responsible for coordinating U.S. mainland air and coastal defense. The Commission was particularly concerned that the North American Air Defense Command, a major component of NORTHCOM, expand its focus to include threats from terrorist use of domestic civil aircraft.

Congressional Responses

Congress has not undertaken any special review of Northern Command, aside from routine oversight exercised in its consideration of the FY2007 DOD appropriations legislation. The North American Air Defense Command and the Federal Aviation Agency have integrated their air traffic control system, allowing NORTHCOM to monitor domestic civilian aircraft.[124]

Homeland Security Oversight: Congressional Options[125]

Commission Concerns and Recommendations

The 9/11 Commission proposed that the House and Senate should each have a single authorizing committee responsible for homeland security, as well as one appropriating subcommittee for homeland security. The commission also suggested that the authorizing panel for homeland security should be a standing committee with a nonpartisan staff. A key objective of the commission was to urge the formation in each chamber of a principal panel responsible for oversight and review of the recently-created Department of Homeland Security (DHS). The report of the commission stated there were at least 88 committees and subcommittees of Congress that had some jurisdiction over DHS. Accordingly, the commission suggested some consolidation of committee jurisdiction to minimize turf conflicts and to reduce the number of panels top DHS officials must appear before as witnesses.

Congressional Responses

Each chamber took steps to address jurisdictional issues related to homeland security. At the start of the 108th Congress, the House created a temporary Select Committee on Homeland Security with both legislative and oversight authority for certain homeland security issues. The Senate kept oversight authority for the new department in its Committee on Governmental Affairs. In addition, early in 2003 the House Appropriations Committee created a new Homeland Security Appropriations Subcommittee, while keeping the total number of subcommittees at the panel's traditional 13. The Senate Appropriations Committee followed suit and also established a counterpart subcommittee on homeland security. Later in the 108th Congress, the Senate adopted a homeland security and intelligence committee reorganization plan (S.Res. 445); it renamed the Governmental Affairs Committee the Homeland Security and Governmental Affairs Committee and assigned it limited legislative and oversight authority over DHS. The committee, too, has broad oversight jurisdiction under Senate Rule XXV over the "efficiency, economy, and effectiveness of all agencies and departments of the Government," which suggests that the panel could oversee a wide range of Federal entities that have some responsibility for homeland security.

When the 109th Congress began, the House transformed its temporary select panel on homeland security into a standing committee. The new permanent committee was assigned, among other matters, jurisdiction for overall homeland security policy and organizational and administrative aspects of DHS. Further, the new committee was granted broad oversight authority over government-wide homeland security matters. Even with creation of a new committee, oversight of DHS is still spread among six other House authorizing committees: Energy and Commerce, Financial Services, Government Reform, Judiciary, Transportation and Infrastructure, and Ways and Means. "We envision a system of purposeful redundancy," said the House Rules Chairman during January 4, 2005, floor debate. "By that, we mean more than one level of oversight and an atmosphere in which the competition of ideas is encouraged." Both the new House standing committee and the renamed Senate committee use a partisan staff model.

Civil Liberties and Government Information Policies and Practices

Driver's Licenses, Personal Identification Cards, Birth Certificates, and Social Security Numbers[126]

Commission Concerns and Recommendations. The 9/11 Commission's final report recommended that "the federal government should set standards for the issuance of birth certificates, and sources of identification, such as drivers' licenses." Specifically noting the rising problem of identification fraud, the Commission also concluded that "sources of identification are the last opportunity to ensure that people are who they say they are and to check whether they are terrorists" (p. 390).

Congressional Responses. ***Drivers Licenses and Personal Identification Cards.*** Congress's initial response to the Commission's report was to adopt language in the Intelligence Reform and Terrorism Prevention Act of 2004 specifically addressing driver's licenses and personal identification cards.[127] The legislation empowered the Secretary of Transportation, in consultation with the Secretary of Homeland Security, state, and local officials, to set minimum standards for federal acceptance of driver's licences and personal identification cards, including anti-tampering and anti-fraud features.[128] These provisions, however, were repealed in May 2005 with the passage of the REAL ID Act of 2005 (REAL ID Act).[129]

The REAL ID Act establishes minimum issuance standards for federal recognition of identification documents.[130] In addition, Section 202©)(2)©) establishes a system of temporary licenses and identification cards that can be issued by the states to applicants who can present evidence that they fall into one of six categories.[131] States are also required to adopt procedures and practices to ensure both the security and retention of identity documents. The Department of Homeland Security was delegated the authority to promulgate regulations regarding the implementation of the REAL ID Act as well as the authority to oversee state and local compliance with the Act.

The REAL ID Act contains language requiring that states, if they elect to issue a driver's license or personal identification card that does not conform to the act, use a unique color identifier or design to alert officials that the document is not to be accepted for any official purpose. Moreover, the Act includes a provision requiring the states to maintain a motor vehicle database that, at a minimum, contains all data fields printed on the driver's license or identification card and all motor vehicle driver history, including violations, suspensions, or points.[132]

Pursuant to the REAL ID Act, the Secretary of Homeland Security is authorized to make grants to states and promulgate regulations and standards (in consultation with both the Secretary of Transportation as well as with the states). As of this writing, the regulations required by the statute have not been promulgated. As a result, it is unclear what the current implementation status is of these provisions.

Birth Certificates. The Intelligence Reform and Terrorism Prevention Act of 2004 required the Secretary of Health and Human Services to promulgate, within a year of enactment, minimum standards for birth certificates to be used by federal agencies for official purposes, with the effective date delayed until 2 years after the regulations are issued.[133] The regulations are to require measures "designed to prevent tampering, counterfeiting, or otherwise duplicating the birth certificate for fraudulent purposes" and to require "proof and verification of identity as a condition of issuance of a birth certificate, with additional security measures for the issuance of a birth certificate for a person who is not the applicant." Concern has been expressed that this provision may have an impact on genealogical and other historical research. The statute also provides for grants to assist the States in conforming to the new standards. As of this writing, the regulations required by the statute have not been promulgated. As a result, it is unclear what the current implementation status is of these provisions.

Social Security Numbers.[134] The Intelligence Reform and Terrorism Prevention Act of 2004 also required the Commissioner of Social Security to implement the following: restrict the issuance of multiple replacement social security cards to any individual to 3 per year and to 10 for the life of the individual, except where there is a minimal opportunity for fraud; create standards for the verification of documents or records submitted to establish eligibility for original or replacement cards; require independent verification of all records provided by applicants for social security numbers other than at birth; and add death and fraud indicators to the verification system for employers, state agencies and others. In addition, an interagency task force to further improve the security of social security cards and numbers is to be created.

The Commissioner was also directed to improve the system of issuing social security cards to newborn children, including (1) the assignment of social security accounts to unnamed children; (2) the issuance of more than one account number to the same child; and (3) other opportunities to obtain a social security account by means of fraud. The Commissioner is to report to Congress on the improvements made to the newborn applicant process and options for ensuring the security of the enumeration at birth process.

Finally, the law expressly prohibits state and local governments from displaying social security numbers on driver's licenses, motor vehicle registrations, or on any other document issued for identification. As of this writing, the regulations required by the statute have not been promulgated. As a result, it is unclear what the current implementation status is of these provisions.

Future Considerations. Much of the recent debate with respect to the REAL ID Act has focused on two issues, implementation costs and privacy concerns. Until the regulations and requirements are published for public comment, however, there remain many unanswered questions and concerns. No new legislation has been proposed to date, although there are many third-party groups that are recommending a variety of options ranging from repeal of the statute to delaying the effective date pending potential implementation issues. With respect to birth certificates and social security numbers, regulation and implementation has been slow to develop, but we are not aware of any introduced legislation targeted to address either of these issues.

Protection of Civil Liberties[135]

Commission Concerns and Recommendations. The final report of the 9/11 Commission recommended that "there should be a board within the executive branch to oversee adherence to the guidelines we recommend and the commitment the government makes to defend our civil liberties." (p. 395). This recommendation was the third of three made in a section of the report concerning the protection of civil liberties. In the other two, the commission recommended that (1) the President, in the course of determining the guidelines for information sharing among government agencies and by them with the private sector, "should safeguard the privacy of individuals about whom information is shared";[136] and (2) the "burden of proof for retaining a particular governmental power should be on the executive, to explain (a) that the power actually materially enhances security and (b) that there is adequate supervision of the executive's use of the powers to ensure protection of civil liberties. If the power is granted," the report added, "there must be adequate guidelines and oversight to properly confine its use."[137] Read together, these recommendations called for a board to oversee adherence to presidential guidelines on information sharing that safeguard the privacy of individuals about whom information is shared, and adherence to guidelines on the executive's continued use of powers that materially enhance security. The report offered no additional commentary on the composition, structure, or operations of the recommended board. Such a board, however, had been proposed in December 2003 in the fifth and final report of the Advisory Panel to Assess Domestic Response Capabilities for Terrorism Involving Weapons of Mass Destruction, chaired by former Virginia Governor James S. Gilmore III.[138]

On August 27, 2004, President George W. Bush issued E.O. 13353 establishing the President's Board on Safeguarding Americans' Civil Liberties within the Department of Justice.[139] Chaired by the Deputy Attorney General and composed of at least 19 other senior counsels and leaders largely from within the intelligence and homeland security communities, the board was to advise the President regarding civil liberties policy, gather information and make assessments regarding such policy and its implementation, make recommendations to the President, refer information about possible violations of such policy by a federal official or employee for prompt action, enhance cooperation and coordination among federal departments and agencies in implementing such policy, and undertake other efforts to protect civil liberties as the President might direct.

Congressional Responses. When enacting the Intelligence Reform and Terrorism Prevention Act, Congress responded to the commission's recommendations for protecting civil liberties in various regards. Section 1061 created a Privacy and Civil Liberties Oversight Board (PCLOB).[140] Located within the Executive Office of the President, the board consists of a chair, vice chair, and three additional members, all appointed by, and serving at the pleasure of, the President. Nominees for the chair and vice chair positions are subject to Senate approval. While the board does not have subpoena power, it may request the assistance of the Attorney General in obtaining desired information from persons other than federal departments and agencies. It also has broad access to information from federal departments and agencies. On June 10, 2005, the President announced his intention to nominate Carol E. Dinkins to be the chairman of the PCLOB, Alan Charles Raul to be the vice chairman of the board, and Lanny J. Davis, Theodore B. Olsen, and Francis X. Taylor to be members of the panel. Dinkins and Raul were confirmed by the Senate on February 17, 2006. The PCLOB was appropriated $1.5 million for FY2006.[141] Its appropriation for FY2007 has not been finalized.

Section 1062 of the statute expressed "the sense of Congress that each executive department or agency with law enforcement or antiterrorism functions should designate a privacy and civil liberties officer." The obligation of the relevant departments and agencies in this regard was less than mandatory. Other arrangements in this regard, however, were subsequently realized (see below).

Section 103D established a Civil Liberties Protection Officer within the office of the newly created Director of National Intelligence (DNI). This official has various responsibilities for civil liberties and privacy protection within the intelligence community. On December 7, 2005, the DNI announced the appointment of Alexander W. Joel as the Civil Liberties Protection Officer.[142]

Section 1016 requires the President to consult with the Privacy and Civil Liberties Oversight Board when issuing guidelines that protect privacy and civil liberties in the development and utilization of an "information sharing environment" (ISE) for the sharing of information about terrorism "in a manner consistent with national security and with applicable legal standards relating to privacy and civil liberties." The role of the board and sensitivity to protecting privacy and civil liberties in the development of the ISE were reflected in the ISE implementation plan released on November 16, 2006.[143]

On March 15, 2005, Representative Carolyn B. Maloney introduced H.R. 1310, the Protection of Civil Liberties Act, for herself and 23 bipartisan cosponsors. The bill was referred to the Government Reform, Homeland Security, Intelligence, and Judiciary committees. Among other modifications, the legislation, if enacted, would have reconstituted the PCLOB as an independent agency within the executive branch, made all appointments to the board's membership subject to Senate confirmation, and limited the board's partisan composition to not more than three members being from the same political party.[144] As the 109th Congress moved toward final adjournment, the bill remained in committee.

When reporting the Transportation, Treasury and General Government Appropriations Bill, 2005, on September 15, 2004, the Senate Committee on Appropriations indicated that Section 520 of the legislation (S. 2806) "directs each agency to acquire a Chief Privacy Officer to assume primary responsibility for privacy and data protection policy." Section 520 appeared in Title V of the legislation. "Those general provisions that address activities or directives affecting all of the agencies covered in this bill," the committee report explained, "are contained in title V." Thus, the provision appeared to apply only to agencies directly funded by the legislation. "General provisions that are government wide in scope," noted the report, "are contained in title VI of this bill."[145]

Transportation, Treasury and General Government Appropriations were among those which came to be included in the Consolidated Appropriations Act, 2005 (H.R. 4818), and constituted Division H of that legislation.[146] Within that division, Section 522 stated: "Each agency shall have a Chief Privacy Officer to assume primary responsibility for privacy and data protection policy," and specified nine particular activities to be undertaken by privacy officers. The section further prescribed privacy and data protection policies and procedures to be established, reviews to be undertaken, and related reports to be made. Located in Title V of the division, the requirements of the section appeared to be applicable only to agencies directly funded by the division. Furthermore, it did not appear that the section created new positions, but, instead, would have the prescribed privacy officer responsibilities assigned to an appropriate individual in an existing position.[147] Subsequently, a February 11, 2005, memorandum to the heads of the executive departments and agencies from Clay Johnson III, Deputy Director for Management, Office of Management and Budget (OMB), appeared to sweep beyond the Section 522 requirement, and asked recipients, within the next 30 days, "to identify to OMB the senior official who has the overall agency-wide responsibility for information privacy issues." Expressing the Administration's commitment "to protecting the information privacy rights of Americans and to ensuring Departments and agencies continue to have effective information privacy management programs in place to carry out this important responsibility," it noted that a Chief Information Officer or "another senior official (at the Assistant Secretary or equivalent level) with agency-wide responsibility for information privacy issues" could be named.[148]

Balancing Security and Information Sharing[149]

Commission Concerns and Recommendations. The Commission recommended a reevaluation of the balance between the security risks and costs of disclosing information against the benefits of sharing information. While recognizing counterintelligence concerns, the 9/11 Commission encouraged a shift to a culture that provided incentives for sharing information so as to maximize the likelihood of "connecting the dots" in intelligence analysis of a given situation. (p. 416-7).

Congressional and Administrative Responses. The trend toward information sharing has been reflected in legislation,[150] executive orders,[151] a Homeland Security Presidential Directive,[152] and Attorney General guidelines.[153] For example, the Foreign Intelligence Surveillance Act (FISA)[154] may be used to gather information where a significant purpose of the investigation is to obtain foreign intelligence information, even if the primary purpose is for law enforcement purposes.[155] Federal officers conducting electronic surveillance or physical searches under FISA may consult with federal law enforcement officers or state, or local law enforcement personnel to coordinate against actual or potential attack or other grave hostile acts of a foreign power or its agent; sabotage or international terrorism by a foreign power or its agent, or clandestine intelligence activities by an intelligence service or network of a foreign power or its agent. 50 U.S.C. §§ 1806, 1825.[156]

In P.L. 107-296, the Homeland Security Act of 2002 (November 25, 2002), the Directorate for Information Analysis and Infrastructure Protection (IAIP) within the Department of Homeland Security (DHS) was given responsibility to access, receive, and analyze law enforcement information, intelligence information, and other information from federal, state, and local government agencies and private sector entities and to integrate that information to identify and assess terrorist threats to the United States; to make recommendations for improvements in the sharing of law enforcement information, intelligence information, intelligence-related information, and other homeland security-related information within the federal government and between federal, state, and local government agencies and authorities; and to address appropriate dissemination of information analyzed by DHS to other federal government agencies, state and local governments, and private entities with homeland security responsibilities. The Secretary of DHS, in consultation with certain others, is charged with developing procedures for sharing and protecting such information. The President is directed to prescribe and implement procedures under which relevant federal agencies share homeland security information with other federal agencies and appropriate state and local personnel through information sharing systems.

Under the Intelligence Reform and Terrorism Prevention Act of 2004, P.L. 108-458 (December 17, 2004), the Director of National Intelligence (DNI) is given the principal authority to ensure maximum availability of and access to intelligence information within the intelligence community consistent with national security requirements.[157] The President is directed, among other things, to create an information sharing environment (ISE) for the sharing of terrorism information in a manner consistent with national security and with applicable legal standards relating to privacy and civil liberties, and to leverage all ongoing efforts consistent with establishment of the ISE and to issue guidelines for acquiring, accessing, sharing and using information; requiring federal department and agency heads to promote an information sharing culture by reducing disincentives and providing affirmative incentives in furtherance of this goal. A program manager is to be designated to handle information sharing across the federal government, and an Information Sharing Council (built upon the Information Systems Council established in E.O. 13356) is established to assist in furthering these goals. The Director of the National Counterterrorism Center (NCTC)[158]is required to submit to Congress within one year of passage of the Act, a strategy to counter terrorist travel, including, among other things, a program for collecting, analyzing, disseminating, and utilizing terrorist travel information and intelligence.[159] The President has issued a series of Executive Orders and a Homeland Security Presidential Directive, which address various aspects of information sharing. In E.O. 13311 (July 29, 2003), which predated the release of the *Final Report of the National Commission on Terrorist Attacks Upon the United States* on July 22, 2004, the President directed the Secretary of DHS to carry out most of the information sharing responsibilities under Section 892 of the Homeland Security Act.

E.O. 13355, *Strengthened Management of the Intelligence Community* (August 27, 2004) amended subsection 1.5 of E.O. 12333 (December 4, 1981), as amended, which deals with *United States Intelligence Activities*. Under the E.O. 13355 amendments, the Director of Central Intelligence (DCI), among other responsibilities, was directed to develop objectives and guidance for the Intelligence Community necessary to ensure timely and effective collection, processing, analysis, and dissemination of intelligence concerning current and potential threats to the security of the United States and its interests; and, working with the Intelligence Community, so that U.S. intelligence collection activities are integrated, among other things, "to ensure that all collected data is available to the maximum extent practicable for integration, analysis, and dissemination to those who can act on, add value to, or otherwise apply it to mission needs." E.O. 12333, subsection 1.5, as amended by E.O. 13355, also directed the DCI to "establish common security and access standards for managing and handling intelligence systems, information, and procedures" with special emphasis on facilitating "the fullest and most prompt sharing of information practicable, assigning the highest priority to detecting, preventing, preempting, and disrupting terrorist threats against our homeland, our people, our allies and our interests;" and "the establishment of interface standards for an interoperable information sharing enterprise that facilitates the automated sharing of intelligence information among the agencies within the Intelligence Community."

E.O. 13356, *Strengthening the Sharing of Terrorism Information to Protect Americans* (August 27, 2004), which was later revoked by E.O. 13388, imposed a duty upon the heads of agencies possessing or acquiring terrorism information to promptly provide access to that information to other agencies with counterterrorism functions under standards developed pursuant to the order. E.O. 13356 also directed the DCI, in consultation with the Attorney General and other agency heads within the Intelligence Community, within 90 days, to develop common standards for sharing terrorism information with other agencies within the Intelligence Community, other agencies with counterterrorism functions, and, through coordination with DHS, appropriate state and local governmental authorities. Further, the executive order required the establishment of an Information Systems Council to plan for and oversee the establishment of an interoperable terrorism information sharing environment to facilitate automatic sharing of terrorism information among appropriate agencies.

Homeland Security Presidential Directive-11, *Comprehensive Terrorist-Related Screening Procedures* (HSPD-11), also issued on August 27, 2004, required the Secretary of Homeland Security, in coordination with the heads of other federal departments and agencies, within 75 days, to report to the President on plans and progress for enhancing terrorist-related screening, including mechanisms for sharing information among screeners and relevant government agencies.

E.O. 13388, *Strengthening the Sharing of Terrorism Information to Protect Americans* (October 25, 2005), set out the information sharing duties of heads of federal agencies possessing or acquiring terrorism information and requirements for collection of such information within the United States. It also established the Information Sharing Council,[160] chaired by the ISE Program Manager, to provide advice and information concerning the establishment of an interoperable terrorism information sharing environment to facilitate automated sharing of terrorism information among appropriate agencies to implement the policy set forth in section 1 of the order; and to perform the duties set forth in section 1016(g) of the Intelligence Reform and Terrorism Prevention Act of 2004.

On March 31, 2005, the Commission on the Intelligence Capabilities of the United States Regarding Weapons of Mass Destruction issued its report. In Chapter 9 of the report, it stated, "The confused lines of authority over information sharing created by the intelligence reform act should be resolved." It recommended that "[t]he overlapping authorities of the [DNI] and the Program Manager [designated under Section 1016 of IRTPA] should be reconciled and coordinated–a result most likely to be achieved by requiring the Program Manager to report to the DNI." On June 2, 2005, President Bush issued a Memorandum for the Heads of Executive Departments and Agencies on "Strengthening Information Sharing, Access, and Integration B Organizational, Management, and Policy Development Structures for Creating the Terrorism Information Sharing Environment," which, in part, placed the Program Manager under the DNI throughout the initial 2 year term of the Program Manager.[161]

On November 16, 2006, Director of National Intelligence (DNI) John Negroponte submitted to Congress the *Implementation Plan Report for the Information Sharing Environment (ISE)*, which includes "a description of the functions, capabilities, resources, and conceptual design of the ISE;" "a plan for designing, testing, integrating, deploying and operating the ISE;" and "a process for measuring progress made toward implementing the ISE, as well as its performance once established."[162] In the news release accompanying its submission to Congress, ISE Program Manager Ambassador Thomas McNamara described the report as "provid[ing] a roadmap for the successful implementation of the ISE" and "respond[ing] to the recommendations of the 9/11 Commission." In producing the report, the Program Manager worked closely with officials from the Department of Justice, the Department of Homeland Security, the Department of Defense, the Department of State, and 10 other agencies on the Information Sharing Council, and received input from state, local, and tribal officials and representatives from the private sector.[163]

DHS Reorganization Related to Information Sharing. On July 13, 2005, Secretary of DHS Chertoff proposed a reorganization of the Department, including elevation of the Information Analysis part of IAIP to become a stand-alone office reporting directly to the Secretary. This Office of Intelligence and Analysis would provide intelligence information in support of DHS, and would disseminate information and intelligence to state, local, and tribal partners and other federal agencies, including the Director of National Intelligence (DNI). Under the proposal, it would work closely with Infrastructure Protection and with the intelligence capabilities of other DHS components, and would provide intelligence analyses throughout DHS and the Intelligence Community.

P.L. 109-90, the *Department of Homeland Security Appropriations Act, 2006*, was enacted into law on October 18, 2005. In the accompanying conference report, H.Rept. 109-241, the conference committee accepted the majority of a series of budget amendments proposed in a letter from President Bush dated July 22, 2005. These proposals reconfigured the Department of Homeland Security budget accounts in a manner that was consistent with Secretary Chertoff's proposed departmental reorganization. One of the proposed changes accepted by the conference committee divided IAIP into two new components—Intelligence Analysis and Operations and a Preparedness Directorate. The position of Assistant Secretary for Information Analysis/Chief Intelligence Officer was moved from the former IAIP to the Office of Intelligence and Analysis, a stand-alone office established by the Homeland Security Act reporting directly to the Secretary of DHS. In testimony before the House Committee on Homeland Security, Subcommittee on Intelligence, Information Sharing, and Terrorism Risk Assessment on October 19, 2005, the Chief Intelligence Officer, Charles Allen, indicated that he had been directed by the Secretary of DHS "to integrate all of the Department's intelligence capabilities, not just those of the Office of Intelligence and Analysis," and to "marshal all the intelligence and information in Homeland Security's component agencies and deliver it to [the Secretary] in a way he can use to make timely, risk-based decisions about how to deploy the Department's human and material resources."[164]

Endnotes

[1] Prepared by Richard A. Best, Jr., Specialist in National Defense, Foreign Affairs, Defense and Trade Division.

[2] Prepared by Walter J. Oleszek, Senior Specialist in the Legislative Process, Government and Finance Division.

[3] For further information generally, see CRS Report RS21955, *S.Res. 445: Senate Committee Reorganization for Homeland Security and Intelligence Matters*, by Paul Rundquist and Christopher Davis. For historical background on the public disclosure issue, see CRS Report 94-261, *Intelligence Spending: Public Disclosure Issues*, by Richard A. Best, Jr. and Elizabeth B. Bazan.

[4] Prepared by Henry B. Hogue, Analyst in American National Government, and Frederick M. Kaiser, Specialist in American National Government, Government and Finance Division.

[5] U.S. National Commission on Terrorist Attacks Upon the United States, *The 9/11 Commission Report* (Washington: GPO, 2004), p. 422.

[6] *9/11 Commission Report*, p. 198.

[7] *9/11 Commission Report*, p. 422.

[8] The phrase "national security team" was not defined in the report.

[9] *9/11 Commission Report*, p. 422.

[10] P.L. 108-458, 118 Stat. 3638.

[11] P.L. 108-458, Sec. 7601(a).

[12] P.L. 108-458, Sec. 7601©).

[13] P.L. 108-458, Sec. 7601(b).

[14] U.S. House Committee on Government Reform, *What's the Hold Up? A Review of Security Clearance Backlog and Reciprocity Issues Plaguing Today's Government and Private Sector Workforce*, hearings, 108th Congress, 2nd sess. (Washington: GPO, 2004). At the same time, the Department of Defense transferred the background investigation function and related personnel to the Office of Personnel Management, which now handles about 90% of all federal background investigations.

[15] P.L. 108-458, Title III, Sec. 3001©).

[16] Executive Order 13381, "Strengthening Processes Relating to Determining Eligibility for Access to Classified National Security Information," issued by President George W. Bush, June 27, 2005, 70 *Federal Register* 37953, June 30, 2005.

[17] Ibid., Sec. 1. In developing the plan, the OMB Deputy Director was required to consult with the heads of the Departments of State, Defense, Justice, Energy, and Homeland Security, as well as the Director of the Office of Personnel Management (OPM) and the Director of National Intelligence (DNI). The OMB Director issued guidelines and instructions to the heads of agencies to ensure such goals. A separate section covers Sensitive Compartmented Information, that information generated by way of intelligence sources and methods, and special access programs pertaining to intelligence activities, including special activities or covert operations. The Deputy Director for Management at OMB has been delegated responsibility for carrying out the order. Along with this, specialized areas of responsibility have been assigned to the Directors of OPM and of National Intelligence as well as to the Assistant to the President for National Security Affairs. The particulars of the plan and its production are covered in several executive reports, testimony before Congress, and a Government Accountability Office (GAO) report. See U.S. Office of Management and Budget, *Report on the Status of Executive Branch Efforts to Improve the Security Clearance Process Required under Title III of Public Law 108-458* (Washington: OMB, 2006), and *Plan for Improving the Personnel Security Clearance Process* (Washington: OMB, 2005); and Kathy L. Dillaman, Associate Director, Federal Investigative Services Division, OPM, testimony on *Human Capital Issues and Security Clearance Procedures*, before the Subcommittee on Management, Integration, and Oversight, House Committee on Homeland Security, May 18, 2006. GAO, however, has found continuing weaknesses in this area; see U.S. Government Accountability Office, *DOD Personnel Clearances: Additional OMB Actions Are Needed to Improve the Security Clearance Process*, GAO-06-1070 (Washington: GAO, 2006).

[18] P.L. 108-458, Sec. 8403.

[19] OGE submitted this report on March 17, 2005. It is available at [http://www.usoge.gov/pages/forms_pubs_otherdocs/fpo_files/ reports_plans/rpogc_fin_dis_03_05.pdf].

[20] At the end of the 109th Congress, staffers for both of the congressional committees indicated that only a few agencies had submitted the required PAS position reduction plans.

[21] OGE submitted this report in Jan. 2006. It is available at [http://www.usoge.gov/pages/forms_pubs_otherdocs/fpo_files/reports_plans/rpt_title18.pdf].

[22] See 108th Cong., H.R. 10, § 5042.

[23] Prepared by Kenneth Katzman, Specialist in Middle Eastern Affairs, Foreign Affairs, Defense, and Trade Division.

[24] For further information on U.S. efforts to stabilize Afghanistan, see CRS Report RL30588, *Afghanistan: Post-War Governance, Security, and U.S. Policy*, by Kenneth Katzman.

[25] See The 9/11 Commission Report, Section 12.2, Recommendation No. 3.

[26] Prepared by K. Alan Kronstadt, Specialist in Asian Affairs, Foreign Affairs, Defense, and Trade Division. See also CRS Report RL33498, *Pakistan-U.S. Relations*, CRS Report RL32259, *Terrorism in South Asia*, CRS Report RL32615, *Pakistan's Domestic Political Developments*, and CRS Report RS22009, *Education Reform in Pakistan*, all by K. Alan Kronstadt; and CRS Report RL32745, *Pakistan's Nuclear Proliferation Activities and the Recommendations of the 9/11 Commission*, by Richard Cronin, K. Alan Kronstadt, and Sharon Squassoni.

[27] See Sections 12.1 and 12.2 (p. 361-374) of *The 9/11 Commission Report*. The concept of "enlightened moderation," as expounded by Musharraf himself, is a direct response to a growing world perception that Islam is linked to fundamentalism, and thus to extremism, and thus to terrorism. It is a strategy meant to both shun the militancy that is rooted in "political injustice, denial, and deprivation,"and to bring "socioeconomic uplift"in the Muslim world. Musharraf has called upon Muslims to "adopt a path of moderation and a conciliatory approach to fight the common belief that Islam is a religion of militancy in conflict with modernization, democracy, and secularism" (Pervez Musharraf, "A Plea for Enlightened Moderation," *Washington Post*, June 1, 2004).

[28] Other major government-to-government arms sales and grants in recent years have included C-130 military transport aircraft, P-3C Orion maritime patrol aircraft, AH-1F Cobra attack helicopters, F-16 combat aircraft, surveillance radars, air traffic control systems, military radio systems, Harpoon anti-ship missiles, Phalanx guns, and TOW anti-armor missiles. Other pending sales include Sidewinder air-to-air missiles and self-propelled howitzers.

[29] Prepared by Alfred B. Prados, Specialist in Middle East Affairs, and Christopher M. Blanchard, Analyst in Middle East Affairs, Foreign Affairs, Defense, and Trade Division.

[30] For additional information, see CRS Report RL33533, *Saudi Arabia: Current Issues and U.S. Relations* and CRS Report RL32499, *Saudi Arabia: Terrorist Financing Issues*, both by Alfred B. Prados and Christopher M. Blanchard.

[31] House Committee on International Relations, Survey of Activities, Week of September 6, 2005: Letter Transmitting Report—September 7, 2005, CLASSIFIED, Department of State, pursuant to Sec. 7120 of the Intelligence Reform and Terrorism Prevention Act, 2004 (P.L. 108-458); Ex. Comm. 3684.

[32] Section 7120 of the Intelligence Reform and Terrorism Prevention Act of 2004 (P.L. 108-458)—required the President to submit a strategy as part of a larger reporting requirement within 180 rather than 90 days, as explained above.

[33] Prepared by Raphael Perl, Specialist in International Affairs, Foreign Affairs, Defense, and Trade Division.

[34] Prepared by Jeremy M. Sharp, Middle East Policy Analyst, Foreign Affairs, Defense, and Trade Division.

[35] For more information, see CRS Report RL33166, *Muslims in Europe: Integration in Selected Countries*, by Paul Gallis, Kristin Archick, Francis T. Miko, and Steven Woehrel.

[36] Prepared by Francis T. Miko, Specialist in International Relations, Foreign Affairs, Defense, and Trade Division.

[37] Prepared by Susan B. Epstein, Specialist in Foreign Policy and Trade, Foreign Affairs, Defense, and Trade Division.

[38] Prepared by Martin A. Weiss, Analyst in International Trade and Finance, Foreign Affairs, Defense and Trade.

[39] According to Commission Chairman Thomas Kean, "Right now we have been spending a lot of energy in the government trying to dry up sources of funding..., obviously if you can dry up money, you dry it up, but we believe one thing we didn't do effectively is follow the money. That's what we have to do." Quoted in Laura Sullivan, "U.S. Split on Tracing, Freezing Terror Funds," *Baltimore Sun*, Aug. 2, 2004.

[40] See Nikos Passos, "Hawala and Other Informal Value Transfer Systems: How to Regulate Them?" available at [http://usinfo.state.gov/eap/Archive_Index/ Hawala_and_Other_Informal_Value_Transfer_Systems_How_to_Regulate_Them.html]

[41] CRS Report RS22469: *Treasury's Terrorist Finance Program's Access to Information Held by the Society for Worldwide Interbank Financial Telecommunication (SWIFT)*, by Jennifer K. Elsea and M. Maureen Murphy.

[42] *Terrorist Financing: Better Strategic Planning Needed to Coordinate U.S. Efforts to Deliver Counter-Terrorism Financing Training and Technical Assistance Abroad*, United States Government Accountability Office, October 2005, GAO 06-19.

[43] "2003 National Money Laundering Strategy Report," Department of the Treasury, available at [http://www.ustreas.gov/offices/enforcement/publications/ml2003.pdf].

[44] *FinCEN Halts BSA Direct Retrieval and Sharing Project*, Treasury Press Release, July 13, 2006, available at [http://www.fincen.gov/bsa_direct_nr.html].

[45] Statement of Robert W. Werner, Director, Financial Crimes Enforcement Network United States Department Of The Treasury before The Senate Banking Committee, September 12, 2006, available at [http://www.ustreas.gov/press/releases/hp101.htm].

[46] *FinCEN seeks industry input on feasibility of collection of cross-border wire transfer data*, Treasury Press Release, March 10, 2006, available at [http://www.fincen.gov /fincennewsrelease03102006.html].

[47] Phone discussion with Treasury Legislative Affairs, November 29, 2006.

[48] "IMF Executive Board Reviews the Quality and Consistency of Assessment Reports for Anti-Money Laundering and Combating the Financing of Terrorism and the Effectiveness of Coordination," *International Monetary Fund Public Information Notice (PIN) No. 06/72.*

[49] The Financial Action Task Force is an inter-governmental body whose purpose is the development and promotion of national and international policies to combat money laundering and terrorist financing. For more information on the Financial Action Task Force, see *Financial Action Task Force Annual Report 2005-2006*,available at [http://www.fatf-gafi.org/dataoecd/38/56/37041969.pdf] and CRS Report RS21904: *The Financial Action Task Force: An Overview*, by James K. Jackson.

[50] Testimony of Daniel Glaser, Deputy Assistant Secretary for Terrorist Financing and Financial Crimes before the Senate Committee on Banking, Housing, and Urban Affairs, September 12, 2006, available at [http://banking.senate.gov/_files/glaser.pdf].

[51] Prepared by Andrew Feickert, Specialist in National Defense, Foreign Affairs, Defense, and Trade Division.

[52] Ann Scott Tyson, "Study Urges CIA Not to Cede Paramilitary Functions to Pentagon," *Washington Post*, Feb. 5, 2005, p. 8.

[53] Transcripts, Senate Select Committee on Intelligence, Subject: National Security Threats to the United States, Federal New Service, February 16, 2005, p. 29.

[54] John J. Lumpkin, "Rumsfeld, Goss Oppose DOD Assumption of CIA Paramilitary Covert Operations," *Army Times*, June 29, 2005.

[55] Douglas Jehl, "White House is Said to Reject Panel's Call for a Greater Pentagon Role in Covert Operations," *New York Times*, June 28, 2005.

[56] Prepared by Steve Bowman and Sharon Squassoni, Specialists in National Defense, Foreign Affairs, Defense, and Trade Division.

[57] The PSI is an agreement among some nations to cooperate in the detection and interdiction of illicit WMD-related materiel shipments. Currently, sixteen nations are PSI participants. See also CRS Report RS21881, *Proliferation Security Initiative (PSI)*, by Sharon Squassoni.

[58] See also, CRS Report RL32359, *Globalizing Cooperative Threat Reduction: A Survey of Options*, by Sharon Squassoni.

[59] Prepared by Ruth Ellen Wasem, Specialist in Immigration Policy, Domestic Social Policy Division.

[60] For further analysis, see CRS Report RL32616, *9/11 Commission: Current Legislative Proposals for U.S. Immigration Law and Policy*, by Michael John Garcia and Ruth Ellen Wasem.

[61] For background and analysis, see CRS Report RL32234, *U.S. Visitor and Immigrant Status Indicator Technology Program (US-VISIT)*, by Lisa Seghetti and Stephen Vina.

[62] For background and analysis, see CRS Report RL31512, *Visa Issuances: Policy, Issues, and Legislation*, by Ruth Ellen Wasem.

[63] For further discussion, see CRS Report RL33125, *Immigration Legislation and Issues in the 109th Congress*, coordinated by Andorra Bruno. For a legal analysis of the REAL ID Act, see CRS Report RL32754, *Immigration: Analysis of the Major Provisions of the REAL ID Act of 2005*, by Michael Garcia, Margaret Mikyung Lee, and Todd Tatelman.

[64] For more information on border fencing, see CRS Report RL33659, *Border Security: Barriers Along the U.S. International Border*, by Blas Nuñez-Neto and Stephen R. ViZa.

[65] Prepared by William J. Krouse, Specialist in Domestic Security, Domestic Social Policy Division.

[66] National Commission on Terrorist Attacks upon the United States, "Three 9/11 Hijackers: Identification, Watchlisting, and Tracking," Staff Statement no. 2, (Washington, 2004), p. 1.

[67] National Commission on Terrorist Attacks upon the United States, *The 9/11 Commission Report*, p. 387.

[68] Sara Kehaulani Goo, "Committee Chairman Runs Into Watch-List Problem: Name Similarity Led to Questioning at Anchorage and Seattle Airports, Alaska Congressman Says," *Washington Post*, Sept. 30, 2004, p. A17, and "Hundreds Report Watch-List Trials: Some Ended Hassles at Airports by Making Slight Change to Name," *Washington Post*, Aug. 21, 2004, p. A08.

[69] According to the FBI, the "No Fly" and "Automatic Selectee" lists have been consolidated in the TSDB and the lookout records on those lists are being expanded and improved. U.S. Department of Justice, Federal Bureau of Investigation, Criminal Justice Information Services (CJIS) Division, "Terrorist Screening Center Consolidates Data for Law Enforcement Needs," *The CJIS LINK*, vol. 7, No. 4, October 2004, pp. 1-2.

[70] The TSC was established under HSPD-6. See, The White House, *Homeland Security Presidential Directive/HSPD-6, Subject: Integration and Use of Screening Information* (Washington, Sept. 16, 2003). Available at [http://www.whitehouse.gov/ news/releases/2003/09/20030916-5.html].

[71] For further information, see CRS Report RL32366, *Terrorist Identification, Screening, and Tracking Under Homeland Presidential Directive 6*, by William J. Krouse.

[72] U.S. Department of Homeland Security, *DHS Privacy Office Report on Assessing the Impact of the Automatic Selectee and No Fly Lists on Privacy and Civil Liberties as Required Under Section 4012(b) of the Intelligence Reform and Terrorism Prevention Act of 2004*, April 27, 2006, 22 pp.

[73] Ibid., p. 8.

[74] Ibid., p. 9.

[75] Ibid.

[76] U.S. Government Accountability Office, *Terrorism Watch List Screening: Efforts to Help Reduce Adverse Effects on the Public*, GAO-06-1031, Sept. 2006, p. 55.

[77] Ibid., p. 12.

[78] Prepared by Blas Nuñez-Neto, Analyst in Domestic Security, Domestic Social Policy Division.

[79] Ibid, pp. 388-389.

[80] For further information on the U.S. VISIT program and immigration-related border security measures passed by Congress, see CRS Report RL32234, *U.S. Visitor and Immigrant Status Indicator Technology (U.S.-VISIT) Program*, by Lisa M. Seghetti and Stephen R. Vina; and CRS Report RL31727, *Border Security: Immigration Issues in the 108th Congress*, by Lisa M. Seghetti.

[81] Subsequent legislation amended §110 of IIRIRA by either changing the scope of categories of aliens who would be subjected to entry and exit controls, or delayed implementation of the system. See the INS Data Management Improvement Act (DMIA; P.L. 106-215); the Visa Waiver Permanent Program Act (VWPPA; P.L. 106-396).

[82] Prepared by Ruth Ellen Wasem, Specialist in Immigration Policy, and Blas Nuñez-Neto, Analyst in Domestic Security, Domestic Social Policy Division.

[83] For further discussion, see CRS Report RL32722, *Intelligence Reform and Terrorism Prevention Act of 2004: National Standards for Driver's Licenses, Social Security Cards, and Birth Certificates*, by Todd Tatelman.

[84] For a legal analysis of the REAL ID Act, see CRS Report RL32754, *Immigration: Analysis of the Major Provisions of the REAL ID Act of 2005*, by Michael Garcia, Margaret Mikyung Lee, and Todd Tatelman.

[85] For further discussion, see CRS Report RL33125, *Immigration Legislation and Issues in the 109th Congress*, coordinated by Andorra Bruno.

[86] Prepared by Ruth Ellen Wasem, Specialist in Immigration Policy, Domestic Social Policy Division.

[87] U.S. National Commission on Terrorist Attacks upon the United States, *The 9/11 Commission Report*, Executive Summary, p. 14, July 2004 (hereafter *The 9/11 Commission Report*).

[88] For a discussion of these recommendations, see *The 9/11 Commission Report*, Chapter 12.4, pp. 383-389, July 2004.

[89] For further analysis, see CRS Report RL32616, *9/11 Commission: Current Legislative Proposals for U.S. Immigration Law and Policy*, by Michael John Garcia and Ruth Ellen Wasem.

[90] For more information on border fencing, see CRS Report RL33659, *Border Security: Barriers Along the U.S. International Border*, by Blas Nuñez-Neto and Stephen R. ViZa.

[91] Prepared by Bart Elias, Specialist in Aviation Safety, Security, and Technology, Resources, Science, and Industry Division.

[92] For more information see CRS Report RL32541, *Aviation Security-Related Findings and Recommendations of the 9/11 Commission*, by Bart Elias.

[93] In addition to CAPPS, current prescreening procedures involve checking passenger name records against "automatic-selectee" and "no-fly" lists provided to the airlines by the Transportation Security Administration (TSA).

[94] For further discussion, see CRS Report RL32498, *Vision 100: Historical Review of the Century of Aviation Reauthorization Act (P.L. 108-176)*, by Bart Elias, John W. Fischer, and Robert S. Kirk.

[95] Prepared by John Frittelli, Specialist in Transportation, Resources, Science, and Industry Division.

[96] Another commission, The Interagency Commission on Crime and Security in U.S. Seaports, that was established by the Clinton Administration in April 1999 and which reported their findings in the fall of 2000, made 20 specific recommendations for improving port security, most of which have been acted upon since September 11, 2001. This commission's report is available at [http://www.securitymanagement.com/library/seaport1200.pdf].

[97] *The 9/11 Commission Report*, p. 391.

[98] Ibid., pp. 391-92.

[99] See [http://www.whitehouse.gov/homeland/maritime-security.html#annex].

[100] This document is designated as "Sensitive Security Information."

[101] U.S. CBP, *CSI Fact Sheet*, September 28, 2006.

[102] DHS, *Fact Sheet: Protecting the Homeland Post September 11*, September 11, 2006.

[103] Ibid.

[104] Prepared by David Randall Peterman, Analyst in Transportation, Resources, Science, and Industry Division.

[105] 9/11 Public Discourse Project, *Final Report on 9/11 Commission Recommendations*, December 5, 2005. Available at [http://www.9-11pdp.org/press/2005-12-05_report.pdf] (viewed 11/29/2006).

[106] Government Accountability Office, *Risk Management: Further Refinements Needed to Assess Risks and Prioritize Protective Measures at Ports and Other Critical Infrastructure*, GAO-06-91, December 15, 2005.

[107] Government Accountability Office, *Critical Infrastructure Protection: Progress Coordinating Government and Private Sector Efforts Varies by Sectors' Characteristics*, GAO-07-39, October 16, 2006, p. 2-3.

[108] Government Accountability Office, *Critical Infrastructure Protection: Progress Coordinating Government and Private Sector Efforts Varies by Sectors' Characteristics*, GAO-07-39, October 16, 2006, p. 15.

[109] Prepared by John Moteff, Specialist in Science and Technology Policy, Resources, Science, and Industry Division.

[110] According to a DHS Inspector General's report, DHS itself considered its initial priority list unreliable. See, Department of Homeland Security. Office of the Inspector General. *Progress in Developing the National Asset Database*. OIG-06-04. June 2006. p. 16.

[111] Threat information is provided by DHS's Homeland Infrastructure Threat and Risk Analysis Center, which provides an up-to-date set of threat scenarios for each sector.

[112] Prepared by Keith Bea, Specialist in American National Government, Government and Finance Division, with contributions by Shawn Reese, Analyst in American National Government, Government and Finance Division, and Linda Moore, Analyst in Telecommunications Policy, Resources, Science and Industry Division.

[113] The Commission noted, however, that liability and indemnification concerns impeded some of the response at the Pentagon and exist throughout the nation. Also of note, the less disastrous results of the Pentagon attack can be explained to a large extent by target and population differences—the jet that struck the Pentagon occurred in a relatively isolated area and directly affected just one building, whereas the jets that destroyed the World Trade Center towers destroyed a significant part of a major metropolitan area. These differences alone meant that the emergency responders in New York City faced a more complex task than those in Virginia.

[114] Four years after the attacks, some of the concerns raised by the Commission in the final report appeared to remain unresolved. Problems identified in the response to Hurricane Katrina (August 2005) indicate that federal and non-federal preparations for catastrophic incidents require further improvement.

[115] For information on proposals in the 108th Congress related to the distribution of federal funds to emergency responders, see CRS Report RL33583, *Homeland Security Grants: Evolution of Program Guidance and Grant Allocation Methods*, by Shawn Reese.

[116] This text reflects language approved by the Senate. The House language, not approved by conferees, would have authorized all local, state, or federal officials to negotiate mutual aid agreements for emergency assistance. Matters of liability, worker compensation, and judicial review would also have been addressed by the House approved text.

[117] P.L. 109-171, Sec. 3002 (a) (1) (B).

[118] *Report to Congress; on the study to assess short-term and long-term needs for allocations of additional portions of the electromagnetic spectrum for federal, state and local emergency response providers,* Federal Communications Commission, December 19, 2005, at

[http://hraunfoss.fcc.gov/edocs_public/attachmatch/DOC-262865A1.pdf]. Viewed December 27, 2005.

[119] P.L. 109-295, Title VI, Sec. 671(b), Title XVIII, Sec. 1803 (a).

[120] P.L. 109-295, Title VI, Sec. 671(b), Title XVIII, Sec. 1803 (a) (5).

[121] P.L. 107-56, Sec. 1014, (USA PATRIOT Act).

[122] U.S. Department of Homeland Security, Office for Grants and Training, *FY2006 HSGP Fact Sheet: Risk Analysis* (Washington: May 2006), p. 2.

[123] Prepared by Steve Bowman, Specialist in National Defense, Foreign Affairs, Defense, and Trade Division.

[124] For further information, see CRS Report RS21322, *Homeland Security: Evolving Roles and Missions for United States Northern Command*, by Steve Bowman and James Crowhurst.

[125] Prepared by Walter J. Oleszek, Senior Specialist in the Legislative Process, Government and Finance Division.

[126] Prepared by Todd B. Tatelman, Legislative Attorney, American Law Division.

[127] Intelligence Reform and Terrorism Prevention Act of 2004, P.L. 108-458 §§ 7211-7214, 118 Stat. 3638, 3825-3832 (2004).

[128] *Id.* at § 7212.

[129] Emergency Supplemental Appropriations Act for Defense, the Global War on Terror, and Tsunami Relief, 2005, P.L. 109-13 Division B, 119 Stat. 231, 302 (2005).

[130] Before a state can issue a driver's license or photo identification card, a state will have to verify with the issuing agency, the issuance, validity and completeness of: (1) a photo identification document or a non-photo document containing both the individual's full legal name and date of birth; (2) date of birth; (3) proof of a social security number (SSN) or verification of the individual's ineligibility for a SSN; and (4) name and address of the individual's principal residence.

[131] Persons are only eligible for temporary driver's licenses or identification cards if evidence is presented that they: (1) have a valid, unexpired non-immigrant visa or non-immigrant visa status for entry into the United States; (2) have a pending or approved application for asylum in the U.S.; (3) have entered into the U.S. in refugee status; (4) have a pending or approved application for temporary protected status in the United States; (5) have approved deferred action status; or (6) have a pending application for adjustment of status to that of an alien lawfully admitted for permanent residence in the United States or conditional permanent resident status in the United States.

[132] For a more complete discussion of the provisions of the REAL ID Act, *see* CRS Report RL32754, *Immigration: Analysis of the Major Provisions of the REAL ID Act of 2005*, by Michael Garcia, Margaret Mikyung Lee, and Todd B. Tatelman.

[133] Intelligence Reform and Terrorism Prevention Act of 2004, *supra* note 127 at § 7211.

[134] *Id.* at § 7213.

[135] Prepared by Harold C. Relyea, Specialist in American National Government, Government and Finance Division.

[136] Section 892 of the Homeland Security Act of 2002 directs the President to prescribe and implement procedures for sharing relevant and appropriate homeland security information with other federal agencies, as well as state and local government personnel. 116 Stat. 2253; 6 U.S.C. § 482.

[137] U.S. National Commission on Terrorist Attacks Upon the United States, *The 9/11 Commission Report*, pp. 394-395.

[138] U.S. Advisory Panel to Assess Domestic Response Capabilities for Terrorism Involving Weapons of Mass Destruction, *V. Forging America's New Normalcy: Securing Our Homeland, Preserving Our Liberty* (Arlington, VA: Rand Corporation, 2003), pp. 22-23.

[139] *Federal Register*, vol. 69, Sept. 1, 2004, pp. 53585-53587.

[140] 118 Stat. 3684.

[141] 119 Stat. 2396.

[142] U.S. Office of the Director of National Intelligence, ODNI Announces Senior Leadership Positions, ODNI New Release No. 7-05 (Washington: Dec. 7, 2005).

[143] U.S. Office of the Director of National Intelligence, Program Manager, Information Sharing Environment, *Information Sharing Environment Implementation Plan* (Washington: Nov. 2006), pp. 21-22, 39, 89-92.

[144] See *Congressional Record*, daily edition, vol. 151, Mar. 16, 2005, p. E456.

[145] U.S. Congress, Senate Committee on Appropriations, *Transportation, Treasury and General Government Appropriations Bill, 2005*, S.Rept. 108-342, report to accompany S. 2806, 108th Cong., 2nd sess. (Washington: GPO, 2004), pp. 200, 202.

[146] 118 Stat. 2809.

[147] *Congressional Record*, daily edition, vol. 150, Nov. 19, 2004, pp. H10358-H10359.

[148] U.S. Office of Management and Budget, "Designation of Senior Agency Officials for Privacy," Memorandum for Heads of Executive Departments and Agencies from Clay Johnson III, Deputy Director for Management (Washington: Feb. 11, 2005).

[149] Prepared by Elizabeth B. Bazan, Legislative Attorney, American Law Division.

[150] See, e.g., P.L. 107-56, §§ 203, 218, 504, 314, 701, 115 Stat. 272 (Oct. 26, 2001); P.L. 107-71, §§ 102, 137 (Nov. 19, 2001) 115. Stat. 597; P.L. 107-173, §§ 201-204 (May 14, 2002), 115 Stat. 543; P.L. 107-296, §§ 214,221, 891-899 (Nov. 25, 2002), 116 Stat. 2135; P.L. 107-306, title VII (Nov. 27, 2002), 116 Stat. 2383); P.L. 108-177, §§ 316, 354, 359 (Dec. 13, 2003), 117 Stat. 2599; P.L. 108-447, Div. H, Title V, § 552 (Dec. 8, 1004), 118 Stat. 2809; P.L. 108-458, §§ 1013, 1016, 6501, 7201 (Dec. 17, 2004), 118 Stat. 3638.

[151] See, e.g., E.O. 13311, E.O. 13355, E.O. 13356, E.O. 13388, discussed *infra*.

[152] HSPD-11, issued August 27, 2004.

[153] See the following guidelines issued by the Attorney General: "Guidelines for Disclosure of Grand Jury and Electronic, Wire, and Oral Interception information identifying United States Persons" (Sept. 23, 2002); "Guidelines Regarding Disclosure to the Director of Central Intelligence and Homeland Security Officials of Foreign Intelligence Acquired in the Course of a Criminal Investigation" (Sept. 23, 2002); "Guidelines Regarding Prompt Handling of Reports of Possible Criminal Activity Involving Foreign Intelligence Sources" (Sept. 23, 2002); "Coordination of Information Relating to Terrorism" (April 11, 2002); "Cooperation with State and Local Officials in the Fight Against Terrorism" (Nov. 13, 2001); "Disseminating Information to Enhance Public Safety and National Security" (Sept. 21, 2001).

[154] P.L. 95-511 (October 25, 1978), as amended, 50 U.S.C. § 1801 *et seq.*

[155] This standard was changed from "the purpose" by the Section 218 of the USA PATRIOT Act, P.L. 107-56.

[156] P.L. 107-56, Section 504.

[157] On August 27, 2004, President Bush issued E.O. 13355, "Strengthening Management of the Intelligence Community" which gave the Director of Central Intelligence authority to develop objectives and guidance for the Intelligence Community to ensure timely and effective collection, processing, and dissemination of intelligence concerning current and potential threats to the United States and its interests; and to address prompt sharing of information and establishment of interoperable information sharing enterprise. In the

wake of passage of P.L. 108-458, many of these responsibilities now appear to rest upon the DNI or the President.

[158] By E.O. 13354, the President created an NCTC as the primary federal organization for analyzing and integrating all intelligence pertaining to terrorism and counterterrorism, except purely domestic counterterrorism information, and giving it the authority, among other things, to receive, retain, and disseminate information from any source to fulfill its responsibilities. Section 1021 of P.L. 108-458 also establishes an NCTC with somewhat similar but not identical responsibilities.

[159] Other legislation has addressed information sharing in particular contexts. For example, Section 332 of P.L. 107-188, the Public Health Security and Bioterrorism Preparedness and Response Act of 2002 (June 12, 2002), 21 U.S.C.A. § 679c(a)(3) and (4), authorizes the Secretary of Agriculture to utilize existing authorities to give high priority to enhancing and expanding the capacity of the Food Safety Inspection Service to conduct activities to, among other things, "strengthen the ability of the Service to collaborate with relevant agencies within the Department of Agriculture and with other entities in the Federal Government, the States, and Indian tribes (as defined in section 450b(e) of Title 25) through the sharing of information and technology;" and " otherwise expand the capacity of the Service to protect against the threat of bioterrorism."

Section 108(a) of the Security and Accountability for Every Port Act of 2006 (SAFE Port Act of 2006), P.L. 109-347 (October 13, 2006), 46 U.S.C.A. § 70107A, provides for the establishment of interagency operational centers for port security at all high-priority ports not later than 3 years after the date of the enactment of the SAFE Port Act. Under this subsection, among other things, such interagency operational centers are to be incorporated in the implementation and administration of maritime intelligence activities under 46 U.S.C. § 70113 and information sharing activities consistent with section 1016 of the Intelligence Reform and Terrorism Prevention Act of 2004 (6 U.S.C. 485) and the Homeland Security Information Sharing Act (6 U.S.C. 481 et seq.).

The Maritime Transportation Security Act of 2002, P.L. 107-295, addressed a range of homeland security requirements relating to port security. Section 102 of that Act, 46 U.S.C. § 70112(a)(2), authorized the creation of area maritime security advisory committees applicable to individual ports. For further discussion of information sharing in the maritime security context, see General Accountability Office, *Testimony before the Subcommittee on Government Management, Finance, Accountability, Committee on Government Reform, House of Representatives, on Maritime Security, Information-Sharing Efforts Are Improving*, GAO-06-933T (July 10, 2006).

Section 303 of P.L. 109-13, the Emergency Supplemental Appropriations Act for Defense, the Global War on Terror, and Tsunami Relief, 2005 (May 11, 2005), required the Secretary of Homeland Security, acting through the Under Secretary of Homeland Security for Border and Transportation Security, in consultation with the Under Secretary of Homeland Security for Science and Technology, the Under Secretary for Information Analysis and Infrastructure Protection, the Assistant Secretary of Commerce for Communications and Information, and other appropriate federal, state, local, and tribal agencies, within 180 days of enactment of Division A of that Act, to improve federal communications systems to facilitate integration of communications among the federal agencies and departments, and state, local, and Indian tribal agencies on border security matters; and to enhance information sharing among federal departments and agencies, state and local governmental agencies, and Indian tribal agencies on such matters. Within one year, the Secretary of Homeland Security is also required to submit a copy of the plan and a report on the plan with any recommendations to the Senate Committee on Commerce, Science, and Transportation, the House Committee on Science, the House Committee on Homeland Security and the House Committee on the Judiciary.

Section 1035 of P.L. 109-364, the John Warner National Defense Authorization Act for Fiscal Year 2007 (October 17, 2006), requires the President, not later than April 1, 2007, to report to Congress on building interagency capacity and enhancing the integration of civilian capabilities of the executive branch with the capabilities of the Armed forces to enhance the achievement of U.S. national security goals and objectives. One element of the report is to address information sharing policies, practices, and systems. *Cf.* Government Accountability Office, *Information Sharing, the Federal Government Needs to Establish Policies and Processes for Sharing Terrorism-Related and Sensitive but Unclassified Information,* GAO-06-385 (March 2006).

[160] Section 5(a) of E.O. 13388 stated that Information Sharing Council membership was to be composed exclusively of designees of: the Secretaries of State, the Treasury, Defense, Commerce, Energy, and Homeland Security; the Attorney General; the Director of National Intelligence; the Director of the Central Intelligence Agency; the Director of the Office of Management and Budget; the Director of the Federal Bureau of Investigation; the Director of the National Counterterrorism Center; and such other heads of departments or agencies as the Director of National Intelligence may designate.

[161] For additional information, see CRS Report RL33042, *Department of Homeland Security Reorganization: The 2SR Initiative,* by Harold C. Relyea and Henry B. Hogue.

[162] News Release from the Office of the Director of National Intelligence Public Affairs Office, ODNI News Release No. 21-06 (November 16, 2006).

[163] *Id.*

[164] Prepared statement of Charles Allen for the House Committee on Homeland Security, Subcommittee on Intelligence, Information Sharing, and Terrorism Risk Assessment, Washington, DC (October 19, 2005). See CRS Report RL33042, *Department of Homeland Security Reorganization: The 2SR Initiative,* by Harold C. Relyea and Henry B. Hogue.

SUBJECT INDEX

Doc/Pg

Congressional Research Service (CRS) Reports

Doc/Pg

Critical Infrastructure Protection

First Responders

Government Accountability Office (GAO) Reports 7/187

Homeland Security

House Homeland Security Committee

Immigration

Maritime Security

National Security – Threats to

9/11 Commission

Senate Commerce, Science and Transportation Committee

Senate Intelligence Committee

Transportation Security

Visas

Printed and bound in the UK by
CPI Antony Rowe, Eastbourne

The manufacturer's authorised representative in the EU for product
safety is Oxford University Press España S.A. of El Parque Empresarial
San Fernando de Henares, Avenida de Castilla, 2 - 28830 Madrid
(www.oup.es/en or product.safety@oup.com). OUP España S.A. also acts
as importer into Spain of products made by the manufacturer.
Printed and bound by CPI Group (UK) Ltd, Croydon, CR0 4YY
14/09/2026
02216308-0020